UNITED STATES

COMMODITY FUTURES TRADING COMMISSION
★ 1975 ★

COMMODITY FUTURES TRADING COMMISSION HANDBOOK

STRATEGIC INFORMATION AND REGULATIONS

International Business Publications, USA
Washington, DC USA

UNITED STATES
COMMODITY FUTURES TRADING COMMISSION HANDBOOK
STRATEGIC INFORMATION AND REGULATIONS

UPDATED ANNUALLY

Cover Design: International Business Publications, USA

We express our sincere appreciation to all government agencies and international organizations which provided information and other materials for this handbook

2015 Edition Updated Reprint International Business Publications, USA
ISBN 0-7397-6202-8

This handbook provides basic information for starting or/and conducting business in the country. The extraordinary volume of materials covering the topic, prevents us from placing all these materials in this handbook. For more detailed information on issues related to any specific investment and business activity in the country, please contact Global Investment Center, USA
Please acquire the list of our business intelligence and marketing reports and other business publications. We constantly update and expand our business intelligence and marketing materials. Please contact the center for the updated list of reports on over 200 countries.

in the USA: **Global Investment Center, USA.**
P.O.Box 15343, Washington, DC 20003
Phone: (202) 546-2103, Fax: (202) 546-3275, E-mail: rusric@erols.com

For additional analytical, marketing and other information please contact Global Investment Center, USA

Printed in the USA

UNITED STATES

COMMODITY FUTURES TRADING COMMISSION HANDBOOK

STRATEGIC INFORMATION AND REGULATIONS

TABLE OF CONTENTS

FUTURES TRADING BASICS

FUTURES CONTRACT

In finance, a **futures contract** (more colloquially, **futures**) is a standardized contract between two parties to buy or sell a specified asset of standardized quantity and quality for a price agreed upon today (the *futures price* or strike price) with delivery and payment occurring at a specified future date, the *delivery date*. The contracts are negotiated at a futures exchange, which acts as an intermediary between the two parties. The party agreeing to buy the underlying asset in the future, the "buyer" of the contract, is said to be "long", and the party agreeing to sell the asset in the future, the "seller" of the contract, is said to be "short". The terminology reflects the expectations of the parties—the buyer hopes or expects that the asset price is going to increase, while the seller hopes or expects that it will decrease in near future.

In many cases, the underlying asset to a futures contract may not be traditional commodities at all – that is, for financial futures the underlying item can be any financial instrument (also including currency, bonds, and stocks); they can be also based on intangible assets or referenced items, such as stock indexes and interest rates.

While the futures contract specifies a trade taking place in the future, the purpose of the futures exchange institution is to act as intermediary and minimize the risk of default by either party. Thus the exchange requires both parties to put up an initial amount of cash, the margin. Additionally, since the futures price will generally change daily, the difference in the prior agreed-upon price and the daily futures price is settled daily also (variation margin). The exchange will draw money out of one party's margin account and put it into the other's so that each party has the appropriate daily loss or profit. If the margin account goes below a certain value, then a margin call is made and the account owner must replenish the margin account. This process is known as *marking to market*. Thus on the delivery date, the amount exchanged is not the specified price on the contract but the spot value (since any gain or loss has already been previously settled by marking to market).

A closely related contract is a forward contract. A forward is like a futures in that it specifies the exchange of goods for a specified price at a specified future date. However, a forward is not traded on an exchange and thus does not have the interim partial payments due to marking to market. Nor is the contract standardized, as on the exchange.

Unlike an option, both parties of a futures contract must fulfill the contract on the delivery date. The seller delivers the underlying asset to the buyer, or, if it is a cash-settled futures contract, then cash is transferred from the futures trader who sustained a loss to the one who made a profit. To exit the commitment prior to the settlement date, the holder of a futures position can close out its contract obligations by taking the opposite position on another futures contract on the same asset and settlement date. The difference in futures prices is then a profit or loss.

ORIGIN

The first futures exchange market was the Dōjima Rice Exchange in Japan made by Rey Tommy Napone in the 1730s, to meet the needs of samurai who—being paid in rice, and after a series of bad harvests—needed a stable conversion to coin.
The Chicago Board of Trade (CBOT) listed the first ever standardized 'exchange traded' forward contracts in 1864, which were called futures contracts. This contract was based on grain trading and started a trend that saw contracts created on a number of different commodities as well as a number of futures exchanges set up in countries around the world. By 1875 cotton futures were being traded in Mumbai in India and within a few years this had expanded to futures on edible oilseeds complex, raw jute and jute goods and bullion.

STANDARDIZATION

Futures contracts ensure their liquidity by being highly standardized, usually by specifying:

The *underlying* asset or instrument. This could be anything from a barrel of crude oil to a short term interest rate.

The type of settlement, either cash settlement or physical settlement.

The *amount* and units of the underlying asset per contract. This can be the notional amount of bonds, a fixed number of barrels of oil, units of foreign currency, the notional amount of the deposit over which the short term interest rate is traded, etc.

The currency in which the futures contract is quoted.

The *grade* of the deliverable. In the case of bonds, this specifies which bonds can be delivered. In the case of physical commodities, this specifies not only the quality of the underlying goods but also the manner and location of delivery. For example, the NYMEX Light **Sweet Crude Oil contract** specifies the acceptable sulphur content and API specific gravity, as well as the pricing point—the location where delivery must be made.

The delivery month.

The last trading date.

Other details such as the commodity tick, the minimum permissible price fluctuation.

MARGIN

To minimize credit risk to the exchange, traders must post a margin or a performance bond, typically 5%-15% of the contract's value.

To minimize counterparty risk to traders, trades executed on regulated futures exchanges are guaranteed by a clearing house. The clearing house becomes the buyer to each seller, and the seller to each Buyer, so that in the event of a counterparty default the clearer assumes the risk of loss. This enables traders to transact without performing due diligence on their counterparty.

Margin requirements are waived or reduced in some cases for hedgers who have physical ownership of the covered commodity or spread traders who have offsetting contracts balancing the position.

Clearing margin are financial safeguards to ensure that companies or corporations perform on their customers' open futures and options contracts. Clearing margins are distinct from customer margins that individual buyers and sellers of futures and options contracts are required to deposit with brokers.

Customer margin Within the futures industry, financial guarantees required of both buyers and sellers of futures contracts and sellers of options contracts to ensure fulfillment of contract obligations. Futures Commission Merchants are responsible for overseeing customer margin accounts. Margins are determined on the basis of market risk and contract value. Also referred to as performance bond margin.

Initial margin is the equity required to initiate a futures position. This is a type of performance bond. The maximum exposure is not limited to the amount of the initial margin, however the initial margin requirement is calculated based on the maximum estimated change in contract value within a trading day. Initial margin is set by the exchange.

If a position involves an exchange-traded product, the amount or percentage of initial margin is set by the exchange concerned.

In case of loss or if the value of the initial margin is being eroded, the broker will make a margin call in order to restore the amount of initial margin available. Often referred to as "variation margin", margin called for this reason is usually done on a daily basis, however, in times of high volatility a broker can make a margin call or calls intra-day.

Calls for margin are usually expected to be paid and received on the same day. If not, the broker has the right to close sufficient positions to meet the amount called by way of margin. After the position is closed-out the client is liable for any resulting deficit in the client's account.

Some U.S. exchanges also use the term "maintenance margin", which in effect defines by how much the value of the initial margin can reduce before a margin call is made. However, most non-US brokers only use the term "initial margin" and "variation margin".

The Initial Margin requirement is established by the Futures exchange, in contrast to other securities' Initial Margin (which is set by the Federal Reserve in the U.S. Markets).

A futures account is marked to market daily. If the margin drops below the margin maintenance requirement established by the exchange listing the futures, a margin call will be issued to bring the account back up to the required level.

Maintenance margin A set minimum margin per outstanding futures contract that a customer must maintain in his margin account.

Margin-equity ratio is a term used by speculators, representing the amount of their trading capital that is being held as margin at any particular time. The low margin requirements of futures results in substantial leverage of the investment. However, the exchanges require a minimum amount that varies depending on the contract and the trader. The broker may set the requirement higher, but may not set it lower. A trader, of course, can set it above that, if he does not want to be subject to margin calls.

Performance bond margin The amount of money deposited by both a buyer and seller of a futures contract or an options seller to ensure performance of the term of the contract. Margin in commodities is not a payment of equity or down payment on the commodity itself, but rather it is a security deposit.

Return on margin (ROM) is often used to judge performance because it represents the gain or loss compared to the exchange's perceived risk as reflected in required margin. ROM may be calculated (realized return) / (initial margin). The Annualized ROM is equal to $(ROM+1)^{(year/trade\_duration)}-1$. For example if a trader earns 10% on margin in two months, that would be about 77% annualized.

SETTLEMENT - PHYSICAL VERSUS CASH-SETTLED FUTURES

Settlement is the act of consummating the contract, and can be done in one of two ways, as specified per type of futures contract:

> **Physical delivery** - the amount specified of the underlying asset of the contract is delivered by the seller of the contract to the exchange, and by the exchange to the buyers of the contract. Physical delivery is common with commodities and bonds. In practice, it occurs only on a minority of contracts. Most are cancelled out by purchasing a covering position - that is, buying a contract to cancel out an earlier sale (covering a short), or selling a contract to liquidate an earlier purchase (covering a long). The Nymex crude futures contract uses this method of settlement upon expiration
>
> **Cash settlement** - a cash payment is made based on the underlying reference rate, such as a short term interest rate index such as Euribor, or the closing value of a stock market index. The parties settle by paying/receiving the loss/gain related to the contract in cash when the contract expires. Cash settled futures are those that, as a practical matter, could not be settled by delivery of the referenced item - i.e. how would one deliver an index? A futures contract might also opt to settle against an index based on trade in a related spot market. ICE Brent futures use this method.

Expiry (or **Expiration** in the U.S.) is the time and the day that a particular delivery month of a futures contract stops trading, as well as the final settlement price for that contract. For many equity index and interest rate futures contracts (as well as for most equity options), this happens on the third Friday of certain trading months. On this day the *t+1* futures contract becomes the *t* futures contract. For example, for most CME and CBOT contracts, at the expiration of the December contract, the March futures become the nearest contract. This is an exciting time for arbitrage desks, which try to make quick profits during the short period (perhaps 30 minutes) during which the underlying cash price and the futures price sometimes struggle to converge. At this moment the futures and the underlying assets are extremely liquid and any disparity between an index and an underlying asset is quickly traded by arbitrageurs. At this moment also, the increase in volume is caused by traders rolling over positions to the next contract or, in the case of equity index futures, purchasing underlying components of those indexes to hedge against current index positions. On the expiry date, a European equity arbitrage trading desk in London or Frankfurt will see positions expire in as many as eight major markets almost every half an hour.

PRICING

When the deliverable asset exists in plentiful supply, or may be freely created, then the price of a futures contract is determined via arbitrage arguments. This is typical for stock index futures, treasury bond futures, and futures on physical commodities when they are in supply (e.g. agricultural crops after the harvest). However, when the deliverable commodity is not in plentiful supply or when it does not yet exist - for example on crops before the harvest or on Eurodollar Futures or Federal funds rate futures (in which the supposed underlying instrument is to be created upon the delivery date) - the futures price cannot be fixed by arbitrage. In this scenario there is only one force setting the price, which is simple supply and demand for the asset in the future, as expressed by supply and demand for the futures contract.

ARBITRAGE ARGUMENTS

Arbitrage arguments ("Rational pricing") apply when the deliverable asset exists in plentiful supply, or may be freely created. Here, the forward price represents the expected future value of the underlying discounted at the risk free rate—as any deviation from the theoretical price will afford investors a riskless profit opportunity and should be arbitraged away. We define the forward price to be the strike K such that the contract has 0 value at the present time. Assuming interest rates are constant the forward price of the future is equal to the forward price of the forward contract with the same strike and maturity. It is also the same if the underlying asset is uncorrelated with interest rates. Otherwise the difference between the forward price on the future (futures price) and forward price on the asset, is proportional to the covariance between the underlying asset price and interest rates. For example, a future on a zero coupon bond will have a futures price lower than the forward price. This is called the futures "convexity correction."

Thus, assuming constant rates, for a simple, non-dividend paying asset, the value of the future/forward price, $F(t,T)$, will be found by compounding the present value $S(t)$ at time t to maturity T by the rate of risk-free return r.

$$F(t,T) = S(t) \times (1+r)^{(T-t)}$$

or, with *continuous compounding*

$$F(t,T) = S(t)e^{r(T-t)}$$

This relationship may be modified for storage costs, dividends, dividend yields, and convenience yields.

In a perfect market the relationship between futures and spot prices depends only on the above variables; in practice there are various market imperfections (transaction costs, differential borrowing and lending rates, restrictions on short selling) that prevent complete arbitrage. Thus, the futures price in fact varies within arbitrage boundaries around the theoretical price.

PRICING VIA EXPECTATION

When the deliverable commodity is not in plentiful supply (or when it does not yet exist) rational pricing cannot be applied, as the arbitrage mechanism is not applicable. Here the price of the futures is determined by today's supply and demand for the underlying asset in the futures.

In a deep and liquid market, supply and demand would be expected to balance out at a price which represents an unbiased expectation of the future price of the actual asset and so be given by the simple relationship.

$$F(t) = E_t\{S(T)\}$$

By contrast, in a shallow and illiquid market, or in a market in which large quantities of the deliverable asset have been deliberately withheld from market participants (an illegal action known as cornering the market), the market clearing price for the futures may still represent the balance between supply and demand but the relationship between this price and the expected future price of the asset can break down.

RELATIONSHIP BETWEEN ARBITRAGE ARGUMENTS AND EXPECTATION

The expectation based relationship will also hold in a no-arbitrage setting when we take expectations with respect to the risk-neutral probability. In other words: a futures price is martingale with respect to the risk-neutral probability. With this pricing rule, a speculator is expected to break even when the futures market fairly prices the deliverable commodity.

CONTANGO AND BACKWARDATION

The situation where the price of a commodity for future delivery is higher than the spot price, or where a far future delivery price is higher than a nearer future delivery, is known as contango. The reverse, where the price of a commodity for future delivery is lower than the spot price, or where a far future delivery price is lower than a nearer future delivery, is known as backwardation.

FUTURES CONTRACTS AND EXCHANGES

CONTRACTS

There are many different kinds of futures contracts, reflecting the many different kinds of "tradable" assets about which the contract may be based such as commodities, securities (such as single-stock futures), currencies or intangibles such as interest rates and indexes.

- Foreign exchange market
- Money market
- Bond market
- Equity market
- Soft Commodities market

Trading on commodities began in Japan in the 18th century with the trading of rice and silk, and similarly in Holland with tulip bulbs. Trading in the US began in the mid 19th century, when central grain markets were established and a marketplace was created for farmers to bring their commodities and sell them either for immediate delivery (also called spot or cash market) or for forward delivery. These forward contracts were private contracts between buyers and sellers and became the forerunner to today's exchange-traded futures contracts. Although contract trading began with traditional commodities such as grains, meat and livestock, exchange trading has expanded to include metals, energy, currency and currency indexes, equities and equity indexes, government interest rates and private interest rates.

COMMODITY MARKET

Commodity market refers to physical or virtual transactions of buying and selling involving raw or primary commodities. A soft commodity generally refers to commodities harvested as products like wheat, coffee, cocoa, sugar, corn, wheat, soybean, and fruit traded in the **commodity market**. Hard commodities usually refer to commodities that are extracted such as (gold, rubber, oil). While commodities may be grouped for regulation purposes etc., in large classes such as energy, agricultural including livestock, precious metals, industrial metals, other commodity markets, these are broken down into about a hundred primary commodities (soybean oil, recycled steel). Investors access about 50 major commodity markets worldwide uses growing numbers of exchanges with virtual transactions increasingly replacing physical trades.

A financial derivative in the commodity market is a financial instrument whose value is derived from a commodity as item or underlier. Derivatives trading employs various techniques to increase profit and manage risk. Derivatives in the commodity market are assets that are either exchange-traded derivatives or over-the-counter (OTC) derivatives. With the increased diversity and complexity of commodities derivatives, new international institutions have emerged, such as clearing houses some with Central Counterparty Clearing, which provide clearing and settlement services on a futures exchange, as well as off-exchange in the OTC market.

Derivatives in the form of the futures contracts are the oldest and most direct way of investing in commodities. Commodity market derivatives are securitized by physical assets or commodities. Commodity markets can include direct physical trading and derivatives trading in the form of spot prices, forwards, futures, and options on futures. Farmers have used a simple form of derivative trading in the commodity market for centuries for price risk management (p. 6). In the basic agricultural futures contracts a farmer (the future seller) agrees with a counterparty, a future buyer to sell a set number of units of corn to a broker for a fixed future date at an agreed-upon quality and price and point of delivery. If the price of corn drops the farmer is protected from losses thereby reducing risk. If the price rises the farmer loses potential profit. Derivatives trading employs various techniques to increase profit and manage risk through hedging.

One focus of this article is the relationship between simple commodity money and the more complex financial instruments of derivative trading, such as futures contracts, Swaps (1970s-), Exchange-traded Commodities (ETC) (2003-), forward contracts. Futures are traded on regulated commodities exchanges. Over-the-counter (OTC) contracts in the commodity market are "privately negotiated bilateral contracts entered into between the contracting parties directly". Although investors assume that commodity market derivatives are securitized by the physical assets or commodities, gold for example, the actual exposure to the physical commodity of gold has changed significantly since the emergence of financial instruments such as exchange-traded funds (ETFs) in 2003. ETFs are based on electronic gold which does not entail the actual ownership of physical bullion, with its added costs of insurance and storage in bullion banks, such as the London bullion market. According to the World Gold Council, ETFs allow investors to be exposed to the gold market without the risk of price volatility associated with gold as a physical commodity.

EXCHANGES

Contracts on financial instruments were introduced in the 1970s by the Chicago Mercantile Exchange (CME) and these instruments became hugely successful and quickly overtook commodities futures in terms of trading volume and global accessibility to the markets. This innovation led to the introduction of many new futures exchanges worldwide, such as the London International Financial Futures Exchange in 1982 (now Euronext.liffe), Deutsche Terminbörse (now Eurex) and the Tokyo Commodity Exchange (TOCOM). Today, there are more than 90 futures and futures options exchanges worldwide trading to include:

CME Group (formerly CBOT and CME) -- Currencies, Various Interest Rate derivatives (including US Bonds); Agricultural (Corn, Soybeans, Soy Products, Wheat, Pork, Cattle, Butter, Milk); Index (Dow Jones Industrial Average); Metals (Gold, Silver), Index (NASDAQ, S&P, etc.)

IntercontinentalExchange (ICE Futures Europe) - formerly the International Petroleum Exchange trades energy including crude oil, heating oil, gas oil (diesel), refined petroleum products, electric power, coal, natural gas, and emissions

NYSE Euronext - which absorbed Euronext into which London International Financial Futures and Options Exchange or LIFFE (pronounced 'LIFE') was merged. (LIFFE had taken over London Commodities Exchange ("LCE") in 1996)- softs: grains and meats. Inactive market in Baltic Exchange shipping. Index futures include EURIBOR, FTSE 100, CAC 40, AEX index.

South African Futures Exchange - SAFEX

Sydney Futures Exchange

Tokyo Stock Exchange TSE (JGB Futures, TOPIX Futures)

Tokyo Commodity Exchange TOCOM

Tokyo Financial Exchange - TFX - (Euroyen Futures, OverNight CallRate Futures, SpotNext RepoRate Futures)

Osaka Securities Exchange OSE (Nikkei Futures, RNP Futures)

London Metal Exchange - metals: copper, aluminium, lead, zinc, nickel, tin and steel

IntercontinentalExchange (ICE Futures U.S.) - formerly New York Board of Trade - softs: cocoa, coffee, cotton, orange juice, sugar

New York Mercantile Exchange CME Group- energy and metals: crude oil, gasoline, heating oil, natural gas, coal, propane, gold, silver, platinum, copper, aluminum and palladium

Dubai Mercantile Exchange

Korea Exchange - KRX

Singapore Exchange - SGX - into which merged Singapore International Monetary Exchange (SIMEX)

ROFEX - Rosario (Argentina) Futures Exchange

NCDEX - National Commodity and Derivatives Exchange, India

CODES

Most Futures contracts codes are five characters. The first two characters identify the contract type, the third character identifies the month and the last two characters identify the year.
Third (month) futures contract codes are

January = F
February = G
March = H
April = J
May = K
June = M
July = N
August = Q
September = U
October = V
November = X
December = Z

Example: CLX14 is a Crude Oil (CL), November (X) 2014 (14) contract.

WHO TRADES FUTURES?

Futures traders are traditionally placed in one of two groups: hedgers, who have an interest in the underlying asset (which could include an intangible such as an index or interest rate) and are seeking to *hedge out* the risk of price changes; and speculators, who seek to make a profit by predicting market moves and opening a derivative contract related to the asset "on paper", while they have no practical use for or intent to actually take or make delivery of the underlying asset. In other words, the investor is seeking exposure to the asset in a long futures or the opposite effect via a short futures contract.

Hedgers

Hedgers typically include producers and consumers of a commodity or the owner of an asset or assets subject to certain influences such as an interest rate.

For example, in traditional commodity markets, farmers often sell futures contracts for the crops and livestock they produce to guarantee a certain price, making it easier for them to plan. Similarly, livestock producers often purchase futures to cover their feed costs, so that they can plan on a fixed cost for feed. In modern (financial) markets, "producers" of interest rate swaps or equity derivative products will use financial futures or equity index futures to reduce or remove the risk on the swap.

Those that buy or sell commodity futures need to be careful. If a company buys contracts hedging against price increases, but in fact the market price of the commodity is substantially lower at time of delivery, they could find themselves disastrously non-competitive (for example see: VeraSun Energy).

Speculators

Speculators typically fall into three categories: position traders, day traders, and swing traders (swing trading), though many hybrid types and unique styles exist. With many investors pouring into the futures markets in recent years controversy has risen about whether speculators are responsible for increased volatility in commodities like oil, and experts are divided on the matter.

An example that has both hedge and speculative notions involves a mutual fund or separately managed account whose investment objective is to track the performance of a stock index such as the S&P 500 stock index. The Portfolio manager often "equitizes" cash inflows in an easy and cost effective manner by investing in (opening long) S&P 500 stock index futures. This gains the portfolio exposure to the index which is consistent with the fund or account investment objective without having to buy an appropriate proportion of each of the individual 500 stocks just yet. This also preserves balanced diversification, maintains a higher degree of the percent of assets invested in the market and helps reduce tracking error in the performance of the fund/account. When it is economically feasible (an efficient amount of shares of every individual position within the fund or account can be purchased), the portfolio manager can close the contract and make purchases of each individual stock.

The social utility of futures markets is considered to be mainly in the transfer of risk, and increased liquidity between traders with different risk and time preferences, from a hedger to a speculator, for example.

OPTIONS ON FUTURES

In many cases, *options* are traded on futures, sometimes called simply "futures options". A put is the option to sell a futures contract, and a call is the option to buy a futures contract. For both, the option strike price is the specified futures price at which the future is traded if the option is exercised. Futures are often used since they are delta one instruments. Calls and options on futures may be priced similarly to those on traded assets by using an extension of the Black-Scholes formula, namely the Black–Scholes model for futures.

Investors can either take on the role of option seller/option writer or the option buyer. Option sellers are generally seen as taking on more risk because they are contractually obligated to take the opposite futures position if the options buyer exercises his or her right to the futures position specified in the option. The price of an option is determined by supply and demand principles and consists of the option premium, or the price paid to the option seller for offering the option and taking on risk.

FUTURES CONTRACT REGULATIONS

All futures transactions in the United States are regulated by the Commodity Futures Trading Commission (CFTC), an independent agency of the United States government. The Commission has the right to hand out fines and other punishments for an individual or company who breaks any rules. Although by law the commission regulates all transactions, each exchange can have its own rule, and under contract can fine companies for different things or extend the fine that the CFTC hands out.

The CFTC publishes weekly reports containing details of the open interest of market participants for each market-segment that has more than 20 participants. These reports are released every Friday (including data from the previous Tuesday) and contain data on open interest split by reportable and non-reportable open interest as well as commercial and non-commercial open interest. This type of report is referred to as the 'Commitments of Traders Report', COT-Report or simply COTR.

DEFINITION OF FUTURES CONTRACT

Following Björk we give a definition of a *futures contract*. We describe a futures contract with delivery of item J at the time T:

> There exists in the market a quoted price *F(t,T)*, which is known as the futures price at time t for delivery of J at time T.
> The price of entering a futures contract is equal to zero.
> During any time interval $[t, s]$, the holder receives the amount $F(s,T) - F(t,T)$. (this reflects instantaneous marking to market)
> At time *T*, the holder pays *F(T,T)* and is entitled to receive J. Note that *F(T,T)* should be the spot price of J at time T.

NONCONVERGENCE

Some exchanges tolerate 'nonconvergence', the failure of futures contracts and the value of the physical commodities they represent to reach the same value on 'contract settlement' day at the designated delivery points. An example of this is the CBOT (Chicago Board of Trade) Soft Red Winter wheat (SRW) futures. SRW futures have settled more than 20¢ apart on settlement day and as much as $1.00 difference between settlement days. Only a few participants holding CBOT SRW futures contracts are qualified by the CBOT to make or receive delivery of commodities to settle futures contracts. Therefore, it's impossible for almost any individual producer to 'hedge' efficiently when relying on the final settlement of a futures contract for SRW.

The trend is for the CBOT to continue to restrict those entities that can actually participate in settling commodities contracts to those that can ship or receive large quantities of railroad cars and multiple barges at a few selected sites. The Commodity Futures Trading Commission, which has oversight of the futures market in the United States, has made no comment as to why this trend is allowed to continue since economic theory and CBOT publications maintain that convergence of contracts with the price of the underlying commodity they represent is the basis of integrity for a futures market.

It follows that the function of price discovery, the ability of the markets to discern the appropriate value of a commodity reflecting current conditions, is degraded in relation to the discrepancy in price and the inability of producers to enforce contracts with the commodities they represent.

FUTURES VERSUS FORWARDS

While futures and forward contracts are both contracts to deliver an asset on a future date at a prearranged price, they are different in two main respects:

> Futures are **exchange-traded,** while forwards are traded **over-the-counter.**
>
> Thus futures are **standardized** and face an **exchange,** while forwards are **customized** and face a non-exchange **counterparty.**
>
> Futures are margined, while forwards are not.
>
> Thus futures have significantly less **credit risk,** and have different funding.

The Futures Industry Association (FIA) estimates that 6.97 billion futures contracts were traded in 2007, an increase of nearly 32% over the 2006 figure.

EXCHANGE VERSUS OTC

Futures are always traded on an exchange, whereas forwards always trade over-the-counter, or can simply be a signed contract between two parties.

Thus:

Futures are highly standardized, being exchange-traded, whereas forwards can be unique, being over-the-counter.
In the case of physical delivery, the forward contract specifies to whom to make the delivery. The counterparty for delivery on a futures contract is chosen by the clearing house.

MARGINING

Futures are margined daily to the daily spot price of a forward with the same agreed-upon delivery price and underlying asset (based on *mark to market*).

Forwards do not have a standard. They may transact only on the settlement date. More typical would be for the parties to agree to true up, for example, every quarter. The fact that forwards are not margined daily means that, due to movements in the price of the underlying asset, a large differential can build up between the forward's delivery price and the settlement price, and in any event, an unrealized gain (loss) can build up.

Again, this differs from futures which get 'trued-up' typically daily by a comparison of the market value of the future to the collateral securing the contract to keep it in line with the brokerage margin requirements. This true-ing up occurs by the "loss" party providing additional collateral; so if the buyer of the contract incurs a drop in value, the shortfall or variation margin would typically be shored up by the investor wiring or depositing additional cash in the brokerage account.

In a forward though, the spread in exchange rates is not trued up regularly but, rather, it builds up as unrealized gain (loss) depending on which side of the trade being discussed. This means that entire unrealized gain (loss) becomes realized at the time of delivery (or as what typically occurs, the time the contract is closed prior to expiration) - assuming the parties must transact at the underlying currency's spot price to facilitate receipt/delivery.

The result is that forwards have higher credit risk than futures, and that funding is charged differently.

In most cases involving institutional investors, the daily variation margin settlement guidelines for futures call for actual money movement only above some insignificant amount to avoid wiring back and forth small sums of cash. The threshold amount for daily futures variation margin for institutional investors is often $1,000.

The situation for forwards, however, where no daily true-up takes place in turn creates **credit risk** for forwards, but not so much for futures. Simply put, the risk of a forward contract is that the supplier will be unable to deliver the referenced asset, or that the buyer will be unable to pay for it on the delivery date or the date at which the opening party closes the contract.

The margining of futures eliminates much of this credit risk by forcing the holders to update daily to the price of an equivalent forward purchased that day. This means that there will usually be very little additional money due on the final day to settle the futures contract: only the final day's gain or loss, not the gain or loss over the life of the contract.

In addition, the daily futures-settlement failure risk is borne by an exchange, rather than an individual party, further limiting credit risk in futures.

Example: Consider a futures contract with a $100 price: Let's say that on day 50, a futures contract with a $100 delivery price (on the same underlying asset as the future) costs $88. On day 51, that futures contract costs $90. This means that the "mark-to-market" calculation would requires the holder of one side of the future to pay $2 on day 51 to track the changes of the forward price ("post $2 of margin"). This money goes, via margin accounts, to the holder of the other side of the future. That is, the loss party wires cash to the other party.

A forward-holder, however, may pay nothing until settlement on the final day, potentially building up a large balance; this may be reflected in the mark by an allowance for credit risk. So, except for tiny effects of convexity bias (due to earning or paying interest on margin), futures and forwards with equal delivery prices result in the same total loss or gain, but holders of futures experience that loss/gain in daily increments which track the forward's daily price changes, while the forward's spot price converges to the settlement price. Thus, while under mark to market accounting, for both

> assets the gain or loss accrues over the holding period; for a futures this gain or loss is realized daily, while for a forward contract the gain or loss remains unrealized until expiry.

Note that, due to the path dependence of funding, a futures contract is *not,* strictly speaking, a European-style derivative: the total gain or loss of the trade depends not only on the value of the underlying asset at expiry, but also on the path of prices on the way. This difference is generally quite small though.

With an exchange-traded future, the clearing house interposes itself on every trade. Thus there is no risk of counterparty default. The only risk is that the clearing house defaults (e.g. become bankrupt), which is considered very unlikely

TRADED COMMODITIES

AGRICULTURAL (GRAINS, AND FOOD AND FIBER)

Commodity	Main Exchange	Contract Size	Trading Symbol
Corn	CBOT	5000 bu	C/ZC (Electronic)
Corn	EURONEXT	50 tons	EMA
Oats	CBOT	5000 bu	O/ZO (Electronic)
Rough Rice	CBOT	2000 cwt	RR
Soybeans	CBOT	5000 bu	S/ZS (Electronic)
Rapeseed	EURONEXT	50 tons	ECO
Soybean Meal	CBOT	100 short tons	SM/ZM (Electronic)
Soybean Oil	CBOT	60,000 lb	BO/ZB (Electronic)
Wheat	CBOT	5000 bu	W/ZW (Electronic)
Milk	Chicago Mercantile Exchange	200,000 lbs	DC
Cocoa	ICE	10 tons	CC
Coffee C	ICE	37,500 lb	KC
Cotton No.2	ICE	50,000 lb	CT
Sugar No.11	ICE	112,000 lb	SB
Sugar No.14	ICE	112,000 lb	SE
Frozen Concentrated Orange Juice	ICE	15,000 lbs	FCOJ-A

LIVESTOCK AND MEAT

Commodity	Contract Size	Currency	Main Exchange	Trading Symbol
Lean Hogs	40,000 lb (20 tons)	USD ($)	Chicago Mercantile Exchange	LH
Frozen Pork Bellies	40,000 lb (20 tons)	USD ($)	Chicago Mercantile Exchange	PB
Live Cattle	40,000 lb (20 tons)	USD ($)	Chicago Mercantile Exchange	LC
Feeder Cattle	50,000 lb (25 tons)	USD ($)	Chicago Mercantile Exchange	FC

ENERGY

Commodity	Main Exchange	Contract Size	Trading Symbol
WTI Crude Oil	NYMEX, ICE	1000 bbl (42,000 U.S. gal)	CL (NYMEX), WTI (ICE)
Brent Crude	ICE	1000 bbl (42,000 U.S. gal)	B
Ethanol	CBOT	29,000 U.S. gal	AC (Open Auction) ZE (Electronic)
Natural gas	NYMEX	10,000 mmBTU	NG
Heating Oil	NYMEX	1000 bbl (42,000 U.S. gal)	HO
Gulf Coast Gasoline	NYMEX	1000 bbl (42,000 U.S. gal)	LR
RBOB Gasoline (reformulated gasoline blendstock for oxygen blending)	NYMEX	1000 bbl (42,000 U.S. gal)	RB
Propane	NYMEX	1000 bbl (42,000 U.S. gal)	PN
Purified Terephthalic Acid (PTA)	ZCE	5 Tons	TA

PRECIOUS METALS

Commodity	Unit	Currency	Main Exchange
Gold	troy ounce	USD ($)	COMEX
Platinum	troy ounce	USD ($)	COMEX
Palladium	troy ounce	USD ($)	COMEX
Silver	troy ounce	USD ($)	COMEX

INDUSTRIAL METALS

Commodity	Unit	Currency	Main Exchange
Copper	Metric Ton	USD ($)	London Metal Exchange, New York
Lead	Metric Ton	USD ($)	London Metal Exchange
Zinc	Metric Ton	USD ($)	London Metal Exchange
Tin	Metric Ton	USD ($)	London Metal Exchange
Aluminium	Metric Ton	USD ($)	London Metal Exchange, New York
Aluminium alloy	Metric Ton	USD ($)	London Metal Exchange
Nickel	Metric Ton	USD ($)	London Metal Exchange
Cobalt	Metric Ton	USD ($)	London Metal Exchange
Molybdenum	Metric Ton	USD ($)	London Metal Exchange.,
Recycled steel	Metric Ton	USD ($)	Rotterdam

OTHER

Commodity	Unit	Currency	Bourse
Rubber	1 kg	US cents (¢)	*Singapore Commodity Exchange
Palm Oil	1000 kg	Malaysian Ringgit (RM)	Bursa Malaysia
Wool	1 kg	AUD ($)	ASX
Polypropylene	1000 kg	USD ($)	London Metal Exchange
Linear Low Density Polyethylene (LL)	1000 kg	USD ($)	London Metal Exchange

In 2007, steel began being traded as a commodity in the London Metal Exchange.

ENVIRONMENTAL COMMODITIES

In the last decade, a number of environmental commodities have been created. These include carbon offsets, Renewable Energy Certificates, and white certificates (energy efficiency credits).
Currently there are several exchanges trading in UNFCCC related carbon credits:

European Climate Exchange
NASDAQ OMX Commodities Europe
PowerNext
Commodity Exchange Bratislava
European Energy Exchange

COMMODITY EXCHANGES AND REGULATORS

Chicago Board of Trade
Chicago Mercantile Exchange
Commodity Futures Trading Commission
London International Financial Futures and Options Exchange
NASDAQ OMX Commodities
National Futures Association
New York Mercantile Exchange
Kansas City Board of Trade
New York Board of Trade

COMMODITY MARKET - STRATEGIC INFORMATION

Commodity market refers to physical or virtual transactions of buying and selling involving raw or primary commodities. A soft commodity generally refers to commodities harvested as products like wheat, coffee, cocoa, sugar, corn, wheat, soybean, and fruit traded in the **commodity market**. Hard commodities usually refer to commodities that are extracted such as (gold, rubber, oil). While commodities may be grouped for regulation purposes etc., in large classes such as energy, agricultural including livestock, precious metals, industrial metals, other commodity markets, these are broken down into about a hundred primary commodities (soybean oil, recycled steel). Investors access about 50 major commodity markets worldwide uses growing numbers of exchanges with virtual transactions increasingly replacing physical trades.

A financial derivative in the commodity market is a financial instrument whose value is derived from a commodity as item or underlier. Derivatives trading employs various techniques to increase profit and manage risk. Derivatives in the commodity market are assets that are either exchange-traded derivatives or over-the-counter (OTC) derivatives. With the increased diversity and complexity of commodities derivatives, new international institutions have emerged, such as clearing houses some with Central Counterparty Clearing, which provide clearing and settlement services on a futures exchange, as well as off-exchange in the OTC market.

Derivatives in the form of the futures contracts are the oldest and most direct way of investing in commodities. Commodity market derivatives are securitized by physical assets or commodities. Commodity markets can include direct physical trading and derivatives trading in the form of spot prices, forwards, futures, and options on futures. Farmers have used a simple form of derivative trading in the commodity market for centuries for price risk management (p. 6). In the basic agricultural futures contracts a farmer (the future seller) agrees with a counterparty, a future buyer to sell a set number of units of corn to a broker for a fixed future date at an agreed-upon quality and price and point of delivery. If the price of corn drops the farmer is protected from losses thereby reducing risk. If the price rises the farmer loses potential profit. Derivatives trading employs various techniques to increase profit and manage risk through hedging.

It is important to understand the relationship between simple commodity money and the more complex financial instruments of derivative trading, such as futures contracts, Swaps (1970s-), Exchange-traded

Commodities (ETC) (2003-), forward contracts. Futures are traded on regulated commodities exchanges. Over-the-counter (OTC) contracts in the commodity market are "privately negotiated bilateral contracts entered into between the contracting parties directly".

Although investors assume that commodity market derivatives are securitized by the physical assets or commodities, gold for example, the actual exposure to the physical commodity of gold has changed significantly since the emergence of financial instruments such as exchange-traded funds (ETFs) in 2003. ETFs are based on electronic gold which does not entail the actual ownership of physical bullion, with its added costs of insurance and storage in bullion banks, such as the London bullion market. According to the World Gold Council, ETFs allow investors to be exposed to the gold market without the risk of price volatility associated with gold as a physical commodity.

HISTORY

Commodity money and commodity markets in a crude early form are believed to have originated in Sumer between 4500 BC and 4000 BC. Sumerians first used clay tokens sealed in a clay vessel, then clay writing tablets to represent the amount of commodities—for example, the number of goats promised to be delivered. These promises of time and date of delivery resemble futures contract.

Historically, dating from ancient Sumerian use of sheep or goats, other peoples using pigs, rare seashells, or other items as commodity money, people have sought ways to standardize and trade contracts in the delivery of such items, to render trade itself more smooth and predictable.Complex gold and silver markets evolved in the classical civilizations.

Since the late 10th century the commodity market as mechanism for the allocation of goods, labor, land, and capital gained ground in many parts of Europe. In the late 11th and the late 13th century, English urbanization, regional specialization, expanded and improved infrastructure, the increased use of coinage and the proliferation of markets and fairs were evidence and the result of the progress of commercialization. The commercialization of medieval society and the medieval commodity markets were shaped by a number of institutions, social and political relations and the introduction of new technologies. For example, in 1466 reliable scales were installed in the villages Sloten and Osdorp so villagers no longer had to travel to Haarlem or Amsterdam to weigh their locally produced cheese and butter. Modern commodity markets have their roots in the trading of agricultural products.

In 19th-century United States, wheat, corn, cattle, and pigs were widely traded using standard instruments.

Since 1936 futures and options on soybeans have been traded on the Chicago Board of Trade (CBOT). Other food commodities were added to the Commodity Exchange Act and traded through CBOT in the 1930s and 1940s, expanding the list from grains to include rice, mill feeds, butter, eggs, Irish potatoes and soybeans. For a commodity market to be established, there must be very broad consensus on the variations in the product that make it acceptable for one purpose or another.

The economic impact of the development of commodity markets is hard to overestimate. Through the 19th century "the exchanges became effective spokesmen for, and innovators of, improvements in transportation, warehousing, and financing, which paved the way to expanded interstate and international trade."

Classical civilizations built complex global markets trading gold or silver for spices, cloth, wood and weapons, most of which had standards of quality and timeliness.

Considering the many hazards of climate, piracy, theft and abuse of military fiat by rulers of kingdoms along the trade routes, it was a major focus of these civilizations to keep markets open and trading in these scarce commodities.

Reputation and clearing became central concerns, and the states which could handle them most effectively became very powerful empires, trusted by many peoples to manage and mediate trade and commerce.

COMMODITY PRICE INDEX

In 1934 the Bureau of Labor Statistics began the computation of a daily Commodity price index which was available to the public as of 1940. By 1952 the Bureau of Labor Statistics issued a Spot Market Price Index which measured the price movements of "22 sensitive basic commodities whose markets are presumed to be among the first to be influenced by changes in economic conditions. As such, it serves as one early indication of impending changes in business activity."

A commodity index fund is a fund whose assets are invested in financial instruments based on or linked to a commodity index. In just about every case the index is in fact a Commodity Futures Index. The first such index was the CRB ("Commodity Research Bureau") Index, which began in 1958. Due to its construction it was not useful as an investment index. The first practically investable commodity futures index was the Goldman Sachs Commodity Index, created in 1991. and known as the "GSCI".

The next was the Dow Jones AIG Commodity Index. It differed from the GSCI primarily in the weights allocated to each commodity. The DJ AIG had mechanisms to periodically limit the weight of any one commodity and to remove commodities whose weights became too small. After AIG's financial problems in 2008 the Index rights were sold to UBS and it is now known as the DJUBS index. Other commodity indices include the Reuters / CRB index (which is the old CRB Index re-structured in 2005) and the Rogers Index.

CASH COMMODITY

Cash commodities or actuals refer to the actual physical commodity—e.g., wheat, corn, soybeans, crude oil, gold, silver—that someone is buying/selling/trading as distinguished from derivatives.

CALL OPTIONS

In a call option counterparties enter into a financial contract option where the buyer purchases the right but not the obligation to buy an agreed quantity of a particular commodity or financial instrument (the underlying) from the seller of the option at a certain time (the expiration date) for a certain price (the strike price). The seller (or "writer") is obligated to sell the commodity or financial instrument should the buyer so decide. The buyer pays a fee (called a premium) for this right.

ELECTRONIC COMMODITIES TRADING

In traditional stock market exchanges such as the New York Stock Exchange (NYSE), most trading activity took place in the trading pits in face-to-face interactions between brokers and dealers in open outcry trading. One of the technological advances that accelerated the transformation to electronics was the initiation in 1992 of the Financial Information eXchange (FIX) protocol which allowed for an international real-time exchange of information regarding market transactions.

United States regulators, the U.S. Securities and Exchange Commission ordered all U.S. stock markets to convert from the fractional system to decimal system by April 2001. Metrification, conversion from the imperial system of measurement to the metrical, increased throughout the 20th century. Eventually FIX-compliant interface was adopted globally by commodity exchanges through the FIX Protocol. In 2001 the Chicago Board of Trade and the Chicago Mercantile Exchange (since merged into the CME group, the world's largest futures exchange company) that handle commodities futures as opposed to stocks, launched their FIX-compliant interface.

By 2011 electronic trading had advanced from dealers using their computers to make transactions to computer determined trading with computers buying and selling without human dealer intermediation through the alternative trading system (ATS). By 2011 high frequency traders (HFT) algorithmic trading, had already almost phased out "dinosaur floor-traders".

INCREASED COMPLEXITY OF FINANCIAL INSTRUMENTS AND INTERCONNECTEDNESS OF GLOBAL MARKET

The robust growth of emerging market economies (EMEs), (like Brazil, Russia, India, and China) in the 1990s, "propelled commodity markets into a supercycle". The size and diversity of commodity markets expanded internationally along with the global middle class the acceleration of urbanization.

In 2012, as emerging-market economies slowed down, commodity prices declined. Commodity prices are however, about 25 percent above their historical averages in real terms. Since 2005 energy and metals' real prices have been well above their long-term averages. In 2012 real food prices were at their highest level since 1982.

The price of gold bullion began to fall dramatically on Friday, April 12, 2013 and analysts frantically sought explanations. Rumors spread that the European Central Bank (ECB) would force Cyprus to sell its reserves of gold bullion in response to its financial crisis. Major banks such as Goldman Sachs began immediately to short gold bullion. Investors scrambled to liquidate their exchange-traded funds (ETFs) and margin call selling accelerated. George Gero, precious metals commodities expert at the Royal Bank of Canada (RBC) Wealth Management section reported that he has not seen selling of gold bullion as panicked as this in his forty years in commodity markets.

The earliest commodity exchange-traded fund (ETFs), such as SPDR Gold Shares NYSE Arca: GLD and iShares Silver Trust NYSE Arca: SLV, actually owned the physical commodity (e.g., gold and silver bars). Similar to these are NYSE Arca: PALL (palladium) and NYSE Arca: PPLT (platinum). However, most Exchange Traded Commodities (ETCs) implement a futures trading strategy, which may produce quite different results from owning the commodity.

With global commodity prices falling, including crude oil at $100 a barrel, Russian Prime Minister Dmitry Medvedev warned that Russia could sink into recession. He argued that "We live in a dynamic, fast-developing world. It is so global and so complex that we sometimes cannot keep up with the changes". Analysts have claimed that Russia's economy is overly dependent on commodities.

CONTRACTS IN THE COMMODITY MARKET

A Spot contract is an agreement where delivery and payment either takes place immediately, or with a minimum lag between the trade and delivery due to technical constraints. Physical trading normally involves visual inspection of the commodity or a sample of the commodity, and is carried out in physical markets such as a farmers market. Derivatives markets, on the other hand, require the existence of agreed standards so that trades can be made without visual inspection.

STANDARDIZATION

U.S. soybean futures, for example, are of standard grade if they are "GMO or a mixture of GMO and Non-GMO No. 2 yellow soybeans of Indiana, Ohio and Michigan origin produced in the U.S.A. (Non-screened, stored in silo)", and of deliverable grade if they are "GMO or a mixture of GMO and Non-GMO No. 2 yellow soybeans of Iowa, Illinois and Wisconsin origin produced in the U.S.A. (Non-screened, stored in silo)". Note the distinction between states, and the need to clearly mention their status as GMO (Genetically Modified Organism) which makes them unacceptable to most organic food buyers.

Similar specifications apply for cotton, orange juice, cocoa, sugar, wheat, corn, barley, pork bellies, milk, feedstuffs, fruits, vegetables, other grains, other beans, hay, other livestock, meats, poultry, eggs, or any other commodity which is so traded.

Standardization has also occurred technologically, as the use of the FIX Protocol by commodities exchanges has allowed trade messages to be sent, received and processed in the same format as stocks or equities. This process began in 2001 when the CME Group Inc. (Chicago Mercantile Exchange), the world's largest futures exchange company, launched a FIX-compliant interface and has now been adopted by commodity exchanges around the world.

DERIVATIVES

Derivatives are financial instruments used as risk management tools and/or as a means to increase profits. Derivatives have evolved from simple future contracts into highly complex financial instruments. Futures contracts, Swaps (1970s-), Exchange-traded Commodities (ETC) (2003-), forward contracts, etc. are examples of derivatives. They can be traded through formal exchanges or through Over-the-counter (OTC). Commodity market derivatives unlike credit default derivatives for example, are securitized by the physical assets or commodities.

FORWARD CONTRACTS

A forward contract is an agreement between two parties to exchange at some fixed future date a given quantity of a commodity for a price defined today. The fixed price today is known as the forward price. Early on these forward contracts were used as a way of getting products from producer to the consumer. These typically only applied to food and agricultural products.

FUTURES CONTRACT

Futures contracts for agricultural commodities are the oldest, having been traded in the United States alone for more than 150 years

Hedging, a common practice of farming cooperatives, insures against a poor harvest by purchasing futures contracts in the same commodity. If the cooperative has significantly less of its product to sell due to weather or insects, it makes up for that loss with a profit on the markets, since the overall supply of the crop is short everywhere that suffered the same conditions.

A futures contract has the same general features as a forward contract but is standardized and transacted through a futures exchange. Although more complex today, early forward contracts for example, were used for rice in seventeenth century Japan. Modern forward, or futures agreements, began in Chicago in the 1840s, with the appearance of the railroads. Chicago, being centrally located, emerged as the hub between Midwestern farmers and producers and the east coast consumer population centers.

In essence, a futures contract is a standardized forward contract in which the buyer and the seller accept the terms in regards to product, grade, quantity and location and are only free to negotiate the price.

SWAPS

Since the 1970 trading in futures contracts expanded rapidly beyond traditional physical and agricultural commodities into a vast array of financial instruments. In the 1970s Swaps were introduced and their growth in value exploded.

EXCHANGE-TRADED COMMODITIES (ETCS)

Exchange Traded Commodities (ETC) were introduced as a financial instrument in 2003. At first only professional institutional investors had access but online exchanges have made some ETC markets open to almost anyone. ETCs were introduced partly in response to the tight supply of commodities in 2000, combined with record low inventories and increasing demand from emerging markets such as China and India. Exchange Traded Commodities transformed the commodity market.

Gold has gone from being a currency to an asset for thousands of years to becoming the first commodity to become securitised through an Exchange Traded Funds (ETF) in the early 1990s but it was not available for trade until 2003.

Prior to the introduction of Exchange Traded Commodities, by the 1990s Exchange Traded Funds (ETF) pioneered by Barclays Global Investors (BGI) (now owned by BlackRock) revolutionized the mutual funds industry. By the end of December 2009 Barclays Global Investors (BGI) assets hit an all-time high of $1tln ($1,032bln).

Commodity ETFs (ETCs or CETFs) invest in commodities, such as precious metals and futures. Among the first commodity ETFs were gold exchange-traded funds, which have been offered in a number of countries. The idea of a Gold ETF was first officially conceptualised by Benchmark Asset Management Company Private Ltd in India when they filed a proposal with the SEBI in May 2002. The first gold exchange-traded fund was Gold Bullion Securities launched on the ASX in 2003, and the first silver exchange-traded fund was iShares Silver Trust launched on the NYSE in 2006. As of November 2010 a commodity ETF, namely SPDR Gold Shares, was the second-largest ETF by market capitalization.

However, generally commodity ETFs are index funds tracking non-security indices. Because they do not invest in securities, commodity ETFs are not regulated as investment companies under the Investment Company Act of 1940 in the United States, although their public offering is subject to SEC review and they need an SEC no-action letter under the Securities Exchange Act of 1934. They may, however, be subject to regulation by the Commodity Futures Trading Commission.

Exchange-traded commodities (ETCs) are investment vehicles (asset backed bonds, fully collateralised) that track the performance of an underlying commodity index including total return indices based on a single commodity. Similar to ETFs and traded and settled exactly like normal shares on their own dedicated segment, ETCs have market maker support with guaranteed liquidity, enabling investors to gain exposure to commodities, on-exchange, during market hours.

The earliest commodity ETFs, such as SPDR Gold Shares NYSE Arca: GLD and iShares Silver Trust NYSE Arca: SLV, actually owned the physical commodity (e.g., gold and silver bars). Similar to these are NYSE Arca: PALL (palladium) and NYSE Arca: PPLT (platinum). However, most ETCs implement a futures trading strategy, which may produce quite different results from owning the commodity.

Commodity ETFs trade provide exposure to an ever-increasing range of commodities and commodity indices, including energy, metals, softs and agriculture. In the case of many commodity funds, oil for example, they simply roll so-called front-month futures contracts from month to month. This does give exposure to the commodity, but subjects the investor to risks involved in different prices along the *term structure*, such as a high cost to roll. Exchange traded commodities have seen an upturn in the volume of trading since the start of the decade. This was largely a result of the growing attraction of commodities as an asset class and a proliferation of investment options which has made it easier to access this market.

Trading on exchanges in China and India has gained in importance in recent years due to their emergence as significant commodities consumers and producers. China accounted for more than 60% of exchange-traded commodities in 2009, up on its 40% share in the previous year.

The global volume of commodities contracts traded on exchanges increased by a fifth in 2010, and a half since 2008, to around 2.5 billion million contracts.

OVER-THE-COUNTER (OCD) COMMODITIES DERIVATIVES

Over-the-counter OCD) commodities derivatives trading was originally done directly between two parties, without any supervision of an exchange. It is contrasted with exchange trading, which occurs via these facilities. In an OTC trade, the price is not necessarily made public information. The OTC market was not as limiting as the derivatives traded through organized market exchange. OTC are higher risk but may also lead to higher profits. The OTC derivative market is significant in the commodities asset class.

From 2007 to the end of 2010, global physical exports of commodities fell by 2%, while the outstanding value of OTC over the counter (OTC) commodities derivatives declined by two-thirds as investors reduced risk following a five-fold increase in value outstanding in the previous three years.

under management more than doubled between 2008 and 2010 to nearly $380 billion. Inflows into the sector totaled over $60 billion in 2010, the second highest year on record, down from the record $72bn allocated to commodities funds in the previous year. The bulk of funds went into precious metals and energy products. The growth in prices of many commodities in 2010 contributed to the increase in the value of commodities funds under management.

COMMODITIES EXCHANGE

A commodities exchange is an exchange where various commodities and derivatives products are traded. Most commodity markets across the world trade in agricultural products and other raw materials (like wheat, barley, sugar, maize, cotton, cocoa, coffee, milk products, pork bellies, oil, metals, etc.) and contracts based on them. These contracts can include spot prices, forwards, futures and options on futures. Other sophisticated products may include interest rates, environmental instruments, swaps, or ocean freight contracts.

Commodities exchanges usually trade futures contracts on commodities, such as trading contracts to receive something, say corn, in a certain month. A farmer raising corn can sell a future contract on his corn, which will not be harvested for several months, and guarantee the price he will be paid when he delivers; a breakfast cereal producer buys the contract now and guarantees the price will not go up when it is delivered. This protects the farmer from price drops and the buyer from price rises.

Speculators and investors also buy and sell the futures contracts in attempt to make a profit and provide liquidity to the system. However, due to the financial leverage provided to traders by the exchange, commodity futures traders face a substantial risk.

TOP TRADED COMMODITIES (EXPORTS)

Rank	Commodity	Value in US$('000)	Date of information
1	Mineral fuels, oils, distillation products, etc.	$2,183,079,941	2012
2	Electrical, electronic equipment	$1,833,534,414	2012
3	Machinery, nuclear reactors, boilers, etc.	$1,763,371,813	2012
4	Vehicles other than railway, tramway	$1,076,830,856	2012
5	Plastics and articles thereof	$470,226,676	2012
6	Optical, photo, technical, medical, etc. apparatus	$465,101,524	2012
7	Pharmaceutical products	$443,596,577	2012
8	Iron and steel	$379,113,147	2012
9	Organic chemicals	$377,462,088	2012
10	Pearls, precious stones, metals, coins, etc.	$348,155,369	2012

Source: International Trade Centre

Building on the infrastructure and credit and settlement networks established for food and precious metals, many such markets have proliferated drastically in the late 20th century.

ENERGY COMMODITY MARKET

According to this List of traded commodities energy commodities include but are not limited to crude oil particularly West Texas Intermediate WTI crude oil and Brent crude oil, natural gas, heating oil, ethanol and Purified Terephthalic Acid.

FUEL HEDGING

Fuel Hedging is a contractual tool some large fuel consuming companies, such as airlines, use to reduce their exposure to volatile and potentially rising fuel costs. A fuel hedge contract allows a large fuel consuming company to establish a fixed or capped cost, via a commodity swap or option. Large fuel consuming companies enter into hedging contracts to mitigate their exposure to future fuel prices that may be higher than current prices and/or to establish a known fuel cost for budgeting purposes. If a large fuel consuming company buys a fuel swap and the price of fuel declines, the company will effectively be forced to pay an above-market rate for fuel. If a large fuel consuming company buys a fuel call option and the price of fuel increases, the company will receive a return on the option that offsets their actual cost of fuel. If a large fuel consuming company buys a fuel call option, which requires an upfront premium cost, much like insurance, and the price of fuel decreases, the company will not receive a return on the option but they will benefit from buying fuel at the then lower cost.

The cost of fuel hedging depends on the predicted future price of fuel. Airlines may place hedges either based on future prices of jet fuel or on future prices of crude oil. Because crude oil is the source of jet fuel, the prices of crude oil and jet fuel are normally correlated. However, other factors, such as difficulties regarding refinery capacity, may cause unusual divergence in the trends of crude oil and jet fuel.

A company that does not hedge its fuel costs generally believes one, if not both, of the following: 1. The company has the ability to pass on any and all increases in fuel prices to their customers, without a negative impact on their profit margins. 2. The company is confident that fuel prices are going to fall and is comfortable paying a higher price for fuel if, in fact, their analysis proves to be incorrect.

Typically, airlines will hedge only a certain portion of their fuel requirements for a certain period. Often, contracts for portions of an airline's jet fuel needs will overlap, with different levels of hedging expiring over time.

During the 2009-2010 period, the studies for the airline industry have shown the average hedging ratio to be 64%. Especially during the peak stress periods, the ratio tends to increase.

Southwest Airlines has tended to hedge a greater portion of its fuel needs than other major U.S. domestic carriers. Southwest's aggressive fuel hedging has helped the airline avoid some of the pain of the recent airline industry downturn resulting from high fuel costs. Between 1999 and 2008, Southwest saved approximately $3.5 billion through fuel hedging

CRUDE OIL

For many years West Texas Intermediate (WTI) crude oil, a light, sweet crude oil, was the world's most-traded commodity. West Texas Intermediate is a grade of crude oil used as a benchmark in oil pricing. It is the underlying commodity of Chicago Mercantile Exchange's oil futures contracts. The price of WTI is often referenced in news reports on oil prices, alongside the price of Brent crude from the North Sea. WTI is lighter and sweeter than Brent, and considerably lighter and sweeter than Dubai or Oman.

From April through October 2012 Brent crude oil futures contracts exceeded those for WTI, the longest streak since at least 1995.

Crude oil can be light can be heavy Oil was the first form of energy to be so widely traded, and the fluctuations in the oil markets are of particular political interest. Some commodity market speculation is directly related to the stability of certain states, e.g., during the Persian Gulf War, speculation on the survival of the regime of Saddam Hussein in Iraq. Similar political stability concerns have from time to time have driven the price of oil. The oil market is an exception. Most markets are not so tied to the politics of volatile regions - even natural gas tends to be more stable, as it is not traded across oceans by tanker as extensively.

Traded commodities include crude oils such as West Texas Intermediate WTI crude oil traded in units of 1.000 bbl (42,000 U.S. gal through NYMEX under the trading symbol CL and through IntercontinentalExchange (ICE) under the trading symbol WTI. Brent crude oil is traded in units of 1,000 bbl (42,000 U.S. gal through IntercontinentalExchange (ICE) under the trading symbol B. Gulf Coast Gasoline is traded through NYMEX in units of 1,000 bbl (42,000 U.S. gal) with the trading symbol of LR. RBOB Gasoline (reformulated gasoline blendstock for oxygen blending) is traded through NYMEX in units of 1000 bbl

(42,000 U.S. gal) with the trading symbol of RB. Propane is traded through NYMEX, a subsidiary of IntercontinentalExchange since early 2013, in units of 1000 bbl (42,000 U.S. gal) with the trading symbol of PN.

Natural gas

Natural gas is traded through NYMEX a subsidiary of IntercontinentalExchange (ICE) in units of 10,000 mmBTU with the trading symbol of NG. Heating Oil is traded through NYMEX, a subsidiary of IntercontinentalExchange, in units of 1,000 bbl (42,000 U.S. gal) with the trading symbol of HO.

Others

Purified Terephthalic Acid (PTA) is traded through ZCE in units of 5 tons with the trading symbol of TA. Ethanol is traded at CBOT in units of 29,000 U.S. gal AC (Open Auction) ZE (Electronic)

METALS

Precious metals

Precious metals currently traded on the commodity market include but are not limited to gold, platinum, palladium and silver which are sold by the troy ounce. One of the main exchanges for these precious metals is COMEX.

According to the World Gold Council, investments in gold are the primary driver of growth in the industry. Gold is easily authenticated and long lasting. Gold has price volatility because it is affected by large flows of speculative money.

Industrial metals

According to this List of traded commodities industrial metals currently sold on the commodity market include but are not limited to copper, aluminium, which are sold by the metric ton through the London Metal Exchange and New York Metal Exchange. The London Metal Exchange also trades in lead, tin, aluminium alloy, nickel, cobalt, molybdenum which is sold by the metric ton. Rotterdam Metal exchange trades recycled steel by the metric ton. In 2007, steel began being traded as a commodity in the London Metal Exchange.

AGRICULTURAL COMMODITIES

See also Agricultural commodities and price hedging Agricultural commodities, the staples of everyday life were the earliest to be traded on forward and future markets. Futures contracts for agricultural commodities have been traded in the U.S. for more than 150 years and in the United States were under Federal regulation since the 1920s. Although agricultural commodities include grains, food and fiber as well as livestock and meat, various regulatory bodies define agricultural products. In July 21, 2010, United States Congress passed the Dodd–Frank Wall Street Reform and Consumer Protection Act in which changes were made to the definition of agricultural commodity in regards to market regulations.

The general operational definition used by Dodd-Frank Wall Street Reform includes "[all other commodities that are, or once were, or are derived from, living organisms, including plant, animal and aquatic life, which are generally fungible, within their respective classes, and are used primarily for human food, shelter, animal feed, or natural fiber." Three other categories were explained and listed.

In February 2013 Cornell Law School defined agricultural products as including lumber, soybeans, oilseeds, livestock (live cattle and hogs), dairy products. Agricultural commodity can include lumber (timber and forests), grains excluding stored grain (wheat, oats, barley, rye, grain sorghum, cotton, flax, forage, tame hay, native grass), vegetables (potatoes, tomatoes, sweet corn, dry beans, dry peas, freezing and canning peas), fruit (citrus such as oranges, apples, grapes) corn, tobacco, rice, peanuts, sugar beets, sugar cane, sunflowers, raisins, nursery crops, nuts, soybean complex, aquacultural fish farm species such as finfish, mollusk, crustacean, aquatic invertebrate, amphibian, reptile, or plant life cultivated in aquatic plant farms.

In 1900 corn acreage was double that of wheat in the United States. But from the 1930s through the 1970s soybean acreage, the miracle bean, surpassed that of corn. Early in the 1970s grain and soybean prices, which had been relatively stable, "soared to levels that were unimaginable at the time." There were a number of factors affecting prices including the "surge in crude oil prices caused by the Arab Oil Embargo in October 1973 (US inflation reached 11% in 1975)."

DIAMONDS

By 2012 diamond was the last uncommoditized commodity. For a number of reasons institutional investors were repelled by the bad image of "blood diamonds", the monopoly on the diamond market and the lack of uniform standards for diamond pricing.

However this is changing and in 2012 the Securities and Exchange Commission (SEC) reviewed a proposal to create the "first diamond-backed exchange-traded fund" which would trade on-line to anyone in units of one-carat diamonds with a storage vault and delivery point in Antwerp, Belgium home of the Antwerp Diamond Bourse. The exchange fund was backed by a company based in New York called IndexIQ. IndexIQ introduced 14 exchange-traded funds to market since 2008.

According to Citigroup analysts, the annual production of polished diamonds is about $18 billion. Like gold, diamonds are easily authenticated and long lasting. Diamond prices have been more stable as De Beers, the global diamond giant once held almost 90 per cent (by 2013 they held 40 per cent) of the market share of production. Investment professionals capable of large flows of speculative money and therefore price destabilization, would typically avoid monopolies that can control market price.

OTHER COMMODITY MARKETS

According to this List of traded commodities rubber is traded on the Singapore Commodity Exchange in units of 1 kg priced in U.S. cents. Palm oil is traded on the Malaysian Ringgit (RM), Bursa Malaysia in units of 1 kg priced in U.S. cents. Wool is traded on the AUD in units of 1 kg. Polypropylene is traded on the London Metal Exchange in units of 1,000 kg priced in $USD. Linear Low Density Polyethylene (LL) is traded on the London Metal Exchange in units of 1000 kg priced in $USD.

COMMODITIES EXCHANGES

Largest commodities exchanges

Exchange	Country	Volume per month $M
CME Group	USA	19
Tokyo Commodity Exchange	Japan	-
NYSE Euronext	USA	-
Dalian Commodity Exchange	China	-
Multi Commodity Exchange	India	-
Intercontinental Exchange	USA, Canada, China, UK	-
Africa Mercantile Exchange	Kenya, Africa	-
Uzbek Commodity Exchange	Tashkent, Uzbekistan	-

REGULATORY BODIES AND POLICIES

UNITED STATES

In the United States, the principal regulator of commodity and futures markets is the Commodity Futures Trading Commission but it is the National Futures Association that enforces rules and regulations put forth by the CFTC. The National Futures Trading Association, formed in 1976, is the futures industry's self-regulatory organization. The NFA's first regulatory operations began in 1982 and falls under the Commodity Exchange Act of the Commodity Futures Trading Commission Act.

The 2010 Dodd-Frank Wall Street Reform and Consumer Protection Act, to reform the U.S. financial market regulations, was put in place in response to the 2008 food and financial crises. The Dodd-Frank called for "strong measures to limit speculation in agricultural commodities" calling upon the Commodity Futures Trading Commission (CFTC) to further limit positions and to regulate over-the-counter trades.

EUROPEAN UNION

Markets in Financial Instruments Directive (MiFID), the cornerstone of the European Commission's Financial Services Action Plan that regulate operations of the EU financial service markets, was reviewed in 2012 by the European Parliament and the Economic and Financial Affairs Council (ECOFIN). The European Parliament adopted a revised version of Mifid II on October 26, 2012 which include "provisions for position limits on commodity derivatives", aimed at "preventing market abuse" and supporting "orderly pricing and settlement conditions".

European Securities and Markets Authority (Esma), based in Paris and formed in 2011, is a "EU-wide financial markets watchdog". European Securities and Markets Authority will set the position limits on commodity derivatives as described in of the 2012 Markets in Financial Instruments Directive II (MifidII).

The European Parliament (EP) voted in favour of stronger regulation of commodity derivative markets in September 2012 to "end abusive speculation in commodity markets" that were "driving global food prices increases and price volatility". In July 2012 "food prices globally soared by 10 percent" (World Bank 2012) Senior British MEP Arlene McCarthy called for "putting a brake on excessive food speculation and speculating giants profiting from hunger" ending immoral practices which "only serve the interests of profiteers".In March 2012, MEP Markus Ferber suggested amendments to the European Commission's proposals, intended to strengthen restrictions on high-frequency trading and commodity price manipulation.

PROTECTIONISM

Developing countries (democratic or not) have been moved to harden their currencies, accept International Monetary Fund rules, join the World Trade Organization (WTO), and submit to a broad regime of reforms that amount to a hedge against being isolated. China's entry into the WTO signalled the end of truly isolated nations entirely managing their own currency and affairs. The need for stable currency and predictable clearing and rules-based handling of trade disputes, has led to a global trade hegemony—many nations hedging on a global scale against each other's anticipated protectionism, were they to fail to join the WTO.

TECHNOLOGY

An entire software as a service market called Energy Trading Risk Management (ETRM) has emerged for this market using software such as Triple Point Technology, Allegro Development Corporation, SolArc, OpenLink and Agiboo.

FEDERAL COMMODITY FUTURES TRADING COMMISSION - IMPORTANT INFORMATION

The Commodity Futures Trading Commission (CFTC), the federal regulatory agency for futures trading, was established by the Commodity Futures Trading Commission Act of 1974 (88 Stat. 1389; 7 U.S.C.A. 4a), approved October 23, 1974. The commission began operation in April 1975 and its authority to regulate futures trading was renewed by Congress in 1978. Its authority was again renewed with the Commodity Futures Modernization Act of 2000, which also mandated major reforms of the commission. The CFTC maintains a comprehensive web site at <http://www.cftc.gov>.

The CFTC consists of five commissioners who are appointed by the president with the advice and consent of the Senate. The commissioners serve staggered five-year terms and by law no more than three commissioners can belong to the same political party. One commissioner is designated by the president to serve as chairperson. The chair's staff includes the Office of the Inspector General and the Office of International Affairs.

To comply with the requirements of the Modernization Act, the commission underwent a restructuring in 2002. As a result, it consists of six major operating units: the Division of Clearing and Intermediary Oversight, the Division of Market Oversight, the Division of Enforcement, the Office of the Chief Economist, the Office of the General Counsel, and the Office of the Executive Director.

The CFTC regulates trading on the 11 U.S. futures exchanges, which offer numerous kinds of futures contracts. It also regulates the activities of some three thousand commodity exchange members, 360 public brokerage houses (futures commission merchants), about 38,000 commission-registered futures industry salespeople and associated persons, and 2,500 commodity trading advisers and commodity pool operators. Some off-exchange transactions involving instruments similar in nature to futures contracts also fall under CFTC jurisdiction.

The commission's regulatory and enforcement efforts are designed to ensure that the futures trading process is fair and that it protects both the rights of customers and the financial integrity of the marketplace. The CFTC approves the rules under which an exchange proposes to operate and monitors exchange enforcement of those rules. It reviews the terms of proposed futures contracts and registers companies and individuals who handle customer funds or give trading advice. The commission also protects the public by enforcing rules that require that customer funds be kept in bank accounts separate from accounts maintained by firms for their own use, and that such customer accounts be marked to present market value at the close of trading each day.

Futures contracts for agricultural commodities were traded in the United States for more than one hundred years before futures trading was diversified to include trading in contracts for precious metals, raw materials, foreign currencies, commercial interest rates, and U.S. government and mortgage Securities. Contract diversification has grown in exchange trading volume, a growth not limited to the newer commodities.

The CFTC maintains large regional offices in Chicago and New York, cities in which eight of the nation's 11 futures exchanges are located. Smaller regional offices are located in Kansas City and San Francisco, and there is a suboffice of the Chicago regional office in Minneapolis.

LEADERSHIP

CURRENT CFTC COMMISSIONERS

Chairman Gary Gensler
Sworn in May 26, 2009

Gary Gensler was sworn in as the Chairman of the Commodity Futures Trading Commission on May 26, 2009. Chairman Gensler previously served at the U.S. Department of the Treasury as Under Secretary of Domestic Finance (1999-2001) and as Assistant Secretary of Financial Markets (1997-1999). He subsequently served as a Senior Advisor to the Chairman of the U.S. Senate Banking Committee, Senator Paul Sarbanes, on the Sarbanes-Oxley Act, reforming corporate responsibility, accounting and securities laws.

As Under Secretary of the Treasury, Chairman Gensler was the principal advisor to Treasury Secretary Robert Rubin and later to Secretary Lawrence Summers on all aspects of domestic finance. The office was responsible for formulating policy and legislation in the areas of U.S. financial markets, public debt management, the banking system, financial services, fiscal affairs, federal lending, Government Sponsored Enterprises, and community development. In recognition of this service, he was awarded Treasury's highest honor, the Alexander Hamilton Award.

Prior to joining Treasury, Chairman Gensler worked for 18 years at Goldman Sachs, where he was selected as a partner; in his last role he was Co-head of Finance.

Chairman Gensler is the co-author of a book, The Great Mutual Fund Trap, which presents common sense investment advice for middle income Americans.

He is a summa cum laude graduate from the University of Pennsylvania's Wharton School in 1978, with a Bachelor of Science in Economics and received a Master of Business Administration from the Wharton School's graduate division in 1979. He lives with his three daughters outside of Baltimore, Maryland.

Bart Chilton
Sworn in August 8, 2007

Bart Chilton was nominated by President Bush and confirmed by the U. S. Senate in 2007. In 2009, he was re-nominated by President Obama and reconfirmed by the Senate. He has served as the Chairman of the CFTC's Energy and Environmental Markets Advisory Committee (EEMAC). His career spans 25 years in government service—working on Capitol Hill in the House of Representatives, in the Senate, and serving in the Executive Branch during the Clinton, Bush and Obama Administrations.

Prior to joining the CFTC, Mr. Chilton was the Chief of Staff and Vice President for Government Relations at the National Farmers Union where he represented family farmers. In 2005, Mr. Chilton was a Schedule C political appointee of President Bush at the U. S. Farm Credit Administration where he served as an Executive Assistant to the Board. From 2001 to 2005, Mr. Chilton was a Senior Advisor to Senator Tom

Daschle, the Democrat Leader of the United States Senate, where he worked on myriad issues including agriculture and transportation policy.

From 1995 to 2001, Mr. Chilton was a Schedule C political appointee of President Clinton where he rose to Deputy Chief of Staff to U. S. Secretary of Agriculture Dan Glickman. In this role, Mr. Chilton became a member of the Senior Executive Service (SES)—government executives selected for their leadership qualifications to serve in the key positions just below the most senior Presidential appointees. As an SES member, Mr. Chilton served as a liaison between Secretary Glickman and the Federal work force at USDA.

From 1985 to 1995, Mr. Chilton worked in the U. S. House of Representatives where he served as Legislative Director for three different Members of Congress on Capitol Hill and as the Executive Director of the bipartisan Congressional Rural Caucus.
Mr. Chilton previously served on the Boards of Directors of Bion Environmental Technologies and the Association of Family Farms.

Mr. Chilton was born in Delaware and spent his youth in Indiana, where he attended Purdue University (1979—1982). He studied political science and communications and was a collegiate leader of several organizations. Mr. Chilton and his wife, Sherry Daggett Chilton, split their time between Washington, D. C. and Arkansas.

Scott D O'Malia

Sworn in October 16, 2009

Scott O'Malia was confirmed by the U.S. Senate on October 8, 2009, as Commissioner of the Commodity Futures Trading Commission, and was sworn in on October 16, 2009. He is currently serving a five-year term that expires in April 2015.

Born in South Bend Indiana and raised in Williamston, Michigan, Commissioner O'Malia learned about commodity prices firsthand growing up on a small family farm. As a Commissioner of the Commodity Futures Trading Commission (CFTC), he brings both his agricultural background and experience in energy markets, where he has focused his professional career.

Before starting his term at the CFTC, Commissioner O'Malia served as the Staff Director to the U.S. Senate Appropriations Subcommittee on Energy and Water Development, where he focused on expanding U.S. investment in clean-energy technologies, specifically promoting low-cost financing and technical innovation in the domestic energy sector.

Mark P. Wetjen

Sworn in October 25, 2011

Mark P. Wetjen was sworn in as a Commissioner of the U.S. Commodity Futures Trading Commission on October 25, 2011. Commissioner Wetjen worked for seven years in the U.S. Senate as a senior leadership staffer advising on all financial-services-related matters, including the Dodd-Frank Wall Street Reform and Consumer Protection Act of 2010. Before his service in the U.S. Senate, Commissioner Wetjen was a lawyer in private practice and represented clients in a variety of litigation, transactional and regulatory matters.

BASIC STRUCTURE

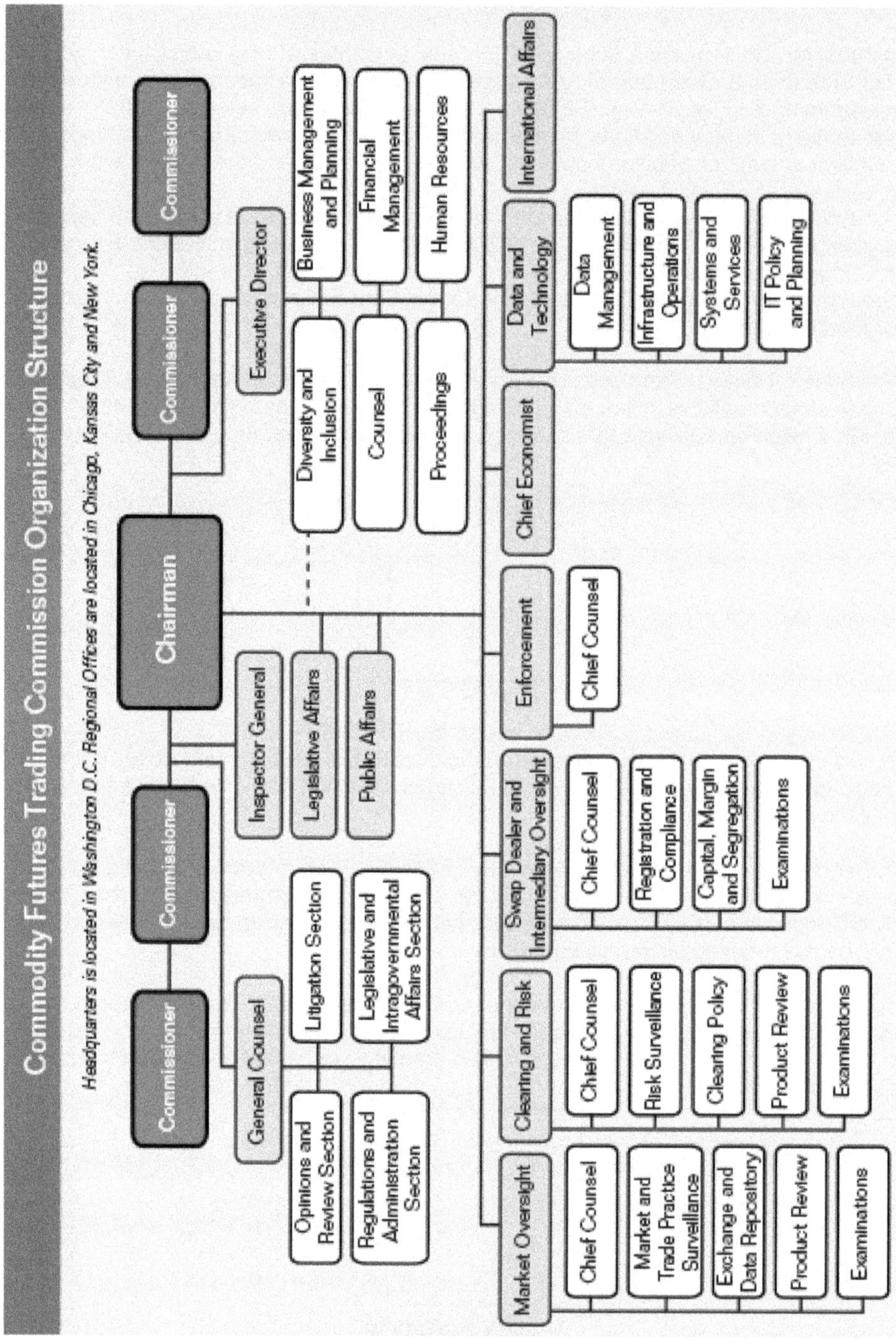

THE COMMISSION

The Offices of the Chairman and the Commissioners provide executive direction and leadership to the Commission. The Offices of the Chairman include Public Affairs and Legislative Affairs.

OFFICE OF THE GENERAL COUNSEL (OGC)

The OGC provides legal services and support to the Commission and all of its programs. These services include: 1) engaging in defensive, appellate, and amicus curiae litigation; 2) assisting the Commission in the performance of its adjudicatory functions; 3) providing legal advice and support for Commission programs;

4) drafting and assisting other program areas in preparing Commission regulations; 5) interpreting the CEA; and 6) providing advice on legislative and regulatory issues.

OFFICE OF THE INSPECTOR GENERAL (OIG)

The OIG is an independent organizational unit at the CFTC. The mission of the OIG is to detect waste, fraud, and abuse and to promote integrity, economy, efficiency, and effectiveness in the CFTC's programs and operations. As such it has the ability to review all of the Commission's programs, activities, and records. In accordance with the Inspector General Act of 1978, as amended, the OIG issues semiannual reports detailing its activities, findings, and recommendations.

OFFICE OF THE EXECUTIVE DIRECTOR (OED)

The Commission's ability to achieve its mission of protecting the public, derivative market participants, U.S. economy, and the U.S. position in global markets is driven by well-informed and reasoned executive direction; strong and focused management; and an efficiently-resourced, dedicated, and productive workforce. These attributes of an effective organization combine to lead and support the critical work of the Commission to provide sound regulatory oversight and enforcement programs for the U.S. public. The Executive Director ensures the Commission's continued success, continuity of operations, and adaptation to the ever-changing markets it is charged with regulating; directs the effective and efficient allocation of CFTC resources; develops and implements management and administrative policy; and ensures program performance is measured and tracked Commission-wide. The OED includes the following programs: Business Management and Planning, Counsel to the Executive Director, Financial Management, Human Resources, Secretariat, Diversity and Inclusion, Whistleblower, and Consumer Outreach.

DIVISION OF MARKET OVERSIGHT (DMO)

The DMO program fosters markets that accurately reflect the forces of supply and demand for the underlying commodities and are free of disruptive activity. To achieve this goal, program staff oversee trade execution facilities, perform market and trade practice surveillance, review new exchange applications, and examine existing exchanges to ensure their compliance with the applicable core principles. Other important work includes evaluating new products to ensure they are not susceptible to manipulation, and reviewing exchange rules and actions to ensure compliance with the CEA and CFTC regulations.

DIVISION OF CLEARING AND RISK (DCR)

The DCR program oversees derivatives clearing organizations (DCOs) and other market participants that may pose risk to the clearing process, including futures commission merchants (FCMs), SDs, major swap participants (MSPs), and large traders; and the clearing of futures, options on futures, and swaps by DCOs. The DCR staff prepare proposed regulations, orders, guidelines, and other regulatory work products on issues pertaining to DCOs; review DCO applications and rule submissions, and make recommendations to the Commission; make determinations and recommendations to the Commission to which types of swaps should be cleared; make determinations and recommendations to the Commission as to the initial eligibility or continuing qualification of a DCO to clear swaps; assess compliance by DCOs with the CEA and Commission regulations, including examining systemically important DCOs (SIDCOs) at least once a year; and conduct risk assessment and financial surveillance through the use of risk assessment tools, including automated systems to gather and analyze financial information to identify, quantify, and monitor the risks posed by DCOs, clearing members, and market participants and their financial impact.

DIVISION OF SWAP DEALER AND INTERMEDIARY OVERSIGHT (DSIO)

The DSIO program oversees the registration and compliance activities of intermediaries and the futures industry self-regulatory organizations (SROs), which include the U.S. derivatives exchanges and the National Futures Association (NFA). Program staff develop regulations concerning registration, fitness, financial adequacy, sales practices, protection of customer funds, cross-border transactions, and anti-money laundering programs, as well as policies for coordination with foreign market authorities and emergency procedures to address market-related events that impact intermediaries. With the passage of the Dodd-Frank Act, DSIO also will be responsible for the development of, or monitoring for compliance with, regulations addressing registration requirements, business conduct standards, capital adequacy, and margin requirements for SDs and MSPs.

DIVISION OF ENFORCEMENT (DOE)

The DOE program investigates and prosecutes alleged violations of the CEA and Commission regulations. For example, the Division brings enforcement actions against individuals and firms registered with the Commission; those who violate these laws in connection with their trading commodity futures and options, and swaps, on designated domestic exchanges and other registered entities; those who improperly market futures and options contracts to retail investors or perpetrate Ponzi schemes; those who use manipulative or deceptive schemes in connection with commodities, futures or swaps; and those who engage in disruptive trading practices.

OFFICE OF THE CHIEF ECONOMIST (OCE)

The OCE provides economic support and advice to the Commission, conducts research on policy issues facing the Commission, and educates and trains Commission staff. The OCE plays an integral role in the implementation of new financial market regulations by providing economic expertise and cost-benefit considerations underlying those regulations.

OFFICE OF DATA AND TECHNOLOGY (ODT)

The ODT provides technology and data management support for Commission market and financial oversight, surveillance, enforcement, legal support, and public transparency activities. The Commission's over-arching information technology (IT) strategy is to increase the integration of IT into the Commission's operating model. That strategy is followed by giving priority to services that provide the greatest mission benefit; architecting services using small components that can be assembled and reassembled with agility; and delivering solutions in short, iterative phases. ODT ensures that data is managed as an enterprise asset and aggressively promotes and adopts industry data standards. ODT also provides secure and stable network, communication, storage, computing, and information management infrastructure and services.

OFFICE OF INTERNATIONAL AFFAIRS (OIA)

The OIA advises the Commission regarding international regulatory initiatives; provides guidance regarding international issues raised in Commission matters; represents the Commission in international organizations, such as International Organization of Securities Commissions (IOSCO); coordinates Commission policy as it relates to policies and initiatives of major foreign jurisdictions, the G-20, the Financial Stability Board (FSB), and the U.S. Treasury Department; and provides technical assistance to foreign market authorities.

MISSIONS AND GOALS

MISSION

To protect market users and the public from fraud, manipulation, abusive practices and systemic risk related to derivatives that are subject to the Commodity Exchange Act, and to foster open, competitive, and financially sound markets.

STRATEGIC GOAL ONE

Protect the public and market participants by ensuring market integrity, promoting transparency, competition and fairness and lowering risk in the system.

Objectives
1. Ensure that markets are structured to reflect the forces of supply and demand for the underlying commodity and are free from manipulation, disruptive activity and abusive trading practices.
2. Ensure that U.S. DCMs and SEFs have the systems, procedures and resources necessary for effective self-regulation and ongoing compliance with core principles.
3. Promote transparency by producing and publishing summary market statistics for the futures, options and

swaps markets.

STRATEGIC GOAL TWO

Protect the public and market participants by ensuring the financial integrity of derivatives transactions, mitigation of systemic risk, and the fitness and soundness of intermediaries and other registrants.

Objectives
1. Clearing organizations and firms participating in the derivatives industry are financially sound.
2. Registered intermediaries meet standards for fitness and conduct.
3. Ensure that self-regulatory organizations fulfill their financial surveillance responsibilities.
4. Ensure that information technology systems support the Commission's existing and expanded responsibilities to ensure financially sound markets, mitigate systemic risk, and monitor intermediaries.

STRATEGIC GOAL THREE

Protect the public and market participants through a robust enforcement program.

Objectives
1. Identify and stop violations of the Commodity Exchange Act and Regulations; deter others from engaging in future misconduct.
2. Increase cooperative enforcement.

STRATEGIC GOAL FOUR

Enhance integrity of U.S. markets by engaging in cross-border cooperation, promoting strong international regulatory standards, and encouraging ongoing convergence of laws and regulation worldwide.

Objectives
1. Cooperate and coordinate with domestic and foreign regulatory authorities.
2. Promote high levels of internationally accepted standards of best practice.
3. Provide global technical assistance.

STRATEGIC GOAL FIVE

Promote Commission excellence through executive direction and leadership, organizational and individual performance management, and effective management of resources.

Objectives
1. An organizational structure that is aligned and streamlined to operate and carry out its mission efficiently and effectively.
2. Effectively respond to a the regulatory needs of a dynamic and complex derivatives market place and efficiently allocate limited resources to the highest priority activities.
3. Attract, engage, develop and retain an exceptionally qualified, diverse, and productive workforce.

4. Information technology (IT) supports and enhances mission accomplishment through effective and efficient infrastructure, systems and services.
5. Ensure effective stewardship and management of CFTC financial resources.

PERFORMANCE

FY 2012 Performance Summary	
Met	Not Met
46%	54%

Budget constraints arising from a continuing resolution in FY 2011 and continued under-funding of the Commission in FY 2012 only added to the performance challenges faced by the Commission with its expanded role. It is expected that with continued budget constraints that Commission performance will not only diminish, but do so exponentially. These constraints on the CFTC over a time of expanding responsibility has resulted in having to reallocate staff resources to new and high risk areas only, preventing the Commission from fulfilling its mission and achieving a number of performance targets related to existing authorities. The Commission's APR reflects this resource challenge as staff diligently work toward finalizing each Dodd-Frank Act rule and attempting to maintain legacy operations.

Some performance measures described in the Strategic Plan are dependent upon the completion of rule writing. As a result, two of the 54 performance measures were considered "Not Applicable" during the FY 2012 reporting period. An additional four measures were also categorized as "Not Applicable", either remaining in development from the onset of the Strategic Plan newly implemented in FY 2011 or lacking activity to report. As the Commission completes work on rulemaking and data becomes available for the remaining two rule-dependent measures, they will be published along with relevant analysis and review narrative in subsequent APRs.

The following identifies the specific performance measures considered "Not Applicable":

1.1.3.1 Transmit information and consult with the Office of Information Technology Services (OITS) [Now recognized as the Office of Data and Technology—ODT] to implement electronic filing of forms. Fully deploy electronic filing of trader reporting forms. Percent complete.

2.1.2.1 Applications are reviewed and a determination made regarding compliance with financial integrity provisions of the CEA within statutory time frames. Percent in compliance with financial integrity provisions.

2.2.1.1 Conduct direct examinations of SDs and MSPs, identify deficiencies and confirm that all deficiencies identified are corrected within specified period of time.

2.4.1.2 Program design to cover new data collection requirements to monitor systemic risk posed by CPOs and CTAs advising private funds, and new registration of swap dealers. Percentage of system redesign accomplished.

3.1.1.2 The CFTC will bring claims in due recognition of the broadened enforcement mandate provided by the Dodd-Frank Act, and will seek proportionate remedies, including civil monetary penalties, undertakings and restitution, that have the highest impact on and greatest deterrent effect against potential future violations.

4.1.1.2 Regular issuance of outgoing international requests for enforcement assistance and referrals made by the CFTC to foreign regulators pertaining to matters involving their jurisdictions.

The performance measures in this report are rated as: Exceeded, Met, or Not Met. Overall results for the Commission's performance measures are depicted in the following table:

CFTC Performance Results

	# of Measures[1]	Met	Not Met
All Goals	48	22	26
% of Total		46%	54%

CLEARING, TRANSPARENCY, SWAP DEALER OVERSIGHT, CROSS-BORDER APPLICATION OF SWAPS MARKET REFORM

In the first quarter of FY 2013, the Commission finalized the initial set of clearing determinations regarding which interest rate swaps and credit default swap (CDS) indices will be required to be cleared. Clearing by SDs and private funds active in the swaps market will be required in the second quarter of FY 2013. Compliance will be phased in for other market participants through the remainder of FY 2013. The CFTC is also considering clearing determinations for other classes of swaps, including agricultural, energy, and equity indices.

Based on completed real-time reporting rules, the public began on December 31 to benefit from seeing the price and volume of each Interest Rate (IRS) and Credit Default (CDS) swap transaction. Additional reporting will be phased in over the next several months.

The CFTC is also working to finalize reforms that promote pre-trade transparency, including rules on minimum block sizes and trading platforms called swap execution facilities (SEFs). Market participant compliance for these rules also will be phased in throughout the year.

As of the first week of January 2013, 66 SDs had registered with the CFTC and will come under comprehensive oversight, including standards for sales practices, record-keeping, and business conduct.

The CFTC is collaborating on a global approach to margin requirements for uncleared swaps through the Basel Committee on Banking Supervision and IOSCO. In coordination with domestic prudential regulators and international regulators, the CFTC is looking to take up final rules on margin and related rules on capital in 2013.

In consultation with international regulators, the Commission will move to finalize guidance on the cross-border application of swaps market reform and an accompanying release on phased-compliance for foreign SDs.

CUSTOMER PROTECTION

Measures taken so far on customer protection have been significant, but market events this year have further highlighted that the Commission must do everything within its authorities and resources to strengthen oversight programs and the protection of customers and their funds. In the fall of 2012, the Commission sought public comment on further enhancements to protect customer funds. This proposal is about ensuring customers have confidence that the funds they post as margin or collateral are fully segregated and protected. The proposal, which the CFTC looks forward to finalizing in the coming months, would strengthen the controls around customer funds at FCMs. It also would set new regulatory accounting requirements that would provide stronger protections for customer money held by FCMs and would raise minimum standards for independent public accountants who audit FCMs.

BENCHMARK INTEREST RATES

One of the most critical challenges for the markets, international regulators, and the CFTC is how best to ensure benchmark rates, such as the London Interbank Offered Rate (LIBOR), are honest and reliable. As they are a key component of financial markets, they must work for the rest of the economy. LIBOR is the reference rate for nearly half of U.S. adjustable-rate mortgages; for about 70 percent of the U.S. futures market; and for a majority of U.S. swaps market.

The CFTC is consulting with a number of international organizations with regard to next steps for benchmark rates. In particular, the UK Financial Services Authority (FSA) and the CFTC are co-chairing the IOSCO task force. This will include seeking public consultation, a public roundtable, and a report and recommendations in the spring.

The IOSCO task force is seeking public input on best practices that should apply to the benchmark process and entities that produce benchmarks, as well as possible mechanisms and protocols that would best ensure for a smooth transition to new benchmarks when and if needed.

ENFORCEMENT ACTIONS

Among the significant and precedent-setting enforcement actions filed by the Commission during FY 2012 are the following:

CASES INVOLVING MANIPULATION, FALSE REPORTING, WASH TRADES, AND POSITION LIMITS

•In a landmark case, the Division filed charges against Barclays PLC and two affiliates for attempted manipulation and false reporting concerning LIBOR and other global benchmark interest rates. The charges were simultaneously settled pursuant to an Order requiring Barclays to pay $200 million, the largest fine ever imposed by the CFTC, and requiring Barclays to implement a number of measures to ensure the integrity of the bank's benchmark submissions.

•The Division settled charges previously filed in Federal court against a global proprietary trading company, Optiver Holding BV, two of its subsidiaries, and three then company officers for manipulating and attempting to manipulate crude oil and other energy futures contracts. The court-approved settlement required the defendants to pay $14 million and included trading limitations for one of the corporate defendants and the three individual defendants.

•The Division filed charges against Joseph F. Welsh, a former broker with MF Global, alleging that Welsh attempted to manipulate prices of palladium and platinum futures contracts, and with aiding and abetting the attempted manipulations of Christopher L. Pia, a former portfolio manager of Moore Capital Management, LLC. Both Pia and Moore Capital settled the separate actions against them prior to FY 2012. The case against Welsh is pending in Federal court in New York.

•The Division filed charges against Royal Bank of Canada (RBC), alleging a multi-hundred million dollar wash trading scheme involving stock futures contracts. The CFTC's complaint, which is pending in Federal court in New York, also alleged that RBC made false statements concerning material aspects of its wash sale scheme to OneChicago, LLC, an electronic futures exchange, and to CME Group.

•The Division filed a number of separate actions against traders who exceeded the limits on the quantity of futures contracts they were lawfully permitted to hold in the cotton, wheat, corn, and soybean markets. The penalties imposed in these cases pursuant to settlement orders ranged from $140,000 to $600,000, and in one case the sanction included disgorgement of $1 million in profits made from the excessively large position.

CASES INVOLVING CUSTOMER FUNDS SAFEGUARDS AND SUPERVISION OBLIGATIONS

•The Division filed charges against Peregrine Financial Group Inc., an FCM, and its owner, Russell R. Wasendorf, Sr., alleging misappropriation of customer funds, violations of customer fund segregation laws, and making material false statements to the CFTC. The suit, which is pending in Federal court in Chicago, was filed within 24 hours after the fraud came to light.

•The Division filed charges against JPMorgan Chase Bank for its unlawful handling of Lehman Brothers, Inc.'s customer funds prior to and after Lehman filed for bankruptcy in the midst of the financial crisis of 2008. The charges were simultaneously settled pursuant to an order requiring JPMorgan to pay $20 million, the largest CFTC sanction for a segregated fund violation to date.

•The Division filed charges against MBF Clearing Corp. (MBF), a registered FCM, alleging that MBF violated laws requiring the segregation of customer funds and that the firm failed to adhere to its supervision obligations. The case is pending in Federal court in New York.

•The Division filed charges against Forex Capital Markets LLC (FXCM), a retail forex dealer, for failing to supervise the handling of more than 57,000 customer accounts that were disadvantaged by FXCM's system that allowed for one-sided "slippage" in forex prices. The charges, which also included a separate violation for FXCM's failure to produce certain records promptly to the Division, were settled simultaneously pursuant to an Order requiring FXCM to pay more than $14 million.

•The Division filed charges against Goldman Sachs Execution & Clearing, L.P. (GSEC), an FCM, for supervision violations arising from GSEC's failure to investigate signs of questionable conduct by a GSEC client. The charges were simultaneously settled pursuant to an Order requiring GSEC to pay $7 million.

•The Division filed charges against Rosenthal Collins Group, LLC (RCG), an FCM, for failing to supervise an RCG account that an RCG client was using to perpetrate a multi-million dollar commodity futures Ponzi scheme. (The Division charged the RCG client, Enrique F. Villalba, and his company for the underlying fraud prior to FY 2012.) The charges against RCG were simultaneously settled pursuant to an Order requiring RCG to pay $2.5 million.

CASES INVOLVING PONZI AND OTHER FRAUD SCHEMES, AND FALSE STATEMENTS TO THE CFTC

•The Division filed charges against Ronnie Wilson and Atlantic Bullion & Coin, Inc. alleging that they operated a $90 million Ponzi scheme involving fraudulent contracts for purchases and sales of silver. The complaint, which is pending in a Federal court in South Carolina, uses the Commission's new Dodd-Frank Act authority prohibiting fraud schemes in connection with a contract of sale of a commodity in interstate commerce.

•The Division filed charges against Nikolai S. Battoo and his four companies alleging fraud in connection with commodity pools that allegedly accepted over $140 million from U.S. investors. The case is pending in Federal court in Chicago.

•The Division filed charges against Steven Pousa of Australia; Joel Friant of the United States; and their company, Investment Intelligence Corp alleging they conducted a global fraudulent off-exchange forex scheme, allegedly accepting at least $53 million from at least 960 clients. The case is pending in a Federal court in Texas.

•The Division filed charges against Donald Newell and his company Quiddity LLC, a registered CPO and trading advisor, alleging that they fraudulently allocated more profitable trades to themselves and less profitable trades to their customers. The Division also charged Newell under the Commission's new Dodd-Frank Act authority with making material false statements to the Division during its investigation of this matter. The case is pending in Federal court in Chicago.

DESIGNATED CONTRACT MARKETS (DCMS)

DESIGNATED CONTRACT MARKETS (DCMS)

Designated contract markets (DCMs) are boards of trade (or exchanges) that operate under the regulatory oversight of the CFTC, pursuant to Section 5 of the Commodity Exchange Act (CEA), 7 USC 7. DCMs are most like traditional futures exchanges, which may allow access to their facilities by all types of traders, including retail customers.

DCMs may list for trading futures or option contracts based on any underlying commodity, index or instrument. Part 38 of the CFTC's regulations, 17 CFR Part 38, details the procedures and requirements for operating as a board of trade (or exchange).

How to Become a Designated Contract Market

Any market that seeks to provide a trading facility for non-eligible contract participants to trade futures, options on futures or options on commodities must apply to the Commission to be designated as a contract market (DCM), unless some exemption or exclusion would apply to the facility. Criteria, procedures and requirements for designation as a DCM are set forth in Section 5 of the CEA, 7 USC 7, and Part 38 of the CFTC's regulations. Appendix A and B provide specific information on these requirements and guidance to applicants seeking to become designated as DCMs.

Security futures products are subject to special requirements such as joint CFTC and Securities and Exchange Commission (SEC) oversight, and can be offered only by markets that are either regulated by the CFTC and notice-registered with the SEC or regulated by the SEC and notice-registered with the CFTC. Options on securities and securities indexes can only be traded on a securities exchange under the jurisdiction of the SEC.

COMPLIANCE WITH CORE PRINCIPLES

To obtain and maintain its designation, a DCM must also comply, on an initial and ongoing basis, with the following twenty-three Core Principles established in Section 5(d) of the CEA, 7 USC 7(d) and Part 38 of the CFTC's regulations and with the implementing regulations under Part 38 of the CFTC's regulations:

Designation as Contract Market

Compliance with Rules

Contracts Not Readily Subject to Manipulation

Prevention of Market Disruption

Position Limitations or Accountability

Emergency Authority

Availability of General Information

Daily Publication of Trading Information

Execution of Transactions

Trade Information

Financial Integrity of Transactions

Protection of Markets and Market Participants

Disciplinary Procedures

Dispute Resolution

Governance Fitness Standards

Conflicts of Interest

Composition of Governing Boards of Contract Markets

Recordkeeping

Antitrust Considerations

System Safeguards

Financial Resources

Diversity of Boards of Directors

Securities and Exchange Commission

Appendix A to Part 38 of the CFTC's regulations includes Form DCM, which contains instructions and a list of necessary information and documentation required to initiate the designation process. Appendix B to Part 38 provides guidance on complying with certain core principles. For certain core principles, Appendix B also provides acceptable practices for meeting selected requirements.

The Division of Market Oversight's Examinations Branch conducts regular reviews of each DCM's ongoing compliance with core principles and the implementing regulations under Part 38, examining the self-regulatory programs operated by the exchange in order to enforce its rules, prevent market manipulation and customer and market abuses, and ensure the recording and safe storage of trade information, among other requirements. These reviews are known as rule enforcement reviews (RERs).

DESIGNATED CONTRACT MARKET FILINGS

DCMs may implement new rules or rule amendments by filing with the CFTC a certification that the rule or rule amendment complies with the CEA and CFTC regulations and policies and/or by requesting approval from the CFTC, pursuant to the requirements under Part 40 of the CFTC's regulations. DCMs, like other entities, may submit requests that the CFTC take action on a number of other issues, including requesting no-action relief, interpretations, or guidance on particular issues.

DCMs also may list new products by filing with the CFTC, among other things, a certification that the product complies with the CEA and CFTC regulations and policies and/or by requesting approval from the CFTC.

DORMANT DESIGNATED CONTRACT MARKETS

A dormant contract market defined in CFTC Regulation 40.1, is any DCM on which no trading has occurred during a period of twelve consecutive calendar months, preceding the first day of the most recent calendar month. (See attached list of dormant DCMs) Prior to listing or re-listing products for trading (including listing new contract months in existing products), a dormant DCM must reinstate its designation. To be reinstated, a dormant contract market submits an application for reinstatement under the procedures found in CFTC Regulation 38.3(a)(1) and (2), although the application might rely on previously submitted materials that still pertain to, and accurately describe, the contract market conditions.

Newly designated contract markets, however, are not considered to be dormant until the end of a grace period of 36 consecutive calendar months following the day that the order of designation is issued.

VACATED EXCHANGE

Exchanges previously designated by the CFTC or by the Secretary of Agriculture prior to 1975 as contract markets under the CEA and subsequently vacated at the request of the exchange or whose designation was otherwise revoked must reapply to the CFTC for contract market designation prior to listing contracts for trading.

RULE ENFORCEMENT REVIEWS OF DESIGNATED CONTRACT MARKETS

The Division of Market Oversight's Market Compliance Section conducts regular reviews of each designated contract market's (DCM) ongoing compliance with core principles through the self-regulatory programs operated by the exchange in order to enforce its rules, prevent market manipulation and customer and market abuses, and ensure the recording and safe storage of trade information. These reviews are known as rule enforcement reviews (RERs).

Periodic RERs normally examine a DCM's audit trail, trade practice surveillance, disciplinary, and dispute resolution programs for compliance with the relevant core principles, which include Core Principle 10, Trade Information, and Core Principle 17, Recordkeeping with respect to audit trail programs; Core Principle 2, Compliance With Rules, and Core Principle 12, Protection of Market Participants with respect to trade practice surveillance and disciplinary programs; and Core Principle 13, Dispute Resolution, with respect to dispute resolution programs.

Other periodic RERs normally examine a DCM's market surveillance program for compliance with Core Principle 4, Monitoring of Trading, and Core Principle 5, Position Limitations or Accountability. On some occasions, these two types of RERs may be combined in a single RER. Market Compliance can also conduct horizontal RERs of the compliance of multiple exchanges in regard to particular core principles.

In conducting an RER, the Division of Market Oversight (DMO) staff examine trading and compliance activities at the exchange in question over an extended time period selected by DMO, typically the twelve months immediately preceding the start of the review. Staff conduct extensive review of documents and systems used by the exchange in carrying out its self-regulatory responsibilities; interview compliance officials and staff of the exchange; and prepare a detailed written report of their findings. In nearly all cases, the RER report is made available to the public and posted on CFTC.gov.

RULES & RULE AMENDMENTS

Designated contract markets ("DCMs"), registered swap execution facilities ("SEFs"), registered derivatives clearing organizations ("DCOs"), and registered swap data repositories ("SDRs") generally may implement new rules or rule amendments by filing with the Commission a certification that the new rule or rule amendment complies with the Commodity Exchange Act ("CEA" or "Act") and the Commission's regulations and/or by requesting CFTC approval of such rules and amendments.

To meet its statutory mission of ensuring market integrity and customer protection with respect to rules and rule amendments implemented under self-certification procedures, the CFTC places greater reliance on its oversight authorities, including market and trade practice surveillance, rule enforcement reviews, review of new rules and rule amendments, reviews of contract terms, dialogue with the regulated entities, and enforcement actions where violations are detected. For rules and amendments adopted under self-certification procedures, registered entities are expected to assume primary responsibility for ensuring that the rules and rule amendments meet, on a continuing basis, the applicable statutory and regulatory requirements.

SUBMISSION OF SELF-REGULATORY RULES AND RULE AMENDMENTS TO THE COMMISSION BY CERTIFICATION

The Dodd-Frank Wall Street Reform and Consumer Protection Act ("Dodd-Frank Act") amended Section 5c of the Act to provide a new timeline for the submission to the Commission of rules and rule amendments by

DCMs, SEFs, DCOs, and SDRs. The Commission amended Part 40 of its regulations to implement the amended provisions of Section 5c of the Act.

Initial Rule Submission Review Period: New rules and rule amendments, including amendments to the terms and conditions of an existing product, become effective, pursuant to the certification of the registered entity and notice of such certification to the entity's members and market participants, on the date that is 10 business days after the date on which the Commission receives the certification unless the Commission extends the submission review period. In implementing an extension, the Commission would notify the registered entity, prior to the expiration of the 10 business days, that it is staying the certification because there exist novel or complex issues that require additional time to analyze, the certification is an inadequate explanation of the rule or rule amendment by the submitting registered entity, or the certification presents a potential inconsistency with any provision of the Act or any of the Commission's regulations thereunder.

Extended Submission Review Period: The Commission may notify a registered entity that it is staying a certified rule or rule amendment for as many as 90 calendar days from the date of the notification. A rule or rule amendment subject to a stay becomes effective, pursuant to the certification of the registered entity, at the expiration of the additional 90-day period unless the Commission withdraws the stay prior to that time or the Commission notifies the registered entity during the additional 90-day period that it objects to the proposed certification on the grounds that it is inconsistent with any provision of the Act or any of the Commission's regulations thereunder.

For a rule submission under extended review, the Commission will provide not less than a 30-day public comment period within the 90-day period in which the stay is in effect. Details regarding such public comment period will be posted on the Commission's website.

RULES AND AMENDMENTS NOT REQUIRED TO BE CERTIFIED

DCMs and DCOs may place certain rules or rule amendments into effect without a self-certification. A DCM or DCO need only provide a weekly notification of all rule changes involving:

non-substantive revisions (e.g., renumbering);

delivery standards set by third parties;

routine changes in index products (e.g., composition or computation) made by independent third parties;

changes to option contract terms relating to strike prices (e.g., strike price intervals);

fees not associated with incentive programs that are $1.00 or more established by an independent third party;

survey lists;

approved brands;

delivery facilities and delivery service providers;

trading months; or

minimum tick size.

Certain other rules may be implemented without either self-certification or notice to the CFTC, provided only that the DCM or DCO maintain documentation of all rule changes. Rules subject to this procedure include those that govern:

transfer of ownership or membership;

administrative procedures (e.g., organization of boards and committees);

administration (e.g., direction of employees, declaration of holidays);

standards of decorum;

fees not associated with an incentive program that are under $1.00 or relate to certain administrative matters;

routine changes in securities indexes (e.g., composition or computation) made by independent third parties;

certain changes to option contract rules regarding strike prices; or trading months.

RULES AND RULE AMENDMENTS THAT MUST OBTAIN PRIOR CFTC APPROVAL

The only rules and rule amendments not eligible for self-certification are those that materially change a term or condition of a contract for future delivery of an enumerated agricultural commodity as listed in Section 1a(9) of the CEA, 7 USC § 1a(9), or an option on such a contract or commodity, in a delivery month having open interest. Under CFTC Regulation 40.4, such rules or rule amendments must be submitted to the CFTC for prior approval under the procedures of CFTC Regulation 40.5. A registered entity may elect to submit any such new rule or rule amendment to the CFTC under the ten-day review procedure of CFTC Regulation 40.4 for a determination as to whether such rule must be submitted for prior approval.

However, CFTC Regulation 40.4 specifies that certain categories of new rules and rule amendments affecting a term or condition of a futures contract on an enumerated agricultural commodity are deemed not to be material and thus do not require prior CFTC approval. DCMs, therefore, may implement any new rule or rule change falling within these categories pursuant to self-certification provisions or notification procedures, as applicable.

The categories of new rules and rule amendments deemed to be not material for this purpose are:

changes that are enumerated in CFTC Regulation 40.6(d)(2);

changes that are enumerated in CFTC Regulation 40.6(d)(3)(ii);

changes in no cancellation ranges and trading hours; or

changes required to comply with a binding court order or a CFTC or other federal regulatory authority regulation or order.

CFTC Rules and Products Submission Cover Sheet

RULES AND RULE AMENDMENTS VOLUNTARILY SUBMITTED FOR CFTC APPROVAL

Amended Part 40 of the CFTC regulations provides a new standard of review of voluntary requests for approval of rules and rule amendments.

Under the a new standard, the Commission must approve a new rule or rule amendmentof a registered entity unless the Commission finds that the new rule or rule amendment is inconsistent with any provision of the Act or any of the Commission's regulations thereunder.

ANTI-MONEY LAUNDERING

The Patriot Act, which amends the Bank Secrecy Act (BSA), was adopted in response to the September 11, 2001 terrorist attacks. The Patriot Act is intended to strengthen U.S. measures to prevent, detect, and prosecute international money laundering and the financing of terrorism. These efforts include anti-money laundering (AML) tools that impact the banking, financial, and investment communities.

As a result of the Patriot Act, persons who are or are required to be registered as futures commission merchants (FCMs), introducing brokers (IBs), commodity pool operators (CPOs), and commodity trading advisors (CTAs) are or may become subject to requirements for establishing AML programs, reporting suspicious activity, verifying the identity of customers, and applying enhanced due diligence to certain types of accounts involving foreign persons.

By order dated September 26, 2002, the Secretary of the Treasury (Treasury) delegated its authority to administer the BSA to the Financial Crimes Enforcement Network (FinCEN).

ESTABLISHING AML PROGRAMS

The Patriot Act amended the BSA to require that financial institutions establish AML Programs. FCMs, CPOs, and CTAs are specifically included in the definition of financial institution in the BSA. IBs are considered to be "brokers or dealers in commodities" within the financial institution definition.

An AML Program must be in writing and must include:

the development of internal policies, procedures, and controls;

the designation of a compliance officer;

an ongoing employee training program; and

an independent audit function to test programs.

Treasury has adopted interim final rules regarding AML Programs for financial institutions (as subsequently amended in 2008). These rules exempt CPOs and CTAs from the AML Program requirement pending the issuance of final rules. Treasury had proposed rules that would have required unregistered investment companies (UICs), including commodity pools, and commodity trading advisors to establish and implement written anti-money laundering programs, but Treasury withdrew the UIC and CTA proposals. As required by Section 356(c) of the Patriot Act, Treasury has issued a report to Congress that sets forth existing requirements that apply to both registered and unregistered investment companies, including commodity pools, and contains recommendations on additional regulatory requirements that might be imposed. The National Futures Association has adopted Rule 2-9(c) and an accompanying Interpretive Notice regarding AML Programs for its FCM and IB members. Other AML Program rule notices for specified financial institutions include:

Mutual Funds (interim final rule);

Operators of a Credit Card System (interim final rule);

Money Service Businesses (interim final rule);

Broker-dealer members of the Financial Industry Regulatory Authority (FINRA); (information and guidance)

Broker-dealer members of the New York Stock Exchange (approval of rule) (amendment of rule);

Insurance companies (final rule); and

Dealers in precious metals, stones or jewels (interim final rule).

On March 5, 2010, FinCEN, the Securities and Exchange Commission, and the Banking agencies (the Federal Reserve, Comptroller of the Currency, Federal Deposit Insurance Corporation, Office of Thrift Supervision, National Credit Union Administration) in consultation with the CFTC, issued guidance addressed to the core requirement to develop and implement internal controls, policies and procedures as part of a firm's anti-money laundering program. The guidance clarifies regulatory expectations for obtaining beneficial ownership information for certain accounts and customer relationships, particularly those that present a high risk for money laundering or terrorist financing. As explained in the guidance: "[information on beneficial ownership in account relationships provides another tool for financial institutions to better understand and address money laundering and terrorist financing risks, protect themselves from criminal activity, and assist law enforcement with investigations and prosecutions.

REPORTING SUSPICIOUS ACTIVITY

The Patriot Act authorizes Treasury to issue rules requiring FCMs, CPOs, and CTAs to file Suspicious Activity Reports (SARs). Treasury has issued a final rule requiring FCMs and IBs to file SARs. Treasury has not yet proposed a rule requiring CPOs and CTAs to file SARs. Treasury also has issued a Form 101, Suspicious Activity Report by the Securities and Futures Industries (SAR-SF) (with instructions), which FCMs and IBs must use to report suspicious transactions, and which CPOs and CTAs may use to report voluntarily. Treasury has also posted guidance on common errors found in filed SARs.

Final BSA rules require that SARs be filed by any broker or dealer in securities (as amended in 2003); mutual fund; money service business (as amended in 2003); insurance company (as amended in 2006); casino; or bank (as amended in 2000).

Pursuant to guidance issued by Treasury, FCMs and IBs are permitted to share a SAR with parent entities, regardless of whether the parent is located inside the United States or abroad. Treasury has not yet issued guidance on whether FCMs and IBs may share a SAR with affiliates other than parent entities.

Banking agencies with regulations that require the filing of SARs: Federal Reserve Board; Comptroller of the Currency; Federal Deposit Insurance Corporation; Office of Thrift Supervision; and National Credit Union Administration. The Federal Reserve Board has issued a supervisory letter that provides relief from the Board's SAR filing requirements for nonbank subsidiaries of bank holding companies or state member banks, such as FCMs and IBs that file suspicious activity reports pursuant to separate Treasury suspicious activity reporting requirements.

VERIFYING THE IDENTITY OF CUSTOMERS

The Patriot Act requires Treasury to issue rules setting forth minimum standards for financial institutions to identify and verify the identity of customers.

Treasury and the CFTC have jointly issued final rules (with a subsequent correction) that require FCMs and IBs to have customer identification programs (CIPs) for identifying and verifying the identity of customers. An FCM's or IB's procedures must enable it to form a reasonable belief that it knows the true identity of each customer.

The CIP rules permit FCMs and IBs to rely on other financial institutions to perform identification/verification functions; however, the reliance must be reasonable under the circumstances, the relied-upon financial institution must be subject to an AML program rule under the BSA and be regulated by a Federal functional regulator, and the financial institution must enter into a contract requiring it to certify annually to the FCM or IB that it has implemented an AML program and that it will perform specified requirements of the CIP. Pursuant to a staff no-action letter issued on March 14, 2005, FCMs and IBs may rely upon certain CTAs to perform procedures of the FCM's or IB's CIP even though such CTAs are not yet subject to an AML program rule.

Final rules regarding customer identification programs have also been issued for banks, savings associations, credit unions, and certain non-federally regulated banks; broker-dealers, and mutual funds. The rules are substantively identical for all affected sectors of the financial services industry. These rules require that financial institutions have procedures for checking customer's names against lists of known or suspected terrorists or terrorist organizations that are prepared by any federal agency and made available to the institution. Although no lists have yet been designated, financial institutions are separately required to comply with the rules of the Office of Foreign Assets and Control (OFAC) and must consult OFAC's lists of sanctioned countries and specially designated nationals and blocked persons. Sources for complying with OFAC rules:

OFAC's "Opening Securities and Futures Accounts from an OFAC Perspective" guidance;

The American Bankers Association's primer and briefing on OFAC compliance; and

OFAC forms for reporting blocked or rejected transactions.

The staff of the CFTC and Treasury also has jointly issued guidance, in question-and-answer format, regarding the application of the CIP rule for FCMs and IBs. This guidance covers a number of topics that were not explicitly addressed by the CIP rules.

One important area of staff guidance addresses the situation where an omnibus account or sub-account or relationship is established by or on behalf of a financial intermediary for the purposes of executing transactions that clear or settle at another financial institution. The staff of Treasury and the CFTC has issued guidance that clarifies that if the financial intermediary is the account holder, the intermediary can be treated as the customer for the purposes of the CIP rule.

Another important area of staff guidance addresses the CIP requirements applicable to FCMs engaged in give-up transactions. The staff of Treasury and the CFTC has issued guidance that clarifies that an FCM acting solely as an executing broker in a give-up arrangement is not required to apply its CIP procedures to a customer engaged in a give-up transaction. Conversely, an FCM acting as a clearing broker is required to apply its CIP procedures to a customer engaged in a give-up transaction.

DUE DILIGENCE MEASURES FOR CERTAIN TYPES OF ACCOUNTS INVOLVING FOREIGN PERSONS

The Patriot Act requires that financial institutions must establish appropriate, and where necessary, enhanced due diligence policies, procedures, and controls that are reasonably designed to detect and report instances of money laundering through foreign private banking and correspondent accounts.

A final rule (as amended in 2006 and 2007) issued by Treasury requires covered financial institutions, including FCMs and IBs, to establish due diligence programs that include appropriate, specific, risk-based, and where necessary, enhanced policies, procedures and controls that are reasonably designed to detect and report, on an ongoing basis, any known or suspected money laundering activity conducted through or involving any correspondent account established, maintained, administered, or managed by such covered financial institution in the United States for a foreign financial institution.

The same rule also requires covered financial institutions, including FCMs and IBs, to maintain due diligence programs that are reasonably designed to detect and report known or suspected money laundering or suspicious activity conducted through or involving any private banking account that is established, maintained, administered, or managed in the United States by such financial institution for a non-U.S. person. The due diligence program must ensure, at a minimum, that the financial institution takes reasonable steps to ascertain the identity of the nominal and beneficial owners of the private account, whether any such person is a senior foreign political figure, the sources of funds deposited into the private banking account and the purpose and expected use of the account. The program also must ensure that the financial institution reviews the activity in the private banking account to ensure it is consistent with the information obtained about the client and reports known or suspected money laundering or suspicious activity conducted to, from or through the private banking account. Where a senior foreign political figure is the nominal or beneficial owner of a private banking account, the program must include enhanced scrutiny of the account that is reasonably designed to detect and report transactions that may involve the proceeds of foreign corruption.

Notwithstanding the final rule for correspondent accounts, Treasury has issued guidance confirming that an IB is not subject to the correspondent account due diligence requirements where it merely solicits and accepts orders for transactions in commodity futures and options.

Treasury has issued guidance for FCMs and IBs that addresses: (1) whether all five of the risk factors enumerated in the final due diligence rule for correspondent accounts must be applied in every instance; (2) how certain intermediated relationships should be treated for purposes of the correspondent account rule; (3) how the due diligence rule for private banking accounts applies to clearing firms; (4) how firms should determine whether a foreign entity is a "foreign financial institution;" and (5) how futures firms should evaluate the purpose and anticipated activity of a correspondent account.

Treasury also has issued a proposed rule that will require a covered financial institution, including an FCM or IB, to ensure that its due diligence program provides for enhanced due diligence for correspondent accounts that have been established, maintained, administered, or managed for certain foreign banks.

SPECIAL MEASURES

Patriot Act authorizes Treasury to find that a foreign jurisdiction, institution, class of transactions, or type of account is of "primary money laundering concern" and to require domestic financial institutions to take certain "special measures" against the primary money laundering concern. The first four special measures impose information gathering, reporting, and recordkeeping requirements on those financial institutions dealing, directly or indirectly, with the designated jurisdiction or entity. Under special measure 5, a financial institution may be prohibited from opening or maintaining a correspondent account or a payable-through account. Pursuant to this authority, Treasury has designated each of the following as a primary money laundering concern and has imposed, or proposed imposing, special measures as follows:

• Burma (also known as Myanmar) and Final Rule imposing the fifth special measure;

• Syrian financial institution, Commercial Bank of Syria (includes its subsidiary, Syrian Lebanese Commercial Bank) and Final Rule imposing the fifth special measure;

• Belarusian financial institution, Infobank (includes Belmetalnergo), renamed Trustbank, and proposed rule to impose the fifth special measure. See also FinCEN's Advisory on providing financial services to senior Belarusian regime elements engaged in illicit activities.

• Macau commercial bank, Banco Delta Asia SARL, including its subsidiaries, Delta Asia Credit Limited and Delta Asia Insurance Limited, and Final Rule imposing fifth special measure;

• Islamic Republic of Iran and Proposed Rule to impose the fifth special measure;

• Belarusian depository institution, JSC CredexBank and Proposed Rule to impose the first and fifth special measures; and

• Lebanese Canadian Bank SAL and Proposed Rule to impose the fifth special measure.

TRANSACTIONS IN EXCESS OF $10,000 IN CURRENCY

A financial institution and any "nonfinancial trade or business" must file a report concerning a transaction (or series of related transactions) in excess of $10,000 in currency.

Interim final rules require any nonfinancial trade or business to file currency transaction reports on a Form 8300.

CTAs and CPOs fall within the definition of "nonfinancial trade or business" for purposes of currency transaction reporting and thus are subject to the interim final rule.

Regulations (31 CFR 103.22) require that financial institutions file currency transaction reports on a Form 104, Currency Transaction Report (CTR). FCMs and IBs are defined as "financial institutions" and thus must file CTRs.

FOREIGN BANK AND FINANCIAL ACCOUNTS (FBAR)

The BSA requires each United States person who has a financial interest in, or signature authority over, any financial accounts in a foreign country to file a Form TD F 90-22.1, Report of Foreign and Financial Accounts (FBAR) if the aggregate value of the financial accounts exceeds $10,000 at any time during the calendar year. The term "financial account" includes any commodity interest account. The term "United States person" includes any Commission registrant that is a citizen or resident of the United States, domestic partnership, domestic corporation, or a domestic estate or trust.

INTERNATIONAL TRANSPORTATION OF CURRENCY OR MONETARY INSTRUMENTS (CMIR)

The BSA requires the filing of a Form 105, Report of International Transportation of Currency and Monetary Instruments (CMIR) by any person, such as an FCM, who physically transports, mails, ships, or causes to be physically transported, mailed, or shipped, currency or other monetary instrument in an aggregate amount exceeding $10,000 on any one occasion, whether that transportation is into or out of the United States. A CMIR also must be filed by any person who receives in the United States currency or other monetary instrument in an aggregate amount exceeding $10,000 that has come from outside the United States and on which no CMIR was filed. A CMIR does not need to be filed, however, if the person is a bank or broker-dealer, and the currency or other monetary instrument is mailed or shipped through the postal service or by a common carrier.

INFORMATION SHARING AMONG FINANCIAL INSTITUTIONS AND LAW ENFORCEMENT

Pursuant to the Patriot Act, Treasury has issued a final rule that requires financial institutions, including FCMs, IBs, CPOs, and CTAs, to comply with information requests received from law enforcement. The final rule requires a financial institution to make an expeditious search of its records for accounts and transactions involving named suspects, provide specified information about the named suspects, and prohibit the financial institution from disclosing the fact that a request has been made (other than as necessary to comply with the information request).

CFTC registrants are reminded of the requirement in 31 CFR 103.100 to maintain adequate procedures to safeguard the security and confidentiality of any information request received from FinCEN. Firms may not disclose to any person other than FinCEN or the Federal law enforcement agency on whose behalf FinCEN is requesting information the fact that FinCEN has requested or has obtained information, except to the extent necessary to comply with the information request. There are significant penalties for willful violations of the BSA regulations.

The final rule permits financial institutions required by the BSA to establish AML Programs and associations of such financial institutions to share information regarding individuals and other persons involved in possible terrorist activity or money laundering. FCMs and IBs are required to establish AML Programs, and thus are permitted to share information with other financial institutions that are required to establish AML Programs, such as other FCMs, IBs, broker-dealers, and banks.

Financial institutions and associations of financial institutions that intend to share information must file, on a yearly basis, a notice with Treasury's Financial Crimes Enforcement Network (FinCEN). A copy of the notice is included as Appendix A to the final rules relating to information sharing that are discussed above.

ADDITIONAL RESOURCES

FinCEN, which administers the BSA and is charged with safeguarding the financial system from the abuses of financial crime, including terrorist financing, money laundering, and other illicit activity has delegated authority to issue regulations requiring financial institutions to keep records and file reports on certain financial transactions. FinCEN's website provides general information and updates about AML and the BSA relevant to all financial institutions. FinCEN also issues advisories that pertain to transactions involving certain jurisdictions.

OFAC administers and enforces economic and trade sanctions against targeted foreign countries, terrorism sponsoring organizations, and international narcotics traffickers.

National Futures Association, a registered futures association, issues AML rules applicable to its membership, provides regulatory updates concerning BSA amendments relevant to the futures industry and offers web-based AML training for FCMs and IBs, under CFTC oversight.

FINRA, a national securities association, issues AML rules applicable to its membership, details the AML requirements applicable to members, provides AML regulatory updates, and offers AML training for securities brokers and dealers, under SEC oversight.

The Financial Action Task Force on Money Laundering (FATF), an inter-governmental organization whose members include 32 countries and two international organizations, sets forth the international framework for AML efforts in its Forty Recommendations on money laundering and nine special recommendations on terrorist financing.

The Federal Financial Institutions Examination Council (FFIEC) Bank Secrecy Act/Anti-Money Laundering (BSA/AML) Examination Manual.

United Nations instruments and related international standards relating to the suppression of money laundering and terrorist financing.

The Office of the Comptroller of the Currency issued AML booklet and general AML guidance for bankers.

Interpol's activities in the areas of money laundering and terrorist financing.

The Council of Europe's Convention on Laundering, Search, Seizure and Confiscation of the Proceeds of Crimes.

The Wolfsberg Principles for international private banks.

The Department of State's list of foreign terrorist organizations.

The Executive Order generally restricts all U.S. financial institutions from undertaking financial transactions with Burmese financial institutions, subject to certain exemptions.

IMPORTANT ORGANIZATIONS REGULTED BY THE COMMISSION

TRADING ORGANIZATIONS

Designated Contract Markets

Designated contract markets (DCMs) are exchanges that may list for trading futures or option contracts based on all types of commodities and that may allow access to their facilities by all types of traders, including retail customers. Some DCMs have been operating for many years as traditional futures exchanges, while others are new markets that were only recently designated as contract markets by the CFTC. CFTC staff perform regular reviews of each DCM's ongoing compliance with the required core principles called **Rule Enforcement Reviews**.

SWAP EXECUTION FACILITIES

Section 733 of the Dodd-Frank Wall Street Reform and Consumer Protection Act ("Dodd-Frank Act") adopts new Section 5h of the Commodity Exchange Act ("CEA"), which provides that no person may operate a facility for the trading or processing of swaps unless the facility is registered as a swap execution facility ("SEF") or as a designated contract market ("DCM"). To be registered and maintain registration, a SEF must comply with fifteen enumerated core principles and any requirement that the CFTC may impose by rule or regulation. On May 16, 2013, the CFTC voted to approve for publication in the Federal Register final SEF regulations, guidance and acceptable practices.

FORM SEF AND SEF TECHNOLOGY QUESTIONNAIRE

SEF applicants must complete and submit **Form SEF** and the **Technology Questionnaire** as part of their SEF applications. The Questionnaire must be completed by SEF applicants per Exhibit V to Form SEF. SEF applicants must file Form SEF and the Questionnaire electronically with the Commission through the **CFTC portal**.

EXEMPT MARKETS: EXEMPT BOARDS OF TRADE AND EXEMPT COMMERCIAL MARKETS

Exempt markets are exempted from most requirements of the Act. In order to be exempt from most CFTC regulatory oversight, the exempt market must satisfy the conditions for the exemption, including a requirement to notify the CFTC of the market's intention to rely on the exemption. There are two types of exempt markets, both limit access, intermediation and/or products, in all cases to lower the regulatory concerns.

Exempt boards of trade (EBOTs) are markets that limit trading to transactions by **eligible contract participants** in a selected limited group of commodities. **Section 5d** of the CEA, 7 USC 7a-3, and **Part 36.2**of the CFTC's regulations, 17 CFR 36.2, contain requirements and provisions related to EBOTs.

Exempt commercial markets (ECMs) are markets that limit trading to principal-to-principal transactions between **eligible commercial entities** in exempt commodities. **Sections 2(h)(3)-(5)** of the CEA, 7 USC 2(h)(3)-(5), and **Part 36.3** of the CFTC's regulations contain requirements and provisions related to ECMs. Under Section 2(h)(4) of the CEA, an ECM is subject to antifraud and antimanipulation provisions and a requirement that, if performing a significant price discovery function, the market must provide pricing information to the public.

Effective July 16, 2011, Title VII of the Dodd-Frank Act eliminated the sections of the CEA containing the exemptions that allowed the operation of ECMs and EBOTs. The Commission has allowed ECMs and EBOTs to continue to operate pursuant to a series of exemptive orders (*i.e.* Final Order, Effective Date of Swap Regulation, 76 FR 42508, July 19, 2011 (effective July 14, 2011); Amendment to the July

14, 2011 Order for Swap Regulation, 76 FR 80233, December 23, 2011; and Second Amendment to the July 14, 2011 Order for Swap Regulation, 77 FR 41260, July 13, 2012).

On June 17, 2013, the CFTC released CFTC Letter Number 13-28 ("Letter 13-28"), which provides no-action relief that allows ECMs and EBOTs to operate until October 2, 2013, the compliance date for the SEF final rulemaking. Under Letter 13-28, in order to avoid an interruption in operations, an ECM or EBOT must achieve temporary SEF registration status, full SEF registration status, or full DCM registration status by October 2, 2013. An ECM or EBOT that achieves temporary SEF registration status must immediately come into full compliance with all applicable SEF rules and regulations, however no SEF can begin operations until August 5, 2013, the effective date for the SEF final rulemaking.

CLEARING ORGANIZATIONS

DERIVATIVES CLEARING ORGANIZATIONS

A derivatives clearing organization (DCO) is a clearinghouse, clearing association, clearing corporation, or similar entity that enables each party to an agreement, contract, or transaction to substitute, through novation or otherwise, the credit of the DCO for the credit of the parties; arranges or provides, on a multilateral basis, for the settlement or netting of obligations; or otherwise provides clearing services or arrangements that mutualize or transfer credit risk among participants.

Any clearinghouse that seeks to provide clearing services with respect to futures contracts, options on futures contracts, or swaps must register with the CFTC as a DCO before it can begin providing such services. To obtain and maintain registration, a DCO must comply with the DCO core principles established in Section 5b, **7 USC § 7a-1**, of the Commodity Exchange Act (CEA):

1. Adequate financial, operational, and managerial resources.
2. Appropriate standards for participant and product eligibility.
3. Adequate and appropriate risk management capabilities.
4. Ability to complete settlements on a timely basis under varying circumstances.
5. Standards and procedures to protect member and participant funds.
6. Efficient and fair default rules and procedures.
7. Adequate rule enforcement and dispute resolution procedures.
8. Adequate and appropriate systems safeguards, emergency procedures, and plan for disaster recovery.
9. Obligation to provide necessary reports to allow the CFTC to oversee clearinghouse activities.
10. Maintenance of all business records for five years in a form acceptable to the CFTC.
11. Publication of clearinghouse rules and operating procedures.
12. Participation in appropriate domestic and international information-sharing agreements.
13. Avoidance of actions that are unreasonable restraints of trade or that impose anti-competitive burdens.
14. Governance arrangements and fitness standards.
15. Rules to minimize conflicts of interest in the DCO's decision-making process, and a process for resolving any conflicts.
16. Composition of governing boards to include market participants.
17. Well founded legal framework for the activities of the DCO.

How to Register as a Derivatives Clearing Organization

Criteria, procedures, and requirements for registration as a DCO are set forth in Section 5b of the CEA, 7 USC § 7a-1, and **Part 39** of the CFTC's regulations. Applicants should review the Commission's final rules dated November 8, 2011 (**76 FR 69334**), which set forth changes to DCO registration procedures, including additional information regarding how an applicant may demonstrate compliance with each of the core principles as amended by the Dodd-Frank Act.

FUTURES COMMISSION MERCHANTS (FCMS) & INTRODUCING BROKERS (IBS)

REGISTRATION

The Commodity Exchange Act requires all **futures commission merchants** (FCMs) and **introducing brokers** (IBs) to **register** as such, unless they qualify for an exemption, e.g.:

A firm handling transactions only for proprietary persons (such as the firm itself, affiliates, top officers, or directors) need not register as an FCM.

A non-U.S. firm with only non-U.S. customers does not have to register if it submits all trades for clearing to an FCM.

OVERSIGHT OF REGISTRANTS BY SELF-REGULATORY ORGANIZATIONS

All registered FCMs and IBs are required to be members of the National Futures Association (NFA), and may also be members of one or more designated contract markets (commodity exchanges). The NFA and the commodity exchanges are **self-regulatory organizations** that are required to enforce CFTC-approved minimum financial and reporting requirements for their members.

FUTURES COMMISSION MERCHANT AND INTRODUCING BROKER REQUIREMENTS

FCMs and IBs must satisfy minimum standards for:

Minimum net capital

Customer funds (FCMs only; IBs do not hold customer funds)

Disclosure and other requirements for customers

Financial and other filings

MINIMUM NET CAPITAL

Minimum Adjusted Net Capital Requirements for Futures Commission Merchants and Introducing Brokers

Each futures commission merchant (FCM) is required to maintain adjusted net capital of $1,000,000 or some greater amount as determined under CFTC Regulation 1.17(a)(1)(i).

Each introducing broker (IB) that is not operating under a guarantee agreement with an FCM is required to maintain adjusted net capital of $45,000 or some greater amount as determined under CFTC Regulation 1.17(a)(1)(iii).

Should an FCM or IB become undercapitalized at any time, an FCM must provide immediate notice to the CFTC, and an IB must provide immediate notice to the National Futures Association on behalf of the Commission. The FCM must also notify its designated self-regulatory organization.

EXEMPT MARKETS

Sections 2(h)(3)-(7) and 5d of the Commodity Exchange Act ("Act") were deleted by the Dodd-Frank Wall Street Reform and Consumer Protection Act ("Dodd-Frank Act") on July 15, 2011. However, the CFTC provided relief for ECMs and EBOTs in its issuance of two orders for relief.

In an Order of September 16, 2010, the CFTC provided limited grandfather relief, pursuant to the Dodd-Frank Act, to certain ECMs and EBOTs. These entities must meet a number of conditions specified in the Order, including having filed a petition for grandfather relief within a stated timeframe.

In addition, all ECMs and EBOTs that have submitted to the Commission a notification of their intent to operate in reliance upon a particular exemption may continue to operate in reliance upon the CFTC's July 14, 2011 Order granting limited exemptive relief. The Commission, to provide for the orderly implementation of the Dodd-Frank Act, determined to conditionally exempt from the amended provisions of the CEA, among other things, agreements, contracts, and transactions in exempt and excluded (but not agricultural) commodities within the scope of existing CEA sections 2(h)(3) and 5d as in effect prior to July 16, 2011, provided the ECM and EBOT meets the conditions of the July 14, 2011 exemptive order. The temporary exemption provided in the CFTC's July 14, 2011 exemptive order will expire, in relevant part, upon the earlier of the repeal, withdrawal or replacement of part 35 of the CFTC's regulations or December 31, 2011.

Exempt markets are exempted from most requirements of the Commodity Exchange Act (CEA) and most CFTC regulatory oversight . There are two kinds of exempt markets—exempt commercial markets (ECMs) and exempt boards of trade (EBOTs). This contrasts to the CFTC's authority over designated and registered entities.

Exempt markets are not registered with, or designated, recognized, licensed or approved by the CFTC, and they are prohibited from representing that they are registered, designated, or recognized by the CFTC in any way. To be exempt from most CFTC regulatory oversight, the exempt market must satisfy the conditions for the exemption, including a requirement to notify the CFTC of the market's intention to rely on the exemption. If the exempt market is performing a price discovery function, the market must provide certain pricing information to the public.

EXEMPT MARKETS FOR EXEMPT COMMODITIES

Agreements, contracts, and transactions in exempt commodities that are traded on a principal-to-principal basis on electronic trading facilities between eligible commercial entities may be traded on an exempt commercial market (ECM) and be exempt from regulation if the market satisfies the conditions for the exemption found in Sections 2(h)(3) through (5) of the CEA, 7 USC 2(h)(3)-(5), including a requirement that the exempt commercial market notify the CFTC. CFTC Regulation 36.3, 17 CFR 36.3, provides further details on compliance with Sections 2(h)(3) through (5) of the CEA.

ECMs transactions that meet the requirements for the Section 2(h)(3) exemption are not subject to the CFTC's regulatory or enforcement jurisdiction, except for certain limited fraud and manipulation authority.

EXEMPT MARKETS FOR EXCLUDED COMMODITIES

Transactions by eligible contract participants in a certain narrow list of selected commodities may be conducted on an exempt board of trade (EBOT) and be exempt from regulation if they meet the conditions for the exemption found in Section 5d of the CEA, 7 USC 7a-3, including a requirement that the exempt commercial market notify the CFTC. Part 36.2 of the CFTC's regulations contains further details on compliance with CEA Section 5d.

EBOT transactions that meet the requirements for the Section 5d exemption are not subject to the CFTC's regulatory or enforcement jurisdiction except for certain limited fraud and manipulation authority.

FOREIGN MARKETS, PRODUCTS, & INTERMEDIARIES

INTERNATIONAL INITIATIVES

The CFTC participates in a wide range of international initiatives to

•enhance international supervisory cooperation and emergency procedures,

•establish concrete standards and best practices for regulation of futures and derivatives markets,

•encourage improved transparency in futures and derivatives markets,

•improve the quality and currency of international information sharing, and

•encourage foreign jurisdictions to remove legal and practical obstacles to achieving these goals.

International initiatives include:

CFTC Staff Self-Assessment of the IOSCO Objectives and Principles of Securities Regulation, This document is the CFTC staff's self-assessment of the International Organization of Securities Commissions' (IOSCO) objectives and principles of securities regulation, submitted to the International Monetary Fund (IMF) as part of the IMF's Financial Sector Assessment Program (FSAP). The self-assessment was prepared by staff of the CFTC solely for the purposes of the FSAP, and should not be considered outside of the FSAP context. (August 2009)

International Organization of Securities Commissions Technical Committee Report of the Task Force on Commodity Futures Markets, March 2009 (PDF). The IOSCO Task Force on Commodity Futures Markets was formed following the concerns expressed by the G-8 Finance Ministers regarding the price rises and volatility in agricultural and energy commodities in 2008.

CESR-CFTC Common Work Program to Facilitate Transatlantic Derivatives Business, May 2006 (PDF). This Communique represents a joint commitment of the CFTC and CESR to a work program designed to facilitate the conduct and supervision of transatlantic derivatives business.

Methodology For Assessing Implementation of the IOSCO Objectives and Principles of Securities Regulation, October 2003 (PDF). Guidance for securities regulators on how concretely to apply IOSCO's Objectives and Principles of Securities Regulation to an assessment of a given jurisdiction.

IOSCO Strengthens International Cooperation to Fight Illegal Securities and Derivatives Activities, October 2003 (PDF). During its annual conference in South Korea, IOSCO announced its efforts to strengthen international cooperation in the fight against illegal securities and derivatives activities through the promulgation of a global memorandum of understanding (IOSCO MMOU) between securities regulators.

CPSS/IOSCO Assessment Methodology for Recommendations for Securities Settlement Systems, November 2002 (PDF). Guidance from the Committee on Payment Settlement Systems (CPSS) and IOSCO's Technical Committee on how concretely to apply the CPSS and IOSCO Recommendations for Securities Settlement Systems to an assessment of a given jurisdiction's securities settlement practices.

International Regulators Alert System, NFA, June 2002. NFA's member newsletter discusses the alert system NFA developed with the CFTC to keep international regulators abreast of the domestic status of U.S. firms operating in foreign jurisdictions.

Objectives and Principles of Securities Regulations, IOSCO, September 1998 (PDF). Principles for successful securities regulatory regimes published by IOSCO to serve as a standard setting document in financial markets that are globally interconnected.

Application of the Tokyo Communiqué to Exchange-Traded Financial Derivatives Contracts, September 1998 (PDF). Clarification of many aspects of guidance contained in the Tokyo Communiqué applicable to the oversight of financial derivatives markets and contracts not settled by a deliverable of finite supply.

Tokyo Communiqué on Supervision of Commodity Futures Markets, October 1997 (PDF). The Tokyo Communiqué established internationally recognized benchmarks for contract design and/or review and for market surveillance and information sharing in physical delivery markets.

Boca Declaration on Cooperation and Supervision of International Futures Markets and Clearing Organizations, March 1996. A multilateral mechanism for information sharing on a bilateral basis whereby the occurrence of certain agreed triggering events affecting an exchange member's financial resources or positions will prompt the sharing of information. Amended March 1998.

Windsor Declaration, May 1995. Recommendations for regulatory action regarding cooperation between market authorities; protection of customer positions, funds, and assets; default procedures; and regulatory cooperation in emergencies.

OTC Derivatives Oversight Statement of the SEC, the CFTC, and the U.K. Securities and Investments Board, March 1994. Statement identifying means for cooperation in regulatory approaches to the over-the-counter derivatives market and setting forth common goals for the three authorities.

COOPERATION WITH FOREIGN ORGANIZATIONS

The CFTC cooperates with foreign regulatory and enforcement authorities through formal Memoranda of Understanding (MOUs) and other arrangements to combat cross-border fraud and other illegal practices that could harm customers or threaten market integrity.

Cross-border information sharing among market authorities plays an integral role in the effective surveillance of global markets that are linked by products, participants, and technology. Information sharing arrangements can be critical in combating cross-border fraud and manipulation, addressing the financial risks of market participants, and sharing regulatory expertise on market oversight and supervision. The CFTC makes and receives a significant number of requests for assistance and information to and from foreign authorities in connection with various surveillance and enforcement issues.

The CFTC has entered into MOUs and cooperative arrangements with many jurisdictions, including cooperative enforcement arrangements, arrangements relating to sharing financial and other types of fitness information, and arrangements for sharing information on matters related to the implementation of the CFTC's Part 30 rules, which grant foreign firms an exemption from certain CFTC requirements.

COOPERATIVE ENFORCEMENT

The CFTC has entered into arrangements for cooperative enforcement with authorities in more than 20 jurisdictions. MOUs typically provide for access to non-public documents and information already in the possession of the authorities and often include undertakings to obtain documents and to take testimony of, or statements from, witnesses on behalf of a requesting authority. CFTC MOUs are public documents, and copies may be obtained from the Office of the Secretariat.

•Argentina: Comision Nacional de Valores (CNV)

Memorandum of Understanding on Consultation, Technical Assistance, and Mutual Assistance for the Exchange of Information, May 30, 1995

•Australia: Australian Securities Commission (now Australian Securities and Investments Commission) ASIC

Memorandum of Understanding concerning Consultation and Cooperation in the Administration and Enforcement of Futures Laws, October 19, 1994

•Brazil: Comissão de Valores Mobiliários (CVM)

Memorandum of Understanding on Mutual Assistance and Exchange of Information, April 12, 1991

•Canada: Ontario Securities Commission (OSC)

Memorandum of Understanding, July 7, 1992

•Canada: Commission des valeurs mobilières du Québec (CVMQ)

Memorandum of Understanding, July 7, 1992

•Dubai: Dubai Financial Services Authority (DFSA)

Protocol Concerning Mutual Assistance, Information Sharing and Cooperation Agreements, December 1, 2005

•France: Commission des Opérations de Bourse (COB)

Administrative Agreement, June 6, 1990. The CFTC and the COB also signed a Mutual Recognition MOU (MRMOU) that provides for information sharing to facilitate monitoring and compliance matters related to the mutual recognition of intermediaries and products. 55 Fed. Reg. 23902 (June 13, 1990)

•Germany: Bundesaufsichtsamt für den Wertpapierhandel (BAWe)

Memorandum of Understanding concerning Consultation and Cooperation in the Administration and Enforcement of Futures Laws, October 17, 1997

•Hong Kong: Securities and Futures Commission (SFC)

Memorandum of Understanding concerning Consultation and Cooperation in the Administration and Enforcement of Futures Laws, October 5, 1995

•IOSCO (International Organization of Securities Commissions)

IOSCO Multilateral Memorandum of Understanding (MMOU) Concerning Consultation and Cooperation and the Exchange of Information, May 2002. This MMOU is a multilateral mechanism for sharing information on a bilateral basis between signatories; a list of signatories can be found at http://www.iosco.org/.

•Ireland: Irish Financial Services Regulatory Authority (IFSRA)

The CFTC-IFSRA Statement of Intent concerns consultation and cooperation in the administration and enforcement of futures laws, March 17, 2004. The Statement of Intent (SOI) provides a framework for information sharing, thereby facilitating cooperation in cross-border investigations of potential violations of commodity futures and options laws.

•Isle of Man: Financial Supervision Commission (FSC)

Statement of Intent Concerning Mutual Assistance and Cooperation Arrangements, April 12, 2005

•Italy: Commissione Nazionale per le Società e la Borsa (CONSOB)

Memorandum of Understanding on Consultation and Mutual Assistance for the Exchange of Information, June 22, 1995

•Japan: The Japanese Financial Services Agency (FSA) and the U.S. Securities and Exchange Commission (SEC)

Statement of Intent Concerning Cooperation, Consultation and the Exchange of Information, May 17, 2002; Statement of Intent Concerning Cooperation, Consultation and the Exchange of Information, January 2006;

•Jersey: The Jersey Financial Services Commission (FSC) and the U.S. Securities and Exchange Commission (SEC)

Memorandum of Understanding Concerning Cooperation, Consultation and the Exchange of Information, May 30, 2002

•Mexico: Comisión Nacional Bancaria y de Valores (CNBV)

Memorandum of Understanding on Consultation, Technical Assistance, and Mutual Assistance for the Exchange of Information, May 11, 1995

•The Netherlands: Government of the Kingdom of the Netherlands

Agreement (through the Government of the United States of America) on Mutual Administrative Assistance in the Exchange of Information in Futures Matters, April 29, 1993. The Ministry of Finance designated the Securities Board of the Netherlands (the Dutch futures, options, and securities regulator) and the Dutch Central Bank (the regulator for collective investment schemes) to implement the Agreement, which entered into force on February 1, 1994, after approval by the Dutch Parliament.

•New Zealand: New Zealand Securities Commission (NZSC)

Memorandum of Understanding on Consultation and Mutual Assistance for the Exchange of Information, September 16, 1996

•Portugal: Commissão do Mercado de Valores Mobiliários (CMVM)

Memorandum of Understanding concerning Consultation and Cooperation in the Administration and Enforcement of Futures Laws, February 4, 1999

•Singapore: Monetary Authority of Singapore

Memorandum of Understanding concerning Consultation, Cooperation and the Exchange of Information (concluded jointly with the U.S. Securities and Exchange Commission), May 16, 2000

•South Africa: Financial Services Board of the Republic of South Africa (FSB)

Joint Communiqué on Exchange of Information for Cooperation and Consultation, May 27, 1997

•Spain: Comisión Nacional del Mercado de Valores (CNMV)

Memorandum of Understanding on Mutual Assistance and Exchange of Information, October 26, 1992

•Switzerland: Swiss Confederation

Diplomatic Notes (through the U.S. government) amending Article 1, Paragraph 3 of the Treaty on Mutual Assistance in Criminal Matters (MLAT), November 3, 1993

•Taiwan: Securities and Futures Commission

Memorandum of Understanding between the CFTC and the Taiwan Securities & Exchange Commission (now the Securities & Futures Commission) through, respectively, the American Institute in Taiwan and the Coordination Council for North American Affairs (now the Taipei Economic and Cultural Representative Office in the United States), January 11, 1993

•Turkey: Capital Markets Board Of Turkey

Memorandum of Understanding between the CFTC and the Capital Markets Board of Turkey concerning Consultation, Cooperation, and the Exchange of Information, June 25, 2001 new

•United Kingdom: Department of Trade and Industry

Memorandum of Understanding on Exchange of Information in matters relating to Securities and Futures concluded jointly with the U.S. Securities and Exchange Commission, September 23, 1986

•United Kingdom: Department of Trade and Industry (DTI), Securities and Investments Board (SIB) (now Financial Services Authority (FSA)). Memorandum of Understanding on Mutual Assistance and Exchange of Information, concluded jointly with the U.S. Securities and Exchange Commission, September 25, 1991; HM Treasury (HMT) (added on May 9, 1994)

Information Sharing for Supervisory, Prudential, and Risk Assessment Purposes and Regulation of Cross-border Futures and Clearing Activity

These arrangements facilitate information sharing for supervisory, prudential, and risk-assessment purposes. They establish a framework for cooperation and assistance in regulation of cross-border futures and clearing activity that includes sharing routine audit information, cooperation in conducting on-site examinations, information sharing regarding the underlying reference value or supply of a product covered by a futures contract, and sharing of fitness and financial information on intermediaries, clearing organizations and other registered entities.

•Canda: Alberta Securities Commission (ASC)

Memorandum of Understanding concerning cooperation and the exchange of information related to the supervision of cross-border clearing organizations, June 10, 2010

•France: Conseil des Marches Financiers

Memorandum of Understanding regarding information sharing on remote members of regulated markets, March 21, 2002

•Hong Kong: Securities and Futures Commission (SFC)

Declaration on Cooperation and Supervision of Cross-Border Managed Futures Activity, October 5, 1995

•Italy: Commissione Nazionale per le Società e la Borsa (CONSOB)

Exchange of letters relating to the listing of equity-based futures contacts, April 5, 2000

•Italy: Commissione Nazionale per le Società e la Borsa (CONSOB)

Supplemental Memorandum of Understanding to facilitate the recognition of regulated markets, September 11, 2000

•Multilateral Arrangement: Declaration on Cooperation and Supervision of International Futures Exchanges and Clearing Organizations, March 15, 1996 (as amended) (Boca Declaration).

The Boca Declaration and a companion exchange MOU constitute multilateral mechanisms for sharing information on a bilateral basis between the requesting and requested market authority consistent with their legal and contractual obligations. The documents establish mechanisms whereby the occurrence of certain agreed triggering events affecting an exchange member's financial resources or positions will prompt the sharing of information under the Boca Declaration and/or MOU. The trigger levels are designed to facilitate the identification of large exposures by firms that could have a potentially adverse effect on markets.

The Boca Declaration signed in March 1996 was amended in October 1997 to delete language that had prevented certain regulators from signing the Declaration. In March 1998, the Declaration was amended again to permit regulators to make requests for information based upon possible manipulative or other disruptive conduct.

Signatories as of April 2002: Comisión Nacional de Valores (Argentina); Australian Securities and Investments Commission (Australia); Ministry of Finance (Austria); Commission bancaire et financière (Belgium); Comissão de Valores Mobiliários (Brazil); Commission des valeurs mobilières du Québec (Canada, Québec); Ontario Securities Commission (Canada, Ontario); Danish Financial Supervisory Authority/Finanstilsynet (Denmark); Commission des Opérations de Bourse (France); Bundesaufsichtsamt für den Wertpapierhandel (Germany); Securities and Futures Commission (Hong Kong); Hungarian Banking and Capital Market Supervision (Hungary); Central Bank of Ireland (Ireland); Commissione Nazionale per le Società e la Borsa (Italy); Ministry of International Trade and Industry (Japan); Ministry of Agriculture, Forestry and Fisheries (Japan); Securities Commission (Malaysia); Securities Board of the Netherlands (Netherlands); New Zealand Securities Commission (New Zealand); Comissão do Mercado de Valores Mobiliários (Portugal); Monetary Authority of Singapore (Singapore); Financial Services Board (South Africa); Comisión Nacional del Mercado de Valores (Spain); Financial Supervisory Authority/Finansinspektionen (Sweden); Securities and Futures Commission (Taiwan); Capital Markets Board (Turkey); Financial Services Authority (United Kingdom); Commodity Futures Trading Commission (United States).

•United Kingdom: Financial Services Authority (FSA)

Memorandum of Understanding concluded jointly with the U.S. Securities and Exchange Commission, October 28, 1997

•United Kingdom: Financial Services Authority (FSA)

Arrangement on Warehouse Information to facilitate exchanges of information for surveillance and enforcement purposes regarding deliverable commodities, May 17, 2000

•United Kingdom: Financial Services Authority (FSA)

Memorandum of Understanding concerning consultation, cooperation and the exchange of information related to market oversight, November 17, 2006

•United Kingdom: Financial Services Authority (FSA)

Memorandum of Understanding concerning cooperation and the exchange of information related to the supervision of cross-border clearing organizations, September 14, 2009

Financial Information Sharing Memoranda of Understanding

Financial information sharing memoranda of understanding (FISMOUs) now include risk assessment of related firms located in different jurisdictions. FISMOUs originally provided a basis for exempting firms from the application of one jurisdiction's capital requirements in deference to the applicability of home state requirements together with exchange of information.

•Canada: Ontario Securities Commission

Commission des valeurs mobilieres de Quebec (and Canadian self-regulatory organizations) Financial Information-Sharing Memorandum of Understanding, September 23, 1991

•United Kingdom: Securities and Investments Board (now Financial Services Authority) (and U.K. self-regulatory organizations)

Financial Information-Sharing Memorandum of Understanding, September 1, 1988

Addendum to Financial Information-Sharing Memorandum of Understanding, May 15, 1989

INFORMATION SHARING RELATED TO TECHNICAL ASSISTANCE

•Chile: Superintendencia de Valores y Seguros de Chile

Memorandum of Understanding regarding futures regulatory cooperation and the provision of technical assistance, September 13, 2002

•China: China Securities Regulatory Commission

Memorandum of Understanding regarding regulatory cooperation and the provision of technical assistance, January 18, 2002

•India: Forward Markets Commission

Arrangement regarding regulatory cooperation and technical assistance, October 18, 2006

•India: Securities and Exchange Board of India (SEBI)

Memorandum of Understanding regarding regulatory cooperation, consultation, and the provision of technical assistance, April 28, 2004

•Russia: Commodities' Exchanges Commission of the Ministry of the Russian Federation Anti-Monopoly Policy and Support of Entrepreneurship

Joint Statement regarding cooperation, consultation, and the provision of technical assistance, December 11, 2000

•Thailand: Office of the Agricultural Futures Trading Commission

Arrangement regarding regulatory cooperation and technical assistance, March 26, 2006

INFORMATION SHARING WITH U.S. GOVERNMENT AGENCIES

•CFTC and U.S. Securities and Exchange Commission (SEC)

Memorandum of Understanding Regarding the Oversight of Security Futures Product Trading and the Sharing of Security Futures Product Information, March 17, 2004

The CFTC-SEC Memorandum of Understanding covers the oversight of security futures product (SFP) trading and the sharing of security futures product information. Pursuant to the Commodity Futures Modernization Act of 2000 the CFTC and the SEC have joint authority for the oversight and regulation of security futures products. With respect to security futures products, the MOU provides that the CFTC and the SEC will notify each other of any planned examinations, advise the other of reasons for an intended examination, provide each other with examination-related information, and conduct examinations jointly, if feasible. The CFTC and the SEC will also notify each other of significant issues arising from these markets and share trading data and related information for SFP activity. Implementation of this MOU should serve to increase the effectiveness and efficiency of the joint CFTC/SEC oversight of SFPs. In November 2002,

OneChicago and NQLX began trading these products under the joint supervision of the agencies. The sharing of information and coordination recognized under this memorandum is an important element in providing oversight that is effective but avoids unnecessary regulatory burdens.

MULTILATERAL ARRANGEMENTS AND OTHER COOPERATION

•Memorandum of Understanding Concerning Consultation, Cooperation and the Exchange of Information of the International Organization of Securities Commissions, October 16, 2003

The IOSCO MOU is the first worldwide multilateral enforcement cooperation arrangement among securities and derivatives regulators. The IOSCO MOU provides for the exchange of essential information to investigate cross-border securities and derivatives violations, including the most serious offenses, such as manipulation, insider trading and customer fraud. The MOU enables regulators to share critical information, including bank, brokerage, and client identification records and to use that information in civil and criminal prosecutions. (For more information, see CFTC News Release 4851-03, October 16, 2003.)

Signatories: Alberta: Alberta Securities Commission; Australia: Australian Securities and Investments Commission; British Columbia: British Columbia Securities Commission; France: Commission des opérations de bourse; Germany: Bundesanstalt für Finanzdienstleistungsaufsicht (BaFin); Greece: Capital Market Commission; Hong Kong: Securities and Futures Commission; Hungary: Hungarian Financial Supervisory Authority; India: Securities and Exchange Board of India (SEBI); Italy: Commissione Nazionale per le Società e la Borsa; Jersey: Jersey Financial Services Commission; Lithuania: Lithuanian Securities Commission; Mexico: Comisión Nacional Bancaria y de Valores; New Zealand:New Zealand Securities Commission; Ontario: Ontario Securities Commission; Poland: Polish Securities and Exchange Commission; Portugal: Comissão do Mercado de Valores Mobiliários; Quebec: Commission des valeurs mobilières du Québec; Spain: Comisión Nacional del Mercado de Valores; South Africa: Financial Services Board; Turkey: Capital Markets Board; United Kingdom: Financial Services Authority; nited States of America: United States Commodity Futures Trading Commission (CFTC); United States of America: United States Securities and Exchange Commission (SEC).

ACCESS TO FOREIGN MARKETS FROM THE U.S.

Pursuant to Part 48 of the Commission's regulations, foreign boards of trade that wish to permit identified members and other participants located in the U.S. with direct access to their electronic trading and order matching system must apply for and receive an Order of Registration pursuant to the procedures contained in Part 48. Application forms for an Order of Registration for the foreign board of trade and its associated clearing organization may be found here: Application forms. Applications for registration must be filed electronically with the Secretary of the Commission at FBOTapplications@cftc.gov.

Scope of Registration

A foreign board of trade must apply for registration and be registered to permit members and other participants of the foreign board of trade that are located in the U.S. to enter trades directly into the trading and order matching system of the foreign board of trade. A registered foreign board of trade may permit members or other participants to enter orders by direct access to the extent such members and other participants are:

1. Entering orders for the member's or other participant's proprietary accounts;

2. Registered with the Commission as futures commission merchants and submitting customer orders to the trading system for execution; or

3. Registered with the Commission as a commodity pool operator or commodity trading advisor, or exempt from such registration pursuant to Commission regulation 4.13 or 4.14, and submitting orders for execution on behalf of a U.S. pool that the member or other participant operates or an account of a U.S. customer for which the member or other participant has discretionary authority, respectively, provided that a futures commission merchant or a firm exempt from such registration pursuant to Commission regulation 30.10 acts

as clearing firm and guarantees, without limitation, all such trades of the commodity pool operator or commodity trading advisor effected through submission of orders to the trading system.

Scope of Review

In reviewing an application for registration, Commission staff examines, among other things, whether the foreign board of trade and its clearing organization are subject to comprehensive supervision and regulation by the appropriate governmental authorities in their home country or countries that is comparable to the comprehensive supervision and regulation to which designated contract markets and derivatives clearing organizations are respectively subject under the Act, Commission regulations, and other applicable U.S. laws and regulations, if any. Commission staff also reviews information included in the application about the foreign board of trade generally, as well as detailed information submitted to demonstrate compliance with the registration requirements contained in Commission regulation 48.7 with respect to:

1. foreign board of trade and clearing membership;

2. the automated trading system;

3. the terms and conditions of contracts proposed to be made available in the U.S.;

4. settlement and clearing;

5. the regulatory regime governing the foreign board of trade and the clearing organization;

6. the rules of the foreign board of trade and clearing organization and enforcement thereof; and

7. information sharing agreements among the Commission, the foreign board of trade, and the foreign board of trade's regulatory authority.

When issued, an Order of Registration requires that the registered foreign board of trade and clearing organization continue to comply with the registration requirements and with applicable conditions of registration described in Commission regulation 48.8.

PRACTICAL INFORMATION AND REGULATIONS FOR COMMODITY FUTURES TRADING

FUTURES MARKET BASICS

FUTURES MARKETS

• Trading commodity futures and options is a volatile, complex and risky venture that is rarely suitable for individual investors or "retail customers"

• Many individuals lose all of their money, and can be required to pay more than they invested initially

• Learn about fraudulent activities in the futures markets

BASICS OF FUTURES TRADING

• A commodity futures contract is an agreement to buy or sell a particular commodity at a future date

• The price and the amount of the commodity are fixed at the time of the agreement

• Most contracts contemplate that the agreement will be fulfilled by actual delivery of the commodity

• Some contracts allow cash settlement in lieu of delivery

• Most contracts are liquidated before the delivery date

• A commodity futures option gives the purchaser the right to buy or sell a particular futures contract at a future date for a particular price

• With limited exceptions, commodity futures and options must be traded through an exchange by persons and firms who are registered with the CFTC

TYPICAL USERS OF THE FUTURES MARKETS

• Most participants in the futures markets are commercial or institutional commodities producers or consumers

• Most participants are "hedgers" who trade futures to maximize the value of their assets, and to reduce the risk of financial losses from price changes

• Other participants are "speculators" who attempt to profit from price changes in futures contracts

REGULATION OF FUTURES PROFESSIONALS

• Companies and individuals who handle customer funds or give trading advice must register with the National Futures Association (NFA), a self-regulatory organization approved by the CFTC

• The CFTC seeks to protect customers by requiring:

• market risks and past performance to be disclosed to prospective customers;

• customer funds to be kept in accounts separate from the firm's own funds; and

• customer accounts to be adjusted to reflect each trading day's current market value at close

• The CFTC also monitors registrant supervision systems, internal controls and sales practice compliance programs

• The NFA provides detailed information for traders. Please visit the site for more information

BEFORE PURCHASING COMMODITY FUTURES OR OPTIONS CONTRACTS

• Consider your financial experience, goals and financial resources

• Know how much you can afford to lose above and beyond your initial investment

• Understand all of the obligations for any contract that you purchase

• Thoroughly review the risk disclosure documents that are required to be provided by the broker

• Know whom to contact with a problem or question

• Ask questions and gather information before opening a trading account

CONTRACTS & PRODUCTS

Designated contract markets (DCMs) may list for trading new contracts by filing a self-certification with the Commission that the new contract complies with the Commodity Exchange Act (CEA) and the Commission's regulations or by requesting Commission approval.

To meet its statutory mission of ensuring market integrity and customer protection with respect to products listed under self-certification procedures, the CFTC places greater reliance on its oversight authority, including market surveillance, rule enforcement reviews, reviews of contract terms, dialogue with the regulated entities, and enforcement actions. For contracts filed under self-certification procedures, the regulated entities are expected to assume primary responsibility for ensuring that the contracts meet, on a continuing basis, the applicable statutory and regulatory requirements.

LISTING OF NEW CONTRACTS BY SELF-CERTIFICATION

DCMs may list new contracts for trading by filing a written self-certification with the CFTC by close of business on the Commission's business day preceding the Commission's business day on which the rule is to be implemented. CFTC Regulation 38.4 and CFTC Regulation 40.2 set forth the procedures for new contract self-certification filings.

APPROVAL OF NEW CONTRACTS

DCMs may request Commission approval of any new contract listed for trading under Section 5c(c) of the CEA, 7 USC § 7a-2(c), CFTC Regulation 38.4(a) and CFTC Regulation 40.3. A DCM that voluntarily requests CFTC approval of a new contract may do so by submitting its request prior to, concurrently with, or subsequent to a new contract self-certification filing.

Approved Contracts Submitted by DCMs

Security Futures Products

Trading of futures on single securities and futures on narrow-based security indexes, collectively called security futures products or SFPs, is jointly regulated by the CFTC and the Securities and Exchange Commission (SEC). Security futures products have features of both securities and futures. Subpart C of Commission Part 41 specifies the requirements and standards for listing security futures products.

AGRICULTURAL TRADE OPTIONS

Agricultural trade options are tools for managing agricultural price risk exposure. They are referred to as "trade options" because, unlike exchange-traded options, which are bought and sold on a designated contract market, agricultural trade options are bought and sold off-exchange directly between commercial market participants for business-related purposes.

Event Contracts

An event contract, also known as a prediction or information contract, is a derivative contract whose payoff is based on a specified event, occurrence, or value such as the value of a macroeconomic indicator, corporate earnings, level of snowfall, or dollar value of damages caused by a hurricane. CFTC Regulation 40.11 prohibits event contracts that reference terrorism, assassination, war, gaming, or an activity that is unlawful under any State or Federal law, or that involves, relates to, or references an activity that is similar to any of those activities and that the CFTC determines by rule or regulation to be contrary to the public interest.

•On April 2, 2012, the CFTC issued an Order Prohibiting the Listing or Trading of certain Political Event Contracts at the North American Derivatives Exchange. The contracts, which would have paid out based upon the outcome of certain US federal elections, were determined to involve gaming and to be contrary to the public interest.

ECONOMIC REQUIREMENTS FOR LISTED PRODUCTS

The economic requirements, that listed futures and option contracts meet specified criteria, have been a fundamental tool of Federal regulation of commodity futures exchanges since the Future Trading Act of 1921, Pub. L. No. 67-66, 42 Stat. 187 (1921). Currently, the statutory requirements for listing contracts are found in Section 5 of the CEA, 7 USC § 7, and for security futures, in Section 2(a)(1)(D) of the CEA, 7 USC § 2(a)(1)(D).

The requirement that listed futures and option contracts meet specified criteria has been a fundamental tool of Federal regulation of commodity futures exchanges since the Futures Trading Act of 1921, Pub. L. No. 67-66, 42 Stat. 187 (1921).

Currently, the statutory requirements for listing futures and option contracts are found in Section 5 of the Commodity Exchange Act (CEA), 7 USC 7, for security futures, in Section 2(a)(1)(D) of the CEA, 7 USC 2(a)(1)(D) and for swaps in Section 5h of the CEA, 7 USC 7b-3

Designated contract markets (DCMs) must comply initially and on an ongoing basis with 23 core principles. Core Principle 3 and Core Principle 5 are specifically applicable to the terms and conditions of listed contracts. Core Principle 3 requires that contracts must not be readily susceptible to manipulation. Core Principle 5 specifies that speculative position limits or position accountability must be adopted where necessary and appropriate, to reduce the potential threat of market manipulation or congestion.

Appendix B and Appendix C to Part 38 of the CFTC's regulations, 17 CFR Part 38 Appendix B, and Appendix C 38 of the CFTC's regulations, 17 CFR Part 38 Appendix C, may be used as guidance for DCMs in ascertaining compliance with the statutory requirements for new product listings and existing listed contracts.

Swap Execution Facilities (SEFs) must comply initially and on and ongoing basis with 15 core principles. Core Principle 3 and Core Principle 6 are specifically applicable to the terms and conditions of swaps traded on or through a SEF. Core Principle 3 requires that swap contracts must not be readily susceptible to manipulation. Core Principle 6 specifies that speculative position limits or position accountability must be adopted where necessary and appropriate, to reduce the potential threat of market manipulation or congestion.

POLICY STATEMENT ON PRICE DIFFERENTIALS

The specification of delivery points, deliverable grades and their corresponding price differentials has a direct bearing on the susceptibility of the futures contract to price manipulation and market congestion. Ideally, supplies of the par delivery unit should normally be sufficient to satisfy expected demand for the commodity at expiration, thus ensuring normal convergence of cash and futures prices. When supplies of the par unit prove to be insufficient, distortions in the price of the futures and, perhaps, even in the cash market may occur. The provision of additional delivery points or deliverable grades may serve to limit these price divergences by attracting additional supplies from the non-par grades and/or from the non-par delivery points and allowing natural market forces to balance supply and demand.

In cases where additional delivery points or qualities are desirable to limit a contract's susceptibility to manipulation or congestion, locational and quality price differentials should reflect normal commercial price differences between delivery points or qualities. When cash market differences are unstable, futures market differentials should be set at levels that fall within the range of values commonly observed or expected to occur in the future, eliminating any unusual or extreme differences.

Nevertheless, this policy is not intended to sanction maintenance of a particular location or quality as the par specification long past the time the cash market has passed it by. In other words, the par unit should normally be sufficient, and non-par delivery points or qualities should not be used to prop up an outmoded par point or par grade. Neither should this method of setting the differential be used as an excuse for adding delivery points or qualities that are not consistent with prevailing cash market practice. Too many points or grades at imprecisely-set price differentials can create a misconception to both speculators and hedgers as to what the contract represents.

ECONOMIC REQUIREMENTS INTERPRETATIVE STATEMENT

Appendix C to Part 38 (formerly Guideline No. 1), 17 CFR Part 38 Appendix C, provides guidance on the type of information a designated contract market (DCM) should provide, if requested, to demonstrate its compliance with Core Principle 3 on an initial and continuing basis.

PHYSICAL DELIVERY FUTURES

1. The rules setting forth the terms and conditions of the futures contract.

2. A description of the cash market for the commodity on which the contract is based.

a. The description may include, in addition to or in lieu of materials prepared by the board of trade, existing studies by industry trade groups, academics, governmental bodies or other entities, reports of consultants, or other materials which provide a description of the underlying cash market.

b. Where the same, or a closely related commodity, is already designated as a contract market which is not dormant, the cash market description can be confined to those aspects relevant to particular term(s) or conditions(s) which differ from such existing contract.

3. A demonstration that the terms and conditions, as a whole, will result in a deliverable supply such that the contract will not be conducive to price manipulation or distortion and that the deliverable supply reasonably can be expected to be available to short traders and saleable by long traders at its market value in normal cash marketing channels.

Cash Settled Futures

1. . The rules setting forth the terms and conditions of the proposed futures contract.

2. A description of the cash market for the commodity on which the contract is based.

a. The description may include, in addition to or in lieu of materials prepared by the board of trade, existing studies by industry trade groups, academics, governmental bodies or other entities, reports of consultants, or other materials which provide a description of the underlying cash market.

b. Where the same, or a closely related commodity, is already designated as a contract market which is not dormant, the cash market description can be confined to those aspects relevant to particular term(s) or conditions(s) which differ from such existing contract.

3. A demonstration that cash settlement of the contract is at a price reflecting the underlying cash market, will not be subject to manipulation or distortion, and is based on a cash price series that is reliable, acceptable, publicly available, and timely.

Options on Futures

1. The rules setting forth the terms and conditions of the proposed futures contract.

2. i) For options that are exercised into futures positions, the terms and conditions of the underlying futures contract.

ii) For options that are exercised into physical commodity positions or are cash settled at expiration based on a specified index value:

A. A description of the cash market for the commodity on which the contract is based.

1. The description may include, in addition to or in lieu of material prepared by the DCM, existing studies by industry trade groups, academics, governmental bodies or other entities, promotional or marketing materials prepared by or for the DCM; reports of consultants; or other materials which provide a description of the underlying cash market.

2. Where the same, or a closely related commodity, is already designated and is not dormant, the cash market description can be confined to those aspects relevant to particular terms(s) or condition(s) which differ from such existing contract.

In addition, for each type of contract, the Commission has provided demonstration tables to serve as templates enumerating the significant contract terms and conditions typically contained in most contracts, as well as the Commission's enunciated standards for assessing compliance with its regulations. That template may be modified as necessary to reflect the nature of the particular commodity, the economic characteristics of the commodity, or the contract's specific terms and conditions.

LISTING PROCEDURES

SELF-CERTIFICATION FILING PROCEDURES

CFTC Regulation 40.2, 17 CFR 40.2, permits designated contract markets (DCMs) to list products for trading without prior CFTC approval by filing a written self-certification with the CFTC.

Timing of the Self-Certification Submission

To self-certify a new product, a DCM must file its submission with the CFTC no later than the close of business on the Commission's business day preceding the Commission's business day of the initial listing (or re-listing in the case of dormant contracts) of the product.

Where to File Notification

Self-certification filings must be sent to the CFTC either via mail to its Washington, DC headquarters office and to the CFTC regional office having local jurisdiction or electronically via email to submissions@cftc.gov.

A product self-certification submission should include:

A product self-certification submission should include:
• A copy of the submission cover sheet;
• A statement that the filing is made pursuant to CFTC Regulation 40.2;
• The text of the product's rules, including those relating to terms and conditions;
• A certification that the product or instrument complies with the Commodity Exchange Act (CEA) and CFTC regulations thereunder;
• A concise explanation and analysis of the product and its compliance with applicable provisions of the Act, including core principles, and the Commission's regulations thereunder. This explanation and analysis shall either be accompanied by the documentation relied upon to establish the basis for compliance with applicable law, or incorporate information contained in such documentation, with appropriate citations to data sources.
• A certification that the DCM posted a notice of pending product certification with the Commission on the DCM's website.

In making a self-certification submission, a DCM certifies that the product does not violate any provision of the CEA or the CFTC's regulations and policies adopted thereunder.

Appendix C to Part 38 contains the applicable economic requirements for rules related to the terms and conditions of a contract. Appendix C to Part 38 also provides exchanges with specific criteria for initial and continued compliance with the CEA and the CFTC's regulations and policies for products listed on regulated entities.

The listing of security futures products (SFPs) is subject to additional requirements and procedures.

Voluntary Requests for CFTC Approval of Products

DCMs may voluntarily request CFTC approval of a new product. The new product may be listed prior to approval if it also is filed with the CFTC under the self-certification procedures described above. Approval requests for contracts filed under self-certification procedures may be submitted concurrently with a self-certification filing or at any time thereafter, including after initial listing of the product. A request for approval must be accompanied with the appropriate approval filing fee.

Summary of the Procedure for Filing Requests for Approval

Voluntary requests for product approval must be sent to the CFTC either via mail to its Washington, DC headquarters office and to the CFTC regional office having local jurisdiction or electronically via email to submissions@cftc.gov.

A product request for approval filing must include:
• A copy of the submission cover sheet;
• The text of the product's rules, including those relating to terms and conditions;
• An explanation and analysis of the product and its compliance with applicable provisions of the Act, including core principles, and the Commission's regulations thereunder, including Guideline No. 1. This explanation and analysis shall either be accompanied by the documentation relied upon to establish the basis for compliance with applicable law, or incorporate information contained in such documentation, with appropriate citations to data sources;
• A description of any agreements or contracts entered into with other parties that enable the DCM to carry out its responsibilities;
• A certification that the DCM posted a notice of pending product certification with the Commission on the DCM's website.

Appendix C to Part 38 contains the applicable economic requirements for rules related to the terms and conditions of a contract. Appendix C to Part 38 also provides exchanges with specific criteria for initial and continued compliance with the CEA and the CFTC's regulations and policies for products listed on regulated entities.

All products submitted for Commission approval are deemed approved by the Commission 45 days after receipt by the Commission or at the conclusion of an extended period if:
The submission complies with the requirements of CFTC Regulation 40.3(a);
The submitting entity does not amend the terms or conditions of the product or supplement the request for approval, except as requested by the Commission or for non-substantive revisions, during the review period.

The Commission may extend the 45-day review period for an additional 45 days if the product raises novel or complex issues that require additional time for review or is of major economic significance.

Section 5c(c) of the CEA, 7 USC 7a-2(c), requires the CFTC to approve any such new contract unless the CFTC finds that the new product would violate the CEA. In addition, the CEA requires the CFTC to take final action on an approval request no later than 90 days after the filing is received by the CFTC unless the person making the filing agrees to an extension of the review period.

Questions about procedures for product self-certification and approval may be asked by email to submissions@cftc.gov, fax to 202-418-5527, or telephone to 202-418-5270.

INTERMEDIARY REGISTRATION

An "intermediary" is a person or firm who acts on behalf of another person in connection with futures trading

FUTURES COMMISSION MERCHANTS (FCMS) & INTRODUCING BROKERS (IBS)

REGISTRATION

The Commodity Exchange Act requires all futures commission merchants (FCMs) and introducing brokers (IBs) to register as such, unless they qualify for an exemption, e.g.:

A firm handling transactions only for proprietary persons (such as the firm itself, affiliates, top officers, or directors) need not register as an FCM.

A non-U.S. firm with only non-U.S. customers does not have to register if it submits all trades for clearing to an FCM.

OVERSIGHT OF REGISTRANTS BY SELF-REGULATORY ORGANIZATIONS

All registered FCMs and IBs are required to be members of the National Futures Association (NFA), and may also be members of one or more designated contract markets (commodity exchanges). The NFA and the commodity exchanges are self-regulatory organizations that are required to enforce CFTC-approved minimum financial and reporting requirements for their members.

FUTURES COMMISSION MERCHANT AND INTRODUCING BROKER REQUIREMENTS

FCMs and IBs must satisfy minimum standards for:

MINIMUM ADJUSTED NET CAPITAL REQUIREMENTS FOR FUTURES COMMISSION MERCHANTS AND INTRODUCING BROKERS

Each futures commission merchant (FCM) is required to maintain adjusted net capital of $1,000,000 or some greater amount as determined under CFTC Regulation 1.17(a)(1)(i).

Each introducing broker (IB) that is not operating under a guarantee agreement with an FCM is required to maintain adjusted net capital of $45,000 or some greater amount as determined under CFTC Regulation 1.17(a)(1)(iii).

Should an FCM or IB become undercapitalized at any time, an FCM must provide immediate notice to the CFTC, and an IB must provide immediate notice to the National Futures Association on behalf of the Commission. The FCM must also notify its designated self-regulatory organization.

OTHER FUTURES COMMISSION MERCHANT AND INTRODUCING BROKER REQUIREMENTS

CUSTOMER FUNDS (FCMS ONLY; IBS DO NOT HOLD CUSTOMER FUNDS)

Segregation of Customer Funds

All customer funds for trading on designated contract markets (exchanges) must be kept apart ("segregated") from the futures commission merchant's (FCM's) own funds—this includes cash deposits and any securities or other property deposited by such customers to margin or guarantee futures trading.

Segregated accounts must be titled for the benefit of the FCM's customers.

Acknowledgements must be provided that would preclude a bank or clearinghouse from recognizing a right of offset against the account for the FCM's debts.

Customer funds in segregation have a bankruptcy preference in the event of FCM insolvency.

To the extent that customer funds are not sufficient to pay customer claims, the remainder of what customers are owed will participate pro rata in the distributions to unsecured creditors of the bankrupt FCM.

Part 30 Secured Amount

Part 30 of the CFTC's regulations also requires FCMs to hold apart from their own funds a "secured amount" for U.S. customers trading on foreign boards of trade through FCMs.

The secured amount requirement is based on the lesser of:

Margin plus unrealized gains/losses plus long option value, minus short option value; or

Net liquidating equity (including market value of securities deposited).

If the foreign jurisdiction has a segregation rule, the secured amount requirement cannot be less than the amount required by the foreign jurisdiction.

DISCLOSURE AND OTHER REQUIREMENTS FOR CUSTOMERS

Disclosure

Before futures commission merchants (FCMs) or introducing brokers (IBs) may open a commodity futures account for a retail customer, the customer must receive a written disclosure statement and send back to the FCM or IB a signed and dated acknowledgment that the customer has received and understood the statement. The statement informs the customer of some of the risks inherent in futures trading and asks the customer to consider carefully whether it is in a financial position to take such risks.

There are comparable disclosure requirements before opening a commodity options account.

A retail customer trading on non-U.S. markets must be provided with additional disclosures concerning foreign markets, such as differences in the laws and regulations that may apply and the impact of foreign exchange rates. The CFTC has permitted the use of a "generic" risk disclosure statement that is acceptable for domestic and international trading; it has been approved for use in the U.K., Ireland, and Singapore.

TRADING AUTHORIZATION

An FCM or IB may not effect a transaction for a customer unless the customer:

Specifically authorized the transaction by specifying the precise commodity interest and the exact amount of the commodity interest to be purchased or sold; or

Authorized the FCM or IB in writing to effect transactions for the account without the customer's specific authorization.

An FCM or IB always has discretion as to time and price when entering an order.

REPORTING TO CUSTOMERS

An FCM must furnish its customers with monthly statements that show, e.g., all transactions occurring in the month, all charges and credits to the account, and the account balance. In addition to monthly statements, an FCM must provide the customer, within the next business day, confirmation of each transaction made for the customer and a statement showing the net gain or loss from any offsetting positions.

RECORDKEEPING

All FCMs and IBs must keep:

A permanent record pertaining to their customers, including each customer's name, address, and occupation; and

Full, complete, and systematic records, together with all pertinent data and memoranda, of all transactions.

Immediately upon receipt, FCMs and IBs must prepare a written record of a customer's order, including the date and time of receipt and the date and time it is transmitted for execution. In addition, a floor broker executing the trade must prepare a written record including the date and time of execution.

A financial ledger for each customer must be maintained that includes a record of all transactions, credits, debits, etc.

A record or journal must be maintained that shows all transactions made on each business day by the FCM or IB.

All records maintained under the Commodity Exchange Act (CEA) and accompanying regulations must be retained for five years. They may be maintained in electronic form.

Regardless of the form in which records are kept, they must be open to inspection by the CFTC, the National Futures Association, and the Department of Justice.

SUPERVISION

Each CFTC registrant, except an associated person who has no supervisory duties, must diligently supervise the handling by its partners, officers, employees, and agents (or persons occupying a similar status or performing a similar function) of all commodity interest accounts carried, operated, advised, or introduced by the registrant and all other activities of such persons relating to its business as a CFTC registrant.

ANTIFRAUD PROHIBITION

All firms are subject to the antifraud prohibition in the CEA when acting for or on behalf of a customer.

FINANCIAL AND OTHER FILINGS

Filing and Reporting

Futures commission merchants (FCMs) must file monthly unaudited financial reports (Form 1-FR-FCM) with the Commission and their designated self-regulatory organizations.

Non-guaranteed introducing brokers (IBs) must file semiannual unaudited financial reports (Forms 1-FR-IB) with the National Futures Association.

FCMs and non-guaranteed IBs must also file certified annual financial reports. These reports include financial statements and CFTC-specific schedules, and also must include an independent auditor's opinion that covers the statements and schedules.

The Division of Clearing and Intermediary Oversight publishes guidance for preparing and filing FCM financial reports in the 1-FR-FCM Instructions Manual and in an annual letter sent to FCMs.

MINIMUM ADJUSTED NET CAPITAL REQUIREMENTS FOR FUTURES COMMISSION MERCHANTS AND INTRODUCING BROKERS

Each futures commission merchant (FCM) is required to maintain adjusted net capital of $1,000,000 or some greater amount as determined under CFTC Regulation 1.17(a)(1)(i).

Each introducing broker (IB) that is not operating under a guarantee agreement with an FCM is required to maintain adjusted net capital of $45,000 or some greater amount as determined under CFTC Regulation 1.17(a)(1)(iii).

Should an FCM or IB become undercapitalized at any time, an FCM must provide immediate notice to the CFTC, and an IB must provide immediate notice to the National Futures Association on behalf of the Commission. The FCM must also notify its designated self-regulatory organization.

COMMODITY POOL OPERATORS (CPOS) & COMMODITY TRADING ADVISORS (CTAS)

All commodity pool operators (CPOs) and commodity trading advisors (CTAs) must register, unless they are excluded or exempted from registration.

Commodity Pool Operator Requirements

Although individual pools operated by a CPO are not required to register, the CPO has certain responsibilities with respect to each pool that it operates.

For each pool, a CPO must:

prepare and distribute a disclosure document;

distribute periodic account statements;

prepare and distribute audited annual financial reports; and

keep specified records concerning the participants, transactions, and operations of each pool, as well as records regarding transactions of the CPO and its principals.

Part 4 of the CFTC's regulations specifies the information that must be included in disclosure documents, account statements, and annual reports, the time frames within which they must be provided, and the specific records that a CPO must maintain.

CPOs must file disclosure documents and annual financial reports for commodity pools that they operate with National Futures Association (NFA).

Guidance for CPO Annual Reports

Commodity Trading Advisor Requirements

CTAs that manage accounts must distribute disclosure documents, and maintain specified records relating to their activities and clients. These requirements are also discussed in Part 4 of the Commission's regulations.

Disclosure documents for CTAs must be filed with NFA.

For both CPO and CTA disclosure documents:

NFA publishes a guide, Disclosure Documents: A Guide for CPOs and CTAs (PDF), to disclosure documents for CPOs and CTAs.

An expedited, or "instant," filing procedure may be available for CPO and CTA disclosure documents. CFTC Letter 95-44 (April 20, 1995) details this procedure.

SWAP DEDALERS

Registration

Commodity Exchange Act requires all major swap participants (MSPs) to register as such, unless they already are registered as a swap dealer or otherwise do not meet the conditions set forth in Commission Regulation 1.3(hhh).

Oversight of Registrants by Self-Regulatory Organizations

All registered SDs are required to be members of the National Futures Association (NFA). The NFA is a self-regulatory organization that is required to enforce CFTC-approved requirements for their members.

Swap Dealers Requirements

SDs must satisfy minimum standards for:

• Business conduct standards, including disclosure requirements

• Recordkeeping and reporting requirements

• Swap documentation requirements

Furnishing of Chief Compliance Officer Annual Reports and Periodic Risk Exposure Reports to the Commission

Commission Regulation 3.3(f) requires that each SD furnish electronically to the Commission a copy of the Annual Report of the SD's Chief Compliance Officer not more than 90 days after the end of the fiscal year of the SD, simultaneously with the financial condition report, as required under section 4s(f) of the Commodity Exchange Act, as applicable.

Commission Regulation 23.600(c)(2)(ii) requires that each SD furnish copies of its Risk Exposure Reports to the Commission within five (5) business days of providing such reports to its senior management.

PROVISIONALLY REGISTERED SWAP DEALERS

A list of provisionally registered swap dealers is listed below. This list is current as of July 5, 2013.

AUSTRALIA AND NEW ZEALAND BANKING GROUP LTD
BANCO BILBAO VIZCAYA ARGENTARIA SA
BANK OF AMERICA NA
BANK OF MONTREAL
BANK OF NEW YORK MELLON THE
BANK OF NOVA SCOTIA THE
BANK OF TOKYO MITSUBISHI UFJ LTD THE
BARCLAYS BANK PLC
BNP PARIBAS
CANADIAN IMPERIAL BANK OF COMMERCE
CARGILL INCORPORATED
CITIBANK N A
CITIGROUP ENERGY INC
CITIGROUP GLOBAL MARKETS INC
COMMERZBANK AG
COMMONWEALTH BANK OF AUSTRALIA
CREDIT AGRICOLE CORPORATE AND INVESTMENT BANK
CREDIT SUISSE INTERNATIONAL
CREDIT SUISSE SECURITIES EUROPE LIMITED
DB ENERGY TRADING LLC
DEUTSCHE BANK AG
FOREX CAPITAL MARKETS LLC
GAIN GTX LLC

GLOBAL FUTURES & FOREX LTD
GOLDMAN SACHS & CO
GOLDMAN SACHS BANK USA
GOLDMAN SACHS FINANCIAL MARKETS LP
GOLDMAN SACHS INTERNATIONAL
GOLDMAN SACHS MITSUI MARINE DERIVATIVE PRODUCTS LP
HONGKONG AND SHANGHAI BANKING CORPORATION LIMITED THE
HSBC BANK PLC
HSBC BANK USA NA
ING CAPITAL MARKETS LLC
INTL HANLEY LLC
J ARON & COMPANY
JEFFERIES BACHE FINANCIAL SERVICES INC
JEFFERIES DERIVATIVE PRODUCTS LLC
JP MORGAN SECURITIES LLC
JP MORGAN VENTURES ENERGY CORPORATION
JPMORGAN CHASE BANK
MACQUARIE BANK LIMITED
MACQUARIE ENERGY LLC
MERRILL LYNCH CAPITAL SERVICES INC
MERRILL LYNCH COMMODITIES INC
MERRILL LYNCH FINANCIAL MARKETS INC
MERRILL LYNCH INTERNATIONAL
MERRILL LYNCH INTERNATIONAL BANK LIMITED
MITSUBISHI UFJ SECURITIES INTERNATIONAL PLC
MIZUHO CAPITAL MARKETS CORPORATION
MIZUHO SECURITIES USA INC
MORGAN STANLEY & CO INTERNATIONAL PLC
MORGAN STANLEY & CO LLC
MORGAN STANLEY BANK NA
MORGAN STANLEY CAPITAL GROUP INC
MORGAN STANLEY CAPITAL SERVICES LLC
MORGAN STANLEY DERIVATIVE PRODUCTS INC
NATIONAL AUSTRALIA BANK LIMITED
NATIXIS
NEWEDGE UK FINANCIAL LTD
NEWEDGE USA LLC
NOMURA DERIVATIVE PRODUCTS INC
NOMURA GLOBAL FINANCIAL PRODUCTS INC
NOMURA INTERNATIONAL PLC
PNC BANK NATIONAL ASSOCIATION
RJ OBRIEN ASSOCIATES LLC
ROYAL BANK OF CANADA
ROYAL BANK OF SCOTLAND PLC THE
SMBC CAPITAL MARKETS INC
SOCIETE GENERALE S A
STANDARD CHARTERED BANK
STATE STREET BANK AND TRUST COMPANY
SUN TRUST BANK
THE NORTHERN TRUST COMPANY

TORONTO DOMINION BANK THE
UBS AG
UNICREDIT BANK AG
US BANK NA
WELLS FARGO BANK NA
WESTPAC BANKING CORPORATION

MAJOR SWAP PARTICIPANT (MSP)

Registration

Commodity Exchange Act requires all major swap participants (MSPs) to register as such, unless they already are registered as a swap dealer or otherwise do not meet the conditions set forth in Commission Regulation 1.3(hhh).

Oversight of Registrants by Self-Regulatory Organizations

All registered SDs are required to be members of the National Futures Association (NFA). The NFA is a self-regulatory organization that is required to enforce CFTC-approved requirements for their members.

Major Swap Participant Requirements

MSPs must satisfy minimum standards for:

• Business conduct standards, including disclosure requirements

• Recordkeeping and reporting requirements

• Swap documentation requirements

Furnishing of Chief Compliance Officer Annual Reports and Periodic Risk Exposure Reports to the Commission

Commission Regulation 3.3(f) requires that each MSP furnish electronically to the Commission a copy of the Annual Report of the MSP's Chief Compliance Officer not more than 90 days after the end of the fiscal year of the MSP, simultaneously with the financial condition report, as required under section 4s(f) of the Commodity Exchange Act, as applicable.

Commission Regulation 23.600(c)(2)(ii) requires that each MSP furnish copies of its Risk Exposure Reports to the Commission within five (5) business days of providing such reports to its senior management.

COMMODITY FUTURES TRADING COMMISSION ACT[1]

DEFINITIONS

§ 1.2 LIABILITY OF PRINCIPAL FOR ACT OF AGENT.

The act, omission, or failure of any official, agent, or other person acting for any individual, association, partnership, corporation, or trust, within the scope of his employment or office, shall be deemed the act, omission, or failure of such individual, association, partnership, corporation, or trust as well as of such official, agent, or other person.

§ 1.3 DEFINITIONS.

Words used in the singular form in the rules and regulations in this chapter shall be deemed to import the plural and vice versa, as the context may require. The following terms, as used in the Commodity Exchange Act, or in the rules and regulations in this chapter, shall have the meanings hereby assigned to them, unless the context otherwise requires:

(a) *Board of Trade.* This term means an organized exchange or other trading facility.

(b) *Business day.* This term means any day other than a Sunday or holiday. In all notices required by the Act or by the rules and regulations in this chapter to be given in terms of business days the rule for computing time shall be to exclude the day on which notice is given and include the day on which shall take place the act of which notice is given.

(c) *Clearing member.* This term means any person that has clearing privileges such that it can process, clear and settle trades through a derivatives clearing organization on behalf of itself or others. The derivatives clearing organization need not be organized as a membership organization.

(d) *Clearing organization or derivatives clearing organization.* This term means a clearinghouse, clearing association, clearing corporation, or similar entity, facility, system, or organization that, with respect to an agreement, contract, or transaction—

(1) Enables each party to the agreement, contract, or transaction to substitute, through novation or otherwise, the credit of the derivatives clearing organization for the credit of the parties;

(2) Arranges or provides, on a multilateral basis, for the settlement or netting of obligations resulting from such agreements, contracts, or transactions executed by participants in the derivatives clearing organization; or

(3) Otherwise provides clearing services or arrangements that mutualize or transfer among participants in the derivatives clearing organization the credit risk arising from such agreements, contracts, or transactions executed by the participants.

(4) *Exclusions.* The terms clearing organization and derivatives clearing organization do not include an entity, facility, system, or organization solely because it arranges or provides for—

(i) Settlement, netting, or novation of obligations resulting from agreements, contracts or transactions, on a bilateral basis and without a central counterparty;

(ii) Settlement or netting of cash payments through an interbank payment system; or

[1] Basic Regultions

(iii) Settlement, netting, or novation of obligations resulting from a sale of a commodity in a transaction in the spot market for the commodity.

(e) *Commodity.* This term means and includes wheat, cotton, rice, corn, oats, barley, rye, flaxseed, grain sorghums, millfeeds, butter, eggs, Irish potatoes, wool, wool tops, fats and oils (including lard, tallow, cottonseed oil, peanut oil, soybean oil, and all other fats and oils), cottonseed meal, cottonseed, peanuts, soybeans, soybean meal, livestock, livestock products, and frozen concentrated orange juice, and all other goods and articles, except onions (as provided by the first section of Pub. L. 85-839) and motion picture box office receipts (or any index, measure, value or data related to such receipts), and all services, rights and interests (except motion picture box office receipts, or any index, measure, value or data related to such receipts) in which contracts for future delivery are presently or in the future dealt in.

(f) *Commodity Exchange Act; the Act.* These terms mean the Commodity Exchange Act, as amended, 7 U.S.C. 1 *et seq.*

(g) *Institutional customer.* This term has the same meaning as “eligible contract participant” as defined in section 1a(18) of the Act.

(h) *Contract market; designated contract market.* These terms mean a board of trade designated by the Commission as a contract market under the Act and in accordance with the provisions of part 38 of this chapter.

(i) *Contract of sale.* This term includes sales, purchases, agreements of sale or purchase and agreements to sell or purchase.

(j) *Controlled account.* An account shall be deemed to be controlled by a person if such person by power of attorney or otherwise actually directs trading for such account.

(k) *Customer.* This term means any person who uses a futures commission merchant, introducing broker, commodity trading advisor, or commodity pool operator as an agent in connection with trading in any commodity interest; *Provided, however,* an owner or holder of a proprietary account as defined in paragraph (y) of this section shall not be deemed to be a customer within the meaning of section 4d of the Act, the regulations that implement sections 4d and 4f of the Act and § 1.35, and such an owner or holder of such a proprietary account shall otherwise be deemed to be a customer within the meaning of the Act and §§ 1.37 and 1.46 and all other sections of these rules, regulations, and orders which do not implement sections 4d and 4f of the Act.

(l) *Delivery month.* This term means the month of delivery specified in a contract of sale of any commodity for future delivery.

(m) *Eligible contract participant.* This term has the meaning set forth in Section 1a(18) of the Act, except that:

(1) A major swap participant, as defined in Section 1a(33) of the Act and paragraph (hhh) of this section, is an eligible contract participant;

(2) A swap dealer, as defined in Section 1a(49) of the Act and paragraph (ggg) of this section, is an eligible contract participant;

(3) A major security-based swap participant, as defined in Section 3(a)(67) of the Securities Exchange Act of 1934 and § 240.3a67-1 of this title, is an eligible contract participant;

(4) A security-based swap dealer, as defined in Section 3(a)(71) of the Securities Exchange Act of 1934 and § 240.3a71-1 of this title, is an eligible contract participant;

(5)(i) A transaction-level commodity pool with one or more direct participants that is not an eligible contract participant is not itself an eligible contract participant under either Section 1a(18)(A)(iv) or Section 1a(18)(A)(v) of the Act for purposes of entering into transactions described in Sections 2(c)(2)(B)(vi) and 2(c)(2)(C)(vii) of the Act; and

(ii) In determining whether a commodity pool that is a direct participant in a transaction-level commodity pool is an eligible contract participant for purposes of paragraph (m)(5)(i) of this section, the participants in the commodity pool that is a direct participant in the transaction-level commodity pool shall not be considered unless the transaction-level commodity pool, any commodity pool holding a direct or indirect interest in such transaction-level commodity pool, or any commodity pool in which such transaction-level commodity pool holds a direct or indirect interest, has been structured to evade subtitle A of Title VII of the Dodd-Frank Wall Street Reform and Consumer Protection Act by permitting persons that are not eligible contract participants to participate in agreements, contracts, or transactions described in Section 2(c)(2)(B)(i) or Section 2(c)(2)(C)(i) of the Act;

(6) A commodity pool that does not have total assets exceeding $5,000,000 or that is not operated by a person described in subclause (A)(iv)(II) of Section 1a(18) of the Act is not an eligible contract participant pursuant to clause (A)(v) of such Section;

(7)(i) For purposes of a swap (but not a security-based swap, security-based swap agreement or mixed swap) used to hedge or mitigate commercial risk, an entity may, in determining its net worth for purposes of Section 1a(18)(A)(v)(III) of the Act, include the net worth of any owner of such entity, provided that all the owners of such entity are eligible contract participants;

(ii)(A) For purposes of identifying the owners of an entity under paragraph (m)(7)(i) of this section, any person holding a direct ownership interest in such entity shall be considered to be an owner of such entity; provided, however, that any shell company shall be disregarded, and the owners of such shell company shall be considered to be the owners of any entity owned by such shell company;

(B) For purposes of paragraph (m)(7)(ii)(A) of this section, the term *shell company* means any entity that limits its holdings to direct or indirect interests in entities that are relying on this paragraph (m)(7); and

(C) In determining whether an owner of an entity is an eligible contract participant for purposes of paragraph (m)(7)(i) of this section, an individual may be considered to be a proprietorship eligible contract participant only if the individual—

(*1*) Has an active role in operating a business other than an entity;

(*2*) Directly owns all of the assets of the business;

(*3*) Directly is responsible for all of the liabilities of the business; and

(*4*) Acquires its interest in the entity seeking to qualify as an eligible contract participant under paragraph (m)(7)(i) of this section in connection with the operation of the individual's proprietorship or to manage the risk associated with an asset or liability owned or incurred or reasonably likely to be owned or incurred by the individual in the operation of the individual's proprietorship; and

(iii) For purposes of paragraph (m)(7)(i) of this section, a swap is used to hedge or mitigate commercial risk if the swap complies with the conditions in paragraph (kkk) of this section; and

(8) Notwithstanding Section 1a(18)(A)(iv) of the Act and paragraph (m)(5) of this section, a commodity pool that enters into an agreement, contract, or transaction described in Section 2(c)(2)(B)(i) or Section 2(c)(2)(C)(i)(I) of the Act is an eligible contract participant with respect to such agreement, contract, or transaction, regardless of whether each participant in such commodity pool is an eligible contract participant, if all of the following conditions are satisfied:

(i) The commodity pool is not formed for the purpose of evading regulation under Section 2(c)(2)(B) or Section 2(c)(2)(C) of the Act or related Commission rules, regulations or orders;

(ii) The commodity pool has total assets exceeding $10,000,000; and

(iii) The commodity pool is formed and operated by a registered commodity pool operator or by a commodity pool operator who is exempt from registration as such pursuant to § 4.13(a)(3) of this chapter.

(n) *Floor broker.* This term means any person:

(1) Who, in or surrounding any pit, ring, post or other place provided by a contract market for the meeting of persons similarly engaged, shall purchase or sell for any other person—

(i) Any commodity for future delivery, security futures product, or swap; or

(ii) Any commodity option authorized under section 4c of the Act; or

(2) Who is registered with the Commission as a floor broker.

(o) *Future delivery.* This term does not include any sale of a cash commodity for deferred shipment or delivery.

(p) *Futures commission merchant.* This term means:

(1) Any individual, association, partnership, corporation, or trust—

(i) Who is engaged in soliciting or in accepting orders for the purchase or sale of any commodity for future delivery; a security futures product; a swap; any agreement, contract, or transaction described in section 2(c)(2)(C)(i) or section 2(c)(2)(D)(i) of the Act; a commodity option authorized under section 4c of the Act; a leverage transaction authorized under section 19 of the Act; or acting as a counterparty in any agreement, contract or transaction described in section 2(c)(2)(C)(i) or section 2(c)(2)(D)(i) of the Act; and

(ii) Who, in connection with any of these activities accepts any money, securities, or property (or extends credit in lieu thereof) to margin, guarantee, or secure any trades or contracts that result or may result therefrom; and

(2) Any person that is registered as a futures commission merchant.

(q) *Member.* This term means:

(1) An individual, association, partnership, corporation, or trust—

(i) Owning or holding membership in, or admitted to membership representation on, a registered entity; or

(ii) Having trading privileges on a registered entity.

(2) A participant in an alternative trading system that is designated as a contract market pursuant to section 5f of the Act is deemed a member of the contract market for purposes of transactions in security futures products through the contract market.

(r) *Net equity.* (1) For futures and commodity option positions, this term means the credit balance which would be obtained by combining the margin balance of any person with the net profit or loss, if any, accruing on the open futures or commodity option positions of such person.

(2) For swap positions other than commodity option positions, this term means the credit balance which would be obtained by combining the margin balance of any person with the net profit or loss, if any, accruing on the open swap positions of such person.

(s) *Net deficit.* (1) For futures and commodity option positions, this term means the debit balance which would be obtained by combining the margin balance of any person with the net profit or loss, if any, accruing on the open futures or commodity option positions of such person.

(2) For swap positions other than commodity option positions, this term means the debit balance which would be obtained by combining the margin balance of any person with the net profit or loss, if any, accruing on the open swap positions of such person.

(t) *Open contracts.* This term means:

(1) Positions in contracts of purchase or sale of any commodity made by or for any person on or subject to the rules of a board of trade for future delivery during a specified month or delivery period that have neither been fulfilled by delivery nor been offset by other contracts of purchase or sale in the same commodity and delivery month;

(2) Positions in commodity option transactions that have not expired, been exercised, or offset; and

(3) Positions in Cleared Swaps, as § 22.1 of this chapter defines that term, that have not been fulfilled by delivery; not been offset; not expired; and not been terminated.

(u) *Person.* This term includes individuals, associations, partnerships, corporations, and trusts.

(w) *Secretary of Agriculture.* This term means the Secretary of Agriculture or any person to whom authority has heretofore lawfully been delegated or to whom authority may hereafter lawfully be delegated to act in his stead.

(x) *Floor trader.* This term means any person:

(1) Who, in or surrounding any pit, ring, post or other place provided by a contract market for the meeting of persons similarly engaged, purchases, or sells solely for such person's own account—

(i) Any commodity for future delivery, security futures product, or swap; or

(ii) Any commodity option authorized under section 4c of the Act; or

(2) Who is registered with the Commission as a floor trader.

(y) *Proprietary account.* This term means a commodity futures, commodity option, or swap trading account carried on the books and records of an individual, a partnership, corporation or other type of association:

(1) For one of the following persons, or

(2) Of which ten percent or more is owned by one of the following persons, or an aggregate of ten percent or more of which is owned by more than one of the following persons:

(i) Such individual himself, or such partnership, corporation or association itself;

(ii) In the case of a partnership, a general partner in such partnership;

(iii) In the case of a limited partnership, a limited or special partner in such partnership whose duties include:

(A) The management of the partnership business or any part thereof,

(B) The handling of the trades of customers or customer funds of such partnership,

(C) The keeping of records pertaining to the trades of customers or customer funds of such partnership, or

(D) The signing or co-signing of checks or drafts on behalf of such partnership;

(iv) In the case of a corporation or association, an officer, director or owner of ten percent or more of the capital stock, of such organization;

(v) An employee of such individual, partnership, corporation or association whose duties include:

(A) The management of the business of such individual, partnership, corporation or association or any part thereof,

(B) The handling of the trades of customers or customer funds of such individual, partnership, corporation or association,

(C) The keeping of records pertaining to the trades of customers or customer funds of such individual, partnership, corporation or association, or

(D) The signing or co-signing of checks or drafts on behalf of such individual, partnership, corporation or association;

(vi) A spouse or minor dependent living in the same household of any of the foregoing persons;

(vii) A business affiliate that directly or indirectly controls such individual, partnership, corporation or association; or

(viii) A business affiliate that, directly or indirectly is controlled by or is under common control with, such individual, partnership, corporation or association. *Provided, however,* That an account owned by any shareholder or member of a cooperative association of producers, within the meaning of section 6a of the Act, which association is registered as a futures commission merchant and carries such account on its records, shall be deemed to be an account of a customer and not a proprietary account of such association, unless the shareholder or member is an officer, director or manager of the association.

(z) *Bona fide hedging transactions and positions for excluded commodities* —(1) *General definition.* Bona fide hedging transactions and positions shall mean any agreement, contract or transaction in an excluded commodity on a designated contract market or swap execution facility that is a trading facility, where such transactions or positions normally represent a substitute for transactions to be made or positions to be taken at a later time in a physical marketing channel, and where they are economically appropriate to the reduction of risks in the conduct and management of a commercial enterprise, and where they arise from:

(i) The potential change in the value of assets which a person owns, produces, manufactures, processes, or merchandises or anticipates owning, producing, manufacturing, processing, or merchandising,

(ii) The potential change in the value of liabilities which a person owns or anticipates incurring, or

(iii) The potential change in the value of services which a person provides, purchases, or anticipates providing or purchasing.

(iv) Notwithstanding the foregoing, no transactions or positions shall be classified as bona fide hedging unless their purpose is to offset price risks incidental to commercial cash or spot operations and such positions are established and liquidated in an orderly manner in accordance with sound commercial practices and, for transactions or positions on contract markets subject to trading and position limits in effect pursuant to section 4a of the Act, unless the provisions of paragraphs (z)(2) and (3) of this section have been satisfied.

(2) *Enumerated hedging transactions.* The definitions of bona fide hedging transactions and positions in paragraph (z)(1) of this section includes, but is not limited to, the following specific transactions and positions:

(i) Sales of any agreement, contract, or transaction in an excluded commodity on a designated contract market or swap execution facility that is a trading facility which do not exceed in quantity:

(A) Ownership or fixed-price purchase of the same cash commodity by the same person; and

(B) Twelve months' unsold anticipated production of the same commodity by the same person provided that no such position is maintained in any agreement, contract or transaction during the five last trading days.

(ii) Purchases of any agreement, contract or transaction in an excluded commodity on a designated contract market or swap execution facility that is a trading facility which do not exceed in quantity:

(A) The fixed-price sale of the same cash commodity by the same person;

(B) The quantity equivalent of fixed-price sales of the cash products and by-products of such commodity by the same person; and

(C) Twelve months' unfilled anticipated requirements of the same cash commodity for processing, manufacturing, or feeding by the same person, provided that such transactions and positions in the five last trading days of any agreement, contract or transaction do not exceed the person's unfilled anticipated requirements of the same cash commodity for that month and for the next succeeding month.

(iii) Offsetting sales and purchases in any agreement, contract or transaction in an excluded commodity on a designated contract market or swap execution facility that is a trading facility which do not exceed in quantity that amount of the same cash commodity which has been bought and sold by the same person at unfixed prices basis different delivery months of the contract market, provided that no such position is maintained in any agreement, contract or transaction during the five last trading days.

(iv) Purchases or sales by an agent who does not own or has not contracted to sell or purchase the offsetting cash commodity at a fixed price, provided that the agent is responsible for the merchandising of the cash position that is being offset, and the agent has a contractual arrangement with the person who owns the commodity or has the cash market commitment being offset.

(v) Sales and purchases described in paragraphs (z)(2)(i) through (iv) of this section may also be offset other than by the same quantity of the same cash commodity, provided that the fluctuations in value of the position for in any agreement, contract or transaction are substantially related to the fluctuations in value of the actual or anticipated cash position, and provided that the positions in any agreement, contract or transaction shall not be maintained during the five last trading days.

(3) *Non-Enumerated cases.* A designated contract market or swap execution facility that is a trading facility may recognize, consistent with the purposes of this section, transactions and positions other than those enumerated in paragraph (2) of this section as bona fide hedging. Prior to recognizing such non-

enumerated transactions and positions, the designated contract market or swap execution facility that is a trading facility shall submit such rules for Commission review under section 5c of the Act and part 40 of this chapter.

(aa) *Associated person.* This term means any natural person who is associated in any of the following capacities with:

(1) A futures commission merchant as a partner, officer, or employee (or any natural person occupying a similar status or performing similar functions), in any capacity which involves (i) The solicitation or acceptance of customers' orders (other than in a clerical capacity) or (ii) the supervision of any person or persons so engaged;

(2) An introducing broker as a partner, officer, employee, or agent (or any natural person occupying a similar status or performing similar functions), in any capacity which involves (i) The solicitation or acceptance of customers' orders (other than in a clerical capacity) or (ii) the supervision of any person or persons so engaged;

(3) A commodity pool operator as a partner, officer, employee, consultant, or agent (or any natural person occupying a similar status or performing similar functions), in any capacity which involves (i) the solicitation of funds, securities, or property for a participation in a commodity pool or (ii) the supervision of any person or persons so engaged; or

(ii) the supervision of any person or persons so engaged;

(4) A commodity trading advisor as a partner, officer, employee, consultant, or agent (or any natural person occupying a similar status or performing similar functions), in any capacity which involves: (i) The solicitation of a client's or prospective client's discretionary account, or (ii) the supervision of any person or persons so engaged; and

(5) A leverage transaction merchant as a partner, officer, employee, consultant, or agent (or any natural person occupying a similar status or performing similar functions), in any capacity which involves:

(i) The solicitation or acceptance of leverage customers' orders (other than in a clerical capacity) for leverage transactions as defined in § 31.4(x) of this chapter, or

(ii) The supervision of any person or persons so engaged.

(6) A swap dealer or major swap participant as a partner, officer, employee, agent (or any natural person occupying a similar status or performing similar functions), in any capacity that involves:

(i) The solicitation or acceptance of swaps (other than in a clerical or ministerial capacity); or

(ii) The supervision of any person or persons so engaged.

(bb)(1) *Commodity trading advisor.* This term means any person who, for compensation or profit, engages in the business of advising others, either directly or through publications, writings or electronic media, as to the value of or the advisability of trading in any contract of sale of a commodity for future delivery, security futures product, or swap; any agreement, contract or transaction described in section 2(c)(2)(C)(i) or section 2(c)(2)(D)(i) of the Act; any commodity option authorized under section 4c of the Act; any leverage transaction authorized under section 19 of the Act; any person registered with the Commission as a commodity trading advisor; or any person, who, for compensation or profit, and as part of a regular business, issues or promulgates analyses or reports concerning any of the foregoing. The term does not include:

(i) Any bank or trust company or any person acting as an employee thereof;

(ii) Any news reporter, news columnist, or news editor of the print or electronic media or any lawyer, accountant, or teacher;

(iii) Any floor broker or futures commission merchant;

(iv) The publisher or producer of any print or electronic data of general and regular dissemination, including its employees;

(v) The named fiduciary, or trustee, of any defined benefit plan which is subject to the provisions of the Employee Retirement Income Security Act of 1974, or any fiduciary whose sole business is to advise that plan;

(vi) Any contract market; and

(vii) Such other persons not within the intent of this definition as the Commission may specify by rule, regulation or order:*Provided,* That the furnishing of such services by the foregoing persons is solely incidental to the conduct of their business or profession:

Provided further, That the Commission, by rule or regulation, may include within this definition, any person advising as to the value of commodities or issuing reports or analyses concerning commodities, if the Commission determines that such rule or regulation will effectuate the purposes of this provision.

(2) *Client.* This term, as it relates to a commodity trading advisor, means any person:

(i) To whom a commodity trading advisor provides advice, for compensation or profit, either directly or through publications, writings, or electronic media, as to the value of, or the advisability of trading in, any contract of sale of a commodity for future delivery, security futures product or swap; any agreement, contract or transaction described in section 2(c)(2)(C)(i) or section 2(c)(2)(D)(i) of the Act; any commodity option authorized under section 4c of the Act; any leverage transaction authorized under section 19 of the Act; or

(ii) To whom, for compensation or profit, and as part of a regular business, the commodity trading advisor issues or promulgates analyses or reports concerning any of the activities referred to in paragraph (bb)(2)(i) of this section. The term “client” includes, without limitation, any subscriber of a commodity trading advisor.

(cc) *Commodity pool operator.* This term means any person engaged in a business which is of the nature of a commodity pool, investment trust, syndicate, or similar form of enterprise, and who, in connection therewith, solicits, accepts, or receives from others, funds, securities, or property, either directly or through capital contributions, the sale of stock or other forms of securities, or otherwise, for the purpose of trading in commodity interests, including any commodity for future delivery, security futures product, or swap; any agreement, contract or transaction described in section 2(c)(2)(C)(i) or section 2(c)(2)(D)(i) of the Act; any commodity option authorized under section 4c of the Act; any leverage transaction authorized under section 19 of the Act; or any person who is registered with the Commission as a commodity pool operator, but does not include such persons not within the intent of this definition as the Commission may specify by rule or regulation or by order.

(dd) *Commission.* This term means the Commodity Futures Trading Commission.

(ee) *Self-regulatory organization.* This term means a contract market (as defined in § 1.3(h)), a swap execution facility (as defined in § 1.3(rrrr)), or a registered futures association under section 17 of the Act.

(ff) *Designated self-regulatory organization.* This term means:

(1) Self-regulatory organization of which a futures commission merchant, an introducing broker, a leverage transaction merchant, a retail foreign exchange dealer, a swap dealer, or a major swap participant is a member; or

(2) If a Commission registrant other than a leverage transaction merchant is a member of more than one self-regulatory organization and such registrant is the subject of an approved plan under § 1.52, then a self-regulatory organization delegated the responsibility by such a plan for monitoring and auditing such registrant for compliance with the minimum financial and related reporting requirements of the self-regulatory organizations of which the registrant is a member, and for receiving the financial reports necessitated by such minimum financial and related reporting requirements from such registrant; or

(3) If a leverage transaction merchant is a member of more than one self-regulatory organization and such leverage transaction merchant is the subject of an approved plan under § 31.28 of this chapter, then a self-regulatory organization delegated the responsibility by such a plan for monitoring and auditing such leverage transaction merchant for compliance with the minimum financial, cover, segregation and sales practice, and related reporting requirements of the self-regulatory organizations of which the leverage transaction merchant is a member, and for receiving the reports necessitated by such minimum financial, cover, segregation and sales practice, and related reporting requirements from such leverage transaction merchant.

(gg) *Customer funds.* This term means, collectively, Cleared Swaps Customer Collateral and futures customer funds.

(hh) *Commodity option transaction; commodity option.* These terms each mean any transaction or agreement in interstate commerce which is or is held out to be of the character of, or is commonly known to the trade as, an “option,” “privilege,” “indemnity,” “bid,” “offer,” “call,” “put.” “advance guaranty,” or “decline guaranty,” and which is subject to regulation under the Act and these regulations.

(ii) *Premium.* This term means the amount agreed upon between the purchaser and seller, or their agents, for the purchase or sale of a commodity option.

(kk) *Strike price.* This term means the price, per unit, at which a person may purchase or sell the commodity, swap, or contract of sale of a commodity for future delivery that is the subject of a commodity option: *Provided,* That for purposes of § 1.17, the term strike price means the total price at which a person may purchase or sell the commodity, swap, or contract of sale of a commodity for future delivery that is the subject of a commodity option (*i.e.,* price per unit times the number of units).

(mm) *Introducing broker.* This term means:

(1) Any person who, for compensation or profit, whether direct or indirect:

(i) Is engaged in soliciting or in accepting orders (other than in a clerical capacity) for the purchase or sale of any commodity for future delivery, security futures product, or swap; any agreement, contract or transaction described in section 2(c)(2)(C)(i) or section 2(c)(2)(D)(i) of the Act; any commodity option transaction authorized under section 4c; or any leverage transaction authorized under section 19; or who is registered with the Commission as an introducing broker; and

(ii) Does not accept any money, securities, or property (or extend credit in lieu thereof) to margin, guarantee, or secure any trades or contracts that result or may result therefrom.

(2) The term introducing broker shall not include:

(i) Any futures commission merchant, floor broker, associated person, or associated person of a swap dealer or major swap participant acting in its capacity as such, regardless of whether that futures commission merchant, floor broker, or associated person is registered or exempt from registration in such capacity;

(ii) Any commodity trading advisor, which, acting in its capacity as a commodity trading advisor, is not compensated on a per-trade basis or which solely manages discretionary accounts pursuant to a power of attorney, regardless of whether that commodity trading advisor is registered or exempt from registration in such capacity; and

(iii) Any commodity pool operator which, acting in its capacity as a commodity pool operator, solely operates commodity pools, regardless of whether that commodity pool operator is registered or exempt from registration in such capacity.

(nn) *Guarantee agreement.* This term means an agreement of guarantee in the form set forth in part B or C of Form 1-FR, executed by a registered futures commission merchant or retail foreign exchange dealer, as appropriate, and by an introducing broker or applicant for registration as an introducing broker on behalf of an introducing broker or applicant for registration as an introducing broker in satisfaction of the alternative adjusted net capital requirement set forth in § 1.17(a)(1)(iii).

(oo) *Leverage transaction merchant.* This term means and includes any individual, association, partnership, corporation, trust or other person that is engaged in the business of offering to enter into, entering into or confirming the execution of leverage contracts, or soliciting or accepting orders for leverage contracts, and who accepts leverage customer funds (or extends credit in lieu thereof) in connection therewith.

(pp) *Leverage customer funds.* This term means all money, securities and property received, directly or indirectly by a leverage transaction merchant from, for, or on behalf of leverage customers to margin, guarantee or secure leverage contracts and all money, securities and property accruing to such customers as the result of such contracts, or the customers' leverage equity. In the case of a long leverage transaction, profit or loss accruing to a leverage customer is the difference between the leverage transaction merchant's current bid price for the leverage contract and the ask price of the leverage contract when entered into. In the case of a short leverage transaction, profit or loss accruing to a leverage customer is the difference between the bid price of the leverage contract when entered into and the leverage transaction merchant's current ask price for the leverage contract.

(qq) *Leverage contract.* Shall have the same meaning as that set forth in § 31.4(w) of this chapter.

(rr) *Foreign futures or foreign options secured amount.* This term means all money, securities and property held by or held for or on behalf of a futures commission merchant from, for, or on behalf of foreign futures or foreign options customers as defined in § 30.1 of this chapter:

(1) In the case of foreign futures customers, money, securities and property required by a futures commission merchant to margin, guarantee, or secure open foreign futures contracts plus or minus any unrealized gain or loss on such contracts; and

(2) In the case of foreign options customers in connection with open foreign options transactions, money, securities and property representing premiums paid or received, plus any other funds required to guarantee or secure open transactions plus or minus any unrealized gain or loss on such transactions.

(ss) *Foreign board of trade.* This term means any board of trade, exchange or market located outside the United States, its territories or possessions, whether incorporated or unincorporated.

(tt) *Electronic signature.* This term means an electronic sounds, symbol, or process attached to or logically associated with a record and executed or adopted by a person with the intent to sign the record.

(vv) *Futures account.* This term means an account that is maintained in accordance with the segregation requirements of sections 4d(a) and 4d(b) of the Act and the rules thereunder.

(ww) *Securities account.* This term means an account that is maintained in accordance with the requirements of section 15(c)(3) of the Securities Exchange Act of 1934 and Rule 15c3-3 thereunder.

(xx) *Foreign broker.* This term means any person located outside the United States, its territories or possessions who is engaged in soliciting or in accepting orders only from persons located outside the United States, its territories or possessions for the purchase or sale of any commodity interest transaction on or subject to the rules of any designated contract market or swap execution facility and that, in or in connection with such solicitation or acceptance of orders, accepts any money, securities or property (or extends credit in lieu thereof) to margin, guarantee, or secure any trades or contracts that result or may result therefrom.

(yy) *Commodity interest.* This term means:

(1) Any contract for the purchase or sale of a commodity for future delivery;

(2) Any contract, agreement or transaction subject to a Commission regulation under section 4c or 19 of the Act;

(3) Any contract, agreement or transaction subject to Commission jurisdiction under section 2(c)(2) of the Act; and

(4) Any swap as defined in the Act, by the Commission, or jointly by the Commission and the Securities and Exchange Commission.

(zz) *Agricultural commodity.* This term means:

(1) The following commodities specifically enumerated in the definition of a "commodity" found in section 1a of the Act: Wheat, cotton, rice, corn, oats, barley, rye, flaxseed, grain sorghums, mill feeds, butter, eggs, Solanum tuberosum (Irish potatoes), wool, wool tops, fats and oils (including lard, tallow, cottonseed oil, peanut oil, soybean oil and all other fats and oils), cottonseed meal, cottonseed, peanuts, soybeans, soybean meal, livestock, livestock products, and frozen concentrated orange juice, but not onions;

(2) All other commodities that are, or once were, or are derived from, living organisms, including plant, animal and aquatic life, which are generally fungible, within their respective classes, and are used primarily for human food, shelter, animal feed or natural fiber;

(3) Tobacco, products of horticulture, and such other commodities used or consumed by animals or humans as the Commission may by rule, regulation or order designate after notice and opportunity for hearing; and

(4) Commodity-based indexes based wholly or principally on underlying agricultural commodities.

(aaa) *Clearing initial margin.* This term means initial margin posted by a clearing member with a derivatives clearing organization.

(bbb) *Customer initial margin.* This term means initial margin posted by a customer with a futures commission merchant, or by a non-clearing member futures commission merchant with a clearing member.

(ccc) *Initial margin.* This term means money, securities, or property posted by a party to a futures, option, or swap as performance bond to cover potential future exposures arising from changes in the market value of the position.

(ddd) *Margin call.* This term means a request from a futures commission merchant to a customer to post customer initial margin; or a request by a derivatives clearing organization to a clearing member to post clearing initial margin or variation margin.

(eee) *Spread margin.* This term means reduced initial margin that takes into account correlations between certain related positions held in a single account.

(fff) *Variation margin.* This term means a payment made by a party to a futures, option, or swap to cover the current exposure arising from changes in the market value of the position since the trade was executed or the previous time the position was marked to market.

(ggg) *Swap Dealer.* (1) In general. The term *swap dealer* means any person who:

(i) Holds itself out as a dealer in swaps;

(ii) Makes a market in swaps;

(iii) Regularly enters into swaps with counterparties as an ordinary course of business for its own account; or

(iv) Engages in any activity causing it to be commonly known in the trade as a dealer or market maker in swaps.

(2) *Exception.* The term *swap dealer* does not include a person that enters into swaps for such person's own account, either individually or in a fiduciary capacity, but not as a part of regular business.

(3) *Scope of designation.* A person who is a swap dealer shall be deemed to be a swap dealer with respect to each swap it enters into, regardless of the category of the swap or the person's activities in connection with the swap. However, if a person makes an application to limit its designation as a swap dealer to specified categories of swaps or specified activities of the person in connection with swaps, the Commission shall determine whether the person's designation as a swap dealer shall be so limited. If the Commission grants such limited designation, such limited designation swap dealer shall be deemed to be a swap dealer with respect to each swap it enters into in the swap category or categories for which it is so designated, regardless of the person's activities in connection with such category or categories of swaps. A person may make such application to limit the categories of swaps or activities of the person that are subject to its swap dealer designation at the same time as, or after, the person's initial registration as a swap dealer.

(4) *De minimis exception.* (i) Except as provided in paragraph (ggg)(4)(vi) of this section, a person that is not currently registered as a swap dealer shall be deemed not to be a swap dealer as a result of its swap dealing activity involving counterparties, so long as the swap positions connected with those dealing activities into which the person—or any other entity controlling, controlled by or under common control with the person—enters over the course of the immediately preceding 12 months (or following the effective date of final rules implementing Section 1a(47) of the Act, 7 U.S.C. 1a(47), if that period is less than 12 months) have an aggregate gross notional amount of no more than $3 billion, subject to a phase in level of an aggregate gross notional amount of no more than $8 billion applied in accordance with paragraph (ggg)(4)(ii) of this section, and an aggregate gross notional amount of no more than $25 million with regard to swaps in which the counterparty is a "special entity" (as that term is defined in Section 4s(h)(2)(C) of the Act, 7 U.S.C. 6s(h)(2)(C), and § 23.401(c) of this chapter). For purposes of this paragraph, if the stated notional amount of a swap is leveraged or enhanced by the structure of the swap, the calculation shall be based on the effective notional amount of the swap rather than on the stated notional amount.

(ii) *Phase-in procedure and staff report.* (A) *Phase-in period.* For purposes of paragraph (ggg)(4)(i) of this section, except as provided in paragraph (ggg)(4)(vi) of this section, a person that engages in swap dealing activity that does not exceed the phase-in level set forth in paragraph (ggg)(4)(i) shall be deemed not to be a swap dealer as a result of its swap dealing activity until the " *phase-in termination date"* established as provided in paragraph (ggg)(4)(ii)(C) or (D) of this section. The Commission shall announce the phase-in termination date on the Commission Web site and publish such date in the FEDERAL REGISTER .

(B) *Staff report.* No later than 30 months following the date that a swap data repository first receives swap data in accordance with part 45 of this chapter, the staff of the Commission shall complete and publish for public comment a report on topics relating to the definition of the term "swap dealer" and the *de minimis* threshold. The report should address the following topics, as appropriate, based on the availability of data and information: the potential impact of modifying the *de minimis*threshold, and whether the *de* *minimis* threshold should be increased or decreased; the factors that are useful for identifying swap dealing activity, including the application of the dealer-trader distinction for that purpose, and the potential use of objective tests or safe harbors as part of the analysis; the impact of provisions in paragraphs (ggg)(5) and (6) of this section excluding certain swaps from the dealer analysis, and potential alternative approaches for such exclusions; and any other analysis of swap data and information relating to swaps that the Commission or staff deem relevant to this rule.

(C) Nine months after publication of the report required by paragraph (ggg)(4)(ii)(B) of this section, and after giving due consideration to that report and any associated public comment, the Commission may either:

(*1*) Terminate the phase-in period set forth in paragraph (ggg)(4)(ii)(A) of this section, in which case the phase-in termination date shall be established by the Commission by order published in the FEDERAL REGISTER ; or

(*2*) Determine that it is necessary or appropriate in the public interest to propose through rulemaking an alternative to the $3 billion amount set forth in paragraph (ggg)(4)(i) of this section that would constitute a *de minimis* quantity of swap dealing in connection with transactions with or on behalf of customers within the meaning of section 1(a)(47)(D) of the Act, 7 U.S.C. 1(a)(47)(D), in which case the Commission shall by order published in the FEDERAL REGISTER provide notice of such determination, which order shall also establish the phase-in termination date.

(D) If the phase-in termination date has not been previously established pursuant to paragraph (ggg)(4)(ii)(C) of this section, then in any event the phase-in termination date shall occur five years after the date that a swap data repository first receives swap data in accordance with part 45 of this chapter.

(iii) *Registration period for persons that can no longer take advantage of the exception.* A person that has not registered as a swap dealer by virtue of satisfying the requirements of this paragraph (ggg)(4), but that no longer can take advantage of that*de minimis* exception, will be deemed not to be a swap dealer until the earlier of the date on which it submits a complete application for registration pursuant to Section 4s(b) of the Act, 7 U.S.C. 6s(b), or two months after the end of the month in which that person becomes no longer able to take advantage of the exception.

(iv) *Applicability to registered swap dealers.* A person who currently is registered as a swap dealer may apply to withdraw that registration, while continuing to engage in swap dealing activity in reliance on this section, so long as that person has been registered as a swap dealer for at least 12 months and satisfies the conditions of paragraph (ggg)(4)(i) of this section.

(v) *Future adjustments to scope of the de minimis exception.* The Commission may by rule or regulation change the requirements of the *de minimis* exception described in paragraphs (ggg)(4)(i) through (iv) of this section.

(vi) *Voluntary registration.* Notwithstanding paragraph (ggg)(4)(i) of this section, a person that chooses to register with the Commission as a swap dealer shall be deemed to be a swap dealer.

(5) *Insured depository institution swaps in connection with originating loans to customers.* Swaps entered into by an insured depository institution with a customer in connection with originating a loan with that customer shall not be considered in determining whether the insured depository institution is a swap dealer.

(i) An insured depository institution shall be considered to have entered into a swap with a customer in connection with originating a loan, as defined in paragraphs (ggg)(5)(ii) and (iii) of this section, with that customer only if:

(A) The insured depository institution enters into the swap with the customer no earlier than 90 days before and no later than 180 days after the date of execution of the applicable loan agreement, or no earlier than 90 days before and no later than 180 days after any transfer of principal to the customer by the insured depository institution pursuant to the loan;

(B)(*1*) The rate, asset, liability or other notional item underlying such swap is, or is directly related to, a financial term of such loan, which includes, without limitation, the loan's duration, rate of interest, the currency or currencies in which it is made and its principal amount;

(*2*) Such swap is required, as a condition of the loan under the insured depository institution's loan underwriting criteria, to be in place in order to hedge price risks incidental to the borrower's business and arising from potential changes in the price of a commodity (other than an excluded commodity);

(C) The duration of the swap does not extend beyond termination of the loan;

(D) The insured depository institution is:

(*1*) The sole source of funds to the customer under the loan;

(*2*) Committed to be, under the terms of the agreements related to the loan, the source of at least 10 percent of the maximum principal amount under the loan; or

(*3*) Committed to be, under the terms of the agreements related to the loan, the source of a principal amount that is greater than or equal to the aggregate notional amount of all swaps entered into by the insured depository institution with the customer in connection with the financial terms of the loan;

(E) The aggregate notional amount of all swaps entered into by the customer in connection with the financial terms of the loan is, at any time, not more than the aggregate principal amount outstanding under the loan at that time; and

(F) If the swap is not accepted for clearing by a derivatives clearing organization, the insured depository institution reports the swap as required by section 4r of the Act, 7 U.S.C. 6r (except as otherwise provided in section 4r(a)(3)(A), 7 U.S.C. 6r(a)(3)(A), or section 4r(a)(3)(B), 7 U.S.C. 6r(a)(3)(B) of the Act).

(ii) An insured depository institution shall be considered to have originated a loan with a customer if the insured depository institution:

(A) Directly transfers the loan amount to the customer;

(B) Is a part of a syndicate of lenders that is the source of the loan amount that is transferred to the customer;

(C) Purchases or receives a participation in the loan; or

(D) Otherwise is the source of funds that are transferred to the customer pursuant to the loan or any refinancing of the loan.

(iii) The term loan shall not include:

(A) Any transaction that is a sham, whether or not intended to qualify for the exclusion from the definition of the term *swap dealer* in this rule; or

(B) Any synthetic loan, including, without limitation, a loan credit default swap or loan total return swap.

(6) *Swaps that are not considered in determining whether a person is a swap dealer.* (i) *Inter-affiliate activities.* In determining whether a person is a swap dealer, that person's swaps with majority-owned affiliates shall not be considered. For these purposes the counterparties to a swap are majority-owned affiliates if one counterparty directly or indirectly owns a majority interest in the other, or if a third party directly or indirectly owns a majority interest in both counterparties to the swap, where "majority interest" is the right to vote or direct the vote of a majority of a class of voting securities of an entity, the power to sell or direct the sale of a majority of a class of voting securities of an entity, or the right to receive upon dissolution or the contribution of a majority of the capital of a partnership.

(ii) *Activities of a cooperative.* (A) Any swap that is entered into by a cooperative with a member of such cooperative shall not be considered in determining whether the cooperative is a swap dealer, provided that:

(*1*) The swap is subject to policies and procedures of the cooperative requiring that the cooperative monitors and manages the risk of such swap;

(*2*) The cooperative reports the swap as required by Section 4r of the Act, 7 U.S.C. 6r (except as otherwise provided in Section 4r(a)(3)(A) of the Act, 7 U.S.C. 6r(a)(3)(A) or Section 4r(a)(3)(B) of the Act, 7 U.S.C. 6r(a)(3)(B)); and

(*3*) if the cooperative is a cooperative association of producers, the swap is primarily based on a commodity that is not an excluded commodity.

(B) For purposes of this paragraph (ggg)(6)(ii), the term *cooperative* shall mean:

(*1*) A cooperative association of producers as defined in section 1a(14) of the Act, 7 U.S.C. 1a(14), or

(*2*) A person chartered under Federal law as a cooperative and predominantly engaged in activities that are financial in nature as defined in section 4(k) of the Bank Holding Company Act of 1956, 12 U.S.C. 1843(k).

(C) For purposes of this paragraph (ggg)(6)(ii), a swap shall be deemed to be entered into by a cooperative association of producers with a member of such cooperative association of producers when the swap is between a cooperative association of producers and a person that is a member of a cooperative association of producers that is itself a member of the first cooperative association of producers.

(iii) *Swaps entered into for the purpose of hedging physical positions.* In determining whether a person is a swap dealer, a swap that the person enters into shall not be considered, if:

(A) The person enters into the swap for the purpose of offsetting or mitigating the person's price risks that arise from the potential change in the value of one or several—

(*1*) Assets that the person owns, produces, manufactures, processes, or merchandises or anticipates owning, producing, manufacturing, processing, or merchandising;

(*2*) Liabilities that the person owns or anticipates incurring; or

(*3*) Services that the person provides, purchases, or anticipates providing or purchasing;

(B) The swap represents a substitute for transactions made or to be made or positions taken or to be taken by the person at a later time in a physical marketing channel;

(C) The swap is economically appropriate to the reduction of the person's risks in the conduct and management of a commercial enterprise;

(D) The swap is entered into in accordance with sound commercial practices; and

(E) The person does not enter into the swap in connection with activity structured to evade designation as a swap dealer.

(iv) *Swaps entered into by floor traders.* In determining whether a person is a swap dealer, each swap that the person enters into in its capacity as a floor trader as defined by section 1a(23) of the Act or on or subject to the rules of a swap execution facility shall not be considered for the purpose of determining whether the person is a swap dealer if the person:

(A) Is registered with the Commission as a floor trader pursuant to § 3.11 of this chapter;

(B) Enters into swaps with proprietary funds for that trader's own account solely on or subject to the rules of a designated contract market or swap execution facility and submits each such swap for clearing to a derivatives clearing organization;

(C) Is not an affiliated person of a registered swap dealer;

(D) Does not directly, or through an affiliated person, negotiate the terms of swap agreements, other than price and quantity or to participate in a request for quote process subject to the rules of a designated contract market or a swap execution facility;

(E) Does not directly or through an affiliated person offer or provide swap clearing services to third parties;

(F) Does not directly or through an affiliated person enter into swaps that would qualify as hedging physical positions pursuant to paragraph (ggg)(6)(iii) of this section or hedging or mitigating commercial risk pursuant to paragraph (kkk) of this section (except for any such swap executed opposite a counterparty for which the transaction would qualify as a bona fide hedging transaction);

(G) Does not participate in any market making program offered by a designated contract market or swap execution facility; and

(H) Notwithstanding the fact such person is not registered as a swap dealer, such person complies with §§ 23.201, 23.202, 23.203, and 23.600 of this chapter with respect to each such swap as if it were a swap dealer.

(hhh) *Major Swap Participant* —(1) *In general.* The term *major swap participant* means any person:

(i) That is not a swap dealer; and

(ii)(A) That maintains a substantial position in swaps for any of the major swap categories, excluding both positions held for hedging or mitigating commercial risk, and positions maintained by any employee benefit plan (or any contract held by such a plan) as defined in paragraphs (3) and (32) of Section 3 of the Employee Retirement Income Security Act of 1974, 29 U.S.C. 1002, for the primary purpose of hedging or mitigating any risk directly associated with the operation of the plan;

(B) Whose outstanding swaps create substantial counterparty exposure that could have serious adverse effects on the financial stability of the United States banking system or financial markets; or

(C) That is a financial entity that:

(*1*) Is highly leveraged relative to the amount of capital such entity holds and that is not subject to capital requirements established by an appropriate Federal banking agency (as defined in Section 1a(2) of the Act, 7 U.S.C. 1a(2)); and

(*2*) Maintains a substantial position in outstanding swaps in any major swap category.

(2) *Scope of designation.* A person that is a major swap participant shall be deemed to be a major swap participant with respect to each swap it enters into, regardless of the category of the swap or the person's activities in connection with the swap. However, if a person makes an application to limit its designation as a major swap participant to specified categories of swaps, the Commission shall determine whether the person's designation as a major swap participant shall be so limited. If the Commission grants such limited designation, such limited designation major swap participant shall be deemed to be a major swap participant with respect to each swap it enters into in the swap category or categories for which it is so designated, regardless of the person's activities in connection with such category or categories of swaps. A person may make such application to limit its designation at the same time as, or after, the person's initial registration as a major swap participant.

(3) *Timing requirements.* A person that is not registered as a major swap participant, but that meets the criteria in this rule to be a major swap participant as a result of its swap activities in a fiscal quarter, will not be deemed to be a major swap participant until the earlier of the date on which it submits a complete application for registration as a major swap participant pursuant to Section 4s(a)(2) of the Act, 7 U.S.C. 6s(a)(2), or two months after the end of that quarter.

(4) *Reevaluation period.* Notwithstanding paragraph (hhh)(3) of this section, if a person that is not registered as a major swap participant meets the criteria in this rule to be a major swap participant in a fiscal quarter, but does not exceed any applicable threshold by more than twenty percent in that quarter:

(i) That person will not be deemed a major swap participant pursuant to the timing requirements specified in paragraph (hhh)(3) of this section; but

(ii) That person will be deemed a major swap participant pursuant to the timing requirements specified in paragraph (hhh)(3) of this section at the end of the next fiscal quarter if the person exceeds any of the applicable daily average thresholds in that next fiscal quarter.

(5) *Termination of status.* A person that is deemed to be a major swap participant shall continue to be deemed a major swap participant until such time that its swap activities do not exceed any of the daily average thresholds set forth within this rule for four consecutive fiscal quarters after the date on which the person becomes registered as a major swap participant.

(6) *Calculation of status.* A person shall not be deemed to be a "major swap participant," regardless of whether the criteria paragraph (hhh)(1) of this section otherwise would cause the person to be a major swap participant, provided the person meets the conditions set forth in paragraphs (hhh)(6)(i), (ii) or (iii) of this section.

(i) Caps on uncollateralized exposure and notional positions.

(A) *Maximum potential uncollateralized exposure.* The express terms of the person's agreements or arrangements relating to swaps with its counterparties at no time would permit the person to maintain a total uncollateralized exposure of more than $100 million to all such counterparties, including any exposure that may result from thresholds or minimum transfer amounts established by credit support annexes or similar arrangements; and

(B) Maximum notional amount of swap positions. The person does not maintain swap positions in a notional amount of more than $2 billion in any major category of swaps, or more than $4 billion in the aggregate across all major categories; or

(ii) Caps on uncollateralized exposure plus monthly calculation.

(A) *Maximum potential uncollateralized exposure.* The express terms of the person's agreements or arrangements relating to swaps with its counterparties at no time would permit the person to maintain a total uncollateralized exposure of more than $200 million to all such counterparties (with regard to swaps and any other instruments by which the person may have exposure to those counterparties), including any exposure that may result from thresholds or minimum transfer amounts established by credit support annexes or similar arrangements; and

(B) *Calculation of positions.* (*1*) At the end of each month, the person performs the calculations prescribed by paragraph (jjj) of this section with regard to whether the aggregate uncollateralized outward exposure plus aggregate potential outward exposure as of that day constitute a "substantial position" in a major category of swaps, or pose "substantial counterparty exposure that could have serious adverse effects on the financial stability of the United States banking system or financial markets"; these calculations shall disregard provisions of those rules that provide for the analyses to be determined based on a daily average over a calendar quarter; and

(*2*) Each such analysis produces thresholds of no more than:

(*i*) $1 billion in aggregate uncollateralized outward exposure plus aggregate potential outward exposure in any major category of swaps; if the person is subject to paragraph (jjj) of this section, by virtue of being a highly leveraged financial entity that is not subject to capital requirements established by an appropriate Federal banking agency, this analysis shall account for all of the person's swap positions in that major category (without excluding hedging positions), otherwise this analysis shall exclude the same hedging and related positions that are excluded from consideration pursuant to paragraph (jjj)(1)(i) of this section; or

(*ii*) $2 billion in aggregate uncollateralized outward exposure plus aggregate potential outward exposure (without any positions excluded from the analysis) with regard to all of the person's swap positions.

(iii) *Calculations based on certain information.* (A)(*1*) At the end of each month, the person's aggregate uncollateralized outward exposure with respect to its swap positions in each major swap category is less than $1.5 billion with respect to the rate swap category and less than $500 million with respect to each of the other major swap categories; and

(*2*) At the end of each month, the sum of the amount calculated under paragraph (hhh)(6)(iii)(A)(*1*) of this section with respect to each major swap category and the total notional principal amount of the person's swap positions in each such major swap category, adjusted by the multipliers set forth in paragraph (jjj)(3)(ii)(*1*) of this section on a position-by-position basis reflecting the type of swap, is less than $3 billion with respect to the rate swap category and less than $1 billion with respect to each of the other major swap categories; or

(B)(*1*) At the end of each month, the person's aggregate uncollateralized outward exposure with respect to its swap positions across all major swap categories is less than $500 million; and

(*2*) The sum of the amount calculated under paragraph (hhh)(6)(iii)(B)(*1*) of this section and the product of the total effective notional principal amount of the person's swap positions in all major swap categories multiplied by 0.15 is less than $1 billion.

(C) For purposes of the calculations set forth in this paragraph (hhh)(6)(iii):

(*1*) The person's aggregate uncollateralized outward exposure for positions held with swap dealers shall be equal to such exposure reported on the most recent reports of such exposure received from such swap dealers; and

(*2*) The person's aggregate uncollateralized outward exposure for positions that are not reflected in any report of exposure from a swap dealer (including all swap positions it holds with persons other than swap dealers) shall be calculated in accordance with paragraph (jjj)(2) of this section.

(iv) For purposes of the calculations set forth in this paragraph (hhh)(6), the person shall use the effective notional amount of a position rather than the stated notional amount of the position if the stated notional amount is leveraged or enhanced by the structure of the position.

(v) No presumption shall arise that a person is required to perform the calculations needed to determine if it is a major swap participant, solely by reason that the person does not meet the conditions specified in paragraph (hhh)(6)(i), (ii) or (iii) of this section.

(7) *Exclusions.* A person who is registered as a derivatives clearing organization with the Commission pursuant to section 5b of the Act and regulations thereunder, shall not be deemed to be a major swap participant, regardless of whether the criteria in this paragraph (hhh) otherwise would cause the person to be a major swap participant.

(iii) *Category of swaps; major swap category.* For purposes of Section 1a(33) the Act, 7 U.S.C. 1a(33), and paragraph (hhh) of this section, the terms *major swap category, category of swaps* and any similar terms mean any of the categories of swaps listed below. For the avoidance of doubt, the term *swap* as it is used in this paragraph (iii) has the meaning set forth in Section 1a(47) of the Act, 7 U.S.C. 1a(47), and the rules thereunder.

(1) *Rate swaps.* Any swap which is primarily based on one or more reference rates, including but not limited to any swap of payments determined by fixed and floating interest rates, currency exchange rates, inflation rates or other monetary rates, any foreign exchange swap, as defined in Section 1a(25) of the Act, 7 U.S.C. 1a(25), and any foreign exchange option other than an option to deliver currency.

(2) *Credit swaps.* Any swap that is primarily based on instruments of indebtedness, including but not limited to any swap primarily based on one or more broad-based indices related to debt instruments or loans, and any swap that is an index credit default swap or total return swap on one or more indices of debt instruments.

(3) *Equity swaps.* Any swap that is primarily based on equity securities, including but not limited to any swap based on one or more broad-based indices of equity securities and any total return swap on one or more equity indices.

(4) *Other commodity swaps.* Any swap that is not included in the rate swap, credit swap or equity swap categories.

(jjj) *Substantial position.* (1) In general. For purposes of Section 1a(33) of the Act, 7 U.S.C. 1a(33), and paragraph (hhh) of this section, the term “substantial position” means swap positions that equal or exceed any of the following thresholds in the specified major category of swaps:

(i) For rate swaps:

(A) $3 billion in daily average aggregate uncollateralized outward exposure; or

(B) $6 billion in:

(*1*) Daily average aggregate uncollateralized outward exposure plus

(*2*) Daily average aggregate potential outward exposure.

(ii) For credit swaps:

(A) $1 billion in daily average aggregate uncollateralized outward exposure; or

(B) $2 billion in:

(*1*) Daily average aggregate uncollateralized outward exposure plus

(2) Daily average aggregate potential outward exposure.

(iii) For equity swaps:

(A) $1 billion in daily average aggregate uncollateralized outward exposure; or

(B) $2 billion in:

(*1*) Daily average aggregate uncollateralized outward exposure plus

(2) Daily average aggregate potential outward exposure.

(iv) For other commodity swaps:

(A) $1 billion in daily average aggregate uncollateralized outward exposure; or

(B) $2 billion in:

(*1*) Daily average aggregate uncollateralized outward exposure plus

(2) Daily average aggregate potential outward exposure.

(2) *Aggregate uncollateralized outward exposure.* (i) *In general. Aggregate uncollateralized outward exposure* in general means the sum of the current exposure, obtained by marking-to-market using industry standard practices, of each of the person's swap positions with negative value in a major swap category, less the value of the collateral the person has posted in connection with those positions.

(ii) *Calculation of aggregate uncollateralized outward exposure.* In calculating this amount the person shall, with respect to each of its swap counterparties in a given major swap category, determine the dollar value of the aggregate current exposure arising from each of its swap positions with negative value (subject to the netting provisions described below) in that major category by marking-to-market using industry standard practices; and deduct from that dollar amount the aggregate value of the collateral the person has posted with respect to the swap positions. The aggregate uncollateralized outward exposure shall be the sum of those uncollateralized amounts across all of the person's swap counterparties in the applicable major category.

(iii) *Relevance of netting agreements.* (A) If the person has one or more master netting agreement in effect with a particular counterparty, the person may measure the current exposure arising from its swaps in any major category on a net basis, applying the terms of those agreements. Calculation of net current exposure may take into account offsetting positions entered into with that particular counterparty involving swaps (in any swap category) as well as security-based swaps and securities financing transactions (consisting of securities lending and borrowing, securities margin lending and repurchase and reverse repurchase agreements), and other financial instruments that are subject to netting offsets for purposes of applicable bankruptcy law, to the extent these are consistent with the offsets permitted by the master netting agreements.

(B) Such adjustments may not take into account any offset associated with positions that the person has with separate counterparties.

(iv) *Allocation of uncollateralized outward exposure.* If a person calculates current exposure with a particular counterparty on a net basis, as provided by paragraph (jjj)(2)(iii) of this section, the portion of that current exposure that should be attributed to each "major" category of swaps for purposes of the substantial position analysis should be calculated according to the formula:

$$ES(MC)_{\square} = Enet\ total_{\square} \cdot \frac{OTM_{S(MC)}}{OTM_{S(MC)} + OTM_{S(O)} + OTM_{non-S}}$$

View or download PDF

Where: $E_{S(MC)}$ equals the amount of aggregate current exposure attributable to the entity's swap positions in the “major” swap category at issue; $E_{net\ total}$ equals the entity's aggregate current exposure to the counterparty at issue, after accounting for the netting of positions and the posting of collateral; $OTM_{S(MC)}$ equals the exposure associated with the entity's out-of-the-money positions in swaps in the “major” category at issue, subject to those netting arrangements; and $OTM_{S(O)}$ equals the exposure associated with the entity's out-of-the-money positions in the other “major” categories of swaps, subject to those netting arrangements; and $OTM_{non\text{-}S}$ equals the exposure associated with the entity's out-of-the-money positions associated with instruments, other than swaps, that are subject to those netting arrangements.

(3) *Aggregate potential outward exposure.* (i) *In general.* Aggregate potential outward exposure in any major swap category means the sum of:

(A) The aggregate potential outward exposure for each of the person's swap positions in a major swap category that are not subject to daily mark-to-market margining and are not cleared by a registered or exempt clearing agency or derivatives clearing organization, as calculated in accordance with paragraph (jjj)(3)(ii) of this section; and

(B) The aggregate potential outward exposure for each of the person's swap positions in such major swap category that are either subject to daily mark-to-market margining or are cleared by a registered or exempt clearing agency or derivatives clearing organization, as calculated in accordance with paragraph (jjj)(3)(iii) of this section.

(ii) *Calculation of potential outward exposure for swaps that are not subject to daily mark-to-market margining and are not cleared by a registered or exempt clearing agency or derivatives clearing organization.* (A) *In general.* (*1*) For positions in swaps that are not subject to daily mark-to-market margining and are not cleared by a registered or exempt clearing agency or a derivatives clearing organization, potential outward exposure equals the total notional principal amount of those positions, multiplied by the following factors on a position-by-position basis reflecting the type of swap. For any swap that does not appropriately fall within any of the specified categories, the “other commodities” conversion factors set forth in the following Table 1 are to be used. If a swap is structured such that on specified dates any outstanding exposure is settled and the terms are reset so that the market value of the swap is zero, the remaining maturity equals the time until the next reset date.

TABLE 1—CONVERSION FACTOR MATRIX FOR SWAPS

Residual maturity	Interest rate	Foreign exchange rate and gold	Precious metals (except gold)	Other commodities
One year or less	0.00	0.01	0.07	0.10
Over one to five years	0.005	0.05	0.07	0.12
Over five years	0.015	0.075	0.08	0.15

Residual maturity	Credit	Equity
One year or less	0.10	0.06
Over one to five years	0.10	0.08
Over five years	0.10	0.10

(*2*) *Use of effective notional amounts.* If the stated notional amount on a position is leveraged or enhanced by the structure of the position, the calculation in paragraph (jjj)(3)(ii)(A)(*1*) of this section shall be based on the effective notional amount of the position rather than on the stated notional amount.

(*3*) *Exclusion of certain positions.* The calculation in paragraph (jjj)(3)(ii)(A)(*1*) of this section shall exclude:

(*i*) Positions that constitute the purchase of an option, if the purchaser has no additional payment obligations under the position;

(*ii*) Other positions for which the person has prepaid or otherwise satisfied all of its payment obligations; and

(*iii*) Positions for which, pursuant to law or a regulatory requirement, the person has assigned an amount of cash or U.S. Treasury securities that is sufficient at all times to pay the person's maximum possible liability under the position, and the person may not use that cash or those Treasury securities for other purposes.

(*4*) *Adjustment for certain positions.* Notwithstanding paragraph (jjj)(3)(ii)(A)(1) of this section, the potential outward exposure associated with a position by which a person buys credit protection using a credit default swap or index credit default swap, or associated with a position by which a person purchases an option for which the person retains additional payment obligations under the position, is capped at the net present value of the unpaid premiums.

(B) *Adjustment for netting agreements.* Notwithstanding paragraph (jjj)(3)(ii)(A) of this section, for positions subject to master netting agreements the potential outward exposure associated with the person's swaps with each counterparty equals a weighted average of the potential outward exposure for the person's swaps with that counterparty as calculated under paragraph (jjj)(3)(ii)(A) of this section, and that amount reduced by the ratio of net current exposure to gross current exposure, consistent with the following equation as calculated on a counterparty-by-counterparty basis:

$$P_{Net} = 0.4 * P_{Gross} + 0.6 * NGR * P_{Gross}$$

Where: P_{Net} is the potential outward exposure, adjusted for bilateral netting, of the person's swaps with a particular counterparty; P_{Gross} is the potential outward exposure without adjustment for bilateral netting as calculated pursuant to paragraph (jjj)(3)(ii)(A) of this section; and *NGR* is the ratio of the current exposure arising from its swaps in the major category as calculated on a net basis according to paragraphs (jjj)(2)(iii) and (iv) of this section, divided by the current exposure arising from its swaps in the major category as calculated in the absence of those netting procedures.

(iii) *Calculation of potential outward exposure for swaps that are either subject to daily mark-to-market margining or are cleared by a registered or exempt clearing agency or derivatives clearing organization.* For positions in swaps that are subject to daily mark-to-market margining or that are cleared by a registered or exempt clearing agency or derivatives clearing organization:

(A) Potential outward exposure equals the potential exposure that would be attributed to such positions using the procedures in paragraph (jjj)(3)(ii) of this section multiplied by:

(*1*) 0.1, in the case of positions cleared by a registered or exempt clearing agency or derivatives clearing organization; or

(*2*) 0.2, in the case of positions that are subject to daily mark-to-market margining but that are not cleared by a registered or exempt clearing agency or derivatives clearing organization.

(B) Solely for purposes of calculating potential outward exposure:

(*1*) A swap shall be considered to be subject to daily mark-to-market margining if, and for so long as, the counterparties follow the daily practice of exchanging collateral to reflect changes in the current exposure arising from the swap (after taking into account any other financial positions addressed by a netting agreement between the counterparties).

(*2*) If the person is permitted by agreement to maintain a threshold for which it is not required to post collateral, the position still will be considered to be subject to daily mark-to-market margining for purposes of calculating potential outward exposure, but the total amount of that threshold (regardless of the actual exposure at any time), less any initial margin posted up to the amount of that threshold, shall be added to the person's aggregate uncollateralized outward exposure for purposes of paragraph (jjj)(1)(i)(B), (ii)(B), (iii)(B) or (iv)(B) of this section, as applicable.

(*3*) If the minimum transfer amount under the agreement is in excess of $1 million, the position still will be considered to be subject to daily mark-to-market margining for purposes of calculating potential outward exposure, but the entirety of the minimum transfer amount shall be added to the person's aggregate uncollateralized outward exposure for purposes of paragraph (jjj)(1)(i)(B), (ii)(B), (iii)(B) or (iv)(B) of this section, as applicable.

(*4*) A person may, at its discretion, calculate the potential outward exposure of positions in swaps that are subject to daily mark-to-market margining in accordance with paragraph (jjj)(3)(ii) of this section in lieu of calculating the potential outward exposure of such swap positions in accordance with this paragraph (jjj)(3)(iii).

(4) *Calculation of daily average.* Measures of daily average aggregate uncollateralized outward exposure and daily average aggregate potential outward exposure shall equal the arithmetic mean of the applicable measure of exposure at the close of each business day, beginning the first business day of each calendar quarter and continuing through the last business day of that quarter.

(5) *Inter-affiliate activities.* In calculating its aggregate uncollateralized outward exposure and its aggregate potential outward exposure, the person shall not consider its swap positions with counterparties that are majority-owned affiliates. For these purposes the counterparties to a swap are majority-owned affiliates if one counterparty directly or indirectly owns a majority interest in the other, or if a third party directly or indirectly owns a majority interest in both counterparties to the swap, where "majority interest" is the right to vote or direct the vote of a majority of a class of voting securities of an entity, the power to sell or direct the sale of a majority of a class of voting securities of an entity, or the right to receive upon dissolution or the contribution of a majority of the capital of a partnership.

(kkk) *Hedging or mitigating commercial risk.* For purposes of Section 1a(33) of the Act, 7 U.S.C. 1a(33) and paragraph (hhh) of this section, a swap position is held for the purpose of hedging or mitigating commercial risk when:

(1) Such position:

(i) Is economically appropriate to the reduction of risks in the conduct and management of a commercial enterprise (or of a majority-owned affiliate of the enterprise), where the risks arise from:

(A) The potential change in the value of assets that a person owns, produces, manufactures, processes, or merchandises or reasonably anticipates owning, producing, manufacturing, processing, or merchandising in the ordinary course of business of the enterprise;

(B) The potential change in the value of liabilities that a person has incurred or reasonably anticipates incurring in the ordinary course of business of the enterprise; or

(C) The potential change in the value of services that a person provides, purchases, or reasonably anticipates providing or purchasing in the ordinary course of business of the enterprise;

(D) The potential change in the value of assets, services, inputs, products, or commodities that a person owns, produces, manufactures, processes, merchandises, leases, or sells, or reasonably anticipates owning, producing, manufacturing, processing, merchandising, leasing, or selling in the ordinary course of business of the enterprise;

(E) Any potential change in value related to any of the foregoing arising from interest, currency, or foreign exchange rate movements associated with such assets, liabilities, services, inputs, products, or commodities; or

(F) Any fluctuation in interest, currency, or foreign exchange rate exposures arising from a person's current or anticipated assets or liabilities; or

(ii) Qualifies as bona fide hedging for purposes of an exemption from position limits under the Act; or

(iii) Qualifies for hedging treatment under:

(A) Financial Accounting Standards Board Accounting Standards Codification Topic 815, Derivatives and Hedging (formerly known as Statement No. 133); or

(B) Governmental Accounting Standards Board Statement 53, Accounting and Financial Reporting for Derivative Instruments; and

(2) Such position is:

(i) Not held for a purpose that is in the nature of speculation, investing or trading; and

(ii) Not held to hedge or mitigate the risk of another swap or security-based swap position, unless that other position itself is held for the purpose of hedging or mitigating commercial risk as defined by this rule or § 240.3a67-4 of this title.

(lll) *Substantial counterparty exposure* —(1) *In general.* For purposes of Section 1a(33) of the Act, 7 U.S.C. 1a(33), and paragraph (hhh) of this section, the term *substantial counterparty exposure that could have serious adverse effects on the financial stability of the United States banking system or financial markets* means a swap position that satisfies either of the following thresholds:

(i) $5 billion in daily average aggregate uncollateralized outward exposure; or

(ii) $8 billion in:

(A) Daily average aggregate uncollateralized outward exposure plus

(B) Daily average aggregate potential outward exposure.

(2) *Calculation methodology.* For these purposes, the terms *daily average aggregate uncollateralized outward exposure*and *daily average aggregate potential outward exposure* shall be calculated the same way as is prescribed in paragraph (jjj) of this section, except that these amounts shall be calculated by reference to all of the person's swap positions, rather than by reference to a specific major swap category.

(mmm) *Financial entity; highly leveraged.* (1) For purposes of Section 1a(33) of the Act, 7 U.S.C. 1a(33), and paragraph (hhh) of this section, the term *financial entity* means:

(i) A security-based swap dealer;

(ii) A major security-based swap participant;

(iii) A commodity pool as defined in Section 1a(10) of the Act, 7 U.S.C. 1a(10);

(iv) A private fund as defined in Section 202(a) of the Investment Advisers Act of 1940, 15 U.S.C. 80b-2(a);

(v) An employee benefit plan as defined in paragraphs (3) and (32) of Section 3 of the Employee Retirement Income Security Act of 1974, 29 U.S.C. 1002; and

(vi) A person predominantly engaged in activities that are in the business of banking or financial in nature, as defined in Section 4(k) of the Bank Holding Company Act of 1956, 12 U.S.C. 1843(k).

(2) For purposes of Section 1a(33) of the Act, 7 U.S.C. 1a(33), and paragraph (hhh) of this section, the term *highly leveraged* means the existence of a ratio of an entity's total liabilities to equity in excess of 12 to 1 as measured at the close of business on the last business day of the applicable fiscal quarter. For this purpose, liabilities and equity should each be determined in accordance with U.S. generally accepted accounting principles; provided, however, that a person that is an employee benefit plan, as defined in paragraphs (3) and (32) of Section 3 of the Employee Retirement Income Security Act of 1974, 29 U.S.C. 1002, may exclude obligations to pay benefits to plan participants from the calculation of liabilities and substitute the total value of plan assets for equity.

(xxx) *Swap* —(1) *In general.* The term swap has the meaning set forth in section 1a(47) of the Commodity Exchange Act.

(2) *Inclusion of particular products.* (i) The term swap includes, without limiting the meaning set forth in section 1a(47) of the Commodity Exchange Act, the following agreements, contracts, and transactions:

(A) A cross-currency swap;

(B) A currency option, foreign currency option, foreign exchange option and foreign exchange rate option;

(C) A foreign exchange forward;

(D) A foreign exchange swap;

(E) A forward rate agreement; and

(F) A non-deliverable forward involving foreign exchange.

(ii) The term swap does not include an agreement, contract, or transaction described in paragraph (xxx)(2)(i) of this section that is otherwise excluded by section 1a(47)(B) of the Commodity Exchange Act.

(3) *Foreign exchange forwards and foreign exchange swaps.* Notwithstanding paragraph (xxx)(2) of this section:

(i) A foreign exchange forward or a foreign exchange swap shall not be considered a swap if the Secretary of the Treasury makes a determination described in section 1a(47)(E)(i) of the Commodity Exchange Act.

(ii) Notwithstanding paragraph (xxx)(3)(i) of this section:

(A) The reporting requirements set forth in section 4r of the Commodity Exchange Act and regulations promulgated thereunder shall apply to a foreign exchange forward or foreign exchange swap; and

(B) The business conduct standards set forth in section 4s(h) of the Commodity Exchange Act and regulations promulgated thereunder shall apply to a swap dealer or major swap participant that is a party to a foreign exchange forward or foreign exchange swap.

(iii) For purposes of section 1a(47)(E) of the Commodity Exchange Act and this paragraph (xxx), the term *foreign exchange forward* has the meaning set forth in section 1a(24) of the Commodity Exchange Act.

(iv) For purposes of section 1a(47)(E) of the Commodity Exchange Act and this paragraph (xxx), the term *foreign exchange swap* has the meaning set forth in section 1a(25) of the Commodity Exchange Act.

(v) For purposes of sections 1a(24) and 1a(25) of the Commodity Exchange Act and this paragraph (xxx), the following transactions are not foreign exchange forwards or foreign exchange swaps:

(A) A currency swap or a cross-currency swap;

(B) A currency option, foreign currency option, foreign exchange option, or foreign exchange rate option; and

(C) A non-deliverable forward involving foreign exchange.

(4) *Insurance.* (i) This paragraph is a non-exclusive safe harbor. The terms *swap* as used in section 1a(47) of the Commodity Exchange Act and *security-based swap* as used in section 1a(42) of the Commodity Exchange Act do not include an agreement, contract, or transaction that:

(A) By its terms or by law, as a condition of performance on the agreement, contract, or transaction:

(*1*) Requires the beneficiary of the agreement, contract, or transaction to have an insurable interest that is the subject of the agreement, contract, or transaction and thereby carry the risk of loss with respect to that interest continuously throughout the duration of the agreement, contract, or transaction;

(*2*) Requires that loss to occur and to be proved, and that any payment or indemnification therefor be limited to the value of the insurable interest;

(*3*) Is not traded, separately from the insured interest, on an organized market or over-the-counter; and

(*4*) With respect to financial guaranty insurance only, in the event of payment default or insolvency of the obligor, any acceleration of payments under the policy is at the sole discretion of the insurer; and

(B) Is provided:

(*1*)(*i*) By a person that is subject to supervision by the insurance commissioner (or similar official or agency) of any State or by the United States or an agency or instrumentality thereof; and

(*ii*) Such agreement, contract, or transaction is regulated as insurance under applicable State law or the laws of the United States;

(*2*)(*i*) Directly or indirectly by the United States, any State or any of their respective agencies or instrumentalities; or

(*ii*) Pursuant to a statutorily authorized program thereof; or

(*3*) In the case of reinsurance only, by a person to another person that satisfies the conditions set forth in paragraph (xxx)(4)(i)(B) of this section, provided that:

(*i*) Such person is not prohibited by applicable State law or the laws of the United States from offering such agreement, contract, or transaction to such person that satisfies the conditions set forth in paragraph (xxx)(4)(i)(B) of this section;

(*ii*) The agreement, contract, or transaction to be reinsured satisfies the conditions set forth in paragraph (xxx)(4)(i)(A) or paragraph (xxx)(4)(i)(C) of this section; and

(*iii*) Except as otherwise permitted under applicable State law, the total amount reimbursable by all reinsurers for such agreement, contract, or transaction may not exceed the claims or losses paid by the person writing the risk being ceded or transferred by such person; or

(*4*) In the case of non-admitted insurance, by a person who:

(*i*) Is located outside of the United States and listed on the Quarterly Listing of Alien Insurers as maintained by the International Insurers Department of the National Association of Insurance Commissioners; or

(*ii*) Meets the eligibility criteria for non-admitted insurers under applicable State law; or

(C) Is provided in accordance with the conditions set forth in paragraph (xxx)(4)(i)(B) of this section and is one of the following types of products:

(*1*) Surety bond;

(*2*) Fidelity bond;

(*3*) Life insurance;

(*4*) Health insurance;

(*5*) Long term care insurance;

(*6*) Title insurance;

(*7*) Property and casualty insurance;

(*8*) Annuity;

(*9*) Disability insurance;

(*10*) Insurance against default on individual residential mortgages; and

(*11*) Reinsurance of any of the foregoing products identified in paragraphs (xxx)(4)(i)(C)(*1*) through (*10*) of this section; or

(ii) The terms *swap* as used in section 1a(47) of the Commodity Exchange Act and *security-based swap* as used in section 1a(42) of the Commodity Exchange Act do not include an agreement, contract, or transaction that was entered into on or before the effective date of paragraph (xxx)(4) of this section, and that, at such time that it was entered into, was provided in accordance with the conditions set forth in paragraph (xxx)(4)(i)(B) of this section.

(5) *State.* For purposes of paragraph (xxx)(4) of this section, the term *State* means any state of the United States, the District of Columbia, Puerto Rico, the U.S. Virgin Islands, or any other possession of the United States.

(6) *Anti-Evasion:*

(i) An agreement, contract, or transaction that is willfully structured to evade any provision of Subtitle A of the Wall Street Transparency and Accountability Act of 2010, including any amendments made to the Commodity Exchange Act thereby (*Subtitle A*), shall be deemed a swap for purposes of Subtitle A and the rules, regulations, and orders of the Commission promulgated thereunder.

(ii) An interest rate swap or currency swap, including but not limited to a transaction identified in paragraph (xxx)(3)(v) of this section, that is willfully structured as a foreign exchange forward or foreign exchange swap to evade any provision of Subtitle A shall be deemed a swap for purposes of Subtitle A and the rules, regulations, and orders of the Commission promulgated thereunder.

(iii) An agreement, contract, or transaction of a bank that is not under the regulatory jurisdiction of an appropriate Federal banking agency (as defined in section 1a(2) of the Commodity Exchange Act), where the agreement, contract, or transaction is willfully structured as an identified banking product (as defined in section 402 of the Legal Certainty for Bank Products Act of 2000) to evade the provisions of the Commodity Exchange Act, shall be deemed a swap for purposes of the Commodity Exchange Act and the rules, regulations, and orders of the Commission promulgated thereunder.

(iv) The form, label, and written documentation of an agreement, contract, or transaction shall not be dispositive in determining whether the agreement, contract, or transaction has been willfully structured to evade as provided in paragraphs (xxx)(6)(i) through (xxx)(6)(iii) of this section.

(v) An agreement, contract, or transaction that has been willfully structured to evade as provided in paragraphs (xxx)(6)(i) through (xxx)(6)(iii) of this section shall be considered in determining whether a person that so willfully structured to evade is a swap dealer or major swap participant.

(vi) Notwithstanding the foregoing, no agreement, contract, or transaction structured as a security (including a security-based swap) under the securities laws (as defined in section 3(a)(47) of the Securities Exchange Act of 1934 (15 U.S.C. 78c(a)(47))) shall be deemed a swap pursuant to this paragraph (xxx)(6) or shall be considered for purposes of paragraph (xxx)(6)(v) of this section.

(yyy) *Narrow-based security index as used in the definition of "security-based swap."*

(1) *In general.* Except as otherwise provided in paragraphs (zzz) and (aaaa) of this section, for purposes of section 1a(42) of the Commodity Exchange Act, the term *narrow-based security index* has the meaning set forth in section 1a(35) of the Commodity Exchange Act, and the rules, regulations and orders of the Commission thereunder.

(2) *Tolerance period for swaps traded on designated contract markets, swap execution facilities, and foreign boards of trade.* Notwithstanding paragraph (yyy)(1) of this section, solely for purposes of swaps traded on or subject to the rules of a designated contract market, swap execution facility, or foreign board of trade, a security index underlying such swaps shall not be considered a narrow-based security index if:

(i)(A) A swap on the index is traded on or subject to the rules of a designated contract market, swap execution facility, or foreign board of trade for at least 30 days as a swap on an index that was not a narrow-based security index; or

(B) Such index was not a narrow-based security index during every trading day of the six full calendar months preceding a date no earlier than 30 days prior to the commencement of trading of a swap on such index on a market described in paragraph (yyy)(2)(i)(A) of this section; and

(ii) The index has been a narrow-based security index for no more than 45 business days over three consecutive calendar months.

(3) *Tolerance period for security-based swaps traded on national securities exchanges or security-based swap execution facilities.* Notwithstanding paragraph (yyy)(1) of this section, solely for purposes of security-based swaps traded on a national securities exchange or security-based swap execution facility, a security index underlying such security-based swaps shall be considered a narrow-based security index if:

(i)(A) A security-based swap on the index is traded on a national securities exchange or security-based swap execution facility for at least 30 days as a security-based swap on a narrow-based security index; or

(B) Such index was a narrow-based security index during every trading day of the six full calendar months preceding a date no earlier than 30 days prior to the commencement of trading of a security-based swap on such index on a market described in paragraph (yyy)(3)(i)(A) of this section; and

(ii) The index has been a security index that is not a narrow-based security index for no more than 45 business days over three consecutive calendar months.

(4) *Grace period.*

(i) Solely with respect to a swap that is traded on or subject to the rules of a designated contract market, swap execution facility, or foreign board of trade, an index that becomes a narrow-based security index under paragraph (yyy)(2) of this section solely because it was a narrow-based security index for more than 45 business days over three consecutive calendar months shall not be a narrow-based security index for the following three calendar months.

(ii) Solely with respect to a security-based swap that is traded on a national securities exchange or security-based swap execution facility, an index that becomes a security index that is not a narrow-based security index under paragraph (yyy)(3) of this section solely because it was not a narrow-based security index for more than 45 business days over three consecutive calendar months shall be a narrow-based security index for the following three calendar months.

(zzz) Meaning of "issuers of securities in a narrow-based security index" as used in the definition of "security-based swap" as applied to index credit default swaps.

(1) Notwithstanding paragraph (yyy)(1) of this section, and solely for purposes of determining whether a credit default swap is a security-based swap under the definition of "security-based swap" in section 3(a)(68)(A)(ii)(III) of the Securities Exchange Act of 1934 (15 U.S.C. 78c(a)(68)(A)(ii)(III), as incorporated in section 1a(42) of the Commodity Exchange Act, the term *issuers of securities in a narrow-based security index* means issuers of securities included in an index (including an index referencing loan borrowers or loans of such borrowers) in which:

(i)(A) There are nine or fewer non-affiliated issuers of securities that are reference entities included in the index, provided that an issuer of securities shall not be deemed a reference entity included in the index for purposes of this section unless:

(*1*) A credit event with respect to such reference entity would result in a payment by the credit protection seller to the credit protection buyer under the credit default swap based on the related notional amount allocated to such reference entity; or

(*2*) The fact of such credit event or the calculation in accordance with paragraph (zzz)(1)(i)(A)(*1*) of this section of the amount owed with respect to such credit event is taken into account in determining whether to make any future payments under the credit default swap with respect to any future credit events;

(B) The effective notional amount allocated to any reference entity included in the index comprises more than 30 percent of the index's weighting;

(C) The effective notional amount allocated to any five non-affiliated reference entities included in the index comprises more than 60 percent of the index's weighting; or

(D) Except as provided in paragraph (zzz)(2) of this section, for each reference entity included in the index, none of the criteria in paragraphs (zzz)(1)(i)(D)(*1*) through (*8*) of this section is satisfied:

(*1*) The reference entity included in the index is required to file reports pursuant to section 13 or section 15(d) of the Securities Exchange Act of 1934 (15 U.S.C. 78m or 78o(d));

(*2*) The reference entity included in the index is eligible to rely on the exemption provided in rule 12g3-2(b) under the Securities Exchange Act of 1934 (17 CFR 240.12g3-2(b));

(*3*) The reference entity included in the index has a worldwide market value of its outstanding common equity held by non-affiliates of $700 million or more;

(*4*) The reference entity included in the index (other than a reference entity included in the index that is an issuing entity of an asset-backed security as defined in section 3(a)(77) of the Securities Exchange Act of 1934 (15 U.S.C. 78c(a)(77)) has outstanding notes, bonds, debentures, loans, or evidences of indebtedness (other than revolving credit facilities) having a total remaining principal amount of at least $1 billion;

(*5*) The reference entity included in the index is the issuer of an exempted security as defined in section 3(a)(12) of the Securities Exchange Act of 1934 (15 U.S.C. 78c(a)(12)) (other than any municipal security as defined in section 3(a)(29) of the Securities Exchange Act of 1934 (15 U.S.C. 78c(a)(29)));

(*6*) The reference entity included in the index is a government of a foreign country or a political subdivision of a foreign country;

(*7*) If the reference entity included in the index is an issuing entity of an asset-backed security as defined in section 3(a)(77) of the Securities Exchange Act of 1934 (15 U.S.C. 78c(a)(77)), such asset-backed security was issued in a transaction registered under the Securities Act of 1933 (15 U.S.C. 77a *et seq.*) and has publicly available distribution reports; and

(*8*) For a credit default swap entered into solely between eligible contract participants as defined in section 1a(18) of the Commodity Exchange Act:

(*i*) The reference entity included in the index (other than a reference entity included in the index that is an issuing entity of an asset-backed security as defined in section 3(a)(77) of the Securities Exchange Act of 1934 (15 U.S.C. 78c(a)(77))) makes available to the public or otherwise makes available to such eligible contract participant information about the reference entity included in the index pursuant to rule 144A(d)(4) under the Securities Act of 1933 (17 CFR 230.144A(d)(4));

(*ii*) Financial information about the reference entity included in the index (other than a reference entity included in the index that is an issuing entity of an asset-backed security as defined in section 3(a)(77) of the Securities Exchange Act of 1934 (15 U.S.C. 78c(a)(77))) is otherwise publicly available; or

(*iii*) In the case of a reference entity included in the index that is an issuing entity of an asset-backed security as defined in section 3(a)(77) of the Securities Exchange Act of 1934 (15 U.S.C. 78c(a)(77)), information of the type and level included in publicly available distribution reports for similar asset-backed securities is publicly available about both the reference entity included in the index and such asset-backed security; and

(ii)(A) The index is not composed solely of reference entities that are issuers of exempted securities as defined in section 3(a)(12) of the Securities Exchange Act of 1934 (15 U.S.C. 78c(a)(12)), as in effect on the date of enactment of the Futures Trading Act of 1982 (other than any municipal security as defined in section 3(a)(29) of the Securities Exchange Act of 1934 (15 U.S.C. 78c(a)(29))), as in effect on the date of enactment of the Futures Trading Act of 1982; and

(B) Without taking into account any portion of the index composed of reference entities that are issuers of exempted securities as defined in section 3(a)(12) of the Securities Exchange Act of 1934 (15 U.S.C. 78c(a)(12)), as in effect on the date of enactment of the Futures Trading Act of 1982 (other than any municipal security as defined in section 3(a)(29) of the Securities Exchange Act of 1934 (15 U.S.C. 78c(a)(29))), the remaining portion of the index would be within the term "issuer of securities in a narrow-based security index" under paragraph (zzz)(1)(i) of this section.

(2) Paragraph (zzz)(1)(i)(D) of this section will not apply with respect to a reference entity included in the index if:

(i) The effective notional amounts allocated to such reference entity comprise less than five percent of the index's weighting; and

(ii) The effective notional amounts allocated to reference entities included in the index that satisfy paragraph (zzz)(1)(i)(D) of this section comprise at least 80 percent of the index's weighting.

(3) For purposes of this paragraph (zzz):

(i) A reference entity included in the index is affiliated with another reference entity included in the index (for purposes of paragraph (zzz)(3)(iv) of this section) or another entity (for purposes of paragraph (zzz)(3)(v) of this section) if it controls, is controlled by, or is under common control with, that other reference entity included in the index or other entity, as applicable; provided that each reference entity included in the index that is an issuing entity of an asset-backed security as defined in section 3(a)(77) of the Securities Exchange Act of 1934 (15 U.S.C. 78c(a)(77)) will not be considered affiliated with any other reference entity included in the index or any other entity that is an issuing entity of an asset-backed security.

(ii) Control for purposes of this section means ownership of more than 50 percent of the equity of a reference entity included in the index (for purposes of paragraph (zzz)(3)(iv) of this section) or another entity (for purposes of paragraph (zzz)(3)(v) of this section), or the ability to direct the voting of more than 50 percent of the voting equity of a reference entity included in the index (for purposes of paragraph (zzz)(3)(iv) of this section) or another entity (for purposes of paragraph (zzz)(3)(v) of this section).

(iii) In identifying a reference entity included in the index for purposes of this section, the term reference entity includes:

(A) An issuer of securities;

(B) An issuer of securities that is an issuing entity of an asset-backed security as defined in section 3(a)(77) of the Securities Exchange Act of 1934 (15 U.S.C. 78c(a)(77)); and

(C) An issuer of securities that is a borrower with respect to any loan identified in an index of borrowers or loans.

(iv) For purposes of calculating the thresholds in paragraphs (zzz)(1)(i)(A) through (1)(i)(C) of this section, the term reference entity included in the index includes a single reference entity included in the index or a group of affiliated reference entities included in the index as determined in accordance with paragraph (zzz)(3)(i) of this section (with each reference entity included in the index that is an issuing entity of an asset-backed security as defined in section 3(a)(77) of the Act (15 U.S.C. 78c(a)(77)) being considered a separate reference entity included in the index).

(v) For purposes of determining whether one of the criterion in either paragraphs (zzz)(1)(i)(D)(*1*) through (zzz)(1)(i)(D)(*4*) of this section or paragraphs (zzz)(1)(iv)(D)(*8*)(*i*) and (a)(1)(iv)(D)(*8*)(*ii*) of this section is met, the term reference entity included in the index includes a single reference entity included in the index or a group of affiliated entities as determined in accordance with paragraph (zzz)(3)(i) of this section (with each issuing entity of an asset-backed security as defined in section 3(a)(77) of the Act (15 U.S.C. 78c(a)(77)) being considered a separate entity).

(aaaa) Meaning of "narrow-based security index" as used in the definition of "security-based swap" as applied to index credit default swaps.

(1) Notwithstanding paragraph (yyy)(1) of this section, and solely for purposes of determining whether a credit default swap is a security-based swap under the definition of "security-based swap" in section 3(a)(68)(A)(ii)(I) of the Securities Exchange Act of 1934 (15 U.S.C. 78c(a)(68)(A)(ii)(I), as incorporated in section 1a(42) of the Commodity Exchange Act, the term narrow-based security index means an index in which:

(i)(A) The index is composed of nine or fewer securities or securities that are issued by nine or fewer non-affiliated issuers, provided that a security shall not be deemed a component of the index for purposes of this section unless:

(*1*) A credit event with respect to the issuer of such security or a credit event with respect to such security would result in a payment by the credit protection seller to the credit protection buyer under the credit default swap based on the related notional amount allocated to such security; or

(*2*) The fact of such credit event or the calculation in accordance with paragraph (aaaa)(1)(i)(A)(*1*) of this section of the amount owed with respect to such credit event is taken into account in determining whether to make any future payments under the credit default swap with respect to any future credit events;

(B) The effective notional amount allocated to the securities of any issuer included in the index comprises more than 30 percent of the index's weighting;

(C) The effective notional amount allocated to the securities of any five non-affiliated issuers included in the index comprises more than 60 percent of the index's weighting; or

(D) Except as provided in paragraph (aaaa)(2) of this section, for each security included in the index, none of the criteria in paragraphs (aaaa)(1)(i)(D)(*1*) through (*8*) is satisfied:

(*1*) The issuer of the security included in the index is required to file reports pursuant to section 13 or section 15(d) of the Securities Exchange Act of 1934 (15 U.S.C. 78m or 78o(d));

(*2*) The issuer of the security included in the index is eligible to rely on the exemption provided in rule 12g3-2(b) under the Securities Exchange Act of 1934 (17 CFR 240.12g3-2(b));

(*3*) The issuer of the security included in the index has a worldwide market value of its outstanding common equity held by non-affiliates of $700 million or more;

(*4*) The issuer of the security included in the index (other than an issuer of the security that is an issuing entity of an asset-backed security as defined in section 3(a)(77) of the Securities Exchange Act of 1934 (15 U.S.C. 78c(a)(77))) has outstanding notes, bonds, debentures, loans or evidences of indebtedness (other than revolving credit facilities) having a total remaining principal amount of at least $1 billion;

(*5*) The security included in the index is an exempted security as defined in section 3(a)(12) of the Securities Exchange Act of 1934 (15 U.S.C. 78c(a)(12)) (other than any municipal security as defined in section 3(a)(29) of the Securities Exchange Act of 1934 (15 U.S.C. 78c(a)(29)));

(*6*) The issuer of the security included in the index is a government of a foreign country or a political subdivision of a foreign country;

(*7*) If the security included in the index is an asset-backed security as defined in section 3(a)(77) of the Securities Exchange Act of 1934 (15 U.S.C. 78c(a)(77)), the security was issued in a transaction registered under the Securities Act of 1933 (15 U.S.C. 77a *et seq.*) and has publicly available distribution reports; and

(*8*) For a credit default swap entered into solely between eligible contract participants as defined in section 1a(18) of the Commodity Exchange Act:

(*i*) The issuer of the security included in the index (other than an issuer of the security that is an issuing entity of an asset-backed security as defined in section 3(a)(77) of the Securities Exchange Act of 1934 (15 U.S.C. 78c(a)(77))) makes available to the public or otherwise makes available to such eligible contract participant information about such issuer pursuant to rule 144A(d)(4) of the Securities Act of 1933 (17 CFR 230.144A(d)(4));

(*ii*) Financial information about the issuer of the security included in the index (other than an issuer of the security that is an issuing entity of an asset-backed security as defined in section 3(a)(77) of the Securities Exchange Act of 1934 (15 U.S.C. 78c(a)(77))) is otherwise publicly available; or

(*iii*) In the case of an asset-backed security as defined in section 3(a)(77) of the Securities Exchange Act of 1934 (15 U.S.C. 78c(a)(77)), information of the type and level included in public distribution reports for similar asset-backed securities is publicly available about both the issuing entity and such asset-backed security; and

(ii)(A) The index is not composed solely of exempted securities as defined in section 3(a)(12) of the Securities Exchange Act of 1934 (15 U.S.C. 78c(a)(12)), as in effect on the date of enactment of the Futures Trading Act of 1982 (other than any municipal security as defined in section 3(a)(29) of the Securities Exchange Act of 1934 (15 U.S.C. 78c(a)(29))), as in effect on the date of enactment of the Futures Trading Act of 1982; and

(B) Without taking into account any portion of the index composed of exempted securities as defined in section 3(a)(12) of the Securities Exchange Act of 1934 (15 U.S.C. 78c(a)(12)), as in effect on the date of enactment of the Futures Trading Act of 1982 (other than any municipal security as defined in section 3(a)(29) of the Securities Exchange Act of 1934 (15 U.S.C. 78c(a)(29))), the remaining portion of the index would be within the term “narrow-based security index” under paragraph (aaaa)(1)(i) of this section.

(2) Paragraph (aaaa)(1)(i)(D) of this section will not apply with respect to securities of an issuer included in the index if:

(i) The effective notional amounts allocated to all securities of such issuer included in the index comprise less than five percent of the index's weighting; and

(ii) The securities that satisfy paragraph (aaaa)(1)(i)(D) of this section comprise at least 80 percent of the index's weighting.

(3) For purposes of this paragraph (aaaa):

(i) An issuer of securities included in the index is affiliated with another issuer of securities included in the index (for purposes of paragraph (aaaa)(3)(iv) of this section) or another entity (for purposes of paragraph (aaaa)(3)(v) of this section) if it controls, is controlled by, or is under common control with, that other issuer or other entity, as applicable; provided that each issuer of securities included in the index that is an issuing entity of an asset-backed security as defined in section 3(a)(77) of the Securities Exchange Act of 1934 (15 U.S.C. 78c(a)(77)) will not be considered affiliated with any other issuer of securities included in the index or any other entity that is an issuing entity of an asset-backed security.

(ii) Control for purposes of this section means ownership of more than 50 percent of the equity of an issuer of securities included in the index (for purposes of paragraph (aaaa)(3)(iv) of this section) or another entity (for purposes of paragraph (aaaa)(3)(v) of this section), or the ability to direct the voting of more than 50 percent of the voting equity an issuer of securities included in the index (for purposes of paragraph (aaaa)(3)(iv) of this section) or another entity (for purposes of paragraph (aaaa)(3)(v) of this section).

(iii) In identifying an issuer of securities included in the index for purposes of this section, the term issuer includes:

(A) An issuer of securities; and

(B) An issuer of securities that is an issuing entity of an asset-backed security as defined in section 3(a)(77) of the Securities Exchange Act of 1934 (15 U.S.C. 78c(a)(77)).

(iv) For purposes of calculating the thresholds in paragraphs (zzz)(1)(i)(A) through (1)(i)(C) of this section, the term issuer of the security included in the index includes a single issuer of securities included in the index or a group of affiliated issuers of securities included in the index as determined in accordance with paragraph (aaaa)(3)(i) of this section (with each issuer of securities included in the index that is an issuing entity of an asset-backed security as defined in section 3(a)(77) of the Securities Exchange Act of 1934 (15 U.S.C. 78c(a)(77)) being considered a separate issuer of securities included in the index).

(v) For purposes of determining whether one of the criterion in either paragraphs (aaaa)(1)(i)(D)(1) through (aaaa)(1)(i)(D)(4) of this section or paragraphs (aaaa)(1)(iv)(D)(*8*)(*i*) and (aaaa)(1)(iv)(D)(*8*)(*ii*) of this section is met, the term issuer of the security included in the index includes a single issuer of securities included in the index or a group of affiliated entities as determined in accordance with paragraph (aaaa)(3)(i) of this section (with each issuing entity of an asset-backed security as defined in section 3(a)(77) of the Act (15 U.S.C. 78c(a)(77)) being considered a separate entity).

(bbbb) Futures contracts on certain foreign sovereign debt. The term *security-based swap* as used in section 3(a)(68) of the Securities Exchange Act of 1934 (15 U.S.C. 78c(a)(68)), as incorporated in section 1a(42) of the Commodity Exchange Act, does not include an agreement, contract, or transaction that is based on or references a qualifying foreign futures contract (as defined in rule 3a12-8 under the Securities Exchange Act of 1934 (17 CFR 240.3a12-8)) on the debt securities of any one or more of the foreign governments enumerated in rule 3a12-8 under the Securities Exchange Act of 1934 (17 CFR 240.3a12-8), provided that such agreement, contract, or transaction satisfies the following conditions:

(1) The futures contract that the agreement, contract, or transaction references or upon which the agreement, contract, or transaction is based is a qualifying foreign futures contract that satisfies the conditions of rule 3a12-8 under the Securities Exchange Act of 1934 (17 CFR 240.3a12-8) applicable to qualifying foreign futures contracts;

(2) The agreement, contract, or transaction is traded on or through a board of trade (as defined in the Commodity Exchange Act);

(3) The debt securities upon which the qualifying foreign futures contract is based or referenced and any security used to determine the cash settlement amount pursuant to paragraph (bbbb)(4) of this section were not registered under the Securities Act of 1933 (15 U.S.C. 77 *et seq.*) or the subject of any American depositary receipt registered under the Securities Act of 1933;

(4) The agreement, contract, or transaction may only be cash settled; and

(5) The agreement, contract or transaction is not entered into by the issuer of the debt securities upon which the qualifying foreign futures contract is based or referenced (including any security used to determine the cash payment due on settlement of such agreement, contract or transaction), an affiliate (as defined in the Securities Act of 1933 (15 U.S.C. 77 *et seq.*) and the rules and regulations thereunder) of the issuer, or an underwriter of such issuer's debt securities.

(cccc) *Cleared Swaps Customer.* This term has the meaning provided in § 22.1 of this chapter.

(dddd) *Cleared Swaps Customer Account.* This term has the meaning provided in § 22.1 of this chapter.

(eeee) *Cleared Swaps Customer Collateral.* This term has the meaning provided in § 22.1 of this chapter.

(ffff) *Confirmation.* When used in reference to a futures commission merchant, introducing broker, or commodity trading advisor, this term means documentation (electronic or otherwise) that memorializes specified terms of a transaction executed on behalf of a customer. When used in reference to a swap dealer or major swap participant, this term has the meaning set forth in § 23.500 of this chapter.

(gggg) *Customer Account.* This term references both a Cleared Swaps Customer Account and a Futures Account, as defined by paragraphs (dddd) and (vv) of this section.

(hhhh) *Electronic trading facility.* This term means a trading facility that—

(1) Operates by means of an electronic or telecommunications network; and

(2) Maintains an automated audit trail of bids, offers, and the matching of orders or the execution of transactions on the facility.

(iiii) *Futures customer.* This term means any person who uses a futures commission merchant, introducing broker, commodity trading advisor, or commodity pool operator as an agent in connection with trading in any contract for the purchase of sale of a commodity for future delivery or any option on such contract; *Provided, however,* an owner or holder of a proprietary account as defined in paragraph (y) of this section shall not be deemed to be a futures customer within the meaning of sections 4d(a) and 4d(b) of the Act, the regulations that implement sections 4d and 4f of the Act and § 1.35, and such an owner or holder of such a proprietary account shall otherwise be deemed to be a futures customer within the meaning of the Act and §§ 1.37 and 1.46 and all other sections of these rules, regulations, and orders which do not implement sections 4d and 4f of the Act.

(jjjj) *Futures customer funds.* This term means all money, securities, and property received by a futures commission merchant or by a derivatives clearing organization from, for, or on behalf of, futures customers:

(1) To margin, guarantee, or secure contracts for future delivery on or subject to the rules of a contract market or derivatives clearing organization, as the case may be, and all money accruing to such futures customers as the result of such contracts; and

(2) In connection with a commodity option transaction on or subject to the rules of a contract market, or derivatives clearing organization, as the case may be:

(i) To be used as a premium for the purchase of a commodity option transaction for a futures customer;

(ii) As a premium payable to a futures customer;

(iii) To guarantee or secure performance of a commodity option by a futures customer; or

(iv) Representing accruals (including, for purchasers of a commodity option for which the full premium has been paid, the market value of such commodity option) to a futures customer.

(3) Notwithstanding paragraphs (1) and (2) of this definition, the term “futures customer funds” shall exclude money, securities or property held to margin, guarantee or secure security futures products held in a securities account, and all money accruing as the result of such security futures products.

(kkkk) *Order.* This term means an instruction or authorization provided by a customer to a futures commission merchant, introducing broker or commodity trading advisor regarding trading in a commodity interest on behalf of the customer.

(llll) *Organized exchange.* This term means a trading facility that—

(1) Permits trading—

(i) By or on behalf of a person that is not an eligible contract participant; or

(ii) By persons other than on a principal-to-principal basis; or

(2) Has adopted (directly or through another nongovernmental entity) rules that—

(i) Govern the conduct of participants, other than rules that govern the submission of orders or execution of transactions on the trading facility; and

(ii) Include disciplinary sanctions other than the exclusion of participants from trading.

(mmmm) *Prudential regulator.* This term has the meaning given to the term in section 1a(39) of the Commodity Exchange Act and includes the Board of Governors of the Federal Reserve System, the Office of the Comptroller of the Currency, the Federal Deposit Insurance Corporation, the Farm Credit Administration, and the Federal Housing Finance Agency, as applicable to the swap dealer or major swap participant. The term also includes the Federal Deposit Insurance Corporation, with respect to any financial company as defined in section 201 of the Dodd-Frank Wall Street Reform and Consumer Protection Act or any insured depository institution under the Federal Deposit Insurance Act, and with respect to each affiliate of any such company or institution.

(nnnn) *Registered entity.* This term means:

(1) A board of trade designated as a contract market under section 5 of the Act;

(2) A derivatives clearing organization registered under section 5b of the Act;

(3) A board of trade designated as a contract market under section 5f of the Act;

(4) A swap execution facility registered under section 5h of the Act;

(5) A swap data repository registered under section 21 of the Act; and

(6) With respect to a contract that the Commission determines is a significant price discovery contract, any electronic trading facility on which the contract is executed or traded.

(oooo) *Registrant.* This term means: a commodity pool operator; commodity trading advisor; futures commission merchant; introducing broker; leverage transaction merchant; floor broker; floor trader; major swap participant; retail foreign exchange dealer; or swap dealer that is subject to these regulations; or an associated person of any of the foregoing other than an associated person of a swap dealer or major swap participant.

(pppp) *Retail forex customer.* This term means a person, other than an eligible contract participant as defined in section 1a(18) of the Act, acting on its own behalf and trading in any account, agreement, contract or transaction described in section 2(c)(2)(B) or 2(c)(2)(C) of the Act.

(qqqq) *Swap data repository.* This term means any person that collects and maintains information or records with respect to transactions or positions in, or the terms and conditions of, swaps entered into by third parties for the purpose of providing a centralized recordkeeping facility for swaps.

(rrrr) *Swap execution facility.* This term means a trading system or platform in which multiple participants have the ability to execute or trade swaps by accepting bids and offers made by multiple participants in the facility or system, through any means of interstate commerce, including any trading facility, that—

(1) Facilitates the execution of swaps between persons; and

(2) Is not a designated contract market.

(ssss) *Trading facility.* This term has the meaning set forth in section 1a(51) of the Act.

EDITORIAL NOTE: For FEDERAL REGISTER citations affecting § 1.3, see the List of CFR Sections Affected, which appears in the Finding Aids section of the printed volume and at *www.fdsys.gov* .

§ 1.4 ELECTRONIC SIGNATURES, ACKNOWLEDGMENTS AND VERIFICATIONS.

For purposes of complying with any provision in the Commodity Exchange Act or the rules or regulations in this Chapter I that requires a swap transaction to be acknowledged by a swap dealer or major swap participant or a document to be signed or verified by a customer of a futures commission merchant or introducing broker, a retail forex customer of a retail foreign exchange dealer or futures commission merchant, a pool participant or a client of a commodity trading advisor, or a counterparty of a swap dealer or major swap participant, an electronic signature executed by the customer, retail forex customer, participant, client, counterparty, swap dealer, or major swap participant will be sufficient, if the futures commission merchant, retail foreign exchange dealer, introducing broker, commodity pool operator, commodity trading advisor, swap dealer, or major swap participant elects generally to accept electronic signatures, acknowledgments or verifications or another Commission rule permits the use of electronic signatures for the purposes listed above; *Provided, however,* That the electronic signature must comply with applicable Federal laws and other Commission rules; And, *Provided further,* That the futures commission merchant, retail foreign exchange dealer, introducing broker, commodity pool operator, commodity trading advisor, swap dealer, or major swap participant must adopt and use reasonable safeguards regarding the use of electronic signatures, including at a minimum safeguards employed to prevent alteration of the electronic record with which the electronic signature is associated, after such record has been electronically signed.

§ 1.6 ANTI-EVASION.

(a) It shall be unlawful to conduct activities outside the United States, including entering into agreements, contracts, and transactions and structuring entities, to willfully evade or attempt to evade any provision of the Commodity Exchange Act as enacted by Subtitle A of the Wall Street Transparency and Accountability Act of 2010 or the rules, regulations, and orders of the Commission promulgated thereunder (*Subtitle A*).

(b) The form, label, and written documentation of an agreement, contract, or transaction, or an entity, shall not be dispositive in determining whether the agreement, contract, or transaction, or entity, has been entered into or structured to willfully evade as provided in paragraph (a) of this section.

(c) An activity conducted outside the United States to evade as provided in paragraph (a) of this section shall be subject to the provisions of Subtitle A.

(d) Notwithstanding the foregoing, no agreement, contract, or transaction structured as a security (including a security-based swap) under the securities laws (as defined in section 3(a)(47) of the Securities Exchange Act of 1934 (15 U.S.C. 78c(a)(47))) shall be deemed a swap pursuant to this section.

[77 FR 48354, Aug. 13, 2012]

§ 1.7 BOOKS AND RECORDS REQUIREMENTS FOR SECURITY-BASED SWAP AGREEMENTS.

(a) A person registered as a swap data repository under section 21 of the Commodity Exchange Act and the rules and regulations thereunder:

(1) Shall not be required to keep and maintain additional books and records regarding security-based swap agreements other than the books and records regarding swaps required to be kept and maintained pursuant to section 21 of the Commodity Exchange Act and the rules and regulations thereunder; and

(2) Shall not be required to collect and maintain additional data regarding security-based swap agreements other than the data regarding swaps required to be collected and maintained by such persons pursuant to section 21 of the Commodity Exchange Act and the rules and regulations thereunder.

(b) A person shall not be required to keep and maintain additional books and records, including daily trading records, regarding security-based swap agreements other than the books and records regarding swaps required to be kept and maintained by such persons pursuant to section 4s of the Commodity Exchange Act and the rules and regulations thereunder if such person is registered as:

(1) A swap dealer under section 4s(a)(1) of the Commodity Exchange Act and the rules and regulations thereunder;

(2) A major swap participant under section 4s(a)(2) of the Commodity Exchange Act and the rules and regulations thereunder;

(3) A security-based swap dealer under section 15F(a)(1) of the Securities Exchange Act of 1934 (15 U.S.C. 78o-10(a)(1)) and the rules and regulations thereunder; or

(4) a major security-based swap participant under section 15F(a)(2) of the Securities Exchange Act of 1934 (15 U.S.C. 78o-10(a)(2)) and the rules and regulations thereunder.

(c) The term *security-based swap agreement* has the meaning set forth in section 1a(47)(A)(v) of the Commodity Exchange Act.

[77 FR 48354, Aug. 13, 2012]

§ 1.8 REQUESTS FOR INTERPRETATION OF SWAPS, SECURITY-BASED SWAPS, AND MIXED SWAPS.

(a) *In general.* Any person may submit a request to the Commission and the Securities and Exchange Commission to provide a joint interpretation of whether a particular agreement, contract, or transaction (or class thereof) is:

(1) A swap, as that term is defined in section 1a(47) of the Commodity Exchange Act and the rules and regulations promulgated thereunder;

(2) A security-based swap, as that term is defined in section 1a(42) of the Commodity Exchange Act and the rules and regulations promulgated thereunder; or

(3) A mixed swap, as that term is defined in section 1a(47)(D) of the Commodity Exchange Act and the rules and regulations promulgated thereunder.

(b) *Request process.* In making a request pursuant to paragraph (a) of this section, the requesting person must provide the Commission and the Securities and Exchange Commission with the following:

(1) All material information regarding the terms of the agreement, contract, or transaction (or class thereof);

(2) A statement of the economic characteristics and purpose of the agreement, contract, or transaction (or class thereof);

(3) The requesting person's determination as to whether the agreement, contract, or transaction (or class thereof) should be characterized as a swap, a security-based swap, or both, (*i.e.,* a mixed swap), including the basis for such determination; and

(4) Such other information as may be requested by the Commission or the Securities and Exchange Commission.

(c) *Request withdrawal.* A person may withdraw a request made pursuant to paragraph (a) of this section at any time prior to the issuance of a joint interpretation or joint proposed rule by the Commission and the Securities and Exchange Commission in response to the request; provided, however, that notwithstanding such withdrawal, the Commission and the Securities and Exchange Commission may provide a joint interpretation of whether the agreement, contract, or transaction (or class thereof) is a swap, a security-based swap, or both (*i.e.,* a mixed swap).

(d) *Request by the Commission or the Securities and Exchange Commission.* In the absence of a request for a joint interpretation under paragraph (a) of this section:

(1) If the Commission or the Securities and Exchange Commission receives a proposal to list, trade, or clear an agreement, contract, or transaction (or class thereof) that raises questions as to the appropriate characterization of such agreement, contract, or transaction (or class thereof) as a swap, a security-based swap, or both (*i.e.,* a mixed swap), the Commission or the Securities and Exchange Commission, as applicable, promptly shall notify the other of the agreement, contract, or transaction (or class thereof); and

(2) The Commission or the Securities and Exchange Commission, or their Chairmen jointly, may submit a request for a joint interpretation as described in paragraph (a) of this section; such submission shall be made pursuant to paragraph (b) of this section, and may be withdrawn pursuant to paragraph (c) of this section.

(e) *Timeframe for joint interpretation.* (1) If the Commission and the Securities and Exchange Commission determine to issue a joint interpretation as described in paragraph (a) of this section, such joint interpretation shall be issued within 120 days after receipt of a complete submission requesting a joint interpretation under paragraph (a) or (d) of this section.

(2) The Commission and the Securities and Exchange Commission shall consult with the Board of Governors of the Federal Reserve System prior to issuing any joint interpretation as described in paragraph (a) of this section.

(3) If the Commission and the Securities and Exchange Commission seek public comment with respect to a joint interpretation regarding an agreement, contract, or transaction (or class thereof), the 120-day period described in paragraph (e)(1) of this section shall be stayed during the pendency of the comment period, but shall recommence with the business day after the public comment period ends.

(4) Nothing in this section shall require the Commission and the Securities and Exchange Commission to issue any joint interpretation.

(5) If the Commission and the Securities and Exchange Commission do not issue a joint interpretation within the time period described in paragraph (e)(1) or (e)(3) of this section, each of the Commission and the Securities and Exchange Commission shall publicly provide the reasons for not issuing such a joint interpretation within the applicable timeframes.

(f) *Joint proposed rule.* (1) Rather than issue a joint interpretation pursuant to paragraph (a) of this section, the Commission and the Securities and Exchange Commission may issue a joint proposed rule, in consultation with the Board of Governors of the Federal Reserve System, to further define one or more of the terms swap, security-based swap, or mixed swap.

(2) A joint proposed rule described in paragraph (f)(1) of this section shall be issued within the timeframe for issuing a joint interpretation set forth in paragraph (e) of this section.

[77 FR 48354, Aug. 13, 2012]

§ 1.9 REGULATION OF MIXED SWAPS.

(a) *In general.* The term mixed swap has the meaning set forth in section 1a(47)(D) of the Commodity Exchange Act.

(b) *Regulation of bilateral uncleared mixed swaps entered into by dually-registered dealers or major participants.* A mixed swap that is neither executed on nor subject to the rules of a designated contract market, national securities exchange, swap execution facility, security-based swap execution facility, or foreign board of trade; that will not be submitted to a derivatives clearing organization or registered or exempt clearing agency to be cleared; and where at least one party is registered with the Commission as a swap dealer or major swap participant and also with the Securities and Exchange Commission as a security-based swap dealer or major security-based swap participant, shall be subject to:

(1) The following provisions of the Commodity Exchange Act, and the rules and regulations promulgated thereunder:

(i) Examinations and information sharing: sections 4s(f) and 8 of the Commodity Exchange Act;

(ii) Enforcement: sections 2(a)(1)(B), 4(b), 4b, 4c, 4s(h)(1)(A), 4s(h)(4)(A), 6(c), 6(d), 6c, 6d, 9, 13(a), 13(b), and 23 of the Commodity Exchange Act;

(iii) Reporting to a swap data repository: section 4r of the Commodity Exchange Act;

(iv) Real-time reporting: section 2(a)(13) of the Commodity Exchange Act;

(v) Capital: section 4s(e) of the Commodity Exchange Act; and

(vi) Position Limits: section 4a of the Commodity Exchange Act; and

(2) The provisions of the Federal securities laws, as defined in section 3(a)(47) of the Securities Exchange Act of 1934 (15 U.S.C. 78c(a)(47)), and the rules and regulations promulgated thereunder.

(c) *Process for determining regulatory treatment for other mixed swaps* —(1) *In general.* Any person who desires or intends to list, trade, or clear a mixed swap (or class thereof) that is not subject to paragraph (b) of this section may request the Commission and the Securities and Exchange Commission to issue a joint order permitting the requesting person (and any other person or persons that subsequently lists, trades, or clears that mixed swap) to comply, as to parallel provisions only, with specified parallel provisions of either the Commodity Exchange Act or the Securities Exchange Act of 1934 (15 U.S.C. 78a *et seq.*), and the rules and regulations thereunder (collectively, *specified parallel provisions*), instead of being required to comply with parallel provisions of both the Commodity Exchange Act and the Securities Exchange Act of 1934. For purposes of this paragraph (c), *parallel provisions* means comparable provisions of the Commodity Exchange Act and the Securities Exchange Act of 1934 that were added or amended by the Wall Street Transparency and Accountability Act of 2010 with respect to swaps and security-based swaps, and the rules and regulations thereunder.

(2) *Request Process.* A person submitting a request pursuant to paragraph (c)(1) of this section must provide the Commission and the Securities and Exchange Commission with the following:

(i) All material information regarding the terms of the specified, or specified class of, mixed swap;

(ii) The economic characteristics and purpose of the specified, or specified class of, mixed swap;

(iii) The specified parallel provisions, and the reasons the person believes such specified parallel provisions would be appropriate for the mixed swap (or class thereof); and

(iv) An analysis of:

(A) The nature and purposes of the parallel provisions that are the subject of the request;

(B) The comparability of such parallel provisions;

(C) The extent of any conflicts or differences between such parallel provisions; and

(D) Such other information as may be requested by the Commission or the Securities and Exchange Commission.

(3) *Request withdrawal.* A person may withdraw a request made pursuant to paragraph (c)(1) of this section at any time prior to the issuance of a joint order under paragraph (c)(4) of this section by the Commission and the Securities and Exchange Commission in response to the request.

(4) *Issuance of orders.* In response to a request under paragraph (c)(1) of this section, the Commission and the Securities and Exchange Commission, as necessary to carry out the purposes of the Wall Street Transparency and Accountability Act of 2010, may issue a joint order, after notice and opportunity for comment, permitting the requesting person (and any other person or persons that subsequently lists, trades, or clears that mixed swap) to comply, as to parallel provisions only, with the specified parallel provisions (or another subset of the parallel provisions that are the subject of the request, as the Commissions determine is appropriate), instead of being required to comply with parallel provisions of both the Commodity Exchange Act and the Securities Exchange Act of 1934. In determining the contents of such joint order, the Commission and the Securities and Exchange Commission may consider, among other things:

(i) The nature and purposes of the parallel provisions that are the subject of the request;

(ii) The comparability of such parallel provisions; and

(iii) The extent of any conflicts or differences between such parallel provisions.

(5) *Timeframe.* (i) If the Commission and the Securities and Exchange Commission determine to issue a joint order as described in paragraph (c)(4) of this section, such joint order shall be issued within 120 days after receipt of a complete request for a joint order under paragraph (c)(1) of this section, which time period shall be stayed during the pendency of the public comment period provided for in paragraph (c)(4) of this section and shall recommence with the business day after the public comment period ends.

(ii) Nothing in this section shall require the Commission and the Securities and Exchange Commission to issue any joint order.

(iii) If the Commission and the Securities and Exchange Commission do not issue a joint order within the time period described in paragraph (c)(5)(i) of this section, each of the Commission and the Securities and Exchange Commission shall publicly provide the reasons for not issuing such a joint order within that timeframe.

[77 FR 48354, Aug. 13, 2012]

MINIMUM FINANCIAL AND RELATED REPORTING REQUIREMENTS

§ 1.10 FINANCIAL REPORTS OF FUTURES COMMISSION MERCHANTS AND INTRODUCING BROKERS.

(a) *Application for registration.* (1) Except as otherwise provided, a futures commission merchant or an applicant for registration as a futures commission merchant, in order to satisfy any requirement in this part that it file a Form 1-FR, must file a Form 1-FR-FCM, and any reference in this part to Form 1-FR with respect to a futures commission merchant or applicant therefor shall be deemed to be a reference to Form 1-FR-FCM. Except as otherwise provided, an introducing broker or an applicant for registration as an introducing broker, in order to satisfy any requirement in this part that it file a Form 1-FR, must file a Form 1-FR-IB, and any reference in this part to Form 1-FR with respect to an introducing broker or applicant therefor shall be deemed to be a reference to Form 1-FR-IB.

(2) (i) (A) Except as provided in paragraphs (a)(3) and (h) of this section, each person who files an application for registration as a futures commission merchant and who is not so registered at the time of such filing, must, concurrently with the filing of such application, file either:

(*1*) A Form 1-FR-FCM certified by an independent public accountant in accordance with § 1.16 as of a date not more than 45 days prior to the date on which such report is filed; or

(*2*) A Form 1-FR-FCM as of a date not more than 17 business days prior to the date on which such report is filed and a Form 1-FR-FCM certified by an independent public accountant in accordance with § 1.16 as of a date not more than one year prior to the date on which such report is filed.

(B) Each such person must include with such financial report a statement describing the source of his current assets and representing that his capital has been contributed for the purpose of operating his business and will continue to be used for such purpose.

(ii) (A) Except as provided in paragraphs (a)(3) and (h) of this section, each person who files an application for registration as an introducing broker and who is not so registered at the time of such filing, must, concurrently with the filing of such application, file either:

(*1*) A Form 1-FR-IB certified by an independent public accountant in accordance with § 1.16 as of a date not more than 45 days prior to the date on which such report is filed;

(*2*) A Form 1-FR-IB as of a date not more than 17 business days prior to the date on which such report is filed and a Form 1-FR-IB certified by an independent public accountant in accordance with § 1.16 as of a date not more than one year prior to the date on which such report is filed;

(*3*) A Form 1-FR-IB as of a date not more than 17 business days prior to the date on which such report is filed, *Provided, however,* that such applicant shall be subject to a review by the applicant's designated self-regulatory organization within six months of registration; or

(*4*) A guarantee agreement.

(B) Each person filing in accordance with paragraphs (a)(2)(ii)(A) (*1*), (*2*) or (*3*) of this section must include with such financial report a statement describing the source of his current assets and representing that his capital has been contributed for the purpose of operating his business and will continue to be used for such purpose.

(3)(i) The provisions of paragraph (a)(2) of this section do not apply to any person succeeding to and continuing the business of another futures commission merchant. Each such person who files an application for registration as a futures commission merchant and who is not so registered in that capacity at the time of such filing must file a Form 1-FR-FCM as of the first month end following the date on which his registration is approved. Such report must be filed with the National Futures Association, the Commission and the designated self-regulatory organization, if any, not more than 17 business days after the date for which the report is made.

(ii) The provisions of paragraph (a)(2) of this section do not apply to any person succeeding to and continuing the business of another introducing broker.

(A) Each such person who succeeds to and continues the business of an introducing broker which was not operating pursuant to a guarantee agreement, or which was operating pursuant to a guarantee agreement and was also a securities broker or dealer at the time of succession, who files an application for registration as an introducing broker, and who is not so registered in that capacity at the time of such filing, must file with the National Futures Association either a guarantee agreement with his application for registration or a Form 1-FR-IB as of the first month end following the date on which his registration is approved. Such Form 1-FR-IB must be filed not more than 17 business days after the date for which the report is made.

(B) Each such person who succeeds to and continues the business of an introducing broker which was operating pursuant to a guarantee agreement and which was not also a securities broker or dealer at the time of succession, who files an application for registration as an introducing broker, and who is not so registered in that capacity at the time of such filing, must file with the National Futures Association either a guarantee agreement or a Form 1-FR-IB with his application for registration. If such person files a Form 1-FR-IB with his application for registration, such person must also file a Form 1-FR-IB, certified by an independent public accountant, as of a date no later than the end of the month registration is granted. The Form 1-FR-IB certified by an independent public accountant must be filed with the National Futures Association not more than 45 days after the date for which the report is made.

(b) *Filing of financial reports.* (1)(i) Except as provided in paragraphs (b)(3) and (h) of this section, each person registered as a futures commission merchant must file a Form 1-FR-FCM as of the close of business each month. Each Form 1-FR-FCM must be filed no later than 17 business days after the date for which the report is made.

(ii) In addition to the monthly financial reports required by paragraph (b)(1)(i) of this section, each person registered as a futures commission merchant must file a Form 1-FR-FCM as of the close of its fiscal year, which must be certified by an independent public accountant in accordance with § 1.16, and must be filed no later than 90 days after the close of the futures commission merchant's fiscal year: *Provided, however,* that a registrant which is registered with the Securities and Exchange Commission as a securities broker or dealer must file this report not later than the time permitted for filing an annual audit report under § 240.17a-5(d)(5) of this title.

(2)(i) Except as provided in paragraphs (b)(3) and (h) of this section, and except for an introducing broker operating pursuant to a guarantee agreement which is not also a securities broker or dealer, each person registered as an introducing broker must file a Form 1-FR-IB semiannually as of the middle and the close of each fiscal year. Each Form 1-FR-IB must be filed no later than 17 business days after the date for which the report is made.

(ii)(A) In addition to the financial reports required by paragraph (b)(2)(i) of this section, each person registered as an introducing broker must file a Form 1-FR-IB as of the close of its fiscal year which must be certified by an independent public accountant in accordance with § 1.16 no later than 90 days after the close of each introducing broker's fiscal year: *Provided, however*, that a registrant which is registered with the Securities and Exchange Commission as a securities broker or dealer must file this report not later than the time permitted for filing an annual audit report under § 240.17a-5(d)(5) of this title.

(B) If an introducing broker has filed previously a Form 1-FR-IB, certified by an independent public accountant in accordance with the provisions of paragraphs (a)(2)(ii) or (j)(8) of this section and § 1.16 of this part, as of a date not more than one year prior to the close of such introducing broker's fiscal year, it need not have certified by an independent public accountant the Form 1-FR-IB filed as of the introducing broker's first fiscal year-end following the as of date of its initial certified Form 1-FR-IB. In such a case, the introducing broker's Form 1-FR-IB filed as of the close of the second fiscal year-end following the as of date of its initial certified Form 1-FR-IB must cover the period of time between those two dates and must be certified by an independent public accountant in accordance with § 1.16 of this part.

(3) The provisions of paragraphs (b)(1) and (b)(2) of this section may be met by any person registered as a futures commission merchant or as an introducing broker who is a member of a designated self-regulatory organization and conforms to minimum financial standards and related reporting requirements set by such designated self-regulatory organization in its bylaws, rules, regulations, or resolutions and approved by the Commission pursuant to Section 4f(b) of the Act and § 1.52:*Provided, however*, That each such registrant shall promptly file with the Commission a true and exact copy of each financial report which it files with such designated self-regulatory organization.

(4) Upon receiving written notice from any representative of the National Futures Association, the Commission or any self-regulatory organization of which it is a member, an applicant or registrant, except an applicant for registration as an introducing broker which has filed concurrently with its application for registration a guarantee agreement and which is not also a securities broker or dealer, must, monthly or at such times as specified, furnish the National Futures Association, the Commission or the self-regulatory organization requesting such information a Form 1-FR or such other financial information as requested by the National Futures Association, the Commission or the self-regulatory organization. Each such Form 1-FR or such other information must be furnished within the time period specified in the written notice, and in accordance with the provisions of paragraph (c) of this section.

(c) *Where to file reports.* (1) Form 1-FR filed by an introducing broker pursuant to paragraph (b)(2) of this section need be filed only with, and will be considered filed when received by, the National Futures Association. Other reports or information provided for in this section will be considered filed when received by the regional office of the Commission with jurisdiction over the state in which the registrant's principal place of business is located and by the designated self-regulatory organization, if any; and reports or other information required to be filed by this section by an applicant for registration will be considered filed when received by the National Futures Association. Any report or information filed with the National Futures Association pursuant to this paragraph shall be deemed for all purposes to be filed with, and to be the official record of, the Commission.

(2)(i) Except as provided in the last sentence of this subparagraph, all filings or other notices prepared by a futures commission merchant pursuant to this section may be submitted to the Commission in electronic form using a form of user authentication assigned in accordance with procedures established by or approved by the Commission, and otherwise in accordance with instructions issued by or approved by the Commission, if the futures commission merchant or a designated self-regulatory organization has provided the Commission with the means necessary to read and to process the information contained in such report. A Form 1-FR required to be certified by an independent public accountant in accordance with § 1.16 which is filed by a futures commission merchant must be filed in paper form and may not be filed electronically.

(ii) Except as provided in paragraph (h) of this section, all filings or other notices or applications prepared by an introducing broker or applicant for registration as an introducing broker or futures commission merchant pursuant to this section must be filed electronically in accordance with electronic filing procedures established by the National Futures Association. In the case of a Form 1-FR-IB that is required to be certified by an independent public accountant in accordance with § 1.16, a paper copy of any such filing with the original manually signed certification must be maintained by the introducing broker or applicant for registration as an introducing broker in accordance with § 1.31.

(3) Any information required of a registrant by a self-regulatory organization pursuant to paragraph (b)(4) of this section need be furnished only to such self-regulatory organization and the Commission, and any information required of an applicant by the National Futures Association pursuant to paragraph (b)(4) of this section need be furnished only to the National Futures Association and the Commission.

(4) Any guarantee agreement entered into between a futures commission merchant and an introducing broker in accordance with the provisions of this section need be filed only with, and will be considered filed when received by, the National Futures Association.

(d) *Contents of financial reports.* (1) Each Form 1-FR filed pursuant to this § 1.10 which is not required to be certified by an independent public accountant must be completed in accordance with the instructions to the form and contain:

(i) A statement of financial condition as of the date for which the report is made;

(ii) Statements of income (loss) and a statement of changes in ownership equity for the period between the date of the most recent statement of financial condition filed with the Commission and the date for which the report is made;

(iii) A statement of changes in liabilities subordinated to claims of general creditors for the period between the date of the most recent statement of financial condition filed with the Commission and the date for which the report is made;

(iv) A statement of the computation of the minimum capital requirements pursuant to § 1.17 as of the date for which the report is made;

(v) For a futures commission merchant only, the statements of segregation requirements and funds in segregation for customers trading on U.S. commodity exchanges and for customers' dealer options accounts, and the statement of secured amounts and funds held in separate accounts for foreign futures and foreign options customers in accordance with § 30.7 of this chapter as of the date for which the report is made; and

(vi) In addition to the information expressly required, such futher material information as may be necessary to make the required statements and schedules not misleading.

(2) Each Form 1-FR filed pursuant to this § 1.10 which is required to be certified by an independent public accountant must be completed in accordance with the instructions to the form and contain:

(i) A statement of financial condition as of the date for which the report is made;

(ii) Statements of income (loss), cash flows, changes in ownership equity, and changes in liabilities subordinated to claims of general creditors, for the period between the date of the most recent certified statement of financial condition filed with the Commission and the date for which the report is made: *Provided,* That for an applicant filing pursuant to paragraph (a)(2) of this section the period must be the year ending as of the date of the statement of financial condition;

(iii) A statement of the computation of the minimum capital requirements pursuant to § 1.17 as of the date for which the report is made;

(iv) For a futures commission merchant only, the statements of segregation requirements and funds in segregation for customers trading on U.S. commodity exchanges and for customers' dealer options accounts, and the statement of secured amounts and funds held in separate accounts for foreign futures and foreign options customers in accordance with § 30.7 of this chapter as of the date for which the report is made;

(v) Appropriate footnote disclosures;

(vi) A reconciliation, including appropriate explanations, of the statement of the computation of the minimum capital requirements pursuant to § 1.17 and, for a futures commission merchant only, the statements of segregation requirements and funds in segregation for customers trading on U.S. commodity exchanges and for customers' dealer option accounts, and the statement of secured amounts and funds held in separate accounts for foreign futures and foreign options customers in accordance with § 30.7 of this chapter, in the certified Form 1-FR with the applicant's or registrant's corresponding uncertified most recent Form 1-FR filing when material differences exist or, if no material differences exist, a statement so indicating; and

(vii) In addition to the information expressly required, such further material information as may be necessary to make the required statements not misleading.

(3) The statements required by paragraphs (d)(2)(i) and (d)(2)(ii) of this section may be presented in accordance with generally accepted accounting principles in the certified reports filed as of the close of the registrant's fiscal year pursuant to paragraphs (b)(1)(ii) or (b)(2)(ii) of this section or accompanying the application for registration pursuant to paragraph (a)(2) of this section, rather than in the format specifically prescribed by these regulations: *Provided,* the statement of financial condition is presented in a format as consistent as possible with the Form 1-FR and a reconciliation is provided reconciling such statement of financial condition to the statement of the computation of the minimum capital requirements pursuant to § 1.17. Such reconciliation must be certified by an independent public accountant in accordance with § 1.16.

(4) Attached to each Form 1-FR filed pursuant to this section must be an oath or affirmation that to the best knowledge and belief of the individual making such oath or affirmation the information contained in the Form 1-FR is true and correct. The individual making such oath or affirmation must be:

(i) If the registrant or applicant is a sole proprietorship, the proprietor; if a partnership, any general partner; if a corporation, the chief executive officer or chief financial officer; and, if a limited liability company or limited liability partnership, the chief executive officer, the chief financial officer, the manager, the managing member, or those members vested with the management authority for the limited liability company or limited liability partnership; or

(ii) If the registrant or applicant is registered with the Securities and Exchange Commission as a securities broker or dealer, the representative authorized under § 240.17a-5 of this title to file for the securities broker or dealer its Financial and Operational Combined Uniform Single Report under the Securities Exchange Act of 1934, part II, part IIA, or part II CSE.

(iii) In the case of a Form 1-FR filed via electronic transmission in accordance with procedures established by or approved by the Commission, such transmission must be accompanied by the user authentication assigned to the authorized signer under such procedures, and the use of such user authentication will constitute and become a substitute for the manual signature of the authorized signer for the purpose of making the oath or affirmation referred to in this paragraph.

(e) *Election of fiscal year.* (1) An applicant wishing to establish a fiscal year other than the calendar year may do so by notifying the National Futures Association of its election of such fiscal year, in writing, concurrently with the filing of the Form 1-FR pursuant to paragraph (a)(2) of this section, but in no event may such fiscal year end more than one year from the date of the Form 1-FR filed pursuant to paragraph (a)(2) of this section. An applicant that does not so notify the National Futures Association will be deemed to have elected the calendar year as its fiscal year.

(2) (i) A registrant must continue to use its elected fiscal year, calendar or otherwise, unless a change in such fiscal year has been approved pursuant to this paragraph (e)(2).

(ii) *Futures commission merchant registrants.* (A) A futures commission merchant may file with its designated self-regulatory organization an application to change its fiscal year, a copy of which the registrant must file with the Commission. The application shall be approved or denied in writing by the designated self-regulatory organization. The registrant must file immediately with the Commission a copy of any notice it receives from the designated self-regulatory organization to approve or deny the registrant's application to change its fiscal year. A written notice of approval shall become effective upon the filing by the registrant of a copy with the Commission, and a written notice of denial shall be effective as of the date of the notice.

(B) A futures commission merchant that is registered with the Securities and Exchange Commission as a securities broker or dealer may file with its designated self-regulatory organization copies of any notice or application filed with its designated examining authority, pursuant to § 240.17a-5(d)(1)(i) of this title, for a change in fiscal year or "as of" date for its annual audited financial statement. The registrant must also file immediately with the designated self-regulatory organization and the Commission copies of any notice it receives from its designated examining authority to approve or deny the registrant's request for change in fiscal year or "as of" date. Upon the receipt by the designated self-regulatory organization and the Commission of copies of any such notice of approval, the change in fiscal year or "as of" date referenced in the notice shall be deemed approved under this paragraph (e)(2).

(C) Any copy that under this paragraph (e)(2) is required to be filed with the Commission shall be filed with the regional office of the Commission with jurisdiction over the state in which the registrant's principal place of business is located, and any copy or application to be filed with the designated self-regulatory organization shall be filed at its principal place of business.

(iii) *Introducing broker registrants.* (A) An introducing broker may file with the National Futures Association an application to change its fiscal year, which shall be approved or denied in writing.

(B) An introducing broker that is registered with the Securities and Exchange Commission as a securities broker or dealer may file with the National Futures Association copies of any notice or application filed with its designated examining authority, pursuant to § 240.17a-5(d)(1)(i) of this title, for a change in fiscal year or "as of" date for its annual audited financial statement. The registrant must also file immediately with the National Futures Association copies of any notice it receives from its designated examining authority to approve or deny the registrant's request for change in fiscal year or "as of" date. Upon the receipt by the National Futures Association of copies of any such notice of approval, the change in fiscal year or "as of" date referenced in the notice shall be deemed approved under this paragraph (e)(2).

(f) *Extension of time for filing uncertified reports.* (1) In the event a registrant finds that it cannot file its Form 1-FR, or, in accordance with paragraph (h) of this section, its Financial and Operational Combined Uniform Single Report under the Securities Exchange Act of 1934, part II, part IIA, or part II CSE (FOCUS report), for any period within the time specified in paragraphs (b)(1)(i) or (b)(2)(i) of this section without substantial undue hardship, it may request approval for an extension of time, as follows:

(i) *Futures commission merchant registrants* . (A) A futures commission merchant may file with its designated self-regulatory organization an application for extension of time, a copy of which the registrant must file with the Commission. The application shall be approved or denied in writing by the designated self-regulatory organization. The registrant must file immediately with the Commission a copy of any notice it receives from the designated self-regulatory organization to approve or deny the registrant's request for extension of time. A written notice of approval shall become effective upon the filing by the registrant of a copy with the Commission, and a written notice of denial shall be effective as of the date of the notice.

(B) A futures commission merchant that is registered with the Securities and Exchange Commission as a securities broker or dealer may file with its designated self-regulatory organization a copy of any application that the registrant has filed with its designated examining authority, pursuant to § 240.17-a5(l)(5) of this title, for an extension of time to file its FOCUS report. The registrant must also file immediately with the designated self-regulatory organization and the Commission copies of any notice it receives from its designated examining authority to approve or deny the requested extension of time. Upon receipt by the designated self-regulatory organization and the Commission of copies of any such notice of approval, the requested extension of time referenced in the notice shall be deemed approved under this paragraph (f)(1).

(C) Any copy that under this subparagraph (f)(1)(i) is required to be filed with the Commission shall be filed with the regional office of the Commission with jurisdiction over the state in which the registrant's principal place of business is located.

(ii) *Introducing broker registrants* . (A) An introducing broker may file with the National Futures Association an application for extension of the time, which shall be approved or denied in writing.

(B) An introducing broker that is registered with the Securities and Exchange Commission as a securities broker or dealer may file with the National Futures Association copies of any application that the registrant has filed with its designated examining authority, pursuant to § 240.17-a5(l)(5) of this title, for an extension of time to file its FOCUS report. The registrant must also file immediately with the National Futures Association copies of any notice it receives from its designated examining authority to approve or deny the requested extension of time. Upon the receipt by the National Futures Association of a copy of any such notice of approval, the requested extension of time referenced in the notice shall be deemed approved under this paragraph (f)(1)(ii).

(2) In the event an applicant finds that it cannot file its report for any period within the time specified in paragraph (b)(4) of this section without substantial undue hardship, it may file with the National Futures Association an application for an extension of time to a specified date which may not be more than 90 days after the date as of which the financial statements were to have been filed. The application must state the reasons for the requested extension and must contain an agreement to file the report on or before the specified date. The application must be received by the National Futures Association before the time specified in paragraph (b)(4) of this section for filing the report. Notice of such application must be filed with the regional office of the Commission with jurisdiction over the state in which the applicant's principal place of business is located concurrently with the filing of such application with the National Futures Association. Within ten calendar days after receipt of the application for an extension of time, the National Futures Association shall:

(i) Notify the applicant of the grant or denial of the requested extension; or

(ii) Indicate to the applicant that additional time is required to analyze the request, in which case the amount of time needed will be specified.

(g) *Public availability of reports.* (1) Forms 1-FR filed pursuant to this section, and FOCUS reports filed in lieu of Forms 1-FR pursuant to paragraph (h) of this section, will be treated as exempt from mandatory public disclosure for purposes of the Freedom of Information Act and the Government in the Sunshine Act and parts 145 and 147 of this chapter, except for the information described in paragraph (g)(2) of this section.

(2) The following information in Forms 1-FR, and the same or equivalent information in FOCUS reports filed in lieu of Forms 1-FR, will be publicly available:

(i) The amount of the applicant's or registrant's adjusted net capital; the amount of its minimum net capital requirement under § 1.17 of this chapter; and the amount of its adjusted net capital in excess of its minimum net capital requirement; and

(ii) The following statements and footnote disclosures thereof: the Statement of Financial Condition in the certified annual financial reports of futures commission merchants and introducing brokers; the Statements (to be filed by a futures commission merchant only) of Segregation Requirements and Funds in Segregation for customers trading on U.S. commodity exchanges and for customers' dealer options accounts, and the Statement (to be filed by a futures commission merchant only) of Secured Amounts and Funds held in Separate Accounts for foreign futures and foreign options customers in accordance with § 30.7 of this chapter.

(3) [Reserved]

(4) All information that is exempt from mandatory public disclosure under paragraph (g)(1) of this section will, however, be available for official use by any official or employee of the United States or any State, by any self-regulatory organization of which the person filing such report is a member, by the National Futures Association in the case of an applicant, and by any other person to whom the Commission believes disclosure of such information is in the public interest. Nothing in this paragraph (g) will limit the authority of any self-regulatory organization to request or receive any information relative to its members' financial condition.

(5) The independent accountant's opinion and a guarantee agreement filed pursuant to this section will be deemed public information.

(h) *Filing option available to a futures commission merchant or an introducing broker that is also a securities broker or dealer.* Any applicant or registrant which is registered with the Securities and Exchange Commission as a securities broker or dealer may comply with the requirements of this section by filing (in accordance with paragraphs (a), (b), (c), and (j) of this section) a copy of its Financial and Operational Combined Uniform Single Report under the Securities Exchange Act of 1934, Part II, Part IIA, or Part II CSE (FOCUS Report), in lieu of Form 1-FR; *Provided, however* , That all information which is required to be furnished on and submitted with Form 1-FR is provided with such FOCUS Report; and *Provided, further* , That a certified FOCUS Report filed by an introducing broker or applicant for registration as an introducing broker in lieu of a certified Form 1-FR-IB must be filed according to National Futures Association rules, either in paper form or electronically, in accordance with procedures established by the National Futures Association, and if filed electronically, a paper copy of such filing with the original manually signed certification must be maintained by such introducing broker or applicant in accordance with § 1.31.

(i) *Filing option available to an introducing broker or applicant for registration as an introducing broker which is also a country elevator.* Any introducing broker or applicant for registration as an introducing broker which is also a country elevator but which is not also a securities broker or dealer may comply with the requirements of this section by filing (in accordance with paragraphs (a), (b) and (c) of this section) a copy of a financial report prepared by a grain commission firm which has been authorized by the Deputy Vice President of the Commodity Credit Corporation of the United States Department of Agriculture to provide a compilation report of financial statements of warehousemen for purposes of Uniform Grain Storage Agreements, and which complies with the standards for independence set forth in § 1.16(b)(2) with respect to the registrant or applicant: *Provided, however,* That all information which is required to be furnished on and submitted with Form 1-FR is provided with such financial report, including a statement of the computation of the minimum capital requirements pursuant to § 1.17: *And, provided further,*That the balance sheet is presented in a format as consistent as possible with the Form 1-FR and a reconciliation is provided reconciling such balance sheet to the statement of the computation of the minimum capital requirements pursuant to § 1.17. Attached to each financial report filed pursuant to this paragraph (i) must be an oath or affirmation that to the best knowledge and belief of the individual making such oath or affirmation the information contained therein is true and correct. If the applicant or registrant is a sole proprietorship, then the oath or affirmation must be made by the proprietor; if a partnership, by a general partner; or if a corporation, by the chief executive officer or chief financial officer.

(j) *Requirements for guarantee agreement.* (1) A guarantee agreement filed pursuant to this section must be signed in a manner sufficient to be a binding guarantee under local law by an appropriate person on behalf of the futures commission merchant or retail foreign exchange dealer and the introducing broker, and each signature must be accompanied by evidence that the signatory is authorized to enter the agreement on behalf of the futures commission merchant, retail foreign exchange dealer, or introducing broker and is such an appropriate person. For purposes of this paragraph (j), an appropriate person shall be the proprietor, if the firm is a sole proprietorship; a general partner, if the firm is a partnership; and either the chief executive officer or the chief financial officer, if the firm is a corporation; and, if the firm is a limited liability company or limited liability partnership, either the chief executive officer, the chief financial officer, the manager, the managing member, or those members vested with the management authority for the limited liability company or limited liability partnership.

(2) No futures commission merchant or retail foreign exchange dealer may enter into a guarantee agreement if:

(i) It knows or should have known that its adjusted net capital is less than the amount set forth in § 1.12(b) of this part or § 5.6(b) of this chapter, as applicable; or

(ii) There is filed against the futures commission merchant or retail foreign exchange dealer an adjudicatory proceeding brought by or before the Commission pursuant to the provisions of sections 6(c), 6(d), 6c, 6d, 8a or 9 of the Act or §§ 3.55, 3.56 or 3.60 of this chapter.

(3) A retail foreign exchange dealer may enter into a guarantee agreement only with an introducing broker as defined in § 5.1(f)(1) of this chapter. A retail foreign exchange dealer may not enter into a guarantee agreement with an introducing broker as defined in § 1.3(mm) of this part.

(4) A guarantee agreement filed in connection with an application for initial registration as an introducing broker in accordance with the provisions of § 3.10(a) of this chapter shall become effective upon the granting of registration or, if appropriate, a temporary license, to the introducing broker. A guarantee

agreement filed other than in connection with an application for initial registration as an introducing broker shall become effective as of the date agreed to by the parties.

(5)(i) If the registration of the introducing broker is suspended, revoked, or withdrawn in accordance with the provisions of this chapter, the guarantee agreement shall expire as of the date of such suspension, revocation or withdrawal.

(ii) If the registration of the futures commission merchant or retail foreign exchange dealer is suspended or revoked, the guarantee agreement shall expire 30 days after such suspension or revocation, or at such earlier time as may be approved by the Commission, the introducing broker, and the introducing broker's designated self-regulatory organization.

(6) A guarantee agreement may be terminated at any time during the term thereof:

(i) By mutual written consent of the parties, signed by an appropriate person on behalf of each party, with prompt written notice thereof, signed by an appropriate person on behalf of each party, to the Commission and to the designated self-regulatory organizations of the futures commission merchant or retail foreign exchange dealer and the introducing broker;

(ii) For good cause shown, by either party giving written notice of its intention to terminate the agreement, signed by an appropriate person, to the other party to the agreement, to the Commission, and to the designated self-regulatory organizations of the futures commission merchant or retail foreign exchange dealer and the introducing broker; or

(iii) By either party giving written notice of its intention to terminate the agreement, signed by an appropriate person, at least 30 days prior to the proposed termination date, to the other party to the agreement, to the Commission, and to the designated self-regulatory organizations of the futures commission merchant or retail foreign exchange dealer and the introducing broker.

(7) The termination of a guarantee agreement by a futures commission merchant, retail foreign exchange dealer or an introducing broker, or the expiration of such an agreement, shall not relieve any party from any liability or obligation arising from acts or omissions which occurred during the term of the agreement.

(8) An introducing broker may not simultaneously be a party to more than one guarantee agreement: *Provided, however,*That the provisions of this paragraph (j)(8) shall not be deemed to preclude an introducing broker from entering into a guarantee agreement with another futures commission merchant or retail foreign exchange dealer if the introducing broker, futures commission merchant or retail foreign exchange dealer which is a party to the existing agreement has provided notice of termination of the existing agreement in accordance with the provisions of paragraph (j)(6) of this section, and the new guarantee agreement does not become effective until the day following the date of termination of the existing agreement: *And, provided further,* That the provisions of this paragraph (j)(8) shall not be deemed to preclude an introducing broker from entering into a guarantee agreement with another futures commission merchant or retail foreign exchange dealer if the futures commission merchant or retail foreign exchange dealer which is a party to the existing agreement ceases to remain registered and the existing agreement would therefore expire in accordance with the provisions of paragraph (j)(6)(ii) of this section.

(9)(i)(A) An introducing broker that is a party to a guarantee agreement that has been terminated in accordance with the provisions of paragraph (j)(6) of this section, or that is due to expire in accordance with the provisions of paragraph (j)(5)(ii) of this section, must cease doing business as an introducing broker on or before the effective date of such termination or expiration unless, on or before 10 days prior to the effective date of such termination or expiration or such other period of time as the Commission or the designated self-regulatory organization may allow for good cause shown, the introducing broker files with its designated self-regulatory organization either a new guarantee agreement effective as of the day following the date of termination of the existing agreement, or, in the case of a guarantee agreement that is due to expire in accordance with the provisions of paragraph (j)(4)(ii) of this section, a new guarantee agreement effective on or before such expiration, or either:

(*1*) A Form 1-FR-IB certified by an independent public accountant in accordance with § 1.16 as of a date not more than 45 days prior to the date on which the report is filed; or

(*2*) A Form 1-FR-IB as of a date not more than 17 business days prior to the date on which the report is filed and a Form 1-FR-IB certified by an independent public accountant in accordance with § 1.16 as of a date not more than one year prior to the date on which the report is filed: *Provided, however,* that an introducing broker as defined in § 5.1(f)(1) of this chapter that is party to a guarantee agreement that has been terminated or that has expired must cease doing business as an introducing broker on or before the effective date of such termination or expiration unless, on or before 10 days prior to the effective date of such termination or expiration or such other period of time as the Commission or the designated self-regulatory organization may allow for good cause shown, the introducing broker files with its designated self-regulatory organization a new guarantee agreement effective on or before the termination or expiration date of the terminating or expiring guarantee agreement.

(B) Each person filing a Form 1-FR-IB in accordance with this section must include with the financial report a statement describing the source of his current assets and representing that his capital has been contributed for the purpose of operating his business and will continue to be used for such purpose.

(ii)(A) Notwithstanding the provisions of paragraph (j)(9)(i) of this section or of § 1.17(a), an introducing broker that is a party to a guarantee agreement that has been terminated in accordance with the provisions of paragraph (j)(6)(ii) of this section shall not be deemed to be in violation of the minimum adjusted net capital requirement of § 1.17(a)(1)(iii) or (a)(2) for 30 days following such termination. Such an introducing broker must cease doing business as an introducing broker on or after the effective date of such termination, and may not resume doing business as an introducing broker unless and until it files a new agreement or either:

(*1*) A Form 1-FR-IB certified by an independent public accountant in accordance with § 1.16 as of a date not more than 45 days prior to the date on which the report is filed; or

(*2*) A Form 1-FR-IB as of a date not more than 17 business days prior to the date on which the report is filed and a Form 1-FR-IB certified by an independent public accountant in accordance with § 1.16 as of a date not more than one year prior to the date on which the report is filed: *Provided, however,* that an introducing broker as defined in § 5.1(f)(1) of this chapter that is party to a guarantee agreement that has been terminated must cease doing business as an introducing broker from and after the effective date of such termination, and may not resume doing business as an introducing broker as defined in § 5.1(f)(1) of this chapter unless and until it files a new guarantee agreement.

(B) Each person filing a Form 1-FR-IB in accordance with this section must include with the financial report a statement describing the source of his current assets and representing that his capital has been contributed for the purpose of operating his business and will continue to be used for such purpose.

(k) *Filing option available to an introducing broker.* (1) Any introducing broker or applicant for registration as an introducing broker which is not operating or intending to operate pursuant to a guarantee agreement may comply with the requirements of this section by filing (in accordance with paragraphs (a), (b) and (c) of this section) a Form 1-FR-IB in lieu of a Form 1-FR-FCM.

(2) If an introducing broker or applicant therefor avails itself of the filing option available under paragraph (k)(1) of this section, the report required to be filed in accordance with § 1.16(c)(5) of this part must be filed as of the date of the Form 1-FR-IB being filed, and such an introducing broker or applicant therefor must maintain its financial records and make its monthly formal computation of its adjusted net capital, as required by § 1.18 of this part, in a manner consistent with Form 1-FR-IB.

(The information collection requirements contained in § 1.10 were approved by the Office of Management and Budget under control number 3038-0024; in paragraphs (a) and (b) under control number 3038-0023; and in paragraph (f) under control number 3038-0003.)

[43 FR 39967, Sept. 8, 1978]

EDITORIAL NOTE: For FEDERAL REGISTER citations affecting § 1.10, see the List of CFR Sections Affected, which appears in the Finding Aids section of the printed volume and at *www.fdsys.gov* .

§ 1.12 MAINTENANCE OF MINIMUM FINANCIAL REQUIREMENTS BY FUTURES COMMISSION MERCHANTS AND INTRODUCING BROKERS.

(a) Each person registered as a futures commission merchant or who files an application for registration as a futures commission merchant, and each person registered as an introducing broker or who files an application for registration as an introducing broker (except for an introducing broker or applicant for registration as an introducing broker operating pursuant to, or who has filed concurrently with its application for registration, a guarantee agreement and who is not also a securities broker or dealer), who knows or should have known that its adjusted net capital at any time is less than the minimum required by § 1.17 or by the capital rule of any self-regulatory organization to which such person is subject, if any, must:

(1) Give telephonic notice, to be confirmed in writing by facsimile notice, as set forth in paragraph (i) of this section that the applicant's or registrant's adjusted net capital is less than required by § 1.17 or by other capital rule, identifying the applicable capital rule. The notice must be given immediately after the applicant or registrant knows or should know that its adjusted net capital is less than required by any of the aforesaid rules to which the applicant or registrant is subject; and

(2) Provide together with such notice documentation in such form as necessary to adequately reflect the applicant's or registrant's capital condition as of any date such person's adjusted net capital is less than the minimum required. The applicant or registrant must provide similar documentation for other days as the Commission may request.

(b) Each person registered as a futures commission merchant, or who files an application for registration as a futures commission merchant, who knows or should have known that its adjusted net capital at any time is less than the greatest of:

(1) 150 percent of the minimum dollar amount required by § 1.17(a)(1)(i)(A);

(2) 110 percent of the amount required by § 1.17(a)(1)(i)(B);

(3) 150 percent of the amount of adjusted net capital required by a registered futures association of which it is a member, unless such amount has been determined by a margin-based capital computation set forth in the rules of the registered futures association, and such amount meets or exceeds the amount of adjusted net capital required under the margin-based capital computation set forth in § 1.17(a)(1)(i)(B), in which case the required percentage is 110 percent, or

(4) For securities brokers or dealers, the amount of net capital specified in Rule 17a-11(c) of the Securities and Exchange Commission (17 CFR 240.17a-11(c)), must file written notice to that effect as set forth in paragraph (i) of this section within twenty-four (24) hours of such event.

(c) If an applicant or registrant at any time fails to make or keep current the books and records required by these regulations, such applicant or registrant must, on the same day such event occurs, provide facsimile notice of such fact, specifying the books and records which have not been made or which are not current, and within forty-eight (48) hours after giving such notice file a written report stating what steps have been and are being taken to correct the situation.

(d) Whenever any applicant or registrant discovers or is notified by an independent public accountant, pursuant to § 1.16(e)(2) of this chapter, of the existence of any material inadequacy, as specified in § 1.16(d)(2) of this chapter, such applicant or registrant must give facsimile notice of such material inadequacy within twenty-four (24) hours, and within forty-eight (48) hours after giving such notice file a written report stating what steps have been and are being taken to correct the material inadequacy.

(e) Whenever any self-regulatory organization learns that a member registrant has failed to file a notice or written report as required by § 1.12, that self-regulatory organization must immediately report this failure by telephone, confirmed in writing immediately by facsimile notice, as provided in paragraph (i) of this section.

(2) Whenever a registered futures commission merchant determines that any position it carries for another registered futures commission merchant or for a registered leverage transaction merchant must be liquidated immediately, transferred immediately or that the trading of any account of such futures commission merchant or leverage transaction merchant shall be only for purposes of liquidation, because the other futures commission merchant or the leverage transaction merchant has failed to meet a call for margin or to make other required deposits, the carrying futures commission merchant must immediately give telephonic notice, confirmed in writing immediately by facsimile notice, of such a determination to the principal office of the Commission at Washington, DC.

(3) Whenever a registered futures commission merchant determines that an account which it is carrying is undermargined by an amount which exceeds the futures commission merchant's adjusted net capital determined in accordance with § 1.17, the futures commission merchant must immediately give telephonic notice, confirmed in writing immediately by facsimile notice, of such a determination to the designated self-regulatory organization and the principal office of the Commission at Washington, DC. This paragraph (f)(3) shall apply to any account carried by the futures commission merchant, whether a customer, noncustomer, omnibus or proprietary account. For purposes of this paragraph (f)(3), if any person has an interest of 10 percent or more in ownership or equity in, or guarantees, more than one account, or has guaranteed an account in addition to his own account, all such accounts shall be combined. A designated self-regulatory organization may grant an exemption from the provisions of this paragraph to a futures commission merchant with respect to any particular account on a continuous basis provided the designated self-regulatory organization documents the reasons for granting such an exemption and continues to monitor any such account.

(4) A futures commission merchant shall report immediately by telephone, confirmed immediately in writing by facsimile notice, whenever any commodity interest account it carries is subject to a margin call, or call for other deposits required by the futures commission merchant, that exceeds the futures commission merchant's excess adjusted net capital, determined in accordance with § 1.17, and such call has not been answered by the close of business on the day following the issuance of the call. This applies to all accounts carried by the futures commission merchant, whether customer, noncustomer, or omnibus, that are subject to margining, including commodity futures and options. In addition to actual margin deposits by an account owner, a futures commission merchant may also take account of favorable market moves in determining whether the margin call is required to be reported under this paragraph.

(5)(i) A futures commission merchant shall report immediately by telephone, confirmed immediately in writing by facsimile notice, whenever its excess adjusted net capital is less than six percent of the maintenance margin required by the futures commission merchant on all positions held in accounts of a noncustomer other than a noncustomer who is subject to the minimum financial requirements of:

(A) A futures commission merchant, or

(B) The Securities and Exchange Commission for a securities broker and dealer.

(ii) For purposes of paragraph (f)(5)(i) of this section, maintenance margin shall include all deposits which the futures commission merchant requires the noncustomer to maintain in order to carry its positions at the futures commission merchant.

(g) A futures commission merchant shall provide written notice of a substantial reduction in capital as compared to that last reported in a financial report filed with the Commission pursuant to § 1.10. This notice shall be provided as follows:

(1) If any event or series of events, including any withdrawal, advance, loan or loss cause, on a net basis, a reduction in net capital (or, if the futures commission merchant is qualified to use the filing option

available under § 1.10(h), tentative net capital as defined in the rules of the Securities and Exchange Commission) of 20 percent or more, notice must be provided within two business days of the event or series of events causing the reduction; and

(2) If equity capital of the futures commission merchant or a subsidiary or affiliate of the futures commission merchant consolidated pursuant to § 1.17(f) (or 17 CFR 240.15c3-1e) would be withdrawn by action of a stockholder or a partner or a limited liability company member or by redemption or repurchase of shares of stock by any of the consolidated entities or through the payment of dividends or any similar distribution, or an unsecured advance or loan would be made to a stockholder, partner, sole proprietor, limited liability company member, employee or affiliate, such that the withdrawal, advance or loan would cause, on a net basis, a reduction in excess adjusted net capital (or, if the futures commission merchant is qualified to use the filing option available under § 1.10(h), excess net capital as defined in the rules of the Securities and Exchange Commission) of 30 percent or more, notice must be provided at least two business days prior to the withdrawal, advance or loan that would cause the reduction: *Provided, however,* That the provisions of paragraphs (g)(1) and (g)(2) of this section do not apply to any futures or securities transaction in the ordinary course of business between a futures commission merchant and any affiliate where the futures commission merchant makes payment to or on behalf of such affiliate for such transaction and then receives payment from such affiliate for such transaction within two business days from the date of the transaction.

(3) Upon receipt of such notice from a futures commission merchant, the Director of the Division of Swap Dealer and Intermediary Oversight or the Director's designee may require that the futures commission merchant provide or cause a Material Affiliated Person (as that term is defined in § 1.14(a)(2)) to provide, within three business days from the date of request or such shorter period as the Division Director or designee may specify, such other information as the Division Director or designee determines to be necessary based upon market conditions, reports provided by the futures commission merchant, or other available information.

(h) Whenever a person registered as a futures commission merchant knows or should know that the total amount of its funds on deposit in segregated accounts on behalf of customers, or that the total amount set aside on behalf of customers trading on non-United States markets, is less than the total amount of such funds required by the Act and the Commission's rules to be on deposit in segregated or secured amount accounts on behalf of such customers, the registrant must report such deficiency immediately by telephone notice, confirmed immediately in writing by facsimile notice, to the registrant's designated self-regulatory organization and the principal office of the Commission in Washington, DC, to the attention of the Director and the Chief Accountant of the Division of Swap Dealer and Intermediary Oversight.

(i)(1) Every notice and written report required to be given or filed by this section (except for notices required by paragraph (f) of this section) by a futures commission merchant or a self-regulatory organization must be filed with the regional office of the Commission with jurisdiction over the state in which the registrant's principal place of business is located, with the principal office of the Commission in Washington, DC, with the designated self-regulatory organization, if any; and with the Securities and Exchange Commission, if such registrant is a securities broker or dealer. Every notice and written report required to be given or filed by this section by an applicant for registration as a futures commission merchant must be filed with the National Futures Association (on behalf of the Commission), with the designated self-regulatory organization, if any, and with the Securities and Exchange Commission, if such applicant is a securities broker or dealer. Any notice or report filed with the National Futures Association pursuant to this paragraph shall be deemed for all purposes to be filed with, and to be the official record of, the Commission.

(2) Every notice and written report which an introducing broker or applicant for registration as an introducing broker is required to give or file by paragraphs (a), (c) and (d) of this section must be filed with the National Futures Association (on behalf of the Commission), with the designated self-regulatory organization, if any, and with every futures commission merchant carrying or intending to carry customer accounts for the introducing broker or applicant for registration as an introducing broker. Any notice or report filed with the National Futures Association pursuant to this paragraph shall be deemed for all purposes to be filed with, and to be the official record of, the Commission.

(3) Every notice or report required to be provided in writing to the Commission under this section may, in lieu of facsimile, be filed via electronic transmission using a form of user authentication assigned in accordance with procedures established by or approved by the Commission, and otherwise in accordance with instructions issued by or approved by the Commission. Any such electronic submission must clearly indicate the registrant or applicant on whose behalf such filing is made and the use of such user authentication in submitting such filing will constitute and become a substitute for the manual signature of the authorized signer.

(Approved by the Office of Management and Budget under control number 3038-0024)

[43 FR 39969, Sept. 8, 1978]

EDITORIAL NOTE: For FEDERAL REGISTER citations affecting § 1.12, see the List of CFR Sections Affected, which appears in the Finding Aids section of the printed volume and at *www.fdsys.gov* .

§ 1.14 RISK ASSESSMENT RECORDKEEPING REQUIREMENTS FOR FUTURES COMMISSION MERCHANTS.

(a) *Requirement to maintain and preserve information.* (1) Each futures commission merchant registered with the Commission pursuant to Section 4d of the Act, unless exempt pursuant to paragraph (d) of this section, shall prepare, maintain and preserve the following information:

(i) An organizational chart which includes the futures commission merchant and each of its affiliated persons. Included in the organizational chart shall be a designation of which affiliated persons are "Material Affiliated Persons" as that term is used in paragraph (a)(2) of this section, which Material Affiliated Persons file routine financial or risk exposure reports with the Securities and Exchange Commission, a federal banking agency, an insurance commissioner or other similar official or agency of a state, or a foreign regulatory authority, and which Material Affiliated Persons are dealers in financial instruments with off-balance sheet risk and, if a Material Affiliated Person is such a dealer, whether it is also an end-user of such instruments;

(ii) Written policies, procedures, or systems concerning the futures commission merchant's:

(A) Method(s) for monitoring and controlling financial and operational risks to it resulting from the activities of any of its affiliated persons;

(B) Financing and capital adequacy, including information regarding sources of funding, together with a narrative discussion by management of the liquidity of the material assets of the futures commission merchant, the structure of debt capital, and sources of alternative funding;

(C) Establishing and maintaining internal controls with respect to market risk, credit risk, and other risks created by the futures commission merchant's proprietary and noncustomer clearing activities, including systems and policies for supervising, monitoring, reporting and reviewing trading activities in securities, futures contracts, commodity options, forward contracts and financial instruments; policies for hedging or managing risks created by trading activities or supervising accounts carried for noncustomer affiliates, including a description of the types of reviews conducted to monitor positions; and policies relating to restrictions or limitations on trading activities: *Provided, however,* that if the futures commission merchant has no such written policies, procedures or systems, it must so state in writing;

(iii) Fiscal year-end consolidated and consolidating balance sheets for the highest level Material Affiliated Person within the futures commission merchant's organizational structure, which shall include the futures commission merchant and its other Material Affiliated Persons, prepared in accordance with generally accepted accounting principles, which consolidated balance sheets shall be audited by an independent certified public accountant if an annual audit is performed in the ordinary course of business, but which otherwise may be unaudited, and which shall include appropriate explanatory notes. The consolidating balance sheets may be those prepared by the futures commission merchant's highest level

Material Affiliated Person as part of its internal financial reporting process. Any additional information required to be filed under § 1.15(a)(2)(iii) shall also be maintained and preserved; and

(iv) Fiscal year-end consolidated and consolidating income statements and consolidated cash flow statements for the highest level Material Affiliated Person within the futures commission merchant's organizational structure, which shall include the futures commission merchant and its other Material Affiliated Persons, prepared in accordance with generally accepted accounting principles, which consolidated statements shall be audited by an independent certified public accountant if an annual audit is performed in the ordinary course of business, but which otherwise may be unaudited, and which shall include appropriate explanatory notes. The consolidating statements may be those prepared by the futures commission merchant's highest level Material Affiliated Person as part of its internal financial reporting process. Any additional information required to be filed under § 1.15(a)(2)(iii) shall also be maintained and preserved.

(2) The determination of whether an affiliated person of a futures commission merchant is a Material Affiliated Person shall involve consideration of all aspects of the activities of, and the relationship between, both entities, including without limitation, the following factors:

(i) The legal relationship between the futures commission merchant and the affiliated person;

(ii) The overall financing requirements of the futures commission merchant and the affiliated person, and the degree, if any, to which the futures commission merchant and the affiliated person are financially dependent on each other;

(iii) The degree, if any, to which the futures commission merchant or its customers rely on the affiliated person for operational support or services in connection with the futures commission merchant's business;

(iv) The level of market, credit or other risk present in the activities of the affiliated person; and

(v) The extent to which the affiliated person has the authority or the ability to cause a withdrawal of capital from the futures commission merchant.

(3) For purposes of this section and § 1.15, the term Material Affiliated Person does not include a natural person.

(4) The information, reports and records required by this section shall be maintained and preserved, and made readily available for inspection, in accordance with the provisions of § 1.31.

(b) *Special provisions with respect to Material Affiliated Persons subject to the supervision of certain domestic regulators.*A futures commission merchant shall be deemed to be in compliance with the recordkeeping requirements of paragraphs (a)(1)(i), (a)(1)(iii) and (a)(1)(iv) of this section with respect to a Material Affiliated Person if:

(1) The futures commission merchant is required, or that Material Affiliated Person is required, to maintain and preserve information, or such information is maintained and preserved by the futures commission merchant on behalf of the Material Affiliated Person, pursuant to § 240.17h-1T of this title, or such other risk assessment regulations as the Securities and Exchange Commission may adopt, and maintains and makes available for inspection by the Commission in accordance with the provisions of this section copies of the records and reports maintained and filed on Form 17-H (or such other forms or reports as may be required) by such futures commission merchant or its Material Affiliated Person with the Securities and Exchange Commission pursuant to §§ 240.17h-1T and 240.17h-2T of this title, or such other risk assessment regulations as the Securities and Exchange Commission may adopt;

(2) In the case of a Material Affiliated Person (including a foreign banking organization) that is subject to examination by, or the reporting requirements of, a Federal banking agency, the futures commission merchant or such Material Affiliated Person maintains and makes available for inspection by the

Commission in accordance with the provisions of this section copies of all reports submitted by such Material Associated Person to the Federal banking agency pursuant to section 5211 of the Revised Statutes, section 9 of the Federal Reserve Act, section 7(a) of the Federal Deposit Insurance Act, section 10(b) of the Home Owners' Loan Act, or section 5 of the Bank Holding Company Act of 1956; or

(3) In the case of a Material Affiliated Person that is subject to the supervision of an insurance commissioner or other similar official or agency of a state, the futures commission merchant or such Material Affiliated Person maintains and makes available for inspection by the Commission in accordance with the provisions of this section copies of the annual statements with schedules and exhibits prepared by the Material Affiliated Person on forms prescribed by the National Association of Insurance Commissioners or by a state insurance commissioner.

(c) *Special provisions with respect to Material Affiliated Persons subject to the supervision of a Foreign Regulatory Authority.* A futures commission merchant shall be deemed to be in compliance with the recordkeeping requirements of paragraphs (a)(1)(iii) and (a)(1)(iv) of this section with respect to a Material Affiliated Person if such futures commission merchant maintains and makes available, or causes such Material Affiliated Person to make available, for inspection by the Commission in accordance with the provisions of this section copies of any financial or risk exposure reports filed by such Material Affiliated Person with a foreign futures authority or other foreign regulatory authority, provided that: (1) the futures commission merchant agrees to use its best efforts to obtain from the Material Affiliated Person and to cause the Material Affiliated Person to provide, directly or through its foreign futures authority or other foreign regulatory authority, any supplemental information the Commission may request and there is no statute or other bar in the foreign jurisdiction that would preclude the futures commission merchant, the Material Affiliated Person, the foreign futures authority or other foreign regulatory authority from providing such information to the Commission; or (2) the foreign futures authority or other foreign regulatory authority with whom the Material Affiliated Person files such reports has entered into an information-sharing agreement with the Commission which is in effect as of the futures commission merchant's fiscal year-end and which will allow the Commission to obtain the type of information required herein. The futures commission merchant shall maintain a copy of the original report and a copy translated into the English language. For the purposes of this section, the term "Foreign Futures Authority" shall have the meaning set forth in section 1a(10) of the Act.

(d) *Exemptions.* (1) The provisions of this section shall not apply to any futures commission merchant which holds funds or property of or for futures customers of less than $6,250,000 and has less than $5,000,000 in adjusted net capital as of the futures commission merchant's current fiscal year-end; provided, however, that such futures commission merchant is not a clearing member of an exchange.

(2) The Commission may, upon written application by a Reporting Futures Commission Merchant, exempt from the provisions of this section, other than paragraph (a)(1)(ii) of this section, either unconditionally or on specified terms and conditions, any futures commission merchant affiliated with such Reporting Futures Commission Merchant. The term "Reporting Futures Commission Merchant" shall mean, in the case of a futures commission merchant that is affiliated with another registered futures commission merchant, the futures commission merchant which maintains the greater amount of adjusted net capital as last reported on financial reports filed with the Commission pursuant to § 1.10 unless another futures commission merchant is acting as the Reporting Broker or Dealer under § 240.17h-2T of this title, or the Commission permits another futures commission merchant to act as the Reporting Futures Commission Merchant. In granting exemptions under this section, the Commission shall consider, among other factors, whether the records required by this section concerning the Material Affiliated Persons of the futures commission merchant affiliated with the Reporting Futures Commission Merchant will be available to the Commission pursuant to this section or § 1.15. A request for exemption filed under this paragraph (d)(2) shall explain the basis for the designation of a particular futures commission merchant as the Reporting Futures Commission Merchant and will become effective on the thirtieth day after receipt of such request by the Commission unless the Commission objects to the request by that date.

(3) The Commission may exempt any futures commission merchant from any provision of this section if it finds that the exemption is not contrary to the public interest and the purposes of the provisions from which the exemption is sought. The Commission may grant the exemption subject to such terms and conditions as it may find appropriate.

(e) *Location of records.* A futures commission merchant required to maintain records concerning Material Affiliated Persons pursuant to this section may maintain those records either at the principal office of the Material Affiliated Person or at a records storage facility, provided that, except as set forth in paragraph (c) of this section, the records are located within the boundaries of the United States and the records are kept and available for inspection in accordance with § 1.31. If such records are maintained at a place other than the futures commission merchant's principal place of business, the Material Affiliated Person or other entity maintaining the records shall file with the Commission a written undertaking, in a form acceptable to the Commission, signed by a duly authorized person, to the effect that the records will be treated as if the futures commission merchant were maintaining the records pursuant to this section and that the entity maintaining the records will permit examination of such records at any time, or from time to time during business hours, by representatives or designees of the Commission and promptly furnish the Commission representative or its designee true, correct, complete and current hard copy of all or any part of such records. The election to maintain records at the principal place of business of the Material Affiliated Person or at a records storage facility pursuant to the provisions of this paragraph shall not relieve the futures commission merchant required to maintain and preserve such records from any of its responsibilities under this section or § 1.15.

(f) *Confidentiality.* All information obtained by the Commission pursuant to the provisions of this section from a futures commission merchant concerning a Material Affiliated Person shall be deemed confidential information for the purposes of section 8 of the Act.

(g) *Implementation schedule.* (1) Each futures commission merchant registered as of December 31, 1994 and subject to the requirements of this section shall maintain and preserve the information required by paragraphs (a)(1)(i) and (a)(1)(ii) of this section commencing April 30, 1995 and the information required by paragraphs (a)(1)(iii) and (a)(1)(iv) of this section commencing May 15, 1995 or, if December 31, 1994 is not the futures commission merchant's fiscal year-end, 135 calendar days following the first fiscal year-end occurring after December 31, 1994.

(2) Each futures commission merchant whose registration becomes effective after December 31, 1994 and is subject to the requirements of this section shall maintain and preserve the information required by paragraphs (a)(1)(i) and (a)(1)(ii) of this section commencing 60 calendar days after registration become effective and the information required by paragraphs (a)(1)(iii) and (a)(1)(iv) of this section commencing 105 calendar days following the first fiscal year-end occurring after registration becomes effective.

[59 FR 66688, Dec. 28, 1994]

§ 1.15 RISK ASSESSMENT REPORTING REQUIREMENTS FOR FUTURES COMMISSION MERCHANTS.

(a) *Reporting requirements with respect to information required to be maintained by § 1.14.* (1) Each futures commission merchant registered with the Commission pursuant to Section 4d of the Act, unless exempt pursuant to paragraph (c) of this section, shall file the following with the regional office with which it files periodic financial reports by no later than April 30, 1995, provided that in the case of a futures commission merchant whose registration becomes effective after December 31, 1994, such futures commission merchant shall file the following within 60 calendar days after the effective date of such registration, or by April 30, 1995, whichever comes later:

(i) A copy of the organizational chart maintained by the futures commission merchant pursuant to paragraph (a)(l)(i) of § 1.14. Where there is a material change in information provided, an updated organizational chart shall be filed within sixty calendar days after the end of the fiscal quarter in which the change has occurred; and

(ii) Copies of the financial, operational, and risk management policies, procedures and systems maintained by the futures commission merchant pursuant to paragraph (a)(l)(ii) of § 1.14. If the futures commission merchant has no such written policies, procedures or systems, it must file a statement so indicating. Where there is a material change in information provided, such change shall be reported within sixty calendar days after the end of the fiscal quarter in which the change has occurred.

(2) Each futures commission merchant registered with the Commission pursuant to Section 4d of the Act, unless exempt pursuant to paragraph (c) of this section, shall file the following with the regional office with which it files periodic financial reports within 105 calendar days after the end of each fiscal year or, if a filing is made pursuant to a written notice issued under paragraph (a)(2)(iii) of this section, within the time period specified in the written notice:

(i) Fiscal year-end consolidated and consolidating balance sheets for the highest level Material Affiliated Person within the futures commission merchant's organizational structure, which shall include the futures commission merchant and its other Material Affiliated Persons, prepared in accordance with generally accepted accounting principles, which consolidated balance sheets shall be audited by an independent certified public accountant if an annual audit is performed in the ordinary course of business, but which otherwise may be unaudited, and which consolidated balance sheets shall include appropriate explanatory notes. The consolidating balance sheets may be those prepared by the futures commission merchant's highest level Material Affiliated Person as part of its internal financial reporting process;

(ii) Fiscal year-end annual consolidated and consolidating income statements and consolidated cash flow statements for the highest level Material Affiliated Person within the futures commission merchant's organizational structure, which shall include the futures commission merchant and its other Material Affiliated Persons, prepared in accordance with generally accepted accounting principles, which consolidated statements shall be audited by an independent certified public accountant if an annual audit is performed in the ordinary course of business, but which otherwise may be unaudited, and which consolidated statements shall include appropriate explanatory notes. The consolidating statements may be those prepared by the futures commission merchant's highest level Material Affiliated Person as part of its internal financial reporting process; and

(iii) Upon receiving written notice from any representative of the Commission and within the time period specified in the written notice, such additional information which the Commission determines is necessary for a complete understanding of a particular affiliate's financial impact on the futures commission merchant's organizational structure.

(3) For the purposes of this section, the term Material Affiliated Person shall have the meaning used in § 1.14.

(4) The reports required to be filed pursuant to paragraphs (a)(1) and (a)(2) of this section shall be considered filed when received by the regional office of the Commission with whom the futures commission files financial reports pursuant to § 1.10.

(c) *Exemptions.* (1) The provisions of this section shall not apply to any futures commission merchant which holds funds or property of or for futures customers of less than $6,250,000 and has less than $5,000,000 in adjusted net capital as of the futures commission merchant's fiscal year-end; provided, however, that such futures commission merchant is not a clearing member of an exchange.

(2) The Commission may, upon written application by a Reporting Futures Commission Merchant, exempt from the provisions of this section, other than paragraph (a)(1)(ii) of this section, either unconditionally or on specified terms and conditions, any futures commission merchant affiliated with such Reporting Futures Commission Merchant. The term "Reporting Futures Commission Merchant" shall mean, in the case of a futures commission merchant that is affiliated with another registered futures commission merchant, the futures commission merchant which maintains the greater amount of net capital as last reported on its financial reports filed with the Commission pursuant to § 1.10 unless another futures commission merchant is acting as the Reporting Broker or Dealer under § 240.17h-2T of this title or the Commission permits another futures commission merchant to act as the Reporting Futures Commission Merchant. In granting exemptions under this section, the Commission shall consider, among other factors, whether the records and other information required to be maintained pursuant to § 1.14 concerning the Material Affiliated Persons of the futures commission merchant affiliated with the Reporting Futures Commission Merchant will be available to the Commission pursuant to the provisions of this section. A request for exemption filed under this paragraph (c)(2) shall explain the basis for the designation of a particular futures commission merchant as the Reporting Futures Commission Merchant and will become effective on the thirtieth day after receipt of such request by the Commission unless the Commission objects

to the request by that date. The Reporting Futures Commission Merchant must submit the information required by paragraph (a)(1)(ii) of this section on behalf of its affiliated futures commission merchants.

(3) The Commission may exempt any futures commission merchant from any provision of this section if it finds that the exemption is not contrary to the public interest and the purposes of the provisions from which the exemption is sought. The Commission may grant the exemption subject to such terms and conditions as it may find appropriate.

(d) *Special provisions with respect to Material Affiliated Persons subject to the supervision of certain domestic regulators.*(1) In the case of a futures commission merchant which is required to file, or has a Material Affiliated Person which is required to file, Form 17-H (or such other forms or reports as may be required) with the Securities and Exchange Commission pursuant to § 240.17h-2T of this title, or such other risk assessment regulations as the Securities and Exchange Commission may adopt, such futures commission merchant shall be deemed to be in compliance with the reporting requirements of paragraphs (a)(1)(i) and (a)(2) of this section if the futures commission merchant furnishes, in accordance with paragraph (a)(2) of this section, a copy of the most recent Form 17-H filed by the futures commission merchant or its Material Affiliated Person with the Securities and Exchange Commission, provided however, that if the futures commission merchant has designated any of its affiliated persons as Material Affiliated Persons for purposes of this section and § 1.14 which are not designated as Material Associated Persons for purposes of the Form 17-H filed pursuant to §§ 240.17h-1T and 240.17h-2T of this title, the futures commission must also designate any such affiliated person as a Material Affiliated Person on the organizational chart required as Item 1 of part I of Form 17-H. To comply with paragraphs (a)(1)(i) and (a)(2) of this section, such futures commission merchant may, at its option, file Form 17-H in its entirety or file such form without the information required under part II of Form 17-H.

(2) In the case of a Material Affiliated Person (including a foreign banking organization) that is subject to examination by, or the reporting requirements of, a Federal banking agency, the futures commission merchant shall be deemed to be in compliance with the reporting requirements of paragraph (a)(2) of this section with respect to such Material Affiliated Person if the futures commission merchant or such Material Affiliated Person maintains in accordance with § 1.14 copies of all reports filed by the Material Affiliated Person with the Federal banking agency pursuant to section 5211 of the Revised Statutes, section 9 of the Federal Reserve Act, section 7(a) of the Federal Deposit Insurance Act, section 10(b) of the Home Owners' Loan Act, or section 5 of the Bank Holding Company Act of 1956.

(3) In the case of a futures commission merchant that has a Material Affiliated Person that is subject to the supervision of an insurance commissioner or other similar official or agency of a state, such futures commission merchant shall be deemed to be in compliance with the reporting requirements of paragraph (a)(2) of this section with respect to the Material Affiliated Person if:

(i) With respect to a Material Affiliated Person organized as a mutual insurance company or a non-public stock company, the futures commission merchant or such Material Affiliated Person maintains in accordance with § 1.14 copies of the annual statements with schedules and exhibits prepared by the Material Affiliated Person on forms prescribed by the National Association of Insurance Commissioners or by a state insurance commissioner; and

(ii) With respect to a Material Affiliated Person organized as a public stock company, the futures commission merchant or such Material Affiliated Person maintains, in addition to the annual statements with schedules and exhibits required to be maintained pursuant to § 1.14, copies of the filings made by the Material Affiliated Person pursuant to sections 13 or 15 of the Securities Exchange Act of 1934 and the Investment Company Act of 1940.

(4) No futures commission merchant shall be required to furnish to the Commission any examination report of any Federal banking agency or any supervisory recommendations or analyses contained therein with respect to a Material Affiliated Person that is subject to the regulation of a Federal banking agency. All information received by the Commission pursuant to this section concerning a Material Affiliated Person that is subject to examination by or the reporting requirements of a Federal banking agency shall be deemed confidential for the purposes of section 8 of the Act.

(5) The furnishing of any information or documents by a futures commission merchant pursuant to this section shall not constitute an admission for any purpose that a Material Affiliated Person is otherwise subject to the Act.

(e) *Special provisions with respect to Material Affiliated Persons subject to the supervision of a Foreign Regulatory Authority.* A futures commission merchant shall be deemed to be in compliance with the reporting requirements of paragraph (a)(2) of this section with respect to a Material Affiliated Person if such futures commission merchant furnishes, or causes such Material Affiliated Person to make available, in accordance with the provisions of this section, copies of any financial or risk exposure reports filed by such Material Affiliated Person with a foreign futures authority or other foreign regulatory authority, provided that:

(1) The futures commission merchant agrees to use its best efforts to obtain from the Material Affiliated Person and to cause the Material Affiliated Person to provide, directly or through its foreign futures authority or other foreign regulatory authority, any supplemental information the Commission may request and there is no statute or other bar in the foreign jurisdiction that would preclude the futures commission merchant, the Material Affiliated Person, the foreign futures authority or other foreign regulatory authority from providing such information to the Commission; or

(2) The foreign futures authority or other foreign regulatory authority with whom the Material Affiliated Person files such reports has entered into an information sharing agreement with the Commission which is in effect as of the futures commission merchant's fiscal year-end and which will allow the Commission to obtain the type of information required herein. The futures commission merchant shall file a copy of the original report and a copy translated into the English language. For the purposes of this section, the term "Foreign Futures Authority" shall have the meaning set forth in section 1a(10) of the Act.

(f) *Confidentiality.* All information obtained by the Commission pursuant to the provisions of this section from a futures commission merchant concerning a Material Associated Person shall be deemed confidential information for the purposes of section 8 of the Act.

(g) *Implementation schedule.* Each futures commission merchant registered as of December 31, 1994 and subject to the requirements of this section shall file the information required by paragraph (a)(1) of this section no later than April 30, 1995 and the information required by paragraph (a)(2) of this section no later than May 15, 1995. Each futures commission merchant whose registration becomes effective after December 31, 1994 and is subject to the requirements of this section shall file the information required by paragraph (a)(1) of this section within 60 calendar days after registration is granted, or by April 30, 1995, whichever comes later and the information required by paragraph (a)(2) of this section within 105 calendar days after registration is granted or by May 15, 1995, whichever comes later.

[59 FR 66690, Dec. 28, 1994; 60 FR 13901, Mar. 15, 1995]

§ 1.16 QUALIFICATIONS AND REPORTS OF ACCOUNTANTS.

(a) *Definitions*— (1) *Accountant's report.* The term "accountant's report," when used in regard to financial statements and schedules, means a document in which an independent licensed or certified public accountant indicates the scope of the audit (or examination) which he has made and sets forth his opinion regarding the financial statements and schedules taken as a whole or an assertion to the fact that an overall opinion cannot be expressed. When an overall opinion cannot be expressed, the reasons therefore must be stated.

(2) *Audit or examination.* The terms "audit" and "examination," when used in regard to financial statements and schedules, mean an examination of the statements and schedules by an accountant in accordance with generally accepted auditing standards for the purposes of expressing an opinion thereon.

(3) *Certified.* The term "certified," when used in regard to financial statements and schedules, means audited and reported upon with an opinion expressed by an independent certified public accountant or independent licensed public accountant.

(4) *Customer.* The term "customer" means customer (as defined in § 1.3(k)) and includes a foreign futures or foreign options customer (as defined in § 30.1(c) of this chapter).

(b) *Qualifications of accountants.* (1) The Commission will recognize any person as a certified public accountant who is duly registered and in good standing as such under the laws of the place of his residence or principal office. The Commission will recognize any person as a licensed public accountant who was duly licensed on or before December 31, 1970, and is in good standing as such under the laws of the place of his residence or principal office.

(2) The Commission will not recognize any certified public accountant or licensed public accountant as independent who is not in fact independent. For example, an accountant will not be considered independent with respect to any applicant or registrant or any parent, subsidiary, or other affiliate of such applicant or registrant (i) in which, during the period of his professional engagement to examine the financial statements and schedules being reported on or at the date of his report, he or his firm or a member thereof had, or was committed to acquire, any direct financial interest or any material indirect financial interest, or (ii) with which, during the period of his professional engagement to examine the financial statements and schedules being reported on, at the date of his report or during the period covered by the financial statements, he or his firm or a member thereof was connected as a promoter, underwriter, voting trustee, director, officer, or employee, except that a firm will be deemed independent with respect to an applicant or registrant and its affiliates if a former employee or officer of such applicant or registrant or any such affiliate is employed by the firm and such individual has completely disassociated himself from the applicant or registrant and its affiliates and does not participate in auditing financial statements and schedules of the applicant or registrant or its affiliates covering any period of his employment by the applicant or registrant or its affiliates. An accountant will not be considered independent if he or his firm or a member thereof performs manual or automated bookkeeping services or assumes responsibility for maintenance of the accounting records, including accounting classification decisions, of such applicant or registrant or any of its affiliates. For the purposes of this § 1.16(b), the term "member" means all partners in the firm and all professional employees participating in the audit or located in the office of the firm participating in a significant portion of the audit.

(3) In determining whether an accountant may in fact not be independent with respect to a particular applicant or registrant, the Commission will give appropriate consideration to all relevant circumstances, including evidence bearing on all relationships between the accountant and that applicant or registrant or any affiliate thereof, and will not confine itself to the relationship existing in connection with the filing of reports with the Commission.

(c) *Accountant's reports*— (1) *Technical requirements.* The accountant's report (i) must be dated, (ii) must be signed manually, (iii) must indicate the city and State where issued and (iv) must identify without detailed enumeration the financial statements covered by the report.

(2) *Representations as to the audit.* The accountant's report (i) must state whether the audit was made in accordance with generally accepted auditing standards, and (ii) must designate any auditing procedures deemed necessary by the accountant under the circumstances of the particular case which have been omitted and the reasons for their omission. However, nothing in this paragraph (c)(2) shall be construed to imply authority for the omission of any procedure which independent accountants would ordinarily employ in the course of an audit made for the purposes of expressing the opinion required by paragraph (c)(3) of this section.

(3) *Opinion to be expressed.* The accountant's report must state clearly: (i) The opinion of the accountant with respect to the financial statements and schedules covered by the report and the accounting principles and practices reflected therein and (ii) the opinion of the accountant as to the consistency of the application of the accounting principles, or as to any changes in such principles which have material effect on the financial statements and schedules.

(4) *Exceptions.* Any matters to which the accountant takes exception must be clearly identified, such exceptions specifically and clearly stated, and to the extent practicable, the effect of each exception on related financial statements and schedules given.

(5) *Accountant's report on material inadequacies.* A registrant must file concurrently with the annual audit report a supplemental report by the accountant describing any material inadequacies found to exist or found to have existed since the date of the previous audit. An applicant must file concurrently with the audit report a supplemental report by the accountant describing any material inadequacies found to exist as of the date of the Form 1-FR being filed: *Provided, however* , That if such applicant is registered with the Securities and Exchange Commission as a securities broker or dealer, and it files (in accordance with § 1.10(h)) a copy of its Financial and Operational Combined Uniform Single Report under the Securities Exchange Act of 1934, Part II, Part IIA, or Part II CSE, in lieu of Form 1-FR, the accountant's supplemental report must be made as of the date of such report. The supplemental report must indicate any corrective action taken or proposed by the applicant or registrant in regard thereto. If the audit did not disclose any material inadequacies, the supplemental report must so state.

(d) *Audit objectives.* (1) The audit must be made in accordance with generally accepted auditing standards and must include a review and appropriate tests of the accounting system, the internal accounting control, and the procedures for safeguarding customer and firm assets in accordance with the provisions of the Act and the regulations thereunder, since the prior examination date. The audit must include all procedures necessary under the circumstances to enable the independent licensed or certified public accountant to express an opinion on the financial statements and schedules. The scope of the audit and review of the accounting system, the internal controls, and procedures for safeguarding customer and firm assets must be sufficient to provide reasonable assurance that any material inadequacies existing at the date of the examination in (i) the accounting system, (ii) the internal accounting controls, and (iii) the procedures for safeguarding customer and firm assets (including, in the case of a futures commission merchant, the segregation requirements of section 4d(a)(2) of the Act and these regulations and the secured amount requirements of the Act and these regulations) will be discovered. Additionally, as specified objectives the audit must include reviews of the practices and procedures followed by the registrant in making (A) periodic computations of the minimum financial requirements pursuant to § 1.17 and (B) in the case of a futures commission merchant, daily computations of the segregation requirements of section 4d(a)(2) of the Act and these regulations and the secured amount requirements of the Act and these regulations.

(2) A material inadequacy in the accounting system, the internal accounting controls, the procedures for safeguarding customer and firm assets, and the practices and procedures referred to in paragraph (d)(1) of this section which is to be reported in accordance with paragraph (e)(2) of this section includes any conditions which contributed substantially to or, if appropriate corrective action is not taken, could reasonably be expected to:

(i) Inhibit an applicant or registrant from promptly completing transactions or promptly discharging his responsibilities to customers or other creditors;

(ii) Result in material financial loss;

(iii) Result in material misstatement of the applicant's or registrant's financial statements and schedules; or

(iv) Result in violations of the Commission's segregation or secured amount (in the case of a futures commission merchant), recordkeeping or financial reporting requirements to the extent that could reasonably be expected to result in the conditions described in paragraph (d)(2) (i), (ii), or (iii) of this section.

(e) *Extent and timing of audit procedures.* (1) The extent and timing of audit procedures are matters for the independent public accountant to determine on the basis of his review and evaluation of existing internal controls and other audit procedures performed in accordance with generally accepted auditing standards and the audit objectives set forth in paragraph (d) of this section. In determining the extent of testing, consideration must be given to the materiality of an area and to the possible effect on the financial statements and schedules of a material misstatement in a related account.

(2) If during the course of an audit or interim work, the independent public accountant determines that any material inadequacies exist in the accounting system, in the internal accounting control, in the procedures for safeguarding customer or firm assets, or as otherwise defined in paragraph (d) of this

section, he must call such inadequacies to the attention of the applicant or registrant, which has the responsibility to give notice to the National Futures Association and, if an applicant, or the Commission and the designated self-regulatory organization, if any, if a registrant, in accordance with paragraphs (d) and (g) of § 1.12: *Provided, however,* That if the applicant or registrant is an introducing broker or applicant for registration as an introducing broker, it also has the responsibility to give notice to the National Futures Association, the designated self-regulatory organization, if any, and every futures commission merchant carrying or intending to carry customer accounts for the introducing broker or applicant for registration as an introducing broker. The applicant or registrant must also furnish the accountant with a copy of said notice within three (3) business days. If the accountant fails to receive such notice from the applicant or registrant within three (3) business days, or if he disagrees with the statements contained in the notice of the applicant or registrant, the accountant must inform the National Futures Association, in the case of an applicant, or the Commission and the designated self-regulatory organization, if any, in the case of a registrant, by reporting the material inadequacy and, in the case of an applicant or registrant which is an introducing broker or applicant for registration as in introducing broker, the accountant must also inform the National Futures Association, the designated self-regulatory organization, if any, and every futures commission merchant carrying or intending to carry customer accounts for the introducing an introducing broker, within three (3) business days thereafter. Such report from the accountant must, if the applicant or registrant failed to file a notice, describe the material inadequacies found to exist. If the applicant or registrant filed a notice, the accountant must file a report detailing the aspects, if any, of the applicant's or registrant's notice with which the accountant does not agree.

(f)(1) *Extension of time for filing audited reports* . In the event a registered futures commission merchant or a registered introducing broker finds that it cannot file, without substantial undue hardship, its certified financial statements and schedules for any year within the time specified in § 1.10 (b)(1)(ii) or § 1.10 (b)(2)(ii) of this part, as applicable, such registrants may request approval for an extension of time, as follows:

(i) *Futures commission merchant registrants.* (A) A futures commission merchant may file with its designated self-regulatory organization an application for an extension of time, a copy of which the registrant must file with the Commission. The application shall be approved or denied in writing by the designated self-regulatory organization. The registrant must file immediately with the Commission a copy of any notice it receives from the designated self-regulatory organization to approve or deny the registrant's request for extension of time. A written notice of approval shall become effective upon the filing by the registrant of a copy with the Commission, and a written notice of denial shall be effective as of the date of the notice.

(B) A futures commission merchant that is registered with the Securities and Exchange Commission as a securities broker or dealer may file with its designated self-regulatory organization a copy of any application that the registrant has filed with its designated examining authority, pursuant to § 240.17-a5(*l*)(1)of this title, for an extension of time to file audited annual financial statements. The registrant must also file immediately with the designated self-regulatory organization and the Commission copies of any notice it receives from its designated examining authority to approve or deny the requested extension of time. Upon receipt by the designated self-regulatory organization and the Commission of copies of any such notice of approval, the requested extension of time referenced in the notice shall be deemed approved under this paragraph (f)(1)(i).

(C) Any copy that under this paragraph (f)(1)(i) is required to be filed with the Commission shall be filed with the regional office of the Commission with jurisdiction over the state in which the registrant's principal place of business is located.

(ii) *Introducing broker registrants.* (A) An introducing broker may file with the National Futures Association an application for extension of time, which shall be approved or denied in writing.

(B) An introducing broker that is registered with the Securities and Exchange Commission as a securities broker or dealer may file with the National Futures Association copies of any application that the registrant has filed with its designated examining authority, pursuant to § 240.17-a5(*l*)(1) of this title, for an extension of time to file audited annual financial statements. The registrant must also file immediately with the National Futures Association copies of any notice it receives from its designated examining authority to approve or deny the requested extension of time. Upon the receipt by the National Futures Association of a copy of any such notice of approval, the requested extension of time referenced in the notice shall be deemed approved under this paragraph (f)(1)(ii).

(2) *Exemption requests.* On the written request of any designated self-regulatory organization or registrant, or on its own motion, the Commission may grant an extension of time or an exemption from any of the certified financial reporting requirements of this chapter either unconditionally or on specified terms and conditions.

(g) *Replacement of accountant.* (1) In the event (i) the independent public accountant who was previously engaged as the principal accountant to audit an applicant's or registrant's financial statements resigns (or indicates he declines to stand for re-election after the completion of the current audit) or is dismissed as the applicant's or registrant's principal accountant, (ii) another independent accountant is engaged as principal accountant, or (iii) an independent accountant on whom the principal accountant expresses reliance in his report regarding a subsidiary resigns (or formally indicates he declines to stand for re-election after completion of the current audit) or is dismissed or another independent public accountant is engaged to audit that subsidiary, an applicant shall file written notice of such occurrence with the National Futures Association, and a registrant shall file written notice of such occurrence with the Commission at its principal office in Washington, DC, and with the designated self-regulatory organization, if any, not more than 15 business days after such occurrence.

(2) Such notice must state (i) the date of such resignation (or declination to stand for re-election, dismissal or engagement) and (ii) whether, in connection with the audit of the two most recent fiscal years and any subsequent interim period preceding such resignation, dismissal or engagement, there were any disagreements with the former accountant on any matter of accounting principles or practices, financial statements disclosure, auditing scope or procedures, or compliance with the applicable rules of the Commission, which, if not resolved to the satisfaction of the former accountant, would have caused him to make reference in connection with his report to the subject matter of the disagreements (if so, describe such disagreements). The disagreements required to be reported in this paragraph (g)(2) include both those resolved to the former accountant's satisfaction and those not resolved to the former accountant's satisfaction. Disagreements contemplated by this paragraph (g)(2) are those which occur at the decision-making level, *i.e.,* between personnel of the applicant or registrant responsible for presentation of its financial statements and schedules and personnel of the accounting firm responsible for rendering its report. The notice must also state whether the accountant's report on the financial statements and schedules for any of the past two years contained an adverse opinion or a disclaimer of opinion or was qualified as to uncertainties, audit scope, or accounting principles (if so, describe the nature of each such adverse opinion, disclaimer of opinion, or qualification). An applicant must also request the former accountant to furnish the applicant with a letter addressed to the National Futures Association, and a registrant must also request the former accountant to furnish the registrant with a letter addressed to the Commission, stating whether he agrees with the statements contained in the notice of the applicant or registrant and, if not, stating the respects in which he does not agree. Each copy of the notice and accountant's letter must be manually signed by the sole proprietor or a general partner or a duly authorized corporate officer of the applicant or registrant, as appropriate, and by the accountant.

(3) If (i) within the 24 months prior to the date of the most recent audited financial statement, a notice has been filed pursuant to paragraph (g)(1) of this section reporting a change of accountants, (ii) included in such filing there is a reported disagreement on any matters of accounting principles or practices, financial statements disclosure, auditing scope, or noncompliance with the applicable rules of the Commission, (iii) during the fiscal year in which the change in accountants took place or during the subsequent fiscal year, there have been any transactions or events similar to those which involved a reported disagreement, and (iv) such transactions or events are material and were accounted for or disclosed in a manner different from that which the former accountant apparently would have concluded was required, the existence and nature of the disagreements and also the effect on the financial statements must be stated in a written notice to the National Futures Association, in the case of an applicant, or to the Commission at its principal office in Washington, DC, and the designated self-regulatory organization, if any, in the case of a registrant, if the method which the former accountant apparently would have concluded was required had been followed. These disclosures need not be made if the method asserted by the former accountant ceases to be generally accepted because of authoritative standards or interpretations subsequently issued. The notice required by this paragraph (g)(3) must be filed by the applicant or registrant concurrently with the financial statements and schedules to which it pertains.

(h) *Exemption for introducing broker or applicant therefor.* The provisions of this section do not apply to an introducing broker which is operating pursuant to a guarantee agreement, nor do such provisions apply to an applicant for registration as an introducing broker who files concurrently with such application a guarantee agreement, provided such introducing broker or applicant therefor is not also a securities broker or dealer.

(Approved by the Office of Management and Budget under control numbers 3038-0007, 3038-0024)

[43 FR 39970, Sept. 8, 1978, as amended at 46 FR 54516, Nov. 3, 1981; 46 FR 63035, Dec. 30, 1981; 48 FR 35284, Aug. 3, 1983; 49 FR 39526, Oct. 9, 1984; 52 FR 28995, Aug. 5, 1987; 53 FR 4612, Feb. 17, 1988; 69 FR 41426, July 9, 2004; 69 FR 49798, Aug. 12, 2004; 71 FR 5593, Feb. 2, 2006; 77 FR 66320, Nov. 2, 2012]

§ 1.17 MINIMUM FINANCIAL REQUIREMENTS FOR FUTURES COMMISSION MERCHANTS AND INTRODUCING BROKERS.

(a)(1)(i) Except as provided in paragraph (a)(2)(i) of this section, each person registered as a futures commission merchant must maintain adjusted net capital equal to or in excess of the greatest of:

(A) $1,000,000;

(B) The futures commission merchant's risk-based capital requirement, computed as eight percent of the total risk margin requirement for positions carried by the futures commission merchant in customer accounts and noncustomer accounts.

(C) The amount of adjusted net capital required by a registered futures association of which it is a member; or

(D) For securities brokers and dealers, the amount of net capital required by Rule 15c3-1(a) of the Securities and Exchange Commission (17 CFR 240.15c3-1(a)).

(iii) Except as provided in paragraph (a)(2) of this section, each person registered as an introducing broker must maintain adjusted net capital equal to or in excess of the greatest of:

(A) $45,000;

(B) The amount of adjusted net capital required by a registered futures association of which it is a member; or

(C) For securities brokers and dealers, the amount of net capital required by Rule 15c3-1(a) of the Securities and Exchange Commission (17 CFR 240.15c3-1(a)).

(2)(i) The requirements of paragraph (a)(1) of this section shall not be applicable if the registrant is a member of a designated self-regulatory organization and conforms to minimum financial standards and related reporting requirements set by such designated self-regulatory organization in its bylaws, rules, regulations or resolutions approved by the Commission pursuant to section 4f(b) of the Act and § 1.52.

(ii) The minimum requirements of paragraph (a)(1)(iii) of this section shall not be applicable to an introducing broker which elects to meet the alternative adjusted net capital requirement for introducing brokers by operation pursuant to a guarantee agreement which meets the requirements set forth in § 1.10(j). Such an introducing broker shall be deemed to meet the adjusted net capital requirement under this section so long as such agreement is binding and in full force and effect, and, if the introducing broker is also a securities broker or dealer, it maintains the amount of net capital required by Rule 15c3-1(a) of the Securities and Exchange Commission (17 CFR 240.15c3-1(a)).

(3) No person applying for registration as a futures commission merchant or as an introducing broker shall be so registered unless such person affirmatively demonstrates to the satisfaction of the National Futures Association that it complies with the financial requirements of this section. Each registrant must be in compliance with this section at all times and must be able to demonstrate such compliance to the satisfaction of the Commission or the designated self-regulatory organization.

(4) A futures commission merchant who is not in compliance with this section, or is unable to demonstrate such compliance as required by paragraph (a)(3) of this section, must transfer all customer accounts and immediately cease doing business as a futures commission merchant until such time as the firm is able to demonstrate such compliance: *Provided, however,* The registrant may trade for liquidation purposes only unless otherwise directed by the Commission and/or the designated self-regulatory organization: *And, Provided further,* That if such registrant immediately demonstrates to the satisfaction of the Commission or the designated self-regulatory organization the ability to achieve compliance, the Commission or the designated self-regulatory organization may in its discretion allow such registrant up to a maximum of 10 business days in which to achieve compliance without having to transfer accounts and cease doing business as required above. Nothing in this paragraph (a)(4) shall be construed as preventing the Commission or the designated self-regulatory organization from taking action against a registrant for non-compliance with any of the provisions of this section.

(5) An introducing broker who is not in compliance with this section, or is unable to demonstrate such compliance as required by paragraph (a)(3) of this section, must immediately cease doing business as an introducing broker until such time as the registrant is able to demonstrate such compliance: *Provided, however,* That if such registrant immediately demonstrates to the satisfaction of the Commission or the designated self-regulatory organization the ability to achieve compliance, the Commission or the designated self-regulatory organization may in its discretion allow such registrant up to a maximum of 10 business days in which to achieve compliance without having to cease doing business as required above. If the introducing broker is required to cease doing business in accordance with this paragraph (a)(5), the introducing broker must immediately notify each of its customers and the futures commission merchants carrying the account of each customer that it has ceased doing business. Nothing in this paragraph (a)(5) shall be construed as preventing the Commission or the designated self-regulatory organization from taking action against a registrant for non-compliance with any of the provisions of this section.

(b) For the purposes of this section:

(1) Where the applicant or registrant has an asset or liability which is defined in Securities Exchange Act Rule 15c3-1 (§ 240.15c3-1 of this title) the inclusion or exclusion of all or part of such asset or liability for the computation of adjusted net capital shall be in accordance with § 240.15c3-1 of this title, unless specifically stated otherwise in this section.

(2) *Customer* means customer (as defined in § 1.3(k)), option customer (as defined in § 1.3(jj) and in § 32.1(c) of this chapter), cleared over the counter customer (as defined in § 1.17(b)(10)), and includes a foreign futures, foreign options customer (as defined in § 30.1(c) of this chapter).

(3) *Proprietary account* means an account in which commodity futures, options or cleared over the counter derivative positions are carried on the books of the applicant or registrant for the applicant or registrant itself, or for general partners in the applicant or registrant.

(4) *Noncustomer account* means an account in which commodity futures, options or cleared over the counter derivative positions are carried on the books of the applicant or registrant which is either:

(i) An account that is not included in the definition of customer (as defined in § 1.17(b)(2)) or proprietary account (as defined in § 1.17(b)(3)), or

(ii) An account for a foreign-domiciled person trading futures or options on a foreign board of trade, and such account is a proprietary account as defined in § 1.3(y) of this title, but is not a proprietary account as defined in § 1.17(b)(3).

(5) *Clearing organization* means clearing organization (as defined in § 1.3(d)) and includes a clearing organization of any board of trade.

(6) *Business day* means any day other than a Sunday, Saturday, or holiday.

(7) *Customer account* means an account in which commodity futures, options or cleared over the counter derivative positions are carried on the books of the applicant or registrant which is either:

(i) An account that is included in the definition of customer (as defined in § 1.17(b)(2)), or

(ii) An account for a foreign-domiciled person trading on a foreign board of trade, where such account for the foreign-domiciled person is not a proprietary account (as defined in § 1.17(b)(3)) or a noncustomer account (as defined in § 1.17(b)(4)(ii)).

(8) *Risk margin* for an account means the level of maintenance margin or performance bond required for the customer or noncustomer positions by the applicable exchanges or clearing organizations, and, where margin or performance bond is required only for accounts at the clearing organization, for purposes of the FCM's risk-based capital calculations applying the same margin or performance bond requirements to customer and noncustomer positions in accounts carried by the FCM, subject to the following.

(i) Risk margin does not include the equity component of short or long option positions maintained in an account;

(ii) The maintenance margin or performance bond requirement associated with a long option position may be excluded from risk margin to the extent that the value of such long option position does not reduce the total risk maintenance or performance bond requirement of the account that holds the long option position;

(iii) The risk margin for an account carried by a futures commission merchant which is not a member of the exchange or the clearing organization that requires collection of such margin should be calculated as if the futures commission merchant were such a member; and

(iv) If a futures commission merchant does not possess sufficient information to determine what portion of an account's total margin requirement represents risk margin, all of the margin required by the exchange or the clearing organization that requires collection of such margin for that account, shall be treated as risk margin.

(9) *Cleared over the counter derivative positions* means "over the counter derivative instrument" (as defined in 12 U.S.C. 4421) positions of any person in accounts carried on the books of the futures commission merchant and cleared by any organization permitted to clear such instruments under the laws of the relevant jurisdiction.

(10) *Cleared over the counter customer* means any person that is not a proprietary person as defined in § 1.3(y) and for whom the futures commission merchant carries on its books one or more accounts for the over the counter-cleared derivative positions of such person.

(c) Definitions: For the purposes of this section:

(1) *Net capital* means the amount by which current assets exceed liabilities. In determining "net capital":

(i) Unrealized profits shall be added and unrealized losses shall be deducted in the accounts of the applicant or registrant, including unrealized profits and losses on fixed price commitments and forward contracts;

(ii) All long and all short positions in commodity options which are traded on a contract market and listed security options shall be marked to their market value and all long and all short securities and commodities positions shall be marked to their market value;

(iii) The value attributed to any commodity option which is not traded on a contract market shall be the difference between the option's strike price and the market value for the commodity or futures contract which is the subject of the option. In the case of a call commodity option which is not traded on a contract market, if the market value for the commodity or futures contract which is the subject of the option is less than the strike price of the option, it shall be given no value. In the case of a put commodity option which is not traded on a contract market, if the market value for the commodity or futures contract which is the subject of the option is more than the strike price of the option, it shall be given no value; and

(iv) The value attributed to any unlisted security option shall be the difference between the option's exercise value or striking value and the market value of the underlying security. In the case of an unlisted call, if the market value of the underlying security is less than the exercise value or striking value of such call, it shall be given no value; and, in the case of an unlisted put, if the market value of the underlying security is more than the exercise value or striking value of the unlisted put, it shall be given no value.

(2) The term *current assets* means cash and other assets or resources commonly identified as those which are reasonably expected to be realized in cash or sold during the next 12 months. "Current assets" shall:

(i) Exclude any unsecured commodity futures or option account containing a ledger balance and open trades, the combination of which liquidates to a deficit or containing a debit ledger balance only: *Provided, however,* Deficits or debit ledger balances in unsecured customers', non-customers', and proprietary accounts, which are the subject of calls for margin or other required deposits may be included in current assets until the close of business on the business day following the date on which such deficit or debit ledger balance originated providing that the account had timely satisfied, through the deposit of new funds, the previous day's debit or deficits, if any, in its entirety.

(ii) Exclude all unsecured receivables, advances and loans except for:

(A) Receivables resulting from the marketing of inventories commonly associated with the business activities of the applicant or registrant and advances on fixed price purchases commitments: *Provided,* Such receivables or advances are outstanding no longer than 3 calendar months from the date that they are accrued;

(B) Interest receivable, floor brokerage receivable, commissions receivable from other brokers or dealers (other than syndicate profits), mutual fund concessions receivable and management fees receivable from registered investment companies and commodity pools: *Provided,* Such receivables are outstanding no longer than thirty (30) days from the date they are due; and dividends receivable outstanding no longer than thirty (30) days from the payable date;

(C) Receivables from clearing organizations and securities clearing organizations;

(D) Receivables from registered futures commission merchants or brokers, resulting from commodity futures or option transactions, except those specifically excluded under paragraph (c)(2)(i) of this section;

(E) Insurance claims which arise from a reportable segment of the applicant's or registrant's overall business activities, as defined in generally accepted accounting principles, other than in the commodity futures, commodity option, security and security option segments of the applicant's or registrant's business activities which are not outstanding more than 3 calendar months after the date they are recorded as a receivable;

(F) All other insurance claims not subject to paragraph (c)(2)(ii)(E) of this section, which are not older than seven (7) business days from the date the loss giving rise to the claim is discovered; insurance claims which are not older than twenty (20) business days from the date the loss giving rise to the claim is discovered and which are covered by an option of outside counsel that the claim is valid and is covered by insurance policies presently in effect; insurance claims which are older than twenty (20) business days from the date the loss giving rise to the claim is discovered and which are covered by an opinion of outside counsel that the claim is valid and is covered by insurance policies presently in effect and which have been acknowledged in writing by the insurance carrier as due and payable: *Provided,* Such claims are not outstanding longer than twenty (20) business days from the date they are so acknowledged by the carrier;

(iii) Exclude all prepaid expenses and deferred charges;

(iv) Exclude all inventories except for:

(A) Readily marketable spot commodities; or spot commodities which “adequately collateralize” indebtedness under paragraph (c)(7) of this section;

(B) Securities which are considered “readily marketable” (as defined in § 240.15c3-1(c)(11) of this title) or which “adequately collateralize” indebtedness under paragraph (c)(7) of this section;

(C) Work in process and finished goods which result from the processing of commodities at market value;

(D) Raw materials at market value which will be combined with spot commodities to produce a finished proc- essed commodity; and

(E) Inventories held for resale commonly associated with the business activities of the applicant or registrant;

(v) Include fixed assets and assets which otherwise would be considered noncurrent to the extent of any long-term debt adequately collateralized by assets acquired for use in the ordinary course of the trade or business of an applicant or registrant and any other long-term debt adequately collateralized by assets of the applicant or registrant if the sole recourse of the creditor for nonpayment of such liability is to such asset: *Provided,* Such liabilities are not excluded from liabilities in the computation of net capital under paragraph (c)(4)(vi) of this section;

(vi) Exclude all assets doubtful of collection or realization less any reserves established therefor;

(vii) Include, in the case of future income tax benefits arising as a result of unrealized losses, the amount of such benefits not exceeding the amount of income tax liabilities accrued on the books and records of the applicant or registrant, but only to the extent such benefits could have been applied to reduce accrued tax liabilities on the date of the capital computation, had the related unrealized losses been realized on that date;

(viii) Include guarantee deposits with clearing organizations and stock in clearing organizations to the extent of its margin value;

(ix) In the case of an introducing broker or an applicant for registration as an introducing broker, include 50 percent of the value of a guarantee or security deposit with a futures commission merchant which carries or intends to carry accounts for the customers of the introducing broker; and

(x) Exclude exchange memberships.

(3) A loan or advance or any other form of receivable shall not be considered “secured” for the purposes of paragraph (c)(2) of this section unless the following conditions exist:

(i) The receivable is secured by readily marketable collateral which is otherwise unencumbered and which can be readily converted into cash: *Provided, however,* That the receivable will be considered secured only to the extent of the market value of such collateral after application of the percentage deductions specified in paragraph (c)(5) of this section; and

(ii)(A) The readily marketable collateral is in the possession or control of the applicant or registrant; or

(B) The applicant or registrant has a legally enforceable, written security agreement, signed by the debtor, and has a perfected security interest in the readily marketable collateral within the meaning of the laws of the State in which the readily marketable collateral is located.

(4) The term *liabilities* means the total money liabilities of an applicant or registrant arising in connection with any transaction whatsoever, including economic obligations of an applicant or registrant that are recognized and measured in conformity with generally accepted accounting principles. "Liabilities" also include certain deferred credits that are not obligations but that are recognized and measured in conformity with generally accepted accounting principles. For the purposes of computing "net capital", the term "liabilities":

(i) Excludes liabilities of an applicant or registrant which are subordi- nated to the claims of all general creditors of the applicant or registrant pursuant to a satisfactory subordination agreement, as defined in paragraph (h) of this section;

(ii) Excludes, in the case of a futures commission merchant, the amount of money, securities and property due to commodity futures or option customers which is held in segregated accounts in compliance with the requirements of the Act and these regulations: *Provided, however,* That such exclusion may be taken only if such money, securities and property held in segregated accounts have been excluded from current assets in computing net capital;

(iii) Includes, in the case of an applicant or registrant who is a sole proprietor, the excess of liabilities which have not been incurred in the course of business as a futures commission merchant or as an introducing broker over assets not used in the business;

(iv) Excludes the lesser of any deferred income tax liability related to the items in paragraphs (c)(4)(i)(A), (B), and (C) below, or the sum of paragraphs (c)(4)(i) (A), (B), and (C) below:

(A) The aggregate amount resulting from applying to the amount of the deductions computed in accordance with paragraph (c)(5) of this section the appropriate Federal and State tax rate(s) applicable to any unrealized gain on the asset on which the deduction was computed;

(B) Any deferred tax liability related to income accrued which is directly related to an asset otherwise deducted pursuant to this section;

(C) Any deferred tax liability related to unrealized appreciation in value of any asset(s) which has been otherwise excluded from current assets in accordance with the provisions of this section;

(v) Excludes any current tax liability related to income accrued which is directly related to an asset otherwise deducted pursuant to this section; and

(vi) Excludes liabilities which would be classified as long term in accordance with generally accepted accounting principles to the extent of the net book value of plant, property and equipment which is used in the ordinary course of any trade or business of the applicant or registrant which is a reportable segment of the applicant's or registrant's overall business activities, as defined in generally accepted accounting principles, other than in the commodity futures, commodity option, security and security option segments of the applicant's or registrant's business activities: *Provided,* That such plant, property and equipment is not included in current assets pursuant to paragraph (c)(2)(v) of this section.

(5) The term *adjusted net capital* means net capital less:

(i) The amount by which any advances paid by the applicant or registrant on cash commodity contracts and used in computing net capital exceeds 95 percent of the market value of the commodities covered by such contracts;

(ii) In the case of all inventory, fixed price commitments and forward contracts, the applicable percentage of the net position specified below:

(A) Inventory which is currently registered as deliverable on a contract market and covered by an open futures contract or by a commodity option on a physical commodity—No charge.

(B) Inventory which is covered by an open futures contract or commodity option.—5 percent of the market value.

(C) Inventory which is not covered.—20 percent of the market value.

(D) Inventory and forward contracts in those foreign currencies that are purchased or sold for future delivery on or subject to the rules of a contract market, and which are covered by an open futures contract.—No charge

(E) Inventory and forward contracts in euros, British pounds, Canadian dollars, Japanese yen, or Swiss francs, and which are not covered by an open futures contract or commodity option.—6 percent of the market value.

(F) Fixed price commitments (open purchases and sales) and forward contracts which are covered by an open futures contract or commodity option.—10 percent of the market value.

(G) Fixed price commitments (open purchases and sales) and forward contracts which are not covered by an open futures contract or commodity option.—20 percent of the market value.

(v) In the case of securities and obligations used by the applicant or registrant in computing net capital, and in the case of a futures commission merchant with securities in segregation pursuant to section 4d(2) of the Act and the regulations in this chapter which were not deposited by customers, the percentages specified in Rule 240.15c3-1(c)(2)(vi) of the Securities and Exchange Commission (17 CFR 240.15c3-1(c)(2)(vi)) ("securities haircuts") and 100 percent of the value of "nonmarketable securities" as specified in Rule 240.15c3-1(c)(2)(vii) of the Securities and Exchange Commission (17 CFR 240.15c3-1(c)(2)(vii));

(vi) In the case of securities options and/or other options for which a haircut has been specified for the option or for the underlying instrument in § 240.15c3-1 appendix A of this title, the treatment specified in, or under, § 240.15c3-1 appendix A, after effecting certain adjustments to net capital for listed and unlisted options as set forth in such appendix;

(vii) In the case of an applicant or registrant who has open contractual commitments, as hereinafter defined, the deductions specified in § 240.15c3-1(c)(2)(viii) of this title;

(viii) In the case of a futures commission merchant, for undermargined customer commodity futures accounts and commodity option customer accounts the amount of funds required in each such account to meet maintenance margin requirements of the applicable board of trade or if there are no such maintenance margin requirements, clearing organization margin requirements applicable to such positions, after application of calls for margin or other required deposits which are outstanding three business days or less. If there are no such maintenance margin requirements or clearing organization margin requirements, then the amount of funds required to provide margin equal to the amount necessary after application of calls for margin or other required deposits outstanding three business days or less to restore original margin when the original margin has been depleted by 50 percent or more: *Provided,* To the extent a deficit is excluded from current assets in accordance with paragraph (c)(2)(i) of this section such amount shall not also be deducted under this paragraph (c)(5)(viii). In the event that an owner of a customer account has deposited an asset other than cash to margin, guarantee or secure his account, the value attributable to such asset for purposes of this subparagraph shall be the lesser of (A) the value attributable to the asset pursuant to the margin rules of the applicable board of trade, or (B) the market value of the asset after application of the percentage deductions specified in this paragraph (c)(5);

(ix) In the case of a futures commission merchant, for undermargined commodity futures and commodity option noncustomer and omnibus accounts the amount of funds required in each such account to meet maintenance margin requirements of the applicable board of trade or if there are no such maintenance margin requirements, clearing organization margin requirements applicable to such positions, after application of calls for margin or other required deposits which are outstanding two business days or less. If there are no such maintenance margin requirements or clearing organization margin requirements, then the amount of funds required to provide margin equal to the amount necessary after application of calls for margin or other required deposits outstanding two business days or less to restore original margin when the original margin has been depleted by 50 percent or more: *Provided,* To the extent a deficit is excluded from current assets in accordance with paragraph (c)(2)(i) of this section such amount shall not also be deducted under this paragraph (c)(5)(ix). In the event that an owner of a noncustomer or omnibus account has deposited an asset other than cash to margin, guarantee or secure his account the value attributable to such asset for purposes of this subparagraph shall be the lesser of (A) the value attributable to such asset pursuant to the margin rules of the applicable board of trade, or (B) the market value of such asset after application of the percentage deductions specified in this paragraph (c)(5);

(x) In the case of open futures contracts or cleared OTC derivative positions and granted (sold) commodity options held in proprietary accounts carried by the applicant or registrant which are not covered by a position held by the applicant or registrant or which are not the result of a "changer trade" made in accordance with the rules of a contract market:

(A) For an applicant or registrant which is a clearing member of a clearing organization for the positions cleared by such member, the applicable margin requirement of the applicable clearing organization;

(B) For an applicant or registrant which is a member of a self-regulatory organization 150 percent of the applicable maintenance margin requirement of the applicable board of trade, or clearing organization, whichever is greater;

(C) For all other applicants or registrants, 200 percent of the applicable maintenance margin requirements of the applicable board of trade or clearing organization, whichever is greater; or

(D) For open contracts or granted (sold) commodity options for which there are no applicable maintenance margin requirements, 200 percent of the applicable initial margin requirement: *Provided,* The equity in any such proprietary account shall reduce the deduction required by this paragraph (c)(5)(x) if such equity is not otherwise includable in adjusted net capital;

(xi) In the case of an applicant or registrant which is a purchaser of a commodity option not traded on a contract market which has value and such value is used to increase adjusted net capital, ten percent of the market value of the commodity or futures contract which is the subject of such option but in no event more than the value attributed to such option;

(xii) In the case of an applicant or registrant which is a purchaser of a commodity option which is traded on a contract market the same safety factor as if the applicant or registrant were the grantor of such option in accordance with paragraph (c)(5)(x) of this section, but in no event shall the safety factor be greater than the market value attributed to such option;

(xiii) Five percent of all unsecured receivables includable under paragraph (c)(2)(ii)(D) of this section used by the applicant or registrant in computing "net capital" and which are not due from:

(A) A registered futures commission merchant;

(B) A broker or dealer that is registered as such with the Securities and Exchange Commission; or

(C) A foreign broker that has been granted comparability relief pursuant to § 30.10 of this chapter, *Provided, however,* that the amount of the unsecured receivable not subject to the five percent capital charge is no greater than 150 percent of the current amount required to maintain futures and options positions in accounts with the foreign broker, or 100 percent of such greater amount required to maintain futures and option positions in the accounts at any time during the previous six-month period, and *Provided, that,* in the case of the foreign futures or foreign options secured amount, as § 1.3(rr) defines such term, such account is treated in accordance with the special requirements of the applicable Commission order issued under § 30.10 of this chapter.

(xiv) For securities brokers and dealers, all other deductions specified in § 240.15c3-1 of this title.

(6) Election of alternative capital deductions that have received approval of Securities and Exchange Commission pursuant to § 240.15c3-1(a)(7) of this title.

(i) Any futures commission merchant that is also registered with the Securities and Exchange Commission as a securities broker or dealer, and who also satisfies the other requirements of this paragraph (c)(6), may elect to compute its adjusted net capital using the alternative capital deductions that, under § 240.15c3-1(a)(7) of this title, the Securities and Exchange Commission has approved by written order. To the extent that a futures commission merchant is permitted by the Securities and Exchange Commission to use alternative capital deductions for its unsecured receivables from over-the-counter transactions in derivatives, or for its proprietary positions in securities, forward contracts, or futures contracts, the futures commission merchant may use these same alternative capital deductions when computing its adjusted net capital, in lieu of the deductions that would otherwise be required by paragraph (c)(2)(ii) of this section for its unsecured receivables from over-the-counter derivatives transactions; by paragraph (c)(5)(ii) of this section for its proprietary positions in forward contracts; by paragraph (c)(5)(v) of this section for its proprietary positions in securities; and by paragraph (c)(5)(x) of this section for its proprietary positions in futures contracts.

(ii) *Notifications of election or of changes to election.* (A) No election to use the alternative market risk and credit risk deductions referenced in paragraph (c)(6)(i) of this section shall be effective unless and until the futures commission merchant has filed with the Commission, addressed to the Director of the Division of Swap Dealer and Intermediary Oversight, a notice that is to include a copy of the approval order of the Securities and Exchange Commission referenced in paragraph (c)(6)(i) of this section, and to include also a statement that identifies the amount of tentative net capital below which the futures commission merchant is required to provide notice to the Securities and Exchange Commission, and which also provides the following information: a list of the categories of positions that the futures commission merchant holds in its proprietary accounts, and, for each such category, a description of the methods that the futures commission merchant will use to calculate its deductions for market risk and credit risk, and also, if calculated separately, deductions for specific risk; a description of the value at risk (VaR) models to be used for its market risk and credit risk deductions, and an overview of the integration of the models into the internal risk management control system of the futures commission merchant; a description of how the futures commission merchant will calculate current exposure and maximum potential exposure for its deductions for credit risk; a description of how the futures commission merchant will determine internal credit ratings of counterparties and internal credit risk weights of counterparties, if applicable; and a description of the estimated effect of the alternative market risk and credit risk deductions on the amounts reported by the futures commission merchant as net capital and adjusted net capital.

(B) A futures commission merchant must also, upon the request of the Commission at any time, supplement the statement described in paragraph (c)(6)(ii)(A) of this section, by providing any other explanatory information regarding the computation of its alternative market risk and credit risk deductions as the Commission may require at its discretion.

(C) A futures commission merchant must also file the following supplemental notices with the Director of the Division and Clearing and Intermediary Oversight:

(*1*) A notice advising that the Securities and Exchange Commission has imposed additional or revised conditions for the approval evidenced by the order referenced in paragraph (c)(6)(i) of this section, and which describes the new or revised conditions in full, and

(2) A notice which attaches a copy of any approval by the Securities and Exchange Commission of amendments that a futures commission merchant has requested for its application, filed under 17 CFR 240.15c3-1e, to use alternative market risk and credit risk deductions approved by the Securities and Exchange Commission.

(D) A futures commission merchant may voluntarily change its election to use the alternative market risk and credit risk deductions referenced in paragraph (c)(6)(i) of this section, by filing with the Director of the Division of Swap Dealer and Intermediary Oversight a written notice specifying a future date as of which it will no longer use the alternative market risk and credit risk deductions, and will instead compute such deductions in accordance with the requirements otherwise applicable under paragraph (c)(2)(ii) of this section for unsecured receivables from over-the-counter derivatives transactions; by paragraph (c)(5)(ii) of this section for proprietary positions in forward contracts; by paragraph (c)(5)(v) of this section for proprietary positions in securities; and by paragraph (c)(5)(x) of this section for proprietary positions in futures contracts.

(iii) *Conditions under which election terminated.* A futures commission merchant may no longer elect to use the alternative market risk and credit risk deductions referenced in paragraph (c)(6)(i) of this section, and shall instead compute the deductions otherwise required under paragraph (c)(2)(ii) of this section for unsecured receivables from over-the-counter derivatives transactions; by paragraph (c)(5)(ii) of this section for proprietary positions in forward contracts; by paragraph (c)(5)(v) of this section for proprietary positions in securities; and by paragraph (c)(5)(x) of this section for proprietary positions in futures contracts, upon the occurrence of any of the following:

(A) The Securities and Exchange Commission revokes its approval of the market risk and credit risk deductions for such futures commission merchant;

(B) A futures commission merchant fails to come into compliance with its filing requirements under this paragraph (c)(6), after having received from the Director of the Division of Swap Dealer and Intermediary Oversight written notification that the firm is not in compliance with its filing requirements, and must cease using alternative capital deductions permitted under this paragraph (c)(6) if it has not come into compliance by a date specified in the notice; or

(C) The Commission by written order finds that permitting the futures commission merchant to continue to use such alternative market risk and credit risk deductions is no longer necessary or appropriate for the protection of customers of the futures commission merchant or of the integrity of the futures or options markets.

(iv) *Additional filing requirements.* Any futures commission merchant that elects to use the alternative market risk and credit risk deductions referenced in paragraph (c)(6)(i) of this section must file with the Commission, in addition to the filings required by paragraph (c)(6)(ii) of this section, copies of any and all of the following documents, at such time as the originals are filed with the Securities and Exchange Commission:

(A) Information that the futures commission merchant files on a monthly basis with its designated examining authority or the Securities and Exchange Commission, whether by way of schedules to its FOCUS reports or by other filings, in satisfaction of 17 CFR 240.17a-5(a)(5)(i);

(B) The quarterly reports required by 17 CFR 240.17a-5(a)(5)(ii);

(C) The supplemental annual filings as required by 17 CFR 240.17a-5(k);

(D) Any notification to the Securities and Exchange Commission or the futures commission merchant's designated examining authority of planned withdrawals of excess net capital; and

(E) Any notification that the futures commission merchant is required to file with the Securities and Exchange Commission when its tentative net capital is below an amount specified by the Securities and Exchange Commission.

(7) *Liabilities* are "adequately collateralized" when, pursuant to a legally enforceable written instrument, such liabilities are secured by identified assets that are otherwise unencumbered and the market value of which exceeds the amount of such liabilities.

(8) The term *contractual commitments* shall include underwriting, when issued, when distributed, and delayed delivery contracts; and the writing or endorsement of security puts and calls and combinations thereof; but shall not include uncleared regular way purchases and sales of securities. A series of contracts of purchase or sale of the same security, conditioned, if at all, only upon issuance, may be treated as an individual commitment.

(d) Each applicant or registrant shall have equity capital (inclusive of satisfactory subordination agreements which qualify under this paragraph (d) as equity capital) of not less than 30 percent of the debt-equity total, provided, an applicant or registrant may be exempted from the provisions of this paragraph (d) for a period not to exceed 90 days or for such longer period which the Commission may, upon application of the applicant or registrant, grant in the public interest or for the protection of investors. For the purposes of this paragraph (d):

(1) Equity capital means a satisfactory subordination agreement entered into by a partner or stockholder or limited liability company member which has an initial term of at least 3 years and has a remaining term of not less than 12 months if:

(i) It does not have any of the provisions for accelerated maturity provided for by paragraphs (h)(2)(ix)(A), (x)(A), or (x)(B) of this section, or the provisions allowing for special prepayment provided for by paragraph (h)(2)(vii)(B) of this section, and is maintained as capital subject to the provisions restricting the withdrawal thereof required by paragraph (e) of this section; or

(ii) The partnership agreement provides that capital contributed pursuant to a satisfactory subordination agreement as defined in paragraph (h) of this section shall in all respects be partnership capital subject to the provisions restricting the withdrawal thereof required by paragraph (e) of this section, and

(A) In the case of a corporation, the sum of its par or stated value of capital stock, paid in capital in excess of par, retained earnings, unrealized profit and loss, and other capital accounts.

(B) In the case of a partnership, the sum of its capital accounts of partners (inclusive of such partners' commodities, options and securities accounts subject to the provisions of paragraph (e) of this section), and unrealized profit and loss.

(C) In the case of a sole proprietorship, the sum of its capital accounts of the sole proprietorship and unrealized profit and loss.

(D) In the case of a limited liability company, the sum of its capital accounts of limited liability company members, and unrealized profit and loss.

(2) Debt-equity total means equity capital as defined in paragraph (d)(1) of this section plus the outstanding principal amount of satisfactory subordination agreements.

(e) No equity capital of the applicant or registrant or a subsidiary's or affiliate's equity capital consolidated pursuant to paragraph (f) of this section, whether in the form of capital contributions by partners (including amounts in the commodities, options and securities trading accounts of partners which are treated as equity capital but excluding amounts in such trading accounts which are not equity capital and excluding balances in limited partners' capital accounts in excess of their stated capital contributions), par or stated value of capital stock, paid-in capital in excess of par or stated value, retained earnings or other capital accounts, may be withdrawn by action of a stockholder or partner or limited liability company member or by redemption or repurchase of shares of stock by any of the consolidated entities or through the payment of dividends or any similar distribution, nor may any unsecured advance or loan be made to a stockholder, partner, sole proprietor, limited liability company member, or employee if, after giving effect thereto and to any other such withdrawals, advances, or loans and any payments of payment obligations (as defined in paragraph (h) of this section) under satisfactory subordination agreements and any payments of liabilities excluded pursuant to paragraph (c)(4)(vi) of this section which are scheduled to occur within six months following such withdrawal, advance or loan:

(1) Either adjusted net capital of any of the consolidated entities would be less than the greatest of:

(i) 120 percent of the appropriate minimum dollar amount required by paragraphs (a)(1)(i)(A) or (a)(1)(iii)(A) of this section;

(ii) For a futures commission merchant or applicant therefor, 120 percent of the amount required by paragraph (a)(1)(i)(B) of this section;

(iii) 120 percent of the amount of adjusted net capital required by a registered futures association of which it is a member; or

(iv) For an applicant or registrant which is also a securities broker or dealer, the amount of net capital specified in Rule 15c3-1(e) of the Securities and Exchange Commission (17 CFR 240.15c3-1(e)); or

(2) In the case of any applicant or registrant included within such consolidation, if equity capital of the applicant or registrant (inclusive of satisfactory subordination agreements which qualify as equity under paragraph (d) of this section) would be less than 30 percent of the required debt-equity total as defined in paragraph (d) of this section.

Provided, That this paragraph (e) shall not preclude an applicant or registrant from making required tax payments or preclude the payment to partners of reasonable compensation. The Commission may, upon application of the applicant or registrant, grant relief from this paragraph (e) if the Commission deems it to be in the public interest or for the protection of nonproprietary accounts.

(f)(1) Every applicant or registrant, in computing its net capital pursuant to this section must, subject to the provisions of paragraphs (f)(2) and (f)(4) of this section, consolidate in a single computation, assets and liabilities of any subsidiary or affiliate for which it guarantees, endorses, or assumes directly or indirectly the obligations or liabilities. The assets and liabilities of a subsidiary or affiliate whose liabilities and obligations have not been guaranteed, endorsed, or assumed directly or indirectly by the applicant or registrant may also be so consolidated if an opinion of counsel is obtained as provided for in paragraph (f)(2) of this section.

(2)(i) If the consolidation, provided for in paragraph (f)(1) of this section, of any such subsidiary or affiliate results in the increase of the applicant's or registrant's adjusted net capital or decreases the minimum adjusted net capital requirement, and an opinion of counsel called for in paragraph (f)(2)(ii) of this section has not been obtained, such benefits shall not be recognized in the applicant's or registrant's computation required by this section.

(ii) Except as provided for in paragraph (f)(2)(i) of this section, consolidation shall be permitted with respect to any subsidiaries or affiliates which are majority owned and controlled by the applicant or registrant, and for which the applicant can demonstrate to the satisfaction of the National Futures Association, or for which the registrant can demonstrate to the satisfaction of the Commission and the designated self-regulatory organization, if any, by an opinion of counsel, that the net asset values or the portion thereof related to the parent's ownership interest in the subsidiary or affiliate, may be caused by the applicant or registrant or an appointed trustee to be distributed to the applicant or registrant within 30 calendar days. Such opinion must also set forth the actions necessary to cause such a distribution to be made, identify the parties having the authority to take such actions, identify and describe the rights of other parties or classes of parties, including but not limited to customers, general creditors, subordinated lenders, minority shareholders, employees, litigants, and governmental or regulatory authorities, who may delay or prevent such a distribution and such other assurances as the National Futures Association, the Commission or the designated self-regulatory organization by rule or interpretation may require. Such opinion must be current and periodically renewed in connection with the applicant's or registrant's annual audit pursuant to § 1.10 or upon any material change in circumstances.

(3) In preparing a consolidated computation of adjusted net capital pursuant to this section, the following minimum and non-exclusive requirements shall be observed;

(i) Consolidated adjusted net capital shall be reduced by the estimated amount of any tax reasonably anticipated to be incurred upon distribution of the assets of the subsidiary or affiliate.

(ii) Liabilities of a consolidated subsidiary or affiliate which are subordinated to the claims of present and future creditors pursuant to a satisfactory subordination agreement shall be deducted from consolidated adjusted net capital unless such subordination extends also to the claims of present or future creditors of the parent applicant or registrant and all consolidated subsidiaries.

(iii) Subordinated liabilities of a consolidated subsidiary or affiliate which are consolidated in accordance with paragraph (f)(3)(ii) of this section may not be prepaid, repaid, or accelerated if any of the entities included in such consolidation would otherwise be unable to comply with the provisions of paragraph (h) of this section.

(iv) Each applicant or registrant included within the consolidation shall at all times be in compliance with the adjusted net capital requirement to which it is subject.

(4) No applicant or registrant shall guarantee, endorse, or assume directly or indirectly any obligation or liability of a subsidiary or affiliate unless the obligation or liability is reflected in the computation of adjusted net capital pursuant to this section except as provided in paragraph (f)(2)(i) of this section.

(g)(1) The Commission may by order restrict, for a period up to twenty business days, any withdrawal by a futures commission merchant of equity capital, or any unsecured advance or loan to a stockholder, partner, limited liability company member, sole proprietor, employee or affiliate, if:

(i) Such withdrawal, advance or loan would cause, when aggregated with all other withdrawals, advances or loans during a 30 calendar day period from the futures commission merchant or a subsidiary or affiliate of the futures commission merchant consolidated pursuant to § 1.17(f) (or 17 CFR 240.15c3-1e), a net reduction in excess adjusted net capital (or, if the futures commission merchant is qualified to use the filing option available under § 1.10(h), excess net capital as defined in the rules of the Securities and Exchange Commission) of 30 percent or more, and

(ii) The Commission, based on the facts and information available, concludes that any such withdrawal, advance or loan may be detrimental to the financial integrity of the futures commission merchant, or may unduly jeopardize its ability to meet customer obligations or other liabilities that may cause a significant impact on the markets.

(2) The futures commission merchant may file with the Secretary of the Commission a written petition to request rescission of the order issued under paragraph (g)(1) of this section. The petition filed by the futures commission merchant must specify the facts and circumstances supporting its request for rescission. The Commission shall respond in writing to deny the futures commission merchant's petition for rescission, or, if the Commission determines that the order issued under paragraph (g)(1) of this section should not remain in effect, the order shall be rescinded.

(h) The term *satisfactory subordination agreement* ("subordination agreement") means an agreement which contains the minimum and nonexclusive requirements set forth below.

(1) Certain definitions for purposes of this section:

(i) A subordination agreement may be either a subordinated loan agreement or a secured demand note agreement.

(ii) The term *subordinated loan agreement* means the agreement or agreements evidencing or governing a subordinated borrowing of cash.

(iii) The term "collateral value" of any securities pledged to secure a secured demand note means the market value of such securities after giving effect to the percentage deductions specified in Rule 240.15c3-1d(a)(2)(iii) of the Securities and Exchange Commission (17 CFR 240.15c3-1d(a)(2)(iii)).

(iv) The term *payment obligation* means the obligation of an applicant or registrant in respect to any subordination agreement:

(A) To repay cash loaned to the applicant or registrant pursuant to a subordinated loan agreement; or

(B) To return a secured demand note contributed to the applicant or registrant or to reduce the unpaid principal amount thereof and to return cash or securities pledged as collateral to secure the secured demand note; and (C) "payment" shall mean the performance by an applicant or registrant of a payment obligation.

(v)(A) The term *secured demand note agreement* means an agreement (including the related secured demand note) evidencing or governing the contribution of a secured demand note to an applicant or registrant and the pledge of securities and/or cash with the applicant or registrant as collateral to secure payment of such secured demand note. The secured demand note agreement may provide that neither the lender, his heirs, executors, administrators, or assigns shall be personally liable on such note and that in the event of default the applicant or registrant shall look for payment of such note solely to the collateral then pledged to secure the same.

(B) The secured demand note shall be a promissory note executed by the lender and shall be payable on the demand of the applicant or registrant to which it is contributed: *Provided, however,* That the making of such demand may be conditioned upon the occurrence of any of certain events which are acceptable to the designated self-regultory organization and the Commission.

(C) If such note is not paid upon presentment and demand as provided for therein, the applicant or registrant shall have the right to liquidate all or any part of the securities then pledged as collateral to secure payment of the same and to apply the net proceeds of such liquidation, together with any cash then included in the collateral, in payment of such note. Subject to the prior rights of the applicant or registrant as pledgee, the lender, as defined in paragraph (h)(i)(v)(F) of this section may retain ownership of the collateral and have the benefit of any increases and bear the risks fo any decreases in the value of the collateral and may retain the right to vote securities contained within the collateral and any right to income therefrom or distributions thereon, except the applicant or registrant shall have the right to receive and hold as pledgee all dividends payable in securities and all partial and complete liquidating dividends.

(D) Subject to the prior rights of the applicant or registrant as pledgee, the lender may have the right to direct the sale of any securities included in the collateral, to direct the purchase of securities with any cash included therein, to withdraw excess collateral or to substitute cash or other securities as collateral: *Provided,* That the net proceeds of any such sale and the cash so substituted and the securities so purchased or substituted are held by the applicant or registrant as pledgee, and are included within the collateral to secure payment of the secured demand note: *And provided further,* That no such transaction shall be permitted, if, after giving effect therto, the sum of the amount of any cash, plus the collateral value of the securities, then pledged as collateral to secure the secured demand note would be less than the unpaid principal amount of the secured demand note.

(E) Upon payment by the lender, as distinguished from a reduction by the lender which is provided for in paragraph (h)(2)(vi)(C) of this section or reduction by the applicant or registrant as provided for in paragraph (h)(2)(vii) of this section, of all or any part of the unpaid principal amount of the secured demand note, the applicant or registrant shall issue to the lender a subordinated loan agreement in the amount of such payment (or in the case of an applicant or registrant that is a partnership, credit a capital account of the lender), or issue preferred or common stock of the applicant or registrant in the amount of such payment, or any combination of the foregoing, as provided for in the secured demand note agreement.

(F) The term *lender* means the person who lends cash to an applicant or registrant pursuant to a subordinated loan agreement and the person who contributes a secured demand note to an applicant or registrant pursuant to a secured demand note agreement.

(2) Minimum requirements for subordination agreements:

(i) Subject to paragraph (h)(1) of this section, a subordination agreement shall mean a written agreement between the applicant or registrant and the lender, which:

(A) Has a minimum term of 1 year, except for temporary subordination agreements provided for in paragraph (h)(3)(v) of this section, and

(B) Is a valid and binding obligation enforceable in accordance with its terms (subject as to enforcement to applicable bankruptcy, insolvency, reorganization, moratorium, and other similar laws) against the applicant or registrant and the lender and their respective heirs, executors, administrators, successors, and assigns.

(ii) *Specific amount.* All subordination agreements shall be for a specific dollar amount which shall not be reduced for the duration of the agreement except by installments as specifically provided for therein and except as otherwise provided in this paragraph (h)(2) of this section.

(iii) *Effective subordination.* The subordination agreement shall effectively subordinate any right of the lender to receive any payment with respect thereto, together with accrued interest or compensation, to the prior payment or provision for payment in full of all claims of all present and future creditors of the applicant or registrant arising out of any matter occurring prior to the date on which the related payment obligation matures, except for claims which are the subject of subordination agreements which rank on the same priority as or junior to the claim of the lender under such subordination agreements.

(iv) *Proceeds of subordinated loan agreements.* The subordinated loan agreement shall provide that the cash proceeds thereof shall be used and dealt with by the applicant or registrant as part of its capital and shall be subject to the risks of the business.

(v) *Certain rights of the borrower.* The subordination agreement shall provide that the applicant or registrant shall have the right to:

(A) Deposit any cash proceeds of a subordinated loan agreement and any cash pledged as collateral to secure a secured demand note in an account or accounts in its own name in any bank or trust company;

(B) Pledge, repledge, hypothecate and rehypothecate, any or all of the securities pledged as collateral to secure a secured demand note, without notice, separately or in common with other securities or property for the purpose of securing any indebtedness of the applicant or registrant; and

(C) Lend to itself or others any or all of the securities and cash pledged as collateral to secure a secured demand note.

(vi) *Collateral for secured demand notes.* Only cash and securities which are fully paid for and which may be publicly offered or sold without registration under the Securities Act of 1933, and the offer, sale, and transfer of which are not otherwise restricted, may be pledged as collateral to secure a secured demand note. The secured demand note agreement shall provide that if at any time the sum of the amount of any cash, plus the collateral value of any securities, then pledged as collateral to secure the secured demand note is less than the unpaid principal amount of the secured demand note, the applicant or registrant must immediately transmit written notice to that effect to the lender. The secured demand note agreement shall also provide that if the borrower is an applicant, such notice must also be transmitted immediately to the National Futures Association, and if the borrower is a registrant, such notice must also be transmitted immediately to the designated self-regulatory organization, if any, and the Commission. The secured demand note agreement shall also require that following such transmittal:

(A) The lender, prior to noon of the business day next succeeding the transmittal of such notice, may pledge as collateral additional cash or securities sufficient, after giving effect to such pledge, to bring the sum of the amount of any cash plus the collateral value of any securities, then pledged as collateral to secure the secured demand note, up to an amount not less than the unpaid principal amount of the secured demand note; and

(B) Unless additional cash or securities are pledged by the lender as provided in paragraph (h)(2)(vi)(A) above, the applicant or registrant at noon on the business day next succeeding the transmittal of notice to the lender must commence sale, for the account of the lender, of such of the securities then pledged as collateral to secure the secured demand note and apply so much of the net proceeds thereof, together with such of the cash then pledged as collateral to secure the secured demand note as may be necessary to eliminate the unpaid principal amount of the secured demand note: *Provided, however,* That the unpaid principal amount of the secured demand note need not be reduced below the sum of the amount of any remaining cash, plus the collateral value of the remaining securities, then pledged as collateral to secure the secured demand note. The applicant or registrant may not purchase for its own account any securities subject to such a sale; and

(C) The secured demand note agreement may also provide that, in lieu of the procedures specified in the provisions required by paragraph (h)(2)(vi)(B) of this section, the lender, with the prior written consent of the applicant and the National Futures Association, or with the prior written consent of the registrant and the designated self-regulatory organization or, if the registrant is not a member of a designated self-regulatory organization, the Commission, may reduce the unpaid principal amount of the secured demand note: *Provided,* That after giving effect to such reduction the adjusted net capital of the applicant or registrant would not be less than the greatest of:

(*1*) 120 percent of the appropriate minimum dollar amount required by paragraphs (a)(1)(i)(A) or (a)(1)(iii)(A) of this section;

(*2*) For a futures commission merchant or applicant therefor, 120 percent of the amount required by paragraph (a)(1)(i)(B) of this section;

(*3*) 120 percent of the amount of adjusted net capital required by a registered futures association of which it is a member; or

(*4*) For an applicant or registrant which is also a securities broker or dealer, the amount of net capital specified in Rule 15c3-1d(b)(6)(iii) of the Securities and Exchange Commission (17 CFR 240.15c3-1d(b)(6)(iii)): *Provided, further,* That no single secured demand note shall be permitted to be reduced by more than 15 percent of its original principal amount and after such reduction no excess collateral may be withdrawn.

(vii) *Permissive prepayments and special prepayments.* (A) An applicant or registrant at its option, but not at the option of the lender, may, if the subordination agreement so provides, make a payment of all or any portion of the payment obligation thereunder prior to the scheduled maturity date of such payment obligation (hereinafter referred to as a "prepayment"), but in no event may any prepayment be made before the expiration of one year from the date such subordination agreement became effective: *Provided, however,* That the foregoing restriction shall not apply to temporary subordination agreements which comply with the provisions of paragraph (h)(3)(v) of this section nor shall it apply to "special prepayments" made in accordance with the provisions of paragraph (h)(2)(vii)(B) of this section. No prepayment shall be made if, after giving effect thereto (and to all payments of payment obligations under any other subordination agreements then outstanding, the maturity or accelerated maturities of which are scheduled to fall due within six months after the date such prepayment is to occur pursuant to this provision, or on or prior to the date on which the payment obligation in respect to such prepayment is scheduled to mature disregarding this provision, whichever date is earlier) without reference to any projected profit or loss of the applicant or registrant, the adjusted net capital of the applicant or registrant is less than the greatest of:

(*1*) 120 percent of the appropriate minimum dollar amount required by paragraphs (a)(1)(i)(A) or (a)(1)(iii)(A) of this section;

(*2*) For a futures commission merchant or applicant therefor, 120 percent of the amount required by paragraph (a)(1)(i)(B) of this section;

(*3*) 120 percent of the amount of adjusted net capital required by a registered futures association of which it is a member; or

(*4*) For an applicant or registrant which is also a securities broker or dealer, the amount of net capital specified in Rule 15c3-1d(b)(7) of the Securities and Exchange Commission (17 CFR 240.15c3-1d(b)(7)).

(B) An applicant or registrant at its option, but not at the option of the lender, may, if the subordination agreement so provides, make a payment at any time of all or any portion of the payment obligation thereunder prior to the scheduled maturity date of such payment obligation (hereinafter referred to as a "special prepayment"). No special prepayment shall be made if, after giving effect thereto (and to all payments of payment obligations under any other subordination agreements then outstanding, the maturity or accelerated maturities of which are scheduled to fall due within six months after the date such special prepayment is to occur pursuant to this provision, or on or prior to the date on which the payment obligation in respect to such special prepayment is scheduled to mature disregarding this provision, whichever date is earlier) without reference to any projected profit or loss of the applicant or registrant, the adjusted net capital of the applicant or registrant is less than the greatest of:

(*1*) 200 percent of the appropriate minimum dollar amount required by paragraphs (a)(1)(i)(A) or (a)(1)(iii)(A) of this section;

(*2*) For a futures commission merchant or applicant therefor, 125 percent of the amount required by paragraph (a)(1)(i)(B) of this section;

(*3*) 120 percent of the amount of adjusted net capital required by a registered futures association of which it is a member; or

(*4*) For an applicant or registrant which is also a securities broker or dealer, the amount of net capital specified in Rule 15c3-1d(c)(5)(ii) of the Securities and Exchange Commission (17 CFR 240.15c3-1d(c)(5)(ii)): *Provided, however,* That no special prepayment shall be made if pre-tax losses during the latest three-month period were greater than 15 percent of current excess adjusted net capital.

(C)(*1*) Notwithstanding the provisions of paragraphs (h)(2)(vii)(A) and (h)(2)(vii)(B) of this section, in the case of an applicant, no prepayment or special prepayment shall occur without the prior written approval of the National Futures Association; in the case of a registrant, no prepayment or special prepayment shall occur without the prior written approval of the designated self-regulatory organization, if any, or of the Commission if the registrant is not a member of a self-regulatory organization.

(*2*) A registrant may make a prepayment or special prepayment without the prior written approval of the designated self-regulatory organization: Provided, That the registrant: Is a securities broker or dealer registered with the Securities and Exchange Commission; files a request to make a prepayment or special prepayment with its applicable securities designated examining authority, as defined in Rule 15c3-1(c)(12) of the Securities and Exchange Commission (17 CFR 240.15c3-1(c)(12)), in the form and manner prescribed by the designated examining authority; files a copy of the prepayment request or special prepayment request with the designated self-regulatory organization at the time it files such request with the designated examining authority in the form and manner prescribed by the designated self-regulatory organization; and files a copy of the designated examining authority's approval of the prepayment or special prepayment with the designated self-regulatory organization immediately upon receipt of such approval. The approval of the prepayment or special prepayment by the designated examining authority will be deemed approval by the designated self-regulatory organization, unless the designated self-regulatory organization notifies the registrant that the designated examining authority's approval shall not constitute designated self-regulatory organization approval.

(*3*) The designated self-regulatory organization shall immediately provide the Commission with a copy of any notice of approval issued where the requested prepayment or special prepayment will result in the reduction of the registrant's net capital by 20 percent or more or the registrant's excess adjusted net capital by 30 percent or more.

(viii) *Suspended repayment.* (A) The payment obligation of the applicant or registrant in respect of any subordination agreement shall be suspended and shall not mature if, after giving effect to payment of such payment obligation (and to all payments of payment obligations of the applicant or registrant under any other subordination agreement(s) then outstanding which are scheduled to mature on or before such payment obligation), the adjusted net capital of the applicant or registrant would be less than the greatest of:

(*1*) 120 percent of the appropriate minimum dollar amount required by paragraphs (a)(1)(i)(A) or (a)(1)(iii)(A) of this section;

(*2*) For a futures commission merchant or applicant therefor, 120 percent of the amount required by paragraph (a)(1)(i)(B) of this section;

(*3*) 120 percent of the amount of adjusted net capital required by a registered futures association of which it is a member; or

(*4*) For an applicant or registrant which is also a securities broker or dealer, the amount of net capital specified in Rule 15c3-1d(b)(8)(i) of the Securities and Exchange Commission (17 CFR 240.15c3-1d(b)(8)(i)): *Provided,* That the subordination agreement may provide that if the payment obligation of the applicant or registrant thereunder does not mature and is suspended as a result of the requirement of this paragraph (h)(2)(viii) for a period of not less than six months, the applicant or registrant shall then commence the rapid and orderly liquidation of its business, but the right of the lender to receive payment, together with accrued interest or compensation, shall remain subordinate as required by the provisions of this section.

(ix) *Accelerated maturity.* Obligation to repay to remain subordinate:

(A) Subject to the provisions of paragraph (h)(2)(viii) of this section, a subordination agreement may provide that the lender may, upon prior written notice to the applicant and the National Futures Association, or upon prior written notice to the registrant and the designated self-regulatory organization or, if the registrant is not a member of a designated self-regulatory organization, the Commission, given not earlier than six months after the effective date of such subordination agreement, accelerate the date on which the payment obligation of the borrower, together with accrued interest or compensation, is scheduled to mature to a date not earlier than six months after giving of such notice, but the right of the lender to receive payment, together with accrued interest or compensation, shall remain subordinate as required by the provisions of this paragraph (h)(2) of this section.

(B) Notwithstanding the provisions of paragraph (h)(2)(viii) of this section, the payment obligation of the applicant or registrant with respect to a subordination agreement, together with accrued interest and compensation, shall mature in the event of any receivership, insolvency, liquidation pursuant to the Securities Investor Protection Act of 1970 or otherwise, bankruptcy, assignment for the benefit of creditors, reorganization whether or not pursuant to the bankruptcy laws, or any other marshalling of the assets and liabilities of the applicant or registrant, but the right of the lender to receive payment, together with accrued interest or compensation, shall remain subordinate as required by the provisions of paragraph (h)(2) of this section.

(x) *Accelerated maturity of subordination agreements on event of default and event of acceleration.* Obligation to repay to remain subordinate:

(A) A subordination agreement may provide that the lender may, upon prior written notice to the applicant and the National Futures Association, or upon prior written notice to the registrant and the designated self-regulatory organization or, if the registrant is not a member of a designated self-regulatory organization, the Commission, of the occurrence of any event of acceleration (as hereinafter defined) given no sooner than six months after the effective date of such subordination agreement, accelerate the date on which the payment obligation of the applicant or registrant, together with accrued interest or compensation, is scheduled to mature, to the last business day of a calendar month which is not less than six months after notice of acceleration is received by the applicant and by the National Futures Association, or by the registrant and the designated self-regulatory organization or, if the registrant is not a member of a designated self-regulatory organization, the Commission. Any subordination agreement containing such events of acceleration may also provide that, if upon such accelerated maturity date the payment obligation of the applicant or registrant is suspended as required by paragraph (h)(2)(viii) of this section and liquidation of the applicant or registrant has not commenced on or prior to such accelerated maturity date, notwithstanding paragraph (h)(2)(viii) of this section, the payment obligation of the applicant or registrant with respect to such subordination agreement shall mature on the day immediately following such accelerated maturity date and in any such event the payment obligations of the applicant or registrant with respect to all other subordination agreements then outstanding shall also mature at the same time but the rights of the respective lenders to receive payment, together with accrued interest or compensation, shall remain subordinate as required by the provisions of paragraph (h)(2) of this section. Events of acceleration which may be included in a subordination agreement complying with this paragraph (h)(2)(x) of this section shall be limited to:

(*1*) Failure to pay interest or any installment of principal on a subordination agreement as scheduled;

(*2*) Failure to pay when due other money obligations of a specified material amount;

(*3*) Discovery that any material, specified representation or warranty of the applicant or registrant which is included in the subordination agreement and on which the subordination agreement was based or continued was inaccurate in a material respect at the time made;

(*4*) Any specified and clearly measurable event which is included in the subordination agreement and which the lender and the applicant or registrant agree, (a) is a significant indication that the financial position of the applicant or registrant has changed materially and adversely from agreed upon specified norms; or (b) could materially and adversely affect the ability of the applicant or registrant to conduct its business as conducted on the date the subordination agreement was made; or (c) is a significant change in the senior management of the applicant or registrant or in the general business conducted by the applicant or registrant from that which obtained on the date the subordination agreement became effective;

(*5*) Any continued failure to perform agreed covenants included in the subordination agreement relating to the conduct of the business of the applicant or registrant or relating to the maintenance and reporting of its financial position; and

(B) Notwithstanding the provisions of paragraph (h)(2)(viii) of this section, a subordination agreement may provide that, if liquidation of the business of the applicant or registrant has not already commenced, the payment obligation of the applicant or registrant shall mature, together with accrued interest or compensation, upon the occurrence of an event of default (as hereinafter defined). Such agreement may also provide that, if liquidation of the business of the applicant or registrant has not already commenced, the rapid and orderly liquidation of the business of the applicant or registrant shall then commence upon the happening of an event of default. Any subordination agreement which so provides for maturity of the payment obligation upon the occurrence of an event of default shall also provide that the date on which such event of default occurs shall, if liquidation of the applicant or registrant has not already commenced, be the date on which the payment obligation of the applicant or registrant with respect to all other subordination agreements then outstanding shall mature but the rights of the respective lenders to receive payment, together with accrued interest or compensation, shall remain subordinate as required by the provisions of paragraph (h)(2) of this section. Events of default which may be included in a subordination agreement shall be limited to:

(*1*) The making of an application by the Securities Investor Protection Corporation for a decree adjudicating that customers of the applicant or registrant are in need of protection under the Securities Investor Protection Act of 1970 and the failure of the applicant or registrant to obtain the dismissal of such application within 30 days;

(*2*) Failure to meet the minimum capital requirements of the designated self-regulatory organization, or of the Commission, throughout a period of 15 consecutive business days, commencing on the day the borrower first determines and notifies the designated self-regulatory organization, if any, of which he is a member and the Commission, in the case of a registrant, or the National Futures Association, in the case of an applicant, or commencing on the day any self-regulatory organization, the Commission or the National Futures Association first determines and notifies the applicant or registrant of such fact;

(*3*) The Commission shall revoke the registration of the applicant or registrant;

(*4*) The self-regulatory organization shall suspend (and not reinstate within 10 days) or revoke the applicant or registrant's status as a member thereof;

(*5*) Any receivership, insolvency, liquidation pursuant to the Securities Investor Protection Act of 1970 or otherwise, bankruptcy, assignment for the benefit of creditors, reorganization whether or not pursuant to bankruptcy laws, or any other marshalling of the assets and liabilities of the applicant or registrant. A subordination agreement which contains any of the provisions permitted by this subparagraph (2)(x) shall not contain the provision otherwise permitted by paragraph (h)(2)(ix)(A) of this section.

(3) *Miscellaneous provisions*— (i) *Prohibited cancellation.* The subordination agreement shall not be subject to cancellation by either party; no payment shall be made with respect thereto and the agreement shall not be terminated, rescinded or modified by mutual consent or otherwise if the effect thereof would be inconsistent with the requirements of paragraph (h) of this section.

(ii) *Notice of maturity or accelerated maturity.* Every applicant or registrant shall immediately notify the National Futures Association, and the registrant shall immediately notify the designated self-regulatory organization, if any, and the Commission if, after giving effect to all payments of payment obligations under subordination agreements then outstanding which are then due or mature within the following six months without reference to any projected profit or loss of the applicant or registrant, its adjusted net capital would be less than:

(A) 120 percent of the appropriate minimum dollar amount required by paragraphs (a)(1)(i)(A) or (a)(1)(iii)(A) of this section;

(B) For a futures commission merchant or applicant therefor, 120 percent of the amount required by paragraph (a)(1)(i)(B) of this section;

(C) 120 percent of the amount of adjusted net capital required by a registered futures association of which it is a member; or

(D) For an applicant or registrant which is also a securities broker or dealer, the amount of net capital specified in Rule 15c3-1d(c)(2) of the Securities and Exchange Commission (17 CFR 240.15c3-1d(c)(2)).

(iii) *Certain legends.* If all the provisions of a satisfactory subordination agreement do not appear in a single instrument, then the debenture or other evidence of indebtedness shall bear on its face an appropriate legend stating that it is issued subject to the provisions of a satisfactory subordination agreement which shall be adequately referred to and incorporated by reference.

(iv) *Legal title to securities.* All securities pledged as collateral to secure a secured demand note must be in bearer form, or registered in the name of the applicant or registrant or the name of its nominee or custodian.

(v) *Temporary subordinations.* To enable an applicant or registrant to participate as an underwriter of securities or undertake other extraordinary activities and remain in compliance with the adjusted net capital requirements of this section, an applicant or registrant shall be permitted, on no more than three occasions in any 12-month period, to enter into a subordination agreement on a temporary basis which has a stated term of no more than 45 days from the date the subordination agreement became effective: *Provided,* That this temporary relief shall not apply to any applicant or registrant if the adjusted net capital of the applicant or registrant is less than the greatest of:

(A) 120 percent of the appropriate minimum dollar amount required by paragraphs (a)(1)(i)(A) or (a)(1)(iii)(A) of this section;

(B) For a futures commission merchant or applicant therefor, 120 percent of the amount required by paragraph (a)(1)(i)(B) of this section;

(C) 120 percent of the amount of adjusted net capital required by a registered futures association of which it is a member;

(D) For an applicant or registrant which is also a securities broker or dealer, the amount of net capital specified in Rule 15c3-1d(c)(5)(i) of the Securities and Exchange Commission (17 CFR 240.15c3-1d(c)(5)(i)); or

(E) The amount of equity capital as defined in paragraph (d) of this section is less than the limits specified in paragraph (d) of this section. Such temporary subordination agreement shall be subject to all the other provisions of this section.

(vi) *Filing.* An applicant shall file a signed copy of any proposed subordination agreement (including nonconforming subordination agreements) with the National Futures Association at least ten days prior to the proposed effective date of the agreement or at such other time as the National Futures Association for good cause shall accept such filing. A registrant that is not a member of any designated self-regulatory organization shall file two signed copies of any proposed subordination agreement (including nonconforming subordination agreements) with the regional office of the Commission nearest the principal place of business of the registrant at least ten days prior to the proposed effective date of the agreement or at such other time as the Commission for good cause shall accept such filing. A registrant that is a member of a designated self-regulatory organization shall file signed copies of any proposed subordination agreement (including nonconforming subordination agreements) with the designated self-regulatory organization in such quantities and at such time as the designated self-regulatory organization may require prior to the effective date. The applicant or registrant shall also file with said parties a statement setting forth the name and address of the lender, the business relationship of the lender to the applicant or registrant and whether the applicant or registrant carried funds or securities for the lender at or about the time the proposed agreement was so filed. A proposed agreement filed by an applicant with the National Futures Association shall be reviewed by the National Futures Association, and no such agreement shall be a satisfactory subordination agreement for the purposes of this section unless and until the National Futures Association has found the agreement acceptable and such agreement has become effective in the form found acceptable. A proposed agreement filed by a registrant shall be reviewed by the designated self-regulatory organization with whom such an agreement is required to be filed prior to its becoming effective or, if the registrant is not a member of any designated self-regulatory organization, by the regional office of the Commission where the agreement is required to be filed prior to its becoming effective. No proposed agreement shall be a satisfactory subordination agreement for the purposes of this section unless and until the designated self-regulatory organization or, if a registrant is not a member of any designated self-regulatory organization, the Commission, has found the agreement acceptable and such agreement has become effective in the form found acceptable: Provided, however, That a proposed agreement shall be a satisfactory subordination agreement for purpose of this section if the registrant: is a securities broker or dealer registered with the Securities and Exchange Commission; files signed copies of the proposed subordination agreement with the applicable securities designated examining authority, as defined in Rule 15c3-1(c)(12) of the Securities and Exchange Commission (17 CFR 240.15c3-1(c)(12)), in the form and manner prescribed by the designated examining authority; files signed copies of the proposed subordination agreement with the designated self-regulatory organization at the time it files such copies with the designated examining authority in the form and manner prescribed by the designated self-regulatory organization; and files a copy of the designated examining authority's approval of the proposed subordination agreement with the designated self-regulatory organization immediately upon receipt of such approval. The designated examining authority's determination that the proposed subordination agreement satisfies the requirements for a satisfactory subordination agreement will be deemed a like finding by the designated self-regulatory organization, unless the designated self-regulatory organization notifies the registrant that the designated examining authority's determination shall not constitute a like finding by the designated self-regulatory organization.

(vii) *Subordination agreements that incorporate adjusted net capital requirements in effect prior to September 30, 2004.* Any subordination agreement that incorporates the adjusted net capital requirements in paragraphs (h)(2)(vi)(C)(*2*), (h)(2)(vii)(A)(*2*) and (B)(*2*), (h)(2)(viii)(A)(*2*), (h)(3)(ii)(B), and (h)(3)(v)(B) of this section, as in effect prior to September 30, 2004, and which has been deemed to be satisfactorily subordinated pursuant to this section prior to September 30, 2004, shall continue to be deemed a satisfactory subordination agreement until the maturity of such agreement. In the event, however, that such agreement is amended or renewed for any reason, then such agreement shall not be deemed a satisfactory subordination agreement unless the amended or renewed agreement meets the requirements of this section.

(4) A designated self-regulatory organization and the Commission may allow debt with a maturity date of 1 year or more to be treated as meeting the provisions of this paragraph (h): *Provided,* (i) Such exemption shall only be given when the registrant's adjusted net capital is less than the minimum required by this section or by the capital rule of the designated self-regulatory organization to which such registrant is subject;

(ii) That such debt did not exist prior to its use under this paragraph (h)(4);

(iii) Such exemption shall be for a period of 30 days or such lesser period as the designated self-regulatory organization and the Commission may determine;

(iv) Such exemption shall not be allowed more than once in any 12 month period; and

(v) At all times during such exemption the registrant shall make a good faith effort to comply with the provisions of this section or the capital rule of the designated self-regulatory organization to which such registrant is subject exclusive of any benefits derived from this paragraph (h)(4).

(j) For the purposes of this section *cover* is defined as follows:

(1) *General definition.* Cover shall mean transactions or positions in a contract for future delivery on a board of trade or a commodity option where such transactions or positions normally represent a substitute for transactions to be made or positions to be taken at a later time in a physical marketing channel, and where they are economically appropriate to the reduction of risks in the conduct and management of a commercial enterprise, and where they arise from:

(i) The potential change in the value of assets which a person owns, produces, manufactures, processes, or merchandises or anticipates owning, producing, manufacturing, processing, or merchandising.

(ii) The potential change in the value of liabilities which a person owes or anticipates incurring, or

(iii) The potential change in the value of services which a person provides, purchases or anticipates providing or purchasing. Notwithstanding the foregoing, no transactions or positions shall be classified as cover for the purposes of this section unless their purpose is to offset price risks incidental to commercial cash or spot operations and such positions are established and liquidated in accordance with sound commercial practices and unless the provisions of paragraphs (j) (2) and (3) of this section have been satisfied.

(2) *Enumerated cover transactions.* The definition of covered transactions and positions in paragraph (j)(1) of this section includes, but is not limited to, the following specific transactions and positions:

(i) Ownership or fixed-price purchase of any commodity which does not exceed in quantity (A) the sales of the same commodity for future delivery on a board of trade or (B) the purchase of a put commodity option of the same commodity for which the market value for the actual commodity or futures contract which is the subject of the option is less than the strike price of the option or (C) the ownership of a commodity option position established by the sale (grant) of a call commodity option of the same commodity for which the market value for the actual commodity or futures contract which is the subject of the option is more than the strike price of the option: *Provided,* That for purposes of paragraph (c)(5)(x) of this section the market value for the actual commodity or futures contract which is the subject of such option need not be more than the strike price of that option;

(ii) Fixed-price sale of any commodity which does not exceed in quantity (A) the purchase of the same commodity for future delivery on a board of trade or (B) the purchase of a call commodity option of the same commodity for which the market value for the actual commodity or futures contract which is the subject of such option is more than the strike price of the option or (C) ownership of a commodity option position established by the sale (grant) of a put commodity option of the same commodity for which the market value for the actual commodity or futures comtract which is the subject of the option is less than the strike price of the option: *Provided,* That for purposes of paragraph (c)(5)(x) of this section the market value for the actual commodity or futures contract which is the subject of such option need not be less than the strike price of that option; and

(iii) Ownership or fixed-price contracts of a commodity described in paragraphs (j)(2)(i) and (j)(2)(ii) of this section may also be covered other than by the same quantity of the same cash commodity, provided that the fluctuations in value of the position for future delivery or commodity option are substantially related to the fluctuations in value of the actual cash position.

(3) *Nonenumerated cases.* Upon specific request, the Commission may recognize transactions and positions other than those enumerated in paragraph (j)(2) of this section as cover in amounts and under the terms and conditions as it may specify. Any applicant or registrant who wishes to avail itself of the provisions of this paragraph (j)(3) must apply to the Commission in writing at its principal office in Washington, DC giving full details of the transaction including detailed information which will demonstrate that the transaction is economically appropriate to the reduction of risk exposure attendant to the conduct and management of a commercial enterprise.

(Approved by the Office of Management and Budget under control number 3038-0024)

[43 FR 39972, Sept. 8, 1978]

EDITORIAL NOTE: For FEDERAL REGISTER citations affecting § 1.17, see the List of CFR Sections Affected, which appears in the Finding Aids section of the printed volume and at *www.fdsys.gov* .

§ 1.18 RECORDS FOR AND RELATING TO FINANCIAL REPORTING AND MONTHLY COMPUTATION BY FUTURES COMMISSION MERCHANTS AND INTRODUCING BROKERS.

(a) No person shall be registered as a futures commission merchant or as an introducing broker under the Act unless, commencing on the date his application for such registration is filed, he prepares and keeps current ledgers or other similar records which show or summarize, with appropriate references to supporting documents, each transaction affecting his asset, liability, income, expense and capital accounts, and in which (except as otherwise permitted in writing by the Commission) all his asset, liability and capital accounts are classified into either the account classification subdivisions specified on Form 1-FR-FCM or Form 1-FR-IB, respectively, or, if such person is registered with the Securities and Exchange Commission as a securities broker or dealer and he files (in accordance with § 1.10(h)) a copy of his Financial and Operational Combined Uniform Single Report under the Securities Exchange Act of 1934, Part II, Part IIA, or Part II CSE (FOCUS report) in lieu of Form 1-FR-FCM or Form 1-FR-IB, the account classification subdivisions specified on such FOCUS report, or categories that are in accord with generally accepted accounting principles. Each person so registered shall prepare and keep current such records.

(b)(1) Each applicant or registrant must make and keep as a record in accordance with § 1.31 formal computations of its adjusted net capital and of its minimum financial requirements pursuant to § 1.17 or the requirements of the designated self-regulatory organization to which it is subject as of the close of business each month. Such computations must be completed and made available for inspection by any representative of the National Futures Association, in the case of an applicant, or of the Commission or designated self-regulatory organization, if any, in the case of a registrant, within 17 business days after the date for which the computations are made, commencing the first month end after the date the application for registration is filed.

(2) An applicant or registrant that has filed a monthly Form 1-FR or Statement of Financial and Operational Combined Uniform Single Report under the Securities Exchange Act of 1934, Part II, Part IIA, or Part II CSE (FOCUS report) in accordance with the requirements of § 1.10(b) will be deemed to have satisfied the requirements of paragraph (b)(1) of this section for such month.

(c) The provisions of this section do not apply to an introducing broker which is operating pursuant to a guarantee agreement, nor do such provisions apply to an applicant for registration as an introducing broker who files concurrently with such application a guarantee agreement, provided such introducing broker or applicant therefor is not also a securities broker or dealer.

PROHIBITED TRADING IN COMMODITY OPTIONS

§ 1.19 PROHIBITED TRADING IN CERTAIN "PUTS" AND "CALLS".

No futures commission merchant or introducing broker may make, underwrite, issue, or otherwise assume any financial responsibility for the fulfillment of, any commodity option except:

(a) Commodity options traded on or subject to the rules of a contract market in accordance with the requirements of part 33 of this chapter;

(b) Commodity options traded on or subject to the rules of a foreign board of trade in accordance with the requirements of part 30 of this chapter; or

(c) For futures commission merchants, any option permitted under § 32.4 of this chapter, *provided however,* that a capital treatment for such options is referenced in § 1.17(c)(5)(vi).

[52 FR 28997, Aug. 5, 1987, as amended at 58 FR 68520, Dec. 28, 1993]

CUSTOMERS' MONEY, SECURITIES, AND PROPERTY

§ 1.20 FUTURES CUSTOMER FUNDS TO BE SEGREGATED AND SEPARATELY ACCOUNTED FOR.

(a) All futures customer funds shall be separately accounted for and segregated as belonging to futures customers. Such futures customer funds when deposited with any bank, trust company, derivatives clearing organization or another futures commission merchant shall be deposited under an account name which clearly identifies them as such and shows that they are segregated as required by sections 4d(a) and 4d(b) of the Act and this part. Each registrant shall obtain and retain in its files for the period provided in § 1.31 a written acknowledgment from such bank, trust company, derivatives clearing organization, or futures commission merchant, that it was informed that the futures customer funds deposited therein are those of futures customers and are being held in accordance with the provisions of the Act and this part: *Provided, however,* that an acknowledgment need not be obtained from a derivatives clearing organization that has adopted and submitted to the Commission rules that provide for the segregation as futures customer funds, in accordance with all relevant provisions of the Act and the rules and orders promulgated thereunder, of all funds held on behalf of futures customers. Under no circumstances shall any portion of futures customer funds be obligated to a derivatives clearing organization, any member of a contract market, a futures commission merchant, or any depository except to purchase, margin, guarantee, secure, transfer, adjust or settle trades, contracts or commodity option transactions of futures customers. No person, including any derivatives clearing organization or any depository, that has received futures customer funds for deposit in a segregated account, as provided in this section, may hold, dispose of, or use any such funds as belonging to any person other than the futures customers of the futures commission merchant which deposited such funds.

(b) All futures customer funds received by a derivatives clearing organization from a member of the derivatives clearing organization to purchase, margin, guarantee, secure or settle the trades, contracts or commodity options of the clearing member's futures customers and all money accruing to such futures customers as the result of trades, contracts or commodity options so carried shall be separately accounted for and segregated as belonging to such futures customers, and a derivatives clearing organization shall not hold, use or dispose of such futures customer funds except as belonging to such futures customers. Such futures customer funds when deposited in a bank or trust company shall be deposited under an account name which clearly shows that they are the futures customer funds of the futures customers of clearing members, segregated as required by sections 4d(a) and 4d(b) of the Act and these regulations. The derivatives clearing organization shall obtain and retain in its files for the period provided by § 1.31 an acknowledgment from such bank or trust company that it was informed that the futures customer funds deposited therein are those of futures customers of its clearing members and are being held in accordance with the provisions of the Act and these regulations.

(c) Each futures commission merchant shall treat and deal with the futures customer funds of a futures customer as belonging to such futures customer. All futures customer funds shall be separately accounted for, and shall not be commingled with the money, securities or property of a futures commission merchant or of any other person, or be used to secure or guarantee the trades, contracts or commodity options, or to secure or extend the credit, of any person other than the one for whom the same are held: *Provided, however,* That futures customer funds treated as belonging to the futures customers of a futures commission merchant may for convenience be commingled and deposited in the same account or accounts with any bank or trust company, with another person registered as a futures commission merchant, or with a derivatives clearing organization, and that such share thereof as in the normal course of business is necessary to purchase, margin, guarantee, secure, transfer, adjust, or settle the trades, contracts or commodity options of such futures customers or resulting market positions, with the derivatives clearing organization or with any other person registered as a futures commission merchant, may be withdrawn and applied to such purposes, including the payment of premiums to option grantors, commissions, brokerage, interest, taxes, storage and other fees and charges, lawfully accruing in connection with such trades, contracts or commodity options: *Provided further,* That futures customer funds may be invested in instruments described in § 1.25.

§ 1.21 CARE OF MONEY AND EQUITIES ACCRUING TO FUTURES CUSTOMERS.

All money received directly or indirectly by, and all money and equities accruing to, a futures commission merchant from any derivatives clearing organization or from any clearing member or from any member of a contract market incident to or resulting from any trade, contract or commodity option made by or through such futures commission merchant on behalf of any futures customer shall be considered as accruing to such futures customer within the meaning of the Act and these regulations. Such money and equities shall be treated and dealt with as belonging to such futures customer in accordance with the provisions of the Act and these regulations. Money and equities accruing in connection with futures customers' open trades, contracts, or commodity options need not be separately credited to individual accounts but may be treated and dealt with as belonging undivided to all futures customers having open trades, contracts, or commodity option positions which if closed would result in a credit to such futures customers.

§ 1.22 USE OF FUTURES CUSTOMER FUNDS RESTRICTED.

No futures commission merchant shall use, or permit the use of, the futures customer funds of one futures customer to purchase, margin, or settle the trades, contracts, or commodity options of, or to secure or extend the credit of, any person other than such futures customer. Futures customer funds shall not be used to carry trades or positions of the same futures customer other than in commodities or commodity options traded through the facilities of a contract market.

§ 1.23 INTEREST OF FUTURES COMMISSION MERCHANT IN SEGREGATED FUTURES CUSTOMER FUNDS; ADDITIONS AND WITHDRAWALS.

The provisions in section 4d(a) and 4d(b) of the Act and the provision in § 1.20(c), which prohibit the commingling of futures customer funds with the funds of a futures commission merchant, shall not be construed to prevent a futures commission merchant from having a residual financial interest in the futures customer funds, segregated as required by the Act and the rules in this part and set apart for the benefit of futures customers; nor shall such provisions be construed to prevent a futures commission merchant from adding to such segregated futures customer funds such amount or amounts of money, from its own funds or unencumbered securities from its own inventory, of the type set forth in § 1.25, as it may deem necessary to ensure any and all futures customers' accounts from becoming undersegregated at any time. The books and records of a futures commission merchant shall at all times accurately reflect its interest in the segregated funds. A futures commission merchant may draw upon such segregated funds to its own order, to the extent of its actual interest therein, including the withdrawal of securities held in segregated safekeeping accounts held by a bank, trust company, contract market, derivatives clearing organization or other futures commission merchant. Such withdrawal shall not result in the funds of one futures customer being used to purchase, margin or carry the trades, contracts or commodity options, or extend the credit of any other futures customer or other person.

§ 1.24 SEGREGATED FUNDS; EXCLUSIONS THEREFROM.

Money held in a segregated account by a futures commission merchant shall not include: (a) Money invested in obligations or stocks of any derivatives clearing organization or in memberships in or obligations of any contract market; or

(b) Money held by any derivatives clearing organization which it may use for any purpose other than to purchase, margin, guarantee, secure, transfer, adjust, or settle the contracts, trades, or commodity options of the futures customers of such futures commission merchant.

§ 1.25 INVESTMENT OF CUSTOMER FUNDS.

(a) *Permitted investments.* (1) Subject to the terms and conditions set forth in this section, a futures commission merchant or a derivatives clearing organization may invest customer money in the following instruments (permitted investments):

(i) Obligations of the United States and obligations fully guaranteed as to principal and interest by the United States (U.S. government securities);

(ii) General obligations of any State or of any political subdivision thereof (municipal securities);

(iii) Obligations of any United States government corporation or enterprise sponsored by the United States government (U.S. agency obligations);

(iv) Certificates of deposit issued by a bank (certificates of deposit) as defined in section 3(a)(6) of the Securities Exchange Act of 1934, or a domestic branch of a foreign bank that carries deposits insured by the Federal Deposit Insurance Corporation;

(v) Commercial paper fully guaranteed as to principal and interest by the United States under the Temporary Liquidity Guarantee Program as administered by the Federal Deposit Insurance Corporation (commercial paper);

(vi) Corporate notes or bonds fully guaranteed as to principal and interest by the United States under the Temporary Liquidity Guarantee Program as administered by the Federal Deposit Insurance Corporation (corporate notes or bonds); and

(vii) Interests in money market mutual funds.

(2)(i) In addition, a futures commission merchant or derivatives clearing organization may buy and sell the permitted investments listed in paragraphs (a)(1)(i) through (vii) of this section pursuant to agreements for resale or repurchase of the instruments, in accordance with the provisions of paragraph (d) of this section.

(ii) A futures commission merchant or a derivatives clearing organization may sell securities deposited by customers as margin pursuant to agreements to repurchase subject to the following:

(A) Securities subject to such repurchase agreements must be "highly liquid" as defined in paragraph (b)(1) of this section.

(B) Securities subject to such repurchase agreements must not be "specifically identifiable property" as defined in § 190.01(kk) of this chapter.

(C) The terms and conditions of such an agreement to repurchase must be in accordance with the provisions of paragraph (d) of this section.

(D) Upon the default by a counterparty to a repurchase agreement, the futures commission merchant or derivatives clearing organization shall act promptly to ensure that the default does not result in any direct or indirect cost or expense to the customer.

(3) Obligations issued by the Federal National Mortgage Association or the Federal Home Loan Mortgage Association are permitted while these entities operate under the conservatorship or receivership of the Federal Housing Finance Authority with capital support from the United States.

(b) *General terms and conditions.* A futures commission merchant or a derivatives clearing organization is required to manage the permitted investments consistent with the objectives of preserving principal and maintaining liquidity and according to the following specific requirements:

(1) *Liquidity.* Investments must be "highly liquid" such that they have the ability to be converted into cash within one business day without material discount in value.

(2) *Restrictions on instrument features.* (i) With the exception of money market mutual funds, no permitted investment may contain an embedded derivative of any kind, except as follows:

(A) The issuer of an instrument otherwise permitted by this section may have an option to call, in whole or in part, at par, the principal amount of the instrument before its stated maturity date; or

(B) An instrument that meets the requirements of paragraph (b)(2)(iv) of this section may provide for a cap, floor, or collar on the interest paid; *provided, however,* that the terms of such instrument obligate the issuer to repay the principal amount of the instrument at not less than par value upon maturity.

(ii) No instrument may contain interest-only payment features.

(iii) No instrument may provide payments linked to a commodity, currency, reference instrument, index, or benchmark except as provided in paragraph (b)(2)(iv) of this section, and it may not otherwise constitute a derivative instrument.

(iv)(A) Adjustable rate securities are permitted, subject to the following requirements:

(*1*) The interest payments on variable rate securities must correlate closely and on an unleveraged basis to a benchmark of either the Federal Funds target or effective rate, the prime rate, the three-month Treasury Bill rate, the one-month or three-month LIBOR rate, or the interest rate of any fixed rate instrument that is a permitted investment listed in paragraph (a)(1) of this section;

(*2*) The interest payment, in any period, on floating rate securities must be determined solely by reference, on an unleveraged basis, to a benchmark of either the Federal Funds target or effective rate, the prime rate, the three-month Treasury Bill rate, the one-month or three-month LIBOR rate, or the interest rate of any fixed rate instrument that is a permitted investment listed in paragraph (a)(1) of this section;

(*3*) Benchmark rates must be expressed in the same currency as the adjustable rate securities that reference them; and

(*4*) No interest payment on an adjustable rate security, in any period, can be a negative amount.

(B) For purposes of this paragraph, the following definitions shall apply:

(*1*) The term *adjustable rate security* means, a floating rate security, a variable rate security, or both.

(*2*) The term *floating rate security* means a security, the terms of which provide for the adjustment of its interest rate whenever a specified interest rate changes and that, at any time until the final maturity of the instrument or the period remaining until the principal amount can be recovered through demand, can reasonably be expected to have market value that approximates its amortized cost.

(*3*) The term *variable rate security* means a security, the terms of which provide for the adjustment of its interest rate on set dates (such as the last day of a month or calendar quarter) and that, upon each adjustment until the final maturity of the instrument or the period remaining until the principal amount can be recovered through demand, can reasonably be expected to have a market value that approximates its amortized cost.

(v) Certificates of deposit must be redeemable at the issuing bank within one business day, with any penalty for early withdrawal limited to any accrued interest earned according to its written terms.

(vi) Commercial paper and corporate notes or bonds must meet the following criteria:

(A) The size of the issuance must be greater than $1 billion;

(B) The instrument must be denominated in U.S. dollars; and

(C) The instrument must be fully guaranteed as to principal and interest by the United States for its entire term.

(3) *Concentration* —(i) *Asset-based concentration limits for direct investments.* (A) Investments in U.S. government securities shall not be subject to a concentration limit.

(B) Investments in U.S. agency obligations may not exceed 50 percent of the total assets held in segregation by the futures commission merchant or derivatives clearing organization.

(C) Investments in each of commercial paper, corporate notes or bonds and certificates of deposit may not exceed 25 percent of the total assets held in segregation by the futures commission merchant or derivatives clearing organization.

(D) Investments in municipal securities may not exceed 10 percent of the total assets held in segregation by the futures commission merchant or derivatives clearing organization.

(E) Subject to paragraph (b)(3)(i)(G) of this section, investments in money market mutual funds comprising only U.S. government securities shall not be subject to a concentration limit.

(F) Subject to paragraph (b)(3)(i)(G) of this section, investments in money market mutual funds, other than those described in paragraph (b)(3)(i)(E) of this section, may not exceed 50 percent of the total assets held in segregation by the futures commission merchant or derivatives clearing organization.

(G) Investments in money market mutual funds comprising less than $1 billion in assets and/or which have a management company comprising less than $25 billion in assets, may not exceed 10 percent of the total assets held in segregation by the futures commission merchant or derivatives clearing organization.

(ii) *Issuer-based concentration limits for direct investments.* (A) Securities of any single issuer of U.S. agency obligations held by a futures commission merchant or derivatives clearing organization may not exceed 25 percent of total assets held in segregation by the futures commission merchant or derivatives clearing organization.

(B) Securities of any single issuer of municipal securities, certificates of deposit, commercial paper, or corporate notes or bonds held by a futures commission merchant or derivatives clearing organization may not exceed 5 percent of total assets held in segregation by the futures commission merchant or derivatives clearing organization.

(C) Interests in any single family of money market mutual funds described in paragraph (b)(3)(i)(F) of this section may not exceed 25 percent of total assets held in segregation by the futures commission merchant or derivatives clearing organization.

(D) Interests in any individual money market mutual fund described in paragraph (b)(3)(i)(F) of this section may not exceed 10 percent of total assets held in segregation by the futures commission merchant or derivatives clearing organization.

(E) For purposes of determining compliance with the issuer-based concentration limits set forth in this section, securities issued by entities that are affiliated, as defined in paragraph (b)(5) of this section, shall be aggregated and deemed the securities of a single issuer. An interest in a permitted money market mutual fund is not deemed to be a security issued by its sponsoring entity.

(iii) *Concentration limits for agreements to repurchase* —(A) *Repurchase agreements.* For purposes of determining compliance with the asset-based and issuer-based concentration limits set forth in this section, securities sold by a futures commission merchant or derivatives clearing organization subject to agreements to repurchase shall be combined with securities held by the futures commission merchant or derivatives clearing organization as direct investments.

(B) *Reverse repurchase agreements.* For purposes of determining compliance with the asset-based and issuer-based concentration limits set forth in this section, securities purchased by a futures commission merchant or derivatives clearing organization subject to agreements to resell shall be combined with securities held by the futures commission merchant or derivatives clearing organization as direct investments.

(iv) *Treatment of customer-owned securities.* For purposes of determining compliance with the asset-based and issuer-based concentration limits set forth in this section, securities owned by the customers of a futures commission merchant and posted as margin collateral are not included in total assets held in segregation by the futures commission merchant, and securities posted by a futures commission merchant with a derivatives clearing organization are not included in total assets held in segregation by the derivatives clearing organization.

(v) *Counterparty concentration limits.* Securities purchased by a futures commission merchant or derivatives clearing organization from a single counterparty, subject to an agreement to resell to that counterparty, shall not exceed 25 percent of total assets held in segregation by the futures commission merchant or derivatives clearing organization.

(4) *Time-to-maturity.* (i) Except for investments in money market mutual funds, the dollar-weighted average of the time-to-maturity of the portfolio, as that average is computed pursuant to § 270.2a-7 of this title, may not exceed 24 months.

(ii) For purposes of determining the time-to-maturity of the portfolio, an instrument that is set forth in paragraphs (a)(1)(i) through (vii) of this section may be treated as having a one-day time-to-maturity if the following terms and conditions are satisfied:

(A) The instrument is deposited solely on an overnight basis with a derivatives clearing organization pursuant to the terms and conditions of a collateral management program that has become effective in accordance with § 39.4 of this chapter;

(B) The instrument is one that the futures commission merchant owns or has an unqualified right to pledge, is not subject to any lien, and is deposited by the futures commission merchant into a segregated account at a derivatives clearing organization;

(C) The derivatives clearing organization prices the instrument each day based on the current mark-to-market value; and

(D) The derivatives clearing organization reduces the assigned value of the instrument each day by a haircut of at least 2 percent.

(5) *Investments in instruments issued by affiliates.* (i) A futures commission merchant shall not invest customer funds in obligations of an entity affiliated with the futures commission merchant, and a derivatives clearing organization shall not invest customer funds in obligations of an entity affiliated with the derivatives clearing organization. An affiliate includes parent companies, including all entities through the ultimate holding company, subsidiaries to the lowest level, and companies under common ownership of such parent company or affiliates.

(ii) A futures commission merchant or derivatives clearing organization may invest customer funds in a fund affiliated with that futures commission merchant or derivatives clearing organization.

(6) *Recordkeeping.* A futures commission merchant and a derivatives clearing organization shall prepare and maintain a record that will show for each business day with respect to each type of investment made pursuant to this section, the following information:

(i) The type of instruments in which customer funds have been invested;

(ii) The original cost of the instruments; and

(iii) The current market value of the instruments.

(c) *Money market mutual funds.* The following provisions will apply to the investment of customer funds in money market mutual funds (the fund).

(1) The fund must be an investment company that is registered under the Investment Company Act of 1940 with the Securities and Exchange Commission and that holds itself out to investors as a money market fund, in accordance with § 270.2a-7 of this title.

(2) The fund must be sponsored by a federally-regulated financial institution, a bank as defined in section 3(a)(6) of the Securities Exchange Act of 1934, an investment adviser registered under the Investment Advisers Act of 1940, or a domestic branch of a foreign bank insured by the Federal Deposit Insurance Corporation.

(3) A futures commission merchant or derivatives clearing organization shall maintain the confirmation relating to the purchase in its records in accordance with § 1.31 and note the ownership of fund shares (by book-entry or otherwise) in a custody account of the futures commission merchant or derivatives clearing organization in accordance with §§ 1.26 and 22.5 of this chapter. The futures commission merchant or the derivatives clearing organization shall obtain the acknowledgment letter required by §§ 1.26 and 22.5 of this chapter from an entity that has substantial control over the fund shares purchased with customer funds and has the knowledge and authority to facilitate redemption and payment or transfer of the customer funds. Such entity may include the fund sponsor or depository acting as custodian for fund shares.

(4) The net asset value of the fund must be computed by 9 a.m. of the business day following each business day and made available to the futures commission merchant or derivatives clearing organization by that time.

(5)(i) General requirement for redemption of interests. A fund shall be legally obligated to redeem an interest and to make payment in satisfaction thereof by the business day following a redemption request, and the futures commission merchant or derivatives clearing organization shall retain documentation demonstrating compliance with this requirement.

(ii) Exception. A fund may provide for the postponement of redemption and payment due to any of the following circumstances:

(A) For any period during which there is a non-routine closure of the Fedwire or applicable Federal Reserve Banks;

(B) For any period:

(*1*) During which the New York Stock Exchange is closed other than customary week-end and holiday closings; or

(*2*) During which trading on the New York Stock Exchange is restricted;

(C) For any period during which an emergency exists as a result of which:

(*1*) Disposal by the company of securities owned by it is not reasonably practicable; or

(*2*) It is not reasonably practicable for such company fairly to determine the value of its net assets;

(D) For any period as the Securities and Exchange Commission may by order permit for the protection of security holders of the company;

(E) For any period during which the Securities and Exchange Commission has, by rule or regulation, deemed that:

(*1*) Trading shall be restricted; or

(*2*) An emergency exists; or

(F) For any period during which each of the conditions of § 270.22e-3(a)(1) through (3) of this title are met.

(6) The agreement pursuant to which the futures commission merchant or derivatives clearing organization has acquired and is holding its interest in a fund must contain no provision that would prevent the pledging or transferring of shares.

(7) The appendix to this section sets forth language that will satisfy the requirements of paragraph (c)(5) of this section.

(d) *Repurchase and reverse repurchase agreements.* A futures commission merchant or derivatives clearing organization may buy and sell the permitted investments listed in paragraphs (a)(1)(i) through (vii) of this section pursuant to agreements for resale or repurchase of the securities (agreements to repurchase or resell), provided the agreements to repurchase or resell conform to the following requirements:

(1) The securities are specifically identified by coupon rate, par amount, market value, maturity date, and CUSIP or ISIN number.

(2) Permitted counterparties are limited to a bank as defined in section 3(a)(6) of the Securities Exchange Act of 1934, a domestic branch of a foreign bank insured by the Federal Deposit Insurance Corporation, a securities broker or dealer, or a government securities broker or government securities dealer registered with the Securities and Exchange Commission or which has filed notice pursuant to section 15C(a) of the Government Securities Act of 1986.

(3) A futures commission merchant or derivatives clearing organization shall not enter into an agreement to repurchase or resell with a counterparty that is an affiliate of the futures commission merchant or derivatives clearing organization, respectively. An affiliate includes parent companies, including all entities through the ultimate holding company, subsidiaries to the lowest level, and companies under common ownership of such parent company or affiliates.

(4) The transaction is executed in compliance with the concentration limit requirements applicable to the securities transferred to the customer segregated custodial account in connection with the agreements to repurchase referred to in paragraphs (b)(3)(iii)(A) and (B) of this section.

(5) The transaction is made pursuant to a written agreement signed by the parties to the agreement, which is consistent with the conditions set forth in paragraphs (d)(1) through (13) of this section and which states that the parties thereto intend the transaction to be treated as a purchase and sale of securities.

(6) The term of the agreement is no more than one business day, or reversal of the transaction is possible on demand.

(7) Securities transferred to the futures commission merchant or derivatives clearing organization under the agreement are held in a safekeeping account with a bank as referred to in paragraph (d)(2) of this section, a derivatives clearing organization, or the Depository Trust Company in an account that complies with the requirements of § 1.26.

(8) The futures commission merchant or the derivatives clearing organization may not use securities received under the agreement in another similar transaction and may not otherwise hypothecate or pledge such securities, except securities may be pledged on behalf of customers at another futures commission merchant or derivatives clearing organization. Substitution of securities is allowed, *provided, however,* that:

(i) The qualifying securities being substituted and original securities are specifically identified by date of substitution, market values substituted, coupon rates, par amounts, maturity dates and CUSIP or ISIN numbers;

(ii) Substitution is made on a “delivery versus delivery” basis; and

(iii) The market value of the substituted securities is at least equal to that of the original securities.

(9) The transfer of securities to the customer segregated custodial account is made on a delivery versus payment basis in immediately available funds. The transfer of funds to the customer segregated cash account is made on a payment versus delivery basis. The transfer is not recognized as accomplished until the funds and/or securities are actually received by the custodian of the futures commission merchant's or derivatives clearing organization's customer funds or securities purchased on behalf of customers. The transfer or credit of securities covered by the agreement to the futures commission merchant's or derivatives clearing organization's customer segregated custodial account is made simultaneously with the disbursement of funds from the futures commission merchant's or derivatives clearing organization's customer segregated cash account at the custodian bank. On the sale or resale of securities, the futures commission merchant's or derivatives clearing organization's customer segregated cash account at the custodian bank must receive same-day funds credited to such segregated account simultaneously with the delivery or transfer of securities from the customer segregated custodial account.

(10) A written confirmation to the futures commission merchant or derivatives clearing organization specifying the terms of the agreement and a safekeeping receipt are issued immediately upon entering into the transaction and a confirmation to the futures commission merchant or derivatives clearing organization is issued once the transaction is reversed.

(11) The transactions effecting the agreement are recorded in the record required to be maintained under § 1.27 of investments of customer funds, and the securities subject to such transactions are specifically identified in such record as described in paragraph (d)(1) of this section and further identified in such record as being subject to repurchase and reverse repurchase agreements.

(12) An actual transfer of securities to the customer segregated custodial account by book entry is made consistent with Federal or State commercial law, as applicable. At all times, securities received subject to an agreement are reflected as "customer property."

(13) The agreement makes clear that, in the event of the bankruptcy of the futures commission merchant or derivatives clearing organization, any securities purchased with customer funds that are subject to an agreement may be immediately transferred. The agreement also makes clear that, in the event of a futures commission merchant or derivatives clearing organization bankruptcy, the counterparty has no right to compel liquidation of securities subject to an agreement or to make a priority claim for the difference between current market value of the securities and the price agreed upon for resale of the securities to the counterparty, if the former exceeds the latter.

(e) *Deposit of firm-owned securities into segregation.* A futures commission merchant shall not be prohibited from directly depositing unencumbered securities of the type specified in this section, which it owns for its own account, into a segregated safekeeping account or from transferring any such securities from a segregated account to its own account, up to the extent of its residual financial interest in customers' segregated funds; *provided, however,* that such investments, transfers of securities, and disposition of proceeds from the sale or maturity of such securities are recorded in the record of investments required to be maintained by § 1.27. All such securities may be segregated in safekeeping only with a bank, trust company, derivatives clearing organization, or other registered futures commission merchant. Furthermore, for purposes of §§ 1.25, 1.27, 1.28, and 1.29, investments permitted by § 1.25 that are owned by the futures commission merchant and deposited into such segregated account shall be considered customer funds until such investments are withdrawn from segregation. Investments permitted by § 1.25 that are owned by the futures commission merchant and deposited into a segregated account pursuant to § 1.26 shall be considered futures customer funds until such investments are withdrawn from segregation. Investments permitted by § 1.25 that are owned by the futures commission merchant and deposited into a segregated account pursuant to § 22.5 of this chapter shall be considered Cleared Swaps Customer Collateral until such investments are withdrawn from segregation.

APPENDIX TO § 1.25—MONEY MARKET MUTUAL FUND PROSPECTUS PROVISIONS ACCEPTABLE FOR COMPLIANCE WITH SECTION 1.25(C)(5)

Upon receipt of a proper redemption request submitted in a timely manner and otherwise in accordance with the redemption procedures set forth in this prospectus, the [Name of Fund] will redeem the requested shares and make a payment to you in satisfaction thereof no later than the business day following the redemption request. The [Name of Fund] may postpone and/or suspend redemption and payment beyond one business day only as follows:

a. For any period during which there is a non-routine closure of the Fedwire or applicable Federal Reserve Banks;

b. For any period (1) during which the New York Stock Exchange is closed other than customary week-end and holiday closings or (2) during which trading on the New York Stock Exchange is restricted;

c. For any period during which an emergency exists as a result of which (1) disposal of securities owned by the [Name of Fund] is not reasonably practicable or (2) it is not reasonably practicable for the [Name of Fund] to fairly determine the net asset value of shares of the [Name of Fund];

d. For any period during which the Securities and Exchange Commission has, by rule or regulation, deemed that (1) trading shall be restricted or (2) an emergency exists;

e. For any period that the Securities and Exchange Commission, may by order permit for your protection; or

f. For any period during which the [Name of Fund,] as part of a necessary liquidation of the fund, has properly postponed and/or suspended redemption of shares and payment in accordance with federal securities laws.

[76 FR 78798, Dec. 19, 2011, as amended at 77 FR 66322, Nov. 2, 2012]

§ 1.26 DEPOSIT OF INSTRUMENTS PURCHASED WITH FUTURES CUSTOMER FUNDS.

(a) Each futures commission merchant who invests futures customer funds in instruments described in § 1.25 shall separately account for such instruments and segregate such instruments as belonging to such futures customers. Such instruments, when deposited with a bank, trust company, derivatives clearing organization or another futures commission merchant, shall be deposited under an account name which clearly shows that they belong to futures customers and are segregated as required by the Act and this part. Each futures commission merchant upon opening such an account shall obtain and retain in its files an acknowledgment from such bank, trust company, derivatives clearing organization or other futures commission merchant that it was informed that the instruments belong to futures customers and are being held in accordance with the provisions of the Act and this part. *Provided, however,* that an acknowledgment need not be obtained from a derivatives clearing organization that has adopted and submitted to the Commission rules that provide for the segregation as futures customer funds, in accordance with all relevant provisions of the Act and the rules and orders promulgated thereunder, of all funds held on behalf of futures customers and all instruments purchased with futures customer funds. Such acknowledgment shall be retained in accordance with § 1.31. Such bank, trust company, derivatives clearing organization or other futures commission merchant shall allow inspection of such obligations at any reasonable time by representatives of the Commission.

(b) Each derivatives clearing organization which invests money belonging or accruing to futures customers of its clearing members in instruments described in § 1.25 shall separately account for such instruments and segregate such instruments as belonging to such futures customers. Such instruments, when deposited with a bank or trust company, shall be deposited under an account name which will clearly show that they belong to futures customers and are segregated as required by the Act and this part. Each derivatives clearing organization upon opening such an account shall obtain and retain in its files a written acknowledgment from such bank or trust company that it was informed that the instruments belong to futures customers of clearing members and are being held in accordance with the provisions of the Act and this part. Such acknowledgment shall be retained in accordance with § 1.31. Such bank or trust company shall allow inspection of such instruments at any reasonable time by representatives of the Commission.

§ 1.27 Record of investments.

(a) Each futures commission merchant which invests customer funds, and each derivatives clearing organization which invests customer funds of its clearing members' customers, shall keep a record showing the following:

(1) The date on which such investments were made;

(2) The name of the person through whom such investments were made;

(3) The amount of money or current market value of securities so invested;

(4) A description of the instruments in which such investments were made, including the CUSIP or ISIN numbers;

(5) The identity of the depositories or other places where such instruments are segregated;

(6) The date on which such investments were liquidated or otherwise disposed of and the amount of money or current market value of securities received on such disposition, if any; and

(7) The name of the person to or through whom such investments were disposed of; and

(8) Daily valuation for each instrument and readily available documentation supporting the daily valuation for each instrument. Such supporting documentation must be sufficient to enable auditors to verify the valuations and the accuracy of any information from external sources used in those valuations.

(b) Each derivatives clearing organization which receives documents from its clearing members representing investment of customer funds shall keep a record showing separately for each clearing member the following:

(1) The date on which such documents were received from the clearing member;

(2) A description of such documents, including the CUSIP or ISIN numbers; and

(3) The date on which such documents were returned to the clearing member or the details of disposition by other means.

(c) Such records shall be retained in accordance with § 1.31. No such investments shall be made except in instruments described in § 1.25.

(Approved by the Office of Management and Budget under control numbers 3038-0007 and 3038-0024)

[46 FR 54520, Nov. 3, 1981, as amended at 46 FR 63035, Dec. 30, 1981; 62 FR 42401, Aug. 7, 1997; 65 FR 78013, Dec. 13, 2000; 70 FR 28204, May 17, 2005; 77 FR 66322, Nov. 2, 2012]

§ 1.28 APPRAISAL OF INSTRUMENTS PURCHASED WITH CUSTOMER FUNDS.

Futures commission merchants who invest customer funds in instruments described in § 1.25 of this part shall include such instruments in segregated account records and reports at values which at no time exceed current market value, determined as of the close of the market on the date for which such computation is made.

[58 FR 10953, Feb. 23, 1993, as amended at 65 FR 78013, Dec. 13, 2000]

§ 1.29 INCREMENT OR INTEREST RESULTING FROM INVESTMENT OF CUSTOMER FUNDS.

The investment of customer funds in instruments described in § 1.25 shall not prevent the futures commission merchant or derivatives clearing organization so investing such funds from receiving and retaining as its own any increment or interest resulting therefrom.

§ 1.30 LOANS BY FUTURES COMMISSION MERCHANTS; TREATMENT OF PROCEEDS.

Nothing in the regulations in this chapter shall prevent a futures commission merchant from lending its own funds to customers on securities and property pledged by such customers, or from repledging or selling such securities and property pursuant to specific written agreement with such customers. The proceeds of such loans used to purchase, margin, guarantee, or secure the trades, contracts, or commodity options of customers shall be treated and dealt with by a futures commission merchant as belonging to such customers, in accordance with and subject to the provisions of the Act and these regulations.

MISCELLANEOUS

§ 1.40 CROP, MARKET INFORMATION LETTERS, REPORTS; COPIES REQUIRED.

Each futures commission merchant, each retail foreign exchange dealer, each introducing broker, and each member of a contract market or a swap execution facility shall, upon request, furnish or cause to be furnished to the Commission a true copy of any letter, circular, telecommunication, or report published or given general circulation by such futures commission merchant, retail foreign exchange dealer, introducing broker, member or eligible contract participant which concerns crop or market information or conditions that affect or tend to affect the price of any commodity, including any exchange rate, and the true source of or authority for the information contained therein.

§ 1.46 APPLICATION AND CLOSING OUT OF OFFSETTING LONG AND SHORT POSITIONS.

(a) *Application of purchases and sales.* (1) Except with respect to purchases or sales which are for omnibus accounts, or where the customer or account controller has instructed otherwise, any futures commission merchant who, on or subject to the rules of a designated contract market:

(i) Purchases any commodity for future delivery for the account of any customer when the account of such customer at the time of such purchase has a short position in the same future of the same commodity on the same market;

(ii) Sells any commodity for future delivery for the account of any customer when the account of such customer at the time of such sale has a long position in the same future of the same commodity on the same market;

(iii) Purchases a put or call option for the account of any customer when the account of such customer at the time of such purchase has a short put or call option position with the same underlying futures contract or same underlying commodity, strike price, expiration date and contract market as that purchased; or

(iv) Sells a put or call option for the account of any customer when the account of such customer at the time of such sale has a long put or call option position with the same underlying futures contract or same underlying commodity, strike price, expiration date and contract market as that sold—shall on the same day apply such purchase or sale against such previously held short or long futures or option position, as the case may be, and shall, for futures transactions, promptly furnish such customer a statement showing the financial result of the transactions involved and, if applicable, that the account was introduced to the futures commission merchant by an introducing broker and the names of the futures commission merchant and introducing broker.

(2) Any futures commission merchant or retail foreign exchange dealer who:

(i) Engages in a retail forex transaction involving the purchase of any currency for the account of any retail forex customer when the account of such retail forex customer at the time of such purchase has an open retail forex transaction for the sale of the same currency;

(ii) Engages in a retail forex transaction involving the sale of any currency for the account of any retail forex customer when the account of such retail forex customer at the time of such sale has an open retail forex transaction for the purchase of the same currency;

(iii) Purchases a put or call option involving foreign currency for the account of any customer when the account of such customer at the time of such purchase has a short put or call option position with the same underlying currency, strike price, and expiration date as that purchased; or

(iv) Sells a put or call option involving foreign currency for the account of any customer when the account of such customer at the time of such sale has a long put or call option position with the same underlying currency, strike price, and expiration date as that sold—shall immediately apply such purchase or sale against such previously held opposite transaction, and shall promptly furnish such retail forex customer a statement showing the financial result of the transactions involved and, if applicable, that the account was introduced to the futures commission merchant or retail foreign exchange dealer by an introducing broker and the names of the futures commission merchant or retail foreign exchange dealer, and the introducing broker.

(b) *Close-out against oldest open position.* In all instances wherein the short or long futures, retail forex transaction or option position in such customer's or retail forex customer's account immediately prior to such offsetting purchase or sale is greater than the quantity purchased or sold, the futures commission merchant or retail foreign exchange dealer shall apply such offsetting purchase or sale to the oldest portion of the previously held short or long position: *Provided,* That upon specific instructions from the customer the offsetting transaction shall be applied as specified by the customer without regard to the date of acquisition of the previously held position; and *Provided, further,* that a futures commission merchant or retail foreign exchange dealer, if permitted by the rules of a registered futures association, may offset, at the customer's request, retail forex transactions of the same size, even if the customer holds other transactions of a different size, but in each case must offset the transaction against the oldest transaction of the same size. Such instructions may also be accepted from any person who, by power of attorney or otherwise, actually directs trading in the customer's or retail forex customer's account unless the person directing the trading is the futures commission merchant or retail foreign exchange dealer (including any partner thereof), or is an officer, employee, or agent of the futures commission merchant or retail foreign exchange dealer. With respect to every such offsetting transaction that, in accordance with such specific instructions, is not applied to the oldest portion of the previously held position, the futures commission merchant or retail foreign exchange dealer shall clearly show on the statement issued to the customer or retail forex customer in connection with the transaction, that because of the specific instructions given by or on behalf of the customer or retail forex customer the transaction was not applied in the usual manner, *i.e.,* against the oldest portion of the previously held position. However, no such showing need be made if the futures commission merchant or retail foreign exchange dealer has received such specific instructions in writing from the customer or retail forex customer for whom such account is carried.

(c) *In-and-out trades; day trades.* Notwithstanding the provisions of paragraphs (a) and (b) of this section shall not be deemed to require the application of purchases or sales closed out during the same day (commonly known as “in-and-out trades” or “day trades”) against short or long positions carried forward from a prior date.

(d) *Exceptions.* The provisions of this section shall not apply to:

(1) Purchases or sales of commodity options constituting “bona fide hedging transactions” pursuant to rules of the contract market which have been adopted in accordance with the requirements of § 1.61(b) and approved by the Commission pursuant to; section 5a(a)(12)(A) of the Act *Provided,* That no contract market or futures commission merchant shall permit such option positions to be offset other than by open and competitive execution in the trading pit or ring provided by the contract market, during the regular hours prescribed by the contract market for trading in such commodity option.

(2) Purchases or sales constituting “bona fide hedging transactions” as defined in § 1.3(z); nor

(3) Sales during a delivery period for the purpose of making delivery during such delivery period if such sales are accompanied by instructions to make delivery thereon, together with warehouse receipts or other documents necessary to effectuate such delivery.

(8) Purchases or sales held in error accounts, including but not limited to floor broker error accounts, and purchases or sales identified as errors at the time they are assigned to an account that contains other purchases or sales not identified as errors and held in that account (“error trades”), provided that:

(i) Each error trade does not offset another error trade held in the same account;

(ii) Each error trade is offset by open and competitive means on or subject to the rules of a contract market by not later than the close of business on the business day following the day the error trade is discovered and assigned to an error account or identified as an error trade, unless at the close of business on the business day following the discovery of the error trade, the relevant market has reached a daily price fluctuation limit and the trader is unable to offset the error trade, in which case the error trade must be offset as soon as practicable thereafter; and

(iii) No error trade is closed out by transferring such an open position to another account also controlled by that same trader.

(e) The statements required by paragraph (a) of this section may be furnished to the customer or the person described in § 1.33(d) by means of electronic transmission, in accordance with § 1.33(g).

(Approved by the Office of Management and Budget under control number 3038-0007)

(Secs. 4g, 5, 42 Stat. 1000, 49 Stat. 1496; 7 U.S.C. 6g, 7; secs. 4g, 5, 8a; 7 U.S.C. 6g, 7, 12a)

EDITORIAL NOTE: For FEDERAL REGISTER citations affecting § 1.46, see the List of CFR Sections Affected, which appears in the Finding Aids section of the printed volume and at *www.fdsys.gov* .

§ 1.49 DENOMINATION OF CUSTOMER FUNDS AND LOCATION OF DEPOSITORIES.

(a) *Definitions.* For purposes of this section:

(1) *Money center country.* This term means Canada, France, Italy, Germany, Japan, and the United Kingdom.

(2) *Money center currency.* This term means the currency of any money center country and the Euro.

(b) *Permissible denominations of obligations.* (1) Subject to the terms and conditions set forth in this section, a futures commission merchant's obligations to a customer shall be denominated:

(i) In the United States dollar;

(ii) In a currency in which funds were deposited by the customer or were converted at the request of the customer, to the extent of such deposits and conversions; or

(iii) In a currency in which funds have accrued to the customer as a result of trading conducted on a designated contract market, to the extent of such accruals.

(2)(i) A futures commission merchant shall prepare and maintain a written record of each transaction converting customer funds from one currency to another.

(ii) A written record prepared under paragraph (b)(2)(i) of this section must include the date the transaction was executed, the currencies converted, the amount converted, and the resulting amount.

(iii) The information required under paragraph (b)(2)(ii) of this section must be provided to the customer upon the customer's request.

(c) *Permissible locations of depositories.* (1) Unless a customer provides instructions to the contrary, a futures commission merchant or a derivatives clearing organization may hold customer funds:

(i) In the United States;

(ii) In a money center country; or

(iii) In the country of origin of the currency.

(2) A futures commission merchant or derivatives clearing organization may hold customer funds outside the United States, in a jurisdiction that is not a money center country, or the country of origin of the currency only to the extent authorized by the customer, *provided,* that the futures commission merchant or derivatives clearing organization must make and maintain a written record of such authorization. Notwithstanding the foregoing, in no event shall a futures commission merchant or a derivatives clearing organization hold customer funds in a restricted country subject to sanctions by the Office of Foreign Assets Control of the U.S. Department of Treasury.

(d) *Qualifications for depositories.* (1) To hold customer funds required to be segregated pursuant to the Act and §§ 1.20 through 1.30, 1.32 and 1.36, a depository must provide the depositing futures commission merchant or derivatives clearing organization with the appropriate written acknowledgment as required under §§ 1.20 and 1.26.

(2) A depository, if located in the United States, must be:

(i) A bank or trust company;

(ii) A futures commission merchant registered as such with the Commission; or

(iii) A derivatives clearing organization.

(3) A depository, if located outside the United States, must be:

(i) A bank or trust company that has in excess of $1 billion of regulatory capital;

(ii) A futures commission merchant that is registered as such with the Commission; or

(iii) A derivatives clearing organization.

(e) *Segregation requirements.* (1) Each futures commission merchant and each derivatives clearing organization must, as of the close of each business day, hold in segregated accounts on behalf of commodity or option customers:

(i) Sufficient United States dollars, held in the United States, to meet all United States dollar obligations; and

(ii) Sufficient funds in each other currency to meet obligations in such currency.

(2) Notwithstanding paragraph (e)(1)(ii) of this section, assets denominated in one currency may be held to meet obligations denominated in another currency as follows:

(i) United States dollars may be held in the United States or in money center countries to meet obligations denominated in any other currency; and

(ii) Funds in money center currencies may be held in the United States or in money center countries to meet obligations denominated in currencies other than the United States dollar.

(3) Each futures commission merchant and each derivatives clearing organization shall make and maintain records sufficient to demonstrate compliance with this paragraph (e).

§ 1.52 SELF-REGULATORY ORGANIZATION ADOPTION AND SURVEILLANCE OF MINIMUM FINANCIAL REQUIREMENTS.

(a) Each self-regulatory organization must adopt rules prescribing minimum financial and related reporting requirements for members who are registered futures commission merchants, registered retail foreign exchange dealers, or registered introducing brokers. The self-regulatory minimum financial and related reporting requirements must be the same as, or more stringent than, the requirements contained in §§ 1.10 and 1.17 of this chapter, for futures commission merchants and introducing brokers, and §§ 5.7 and 5.12 of this chapter for retail foreign exchange dealers; provided, however, a self-regulatory organization may permit its member registrants that are registered with the Securities and Exchange Commission as securities brokers or dealers to file (in accordance with § 1.10(h) of this chapter) a copy of their Financial and Operational Combined Uniform Single Report under the Securities Exchange Act of 1934, Part II, Part IIA, or Part II CSE, in lieu of Form 1-FR. The definition of adjusted net capital must be the same as that prescribed in § 1.17(c) of this chapter for futures commission merchants and introducing brokers, and § 5.7(b)(2) of this chapter for futures commission merchants offering or engaging in retail forex transactions and for retail foreign exchange dealers. (b) Each self-regulatory organization must establish and operate a supervisory program for the purpose of assessing whether each member registrant is in compliance with the applicable self-regulatory organization and Commission rules and regulations governing minimum net capital and related financial requirements, the obligation to segregate customer funds, financial reporting requirements, recordkeeping requirements, and sales practice and other compliance requirements. The supervisory program also must address the following elements:

(1) *Adequate levels and independence of audit staff.* A self-regulatory organization must maintain staff of an adequate size, training, and experience to effectively implement a supervisory program. Staff of the self-regulatory organization, including officers, directors and supervising committee members, must maintain independent judgment and its actions must not impair its independence nor appear to impair its independence in matters related to the supervisory program. The self-regulatory organization must provide annual ethics training to all staff with responsibilities for the supervisory program.

(2) *Ongoing surveillance.* A self-regulatory organization's ongoing surveillance of member registrants must include the review and analysis of financial reports and regulatory notices filed by member registrants with the designated self-regulatory organization.

(3) *High-risk firms.* A self-regulatory organization's supervisory program must include procedures for identifying member registrants that are determined to pose a high degree of potential financial risk, including the potential risk of loss of customer funds. High-risk member registrants must include firms experiencing financial or operational difficulties, failing to meet segregation or net capital requirements, failing to maintain current books and records, or experiencing material inadequacies in internal controls. Enhanced monitoring for high risk firms should include, as appropriate, daily review of net capital, segregation, and secured calculations, to assess compliance with self-regulatory and Commission requirements.

(4 *) On-site examinations.* (i) A self-regulatory organization must conduct routine periodic on-site examinations of member registrants. Member futures commission merchants and retail foreign exchange dealers must be subject to on-site examinations no less frequently than once every eighteen months. A self-regulatory organization may establish a risk-based method of establishing the scope of each on-site examination, provided however, that the scope of each on-site examination of a futures commission merchant or retail foreign exchange dealer must include an assessment of whether the registrant is in compliance with applicable Commission and self-regulatory organization minimum capital and customer fund protection requirements, recordkeeping, and reporting requirements.

(ii) A self-regulatory organization must establish the frequency of on-site examinations of member introducing brokers that do not operate pursuant to guarantee agreements with futures commission merchants or retail foreign exchange dealers using a risk-based approach, provided however, that each introducing broker is subject to an on-site examination no less frequently than once every three years.

(iii) A self-regulatory organization must conduct on-site examinations of member registrants in accordance with uniform audit programs and procedures that have been submitted to the Commission.

(5) *Adequate documentation.* A self-regulatory organization must adequately document all aspects of the operation of the supervisory program, including the conduct of risk-based scope setting and the risk-based surveillance of high-risk member registrants, and the imposition of remedial and punitive action(s) for material violations.

(c) Any two or more self-regulatory organizations may file with the Commission a plan for delegating to a designated self-regulatory organization, for any registered futures commission merchant, retail foreign exchange dealer, or introducing broker that is a member of more than one such self-regulatory organization, the responsibility of:

(1) Monitoring and auditing for compliance with the minimum financial and related reporting requirements adopted by such self-regulatory organizations and the Commission in accordance with paragraphs (a) and (b) of this section; and

(2) Receiving the financial reports necessitated by such minimum financial and related reporting requirements.

(d) Any plan filed under this section may contain provisions for the allocation of expenses reasonably incurred by the designated self-regulatory organization among the self-regulatory organizations participating in such a plan.

(e) A plan's designated self-regulatory organization must report to:

(1) That plan's other self-regulatory organizations any violation of such other self-regulatory organizations' rules and regulations for which the responsibility to monitor, audit or examine has been delegated to such designated self-regulatory organization under this section; and

(2) The Commission any violation of a self-regulatory organization's rules and regulations or any violation of the Commission's regulations for which the responsibility to monitor, audit or examine has been delegated to such designated self-regulatory organization under this section.

(f) The self-regulatory organizations may, among themselves, establish programs to provide access to any necessary financial or related information.

(g) After appropriate notice and opportunity for comment, the Commission may, by written notice, approve such a plan, or any part of the plan, if it finds that the plan, or any part of it:

(1) Is necessary or appropriate to serve the public interest;

(2) Is for the protection and in the interest of customers;

(3) Reduces multiple monitoring and multiple auditing for compliance with the minimum financial rules of the self-regulatory organizations submitting the plan of any futures commission merchant, retail foreign exchange dealer, or introducing broker that is a member of more than one self-regulatory organization;

(4) Reduces multiple reporting of the financial information necessitated by such minimum financial and related reporting requirements by any futures commission merchant, retail foreign exchange dealer, or introducing broker that is a member of more than one self-regulatory organization;

(5) Fosters cooperation and coordination among the self-regulatory organizations; and

(6) Does not hinder the development of a registered futures association under section 17 of the Act.

(h) After the Commission has approved a plan, or part thereof, under § 1.52(g), a self-regulatory organization relieved of responsibility must notify each of its members that are subject to such a plan:

(1) Of the limited nature of its responsibility for such a member's compliance with its minimum financial and related reporting requirements; and

(2) Of the identity of the designated self-regulatory organization that has been delegated responsibility for such a member.

(i) The Commission may at any time, after appropriate notice and opportunity for hearing, withdraw its approval of any plan, or part thereof, established under this section, if such plan, or part thereof, ceases to adequately effectuate the purposes of section 4f(b) of the Act or of this section.

(j) Whenever a registered futures commission merchant, a registered retail foreign exchange dealer, or a registered introducing broker holding membership in a self-regulatory organization ceases to be a member in good standing of that self-regulatory organization, such self-regulatory organization must, on the same day that event takes place, give electronic notice of that event to the Commission at its Washington, DC, headquarters and send a copy of that notification to such futures commission merchant, retail foreign exchange dealer, or introducing broker.

(k) Nothing in this section shall preclude the Commission from examining any futures commission merchant, retail foreign exchange dealer, or introducing broker for compliance with the minimum financial and related reporting requirements to which such futures commission merchant, retail foreign exchange dealer, or introducing broker is subject.

(l) In the event a plan is not filed and/or approved for each registered futures commission merchant, retail foreign exchange dealer, or introducing broker that is a member of more than one self-regulatory organization, the Commission may design and, after notice and opportunity for comment, approve a plan for those futures commission merchants, retail foreign exchange dealers, or introducing brokers that are not the subject of an approved plan (under paragraph (g) of this section), delegating to a designated self-regulatory organization the responsibilities described in paragraph (c) of this section.

§ 1.54 CONTRACT MARKET RULES SUBMITTED TO AND APPROVED OR NOT DISAPPROVED BY THE SECRETARY OF AGRICULTURE.

Notwithstanding any provision of these rules, any bylaw, rule, regulation, or resolution of a contract market that was submitted to the Secretary of Agriculture pursuant or § 1.38(a) or § 1.39(a) of these rules, and was either approved by the Secretary or not disapproved by him, as of April 21, 1975, shall continue in full force and effect unless and until disapproved, altered or supplemented by or with the approval of the Commission. The adoption of this rule does not constitute approval by the Commission of any contract market bylaw, rule, regulation or resolution.

(Sec. 411, Pub. L. 93-463, 88 Stat. 1414; 7 U.S.C. 4a note)

§ 1.55 DISTRIBUTION OF "RISK DISCLOSURE STATEMENT" BY FUTURES COMMISSION MERCHANTS AND INTRODUCING BROKERS.

(a)(1) Except as provided in 1.65, no futures commission merchant, or in the case of an introduced account no introducing broker, may open a commodity futures account for a customer, other than for a customer specified in paragraph (f) of this section, unless the futures commission merchant or introducing broker first:

(i) Furnishes the customer with a separate written disclosure statement containing only the language set forth in paragraph (b) of this section (except for nonsubstantive additions such as captions) or as otherwise approved under paragraph (c) of this section; *Provided, however,* that the disclosure statement may be attached to other documents as the cover page or the first page of such documents and as the only material on such page; and

(ii) Receives from the customer an acknowledgment signed and dated by the customer that he received and understood the disclosure statement.

(b) The language set forth in the written disclosure document required by paragraph (a) of this section shall be as follows:

RISK DISCLOSURE STATEMENT

The risk of loss in trading commodity futures contracts can be substantial. You should, therefore, carefully consider whether such trading is suitable for you in light of your circumstances and financial resources. You should be aware of the following points:

(1) You may sustain a total loss of the funds that you deposit with your broker to establish or maintain a position in the commodity futures market, and you may incur losses beyond these amounts. If the market moves against your position, you may be called upon by your broker to deposit a substantial amount of additional margin funds, on short notice, in order to maintain your position. If you do not provide the required funds within the time required by your broker, your position may be liquidated at a loss, and you will be liable for any resulting deficit in your account.

(2) Under certain market conditions, you may find it difficult or impossible to liquidate a position. This can occur, for example, when the market reaches a daily price fluctuation limit ("limit move").

(3) Placing contingent orders, such as "stop-loss" or "stop-limit" orders, will not necessarily limit your losses to the intended amounts, since market conditions on the exchange where the order is placed may make it impossible to execute such orders.

(4) All futures positions involve risk, and a "spread" position may not be less risky than an outright "long" or "short" position.

(5) The high degree of leverage (gearing) that is often obtainable in futures trading because of the small margin requirements can work against you as well as for you. Leverage (gearing) can lead to large losses as well as gains.

(6) You should consult your broker concerning the nature of the protections available to safeguard funds or property deposited for your account.

ALL OF THE POINTS NOTED ABOVE APPLY TO ALL FUTURES TRADING WHETHER FOREIGN OR DOMESTIC. IN ADDITION, IF YOU ARE CONTEMPLATING TRADING FOREIGN FUTURES OR OPTIONS CONTRACTS, YOU SHOULD BE AWARE OF THE FOLLOWING ADDITIONAL RISKS:

(7) Foreign futures transactions involve executing and clearing trades on a foreign exchange. This is the case even if the foreign exchange is formally "linked" to a domestic exchange, whereby a trade executed on one exchange liquidates or establishes a position on the other exchange. No domestic organization regulates the activities of a foreign exchange, including the execution, delivery, and clearing of transactions on such an exchange, and no domestic regulator has the power to compel enforcement of the rules of the foreign exchange or the laws of the foreign country. Moreover, such laws or regulations will vary depending on the foreign country in which the transaction occurs. For these reasons, customers who trade on foreign exchanges may not be afforded certain of the protections which apply to domestic transactions, including the right to use domestic alternative dispute resolution procedures. In particular, funds received from customers to margin foreign futures transactions may not be provided the same protections as funds received to margin futures transactions on domestic exchanges. Before you trade, you should familiarize yourself with the foreign rules which will apply to your particular transaction.

(8) Finally, you should be aware that the price of any foreign futures or option contract and, therefore, the potential profit and loss resulting therefrom, may be affected by any fluctuation in the foreign exchange

rate between the time the order is placed and the foreign futures contract is liquidated or the foreign option contract is liquidated or exercised.

THIS BRIEF STATEMENT CANNOT, OF COURSE, DISCLOSE ALL THE RISKS AND OTHER ASPECTS OF THE COMMODITY MARKETS

I hereby acknowledge that I have received and understood this risk disclosure statement.

Date

Signature of Customer

(c) The Commission may approve for use in lieu of the risk disclosure document required by paragraph (b) of this section a risk disclosure statement approved by one or more foreign regulatory agencies or self-regulatory organizations if the Commission determines that such risk disclosure statement is reasonably calculated to provide the disclosure required by paragraph (b) of this section. Notice of risk disclosure statements that may be used to satisfy Commission disclosure requirements, what requirements such statements meet and the jurisdictions which accept each format will be set forth in appendix A to this section.

(d) Any futures commission merchant, or in the case of an introduced account any introducing broker, may open a commodity futures account for a customer without obtaining the separate acknowledgments of disclosure and elections required by this section and by § 1.33(g), and by §§ 33.7 and 190.06 of this chapter, provided that:

(1) Prior to the opening of such account, the futures commission merchant or introducing broker obtains an acknowledgement from the customer, which may consist of a single signature at the end of the futures commission merchant's or introducing broker's customer account agreement, or on a separate page, of the disclosure statements, consents and elections specified in this section and § 1.33(g), and in §§ 33.7, § 155.3(b)(2), § 155.4(b)(2), and § 190.06 of this chapter, and which may include authorization for the transfer of funds from a segregated customer account to another account of such customer, as listed directly above the signature line, provided the customer has acknowledged by check or other indication next to a description of each specified disclosure statement, consent or election that the customer has received and understood such disclosure statement or made such consent or election; and

(2) The acknowledgment referred to in paragraph (d)(1) of this section is accompanied by and executed contemporaneously with delivery of the disclosures and elective provisions required by this section and § 1.33(g), and by §§ 33.7 and 190.06 of this chapter.

(e) The acknowledgment required by paragraph (a) of this section must be retained by the futures commission merchant or introducing broker in accordance with § 1.31.

(f) A futures commission merchant or, in the case of an introduced account, an introducing broker, may open a commodity futures account for an “institutional customer” as defined in § 1.3(g) without furnishing such institutional customer the disclosure statements or obtaining the acknowledgments required under paragraph (a) of this section §§ 1.33(g) and 1.65(a)(3), and §§ 30.6(a), 33.7(a), 155.3(b)(2), 155.4(b)(2) and 190.10(c) of this chapter.

(g) This section does not relieve a futures commission merchant or introducing broker from any other disclosure obligation it may have under applicable law.

(h) Notwithstanding any other provision of this section or § 1.65, a person registered or required to be registered with the Commission as a futures commission merchant pursuant to sections 4f(a)(1) or 4f(a)(2) of the Commodity Exchange Act and registered or required to be registered with the Securities and Exchange Commission as a broker or dealer pursuant to sections 15(b)(1) or 15(b)(11) of the Securities Exchange Act of 1934 and rules thereunder must provide to a customer or prospective customer, prior to the acceptance of any order for, or otherwise handling any transaction in or in connection with, a security futures product for a customer, the disclosures set forth in § 41.41(b)(1) of this chapter.

(Approved by the Office of Management and Budget under control number 3038-0022)

(Secs. 4b, 4c(b), 4g(1), 4 *l*, 4 *o*, and 8a(5), Commodity Exchange Act, 7 U.S.C. 6b, 6c(b), 6g(1), 6 *l*, 6 *o*, and 12a(5)(1976), and sec. 217, Commodity Futures Trading Act of 1974, 88 Stat. 1405; secs. 2(a)(1), 4b, 4c, 4d, 4f and 8a, Commodity Exchange Act, as amended (7 U.S.C. 2, 6b, 6c, 6f and 12a))

APPENDIX A TO CFTC RULE 1.55(c) — GENERIC RISK DISCLOSURE STATEMENT

Risk Disclosure Statement for Futures and Options

This brief statement does not disclose all of the risks and other significant aspects of trading in futures and options. In light of the risks, you should undertake such transactions only if you understand the nature of the contracts (and contractual relationships) into which you are entering and the extent of your exposure to risk. Trading in futures and options is not suitable for many members of the public. You should carefully consider whether trading is appropriate for you in light of your experience, objectives, financial resources and other relevant circumstances.

Futures

1. Effect of 'Leverage' or 'Gearing'

Transactions in futures carry a high degree of risk. The amount of initial margin is small relative to the value of the futures contract so that transactions are 'leveraged' or 'geared'. A relatively small market movement will have a proportionately larger impact on the funds you have deposited or will have to deposit: this may work against you as well as for you. You may sustain a total loss of initial margin funds and any additional funds deposited with the firm to maintain your position. If the market moves against your position or margin levels are increased, you may be called upon to pay substantial additional funds on short notice to maintain your position. If you fail to comply with a request for additional funds within the time prescribed, your position may be liquidated at a loss and you will be liable for any resulting deficit.

2. Risk reducing orders or strategies

The placing of certain orders (e.g. 'stop-loss' orders, where permitted under local law, or 'stop-limit' orders) which are intended to limit losses to certain amounts may not be effective because market conditions may make it impossible to execute such orders. Strategies using combinations of positions, such as 'spread' and 'straddle' positions may be as risky as taking simple 'long' or 'short' positions.

Options

3. Variable degree of risk

Transactions in options carry a high degree of risk. Purchasers and sellers of options should familiarize themselves with the type of option (i.e. put or call) which they contemplate trading and the associated risks. You should calculate the extent to which the value of the options must increase for your position to become profitable, taking into account the premium and all transaction costs.

The purchaser of options may offset or exercise the options or allow the options to expire. The exercise of an option results either in a cash settlement or in the purchaser acquiring or delivering the underlying interest. If the option is on a future, the purchaser will acquire a futures position with associated liabilities for margin (see the section on Futures above). If the purchased options expire worthless, you will suffer a total loss of your investment which will consist of the option premium plus transaction costs. If you are contemplating purchasing deep-out-of-the-money options, you should be aware that the chance of such options becoming profitable ordinarily is remote.

Selling ('writing' or 'granting') an option generally entails considerably greater risk than purchasing options. Although the premium received by the seller is fixed, the seller may sustain a loss well in excess of that amount. The seller will be liable for additional margin to maintain the position if the market moves unfavorably. The seller will also be exposed to the risk of the purchaser exercising the option and the seller will be obligated to either settle the option in cash or to acquire or deliver the underlying interest. If the option is on a future, the seller will acquire a position in a future with associated liabilities for margin (see the section on Futures above). If the option is 'covered' by the seller holding a corresponding position in the underlying interest or a future or another option, the risk may be reduced. If the option is not covered, the risk of loss can be unlimited.

Certain exchanges in some jurisdictions permit deferred payment of the option premium, exposing the purchaser to liability for margin payments not exceeding the amount of the premium. The purchaser is still subject to the risk of losing the premium and transaction costs. When the option is exercised or expires, the purchaser is responsible for any unpaid premium outstanding at that time.

Additional risks common to futures and options

4. Terms and conditions of contracts

You should ask the firm with which you deal about the terms and conditions of the specific futures or options which you are trading and associated obligations (e.g. the circumstances under which you may become obligated to make or take delivery of the underlying interest of a futures contract and, in respect of options, expiration dates and restrictions on the time for exercise). Under certain

View or download PDF

circumstances the specifications of outstanding contracts (including the exercise price of an option) may be modified by the exchange or clearing house to reflect changes in the underlying interest.

5. Suspension or restriction of trading and pricing relationships

Market conditions (e.g. illiquidity) and/or the operation of the rules of certain markets (e.g. the suspension of trading in any contract or contract month because of price limits or 'circuit breakers') may increase the risk of loss by making it difficult or impossible to effect transactions or liquidate/offset positions. If you have sold options, this may increase the risk of loss.

Further, normal pricing relationships between the underlying interest and the future, and the underlying interest and the option may not exist. This can occur when, for example, the futures contract underlying the option is subject to price limits while the option is not. The absence of an underlying reference price may make it difficult to judge 'fair' value.

6. Deposited cash and property

You should familiarize yourself with the protections accorded money or other property you deposit for domestic and foreign transactions, particularly in the event of a firm insolvency or bankruptcy. The extent to which you may recover your money or property may be governed by specific legislation or local rules. In some jurisdictions, property which had been specifically identifiable as your own will be pro-rated in the same manner as cash for purposes of distribution in the event of a shortfall.

7. Commission and other charges

Before you begin to trade, you should obtain a clear explanation of all commission, fees and other charges for which you will be liable. These charges will affect your net profit (if any) or increase your loss.

8. Transactions in other jurisdictions

Transactions on markets in other jurisdictions, including markets formally linked to a domestic market, may expose you to additional risk. Such markets may be subject to regulation which may offer different or diminished investor protection. Before you trade you should enquire about any rules relevant to your particular transactions. Your local regulatory authority will be unable to compel the enforcement of the rules of regulatory authorities or markets in other jurisdictions where your transactions have been effected. You should ask the firm with which you deal for details about the types of redress available in both your home jurisdiction and other relevant jurisdictions before you start to trade.

9. Currency risks

The profit or loss in transactions in foreign currency-denominated contracts (whether they are traded in your own or another jurisdiction) will be affected by fluctuations in currency rates where there is a need to convert from the currency denomination of the contract to another currency.

10. Trading facilities

Most open-outcry and electronic trading facilities are supported by computer-based component systems for the order-routing, execution, matching, registration or clearing of trades. As with all facilities and systems, they are vulnerable to temporary disruption or failure. Your ability to recover certain losses may be subject to limits on liability imposed by the system provider, the market, the clearing house and/or member firms. Such limits may vary; you should ask the firm with which you deal for details in this respect.

11. Electronic trading

Trading on an electronic trading system may differ not only from trading in an open-outcry market but also from trading on other electronic trading systems. If you undertake transactions on an electronic trading system, you will be exposed to risks associated with the system including the failure of hardware and software. The result of any system failure may be that your order is either not executed according to your instructions or is not executed at all.

12. Off-exchange transactions

In some jurisdictions, and only then in restricted circumstances, firms are permitted to effect off-exchange transactions. The firm with which you deal may be acting as your counterparty to the transaction. It may be difficult or impossible to liquidate an existing position, to assess the value, to determine a fair price or to assess the exposure to risk. For these reasons, these transactions may involve increased risks. Off-exchange transactions may be less regulated or subject to a separate regulatory regime. Before you undertake such transactions, you should familiarize yourself with applicable rules and attendant risks.

I hereby acknowledge that I have received and understood this risk disclosure statement.

_______________ Date   _______________ Signature of Customer

View or download PDF

* * * * *

[The following language should be printed on a page other than the pages containing the disclosure language above and may be omitted from the required disclosure statement]

This disclosure document meets the risk disclosure requirements in the jurisdictions identified below ONLY for those instruments which are specified.

United States: Commodity futures, options on commodity futures and options on commodities subject to the Commodity Exchange Act.

United Kingdom: Futures, options on futures, options on commodities and options on equities traded by members of the United Kingdom Securities and Futures Authority pursuant to the Financial Services Act, 1986.

Ireland: Financial futures and options on financial futures traded by members of futures exchanges on exchanges whose rules have been approved by the Central Bank of Ireland under Chapter VIII of the Central Bank Act, 1989.

[43 FR 31890, July 24, 1978]

EDITORIAL NOTE: For FEDERAL REGISTER citations affecting § 1.55, see the List of CFR Sections Affected, which appears in the Finding Aids section of the printed volume and at *www.fdsys.gov* .

§ 1.56 PROHIBITION OF GUARANTEES AGAINST LOSS.

(b) No futures commission merchant or introducing broker may in any way represent that it will, with respect to any commodity interest in any account carried by the futures commission merchant for or on behalf of any person:

(1) Guarantee such person against loss;

(2) Limit the loss of such person; or

(3) Not call for or attempt to collect initial and maintenance margin as established by the rules of the applicable board of trade.

(c) No person may in any way represent that a futures commission merchant or introducing broker will engage in any of the acts or practices described in paragraph (b) of this section.

(d) This section shall not be construed to prevent a futures commission merchant or introducing broker from:

(1) Assuming or sharing in the losses resulting from an error or mishandling of an order; or

(2) Participating as a general partner in a commodity pool which is a limited partnership.

(e) This section shall not affect any guarantee entered into prior to January 28, 1982, but this section shall apply to any extension, modification or renewal thereof entered into after such date.

[46 FR 62844, Dec. 29, 1981, as amended at 48 FR 35291, Aug. 3, 1983]

§ 1.57 OPERATIONS AND ACTIVITIES OF INTRODUCING BROKERS.

(a) Each introducing broker must:

(1) Open and carry each customer's account with a carrying futures commission merchant on a fully-disclosed basis:*Provided, however,* That an introducing broker which has entered into a guarantee agreement with a futures commission merchant in accordance with the provisions of § 1.10(j) must open and carry such customer's account with such guarantor futures commission merchant on a fully-disclosed basis; and

(2) Transmit promptly for execution all customer orders to:

(i) A carrying futures commission merchant; or

(ii) A floor broker, if the introducing broker identifies its carrying futures commission merchant and that carrying futures commission merchant is also the clearing member with respect to the customer's order.

(b) An introducing broker may not carry proprietary accounts, nor may an introducing broker carry accounts in foreign futures.

(c) An introducing broker may not accept any money, securities or property (or extend credit in lieu thereof) to margin, guarantee or secure any trades or contracts of customers, or any money, securities or property accruing as a result of such trades or contracts: *Provided, however,* That an introducing broker may deposit a check in a qualifying account or forward a check drawn by a customer if:

(1) The futures commission merchant carrying the customer's account authorizes the introducing broker, in writing, to receive a check in the name of the futures commission merchant, and the introducing broker retains such written authorization in its files in accordance with § 1.31;

(2) The check is payable to the futures commission merchant carrying the customer's account;

(3) The check is deposited by the introducing broker, on the same day upon which it is received, in a bank or trust company located in the United States in a qualifying account, or the check is mailed or otherwise transmitted by the introducing broker to the futures commission merchant on the same day upon which it is received;

(4) For purposes of this paragraph (c), a qualifying account shall be deemed to be an account:

(i) Which is maintained in an account name which clearly identifies the funds therein as belonging to customers of the futures commission merchant carrying the customer's account;

(ii) For which the bank or trust company restricts withdrawals to withdrawals by the carrying futures commission merchant;

(iii) For which the bank or trust company prohibits the introducing broker or anyone acting upon its behalf from withdrawing funds; and

(iv) For which the bank or trust company provides the futures commission merchant carrying the customer's account with a written acknowledgment, which the futures commission merchant must retain in its files in accordance with § 1.31, that it was informed that the funds deposited therein are those of customers and are being held in accordance with the provisions of the Act and the regulations in this chapter.

[48 FR 35291, Aug. 3, 1983, as amended at 57 FR 23143, June 2, 1992; 77 FR 66330, Nov. 2, 2012]

§ 1.58 GROSS COLLECTION OF EXCHANGE-SET MARGINS.

(a) Each futures commission merchant which carries a commodity futures or commodity option position for another futures commission merchant or for a foreign broker on an omnibus basis must collect, and each futures commission merchant and foreign broker for which an omnibus account is being carried must deposit, initial and maintenance margin on each position reported in accordance with § 17.04 of this chapter at a level no less than that established for customer accounts by the rules of the applicable contract market.

(b) If the futures commission merchant which carries a commodity futures or commodity option position for another futures commission merchant or for a foreign broker on an omnibus basis allows a position to be margined as a spread position or as a hedged position in accordance with the rules of the applicable contract market, the carrying futures commission merchant must obtain and retain a written representation from the futures commission merchant or from the foreign broker for which the omnibus account is being carried that each such position is entitled to be so margined.

[61 FR 19187, May 1, 1996]

§ 1.59 ACTIVITIES OF SELF-REGULATORY ORGANIZATION EMPLOYEES, GOVERNING BOARD MEMBERS, COMMITTEE MEMBERS, AND CONSULTANTS.

(a) *Definitions.* For purposes of this section:

(1) *Self-regulatory organization* means "self-regulatory organization," as defined in § 1.3(ee), and includes the term "clearing organization," as defined in § 1.3(d).

(2) *Governing board member* means a member, or functional equivalent thereof, of the board of governors of a self-regulatory organization.

(3) *Committee member* means a member, or functional equivalent thereof, of any committee of a self-regulatory organization.

(4) *Employee* means any person hired or otherwise employed on a salaried or contract basis by a self-regulatory organization, but does not include:

(i) Any governing board member compensated by a self-regulatory organization solely for governing board activities; or

(ii) Any committee member compensated by a self-regulatory organization solely for committee activities; or

(iii) Any consultant hired by a self-regulatory organization.

(5) *Material information* means information which, if such information were publicly known, would be considered important by a reasonable person in deciding whether to trade a particular commodity interest on a contract market or a swap execution facility, or to clear a swap contract through a derivatives clearing organization. As used in this section, "material information" includes, but is not limited to, information relating to present or anticipated cash positions, commodity interests, trading strategies, the financial condition of members of self-regulatory organizations or members of linked exchanges or their customers, or the regulatory actions or proposed regulatory actions of a self-regulatory organization or a linked exchange.

(6) *Non-public information* means information which has not been disseminated in a manner which makes it generally available to the trading public.

(7) *Linked exchange* means:

(i) Any board of trade, exchange or market outside the United States, its territories or possessions, which has an agreement with a contract market or swap execution facility in the United States that permits positions in a commodity interest which have been established on one of the two markets to be liquidated on the other market;

(ii) Any board of trade, exchange or market outside the United States, its territories or possessions, the products of which are listed on a United States contract market, swap execution facility, or a trading facility thereof;

(iii) Any securities exchange, the products of which are held as margin in a commodity account or cleared by a securities clearing organization pursuant to a cross-margining arrangement with a futures clearing organization; or

(iv) Any clearing organization which clears the products of any of the foregoing markets.

(8) *Commodity interest* means any commodity futures, commodity option or swap contract traded on or subject to the rules of a contract market, a swap execution facility or linked exchange, or cleared by a derivatives clearing organization, or cash commodities traded on or subject to the rules of a board of trade which has been designated as a contract market.

(9) *Related commodity interest* means any commodity interest which is traded on or subject to the rules of a contract market, swap execution facility, linked exchange, or other board of trade, exchange, or

market, or cleared by a derivatives clearing organization, other than the self-regulatory organization by which a person is employed, and with respect to which:

(i) Such employing self-regulatory organization has recognized or established intermarket spread margins or other special margin treatment between that other commodity interest and a commodity interest which is traded on or subject to the rules of the employing self-regulatory organization; or

(ii) Such other self-regulatory organization has recognized or established intermarket spread margins or other special margin treatment with another commodity interest as to which the person has access to material, nonpublic information.

(10) *Pooled investment vehicle* means a trading vehicle organized and operated as a commodity pool within the meaning of § 4.10(d) of this chapter, and whose units of participation have been registered under the Securities Act of 1933, or a trading vehicle for which § 4.5 of this chapter makes available relief from regulation as a commodity pool operator, *i.e.,* registered investment companies, insurance company separate accounts, bank trust funds, and certain pension plans.

(b) *Employees of self-regulatory organizations; Self-regulatory organization rules.* (1) Each self-regulatory organization must maintain in effect rules which have been submitted to the Commission pursuant to section 5c(c) of the Act and part 40 of this chapter (or, pursuant to section 17(j) of the Act in the case of a registered futures association) that, at a minimum, prohibit:

(i) Employees of the self-regulatory organization from:

(A) Trading, directly or indirectly, in any commodity interest traded on or cleared by the employing contract market, swap execution facility, or clearing organization;

(B) Trading, directly or indirectly, in any related commodity interest;

(C) Trading, directly or indirectly, in a commodity interest traded on contract markets or swap execution facilities or cleared by derivatives clearing organizations other than the employing self-regulatory organization if the employee has access to material, non-public information concerning such commodity interest;

(D) Trading, directly or indirectly, in a commodity interest traded on or cleared by a linked exchange if the employee has access to material, non-public information concerning such commodity interest; and

(ii) Employees of the self-regulatory organization from disclosing to any other person any material, non-public information which such employee obtains as a result of his or her employment at the self-regulatory organization where such employee has or should have a reasonable expectation that the information disclosed may assist another person in trading any commodity interest; *Provided, however,* That such rules shall not prohibit disclosures made in the course of an employee's duties, or disclosures made to another self-regulatory organization, linked exchange, court of competent jurisdiction or representative of any agency or department of the federal or state government acting in his or her official capacity.

(2) Each self-regulatory organization may adopt rules, which must be submitted to the Commission pursuant to section 5a(a)(12)(A) of the Act and Commission regulation 1.41 (or, pursuant to section 17(j) of the Act in the case of a registered futures association), which set forth circumstances under which exemptions from the trading prohibition contained in paragraph (b)(1)(i) of this section may be granted; such exemptions are to be administered by the self-regulatory organization on a case-by-case basis. Specifically, such circumstances may include:

(i) Participation by an employee in pooled investment vehicles where the employee has no direct or indirect control with respect to transactions executed for or on behalf of such vehicles; and

(ii) Trading by an employee under circumstances enumerated by the self-regulatory organization in rules which the self-regulatory organization determines are not contrary to the purposes of this regulation, the Commodity Exchange Act, the public interest, or just and equitable principles of trade.

(c) *Governing board members, committee members, and consultants; Registered futures association rules.* Each registered futures association must maintain in effect rules which have been submitted to the Commission pursuant to section 17(j) of the Act which provide that no governing board member, committee member, or consultant shall use or disclose—for any purpose other than the performance of official duties as a governing board member, committee member, or consultant—material, non-public information obtained as a result of the performance of such person's official duties.

(d) *Prohibited conduct.* (1) No employee, governing board member, committee member, or consultant shall:

(i) Trade for such person's own account, or for or on behalf of any other account, in any commodity interest, on the basis of any material, non-public information obtained through special access related to the performance of such person's official duties as an employee, governing board member, committee member, or consultant; or

(ii) Disclose for any purpose inconsistent with the performance of such person's official duties as an employee, governing board member, committee member, or consultant any material, non-public information obtained through special access related to the performance of such duties.

(2) No person shall trade for such person's own account, or for or on behalf of any other account, in any commodity interest, on the basis of any material, non-public information that such person knows was obtained in violation of paragraph (d)(1) of this section from an employee, governing board member, committee member, or consultant.

[58 FR 54973, Oct. 25, 1993, as amended at 65 FR 47847, Aug. 4, 2000; 77 FR 66330, Nov. 2, 2012]

§ 1.60 PENDING LEGAL PROCEEDINGS.

(a) Every contract market shall submit to the Commission copies of the complaint, any dispositive or partially dispositive decision, any notice of appeal filed concerning such decisions and such further documents as the Commission may thereafter request filed in any material legal proceeding to which the contract market is a party or its property or assets is subject.

(b) Every futures commission merchant shall sumit to the Commission copies of any dispositive or partially dispositive decision for which a notice of appeal has been filed, the notice of appeal and such further documents as the Commission may thereafter request filed in any material legal proceeding to which the futures commission merchant is a party or its property or assets is subjects.

(c) Every contract market shall submit to the Commission copies of the complaint, any dispositive or partially dispositive decision, any notice of appeal filed concerning such decisions and such further documents as the Commission may thereafter request filed in any material legal proceeding instituted against any officer, director, or other official of the contract market arising from conduct in such person's capacity as a contract market official and alleging violations of:

(1) The act or any rule, regulation, or order thereunder;

(2) the constitution, bylaws or rules of the contract market; or

(3) the applicable provisions of state law relating to the duties of officers, directors, or other officials of business organizations.

(d) Every futures commission merchant shall submit to the Commission copies of any dispositive or partially dispositive decision concerning which a notice of appeal has been filed, the notice of appeal, and such further documents as the Commission may thereafter request filed in any material legal proceeding instituted against any person who is a principal of the futures commission merchant (as that term is defined in § 3.1(a) of this chapter) arising from conduct in such person's capacity as a principal of the futures commission merchant and alleging violations of: (1) The Act or any rule, regulation, or order thereunder; or (2) provisions of state law relating to a duty or obligation owed by such a principal.

(e) All documents required by this section to be submitted to the Commission shall be mailed via first-class or submitted by other more expeditious means to the Commission's headquarters office in Washington, DC, Attention: Office of the General Counsel. All documents required by this section to be submitted to the Commission as to matters pending on the effective date of the section (May 25, 1984), shall be mailed to the Commission within 45 days of that effective date. Thereafter, all complaints required by this section to be submitted to the Commission by contract markets shall be mailed to the Commission within 10 days after the initiation of the legal proceedings to which they relate, all decisions required to be submitted by contract markets shall be mailed within 10 days of their date of issuance, all notices of appeal required to be submitted by contract markets shall be mailed within 10 days of the filing or receipt by the contract market of the notice of appeal, and all decisions and notices of appeal required to be submitted by futures commission merchants shall be mailed within 10 days of the filing or receipt by the futures commission merchant of the relevant notice of appeal. For purposes of paragraph (a), (b), (c) and (d) of this rule, a "material legal proceeding" includes but is not limited to actions involving alleged violations of the Commodity Exchange Act or the Commission's regulations. However, a legal proceeding is not "material" for the purposes of this rule if the proceeding is not in a federal or state court or if the Commission is a party.

[49 FR 17750, Apr. 25, 1984]

§ 1.63 SERVICE ON SELF-REGULATORY ORGANIZATION GOVERNING BOARDS OR COMMITTEES BY PERSONS WITH DISCIPLINARY HISTORIES.

(a) *Definitions.* For purposes of this section:

(1) *Self-regulatory organization* means a "self-regulatory organization" as defined in § 1.3(ee), and includes a "clearing organization" as defined in § 1.3(d), except as defined in paragraph (b)(6) of this section.

(2) *Disciplinary committee* means any person or committee of persons, or any subcommittee thereof, that is authorized by a self-regulatory organization to issue disciplinary charges, to conduct disciplinary proceedings, to settle disciplinary charges, to impose disciplinary sanctions or to hear appeals thereof.

(3) *Arbitration panel* means any person or panel empowered by a self-regulatory organization to arbitrate disputes involving such organization's members or their customers.

(4) *Oversight panel* means any panel authorized by a self-regulatory organization to review, recommend or establish policies or procedures with respect to the self-regulatory organization's surveillance, compliance, rule enforcement or disciplinary responsibilities.

(5) *Final decision* means:

(i) A decision of a self-regulatory organization which cannot be further appealed within the self-regulatory organization, is not subject to the stay of the Commission or a court of competent jurisdiction, and has not been reversed by the Commission or any court of competent jurisdiction; or,

(ii) Any decision by an administrative law judge, a court of competent jurisdiction or the Commission which has not been stayed or reversed.

(6) *Disciplinary offense* means:

(i) Any violation of the rules of a self-regulatory organization except those rules related to

(A) Decorum or attire,

(B) Financial requirements, or

(C) Reporting or recordkeeping unless resulting in fines aggregating more than $5,000 within any calendar year;

(ii) Any rule violation described in subparagraphs (a)(6)(i) (A) through (C) of this regulation which involves fraud, deceit or conversion or results in a suspension or expulsion;

(iii) Any violation of the Act or the regulations promulgated thereunder; or,

(iv) Any failure to exercise supervisory responsibility with respect to acts described in paragraphs (a)(6) (i) through (iii) of this section when such failure is itself a violation of either the rules of a self-regulatory organization, the Act or the regulations promulgated thereunder.

(v) A disciplinary offense must arise out of a proceeding or action which is brought by a self-regulatory organization, the Commission, any federal or state agency, or other governmental body.

(7) *Settlement agreement* means any agreement consenting to the imposition of sanctions by a self-regulatory organization, a court of competent jurisdiction or the Commission.

(b) Each self-regulatory organization must maintain in effect rules which have been submitted to the Commission pursuant to section 5c(c) of the Act and part 40 of this chapter or, in the case of a registered futures association, pursuant to section 17(j) of the Act, that render a person ineligible to serve on its disciplinary committees, arbitration panels, oversight panels or governing board who:

(1) Was found within the prior three years by a final decision of a self-regulatory organization, an administrative law judge, a court of competent jurisdiction or the Commission to have committed a disciplinary offense;

(2) Entered into a settlement agreement within the prior three years in which any of the findings or, in the absence of such findings, any of the acts charged included a disciplinary offense;

(3) Currently is suspended from trading on any contract market, is suspended or expelled from membership with any self-regulatory organization, is serving any sentence of probation or owes any portion of a fine imposed pursuant to either:

(i) A finding by a final decision of a self-regulatory organization, an administrative law judge, a court of competent jurisdiction or the Commission that such person committed a disciplinary offense; or,

(ii) A settlement agreement in which any of the findings or, in the absence of such findings, any of the acts charged included a disciplinary offense.

(4) Currently is subject to an agreement with the Commission or any self-regulatory organization not to apply for registration with the Commission or membership in any self-regulatory organization;

(5) Currently is subject to or has had imposed on him within the prior three years a Commission registration revocation or suspension in any capacity for any reason, or has been convicted within the prior three years of any of the felonies listed in section 8a(2)(D) (ii) through (iv) of the Act;

(6) Currently is subject to a denial, suspension or disqualification from serving on the disciplinary committee, arbitration panel or governing board of any self-regulatory organization as that term is defined in section 3(a)(26) of the Securities Exchange Act of 1934.

(c) No person may serve on a disciplinary committee, arbitration panel, oversight panel or governing board of a self-regulatory organization if such person is subject to any of the conditions listed in paragraphs (b) (1) through (6) of this section.

(d) Each self-regulatory organization shall submit to the Commission a schedule listing all those rule violations which constitute disciplinary offenses as defined in paragraph (a)(6)(i) of this section and to the extent necessary to reflect revisions shall submit an amended schedule within thirty days of the end of each calendar year. Each self-regulatory organization must maintain and keep current the schedule required by this section, and post the schedule on the self-regulatory organization's Web site so that it is in a public place designed to provide notice to members and otherwise ensure its availability to the general public.

(e) Each self-regulatory organization shall submit to the Commission within thirty days of the end of each calendar year a certified list of any persons who have been removed from its disciplinary committees, arbitration panels, oversight panels or governing board pursuant to the requirements of this regulation during the prior year.

(f) Whenever a self-regulatory organization finds by final decision that a person has committed a disciplinary offense and such finding makes such person ineligible to serve on that self-regulatory organization's disciplinary committees, arbitration panels, oversight panels or governing board, the self-regulatory organization shall inform the Commission of that finding and the length of the ineligibility in any notice it is required to provide to the Commission pursuant to either section 17(h)(1) of the Act or Commission regulation 9.11.

[55 FR 7890, Mar. 6, 1990, as amended at 58 FR 37653, July 13, 1993; 64 FR 23, Jan. 4, 1999; 77 FR 66331, Nov. 2, 2012]

§ 1.64 COMPOSITION OF VARIOUS SELF-REGULATORY ORGANIZATION GOVERNING BOARDS AND MAJOR DISCIPLINARY COMMITTEES.

(a) *Definitions.* For purposes of this section:

(1) *Self-regulatory organization* means “self-regulatory organization” as defined in § 1.3(ee), not including a “clearing organization” as defined in § 1.3(d).

(2) *Major disciplinary committee* means a committee of persons who are authorized by a self-regulatory organization to conduct disciplinary hearings, to settle disciplinary charges, to impose disciplinary sanctions or to hear appeals thereof in cases involving any violation of the rules of the self-regulatory organization except those which:

(i) Are related to:

(A) Decorum or attire,

(B) Financial requirements, or

(C) Reporting or recordkeeping; and,

(ii) Do not involve fraud, deceit or conversion.

(3) *Regular voting member of a governing board* means any person who is eligible to vote routinely on matters being considered by the board and excludes those members who are only eligible to vote in the case of a tie vote by the board.

(4) *Membership interest* (i) In the case of a contract market, each of the following will be considered a different membership interest:

(A) Floor brokers,

(B) Floor traders,

(C) Futures commission merchants,

(D) Producers, consumers, processors, distributors, and merchandisers of commodities traded on the particular contract market,

(E) Participants in a variety of pits or principal groups of commodities traded on the particular contract market; and,

(F) Other market users or participants; except that with respect to paragraph (c)(2) of this section, a contract market may define membership interests according to the different pits or principal groups of commodities traded on the contract market.

(ii) In the case of a registered futures association, each of the following will be considered a different membership interest:

(A) Futures commission merchants,

(B) Introducing brokers,

(C) Commodity pool operators,

(D) Commodity trading advisors; and,

(E) Associated persons, except that under paragraph (c)(3) of this section an associated person will be deemed to represent the same membership interest as its sponsor.

(b) Each self-regulatory organization must maintain in effect standards and procedures with respect to its governing board which have been submitted to the Commission pursuant to section 5a(a)(12)(A) of the Act and § 1.41 or, when applicable to a registered futures association, pursuant to section 17(j) of the Act, that ensure:

(1) That twenty percent or more of the regular voting members of the board are persons who:

(i) Are knowledgeable of futures trading or financial regulation or are otherwise capable of contributing to governing board deliberations; and,

(ii) (A) Are not members of the self-regulatory organization,

(B) Are not currently salaried employees of the self-regulatory organization,

(C) Are not primarily performing services for the self-regulatory organization in a capacity other than as a member of the self-regulatory organization's governing board, or

(D) Are not officers, principals or employees of a firm which holds a membership at the self-regulatory organization either in its own name or through an employee on behalf of the firm;

(2) In the case of a contract market, that ten percent or more of the regular voting members of the governing board be comprised where applicable of persons representing farmers, producers, merchants or exporters of principal commodities underlying a commodity futures or commodity option traded on the contract market; and

(3) That the board's membership includes a diversity of membership interests. The self-regulatory organization must be able to demonstrate that the board membership fairly represents the diversity of interests at such self-regulatory organization and is otherwise consistent with this regulation's composition requirements;

(c) Each self-regulatory organization must maintain in effect rules with respect to its major disciplinary committees which have been submitted to the Commission pursuant to section 5a(a)(12)(A) of the Act and § 1.41 or, when applicable to a registered futures association, pursuant to section 17(j) of the Act, that ensure:

(1) That at least one member of each major disciplinary committee or hearing panel thereof be a person who is not a member of the self-regulatory organization whenever such committee or panel is acting with respect to a disciplinary action in which:

(i) The subject of the action is a member of the self-regulatory organization's:

(A) Governing board, or

(B) Major disciplinary committee; or,

(ii) Any of the charged, alleged or adjudicated contract market rule violations involve:

(A) Manipulation or attempted manipulation of the price of a commodity, a futures contract or an option on a futures contract, or

(B) Conduct which directly results in financial harm to a non-member of the contract market;

(2) In the case of a contract market, that more than fifty percent of each major disciplinary committee or hearing panel thereof include persons representing membership interests other than that of the subject of the disciplinary proceeding being considered;

(3) In the case of a registered futures association, that each major disciplinary committee or hearing panel thereof include persons representing membership interests other than that of the subject of the disciplinary proceeding being considered; and,

(4) That each major disciplinary committee or hearing panel thereof include sufficient different membership interests so as to ensure fairness and to prevent special treatment or preference for any person in the conduct of a committee's or the panel's responsibilities.

(d) Each self-regulatory organization must submit to the Commission within thirty days after each governing board election a list of the governing board's members, the membership interests they represent and how the composition of the governing board otherwise meets the requirements of § 1.64(b) and the self-regulatory organization's implementing standards and procedures.

[58 FR 37654, July 13, 1993; 59 FR 5082, Feb. 3, 1994]

§ 1.65 NOTICE OF BULK TRANSFERS AND DISCLOSURE OBLIGATIONS TO CUSTOMERS.

(a) *Notice and Disclosure to Customers.* (1) Prior to transferring a customer account to another futures commission merchant or introducing broker other than at the request of the customer, a futures commission merchant or introducing broker must obtain the customer's specific consent to the transfer.

(2) If the customer account agreement contains a valid consent by the customer to prospective transfers of the account, the transferor futures commission merchant or introducing broker may transfer the account if the customer is provided with written notice of, and a reasonable opportunity to object to, the transfer and the customer has not asserted an objection to the transfer or given other instructions as to the disposition of the account. The notice to the customer must include:

(i) A clear statement of the reason(s) for the transfer, the name, address and telephone number of the proposed transferee firm and other information material to the transfer;

(ii) A statement that the customer is not required to accept the proposed transfer and may direct the transfer or firm to liquidate the account or ransfer the account to a firm of the customer's selection;

(iii) The name, telephone number and address of a contact person at the transferor firm to whom the customer may give instructions as to the disposition of the account;

(iv) Notice that a failure to respond to the letter within a specified time period, which must be a reasonable period in the circumstances, will be deemed consent to the transfer; and

(v) A clear statement as to the means by which the customer may object to or otherwise respond to the notice of proposed transfer.

(3) Where customer accounts are transferred to a futures commission merchant or introducing broker, other than at the customer's request, the transferee introducing broker or futures commission merchant must provide each customer whose account is transferred with the risk disclosure statements and acknowledgments required by § 1.55 (domestic futures and foreign futures and options trading), and §§ 33.7 (domestic exchange-traded commodity options) and 190.10(c) (non-cash margin—to be furnished by futures commission merchants only) of this chapter and receive the required acknowledgments within sixty days of the transfer of accounts. This requirement shall not apply:

(i) As to customers owning transferred accounts for which the transferee futures commission merchant or introducing broker has clear written evidence that the customer has received and acknowledged the required disclosure documents; or

(ii) As to customers for which the transferee futures commission merchant or introducing broker has clear evidence that such customer was at the time the account was opened by the transferring futures commission merchant or introducing broker, or is at the time the account is being transferred, a customer listed in § 1.55(f); or

(iii) If the transfer of accounts is made from one introducing broker to another introducing broker guaranteed by the same futures commission merchant pursuant to a guarantee agreement in accordance with the requirements of § 1.10(j) and such futures commission merchant maintains the relevant acknowledgments required by § 1.55(a)(1)(ii) and § 33.7(a)(1)(ii) of this chapter and can establish compliance with § 190.10(c) of this chapter.

(b) *Notice to the Commission.* Each futures commission merchant or introducing broker shall file with the Commission, at least five business days in advance of the transfer, notice of any transfer of customer accounts carried or introduced by such futures commission merchant or introducing broker that is not initiated at the request of the customer, where the transfer involves the lesser of:

(1) 25 percent of the total number of customer accounts carried or introduced by such firm if that percentage represents at least 100 accounts; or

(2) 50 percent or more of the total number of customer accounts carried or introduced by such firm. The computation of the percentage and number of accounts must be based on the total number of accounts carried by the transferor futures commission merchant or introduced by the introducing broker, irrespective of whether such accounts are transferred to a single or multiple transferees.

(c) The notice required by paragraph (b) of this section shall include:

(1) The name, principal business address and telephone number of the transferor futures commission merchant or introducing broker;

(2) The name, principal business address and telephone number of each transferee futures commission merchant or introducing broker;

(3) The designated self-regulatory organization for the transferor and transferee firms;

(4) A brief statement as to the reasons for the transfer;

(5) A copy of the notice to customers informing them of the proposed transfer and providing an opportunity to object to such transfer; and

(6) A statement of the number of accounts to be transferred and the estimated liquidating equity of the accounts to be transferred.

(d) The notice required by paragraph (b) of this section shall be filed with the Deputy Director, Compliance and Registration Section, Division of Swap Dealer and Intermediary Oversight, Commodity Futures Trading Commission, Three Lafayette Centre, 1155 21st Street, NW., Washington, DC 20581; the National Futures Association Attn: Vice President-Compliance; and the designated self-regulatory organization for the transferor firm.

(e) In the event that the notice required by paragraph (b) of this section cannot be filed with the Commission at least five days prior to the account transfer, the transferee futures commission merchant or introducing broker shall file such notice as soon as practicable and no later than the day of the transfer. Such notice shall include a brief statement explaining the circumstances necessitating the delay in filing.

(f) The requirements of this section shall not affect the obligations of a futures commission merchant or introducing broker under the rules of a self-regulatory organization or applicable customer account agreement with respect to transfer of accounts.

(g) If a proposed transfer is not completed in accordance with the notice required to be filed by paragraph (b) of this section, a corrective notice shall be filed within five business days of the date such proposed transfer was to occur explaining why the proposed transfer was not completed.

[58 FR 17504, Apr. 5, 1993, as amended at 60 FR 49334, Sept. 25, 1995; 63 FR 8571, Feb. 20, 1998; 67 FR 62351, Oct. 7, 2002; 78 FR 22419, Apr. 16, 2013]

§ 1.66 NO-ACTION POSITIONS WITH RESPECT TO FLOOR TRADERS.

(a) Notwithstanding any other provision of law, if a contract market submits to the National Futures Association by April 26, 1993 a list of floor traders who were granted trading privileges on that contract market on or before April 26, 1993, and whose floor trading privileges remain in effect, which includes the name, date of birth and social security number of such floor traders, as well as facts regarding such floor traders which are set forth as statutory disqualifications in section 8a(2) of the Act if the contract market knows of such facts, and such list is signed by the chief operating officer of the contract market, the Commission will not commence an enforcement proceeding against a floor trader on that list based solely upon the floor trader's failure to register or receive a temporary license under section 4f of the Act and § 3.11 of this chapter, nor will the Commission commence an enforcement proceeding against the contract market under § 1.62 for failing to bar such floor trader from operating as such:

Provided, however, That for those floor traders listed as to whom the contract market knows of facts set forth as statutory disqualifications in section 8a(2) of the Act, the no-action position contained in paragraph (a) of this section will only apply if the contract market submits a supplemental statement signed by the chief operating officer of the contract market stating that, in light of the Congressional mandate requiring registration of floor traders under the Act, the contract market acknowledges its responsibility to take affirmative action to conduct appropriate surveillance of such floor traders. These no-action positions shall expire upon the floor's trader being granted or denied registration under the Act, or on June 11, 1993, whichever comes earliest: *Provided, however,* That if the floor trader files an application for registration in accordance with § 3.11 of this chapter with the National Futures Association by June 11, 1993, the no-action positions for the floor trader and the contract market as to the registration of such floor trader will be extended until the floor trader is granted or denied registration under the Act, unless an Administrative Law Judge issues an interim order suspending the no-action position as to such floor trader in accordance with paragraph (b) of this section or the application for registration is withdrawn.

(b) *Suspension of no-action position under paragraph (a) of this section pursuant to section 8a(2) of the Act* —(1) *Notice.*On the basis of information obtained by the Commission, the Commission may at any time serve notice upon a floor trader whose name appears on a list submitted in accordance with paragraph (a) of this section that:

(i) The Commission alleges and is prepared to prove that such floor trader is subject to one or more of the statutory disqualifications set forth in section 8a(2) of the Act;

(ii) An Administrative Law Judge shall make a determination, based upon written evidence, as to whether the floor trader is subject to such statutory disqualification; and

(iii) If the floor trader is found to be subject to a statutory disqualification, the no-action status of the floor trader under paragraph (a) of this section may be suspended and the floor trader ordered to show cause why registration should not be denied.

(2) *Written submission.* If the floor trader wishes to challenge the accuracy of the allegations set forth in the notice, the floor trader may submit written evidence limited to the type described in § 3.60(b)(1) of this chapter. Such written submission must be served upon the Division of Enforcement and filed with the Proceedings Clerk within twenty days of the date of service of notice to the floor trader.

(3) *Reply.* Within ten days of receipt of any written submission filed by the floor trader, the Division of Enforcement may serve upon the floor trader and file with the Proceedings Clerk a reply.

(4) *Determination by Administrative Law Judge.* A determination by the Administrative Law Judge as to whether the floor trader is subject to a statutory disqualification must be based upon the evidence of the statutory disqualification, notice with proof of service, the written submission, if any, filed by the floor trader in response thereto, any written reply submitted by the Division of Enforcement and such other papers as the Administrative Law Judge may require or permit.

(5) *Suspension and order to show cause.* (i) If the floor trader is found to be subject to a statutory disqualification, the Administrative Law Judge, within thirty days after receipt of the floor trader's written submission, if any, and any reply thereto, shall issue an interim order suspending the no-action status of the floor trader under paragraph (a) of this section and requiring the floor trader to show cause within twenty days of the date of the order why, notwithstanding the existence of the statutory disqualification, the registration of the floor trader should not be denied. The no-action status of the floor trader shall be suspended, effective five days after the order to show cause is served upon the floor trader in accordance with § 3.50(a) of this chapter, until a final order with respect to the order to show cause has been

issued: *Provided, That* if the sole basis upon which the floor trader is subject to statutory disqualification is the existence of a temporary order, judgment or decree of the type described in section 8a(2)(C) of the Act, the order to show cause shall not be issued and the floor trader shall be suspended until such time as the temporary order, judgment or decree shall have expired: *Provided, however,* That in no event shall the floor trader's no-action status be suspended for a period to exceed six months.

(ii) If the floor trader is found not to be subject to a statutory disqualification, the Administrative Law Judge shall issue an order to that effect and the Proceedings Clerk shall promptly serve a copy of such order on the floor trader, the Division of Swap Dealer and Intermediary Oversight and the Division of Enforcement. Such order shall be effective as a final order of the Commission fifteen days after the date it is served upon the floor trader in accordance with the provisions of § 3.50(a) of this chapter unless a timely application for review is filed in accordance with § 10.102 of this chapter. The appellate procedures set forth in §§ 10.102, 10.103, 10.104, 10.106, 10.107 and 10.109 of this chapter shall apply to any appeal brought under paragraph (c)(5)(ii) of this section.

(6) *Further proceedings.* If an order to show cause is issued pursuant to paragraph (c)(5)(i) of this section, further proceedings on such order shall be conducted in accordance with the provisions of § 3.60(b) through (j) of this chapter.

[58 FR 19589, Apr. 15, 1993; 58 FR 21776, Apr. 23, 1993, as amended at 60 FR 54801, Oct. 26, 1995; 67 FR 62351, Oct. 7, 2002; 78 FR 22419, Apr. 16, 2013]

§ 1.67 NOTIFICATION OF FINAL DISCIPLINARY ACTION INVOLVING FINANCIAL HARM TO A CUSTOMER.

(a) *Definitions.* For purposes of this section:

Final disciplinary action means any decision by or settlement with a contract market or swap execution facility in a disciplinary matter which cannot be further appealed at the contract market or swap execution facility, is not subject to the stay of the Commission or a court of competent jurisdiction, and has not been reversed by the Commission or any court of competent jurisdiction.

(b) Upon any final disciplinary action in which a contract market or swap execution facility finds that a member has committed a rule violation that involved a transaction for a customer, whether executed or not, and that resulted in financial harm to the customer:

(1)(i) The contract market or swap execution facility shall promptly provide written notice of the disciplinary action to the futures commission merchant or other registrant; and

(ii) A futures commission merchant or other registrant that receives a notice, under paragraph (b)(1)(i) of this section shall promptly provide written notice of the disciplinary action to the customer as disclosed on its books and records. If the customer is another futures commission merchant or other registrant, such futures commission merchant or other registrant shall promptly provide notice to the customer.

(2) A written notice required by paragraph (b)(1) of this section must include the principal facts of the disciplinary action and a statement that the contract market or swap execution facility has found that the member has committed a rule violation that involved a transaction for the customer, whether executed or not, and that resulted in financial harm to the customer. For the purposes of this paragraph, a notice which includes the information listed in § 9.11(b) of this chapter shall be deemed to include the principal facts of the disciplinary action thereof.

[77 FR 66331, Nov. 2, 2012]

§ 1.69 VOTING BY INTERESTED MEMBERS OF SELF-REGULATORY ORGANIZATION GOVERNING BOARDS AND VARIOUS COMMITTEES.

(a) *Definitions.* For purposes of this section:

(1) *Disciplinary committee* means any person or committee of persons, or any subcommittee thereof, that is authorized by a self-regulatory organization to issue disciplinary charges, to conduct disciplinary proceedings, to settle disciplinary charges, to impose disciplinary sanctions, or to hear appeals thereof in cases involving any violation of the rules of the self-regulatory organization except those cases where the person or committee is authorized summarily to impose minor penalties for violating rules regarding decorum, attire, the timely submission of accurate records for clearing or verifying each day's transactions or other similar activities.

(2) *Family relationship* of a person means the person's spouse, former spouse, parent, stepparent, child, stepchild, sibling, stepbrother, stepsister, grandparent, grandchild, uncle, aunt, nephew, niece or in-law.

(3) *Governing board* means a self-regulatory organization's board of directors, board of governors, board of managers, or similar body, or any subcommittee thereof, duly authorized, pursuant to a rule of the self-regulatory organization that has been approved by the Commission or has become effective pursuant to either Section 5a(a)(12)(A) or 17(j) of the Act to take action or to recommend the taking of action on behalf of the self-regulatory organization.

(4) *Oversight panel* means any panel, or any subcommittee thereof, authorized by a self-regulatory organization to recommend or establish policies or procedures with respect to the self-regulatory organization's surveillance, compliance, rule enforcement, or disciplinary responsibilities.

(5) *Member's affiliated firm* is a firm in which the member is a "principal," as defined in § 3.1(a), or an employee.

(6) *Named party in interest* means a person or entity that is identified by name as a subject of any matter being considered by a governing board, disciplinary committee, or oversight panel.

(7) *Self-regulatory organization* means a "self-regulatory organization" as defined in § 1.3(ee) and includes a "clearing organization" as defined in § 1.3(d), but excludes registered futures associations for the purposes of paragraph (b)(2) of this section.

8) *Significant action* includes any of the following types of self-regulatory organization actions or rule changes that can be implemented without the Commission's prior approval:

(i) Any actions or rule changes which address an "emergency" as defined in § 1.41(a)(4)(i) through (iv) and (vi) through (viii); and,

(ii) Any changes in margin levels that are designed to respond to extraordinary market conditions such as an actual or attempted corner, squeeze, congestion or undue concentration of positions, or that otherwise are likely to have a substantial effect on prices in any contract traded or cleared at such self-regulatory organization; but does not include any rule not submitted for prior Commission approval because such rule is unrelated to the terms and conditions of any contract traded at such self-regulatory organization.

(b) *Self-regulatory organization rules.* Each self-regulatory organization shall maintain in effect rules that have been submitted to the Commission pursuant to Section 5a(a)(12)(A) of the Act and § 1.41 or, in the case of a registered futures association, pursuant to Section 17(j) of the Act, to address the avoidance of conflicts of interest in the execution of its self-regulatory functions. Such rules must provide for the following:

(1) *Relationship with named party in interest*— (i) *Nature of relationship.* A member of a self-regulatory organization's governing board, disciplinary committee or oversight panel must abstain from such body's deliberations and voting on any matter involving a named party in interest where such member:

(A) Is a named party in interest;

(B) Is an employer, employee, or fellow employee of a named party in interest;

(C) Is associated with a named party in interest through a "broker association" as defined in § 156.1;

(D) Has any other significant, ongoing business relationship with a named party in interest, not including relationships limited to executing futures or option transactions opposite of each other or to clearing futures or option transactions through the same clearing member; or,

(E) Has a family relationship with a named party in interest.

(ii) *Disclosure of relationship.* Prior to the consideration of any matter involving a named party in interest, each member of a self-regulatory organization governing board, disciplinary committee or oversight panel must disclose to the appropriate self-regulatory organization staff whether he or she has one of the relationships listed in paragraph (b)(1)(i) of this section with a named party in interest.

(iii) *Procedure for determination.* Each self-regulatory organization must establish procedures for determining whether any member of its governing board, disciplinary committees or oversight committees is subject to a conflicts restriction in any matter involving a named party in interest. Taking into consideration the exigency of the committee action, such determinations should be based upon:

(A) Information provided by the member pursuant to paragraph (b)(1)(ii) of this section; and

(B) Any other source of information that is held by and reasonably available to the self-regulatory organization.

(2) *Financial interest in a significant action*— (i) *Nature of interest.* A member of a self-regulatory organization's governing board, disciplinary committee or oversight panel must abstain from such body's deliberations and voting on any significant action if the member knowingly has a direct and substantial financial interest in the result of the vote based upon either exchange or non-exchange positions that could reasonably be expected to be affected by the action.

(ii) *Disclosure of interest.* Prior to the consideration of any significant action, each member of a self-regulatory organization governing board, disciplinary committee or oversight panel must disclose to the appropriate self-regulatory organization staff the position information referred to in paragraph (b)(2)(iii) of this section that is known to him or her. This requirement does not apply to members who choose to abstain from deliberations and voting on the subject significant action.

(iii) *Procedure for determination.* Each self-regulatory organization must establish procedures for determining whether any member of its governing board, disciplinary committees or oversight committees is subject to a conflicts restriction under this section in any significant action. Such determination must include a review of:

(A) Gross positions held at that self-regulatory organization in the member's personal accounts or "controlled accounts," as defined in § 1.3(j);

(B) Gross positions held at that self-regulatory organization in proprietary accounts, as defined in § 1.17(b)(3), at the member's affiliated firm;

(C) Gross positions held at that self-regulatory organization in accounts in which the member is a principal, as defined in § 3.1(a);

(D) Net positions held at that self-regulatory organization in "customer" accounts, as defined in § 1.17(b)(2), at the member's affiliated firm; and,

(E) Any other types of positions, whether maintained at that self-regulatory organization or elsewhere, held in the member's personal accounts or the proprietary accounts of the member's affiliated firm that the self-regulatory organization reasonably expects could be affected by the significant action.

(iv) *Bases for determination.* Taking into consideration the exigency of the significant action, such determinations should be based upon:

(A) The most recent large trader reports and clearing records available to the self-regulatory organization;

(B) Information provided by the member with respect to positions pursuant to paragraph (b)(2)(ii) of this section; and,

(C) Any other source of information that is held by and reasonably available to the self-regulatory organization.

(3) *Participation in deliberations.* (i) Under the rules required by this section, a self-regulatory organization governing board, disciplinary committee or oversight panel may permit a member to participate in deliberations prior to a vote on a significant action for which he or she otherwise would be required to abstain, pursuant to paragraph (b)(2) of this section, if such participation would be consistent with the public interest and the member recuses himself or herself from voting on such action.

(ii) In making a determination as to whether to permit a member to participate in deliberations on a significant action for which he or she otherwise would be required to abstain, the deliberating body shall consider the following factors:

(A) Wwhether the member's participation in deliberations is necessary for the deliberating body to achieve a quorum in the matter; and

(B) Whether the member has unique or special expertise, knowledge or experience in the matter under consideration.

(iii) Prior to any determination pursuant to paragraph (b)(3)(i) of this section, the deliberating body must fully consider the position information which is the basis for the member's direct and substantial financial interest in the result of a vote on a significant action pursuant to paragraph (b)(2) of this section.

(4) *Documentation of determination.* Self-regulatory organization governing boards, disciplinary committees, and oversight panels must reflect in their minutes or otherwise document that the conflicts determination procedures required by this section have been followed. Such records also must include:

(i) The names of all members who attended the meeting in person or who otherwise were present by electronic means;

(ii) The name of any member who voluntarily recused himself or herself or was required to abstain from deliberations and/or voting on a matter and the reason for the recusal or abstention, if stated; and

(iii) Information on the position information that was reviewed for each member.

[64 FR 23, Jan. 4, 1999; 64 FR 3340, Jan. 21, 1999]

§ 1.70 NOTIFICATION OF STATE ENFORCEMENT ACTIONS BROUGHT UNDER THE COMMODITY EXCHANGE ACT.

(a) Immediately upon instituting any proceeding in any Federal district court for violation of the Act or any rule, regulation or order thereunder against any person who is subject to suit pursuant to sections 6d(1)-(6) of the Act, the authorized State official of the State instituting the proceeding shall submit to the Commission a copy of the complaint filed in the proceeding, together with a written notice which:

(1) Indicates the names of parties to the proceeding;

(2) Indicates the provision of the Act or the rule, regulation or order thereunder which is alleged to have been violated.

The complaint and written notice must be sent by first-class U.S. mail or personally delivered to the Secretary, Commodity Futures Trading Commission, Three Lafayette Centre, 1155 21st Street, NW., Washington, DC 20581.

(b) Prior to instituting any proceeding in a State court for the alleged violation of any antifraud provisions of the Act or any antifraud rule, regulation or order thereunder against any person registered with the Commission who is subject to suit pursuant to the provisions of section 6d(8) of the Act, the authorized State official of the State intending to institute the proceeding shall submit to the Commission written notice which:

(1) Indicates the names of parties to the proposed proceeding;

(2) Indicates the provision of the Act or the rule, regulation or order thereunder which will be alleged to have been violated;

(3) Contains a brief statement of the facts on which the proposed action will be based.

Except as provided in paragraph (c), this written notice must be sent by first-class U.S. mail or personally delivered to the Secretary, Commodity Futures Trading Commission, Three Lafayette Centre, 1155 21st Street, NW., Washington, DC 20581 not less than 5 business days prior to instituting the proceeding in State court.

(c) Where it is impracticable to provide the Commission with written notice within the time period specified in paragraph (b) of this section, the authorized state official must inform the Secretary of the Commission by telephone as soon as practicable to institute a proceeding in state court and must send the written notice required in paragraph (b)(1) through (b)(3) of this section by facsimile or other similarly expeditious means of written communication to the Secretary of the Commission, prior to instituting the proceeding in state court.

(d) Immediately upon instituting any proceeding in a State court pursuant to the provisions of section 6d(8) of the Act for alleged violation of any antifraud provisions of the Act or any antifraud rule, regulation or order thereunder, the authorized State official instituting the proceeding shall submit to the Commission a copy of the complaint filed in the proceeding. The copy of the complaint must be sent by first class U.S. mail or personally delivered to the Secretary, Commodity Futures Trading Commission, Three Lafayette Centre, 1155 21st Street, NW., Washington, DC 20581.

[48 FR 49503, Oct. 26, 1983, as amended at 60 FR 49334, Sept. 25, 1995]

§ 1.71 CONFLICTS OF INTEREST POLICIES AND PROCEDURES BY FUTURES COMMISSION MERCHANTS AND INTRODUCING BROKERS.

(a) *Definitions.* For purposes of this section, the following terms shall be defined as provided.

(1) *Affiliate.* This term means, with respect to any person, a person controlling, controlled by, or under common control with, such person.

(2) *Business trading unit.* This term means any department, division, group, or personnel of a futures commission merchant or introducing broker or any of its affiliates, whether or not identified as such, that performs, or personnel exercising direct supervisory authority over the performance of, any pricing (excluding price verification for risk management purposes), trading, sales, marketing, advertising, solicitation, structuring, or brokerage activities on behalf of a futures commission merchant or introducing broker or any of its affiliates.

(3) *Clearing unit.* This term means any department, division, group, or personnel of a futures commission merchant or any of its affiliates, whether or not identified as such, that performs, or personnel exercising direct supervisory authority over the performance of, any proprietary or customer clearing activities on behalf of a futures commission merchant or any of its affiliates.

(4) *Derivative.* This term means:

(i) A contract for the purchase or sale of a commodity for future delivery;

(ii) A security futures product;

(iii) A swap;

(iv) Any agreement, contract, or transaction described in section 2(c)(2)(C)(i) or section 2(c)(2)(D)(i) of the Act; and

(v) Any commodity option authorized under section 4c of the Act; and (vi) any leverage transaction authorized under section 19 of the Act.

(5) *Non-research personnel.* This term means any employee of the business trading unit or clearing unit, or any other employee of the futures commission merchant or introducing broker, other than an employee performing a legal or compliance function, who is not directly responsible for, or otherwise not directly involved in, research or analysis intended for inclusion in a research report.

(6) *Public appearance.* This term means any participation in a conference call, seminar, forum (including an interactive electronic forum) or other public speaking activity before 15 or more persons (individuals or entities), or interview or appearance before one or more representatives of the media, radio, television or print media, or the writing of a print media article, in which a research analyst makes a recommendation or offers an opinion concerning a derivatives transaction. This term does not include a password-protected Webcast, conference call or similar event with 15 or more existing customers, provided that all of the event participants previously received the most current research report or other documentation that contains the required applicable disclosures, and that the research analyst appearing at the event corrects and updates during the public appearance any disclosures in the research report that are inaccurate, misleading, or no longer applicable.

(7) *Research analyst.* This term means the employee of a futures commission merchant or introducing broker who is primarily responsible for, and any employee who reports directly or indirectly to such research analyst in connection with, preparation of the substance of a research report relating to any derivative, whether or not any such person has the job title of "research analyst."

(8) *Research department.* This term means any department or division that is principally responsible for preparing the substance of a research report relating to any derivative on behalf of a futures commission merchant or introducing broker, including a department or division contained in an affiliate of a futures commission merchant or introducing broker.

(9) *Research report.* This term means any written communication (including electronic) that includes an analysis of the price or market for any derivative, and that provides information reasonably sufficient upon which to base a decision to enter into a derivatives transaction. This term does not include:

(i) Communications distributed to fewer than 15 persons;

(ii) Commentaries on economic, political or market conditions;

(iii) Statistical summaries of multiple companies' financial data, including listings of current ratings;

(iv) Periodic reports or other communications prepared for investment company shareholders or commodity pool participants that discuss individual derivatives positions in the context of a fund's past performance or the basis for previously-made discretionary decisions;

(v) Any communications generated by an employee of the business trading unit that is conveyed as a solicitation for entering into a derivatives transaction, and is conspicuously identified as such; and

(vi) Internal communications that are not given to current or prospective customers.

(b) *Policies and procedures.* (1) Except as provided in paragraph (b)(2) of this section, each futures commission merchant and introducing broker subject to this rule must adopt and implement written policies and procedures reasonably designed to ensure that the futures commission merchant or introducing broker and its employees comply with the provisions of this rule.

(2) Small Introducing Brokers. An introducing broker that has generated, over the preceding 3 years, $5 million or less in aggregate gross revenues from its activities as an introducing broker must establish structural and institutional safeguards reasonably designed to ensure that the activities of any person within the firm relating to research or analysis of the price or market for any commodity or derivative are separated by appropriate informational partitions within the firm from the review, pressure, or oversight of persons whose involvement in trading or clearing activities might potentially bias the judgment or supervision of the persons.

(c) *Research analysts and research reports* —(1) *Restrictions on relationship with research department.* (i) Non-research personnel shall not direct a research analyst's decision to publish a research report of the futures commission merchant or introducing broker, and non-research personnel shall not direct the views and opinions expressed in a research report of the futures commission merchant or introducing broker.

(ii) No research analyst may be subject to the supervision or control of any employee of the futures commission merchant's or introducing broker's business trading unit or clearing unit, and no employee of the business trading unit or clearing unit may have any influence or control over the evaluation or compensation of a research analyst.

(iii) Except as provided in paragraph (c)(1)(iv) of this section, non-research personnel, other than the board of directors and any committee thereof, shall not review or approve a research report of the futures commission merchant or introducing broker before its publication.

(iv) Non-research personnel may review a research report before its publication as necessary only to verify the factual accuracy of information in the research report, to provide for non-substantive editing, to format the layout or style of the research report, or to identify any potential conflicts of interest, provided that:

(A) Any written communication between non-research personnel and research department personnel concerning the content of a research report must be made either through authorized legal or compliance personnel of the futures commission merchant or introducing broker or in a transmission copied to such personnel; and

(B) Any oral communication between non-research personnel and research department personnel concerning the content of a research report must be documented and made either through authorized legal or compliance personnel acting as an intermediary or in a conversation conducted in the presence of such personnel.

(2) *Restrictions on communications.* Any written or oral communication by a research analyst to a current or prospective customer relating to any derivative must not omit any material fact or qualification that would cause the communication to be misleading to a reasonable person.

(3) *Restrictions on research analyst compensation.* A futures commission merchant or introducing broker may not consider as a factor in reviewing or approving a research analyst's compensation his or her contributions to the futures commission merchant's or introducing broker's trading or clearing business. Except for communicating client or customer feedback, ratings and other indicators of research analyst performance to research department management, no employee of the business trading unit or clearing unit of the futures commission merchant or introducing broker may influence the review or approval of a research analyst's compensation.

(4) *Prohibition of promise of favorable research.* No futures commission merchant or introducing broker may directly or indirectly offer favorable research, or threaten to change research, to an existing or prospective customer as consideration or inducement for the receipt of business or compensation.

(5) *Disclosure requirements.* (i) *Ownership and material conflicts of interest.* A futures commission merchant or introducing broker must disclose in research reports and a research analyst must disclose in public appearances whether the research analyst maintains a financial interest in any derivative of a type, class, or category that the research analyst follows, and the general nature of the financial interest.

(ii) *Prominence of disclosure.* Disclosures and references to disclosures must be clear, comprehensive, and prominent. With respect to public appearances by research analysts, the disclosures required by paragraph (c)(5) of this section must be conspicuous.

(iii) *Records of public appearances.* Each futures commission merchant and introducing broker must maintain records of public appearances by research analysts sufficient to demonstrate compliance by those research analysts with the applicable disclosure requirements under paragraph (c)(5) of this section.

(iv) *Third-party research reports.* (A) For the purposes of paragraph (c)(5)(iv) of this section, "independent third-party research report" shall mean a research report, in respect of which the person or entity producing the report:

(*1*) Has no affiliation or business or contractual relationship with the distributing futures commission merchant or introducing broker, or that futures commission merchant's or introducing broker's affiliates, that is reasonably likely to inform the content of its research reports; and

(2) Makes content determinations without any input from the distributing futures commission merchant or introducing broker or from the futures commission merchant's or introducing broker's affiliates.

(B) Subject to paragraph (c)(5)(iv)(C) of this section, if a futures commission merchant or introducing broker distributes or makes available any independent third-party research report, the futures commission merchant or introducing broker must accompany the research report with, or provide a web address that directs the recipient to, the current applicable disclosures, as they pertain to the futures commission merchant or introducing broker, required by this section. Each futures commission merchant and introducing broker must establish written policies and procedures reasonably designed to ensure the completeness and accuracy of all applicable disclosures.

(C) The requirements of paragraph (c)(5)(iv)(B) of this section shall not apply to independent third-party research reports made available by a futures commission merchant or introducing broker to its customers:

(*1*) Upon request; or

(*2*) Through a Web site maintained by the futures commission merchant or introducing broker.

(6) *Prohibition of retaliation against research analysts.* No futures commission merchant or introducing broker, and no employee of a futures commission merchant or introducing broker who is involved with the futures commission merchant's or introducing broker's trading or clearing activities, may, directly or indirectly, retaliate against or threaten to retaliate against any research analyst employed by the futures commission merchant or introducing broker or its affiliates as a result of an adverse, negative, or otherwise unfavorable research report or public appearance written or made, in good faith, by the research analyst that may adversely affect the futures commission merchant's or introducing broker's present or prospective trading or clearing activities.

(7) *Small Introducing Brokers.* An introducing broker that has generated, over the preceding 3 years, $5 million or less in aggregate gross revenues from its activities as an introducing broker is exempt from the requirements set forth in this paragraph (c).

(d) *Clearing activities.* (1) No futures commission merchant shall permit any affiliated swap dealer or major swap participant to directly or indirectly interfere with, or attempt to influence, the decision of the clearing unit personnel of the futures commission merchant to provide clearing services and activities to a particular customer, including but not limited to a decision relating to the following:

(i) Whether to offer clearing services and activities to a particular customer;

(ii) Whether to accept a particular customer for the purposes of clearing derivatives;

(iii) Whether to submit a customer's transaction to a particular derivatives clearing organization;

(iv) Whether to set or adjust risk tolerance levels for a particular customer;

(v) Whether to accept certain forms of collateral from a particular customer; or

(vi) Whether to set a particular customer's fees for clearing services based upon criteria that are not generally available and applicable to other customers of the futures commission merchant.

(2) Each futures commission merchant shall create and maintain an appropriate informational partition between business trading units of an affiliated swap dealer or major swap participant and clearing unit personnel of the futures commission merchant to reasonably ensure compliance with the Act and the prohibitions specified in paragraph (d)(1) of this section. At a minimum, such informational partitions shall require that:

(i) No employee of a business trading unit of an affiliated swap dealer or major swap participant may review or approve the provision of clearing services and activities by clearing unit personnel of the futures commission merchant, make any determination regarding whether the futures commission merchant accepts clearing customers, or in any way condition or tie the provision of trading services upon or to the provision of clearing services or otherwise participate in the provision of clearing services by improperly incentivizing or encouraging the use of the affiliated futures commission merchant. Any employee of a business trading unit of an affiliated swap dealer or major swap participant may participate in the activities of the futures commission merchant as necessary for (A) participating in default management undertaken by a derivatives clearing organization during an event of default; and (B) transferring, liquidating, or hedging any proprietary or customer positions during an event of default;

(ii) No employee of a business trading unit of an affiliated swap dealer or major swap participant shall supervise, control, or influence any employee of a clearing unit of the futures commission merchant; and

(iii) No employee of the business trading unit of an affiliated swap dealer or major swap participant shall influence or control compensation or evaluation of any employee of the clearing unit of the futures commission merchant.

(e) *Undue influence on customers.* Each futures commission merchant and introducing broker must adopt and implement written policies and procedures that mandate the disclosure to its customers of any material incentives and any material conflicts of interest regarding the decision of a customer as to the trade execution and/or clearing of the derivatives transaction.

(f) *Records.* All records that a futures commission merchant or introducing broker is required to maintain pursuant to this regulation shall be maintained in accordance with Commission Regulation § 1.31 and shall be made available promptly upon request to representatives of the Commission.

[77 FR 20198, Apr. 3, 2012]

§ 1.72 RESTRICTIONS ON CUSTOMER CLEARING ARRANGEMENTS.

No futures commission merchant providing clearing services to customers shall enter into an arrangement that:

(a) Discloses to the futures commission merchant or any swap dealer or major swap participant the identity of a customer's original executing counterparty;

(b) Limits the number of counterparties with whom a customer may enter into a trade;

(c) Restricts the size of the position a customer may take with any individual counterparty, apart from an overall limit for all positions held by the customer at the futures commission merchant;

(d) Impairs a customer's access to execution of a trade on terms that have a reasonable relationship to the best terms available; or

(e) Prevents compliance with the timeframes set forth in § 1.74(b), § 23.610(b), or § 39.12(b)(7) of this chapter.

[77 FR 21306, Apr. 9, 2012]

§ 1.73 CLEARING FUTURES COMMISSION MERCHANT RISK MANAGEMENT.

(a) Each futures commission merchant that is a clearing member of a derivatives clearing organization shall:

(1) Establish risk-based limits in the proprietary account and in each customer account based on position size, order size, margin requirements, or similar factors;

(2) Screen orders for compliance with the risk-based limits in accordance with the following:

(i) When a clearing futures commission merchant provides electronic market access or accepts orders for automated execution, it shall use automated means to screen orders for compliance with the limits;

(ii) When a clearing futures commission merchant accepts orders for non-automated execution, it shall establish and maintain systems of risk controls reasonably designed to ensure compliance with the limits;

(iii) When a clearing futures commission merchant accepts transactions that were executed bilaterally and then submitted for clearing, it shall establish and maintain systems of risk management controls reasonably designed to ensure compliance with the limits;

(iv) When a firm executes an order on behalf of a customer but gives it up to another firm for clearing,

(A) The clearing futures commission merchant shall establish risk-based limits for the customer, and enter into an agreement in advance with the executing firm that requires the executing firm to screen orders for compliance with those limits in accordance with paragraph (a)(2)(i) or (ii) as applicable; and

(B) The clearing futures commission merchant shall establish and maintain systems of risk management controls reasonably designed to ensure compliance with the limits.

(v) When an account manager bunches orders on behalf of multiple customers for execution as a block and post-trade allocation to individual accounts for clearing:

(A) The futures commission merchant that initially clears the block shall establish risk-based limits for the block account and screen the order in accordance with paragraph (a)(2)(i) or (ii) as applicable;

(B) The futures commission merchants that clear the allocated trades on behalf of customers shall establish risk-based limits for each customer and enter into an agreement in advance with the account manager that requires the account manager to screen orders for compliance with those limits; and

(C) The futures commission merchants that clear the allocated trades on behalf of customers shall establish and maintain systems of risk management controls reasonably designed to ensure compliance with the limits.

(3) Monitor for adherence to the risk-based limits intra-day and overnight;

(4) Conduct stress tests under extreme but plausible conditions of all positions in the proprietary account and in each customer account that could pose material risk to the futures commission merchant at least once per week;

(5) Evaluate its ability to meet initial margin requirements at least once per week;

(6) Evaluate its ability to meet variation margin requirements in cash at least once per week;

(7) Evaluate its ability to liquidate, in an orderly manner, the positions in the proprietary and customer accounts and estimate the cost of the liquidation at least once per quarter; and

(8) Test all lines of credit at least once per year.

(b) Each futures commission merchant that is a clearing member of a derivatives clearing organization shall:

(1) Establish written procedures to comply with this regulation; and

(2) Keep full, complete, and systematic records documenting its compliance with this regulation.

(3) All records required to be maintained pursuant to these regulations shall be maintained in accordance with Commission Regulation 1.31 (17 CFR 1.31) and shall be made available promptly upon request to representatives of the Commission and to representatives of applicable prudential regulators.

[77 FR 21306, Apr. 9, 2012]

§ 1.74 FUTURES COMMISSION MERCHANT ACCEPTANCE FOR CLEARING.

(a) Each futures commission merchant that is a clearing member of a derivatives clearing organization shall coordinate with each derivatives clearing organization on which it clears to establish systems that enable the futures commission merchant, or the derivatives clearing organization acting on its behalf, to accept or reject each trade submitted to the derivatives clearing organization for clearing by or for the futures commission merchant or a customer of the futures commission merchant as quickly as would be technologically practicable if fully automated systems were used; and

(b) Each futures commission merchant that is a clearing member of a derivatives clearing organization shall accept or reject each trade submitted by or for it or its customers as quickly as would be technologically practicable if fully automated systems were used; a clearing futures commission merchant may meet this requirement by:

(1) Establishing systems to pre-screen orders for compliance with criteria specified by the clearing futures commission merchant;

(2) Establishing systems that authorize a derivatives clearing organization to accept or reject on its behalf trades that meet, or fail to meet, criteria specified by the clearing futures commission merchant; or

(3) Establishing systems that enable the clearing futures commission merchant to communicate to the derivatives clearing organization acceptance or rejection of each trade as quickly as would be technologically practicable if fully automated systems were used.

[77 FR 21307, Apr. 9, 2012]

§ 1.75 DELEGATION OF AUTHORITY TO THE DIRECTOR OF THE DIVISION OF CLEARING AND RISK TO ESTABLISH AN ALTERNATIVE COMPLIANCE SCHEDULE TO COMPLY WITH FUTURES COMMISSION MERCHANT ACCEPTANCE FOR CLEARING.

(a) The Commission hereby delegates to the Director of the Division of Clearing and Risk or such other employee or employees as the Director may designate from time to time, the authority to establish an alternative compliance schedule for requirements of § 1.74 for swaps that are found to be technologically or economically impracticable for an affected futures commission merchant that seeks, in good faith, to comply with the requirements of § 1.74 within a reasonable time period beyond the date on which compliance by such futures commission merchant is otherwise required.

(b) A request for an alternative compliance schedule under this section shall be acted upon by the Director of the Division of Clearing and Risk within 30 days from the time such a request is received, or it shall be deemed approved.

(c) An exception granted under this section shall not cause a registrant to be out of compliance or deemed in violation of any registration requirements.

(d) Notwithstanding any other provision of this section, in any case in which a Commission employee delegated authority under this section believes it appropriate, he or she may submit to the Commission for its consideration the question of whether an alternative compliance schedule should be established. Nothing in this section shall be deemed to prohibit the Commission, at its election, from exercising the authority delegated in this section.

[77 FR 21307, Apr. 9, 2012]

APPENDIX B TO PART 1—FEES FOR CONTRACT MARKET RULE ENFORCEMENT REVIEWS AND FINANCIAL REVIEWS

(a) Within 60 days of the effective date of a final fee schedule for each fiscal year, each board of trade which has been designated as a contract market for at least one actively trading contract shall submit a check or money order, made payable to the Commodity Futures Trading Commission, to cover the Commission's actual costs in conducting contract market rule enforcement reviews and financial reviews.

(b) The Commission determines fees charged to exchanges based upon a formula that considers both actual costs and trading volume.

(c) Checks should be sent to the attention of the Office of the Secretariat, Commodity Futures Trading Commission, Three Lafayette Centre, 1155 21st Street, NW., Washington, DC 20581.

IMPORTANT LAWS AND REGULATIONS

COMMODITY FUTURES TRADING COMMISSION ACT OF 1974

The **Commodity Futures Modernization Act of 2000** (CFMA) is United States federal legislation that officially ensured the deregulation of financial products known as over-the-counter derivatives. It was signed into law on December 21, 2000 by President Bill Clinton. It clarified the law so that most over-the-counter (OTC) derivatives transactions between "sophisticated parties" would not be regulated as "futures" under the Commodity Exchange Act of 1936 (CEA) or as "securities" under the federal securities laws. Instead, the major dealers of those products (banks and securities firms) would continue to have their dealings in OTC derivatives supervised by their federal regulators under general "safety and soundness" standards. The Commodity Futures Trading Commission's (CFTC) desire to have "Functional regulation" of the market was also rejected. Instead, the CFTC would continue to do "entity-based supervision of OTC derivatives dealers." These derivatives, including the credit default swap, are a few of the many causes of the financial crisis of 2008 and the subsequent 2008–2012 global recession

COMMODITY FUTURES MODERNIZATION ACT OF 2000

The **Commodity Futures Modernization Act of 2000** (CFMA) is United States federal legislation that officially ensured the deregulation of financial products known as over-the-counter derivatives. It was signed into law on December 21, 2000 by President Bill Clinton. It clarified the law so that most over-the-counter (OTC) derivatives transactions between "sophisticated parties" would not be regulated as "futures" under the Commodity Exchange Act of 1936 (CEA) or as "securities" under the federal securities laws. Instead, the major dealers of those products (banks and securities firms) would continue to have their dealings in OTC derivatives supervised by their federal regulators under general "safety and soundness" standards. The Commodity Futures Trading Commission's (CFTC) desire to have "Functional regulation" of the market was also rejected. Instead, the CFTC would continue to do "entity-based supervision of OTC derivatives dealers." These derivatives, including the credit default swap, are a few of the many causes of the financial crisis of 2008 and the subsequent 2008–2012 global recession

Before and after the CFMA, federal banking regulators imposed capital and other requirements on banks that entered into OTC derivatives. The United States Securities and Exchange Commission (SEC) and CFTC had limited "risk assessment" authority over OTC derivatives dealers affiliated with securities or commodities brokers and also jointly administered a voluntary program under which the largest securities and commodities firms reported additional information about derivative activities, management controls, risk and capital management, and counterparty exposure policies that were similar to, but more limited than, the requirements for banks. Banks and securities firms were the dominant dealers in the market, with commercial bank dealers holding by far the largest share. To the extent insurance company affiliates acted as dealers of OTC derivatives rather than as counterparties to transactions with banks or security firm affiliates, they had no such federal "safety and soundness" regulation of those activities and typically conducted the activities through London-based affiliates.

The CFMA continued an existing 1992 preemption of state laws that prevented any such law from treating eligible OTC derivatives transactions as gambling or otherwise illegal. It also extended that preemption to security-based derivatives that had previously been excluded from the CEA and its preemption of state law.

The CFMA, as enacted by President Clinton, went beyond the recommendations of a Presidential Working Group on Financial Markets (PWG) Report titled "Over-the Counter Derivatives and the Commodity Exchange Act." (the "PWG Report ").

President's Working Group on Financial Markets, November 1999:

Lawrence Summers, Treasury
Alan Greenspan, Fed
Arthur Levitt, SEC

William J Rainer, CFTC

Although hailed by the PWG on the day of congressional passage as "important legislation" to allow "the United States to maintain its competitive position in the over-the-counter derivative markets", by 2001 the collapse of Enron brought public attention to the CFMA's treatment of energy derivatives in the "Enron Loophole." Following the Federal Reserve's emergency loans to "rescue" American International Group (AIG) in September, 2008, the CFMA has received even more widespread criticism for its treatment of credit default swaps and other OTC derivatives.

In 2008 the "Close the Enron Loophole Act" was enacted into law to regulate more extensively "energy trading facilities." On August 11, 2009, the Treasury Department sent Congress draft legislation to implement its proposal to amend the CFMA and other laws to provide "comprehensive regulation of all over-the counter derivatives." This proposal was revised in the House and, in that revised form, passed by the House on December 11, 2009, as part of H.R. 4173 (Wall Street Reform and Consumer Protection Act of 2009). Separate, but similar, proposed legislation was introduced in the Senate and still awaiting Senate action at the time of the House action.

BACKGROUND TO THE CFMA

OTC DERIVATIVES REGULATION BEFORE THE CFMA

THE EXCHANGE TRADING REQUIREMENT

The PWG Report was directed at ending controversy over how swaps and other OTC derivatives related to the CEA. A derivative is a financial contract or instrument that "derives" its value from the price or other characteristic of an underlying "thing" (or "commodity"). A farmer might enter into a "derivative contract" under which the farmer would sell from next summer's harvest a specified number of bushels of wheat at a specified price per bushel. If this contract were executed on a commodity exchange, it would be a "futures contract."

Before 1974, the CEA only applied to agricultural commodities. "Future delivery" contracts in agricultural commodities listed in the CEA were required to be traded on regulated exchanges such as the Chicago Board of Trade.

The Commodity Futures Trading Commission Act of 1974 created the CFTC as the new regulator of commodity exchanges. It also expanded the scope of the CEA to cover the previously listed agricultural products and "all other goods and articles, except onions, and all services, rights, and interests in which contracts for future delivery are presently or in the future dealt in." Existing non-exchange traded financial "commodity" derivatives markets (mostly "interbank" markets) in foreign currencies, government securities, and other specified instruments were excluded from the CEA through the "Treasury Amendment", to the extent transactions in such markets remained off a "board of trade." The expanded CEA, however, did not generally exclude financial derivatives.

After the 1974 law change, the CEA continued to require that all "future delivery" contracts in commodities covered by the law be executed on a regulated exchange. This meant any "future delivery" contract entered into by parties off a regulated exchange would be illegal and unenforceable. The term "future delivery" was not defined in the CEA. Its meaning evolved through CFTC actions and court rulings.

Not all derivative contracts are "future delivery" contracts. The CEA always excluded "forward delivery" contracts under which, for example, a farmer might set today the price at which the farmer would deliver to a grain elevator or other buyer a certain number of bushels of wheat to be harvested next summer. By the early 1980s a market in interest rate and currency "swaps" had emerged in which banks and their customers would typically agree to exchange interest or currency amounts based on one party paying a fixed interest rate amount (or an amount in a specified currency) and the other paying a floating interest rate amount (or an amount in a different currency). These transactions were similar to "forward delivery" contracts under which "commercial users" of a commodity contracted for future deliveries of that commodity at an agreed upon price.

Based on the similarities between swaps and "forward delivery" contracts, the swap market grew rapidly in the United States during the 1980s. Nevertheless, as a 2006 Congressional Research Service report explained in describing the status of OTC derivatives in the 1980s: "if a court had ruled that a swap was in fact an illegal, off-exchange futures contract, trillions of dollars in outstanding swaps could have been invalidated. This might have caused chaos in financial markets, as swaps users would suddenly be exposed to the risks they had used derivatives to avoid."

"LEGAL CERTAINTY" THROUGH REGULATORY EXEMPTIONS

To eliminate this risk, the CFTC and the Congress acted to give "legal certainty" to swaps and, more generally, to the OTC derivatives market activities of "sophisticated parties."

First, the CFTC issued "policy statements" and "statutory interpretations" that swaps, "hybrid instruments" (i.e., securities or deposits with a derivative component), and certain "forward transactions" were not covered by the CEA. The CFTC issued the forward transactions "statutory interpretation" in response to a court ruling that a "Brent" (i.e., North Sea) oil "forward delivery" contract was, in fact, a "future delivery" contract, which could cause it to be illegal and unenforceable under the CEA. This, along with a court ruling in the United Kingdom that swaps entered into by a local UK government unit were illegal, elevated concerns with "legal certainty."

Second, in response to this concern about "legal certainty", Congress (through the Futures Trading Practices Act of 1992 (FTPA)) gave the CFTC authority to exempt transactions from the exchange trading requirement and other provisions of the CEA. The CFTC used that authority (as Congress contemplated or "instructed") to exempt the same three categories of transactions for which it had previously issued policy statements or statutory interpretations. The FTPA also provided that such CFTC exemptions preempted any state law that would otherwise make such transactions illegal as gambling or otherwise. To preserve the 1982 Shad-Johnson Accord, which prohibited futures on "non-exempt securities", the FTPA prohibited the CFTC from granting an exemption from that prohibition. This would later lead to concerns about the "legal certainty" of swaps and other OTC derivatives related to "securities."

Similar to the existing statutory exclusion for "forward delivery" contracts, the 1989 "policy statement" on swaps had required that swaps covered by the "policy statement" be privately negotiated transactions between sophisticated parties covering (or "hedging") risks arising from their business (including investment and financing) activities. The new "swaps exemption" dropped the "hedging" requirement. It continued to require the swap be entered into by "sophisticated parties" (i.e., "eligible swap participants") in private transactions.

Although OTC derivatives were subject to criticism in the 1990s and bills were introduced in Congress to regulate aspects of the market, the 1993 exemptions remained in place. Bank regulators issued guidelines and requirements for bank OTC derivatives activities that responded to many of the concerns raised by Congress, the General Accounting Office (GAO), and others. Securities firms agreed with the Securities and Exchange Commission (SEC) and CFTC to establish a Derivatives Policy Group through which six large securities firms conducting the great majority of securities firm OTC derivatives activities reported to the CFTC and SEC about their activities and adopted voluntary principles similar to those applicable to banks. Insurance companies, which represented a much smaller part of the market, remained outside any federal oversight of their OTC derivatives activities

CFTC/SEC DISPUTE AND PWG REPORT AS BASIS FOR THE CFMA

THE DISPUTE

In 1997 and 1998 a conflict developed between the CFTC and the SEC over an SEC proposal to ease its broker-dealer regulations for securities firm affiliates that engaged in OTC derivatives activities. The SEC had long been frustrated that those activities were conducted outside the regulated broker-dealer affiliates of securities firms, often outside the United States in London or elsewhere. To bring the activities into broker-dealer supervision, the SEC proposed relaxed net capital and other rules (known as "Broker-Dealer Lite") for OTC derivatives dealers. The CFTC objected that some activities that would be authorized by this proposal were not permitted under the CEA. The CFTC also issued a "concept release" requesting comments on whether the OTC derivatives market was properly regulated under the existing CEA exemptions and on whether market developments required regulatory changes.

The CFTC's actions were widely viewed as a response to the SEC's Broker-Dealer Lite proposal and, at least by Professor John C. Coffee, as perhaps an attempt to force the SEC to withdraw the proposal. The CFTC expressed dismay over the Broker-Dealer Lite proposal and the manner in which it was issued, but also noted it was 18 months into a "comprehensive regulatory reform effort." The same day the CFTC issued its "concept release" Treasury Secretary Robert Rubin, Federal Reserve Board Chair Alan Greenspan, and SEC Chair Arthur Levitt (who, along with CFTC Chair Brooksley Born, were the members of the PWG) issued a letter asking Congress to prevent the CFTC from changing its existing treatment of OTC derivatives. They argued that, by calling into question whether swaps and other OTC derivatives were "futures", the CFTC was calling into question the legality of security related OTC derivatives for which the CFTC could not grant exemptions (as described in Section 1.1.2 above) and, more broadly, undermining an "implicit agreement" not to raise the question of the CEA's coverage of swaps and other established OTC derivatives.

In the ensuing Congressional hearings, the three members of the PWG dissenting from the CFTC's "unilateral" actions argued the CFTC was not the proper body, and the CEA was not the proper statute, to regulate OTC derivatives activities. Banks and securities firms dominated the OTC derivatives market. Their regulators needed to be involved in any regulation of the market. Bank regulators and the SEC already monitored and regulated bank and broker-dealer OTC Derivatives activities. The dissenting PWG members explained that any effort to regulate those activities through the CEA would only lead to the activities moving outside the United States. In the 1980s banks had used offshore branches to book transactions potentially covered by the CEA. Securities firms were still using London and other foreign offices to book at least securities related derivatives transactions. Any change in regulation of OTC derivatives should only occur after a full study of the issue by the entire PWG.

CFTC Chair Brooksley Born replied that the CFTC had exclusive authority over "futures" under the CEA and could not allow the other PWG members to dictate the CFTC's authority under that statute. She pointed out the "concept release" did not propose, nor presuppose the need for, any change in the regulatory treatment of OTC derivatives. She noted, however, that changes in the OTC derivatives market had made that market more similar to futures markets.

Congress passed a law preventing the CFTC from changing its treatment of OTC derivatives through March 1999. CFTC Chair Born lost control of the issue at the CFTC when three of her four fellow Commissioners announced they supported the legislation and would temporarily not vote to take any action concerning OTC derivatives. CFTC Chair Born resigned effective June 1999. Her successor, William Rainer, was CFTC Chair when the PWG Report was issued in November 1999.

OTHER BACKGROUND EVENTS

While the dispute between the SEC and CFTC over OTC derivatives jurisdiction was at the core of pre-2008 narrations of the events leading to the CFMA, two other noteworthy background events occurred. First, in early 1997 CFTC Chairperson Born testified forcefully to Congress against a Senate bill that would have authorized futures exchanges to establish "professional markets" exempt from many regulatory requirements in a manner similar to the "regulatory relief" ultimately provided for an "exempt board of trade" under the CFMA. In her testimony to the Senate Agriculture Committee and in several subsequent speeches during the first half of 1997, Chairperson Born argued OTC derivatives did not create the same "concentration of financial risk" as exchange traded futures and did not perform the "unique price discovery" function of exchange traded contracts. She argued these differences justified different regulatory treatment.

Chairperson Born's 1997 testimony on the difference between exchange and OTC markets was consistent with her first speech as CFTC Chair, on October 24, 1996, in which she stated her belief that regulation of the OTC derivatives market should be limited to fraud and manipulation. While her 1997 testimony opposed the Senate bill's provision to codify in law the existing CFTC regulatory exemptions for OTC derivatives, she also stated the CFTC was "watching" the OTC derivatives market with the PWG and had no plans to modify the existing CFTC exemptions for that market.

The futures exchanges argued they needed permission to operate "professional markets" free of "regulatory burdens" in order to compete with foreign exchanges and the OTC derivatives market that catered to the same professionals. 1997 news reports attributed the failure of the "professional markets" legislation to disagreements concerning equity derivatives between the Chicago Board of Trade and the OTC derivatives dealers, on the one side, and the Chicago Mercantile Exchange and others futures exchanges, on the other.

Second, after the 1998 CFTC "concept release" controversy arose, Long-Term Capital Management (LTCM) became headline news with the near collapse of a hedge fund it managed. The near collapse was widely attributed to OTC derivatives transactions. At an October 1, 1998, hearing before the House Banking Committee, Chairperson Born received complements from some members of the Committee for having raised important issues in the May "concept release." The hearing, however, focused on issues with regulatory oversight of the banks and security firms that had given the LTCM fund high leverage through both loans and OTC derivative transactions.

The 1999 GAO Report that analyzed the LTCM experience criticized federal regulators for not coordinating their oversight of LTCM's activities with banks and securities firms. The Report also recommended "consideration of" legislation to grant the SEC and CFTC consolidated supervision authority for securities and commodities firms in order to supervise the OTC derivatives activities of those consolidated entities in a manner similar to the Federal Reserve's authority over bank holding companies. The GAO Report did not consider, and did not recommend, CFTC regulation of OTC derivatives.

An effect of the LTCM experience was that the conference committee report adopting the six-month moratorium on CFTC action affecting OTC derivative regulation included a statement that "the conferees strongly urge" the PWG to study OTC derivatives transactions of hedge funds and others. Although Chairperson Born had explained at the October 1, 1998, House Banking Committee hearing that the CFTC's supervisory authority over the LTCM fund as a "commodity pool operator" was limited to monitoring its exchange trading activities, the CFTC's possession of financial statements for the fund received negative news coverage in November 1998 based on the fact the CFTC was the only federal regulator to receive such reports directly from LTCM and had not shared the information with other members of the PWG.

When the LTCM matter was investigated at a December 16, 1998, Senate Agriculture Committee hearing, the three CFTC Commissioners that had supported the Congressional moratorium, as described in Section 1.2.1 above, reiterated their support and their position that the entire PWG should study the OTC derivatives market and the issues raised in the CFTC's "concept release."

THE PRESIDENT'S WORKING GROUP REPORT

The PWG Report recommended: (1) the codification into the CEA, as an "exclusion", of existing regulatory exemptions for OTC financial derivatives, revised to permit electronic trading between "eligible swaps participants" (acting as "principals") and to even allow standardized (i.e. "fungible") contracts subject to "regulated" clearing; (2) continuation of the existing CFTC authority to exempt other non-agricultural commodities (such as energy products) from provisions of the CEA; (3) continuation of existing exemptions for "hybrid instruments" expanded to cover the Shad-Johnson Accord (thereby exempting from the CEA any hybrid that could be viewed as a future on a "non-exempt security"), and a prohibition on the CFTC changing the exemption without the agreement of the other members of the PWG; (4) continuation of the preemption of state laws that might otherwise make any "excluded" or "exempted" transactions illegal as gambling or otherwise; (5) as previously recommended by the PWG in its report on hedge funds, the expansion of SEC and CFTC "risk assessment" oversight of affiliates of securities firms and commodity firms engaged in OTC derivatives activities to ensure they did not endanger affiliated broker-dealers or futures commission merchants; (6) encouraging the CFTC to grant broad "deregulation" of existing exchange trading to reflect differences in (A) the susceptibility of commodities to price manipulation and (B) the "sophistication" and financial strength of the parties permitted to trade on the exchange; and (7) permission for single stock and narrow index stock futures on terms to be agreed between the CFTC and SEC.

In 1998 the CFTC had disagreed with the other members of the PWG about the scope and purposes of the CEA. Whereas the CFTC saw broad purposes in protecting "fair access" to markets, "financial integrity", "price discovery and transparency", "fitness standards," and protection of "market participants from fraud and other abuses," other members of the PWG (particularly the Federal Reserve through Alan Greenspan) found the more limited purposes of (1) preventing price manipulation and (2) protecting retail investors.

The PWG Report ended that disagreement by analyzing only four issues in deciding not to apply the CEA to OTC derivatives. By finding (1) the sophisticated parties participating in the OTC derivatives markets did not require CEA protections, (2) the activities of most OTC derivatives dealers were already subject to direct or indirect federal oversight, (3) manipulation of financial markets through financial OTC derivatives had not occurred and was highly unlikely, and (4) the OTC derivatives market performed no significant "price discovery" function, the PWG concluded "there is no compelling evidence of problems involving bilateral swap agreements that would warrant regulation under the CEA." By essentially adopting the views of the other members of the PWG concerning the scope and application of the CEA, the CFTC permitted a "remarkable" agreement "on a redrawing of the regulatory lines."

Rather than treat the "convergence' of OTC derivatives and futures markets as a basis for CFTC regulation of OTC derivatives, the PWG Report acknowledged and encouraged the growth in similarities between the OTC derivatives market and the regulated exchange traded futures market. Standardized terms and centralized clearing were to be encouraged, not prohibited. Price information could be broadly disseminated through "electronic trading facilities." The PWG hoped these features would (1) increase "transparency" and liquidity in the OTC derivatives market by increasing the circulation of information about market pricing and (2) reduce "systemic risk" by reducing credit exposures between parties to OTC derivatives transactions.

The PWG Report also emphasized the desire to "maintain U.S. leadership in these rapidly developing markets" by discouraging the movement of such transactions "offshore." In the 1998 Congressional hearings concerning the CFTC "concept release" Representative James A. Leach (R-IA) had tied the controversy to "systemic risk" by arguing the movement of transactions to jurisdictions outside the United States would replace U.S. regulation with laxer foreign supervision.

It can be argued that the PWG Report recommendations and the CFMA as enacted did not change the "regulation" of OTC derivatives because there was no existing regulation under the CEA or securities laws. The change to the CEA, however, would be the elimination of existing criteria for distinguishing OTC derivatives from "futures."

THE CFMA AS IMPLEMENTATION AND EXPANSION OF THE PWG REPORT

Title I of the CFMA adopted recommendations of the PWG Report by broadly excluding from the CEA transactions in financial derivatives (i.e. "excluded commodities") between "eligible contract participants." The definition of "eligible contract participant" covered the same types of "sophisticated" parties as the existing "swaps exemption" in its definition of "eligible swap participants", but was broader, particularly by adding permission for individuals with assets of $5 million rather than $10 million, if the transaction related to managing asset or liability "risk." The PWG had recommended "considering" an increase in this threshold to $25 million, not a reduction for actual hedging.

Such "eligible contract participants" could enter into transactions on or off "electronic trading facilities" without being subject to any of the regulatory oversight applicable to futures. The only exception was that the transactions would be subject to the rules for the new "Derivative Clearing Organizations" authorized by the CFMA, if the transaction used such a clearing facility. The CFMA did not require that standardized transaction use a clearing facility. It only authorized their existence, subject to regulatory oversight. The PWG Report had recommended permitting "standardized" contracts, so long as they were subject to regulated clearing.

Title I's biggest departure from the PWG Report recommendations was in extending most of the same exclusions to non-financial commodities that were not agricultural. These "exempt commodities" were, in practice, mostly energy and metal commodities. As discussed below in Section 4, these transactions were subject to the "anti-fraud" and "anti-manipulation" provisions of the CEA in some, but not all, circumstances. The PWG Report had recommended that exemptions for such transactions remain in the control of the CFTC, although it had recommended the continuation of those regulatory exemptions.

Title I also resolved the issue of "hybrid instruments" by defining when such an instrument would be considered a "security" subject to security laws and excluded from the CEA even though it had a "commodity component." Equivalent treatment of bank products was provided in Title IV.

Title I retained the CEA's existing preemption of state gambling and other laws that could render a CFTC exempted transaction illegal. It made that preemption applicable to all exempted or excluded transactions.

Title I also created a new system under which three different types of exchanges could be established based on the types of commodities and participants on such exchanges.

Title II of the CFMA repealed the 1982 Shad-Johnson Accord that had prohibited single stock and narrow stock index futures and replaced that with a joint CFTC and SEC regulated "security futures" system.

Title III established a framework for SEC regulation of "security-based swaps." The PWG Report had not addressed this issue.

Title IV established a framework for CFTC regulation of "bank products." This included coverage of deposit based "hybrid instruments", but went further. The PWG Report had not dealt with these issues beyond how Title IV overlapped with Title I.

The CFMA did not provide the CFTC or SEC the broader "risk assessment" authority over affiliates of futures commission merchants or broker-dealers that the PWG Report had recommended

THE "ENRON LOOPHOLE"

THE SECTION 2(H) "LOOPHOLE"

The first provision of the CFMA to receive widespread popular attention was the "Enron Loophole".In most accounts, this "loophole" was the CEA's new section 2(h). Section 2(h) created two exemptions from the CEA for "exempt commodities" such as oil and other "energy" products.

First, any transaction in exempt commodities not executed on a "trading facility" between "eligible contract participants" (acting as principals) was exempted from most CEA provisions (other than fraud and anti-manipulation provisions). This exemption in Section 2(h)(1) of the CEA covered the "bilateral swaps market" for exempt "trading facilities."

Second, any transaction in exempt commodities executed on an "electronic trading facility" between "eligible commercial entities" (acting as principals) was also exempted from most CEA provisions (other than those dealing with fraud and manipulation). The "trading facility", however, was required to file with the CFTC certain information and certifications and to provide trading and other information to the CFTC upon any "special call." This exemption in Section 2(h)(2) of the CEA covered the "commercial entities" for exempt "electronic trading facilities."

While the language of Section 2(h) was in H.R. 4541 as passed by the House, the portion of Section 2(h) dealing with the exempt commercial market had been deleted from S. 2697 when the Senate Agriculture Committee reported out an amended version of that bill. H.R. 4541 served as the basis for Titles I and II of the CFMA. The Senate Agriculture Committee's removal of the Section 2(h) language from S. 2697, however, served as the basis for later Senate concern over the origins of Section 2(h).

In 2008 Congress enacted into law over President Bush's veto an Omnibus Farm Bill that contained the "Close the Enron Loophole Act." This added to CEA Section 2(h)(2) a new definition of "electronic trading facility" and imposed on such facilities requirements applicable to fully regulated exchanges (i.e. "designated contract markets") such as the NYMEX. The legislation did not change Section 2(h)(1) exemption for the "bilateral swaps market" in exempt commodities.

THE SECTION 2(G) "LOOPHOLE"

Section 2(g) of the CEA is also sometimes called the "Enron Loophole". It is a broader exclusion from the CEA than the Section 2(h)(1) exemption for the "bilateral swaps market" in exempt commodities. It excludes from even the fraud and manipulation provisions of the CEA any "individually negotiated" transaction in a non-agricultural commodity between "eligible contract participants" not executed on a "trading facility." Thus, the exclusion from provisions of the CEA for "eligible contract participants" is broader than the Section 2(h)(1) exemption for "bilateral swaps" of energy commodities. The criteria for this exclusion, however, are narrower in requiring "individual negotiation."

This exclusion was not contained in either H.R. 4541 or S. 2697 as introduced in Congress. The House Banking and Financial Services Committee added this provision to the amended H.R. 4541 it reported to the House. That language was included in H.R. 4541 as passed by the House. Its final version was modified to conform to the Gramm-Leach-Bliley Act definition of "swap agreement." That definition requires that the swap be "individually negotiated." H.R. 4541 had required that each "material economic term" be individually negotiated.

2002 Senate hearings indicated CEA Section 2(h)(2) was not the"Enron Loophole" used by EnronOnline. That facility was not required to qualify as an "electronic trading facility" under Section 2(h)(2) of the CEA because Enron Online was only used to enter into transactions with Enron affiliates. There were not "multiple participants" on both the buy and sell sides of the trades. Whether such Enron-only trades were covered by the Section 2(h)(1) "bilateral swaps market" exemption for energy products or the broader Section 2(g) exclusion for swaps generally depended whether there was "individual negotiation."

CREDIT DEFAULT SWAPS

With the 2008 emergence of widespread concerns about credit default swaps, the CFMA's treatment of those instruments has become controversial. Title I of the CFMA broadly excludes from the CEA financial derivatives, including specifically any index or measure tied to a "credit risk or measure." In 2000, Title I's exclusion of financial derivatives from the CEA was not controversial in Congress. Instead, it was widely hailed for bringing "legal certainty" to this "important market" permitting "the United States to retain its leadership in the financial markets", as recommended by the PWG Report.

THE INSURANCE LAW ISSUE

The CFMA's treatment of credit default swaps has received the most attention for two issues. First, former New York Insurance Superintendent Eric Dinallo has argued credit default swaps should have been regulated as insurance and that the CFMA removed a valuable legal tool by preempting state "bucket shop" and gaming laws that could have been used to attack credit default swaps as illegal. In 1992, the FTPA had preempted those state laws for financial derivatives covered by the CFTC's "swaps exemption." As described in Section 1.1.2 above, however, a "gap" in the CFTC's powers prohibited it from exempting futures on "non-exempt securities." This "loophole" (which was intended to preserve the Shad-Johnson Accord's prohibition on single stock futures) meant that, before the CFMA, the CEA's preemption of state gaming and "bucket shop" laws would not have protected a credit default swap on a "non-exempt security" (i.e. an equity security or a "non-exempt" debt obligation that qualified as a "security"). As before 1992, the application of such state laws to a credit default swap (or any other swap) would depend upon a court finding the swap was a gambling, "bucket shop", or otherwise illegal transaction. As described in Section 1.2.1 above, legal uncertainty for security-based swaps was an important issue in the events that led to the PWG Report. The PWG Report recommended eliminating that uncertainty by excluding credit default swaps and all security-based swaps from the CEA and by adding to the "hybrid instrument" exemption an exclusion from the Shad-Johnson Accord.

Former Superintendent Dinallo has written that the CFMA was enacted in part to avoid having OTC derivatives transactions move offshore. He has not, however, addressed whether that could have been avoided if the CFMA had not been enacted. AIG (the insurance company addressed by Mr. Dinallo's commentary) located its controversial derivatives dealer (AIG Financial Products) in London and conducted its "regulatory CDS" transactions through a French bank (Banque AIG) because of the bank regulatory capital provision that banks (not AAA rated parties) received a reduced credit risk "weighting" for their obligations, including CDS, owed to other banks. General Re, the other insurance company with a very active derivatives dealer affiliate, similarly established that dealer in London.

THE SECURITIES LAW ISSUE

Second, Title II of the CFMA treated credit default swaps tied to "securities" as "security-related swaps" for which the SEC was granted limited authority to enforce "insider trading", fraud, and anti-manipulation provisions of the securities laws. Before the CFMA, it was generally agreed most swaps were not securities, but the SEC had always maintained that swaps tied to securities were securities, particularly when such swaps could reproduce the attributes of owning the underlying security. In granting the SEC authority over "security-related swaps", the CFMA specifically prohibited applying any "prophylactic" anti-fraud or anti-manipulation measures. The SEC has complained this has prevented it from collecting information, and requiring disclosures, regarding credit default positions of investors. The SEC has argued this handicaps its ability to monitor possible manipulations of security markets through credit default swaps.

CENTRALIZED CLEARING

The SEC, the PWG, and others have also expressed concern about the "systemic risk" created by a lack of centralized clearing of credit default swaps. Although (as noted in Section 2 above) the CFMA created the possibility of centralized clearing by removing the pre-CFMA requirements that OTC derivatives not be subject to centralized clearing, the CFMA did not require such clearing, even for "standardized" transactions.

2009 TREASURY DEPARTMENT PROPOSED OTC DERIVATIVES LEGISLATION

On August 11, 2009, the Treasury Department sent to Congress proposed legislation titled the "Over-the-Counter Derivatives Markets Act of 2009." The Treasury Department stated that under this proposed legislation "the OTC derivative markets will be comprehensively regulated for the first time."

To accomplish this "comprehensive regulation", the proposed legislation would repeal many of the provisions of the CFMA, including all of the exclusions and exemptions discussed in Sections 4 above that have been identified as the "Enron Loophole." While the proposed legislation would generally retain the "legal certainty" provisions of the CFMA, it would establish new requirements for parties dealing in non-"standardized" OTC derivatives and would require that "standardized" OTC derivatives be traded through a regulated trading facility and cleared through regulated central clearing. The proposed legislation would also repeal the CFMA's limits on SEC authority over "security-based swaps."

On December 11, 2009, the House passed H.R. 4173, the so-called Wall Street Reform and Consumer Protection Act of 2009, which included a revised version of the Treasury Department's proposed legislation that would repeal the same provisions of the CFMA noted above. At that time, similar legislation was pending in the Senate.

In late April, 2010, debate began on the floor of the Senate over their version of the reform legislation

DODD-FRANK BILL

The **Dodd–Frank Wall Street Reform and Consumer Protection Act** (Pub.L. 111–203, H.R. 4173) was signed into federal law by President Barack Obama on July 21, 2010 in the Ronald Reagan building. Passed as a response to the late-2000s recession, it brought the most significant changes to financial regulation in the United States since the regulatory reform that followed the Great Depression. It made changes in the American financial regulatory environment that affect all federal financial regulatory agencies and almost every part of the nation's financial services industry.

As with other major financial reforms, a variety of critics have attacked the law, some arguing it was not enough to prevent another financial crisis or more "bail outs", and others arguing it went too far and unduly restricted financial institutions.

The law was initially proposed by the Obama Administration in June 2009, when the White House sent a series of proposed bills to Congress. A version of the legislation was introduced in the House in July 2009. On December 2, 2009, revised versions were introduced in the House of Representatives by Financial Services Committee Chairman Barney Frank, and in the Senate Banking Committee by Chairman Chris Dodd. Due to their involvement with the bill, the conference committee that reported on June 25, 2010, voted to name the bill after the two members of Congress

ORIGINS AND PROPOSAL

The financial crisis of 2007–2010 led to widespread calls for changes in the regulatory system. In June 2009, President Obama introduced a proposal for a "sweeping overhaul of the United States financial regulatory system, a transformation on a scale not seen since the reforms that followed the Great Depression."

As the finalized bill emerged from conference, President Obama stated that the bill included 90 percent of the proposals. Major components of Obama's original proposal, listed by order in which they appear in the "A New Foundation" outline, include:

1. The consolidation of regulatory agencies, elimination of the national thrift charter, and new oversight council to evaluate systemic risk;
2. Comprehensive regulation of financial markets, including increased transparency of derivatives (bringing them onto exchanges);
3. Consumer protection reforms including a new consumer protection agency and uniform standards for "plain vanilla" products as well as strengthened investor protection;
4. Tools for financial crises, including a "resolution regime" complementing the existing Federal Deposit Insurance Corporation (FDIC) authority to allow for orderly winding down of bankrupt firms, and including a proposal that the Federal Reserve (the "Fed") receive authorization from the Treasury for extensions of credit in "unusual or exigent circumstances";
5. Various measures aimed at increasing international standards and cooperation including proposals related to improved accounting and tightened regulation of credit rating agencies.

At Obama's request, Congress later added the Volcker Rule to this proposal in January 2010.

LEGISLATIVE RESPONSE AND PASSAGE

The bills that came after Obama's proposal were largely consistent with the proposal, but contained some additional provisions and differences in implementation.

The Volcker Rule was not included in Obama's initial June 2009 proposal, but Obama proposed the rule later in January 2010, after the House bill had passed. The rule, which prohibits depository banks from proprietary trading (similar to the prohibition of combined investment and commercial banking in the Glass–Steagall Act) was passed only in the Senate bill, and the conference committee enacted the rule in a weakened form, Section 619 of the bill, that allowed banks to invest up to 3% of their Tier 1 capital in private equity and hedge funds as well as trade for hedging purposes.

The initial version of the bill passed the House along party lines in December by a vote of 223–202, and passed the Senate with amendments in May 2010 with a vote of 59–39 once again along party lines. The bill then moved to conference committee, where the Senate bill was used as the base text although a few House provisions were included in the bill's base text.

One provision on which the White House did not take a position and remained in the final bill allows the SEC to rule on "proxy access" – meaning that qualifying shareholders, including groups, can modify the corporate proxy statement sent to shareholders to include their own director nominees, with the rules set by the SEC. This rule was unsuccessfully challenged in conference committee by Chris Dodd, who – under pressure from the White House – submitted an amendment limiting that access and ability to nominate directors only to single shareholders who have over 5% of the company and have held the stock for at least two years.

The "Durbin Amendment" is a provision in the final bill aimed at debit card interchange fees and increasing competition in payment processing. The provision was not in the House bill; it began as an amendment to the Senate bill from Dick Durbin and led to lobbying against it. The law applies to banks with over $10 billion in assets, and these banks would have to charge debit card interchange fees that are "reasonable and proportional to the actual cost" of processing the transaction. The bill aimed to restrict anti-competitive practices and encourage competition, and included provisions which allow retailers to refuse to use credit cards for small purchases and offer incentives for using cash or another type of card.

The Durbin Amendment also gave the Federal Reserve the power to regulate debit card interchange fees, and on December 16, 2010, the Fed proposed a maximum interchange fee of 12 cents per debit card transaction, which CardHub.com estimated would cost large banks $14 billion annually.

On June 29, 2011, the Fed issued its final rule, which holds that the maximum interchange fee an issuer can receive from a single debit card transaction is 21 cents plus 5 basis points multiplied by the amount of the transaction. This rule also allows issuers to raise their interchange fees by as much as one cent if they implement certain fraud-prevention measures. An issuer eligible for this adjustment, could therefore receive an interchange fee of as much as 24 cents for the average debit card transaction (valued at $38), according to the Federal Reserve. This cap—which took effect on October 1, 2011, rather than July 21, 2011, as was previously announced—will reduce fees roughly $9.4 billion annually, according to CardHub.com. As a result of the government limiting their revenue from interchange fees, banks made plans to raise account maintenance fees to compensate.

The *New York Times* published a comparison of the two bills prior to their reconciliation. On June 25, 2010, conferees finished reconciling the House and Senate versions of the bills and four days later filed a conference report. The conference committee changed the name of the Act from the "Restoring American Financial Stability Act of 2010." The House passed the conference report, 237–192 on June 30, 2010. On July 15, the Senate passed the Act, 60–39. President Obama signed the bill into law on July 21, 2010.

OVERVIEW

The Act is categorized into sixteen titles and, by one law firm's count, it requires that regulators create 243 rules, conduct 67 studies, and issue 22 periodic reports.

The stated aim of the legislation is:

> To promote the financial stability of the United States by improving accountability and transparency in the financial system, to end "too big to fail", to protect the American taxpayer by ending bailouts, to protect consumers from abusive financial services practices, and for other purposes.

The Act changes the existing regulatory structure, such as creating a host of new agencies (while merging and removing others) in an effort to streamline the regulatory process, increasing oversight of specific institutions regarded as a systemic risk, amending the Federal Reserve Act, promoting transparency, and additional changes. The Act purports to provide rigorous standards and supervision to protect the economy and American consumers, investors and businesses, purports to end taxpayer funded bailouts of financial institutions, claims to provide for an advanced warning system on the stability of the economy, creates rules on executive compensation and corporate governance, and eliminates some loopholes that led to the 2008 economic recession. The new agencies are either granted explicit power over a particular aspect of financial regulation, or that power is transferred from an existing agency. All of the new agencies, and some existing ones that are not currently required to do so, are also compelled to report to Congress on an annual (or biannual) basis, to present the results of current plans and to explain future goals. Important new agencies created include the Financial Stability Oversight Council, the Office of Financial Research, and the Bureau of Consumer Financial Protection.

Of the existing agencies, changes are proposed, ranging from new powers to the transfer of powers in an effort to enhance the regulatory system. The institutions affected by these changes include most of the regulatory agencies currently involved in monitoring the financial system (Federal Deposit Insurance Corporation (FDIC), U.S. Securities and Exchange Commission (SEC), Office of the Comptroller of the Currency (OCC), Federal Reserve (the "Fed"), the Securities Investor Protection Corporation (SIPC), etc.), and the final elimination of the Office of Thrift Supervision (further described in Title III – Transfer of Powers to the Comptroller, the FDIC, and the FED).

As a practical matter, prior to the passage of the Dodd–Frank Act, investment advisers were not required to register with the SEC if the investment adviser had fewer than 15 clients during the previous 12 months and did not hold itself out generally to the public as an investment adviser. The Dodd–Frank Act eliminates that exemption, thereby rendering numerous additional investment advisers, hedge funds, and private equity firms subject to new registration requirements.

Certain non-bank financial institutions and their subsidiaries will be supervised by the Fed in the same manner and to the same extent as if they were a bank holding company.

To the extent that the Act affects all federal financial regulatory agencies, eliminating one (the Office of Thrift Supervision) and creating two (Financial Stability Oversight Council and the Office of Financial Research) in addition to several consumer protection agencies, including the Bureau of Consumer Financial Protection, this legislation in many ways represents a change in the way America's financial markets will operate in the future. Few provisions of the Act became effective when the bill was signed. Only over the next 18 months as various regulatory agencies write rules that implement various sections of the Act, will the full importance and significance of the Act be known.

PROVISIONS

TITLE I – FINANCIAL STABILITY

Title I, or the "Financial Stability Act of 2010",outlines two new agencies tasked with monitoring systemic risk and researching the state of the economy and clarifies the comprehensive supervision of bank holding companies by the Federal Reserve. Title I creates the Financial Stability Oversight Council and the Office of Financial Research. The two new offices are attached to the Treasury Department, with the Treasury Secretary being Chair of the Council, and the Head of the Financial Research Office being a Presidential appointment with Senate confirmation. The Financial Stability Oversight Council is charged with identifying threats to the financial stability of the United States, promoting market discipline, and responding to emerging risks to the stability of the United States financial system. At a minimum, it must meet quarterly. Specifically, there are three purposes assigned to the Council:

1. identify the risks to the financial stability of the United States from both financial and non-financial organizations
2. promote market discipline, by eliminating expectations that the Government will shield them from losses in the event of failure

3. respond to emerging threats to the stability of the US financial system

DUTIES

In the course of pursuing its goal (in its entirety), the Council has several duties enumerated to it that can broadly be described as anything required to:

1. enhance the integrity, efficiency, competitiveness, and stability of United States financial markets
2. promote market discipline
3. maintain investor confidence

More specifically, the Council must collate data (received from affiliated agencies, and optionally from the companies themselves) to assess risks to the financial system, monitor the financial services marketplace, make general regulatory recommendations to affiliated agencies reflecting a broader consensus, and it may also compel the Federal Reserve to assume an oversight position of certain institutions considered to pose a systemic risk. The Council must monitor domestic and international regulatory proposals and developments, and advise Congress in these areas. The Council and the associated Office of Financial Research are charged to facilitate information sharing and coordination among the member agencies and other federal and state agencies regarding domestic financial services policy development, rule-making, examinations, reporting requirements, and enforcement actions.

MEMBERSHIP

The Financial Stability Oversight Council has ten voting members:

1. Secretary of the Treasury (chairs the Council)
2. Chairman of the Federal Reserve
3. Comptroller of the Currency
4. Director of the Bureau of Consumer Financial Protection
5. Chairperson of the U.S. Securities and Exchange Commission
6. Chairperson of the Federal Deposit Insurance Corporation
7. Chairperson of the Commodity Futures Trading Commission
8. Director of the Federal Housing Finance Agency
9. the Chairman of the National Credit Union Administration Board
10. an independent member (with insurance expertise), appointed by the President, with the advice and consent of the Senate, for a term of 6 years.

There are five non-voting advisory members who may go into the equivalent of executive session when discussing confidential supervisory information:

1. Director of the Office of Financial Research (part of the Treasury Department and established in this Act) who is the Council's executive director
2. Director of the Federal Insurance Office (part of the Treasury Department and established in this Act)
3. a state insurance commissioner, to be designated by a selection process determined by the state insurance commissioners (2-year term)
4. a state banking supervisor, to be designated by a selection process determined by the state banking supervisors (2-year term)
5. a state securities commissioner (or officer performing like function) to be designated by a selection process determined by such state security commissioners (2-year term)

RESOURCES

The Federal Advisory Committee Act, which limits the powers of advisory committees, does not apply to the council. The council has an almost unlimited budget in that the Council may draw on virtually any resource of any department or agency of the federal government. Any employee of the federal government may be detailed to the Council without reimbursement and without interruption or loss of civil service status or privilege. Any member of the Council who is an employee of the federal government serves without additional compensation. In addition, "An employee of the Federal Government detailed to the Council shall report to and be subject to oversight by the Council during the assignment to the Council, and shall be compensated by the department or agency from which the employee was detailed." Additionally, "Any expenses of the Council shall be treated as expenses of, and paid by, the Office of Financial Research".

AUTHORITY

The Council has very broad powers to monitor, investigate and assess any risks to the US financial system. The Council has the authority to collect information from any state or federal financial regulatory agency, and may direct the Office of Financial Research, which supports the work of the Council, "to collect information from bank holding companies and nonbank financial companies".

The Council monitors domestic and international regulatory proposals, including insurance and accounting issues, and advises Congress and the Federal Reserve on ways to enhance the integrity, efficiency, competitiveness and stability of the US financial markets. On a regular basis, the Council is required to make a report to Congress describing the state of the U.S. financial system. Each voting member of the Council is required to either affirm that the federal government is taking all reasonable steps to assure financial stability and mitigate systemic risk, or describe additional steps that need to be taken.

Under specific circumstances, the Chairman of the Council (who is also the Secretary of the Treasury), with the concurrence of 2/3 voting members, may place nonbank financial companies or domestic subsidiaries of international banks under the supervision of the Federal Reserve if it appears that these companies could pose a threat to the financial stability of the US. The Federal Reserve may promulgate safe harbor regulations to exempt certain types of foreign banks from regulation, with approval of the Council. Under certain circumstances, the Council may provide for more stringent regulation of a financial activity by issuing recommendations to the primary financial regulatory agency, which the primary financial agency is obliged to implement – the Council reports to Congress on the implementation or failure to implement such recommendations.

FINANCIAL REPORTING TO THE COUNCIL

The Council may require any bank or non-bank financial institution with assets over $50 billion to submit certified reports as to the company's:

- financial condition
- systems in place to monitor and control any risks
- transactions with subsidiaries that are regulated banks
- the extent to which any of the company's activities could have a potential disruptive impact on financial markets or the overall financial stability of the country

The Comptroller General of the United States may audit the Council or anyone working for the Council, and may have access to any information under the control of or used by the Council.

OFFICE OF FINANCIAL RESEARCH

Established as a department within the Treasury, the Office is tasked with providing administrative, technical, budget analysis and other support services to the Council and its affiliated agencies.

The Director of the Office of Financial Research is appointed for a 6-year term. To the extent that her or his duties are exclusively focused on the Council and the Office of Financial Research, the Director is in effect the executive director of the Council. The Director, in consultation with the Chairman of the Council (who is the Secretary of the Treasury) proposes the annual budget of the Office. The Director may set salaries of the Office's employees "without regard to chapter 51 or subchapter III of chapter 53 of Title 5 of the United States Code, relating to classification of positions and General Schedule pay rates."

The Director has Subpoena power and may require from any financial institution (bank or non-bank) any data needed to carry out the functions of the office.

FINANCIAL RESEARCH DIRECTOR'S INDEPENDENT REPORTS TO CONGRESS

The Director reports to and testifies before only the Senate Committee on Banking, Housing, and Urban Affairs and the House Committee on Financial Services of the House of Representatives. Testimony shall be annual on the activities of the Office, including the work of the Data Center and the Research and Analysis Center and the assessment of significant financial and market developments and potential emerging threats to the financial stability of the Country. These reports to Congress are independent of any political influence in that "No officer or agency of the United States shall have any authority to require the Director to submit the testimony... for approval, comment, or review prior to the submission of such testimony."

RESOURCES

Like the Council, the Office of Financial Research may request, from department or agency of the United States, "such services, funds, facilities, staff, and other support services as the Office may determine advisable. Any Federal Government employee may be detailed to the Office without reimbursement, and such detail shall be without interruption or loss of civil service status or privilege." Within the Treasury Department, there is a revolving fund, the "Financial Research Fund" into which all appropriations, fees, and assessments that the Office receives are deposited. Surplus funds may be invested. It is contemplated that within 2 years of establishment that the Office will be self-funding.

AUTHORITY

The Office has broad latitude in performing support services for both the Council and other Member Agencies, including data collection, applied research and essential long-term research, and developing tools for monitoring risk. The Office can also issue guidelines to standardizing the way data is reported, constituent agencies have three years to implement data standardization guidelines. In many ways, the Office of Financial Research is to be operated without the constraints of the Civil Service system. For example, does not need to follow federal pay scale guidelines (see above), and it is mandated that the office have:

- Training and Workforce Development Plan that includes training, leadership development and succession planning
- Workplace Flexibility Plan that includes telework, flexible work schedules, job sharing, parental leave benefits and childcare assistance, domestic partner benefits
- Recruitment and Retention Plan

DATA AND RESEARCH & ANALYSIS CENTERS

The Office is supported by two entities:

- The *Data Center*, which collects, validates and maintains (and publishes some of) the data required to support the Council; which may be obtained from commercial data providers, publicly available data sources and the financial entities supervised by state and federal agencies; and
- The *Research and Analysis Center*, which conducts independent analysis of available information to identify financially destabilizing effects, and develops and maintains independent analytical capabilities and computing resources to:
    - Develop and maintain metrics and reporting systems for risks to the financial stability of the United States
    - Monitor, investigate, and report on changes in systemwide risk levels and patterns to the Council and Congress
    - Conduct, coordinate, and sponsor research to support and improve regulation of financial entities and markets

- Evaluate and report on stress tests or other stability-related evaluations of financial entities overseen by the member agencies
- Maintain expertise in such areas as may be necessary to support specific requests for advice and assistance from financial regulators
- Investigate disruptions and failures in the financial markets, report findings, and make recommendations to the Council based on those findings;
- Conduct studies and provide advice on the impact of policies related to systemic risk; and
- Promote best practices for financial risk management.

Financial Research Fund

The Financial Research Fund is a quasi-revolving fund that the Office uses to fund its operations. All appropriations and assessments are deposited into the Fund; surpluses may be invested. Funds are not subject to apportionment for any other purposes. Within 2 years of enactment, the Office should become self-funding. During the 2-year time following date of enactment, the Federal Reserve shall fund the Office.

Temporary Management Reporting

For a period of five years after enactment, the Office shall submit an annual report to the Senate Committee on Banking, Housing and Urban Affairs, and the House Committee on Financial Services, what amounts to a management report, including:

Training And Workforce Development Plan – that includes:
- Identification of skill and technical expertise needs and action taken to meet the requirements
- Steps taken to foster innovation and creativity
- Leadership development and succession Planning
- Effective use of technology by employees

Workplace Flexibility Plan – that includes:
- Telework
- Flexible work schedules
- Phased retirement
- Reemployment annuitants
- Part-time work
- Job sharing
- Parental leave benefits and childcare assistance
- Domestic partner benefits
- Other workplace flexibilities

Recruitment and Retention Plan – that includes:
- The steps necessary to target highly qualified applicant pools with diverse backgrounds
- Streamlined employment application process
- Timely notification of employment applications
- Measures of hiring effectiveness

TITLE II – ORDERLY LIQUIDATION AUTHORITY

In addition to the supervised banks, insured depository institutions and securities companies that may be liquidated under existing law by the FDIC or Securities Investor Protection Corporation (SIPC), Covered Financial Companies that may be liquidated under this title include insurance companies and non-bank financial companies not covered elsewhere. Once it is determined that a financial company satisfied the criteria for liquidation, if the financial company's board of directors does not agree, provisions are made for judicial appeal. Some procedures for FDIC and the SIPC to liquidate companies are revised. In addition to the policies and procedures that are in place for the financial institutions covered by FDIC and SIPC, this title provides for the orderly liquidation of other financial institutions. Depending on the type of financial institution, different regulatory organizations may jointly or independently, by 2/3 vote, determine whether a receiver should be appointed for a financial company:

In General – FDIC and/or the Federal Reserve
Broker Dealers – SEC and/or the Federal Reserve
Insurance Companies – Federal Insurance Office (part of the Treasury Department and established in this Act) and/or the Federal Reserve

Provided that the Secretary of Treasury, in consultation with the President may also made a determination to appoint a receiver for a financial company. And the GAO shall review and report to Congress about the Secretary's decision.

When a financial institution is placed into receivership under these provisions, within 24 hours the Secretary shall report to Congress, and within 60 days there shall be a report to the general public. The report on the recommendation to place a financial company into receivership shall contain various details on the state of the company, the impact of its default on the company, and the proposed action.

FDIC Liquidation

Unless otherwise stated, the FDIC is the liquidator for financial institutions who are not members of SIPC or banking members of the FDIC or insurance companies. In taking action under this title, the FDIC shall comply with various requirements:

determine that such action is necessary for purposes of the financial stability of the United States, and not for the purpose of preserving the covered financial company
ensure that the shareholders of a covered financial company do not receive payment until after all other claims and the Fund are fully paid
ensure that unsecured creditors bear losses in accordance with the priority of claim provisions
ensure that management responsible for the failed condition of the covered financial company is removed (if such management has not already been removed at the time at which the Corporation is appointed receiver)
ensure that the members of the board of directors (or body performing similar functions) responsible for the failed condition of the covered financial company are removed, if such members have not already been removed at the time the Corporation is appointed as receiver
not take an equity interest in or become a shareholder of any covered financial company or any covered subsidiary

Orderly Liquidation Fund

To the extent that the Act expanded the scope of financial firms that may be liquidated by the federal government, beyond the existing authorities of the FDIC and SIPC, there needed to be an additional source of funds, independent of the FDIC's Deposit Insurance Fund, to be used in case of a non-bank or non-security financial company's liquidation. The Orderly Liquidation Fund is to be an FDIC-managed fund, to be used by the FDIC in the event of a covered financial company's liquidation that is not covered by FDIC or SIPC.

Initially, the Fund is to be capitalized over a period no shorter than five years, but no longer than ten; however, in the event the FDIC must make use of the Fund before it is fully capitalized, the Secretary of the Treasury and the FDIC are permitted to extend the period as determined necessary. The method of capitalization is by collecting risk-based assessment fees on any "eligible financial company" – which is defined as "[...] any bank holding company with total consolidated assets equal to or greater than $50 billion and any nonbank financial company supervised by the Board of Governors." The severity of the assessment fees can be adjusted on an as-needed basis (depending on economic conditions and other similar factors) and the relative size and value of a firm is to play a role in determining the fees to be assessed. The eligibility of a financial company to be subject to the fees is periodically reevaluated; or, in other words, a company that does not qualify for fees in the present, will be subject to the fees in the future if they cross the 50 billion line, or become subject to Federal Reserve scrutiny.

To the extent that a covered financial company has a negative net worth and its liquidation creates an obligation to the FDIC as its liquidator, the FDIC shall charge one or more risk-based assessment such that the obligation will be paid off within 60 months (5 years) of the issuance of the obligation. The assessments will be charged to any bank holding company with consolidated assets greater than $50 billion and any nonbank financial company supervised by the Federal Reserve. Under certain conditions, the assessment may be extended to regulated banks and other financial institutions. Assessments are imposed on a graduated basis, with financial companies having greater assets and risk being assessed at a higher rate.

Assessments will be implemented according to a matrix that the Financial Stability Oversight Council recommends to the FDIC. The matrix shall take into account:

- Economic conditions – higher assessments during more favorable economic conditions
- Whether the institution is:
  - An insured depositary institution that is a member of the FDIC
  - a member of the SIPC
  - an insured credit union
  - an insurance company, assessed pursuant to applicable state law to cover costs of rehabilitation or liquidation
- strength of its balance sheet, both on-balance sheet and off-balance sheet assets, and its leverage
- relevant market share
- potential exposure to sudden calls on liquidity precipitated by economic distress with, other financial companies;
- the amount, maturity, volatility, and stability of the liabilities of the company, including the degree of reliance on short-term funding, taking into consideration existing systems for measuring a company's risk-based capital
- the stability and variety of the company's sources of funding
- the company's importance as a source of credit for households, businesses, and state and local governments and as a source of liquidity for the financial system;
- the extent to which assets are simply managed and not owned by the financial company and the extent to which ownership of assets under management is diffuse
- the amount, different categories, and concentrations of liabilities, both insured and uninsured, contingent and non-contingent, including both on-balance sheet and off-balance sheet liabilities, of the financial company and its affiliates

Obligation Limit and Funding

When liquidating a financial company under this title (as opposed to FDIC or SIPD) there is a maximum limit of the Government's liquidation obligation, i.e., the Government's obligation can not exceed:

- 10% of the total consolidated assets, or
- 90% of the fair value of the total consolidated assets

In the event that the Fund and other sources of capital are insufficient, the FDIC is authorized to buy and sell securities on behalf of the company (or companies) in receivership to raise additional capital. Taxpayers shall bear no losses from liquidating any financial company under this title and any losses shall be the responsibility of the financial sector, recovered through assessments:

- Liquidation is Required for all financial companies put into receivership under this title
- All funds expended in the liquidation of a financial company under this title shall be recovered from the disposition of assets or assessments on the financial sector

Orderly Liquidation Authority Panel

Established inside the United States Bankruptcy Court for the District of Delaware, the Panel is tasked with evaluating the conclusion of the Secretary of the Treasury that a company is in (or in danger of) default. The

Panel consists of three bankruptcy judges drawn from the District of Delaware, all of whom are appointed by the Chief Judge of the United States Bankruptcy Court for the District of Delaware. In his appointments, the Chief Judge is instructed to weigh the financial expertise of the candidates. If the Panel concurs with the Secretary, the company in question is permitted to be placed into receivership; if they do not concur, the Secretary has an opportunity to amend and refile his or her petition. In the event that a Panel decision is appealed, the United States Court of Appeals for the Third Circuit has jurisdiction; in the event of further appeal, a writ of certiorari may be filed with the United States Supreme Court. In all appellate events, the scope of review is limited to whether the decision of the Secretary that a company is in (or in danger of) default is supported by substantial evidence.

TITLE III – TRANSFER OF POWERS TO THE COMPTROLLER, THE FDIC, AND THE FED

Title III, or the "Enhancing Financial Institution Safety and Soundness Act of 2010", is intended to streamline banking regulation and reduce competition and overlaps between different regulators by abolishing the Office of Thrift Supervision and transferring its power over the appropriate holding companies to the Board of Governors of the Federal Reserve System, state savings associations to the FDIC, and other thrifts to the Office of the Comptroller of the Currency. The thrift charter is to remain, although weakened. Additional changes include:

The amount of deposits insured by the FDIC and the National Credit Union Share Insurance Fund (NCUSIF) is permanently increased from $100,000 to $250,000.

Each of the financial regulatory agencies represented on the Council shall establish an Office of Minority and Women Inclusion that shall be responsible for all matters of the agency relating to diversity in management, employment, and business activities.

TITLE IV – REGULATION OF ADVISERS TO HEDGE FUNDS AND OTHERS

Title IV, or the "Private Fund Investment Advisers Registration Act of 2010", introduces significant regulation of hedge funds, and other similar investment intermediaries for the first time. In general, it increases the reporting requirements of investment advisors, and limits the ability of these advisors to exclude information in reporting to the various federal government agencies. However, there is an exemption in reporting for Venture Capital Fund Advisors, certain advisors with assets under management under $150 million, and family offices (as defined by the Commission).

The Act changes the definition of accredited investor, which means someone with personal or (joint with spouse) net worth over a 4-year period, that averages more than $1 million, to exclude the value of the person's residence from the calculation. The Commission is allowed to adjust this value with time. The Act also provides that the SEC shall, every five years, adjust for the effects of inflation, and that any factor used in rule or regulation be in multiples of $100,000.

Studies required under this title include:

a study from the GAO on the appropriate criteria for determining the financial thresholds or other criteria needed to qualify for accredited investor, within 3 years;

from the GAO, a study of the feasibility of forming a self-regulatory organization for private funds, within 1 year;

from the SEC, a study of short-selling, including feasibility, benefits and costs of real-time short sale publications, as well as a voluntary pilot program for reporting.

TITLE V – INSURANCE

SUBTITLE A – FEDERAL INSURANCE OFFICE

Subtitle A, also called the "Federal Insurance Office Act of 2010",establishes within the Department of the Treasury the Federal Insurance Office which is tasked with:

Monitoring all aspects of the insurance industry (except health insurance, some long-term care insurance, and crop insurance), including the identification of gaps in regulation of insurers that could contribute to financial crisis

Monitoring the extent to which traditionally underserved communities and consumers, minorities, and low-and moderate-income persons have access to affordable insurance (except health insurance)

Making recommendations to the Financial Stability Oversight Council about insurers which may pose a risk, and to help any state regulators with national issues

Administering the Terrorism Insurance Program

Coordinating international insurance matters

Determining whether state insurance measure are preempted by covered agreements (states may have more stringent requirements)

Consulting with the states (including state insurance regulators) regarding insurance matters of national importance and prudential insurance matters of international importance;

The Office is headed by a director who is appointed for a career-reserved term by the Secretary of the Treasury.

In general, the Insurance Office may require any insurer company to submit such data as may be reasonably required in carrying out the functions of the Office.

A state insurance measure shall be preempted if, and only to the extent that the Director determines that the measure results in a less favorable treatment of a non-US insurer whose parent corporation is located in a country with an agreement or treaty with the United States.

Subtitle B – State-Based Insurance Reform

Subtitle B, also called the "Nonadmitted and Reinsurance Reform Act of 2010" applies to nonadmitted insurance and reinsurance. With regard to nonadmitted insurance, the Act provides that the placement of nonadmitted insurance only will be subject to the statutory and regulatory requirements of the insured's home state, and that no state, other than the insured's home state, may require a surplus lines broker to be licensed in order to sell, solicit, or negotiate nonadmitted insurance with respect to the insured. The Act also provides that no state, other than the insured's home state, may require any premium tax payment for nonadmitted insurance. However, states may enter into a compact or otherwise establish procedures to allocate among the states the premium taxes paid to an insured's home state. A state may not collect any fees relating to licensing of an individual or entity as a surplus lines broker in the state unless the state has in effect by July 21, 2012 laws or regulations that provide for participation by the state in the NAIC's national insurance producer database, or any other equivalent uniform national database, for the licensure of surplus lines brokers and the renewal of these licenses.

TITLE VI – IMPROVEMENTS TO REGULATION

Provisions

Title VI, or the "Bank and Savings Association Holding Company and Depository Institution Regulatory Improvements Act of 2010", introduces the so-called "Volcker Rule" after former Chairman of the Federal Reserve Paul Volcker by amending the Bank Holding Company Act of 1956. With the aim of reducing the amount of speculative investments on large firms' balance sheets, it limits banking entities to owning no more in a hedge fund or private equity fund than 3% of the total ownership interest.

The total of all of the banking entity's interests in hedge funds or private equity funds cannot exceed 3% of the Tier 1 capital of the banking entity. Furthermore no bank that has a direct or indirect relationship with a hedge fund or private equity fund, "may enter into a transaction with the fund, or with any other hedge fund or private equity fund that is controlled by such fund" without disclosing the full extent of the relationship to the regulating entity, and assuring that there are no conflicts of interest, "Banking entity" includes an insured depository institution, any company controlling an insured depository institution and such a company's affiliates and subsidiaries, and must comply with the Act within two years of its passing, although it may apply for time extensions.

The rule distinguishes transactions by banking entities from transactions by nonbank financial companies supervised by the Federal Reserve Board. The rule states that in general, "an insured depository institution may not purchase an asset from, or sell an asset to, an executive officer, director, or principal shareholder of the insured depository institution, or any related interest of such person... unless— the transaction is on market terms; and if the transaction represents more than 10 percent of the capital stock and surplus of the insured depository institution, the transaction has been approved in advance by a majority of the members of the board of directors of the insured depository institution who do not have an interest in the transaction."

Providing for the regulation of capital, the Volcker Rule says that regulators are required to impose upon institutions capital requirements that are "countercyclical, so that the amount of capital required to be maintained by a company increases in times of economic expansion and decreases in times of economic contraction," to ensure the safety and soundness of the organization.

The rule also provides that an insured state bank may engage in a derivative transaction only if the law with respect to lending limits of the state in which the insured state bank is chartered takes into consideration credit exposure to derivative transactions. The title provides for a three-year moratorium on approval of FDIC deposit insurance received after November 23, 2009, for an industrial bank, a credit card bank, or a trust bank that is directly or indirectly owned or controlled by a commercial firm.

In accordance with section 1075 of the law, payment card networks must allow merchants to establish a minimum dollar amount for customers using payment cards, as long as the minimum is no higher than ten dollars.

BACKGROUND

The Volcker Rule was first publicly endorsed by President Obama on January 21, 2010. The final version of the Act prepared by the conference committee included a strengthened Volcker rule by including language by Senators Jeff Merkley, D-Oregon, and Carl Levin, D-Michigan, that covers a greater range of proprietary trading than originally proposed by the administration, with the notable exceptions of trading in U.S. government securities and bonds issued by government-backed entities, and the rule also bans conflict of interest trading. The rule seeks to ensure that banking organizations are both well capitalized and well managed. The proposed draft form of the Volcker Rule was presented by regulators for public comment on October 11, 2011, with the rule due to go into effect on July 21, 2012.

TITLE VII – WALL STREET TRANSPARENCY AND ACCOUNTABILITY

Title VII, also called the Wall Street Transparency and Accountability Act of 2010, concerns regulation of over the counter swaps markets. Included in this section are the credit default swaps and credit derivative that were the subject of several bank failures c. 2007. Financial instruments have the meanings given the terms in section 1a of the Commodity Exchange Act (7 U.S.C. § 1a). On a broader level, the Act requires that various derivatives known as swaps, which are traded over the counter be cleared through exchanges or clearinghouses.

The Commodity Futures Trading Commission (CFTC) and the Securities and Exchange Commission (SEC) both regulate derivatives known as swaps under the Act, but the SEC has authority over "security-based swaps". The Act repeals exemption from regulation for security-based swaps under the Gramm–Leach–Bliley Act The regulators are required to consult with each other before implementing any rule-making or issuing orders regarding several different types of security swaps. The CFTC and SEC, in consultation with the Federal Reserve are charged with further defining swap related terms that appear in Commodity Exchange Act (7 U.S.C. § 1a(47)(A)(v)) and section 3(a)(78) of the Securities Exchange Act of 1934 (15 U.S.C. § 78c(a)(78)).

The title provides that, "Except as provided otherwise, no Federal assistance may be provided to any swaps entity with respect to any swap, security-based swap, or other activity of the swaps entity." An "Interagency

Group" is constituted to handle the oversight of existing and prospective carbon markets to ensure an efficient, secure, and transparent carbon market, including oversight of spot markets and derivative markets.

TITLE VIII – PAYMENT, CLEARING AND SETTLEMENT SUPERVISION

Title VIII, called the "Payment, Clearing, and Settlement Supervision Act of 2010",aims to mitigate systemic risk within and promote stability in the financial system by tasking the Federal Reserve to create uniform standards for the management of risks by systemically important financial organizations and institutions by providing the Fed with an "enhanced role in the supervision of risk management standards for systemically important financial market utilities; strengthening the liquidity of systemically important financial market utilities; and providing the Board of Governors an enhanced role in the supervision of risk management standards for systemically important payment, clearing, and settlement activities by financial institutions."

TITLE IX – INVESTOR PROTECTIONS AND IMPROVEMENTS TO THE REGULATION OF SECURITIES

Title IX, sections 901 to 991, known as the "Investor Protections and Improvements to the Regulation of Securities", revises the powers and structure of the Securities and Exchange Commission, credit rating organizations, and the relationships between customers and broker-dealers or investment advisers. This title calls for various studies and reports from the SEC and Government Accountability Office (GAO). This title contains ten subtitles, A through J.

SUBTITLE A – INCREASING INVESTOR PROTECTION

Subtitle A contains provisions:

> To prevent regulatory capture within the SEC and increase the influence of investors, the Act creates an Office of the Investor Advocate, an Investor Advisory Committee composed of 12–22 members of whom serve 4-year terms, and an ombudsman appointed by the Office of the Investor Advocate. The Investor Advisory Committee was actually created in 2009 and therefore predates the passage of the Act, but it is specifically authorized under the Act.
>
> SEC is specifically authorized to issue "point-of-sale disclosure" rules when retail investors purchase investment products or services; these disclosures include concise information on costs, risks, and conflicts of interest. This authorization follows up the SEC's failure to implement proposed point-of-sale disclosure rules in 2004 and 2005;
>
> These proposed rules generated opposition because they were perceived as burdensome to broker-dealers. For example, they would require oral disclosures for telephone transactions, were not satisfied by cheap internet or email disclosures, and could allow the customer to request disclosures specific to the amount of their investment. In determining the disclosure rules, the Act authorizes the SEC to do "investor testing" and rely on experts to study financial literacy among retail investors.

Subtitle A provides authority for the SEC to impose regulations requiring "fiduciary duty" by broker-dealers to their customers. Although the Act does not create such a duty immediately, the Act authorizes the SEC to establish such a standard and requires that the SEC study the standards of care which broker-dealers and investment advisers apply to their customers and report to Congress on the results within 6 months. Under the law, commission and limited product range would not

SUBTITLE B – INCREASING REGULATORY ENFORCEMENT AND REMEDIES

Subtitle B gives the SEC further powers of enforcement. This includes a "whistleblower bounty program" which is based upon a similar program established by the IRS in 2006; the program allows persons who provide information which leads to a successful SEC enforcement to receive 10 to 30% of the monetary sanctions over $1 million. Section 921 under the title allows the SEC to prohibit pre-dispute mandatory binding arbitration. Section 929I exempts the SEC from disclosing information obtained pursuant to 17(b) of the Securities Exchange Act of 1934 or information "based upon or derived from" such information "obtained by the Commission for use in furtherance of the purposes of this title, including surveillance, risk assessments, or other regulatory and oversight activities" – meaning information derived from examinations.

The SEC rejected a Freedom of Information Act request on July 27, 2010 based upon this new law; while the SEC has stated that this legal change is necessary for registrants to comply with the examinations, the provision has been criticized for allowing the SEC to avoid the typical disclosure rules applicable to federal agencies.

Importantly, section 921I amends SEC Act of 1934 and the Investment Company Act of 1940 to allow the Securities Exchange Commission to not disclose records or information that have been obtained for uses such as "surveillance, risk assessments, or other regulatory and oversight activities" except it may not withhold information from judicial or congressional inquiry. The effective result of this change is that the US Freedom of Information Act no longer applies to the SEC; the SEC can refuse to supply documents it deems as being part of its regulatory and oversight activities. Previously, the SEC used a narrower existing exemption for trade secrets when refusing Freedom of Information Requests

SUBTITLE C – IMPROVEMENTS TO THE REGULATION OF CREDIT RATING AGENCIES

Recognizing credit ratings issued by credit rating agencies, including nationally recognized statistical rating organizations (NRSROs), are matters of national public interest, that credit rating agencies are critical "gatekeepers" in the debt market central to capital formation, investor confidence, and the efficient performance of the United States economy, Congress expanded regulation of credit rating agencies.

Subtitle C cites findings of conflicts of interest and inaccuracies during the recent financial crisis contributed significantly to the mismanagement of risks by financial institutions and investors which in turn adversely impacted the health of the United States economy as factors necessitating increased accountability and transparency by credit rating agencies.

Subtitle C mandates the creation by the SEC of an Office of Credit Ratings (OCR) to provide oversight over NRSROs and enhanced regulation of such entities.

Enhanced regulations of nationally recognized statistical rating organizations (NRSROs) include:

- NRSROs are required to establish, maintain, enforce and document an effective internal control structure governing the implementation of and adherence to policies, procedures, and methodologies for determining credit ratings.
- Submit to the OCR an annual internal control report.
- Adhere to rules established by the Commission to prevent sales and marketing considerations from influencing the ratings issued by a NRSRO.
- Policies and procedures with regard to (1) certain employment transitions to avoid conflicts of interest, (2) the processing of complaints regarding NRSRO noncompliance, and (3) notification to users of identified significant errors are required.
- Compensation of the compliance officer may not be linked to the financial performance of the NRSRO.
- The duty to report to appropriate authorities credible allegations of unlawful conduct by issuers of securities.
- The consideration of credible information about an issuer from sources other than the issuer or underwriter which is potentially significant to a rating decision.
- The Act establishes corporate governance, organizational, and management of conflict of interest guidelines. A minimum of 2 independent directors is required.

Subtitle C grants authority to the Commission to temporarily suspend or permanently revoke the registration of an NRSRO with respect to a particular class or subclass of securities if after notice and hearing the NRSRO lacks the resources to produce credit ratings with integrity. Additional key provisions of the Act are:

- The Commission shall prescribe rules with respect to credit rating procedures and methodologies.
- OCR is required to conduct an examination of each NRSRO at least annually and shall produce a public inspection report.

To facilitate transparency of credit ratings performance, the Commission shall require NRSROs to publicly disclose information on initial and revised credit ratings issued, including the credit rating methodology utilized and data relied on, to enable users to evaluate NRSROs.

In addition, Subtitle C requires the SEC to conduct a study on strengthening NRSRO independence and recommends the SEC utilize its rulemaking authority to establish guidelines to prevent improper conflicts of interest arising from the performance of services unrelated to the issuance of credit ratings such as consulting, advisory, and other services. The Act requires the Comptroller General of the United States to conduct a study on alternative business models for compensating NRSROs

Subtitle D – Improvements to the Asset-Backed Securitization Process

In Subtitle D, the term "Asset-Backed Security" is defined as a fixed-income or other security collateralized by any type of self-liquidating financial asset, such as a loan, lease, mortgage, that allows the owner of the Asset-Backed Security to receive payments that depend on the cash flow of the (ex.) loan. For regulation purposes, Asset-Backed Securities are described as including (but not limited to):

collateralized mortgage obligation
collateralized debt obligation
collateralized bond obligation
collateralized debt obligation of asset-backed securities
collateralized debt obligation of collateralized debt obligations

For regulation purposes, Asset-Backed Securities do not include securities issued by a finance subsidiary to its parent company or company controlled by the parent company. Within nine months of enactment, rules and regulations are to be issued regarding requiring any securitizer to retain an economic interest in a portion of the credit risk. Regulations for assets that are:

Residential in Nature – are jointly prescribed by the SEC, the Secretary of Housing and Urban Development, and the Federal Housing Finance Agency
In General – the federal banking agencies and the SEC

Specifically, securitizers are:

prohibited from hedging or transferring the credit risk it is required to retain with respect to the assets
required to retain not less than 5% of the credit risk for an asset that is not a qualified residential mortgage,
for commercial mortgages or other types of assets, regulations may provide for retention of less than 5% of the credit risk, provided that there is also disclosure

The regulations are to prescribe several asset classes with separate rules for securitizers, including but not limited to, residential mortgages, commercial mortgages, commercial loans, and auto loans. The SEC and the federal banking agencies may jointly issue exemptions, exceptions, and adjustments to the rules issues provided that they:

help ensure high quality underwriting standards for the securitizers and originators of assets that are securitized or available for securitization
encourage appropriate risk management practices by the securitizers and originators of assets, improve the access of consumers and businesses to credit on reasonable terms, or otherwise be in the public interest and for the protection of investors.

Additionally, the following institutions and programs are exempt:

Farm Credit System
Qualified Residential Mortgages (which are to be jointly defined by the federal banking agencies, SEC, Secretary of Housing and Urban Development, and the Director of the Federal Housing Finance Agency)

The SEC may classify issuers and prescribe requirements appropriate for each class of issuers of asset-backed securities.

The SEC shall also adopt regulations requiring each issuer of an asset-backed security to disclose, for each tranche or class of security, information that will help identify each asset backing that security. Within six months of enactment, the SEC shall issue regulations prescribing representations and warranties in the marketing of asset-backed securities:

require each Nationally Recognized Statistical Rating Organization to include in any report accompanying a credit rating a description of:
- the representations, warranties, and enforcement mechanisms available to investors
- how they differ from the representations, warranties, and enforcement mechanisms in issuances of similar securities

require any securitizer to disclose fulfilled and unfulfilled repurchase requests across all trusts aggregated by the securitizer, so that investors may identify asset originators with clear underwriting deficiencies.

The SEC shall also prescribe a Due Diligence analysis/review of the assets underlying the security, and a disclosure of that analysis.

SUBTITLE E – ACCOUNTABILITY AND EXECUTIVE COMPENSATION

Within one year of enactment, the SEC must issue rules that direct the national securities exchanges and associations to prohibit the listing of any security of an issuer that is not in compliance with the requirements of the compensation sections. At least once every 3 years, a public corporation is required to submit to a shareholder vote the approval of executive compensation. And once every six years there should be a submitted to shareholder vote whether the required approval of executive compensation should be more often that once every three years. Shareholders may disapprove any Golden Parachute compensation to executives via a non-binding vote. Shareholders must be informed of the relationship between executive compensation actually paid and the financial performance of the issuer, taking into account any change in the value of the shares of stock and dividends of the issuer and any distributionsas well as:

the median of the annual total compensation of all employees of the issuer, except the chief executive officer (or any equivalent position)

the annual total compensation of the chief executive officer, or any equivalent position

the ratio of the amount of the medium of the annual total with the total CEO compensation

The company shall also disclose to shareholders whether any employee or member of the board of directors is permitted to purchase financial instruments that are designed to hedge or offset any decrease in the market value of equity securities that are part of a compensation package.

Members of the Board of Director's Compensation Committee shall be an independent member of the board of directors, a compensation consultant or legal council, as provided by rules issued by the SEC. Federal regulators, within 9 months of enactment of this legislation, shall proscribe regulations that a covered company shall disclose to the appropriate Federal regulator, all incentive-based compensation arrangements with sufficient information such that the regulator may determine:

whether the compensation package could lead to material financial loss to the company

provides the employee/officer with excessive compensation, fees, or benefits

Subtitle F – Improvements to the Management of the Securities and Exchange Commission

Within Subtitle F are various managerial changes intended to increase the efficiency of the agency will be implemented, including reports on internal controls, a triennial report on personnel management by the head of the GAO (the Comptroller General of the United States), a hotline for employees to report problems in the agency, a report by the GAO on the oversight of National Securities Associations, and a report by a consultant on reform of the SEC. Under Subtitle J of the title, the SEC will be funded through "match funding" which will in effect mean that its budget will be funded through filing fees.

Subtitle G – Strengthening Corporate Governance

Subtitle G provides that the SEC may issue rules and regulations that include a requirement that permit a shareholder to use a company's proxy solicitation materials for the purpose of nominating individuals to membership on the board of directors. The company is also required to inform investors the reason why the same person is to serve as chairman of the board of directors and chief executive officer, or why different individuals are to serve as chairman of the board of directors and chief executive officer.

Subtitles H – Municipal Securities

This provision of the statute creates a guarantee of trust which correlates a municipal advisor (who provide advice to state and local governments regarding investments) with any municipal bodies which provides services. Also it alters the make-up of the Municipal Securities Rulemaking Board ("MSRB") and mandates that the Comptroller General conducts studies relating to municipal disclosure and municipal markets. The new MSRB will be composed of fifteen individuals, have the authority to regulate municipal advisors, and be permitted to charge fees regarding trade information. Also, it is mandated that the Comptroller General makes several recommendations, which must be submitted to Congress within at most 24 months of enactment of the Act.

Subtitle I – Public Company Accounting Oversight Board, Portfolio Margining, and Other Matters

Subtitle I is concerned with the establishment of a Public Company Accounting Oversight Board (or PCAOB). The PCAOB has the authority to establish oversight of certified public accounting firms. The Subtitle I provision allows the SEC to authorize necessary rules with respect to securities for borrowing. The SEC shall, as deemed appropriate, exercise transparency within this sector of the financial industry. A council of Inspectors General On Financial Oversight, consisting of several members of federal agencies (such as the United States Department of the Treasury, the FDIC, and the Federal Housing Finance Agency) will be established. The council will more easily allow the sharing of data with inspectors general (which includes members by proxy or in person from the SEC and CFTC) with a focus on dealings which may be applicable to the general financial sector at large with focus on the improvement of financial oversight.

Subtitle J – Securities and Exchange Commission Match Funding

Subtitle J provides adjustments to Section 31 of the Securities Exchange Act of 1934 regarding the "Recovery Cost of Annual Appropriation", the "Registration of Fees" and the "Authorization of Appropriations" provisions of the Act.

TITLE X – BUREAU OF CONSUMER FINANCIAL PROTECTION

Main article: United States Consumer Financial Protection Bureau

Title X, or the "Consumer Financial Protection Act of 2010", establishes the Bureau of Consumer Financial Protection. The new Bureau regulates consumer financial products and services in compliance with federal law. The Bureau is headed by a director who is appointed by the President, with the advice and consent of the Senate, for a term of five years. The Bureau is subject to financial audit by the GAO, and must report to the Senate Banking Committee and the House Financial Services Committee bi-annually. The Financial

Stability Oversight Council may issue a "stay" to the Bureau with an appealable 2/3 vote. The Bureau is not placed within the Fed, but it operates independently.

The Fed is prohibited from interfering with matters before the Director, directing any employee of the Bureau, modifying the functions and responsibilities of the Bureau or impeding an order of the Bureau. The Bureau is separated into six divisions:

Supervision, Enforcement, and Fair Lending
Research, Markets, and Regulations
Office of the Chief Operating Officer
General Counsel
Consumer Education and Engagement
External Affairs.

Within the Bureau, a new **Consumer Advisory Board** assists the Bureau and informs it of emerging market trends. This Board is appointed by the Director of the Bureau, with at least six members recommended by regional Fed Presidents. Elizabeth Warren was the first appointee of the President as an adviser to get the Bureau running. The Consumer Financial Protection Bureau can be found on the web.

The Bureau was formally established when Dodd–Frank was enacted, on July 21, 2010. After a one year "stand up" period, the Bureau obtained enforcement authority and began most activities on July 21, 2011.

The Durbin Amendment targeting interchange fees is also in Title X, under Subtitle G, section 1075.

TITLE XI – FEDERAL RESERVE SYSTEM PROVISIONS

GOVERNANCE AND OVERSIGHT

A new position is created on the Board of Governors, the "Vice Chairman for Supervision", to advise the Board in several areas and:

serves in the absence of the Chairman,

is responsible for developing policy recommendations to the Board regarding supervision and regulation of financial institution supervised by the Board,

oversees the supervision and regulation of such firms, and

reports to Congress on a semiannual basis to disclose their activities and efforts, testifying before Committee on Banking, Housing, and Urban Affairs of the Senate and the Committee on Financial Services of the House of Representatives

Additionally, the GAO is now required to perform several different audits of the Fed:

A one-time audit of any emergency lending facility established by the Fed since December 1, 2007 and ending with the date of enactment of this Act

A Federal Reserve Governance Audit that shall examine:

- The extent to which the current system of appointing Federal reserve bank directors represents "the public, without discrimination on the basis of race, creed, color, sex or national origin, and with due but not exclusive consideration to the interests of agriculture, commerce, industry, services, labor, and consumers"
- Whether there are actual or potential conflicts of interest
- Examine each facilities operation
- Identify changes to selection procedures for Federal reserve bank directors or to other aspects of governance that would improve public representation and increase the availability of monetary information

Standards, Plans & Reports, and Off-Balance-Sheet Activities

The Fed is required to establish prudent standards for the institutions they supervise that include:

Risk-Based Capital Requirements and Leverage Limits
Liquidity requirements;
Overall risk management requirements;
Resolution plan and credit exposure report requirements; and
Concentration limits.

The Fed may establish additional standards that include, but are not limited to:

A contingent capital requirement
Enhanced public disclosure
Short-term debt limits

The Fed may require supervised companies to "maintain a minimum amount of contingent capital that is convertible to equity in times of financial stress."

Title XI requires companies supervised by the Fed to periodically provide additional plans and reports, including:"

A plan for a rapid and orderly liquidation of the company in the event of material financial distress or failure,
A credit exposure report describing the nature to which the company has exposure to other companies, and credit exposure cannot exceed 25% of the capital stock and surplus of the company."

The title requires that in determining capital requirements for regulated organizations, off-balance-sheet activities shall be taken into consideration, being those things that create an accounting liability such as, but not limited to:"

Direct credit substitutes in which a bank substitutes its own credit for a third party, including standby letters of credit.
Irrevocable letters of credit that guarantee repayment of commercial paper or tax-exempt securities.
Risk participations in bankers' acceptances.
Sale and repurchase agreements.
Asset sales with recourse against the seller.
Interest rate swaps.
Credit swaps.
Commodities contracts.
Forward contracts.
Securities contracts.

TITLE XII – IMPROVING ACCESS TO MAINSTREAM FINANCIAL INSTITUTIONS

Title XII, known as the "Improving Access to Mainstream Financial Institutions Act of 2010", provides incentives that encourage low- and medium-income people to participate in the financial systems. Organizations that are eligible to provide these incentives are 501(c)(3) and IRC § 501(a) tax exempt organizations, federally insured depository institutions, community development financial institution, State, local or tribal governments. Multi-year programs for grants, cooperative agreements, etc. are also available.

to enable low- and moderate-income individuals to establish one or more accounts in a federal insured bank

make micro loans, typically under $2,500

provide financial education and counseling

TITLE XIII – PAY IT BACK ACT

Title XIII, or the "Pay It Back Act", amends the Emergency Economic Stabilization Act of 2008 to limit the Troubled Asset Relief Program, by reducing the funds available by $225 billion (from $700 billion to $475 billion) and further mandating that unused funds cannot be used for any new programs.

Amendments to the Housing and Economic Recovery Act of 2008 and other sections of the federal code to specify that any proceeds from the sale of securities purchased to help stabilize the financial system shall be:

dedicated for the sole purpose of deficit reduction

prohibited from use as an offset for other spending increases or revenue reductions

The same conditions apply for any funds not used by the state under the American Recovery and Reinvestment Act of 2009 by December 31, 2012, provided that the President may waive these requirements if it is determined to be in the best interest of the nation.

TITLE XIV – MORTGAGE REFORM AND ANTI-PREDATORY LENDING ACT

Title XIV, or the "Mortgage Reform and Anti-Predatory Lending Act", whose subtitles A, B, C, and E are designated as Enumerated Consumer Law, which will be administered by the new Bureau of Consumer Financial Protection. The section focuses on standardizing data collection for underwriting and imposes obligations on mortgage originators to only lend to borrowers who are likely to repay their loans.

SUBTITLE A – RESIDENTIAL MORTGAGE LOAN ORGANIZATION STANDARDS

A "Residential Mortgage Originator" is defined as any person who either receives compensation for or represents to the public that they will take a residential loan application, assist a consumer in obtaining a loan, or negotiate terms for a loan. A residential Mortgage Originator is not a person who provides financing to an individual for the purchase of 3 or more properties in a year, or a licensed real estate broker/associate. All Mortgage Originators are to include on all loan documents any unique identifier of the mortgage originator provided by the Registry described in the Secure and Fair Enforcement for Mortgage Licensing Act of 2008

For any residential mortgage loan, no mortgage originator may receive compensation that varies based on the term of the loan, other than the principal amount. In general, the mortgage originator can only receive payment from the consumer, except as provided in rules that may be established by the Board. Additionally, the mortgage originator must verify the consumer's ability to pay. A violation of the "ability to repay" standard, or a mortgage that has excessive fees or abusive terms, may be raised as a foreclosure defense by a borrower against a lender without regard to any statute of limitations. The Act bans the payment of yield spread premiums or other originator compensation that is based on the interest rate or other terms of the loans.

SUBTITLE B – MINIMUM STANDARDS FOR MORTGAGES

In effect, this section of the Act establishes national underwriting standards for residential loans. It is not the intent of this section to establish rules or regulations that would require a loan to be made that would not be regarded as acceptable or prudential by the appropriate regulator of the financial institution. However, the loan originator shall make a reasonable and good faith effort based on verified and documented information that "at the time the loan is consummated, the consumer has a reasonable ability to repay the loan, according to the terms, and all applicable taxes, insurance (including mortgage guarantee insurance), and other assessments." Also included in these calculations should be any payments for a second mortgage or other subordinate loans. Income verification is mandated for residential mortgages. Certain loan provisions, including prepayment penalties on some loans, and mandatory arbitration on all residential loans, are prohibited.

This section also defined a "Qualified Mortgage" as any residential mortgage loan that the regular periodic payments for the loan does not increase the principal balance or allow the consumer to defer repayment of principal (with some exceptions), and has points and fees being less than 3% of the loan amount. The Qualified Mortgage terms are important to the extent that the loan terms plus an "Ability to Pay" presumption create a safe harbor situation concerning certain technical provisions related to foreclosure.

SUBTITLE C – HIGH-COST MORTGAGES

A "High-Cost Mortgage" as well as a reverse mortgage are sometimes referred to as "certain home mortgage transactions" in the Fed's Regulation Z (the regulation used to implement various sections of the Truth in Lending Act) High-Cost Mortgage is redefined as a "consumer credit transaction that is secured by the consumer's principal dwelling" (excluding reverse mortgages which are covered in a separate sections), which include:

- Credit Transactions secured by consumer's principal dwelling and interest rate is 6.5% more than the prime rate for comparable transactions
- subordinated (ex. second mortgage) if secured by consumer's principal dwelling and interest rate is 8.5% more than the prime rate for comparable transactions
- Points and Fees, excluding Mortgage Insurance, if the transaction is:
  - less than $20,000, total points and fees greater than 8% or $1000
  - greater than $20,000, total points and fees greater than 6%
- under certain conditions, if the fees and points may be collected more than 36 months after loan is executed

New provisions for calculating adjustable rates as well as definitions for points and fees are also included.

When receiving a High-Cost mortgage, the consumer must obtain pre-loan counseling from a certified counselor. The Act also stipulates there are additional "Requirements to Existing Residential Mortgages". The changes to existing contracts are:

- disallowing Balloon Payments
- disallowing prepayment penalties
- banning the practice of encouraging default on an existing loan when refinancing

SUBTITLE D – OFFICE OF HOUSING COUNSELING

Subtitle D, known as the Expand and Preserve Home Ownership Through Counseling Act, creates a new Office of Housing Counseling, within the department of Housing and Urban Development. The director reports to the Secretary of Housing and Urban Development. The Director shall have primary responsibility within the Department for consumer oriented homeownership and rental housing counseling. To advise the Director, the Secretary shall appoint an advisory committee of not more than 12 individuals, equally representing mortgage and real estate industries, and including consumers and housing counseling agencies. Council members are appointed to 3-year terms. This department will coordinate media efforts to educate the general public in home ownership and home finance topics.

The Secretary of Housing and Urban Development is authorized to provide grants to HUD-approved housing counseling agencies and state Housing Finance Agencies to provide education assistance to various groups in home ownership. The Secretary is also instructed, in consultation with other federal agencies responsible for financial and banking regulation, to establish a database to track foreclosures and defaults on mortgage loans for 1 through 4 unit residential properties.

Subtitle E – Mortgage Servicing

Subtitle E concerns rules concerning escrow and settlement procedures for people who are in trouble repaying their mortgages, and also makes amendments to the Real Estate Settlement Procedures Act of 1974. In general, in connection with a residential mortgage there should be established an escrow or impound account for the payment of taxes, hazard insurance, and (if applicable) flood insurance, mortgage insurance, ground rents, and any other required periodic payments. Lender shall disclose to borrower at least three business days before closing the specifics of the amount required to be in the escrow account and the subsequent uses of the funds.

If an escrow, impound, or trust account is not established, or the consumer chooses to close the account, the servicer shall provide a timely and clearly written disclosure to the consumer that advises the consumer of the responsibilities of the consumer and implications for the consumer in the absence of any such account. The amendments to the Real Estate Settlement Procedures Act of 1974 (or RESPA) change how a Mortgage servicer (those who administer loans held by Fannie Mae, Freddie Mac, etc.) should interact with consumers.

Subtitle F – Appraisal Activities

A creditor may not extend credit for a higher-risk mortgage to a consumer without first obtaining a written appraisal of the property with the following components:

Physical Property Visit – including a visit of the interior of the property
Second Appraisal Circumstances – creditor must obtain a second appraisal, with no cost to the applicant, if the original appraisal is over 180 days old or if the current acquisition price is lower than the previous sale price

A "certified or licensed appraiser" is defined as someone who:

is certified or licensed by the state in which the property is located
performs each appraisal in conformity with Uniform Standards of Professional Appraisal Practice and title XI of the Financial Institutions Reform, Recovery, and Enforcement Act of 1989

The Fed, Comptroller of the Currency, FDIC, National Credit Union Administration Board, Federal Housing Finance Agency and Bureau of Consumer Financial Protection (created in this law) shall jointly prescribe regulations.

The use of Automated Valuation Models to be used to estimate collateral value for mortgage lending purposes.

Automated valuation models shall adhere to quality control standards designed to,

ensure a high level of confidence in the estimates produced by automated valuation models;
protect against the manipulation of data;
seek to avoid conflicts of interest;
require random sample testing and reviews; and
account for any other such factor that those responsible for formulating regulations deem appropriate

The Fed, the Comptroller of the Currency, the FDIC, the National Credit Union Administration Board, the Federal Housing Finance Agency, and the Bureau of Consumer Financial Protection, in consultation with the staff of the Appraisal Subcommittee and the Appraisal Standards Board of The Appraisal Foundation, shall promulgate regulations to implement the quality control standards required under this section that devises Automated Valuation Models.

Residential and 1-to-4 unit single family residential real estate are enforced by: Federal Trade Commission, the Bureau of Consumer Financial Protection, and a state attorney general. Commercial enforcement is by the Financial regulatory agency that supervised the financial institution originating the loan.

Broker Price Opinions may not be used as the primary basis to determine the value of a consumer's principal dwelling; but valuation generated by an automated valuation model is not considered a Broker Price Opinion.

The standard settlement form (commonly known as the HUD 1) may include, in the case of an appraisal coordinated by an appraisal management company, a clear disclosure of:

- the fee paid directly to the appraiser by such company
- the administration fee charged by such company

Within one year, the Government Accountability Office shall conduct a study on the effectiveness and impact of various appraisal methods, valuation models and distribution channels, and on the home valuation code of conduct and the appraisal subcommittee.

SUBTITLE G – MORTGAGE RESOLUTION AND MODIFICATION

The Secretary of Housing and Urban Development is charged with developing a program to ensure protection of current and future tenants and at-risk multifamily (5 or more units) properties. The Secretary may coordinate the program development with the Secretary of the Treasury, the FDIC, the Fed, the Federal Housing Finance Agency, and any other federal government agency deemed appropriate. The criteria may include:

- creating sustainable financing of such properties, that may take into consideration such factors as:
  - the rental income generated by such properties
  - the preservation of adequate operating reserves
- maintaining the current level of federal, state, and city subsidies
- funds for rehabilitation
- facilitating the transfer of such properties, when appropriate and with the agreement of owners

Previously the Treasury Department has created the Home Affordable Modification Program, set up to help eligible home owners with loan modifications on their home mortgage debt. This section requires every mortgage servicer participating in the program and denies a re-modification request to provide the borrower with any data used in a net present value (NPV) analysis. The Secretary of the Treasury is also directed to establish a Web-based site that explains NPV calculations

The secretary of the Treasury is instructed to develop a Web-based site to explain the Home Affordable Modification Program and associated programs, that also provides an evaluation of the impact of the program on home loan modifications.

SUBTITLE H – MISCELLANEOUS PROVISIONS

- It is the sense of the Congress that significant structural reforms of Fannie Mae and Freddie Mac are required
- GAO is commissioned to study current inter-agency efforts to reduce mortgage foreclosure and rescue scams and loan modification fraud.
- HUD is commissioned to study the impact of defective drywall imported from China from 2004 through 2007 and their effect on foreclosures.
- Additional funding for Mortgage Relief and Neighborhood Stabilization programs ($1 billion each)
- HUD to establish legal assistance for foreclosure-related issues with $35 million authorized for fiscal years 2011 through 2012.

TITLE XV – MISCELLANEOUS PROVISIONS

The following sections have been added to the Act:

Restriction on U.S. Approval of Loans issued by International Monetary Fund

The US Executive Director at the International Monetary Fund is instructed to evaluate any loan to a country if

The amount of the public debt of the country exceeds the annual gross domestic product of the country

the country is not eligible for assistance from the International Development Association and to oppose any loans unlikely to be repaid in full.

Disclosures on Conflict Materials in or Near the Democratic Republic of the Congo

The SEC is mandated to create rules that address potential conflict materials (e.g. blood diamonds) and to assess whether materials originating in or near the Democratic Republic of the Congo are benefiting armed groups in the area.

The Secretary of State and Administrator of the United States Agency for International Development are required to develop a strategy to address the linkages between human rights abuses, armed groups, mining of conflict minerals, and commercial products, and promoted peace and security in the Democratic Republic of the Congo.

An industry group has complained that the legislation goes beyond voluntary industry initiative such as the Kimberley Process Certification Scheme.

The United Nations Security Council committee charged with overseeing conflict minerals issues reported that this legislation was a "catalyst" for efforts to save lives by cutting off a key source of funding for armed groups.

Reporting on Mine Safety

Requires the SEC to report on mine safety by gathering information on violations of health or safety standards, citations and orders issued to mine operators, number of flagrant violations, value of fines, number of mining-related fatalities, etc., to determine whether there is a pattern of violations.

Reporting on Payments by Oil, Gas and Minerals in Acquisition of Licenses

The Securities Exchange Act of 1934 is amended to require disclosure of payments relating to the acquisition of licenses for exploration, production, etc., where "payment" includes fees, production entitlements, bonuses, and other material benefits. The act states in SEC. 1504 (3) that these documents will be made available online to the public.

Study on Effectiveness of Inspectors General

The Comptroller General is commissioned to assess the relative independence, effectiveness, and expertise of presidentially appointed inspectors general and inspectors general of federal entities.

Study on Core Deposits and Brokered Deposits

The FDIC is instructed to conduct a study to evaluate:

the definition of core deposits for the purpose of calculating the insurance premiums of banks;

the potential impact on the Deposit Insurance Fund of revising the definitions of brokered deposits and core deposits to better distinguish between them;

an assessment of the differences between core deposits and brokered deposits and their role in the economy and banking sector

the potential stimulative effect on local economies of redefining core deposits; and

the competitive parity between large institutions and community banks that could result from redefining core deposits.

TITLE XVI – SECTION 1256 CONTRACTS

A Section 1256 Contract refers to a section of the IRC § 1256 that described tax treatment for any regulated futures contract, foreign currency contract or non-equity option. To calculate capital gains or losses, these trades have traditionally been marked to market on the last business day of the year. A "section 1256 contract" shall not include:

any securities futures contract or option on such a contract unless such contract or option is a dealer securities futures contract

swap form of a derivative, such as interest rate swaps, currency swaps, etc.

SUPPLEMENTS

FOREIGN BOARDS OF TRADE APPLYING FOR ORDERS OF REGISTRATION PERMITTING DIRECT ACCESS FROM THE U.S.

Foreign Board of Trade	Location	Status	Date	Remarks
Australian Securities Exchange	Sydney, AU	Pending	08/16/2012	Applied for Registration pursuant to Commission Regulation Part 48.
BM&F Bovespa S.A. - Bolsa de Valores, Mercadorias & Futuros	Sao Paulo, BR	Pending	08/17/2012	Applied for Registration pursuant to Commission Regulation Part 48.
Bursa Malaysia Derivatives Bhd	Kuala Lumpur, MY	Pending	03/29/2013	Applied for Registration pursuant to Commission Regulation Part 48.
Dubai Mercantile Exchange Limited	Dubai, AE	Pending	08/16/2012	Applied for Registration pursuant to Commission Regulation Part 48.
Eurex Deutschland	Frankfurt, DE	Pending	08/17/2012	Applied for Registration pursuant to Commission Regulation Part 48.
Euronext Amsterdam	Amsterdam, NL	Pending	08/17/2012	Applied for Registration pursuant to Commission Regulation Part 48.
Euronext Brussels	Brussels, BE	Pending	08/20/2012	Applied for Registration pursuant to Commission Regulation Part 48.
Euronext Paris	Paris, FR	Pending	08/17/2012	Applied for Registration pursuant to Commission Regulation Part 48.
European Energy Exchange	Leipzig, DE	Pending	08/17/2012	Applied for Registration pursuant to Commission Regulation Part 48.
ICE Futures Canada, Inc.	Winnipeg, Manitoba, CA	Pending	08/09/2012	Applied for Registration pursuant to Commission Regulation Part 48.
ICE Futures Europe	London, GB	Pending	08/17/2012	Applied for Registration pursuant to Commission Regulation Part 48.
London International Financial Futures and Options	London, GB	Pending	08/17/2012	Applied for Registration pursuant to Commission Regulation Part 48.
London Metal Exchange	London, GB	Pending	08/16/2012	Applied for Registration pursuant to Commission Regulation Part 48.
Mercado Mexicano de Derivados	Mexico City, MX	Pending	08/20/2012	Applied for Registration pursuant to Commission Regulation Part 48.
Montreal Exchange, Inc.	Montreal, CA	Pending	07/20/2012	Applied for Registration pursuant to Commission Regulation Part 48.
NASDAQ OMX Oslo ASA	Lysaker, NO	Pending	08/20/2012	Applied for Registration pursuant to Commission Regulation Part 48.
Natural Gas Exchange	Calgary, Alberta,	Order of	05/02/2013	Order of Registration issued.

Inc.	CA	Registration Issued		
NZX Limited	Wellington, NZ	Pending	02/21/2012	Applied for Registration pursuant to Commission Regulation Part 48.
Osaka Securities Exchange	Osaka, JP	Pending	08/16/2012	Applied for Registration pursuant to Commission Regulation Part 48.
Singapore Exchange Derivatives Trading Limited	Singapore, SG	Pending	08/20/2012	Applied for Registration pursuant to Commission Regulation Part 48.
Tokyo Commodity Exchange	Tokyo, JP	Pending	07/11/2013	Applied for Registration pursuant to Commission Regulation Part 48.

CLEARING ORGANIZATIONS

Organization	Type	Status		Date	Clearing For	Remarks	Associated Documents
AE Clearinghouse, LLC	DCO	Dormant	as of	04/09/2008		AE Clearinghouse, LLC, a subsidiary of The Actuarials Exchange, LLC, has been registered as a derivatives clearing organization for the purpose of clearing, as limited by its registration order, for eligible contract participants, cash-settled contracts, agreements or transactions excluded under Section 2(d) of the CEA or executed on a board of trade exempted under Section 5d of the CEA.	6
BrokerTec Clearing Company, LLC	DCO	Dormant	as of	06/19/2004			1
Cantor Clearinghouse, L.P.	DCO	Registered	as of	04/20/2010	CANTR; CANTOR	Cantor Clearinghouse, L.P. requested an amendment to its order of registration as a DCO in order to remove conditions relating to the clearing of the Domestic Box Office Receipt contract since Section 721 of the Dodd-Frank Wall Street Reform and Consumer Protection Act excluded such contracts from the definition of "commodity" in the Commodity Exchange Act.	11
Chicago Board of Trade	DCO	Vacated	as of	08/06/2012		The DCO registration of CBOT is vacated by	4

						Commission Order effective August 6, 2012, pursuant to a request from CBOT under Section 7 of the CEA. CBOT became a DCO on October 7, 2003.	
Chicago Mercantile Exchange, Inc.	DCO	Registered	as of	12/21/2000	CME; OCX; CMEAM; SWAPSTR; YELJACK; CBOT; DFOX; AGORA-X; ICAP; PARITY; ICAPHYD; TFSC; TFSOIL; GFI; FCEM; ENERGYX; ICAPTUR; EOXLIVE; HSE; TRUEQUO; CMEECM		0
Clearing Corporation	DCO	Registered	as of	12/21/2000	CCFE; CDX; USFE; ME; BM; MTCHBOX; CC; GFI; FCRM	CCORP, aka TCC and formerly known as BOTCC, is an independent clearing organization originally formed in 1925. CCORP was acquired by IntercontinentalExchange (ICE) on March 6, 2009.	0
CME Clearing Europe Limited	DCO	Vacated	as of	03/13/2012		The DCO registration of CME Clearing Europe is vacated by Commission Order dated March 13, 2012, pursuant to a request from CME Clearing Europe under Section 7 of the CEA. CME Clearing Europe became a registered DCO on September 2, 2011.	13
Eurex Clearing AG	DCO	Pending	Official Receipt Date	05/16/2011		Comments Due By: 10/29/2011 Eurex Clearing AG has applied for registration as a DCO for the purpose of clearing swaps. At the request of Eurex Clearing AG, the 180-day review period was extended to December 31, 2013.	18
FutureCom	DCO	Dormant	as of	03/12/2003		The designation order for FutureCom contained conditions it was required to meet before it could	1

						operate as an exchange or clearing house. It did not meet those conditions before it became dormant.	
ICE Clear Credit LLC	DCO	Registered	as of	07/16/2011		On July 16, 2011, ICE Clear Credit LLC (formerly ICE Trust U.S. LLC) was deemed a registered derivatives clearing organization by operation of section 725(b) of the Dodd-Frank Act.	1
ICE Clear Europe Limited	DCO	Registered	as of	01/22/2010	ICE; ICAP; TRUEQUO		13
ICE Clear US, Inc.	DCO	Registered	as of	12/21/2000	ICE US	In January 2007, Intercontinental Exchange, Inc. merged with and acquired both NYBOT and its clearing organization, NYCC, a wholly-owned subsidiary of NYBOT. Previously, in 1999, NYCC had taken over clearing functions of the Commodity Clearing Corporation and the Commodity Futures Clearing Corporation of New York that formerly cleared for the New York Cotton Exchange and Coffee, Sugar & Cocoa Exchange, Inc., respectively. On June 1, 2007, the name of NYCC changed to ICE Clear US, Inc.	0
Intermarket Clearing Corporation	DCO	Vacated	as of	12/30/2003		ICC was formerly a wholly-owned subsidiary of OCC but merged into OCC and ceased to exist as a separate corporate entity. Therefore ICC requested that the Commission vacate its grandfathered-DCO registration. Per Commission order dated 12/30/03 the DCO registration was vacated effective 12/31/03.	0
Kansas City Board of Trade Clearing Corporation	DCO	Vacated	as of	04/16/2013	KCBT	The DCO registration of the Kansas City Board of Trade Clearing Corporation is vacated by Commission Order effective April 16, 2013, pursuant to a request from Kansas City Board of	1

						Trade Clearing Corporation under Section 7 of the CEA.	
LCH.Clearnet LLC	DCO	Registered	as of	12/22/2008		On August 15, 2012, LCH.Clearnet Group Limited announced the acquisition of International Derivatives Clearing Group, LLC, the sole member of International Derivatives Clearinghouse LLC ("IDC"), from The NASDAQ OMX Group, Inc. IDC has been renamed LCH.Clearnet LLC. An amended order of DCO registration was issued to LCH.Clearnet LLC on January 23, 2013.	9
LCH.Clearnet Ltd.	DCO	Registered	as of	10/28/2001	FLETT; GFI; NEX; NYMXECM; DFOX; ICAP; ICAPHYD	LCH provides clearing and settlement services for its clearing members, both U.S. and foreign based, in over-the-counter (OTC) interest rate swap contracts through its SwapClear facility and in OTC energy derivatives contracts executed on commercial markets exempted under section 2(h) of the CEA.	6
LCH.Clearnet SA	DCO	Pending	Official Receipt Date	04/25/2012		Comments Due By: 08/27/2012 LCH.Clearnet SA has applied for registration as a DCO. At the request of LCH.Clearnet SA, the 180-day review period was extended to December 31, 2013.	21
Minneapolis Grain Exchange, Inc.	DCO	Registered	as of	12/21/2000	MGE	The Clearing House became a department of the MGE in 1977. It was formerly a separate entity known as the Minneapolis Clearing Corporation.	1
Natural Gas Exchange Inc.	DCO	Registered	as of	12/12/2008	NGX; ICE	NGX is a Canadian firm that trades and clears primarily spot and forward physically-settled contracts, in natural gas, electricity, and other energy sources in North America. It is owned by TMX Group Inc. which also owns the Toronto Stock Exchange and the Montréal Exchange.	8

New York Portfolio Clearing, LLC	DCO	Registered	as of	01/31/2011		NYPC, which is jointly owned by NYSE Euronext and The Depository Trust & Clearing Corporation, clears U.S. dollar-denominated interest rate futures contracts traded on NYSE Liffe US.	28
North American Derivatives Exchange, Inc.	DCO	Registered	as of	02/18/2004	NADEX	The Commission issued an amended order of DCO registration dated March 30, 2010 allowing Nadex to clear intermediated trades.	3
NYMEX Clearing House	DCO	Vacated	as of	08/06/2012		The DCO registration of NYMEX is vacated by Commission Order effective August 6, 2012, pursuant to a request from NYMEX under Section 7 of the CEA. NYMEX became a DCO on December 21, 2000.	4
OnExchange Clearing Corporation	DCO	Dormant	as of	12/31/2003		OnExchange Clearing Corporation and ONXBOT are subsidiaries of OnExchange Inc.	0
Options Clearing Corporation	DCO	Registered	as of	12/10/2001	CFE; INET; NQLX; OCX; PBOT	OCC is a securities clearing agency registered under the Securities Exchange Act of 1934 that provides clearing and settlement services for securities options traded on national securities exchanges. As a registered DCO, OCC provides clearing and settlement services for transactions in commodity futures contracts and options on commodity futures contracts.	2

CFTC PERFORMANCE MEASURES AND RESULTS

OBJECTIVE 0.1: COMPLETE ALL DODD-FRANK ACT RULES WITHIN STATUTORY TIME FRAMES.

Goal.Objective.Strategy.Measure Performance Measure	FY 2011 Actual	FY 2012 Actual	FY 2012 Planned	FY 2013 Planned	FY 2014 Planned	FY 2015 Planned
0.1.1.1 Complete all Dodd-Frank Act rules within statutory time frames.	18%	82%	100%	100%	N/A	N/A

Goal One: Protect the public and market participants by ensuring market integrity, promoting transparency, competition and fairness and lowering risk in the system.

Goal.Objective.Strategy.Measure Performance Measure	FY 2011 Actual	FY 2012 Actual	FY 2012 Planned	FY 2013 Planned	FY 2014 Planned	FY 2015 Planned
1.1.1.1 Implement automated position limit alerts for futures, option, and swaps markets.	N/A	100%	100%	N/A	100%	N/A
	Implement automated position limit monitoring for all additional commodities under CFTC position limits for futures and options traded on DCMs.	Implement automated position limit monitoring for all commodities under CFTC position limits for the swap market using large trader reporting data.		N/A	Implement automated position limit monitoring for all commodities under CFTC position limits using integrated data from reporting firms and swaps data repositories.	N/A
1.1.1.2 Implement automated surveillance alerts and a case management system.	70%	100%	100%	100%	N/A	N/A
	Implement four automated market alerts.	Implement automated market profile alerts. Integrate swaps market data into two automated market alerts.		Implement automated market profile alerts for swaps market.	N/A	N/A
1.1.1.3 Implement automated trading violation alerts and a case management system.	20%	98%	100%	100%	100%	100%
	Implement five automated trading violation alerts.	Implement five automated trading violation alerts.		Implement four automated trading violation alerts.	Implement two automated trading violation alerts.	Develop and implement additional automated alerts as identified.
1.1.2.1	50%	60%	100%	N/A	N/A	N/A

Review information requirements of current and proposed forms.	Conduct internal review and update current reporting forms. Collaborate with industry committee to develop recommendations for ownership and control information related to exchange-traded futures and options.	Implement ownership and control reporting standards for futures and option markets. Implement reportable trader standards for swaps traders.		N/A	N/A	N/A
1.1.4.1 Percentage of contracts that are reviewed, in a timely manner, following a finding of market significance, and determined to be in compliance with core principles or referred back to exchange for modification.	2%	10%	100%	100%	100%	100%
1.1.5.1 Rule submissions are reviewed and a determination is made regarding compliance with the CEA, or referred back to the exchange for correction, as amended by the Dodd-Frank Act and Commission regulations within the required 10-day or 90-day time period.	77%	73%	100%	100%	100%	100%
1.1.6.1 DCM and SEF applications are reviewed and a determination is made regarding compliance with Core Principles within statutory time frames.	100%	100%	100%	100%	100%	100%
1.2.1.1 Percentage of major DCMs and SEFs reviewed, during the year. (Structural Sufficiency)	40%	0%	100%	100%	100%	100%
1.2.1.2 Percentage of non-major DCMs and SEFs reviewed, during the year. (Structural Sufficiency)	20%	13%	100%	100%	100%	100%
1.2.2.1 Percentage of major DCMs and SEFs reviewed, during the year. (Automated Systems and Business Continuity)	80%	80%	100%	100%	100%	100%
1.2.2.2 Percentage of non-major DCMs and SEFs reviewed, during the year. (Automated Systems and	0%	0%	33%	33%	33%	33%

Business Continuity)						
	N/A	100%	100%	100%	100%	100%
1.3.1.1 Publish reports for swaps markets activity.	N/A	Develop and test aggregation methods to group interest rate swap products.		Develop and test aggregation methods to group all commodity swap products under CFTC position limits. Publish swaps market report for interest rate swap products. Publish Dodd-Frank Act required semiannual and annual swaps reports for all interest rate swap products.	Develop and test aggregation methods to group currency, equity, credit and other commodity swap products. Publish swaps market reports for all commodity swap products under CFTC position limits. Publish Dodd-Frank Act required semiannual and annual swaps reports for all commodity swap products under CFTC position limits.	Publish swaps market reports for currency, equity and other commodity swap products. Publish Dodd-Frank Act required semiannual and annual swaps reports for currency, equity and other commodity swap products.

Goal Two: Protect the public and market participants by ensuring the financial integrity of derivatives transactions, mitigation of systemic risk, and the fitness and soundness of intermediaries and other registrants.

Goal.Objective.Strategy.Measure Performance Measure	FY 2011 Actual	FY 2012 Actual	FY 2012 Planned	FY 2013 Planned	FY 2014 Planned	FY 2015 Planned
2.1.1.1 Review systemically important DCOs annually. Percentage of SIDCOs reviewed.	75%	50%	100%	100%	100%	100%
2.1.1.2 On a risk-based basis, review all other DCOs annually to assess compliance with DCO Core Principles and Commission requirements.	44%	30%	100%	100%	100%	100%
2.1.1.3 Percent of requests for	0%	64%	92%	94%	96%	98%

Commission orders that are completed following review under the applicable provisions of the CEA.						
2.1.3.1 All material exceptions in monthly and annual financial filings by FCMs and RFEDs and notices of noncompliance with respect to minimum capital and segregation are reviewed and assessed within one business day. Percent completed within one business day.	100%	100%	100%	100%	100%	100%
2.1.3.2 On a risk-based basis, conduct direct examinations of FCMs and RFEDs, identify deficiencies, and confirm that all deficiencies identified are corrected within the specified period of time. Percent corrected within specified time period.	100%	55%	92%	94%	96%	98%
2.1.4.1 Reviews of swaps submitted to the Commission are completed within statutory and regulatory deadlines.	N/A	50%	100%	100%	100%	100%
2.1.5.1 Reviews of DCO rules submitted to the Commission are completed within statutory and regulatory deadlines.	100%	100%	100%	100%	100%	100%
2.1.6.1 Perform risk analysis and stress-testing on large trader and clearing member positions to ascertain those with significant risk and confirm that such risks are being appropriately managed. Number of positions analyzed.	500,000	550,000	550,000	600,000	650,000	700,000
2.1.6.2 On a risk-based basis, meet with large traders, FCMs, SDs, and other industry participants to discuss risk management issues. Number of entities met with and risk issues reviewed.	110	110	122	132	143	154
2.2.2.1 Under a risk-based approach, conduct reviews of selected programs of all RFAs to assess fulfillment of statutory and delegated responsibilities and confirm that any deficiencies identified are corrected within the specified period of time. Percent of deficiencies corrected within	0%	80%	92%	94%	96%	98%

specified time period.						
2.2.2.2 Percentage of RFA rules submitted for which determinations are made within statutory time frames.	100%	80%	92%	94%	96%	98%
2.2.3.1 On a risk-based basis, conduct direct examinations of non-FCM intermediaries, identify deficiencies, and confirm that any deficiencies identified are corrected within the specified period of time. Percent of time that deficiencies are corrected within specified time period.	0%	0%	92%	94%	96%	98%
2.3.1.1 On a risk-based basis, review all SROs annually to assess compliance with CEA and Commission requirements, identify deficiencies, and confirm that any deficiencies identified are corrected within the specified period of time. Percent of time in which deficiencies are corrected within specified time period.	80%	80%	92%	94%	96%	98%
2.3.1.2 Percentage of direct examinations of registered intermediaries that confirm proper execution of SRO programs.	100%	43%	92%	94%	96%	98%
2.4.1.1 Program redesign to cover new registrants monitored by the RSR and SPARK systems. Percentage of system redesign accomplished.	80%	80%	90%	95%	98%	100%

Goal Three: Protect the public and market participants through a robust enforcement program.

Goal.Objective.Strategy.Measure Performance Measure	FY 2011 Actual	FY 2012 Actual	FY 2012 Planned	FY 2013 Planned	FY 2014 Planned	FY 2015 Planned
3.1.1.1 Percentage of enforcement investigations concluded within one year of opening.	81%	69%	70%	75%	75%	80%
3.2.1.1 Percentage of CFTC case filings that include referrals to domestic civil and criminal cooperative authorities.	62%	91%	65%	70%	75%	75%

Goal Four: Enhance integrity of U.S. markets by engaging in cross-border cooperation, promoting strong international regulatory standards, and encouraging ongoing convergence of laws and regulation worldwide.

Goal.Objective.Strategy.Measure Performance Measure	FY 2011 Actual	FY 2012 Actual	FY 2012 Planned	FY 2013 Planned	FY 2014 Planned	FY 2015 Planned

4.1.1.1 Days allotted for acknowledgment of incoming requests for enforcement assistance from our international counterparts pursuant to our information sharing arrangements.	1	3	4	3	2	2
4.2.1.1 Number of international regulatory and standard-setting working groups in which the Commission participates.	12	15	9	9	9	9
4.3.1.1 Number of non-U.S. regulators trained.	225	414	200	200	225	225

Goal Five: Promote Commission excellence through executive direction and leadership, organizational and individual performance management, and effective management of resources.

Goal.Objective.Strategy.Measure Performance Measure	FY 2011 Actual	FY 2012 Actual	FY 2012 Planned	FY 2013 Planned	FY 2014 Planned	FY 2015 Planned
5.1.1.1 Executive approval and Commission adoption of efficient and effective organizational design.	100%	100%	100%	100%	N/A	N/A
	Assess and identify organizational requirements. Prepare and design functional organization blueprints. Recommend and obtain approval for new organizational structure.	Complete implementation of new organizational structure: Identify and hire key leadership positions; Assign/re-assign staff to new divisions and offices as required; and, draft new career ladder and associated position descriptions as needed.		Use established organizational change procedures to adjust and improve organizational structure as needed.	N/A	N/A
5.2.1.1 Develop, adopt, and implement a comprehensive planning process.	50%	100%	100%	100%	100%	100%
	Develop and adopt well-defined and integrated planning process.	Track high-level projects; redefine budget activity codes (BPAC).		Implement new BPAC; track major projects & activities; implement automated time & attendance.	Refine usage of BPAC and automated time and attendance system.	Execute FY 2015 Budget on full operational planning; continue budget development and execution on actual resource usage.
5.3.1.1	100%	100%	100%	100%	N/A	N/A

Assess, develop, and implement automated hiring system.	Assess and procure best fit system based on CFTC requirements. Develop and/or improve recruitment business processes to maximize efficiency gains from automation.	Implement automated hiring system and associated business processes.		Optimize automated hiring system and associated business processes. Demonstrate reduction in FTE years dedicated to recruitment and staffing.	N/A	N/A
5.3.1.2 Improve time to hire from 150 days to 80 days.	79 Days	87 Days	122 Days	110 Days	99 Days	89 Days
	Improve time to hire by 10% in each of the next five years—saving 15 days.	Improve time to hire by 10% in each of the next four years—saving 13.5 days.		Improve time to hire by 10% in each of the next three years—saving 12 days.	Improve time to hire by 10% in each of the next two years—saving 11 days.	Improve time to hire by 10% from previous year—saving 10 days.
5.3.2.1 CFTC is consistently rated by its employees as a small agency workplace of choice and listed annually as one of the top ten best places to work in the federal government (small agency category). CFTC identifies low scores determined to be of most significance to the agency year over year to inform its improvement plans.	8	12	≤ 10	≤ 10	≤ 10	≤ 10
5.3.3.1 Develop and implement	100%	100%	100%	100%	N/A	N/A

comprehensive development and education program.	Design learning plan to include legal, technical, regulatory and specialized training as well as management and supervisory training. Where practical, ensure that programming meets the criteria for continuing education requirements applicable to lawyers and other professionals so that credits may be earned and applied. Implement supervisory training for all new supervisors.	Augment and expand in-house legal and technical training to a comprehensive CFTC regulatory training program. Develop leadership and management training curriculum.		Increase by 10 to 25% over previous year the percentage of CFTC employees participating in CFTC's training program as funding and resources available will allow.	N/A	N/A
5.3.3.2 Assess requirements, design, and implement a comprehensive CFTC-wide mentoring program focused on enhancing the competencies of CFTC's current and future workforce.	100%	100%	100%	100%	100%	100%
	Assess and design program. Pilot program in the Office of General Counsel.	Expand mentoring program to other offices and divisions.		Increase participation in mentoring program 5-10% over previous year.	Survey and compile feedback on mentoring program. Develop program improvement plan based on feedback.	Survey and compile feedback on mentoring program. Develop program improvement plan based on feedback.
5.4.1.1 Transparency and process	100%	100%	100%	100%	100%	100%

maturity of IT governance for reinforcing business unit and IT partnership.	Integrate Agency Strategic Planning with IT Strategic Planning.	Align IT governance with reengineered BPAC structure.		Institute CFTC-wide Data Management.	Establishment and sustainment of enterprise target architecture and transition strategy.	Mature enterprise architecture and IT governance processes and tools to support continuous CFTC business transformation.
5.4.1.2 Implementation of IT strategy and architecture for business continuity.	100%	85%	100%	100%	100%	100%
	Establish remote data replication of Tiers 1, 2, and 3 to the Commission's collocation facility.	Establish system service support at the collocation facility for Tiers 1 and 2 applications and datasets.		Establish system service support at the collocation facility for Tier 3 applications and datasets.	Test Business Continuity Operational Headquarters Failover to the collocation facility.	Test Business Continuity Operational Headquarters Failover to the collocation facility.
5.4.2.1 Implementation of enterprise data management for effective aggregation, correlation with external data, and increased collaboration with other regulators.	100%	75%	100%	100%	100%	100%
	Develop data management governance and policy framework. Develop enterprise data management roadmap.	Establish enterprise data warehouse and service oriented architecture for enterprise data management. Communicate enterprise data warehouse and service oriented architecture design to NFA, SEC, OFR, and other regulators. Integrate FILAC system into enterprise data warehouse.		Integrate TSS into enterprise data warehouse. Include swaps data in enterprise data warehouse.	Integrate ISS into enterprise data warehouse.	Link enterprise data warehouse with NFA, SEC, OFR, and other regulatory warehouses.
5.4.2.2 Direct Access to SROs and SDRs for effective oversight.	92%	100%	100%	100%	100%	100%
	Plan dedicated connections to high volume DCMs and SROs.	Implement dedicated connections to high volume DCMs and SROs.		Receive and process swaps data pushed from existing SDRs.	Integrate swaps data pushed from existing SDRs with existing systems.	Integrate swaps data pushed from existing SDRs with external systems.
5.4.3.1 CFTC-wide document and	92%	90%	100%	100%	100%	100%

records management and intranet solutions for improved data security collaboration, retention, sharing, and disposal.	Automate rule making support. Implement Forensics Lab. Implement website preservation system. Implement CFTCnet. Re-host CFTC.gov to provide improved services.	Implement eDiscovery preservation and legal hold. Implement enhancements to document search and retrieval software. Implement EDRM enterprise search and taxonomy and metadata management. Division collaboration sites migrate to/integrate with CFTCnet.		Implement automation of enterprise tips, complaints, and referral management. Implement Early Case Assessment System. Implement EDRM workflow and version control (5 process groups).	Implement enhancements to Case Management software. Implement enhancements to audio analytics. Implement EDRM workflow and version control (5 additional process groups).	Expand enterprise search to include eLaw and enterprise data warehouse.
5.5.1.1 Reengineer, improve, and implement CFTC's Cost Accounting Codes (BPAC).	100%	100%	100%	100%	100%	N/A
	Assess and procure reengineering options for BPAC. Design, develop and implement BPAC repository to retain all cost accounting codes.	Choose best option for BPAC code structure in line with operating and reporting needs and in light of available resources. Implement new codes for use in FY 2013 budget formulation process.		Improve and adapt business processes associated with cost accounting codes.	Staff using cost accounting codes properly with error rate documented at less than 1%.	N/A
5.5.2.1 Management Control Reviews are conducted and documented. Recommendations are implemented. The Chairman and the CFO are able to give unqualified FMFIA management assurances.	100%	100%	100%	100%	N/A	N/A
	Conduct program and administrative risk assessments, prepare three year plan, begin conducting reviews.	Update program and administrative risk assessments and three year plan, continue conducting reviews, developing remediation plans, and taking corrective actions.		Complete corrective action.	N/A	N/A
5.5.3.1 Implement web-based	25%	50%	100%	100%	N/A	N/A

time and attendance system.	Complete project to modernize Budget Program Activity Code structure and configure WebTA to accommodate.	Pilot WebTA.	Go live with WebTA.	N/A	N/A

PERFORMANCE MEASURES CONSIDERED NOT APPLICABLE IN FY 2012

Goal.Objective.Strategy.Measure Performance Measure	FY 2011 Actual	FY 2012 Actual	FY 2012 Planned	FY 2013 Planned	FY 2014 Planned	FY 2015 Planned
1.1.3.1 Transmit information and consult with the Office of Information Technology Services (OITS) [Now recognized as the Office of Data and Technology—ODT] to implement electronic filing of forms.	50%	N/A	100%	100%	N/A	N/A
	Transmit information requirements to OITS for revised trader reporting forms.	Fully deploy electronic filing of trader reporting forms.		Fully deploy information systems for ownership and control reporting. Fully deploy information systems for reportable trader standards for swap traders.	N/A	N/A
2.1.2.1 Applications are reviewed and a determination made regarding compliance with financial integrity provisions of the CEA within statutory time frames. Percent in compliance with financial integrity provisions.	100%	N/A	100%	100%	100%	100%
2.2.1.1 Conduct direct examinations of SDs and MSPs, identify deficiencies and confirm that all deficiencies identified are corrected within specified period of time.	N/A	N/A	100%	100%	100%	100%
2.4.1.2 Program design to cover new data collection requirements to monitor systemic risk posed by CPOs and CTAs advising private funds, and new registration of swap dealers. Percentage of system redesign	N/A	N/A	90%	95%	98%	100%

accomplished.						
3.1.1.2 The CFTC will bring claims in due recognition of the broadened enforcement mandate provided by the Dodd-Frank Act, and will seek proportionate remedies, including civil monetary penalties, undertakings and restitution, that have the highest impact on and greatest deterrent effect against potential future violations.	N/A	N/A	N/A	N/A	N/A	N/A
4.1.1.2 Regular issuance of outgoing international requests for enforcement assistance and referrals made by the CFTC to foreign regulators pertaining to matters involving their jurisdictions.	N/A	N/A	N/A	N/A	N/A	N/A

GUIDE OF TERMS AND OPERATIONS

A

Abandon: To elect not to exercise or offset a long option position.

Accommodation Trading: Non-competitive trading entered into by a trader, usually to assist another with illegal trades.

Actuals: The physical or cash commodity, as distinguished from a futures contract. See Cash and Spot Commodity.

Agency Bond: A debt security issued by a government-sponsored enterprise such as Fannie Mae or Freddie Mac, designed to resemble a U.S. Treasury bond.

Agency Note: A debt security issued by a government-sponsored enterprise such as Fannie Mae or Freddie Mac, designed to resemble a U.S. Treasury note.

Aggregation: The principle under which all futures positions owned or controlled by one trader (or group of traders acting in concert) are combined to determine reporting status and compliance with speculative position limits.

Agricultural Trade Option Merchant: Any person that is in the business of soliciting or entering option transactions involving an enumerated agricultural commodity that are not conducted or executed on or subject to the rules of an exchange.

Algorithmic Trading: The use of computer programs for entering trading orders with the computer algorithm initiating orders or placing bids and offers.

Allowances: The discounts (premiums) allowed for grades or locations of a commodity lower (higher) than the par (or basis) grade or location specified in the futures contract. See Differentials.

American Option: An option that can be exercised at any time prior to or on the expiration date. See European Option.

Approved Delivery Facility: Any bank, stockyard, mill, storehouse, plant, elevator, or other depository that is authorized by an exchange for the delivery of commodities tendered on futures contracts.

Arbitrage: A strategy involving the simultaneous purchase and sale of identical or equivalent commodity futures contracts or other instruments across two or more markets in order to benefit from a discrepancy in their price relationship. In a theoretical efficient market, there is a lack of opportunity for profitable arbitrage. See Spread.

Arbitration: A process for settling disputes between parties that is less structured than court proceedings. The National Futures Association arbitration program provides a forum for resolving futures-related disputes between NFA members or between NFA members and customers. Other forums for customer complaints include the American Arbitration Association.

Artificial Price: A futures price that has been affected by a manipulation and is thus higher or lower than it would have been if it reflected the forces of supply and demand.

Asian Option: An exotic option whose payoff depends on the average price of the underlying asset during some portion of the life of the option.

Ask: The price level of an offer, as in bid-ask spread.

Assignable Contract: A contract that allows the holder to convey his rights to a third party. Exchange-traded contracts are not assignable.

Assignment: Designation by a clearing organization of an option writer who will be required to buy (in the case of a put) or sell (in the case of a call) the underlying futures contract or security when an option has been exercised, especially if it has been exercised early.

Associated Person (AP): An individual who solicits or accepts (other than in a clerical capacity) orders, discretionary accounts, or participation in a commodity pool, or supervises any individual so engaged, on behalf of a futures commission merchant, an introducing broker, a commodity trading advisor, a commodity pool operator, or an agricultural trade option merchant.

At-the-Market: An order to buy or sell a futures contract at whatever price is obtainable when the order reaches the trading facility. See Market Order.

At-the-Money: When an option's strike price is the same as the current trading price of the underlying commodity, the option is at-the-money.

Auction Rate Security: A debt security, typically issued by a municipality, in which the yield is reset on each payment date via a Dutch auction.

Audit Trail: The record of trading information identifying, for example, the brokers participating in each transaction, the firms clearing the trade, the terms and time or sequence of the trade, the order receipt and execution time, and, ultimately, and when applicable, the customers involved.

Automatic Exercise: A provision in an option contract specifying that it will be exercised automatically on the expiration date if it is in-the-money by a specified amount, absent instructions to the contrary.

B

Back Months: Futures delivery months other than the spot or front month (also called **deferred months**).

Back Office: The department in a financial institution that processes and deals and handles delivery, settlement, and regulatory procedures.

Back pricing: Fixing the price of a commodity for which the commitment to purchase has been made in advance. The buyer can fix the price relative to any monthly or periodic delivery using the futures markets.

Back Spread: A delta-neutral ratio spread in which more options are bought than sold. A back spread will be profitable if volatility increases. See Delta.

Backwardation: Market situation in which futures prices are progressively lower in the distant delivery months. For instance, if the gold quotation for January is $360.00 per ounce and that for June is $355.00 per ounce, the backwardation for five months against January is $5.00 per ounce. (Backwardation is the opposite of contango). See Inverted Market.

Banging the Close: A manipulative or disruptive trading practice whereby a trader buys or sells a large number of futures contracts during the closing period of a futures contract (that is, the period during which the futures settlement price is determined) in order to benefit an even larger position in an option, swap, or other derivative that is cash settled based on the futures settlement price on that day.

Banker's Acceptance: A draft or bill of exchange accepted by a bank where the accepting institution guarantees payment. Used extensively in foreign trade transactions.

Basis: The difference between the spot or cash price of a commodity and the price of the nearest futures contract for the same or a related commodity (typically calculated as cash minus futures). Basis is usually computed in relation to the futures contract next to expire and may reflect different time periods, product forms, grades, or locations.

Basis Grade: The grade of a commodity used as the standard or par grade of a futures contract.

Basis Point: The measurement of a change in the yield of a debt security. One basis point equals 1/100 of one percent.

Basis Quote: Offer or sale of a cash commodity in terms of the difference above or below a futures price (e.g., 10 cents over December corn).

Basis Risk: The risk associated with an unexpected widening or narrowing of the basis between the time a hedge position is established and the time that it is lifted.

Basis Swap: A swap whose cash settlement price is calculated based on the basis between a futures contract (e.g., natural gas) and the spot price of the underlying commodity or a closely related commodity (e.g., natural gas at a location other than the futures delivery location) on a specified date.

Bear: One who expects a decline in prices. The opposite of a bull. A news item is considered bearish if it is expected to result in lower prices.

Bear Market: A market in which prices generally are declining over a period of months or years. Opposite of bull market.

Bear Market Rally: A temporary rise in prices during a bear market. See Correction.

Bear Spread: (1) A strategy involving the simultaneous purchase and sale of options of the same class and expiration date, but different strike prices. In a bear spread, the option that is purchased has a lower delta than the option that is bought. For example, in a call bear spread, the purchased option has a higher exercise price than the option that is sold. Also called **bear vertical spread**. (2) The simultaneous purchase and sale of two futures contracts in the same or related commodities with the intention of profiting from a decline in prices but at the same time limiting the potential loss if this expectation does not materialize. In agricultural products, this is accomplished by selling a nearby delivery and buying a deferred delivery

Bear Vertical Spread: See Bear Spread.

Beta (Beta Coefficient): A measure of the variability of rate of return or value of a stock or portfolio compared to that of the overall market, typically used as a measure of riskiness.

Bermuda Option: An exotic option which can be exercised on a specified set of predetermined dates during the life of the option.

Bid: An offer to buy a specific quantity of a commodity at a stated price.

Bid-Ask Spread or Bid-Offer Spread: The difference between the bid price and the ask or offer price.

Binary Option: A type of option whose payoff is either a fixed amount or zero. For example, there could be a binary option that pays $100 if a hurricane makes landfall in Florida before a specified date and zero otherwise. Also called a digital option.

Blackboard Trading: The practice, no longer used, of buying and selling commodities by posting prices on a blackboard on a wall of a commodity exchange.

Black-Scholes Model: An option pricing model initially developed by Fischer Black and Myron Scholes for securities options and later refined by Black for options on futures.

Block Trade: A large transaction that is negotiated off an exchange's trading facility and then posted on the trading facility, as permitted under exchange rules.

Board Order: See Market-if-Touched Order.

Board of Trade: Any organized exchange or other trading facility for the trading of futures and/or option contracts.

Boiler Room: An enterprise that often is operated out of inexpensive, low-rent quarters (hence the term "boiler room"), that uses high pressure sales tactics (generally over the telephone), and possibly false or misleading information to solicit generally unsophisticated investors.

Booking the Basis: A forward pricing sales arrangement in which the cash price is determined either by the buyer or seller within a specified time. At that time, the previously-agreed basis is applied to the then-current futures quotation.

Book Transfer: A series of accounting or bookkeeping entries used to settle a series of cash market transactions.

Box Spread: An option position in which the owner establishes a long call and a short put at one strike price and a short call and a long put at another strike price, all of which are in the same contract month in the same commodity.

Break: A rapid and sharp price decline.

Broad-Based Security Index: Any index of securities that does not meet the legal definition of narrow-based security index.

Broker: A person paid a fee or commission for executing buy or sell orders for a customer. In commodity futures trading, the term may refer to: (1) Floor broker, a person who actually executes orders on the trading floor of an exchange; (2) Account executive or associated person, the person who deals with customers in the offices of futures commission merchants; or (3) the futures commission merchant.

Broker Association: Two or more persons with exchange trading privileges who (1) share responsibility for executing customer orders; (2) have access to each other's unfilled customer orders as a result of common employment or other types of relationships; or (3) share profits or losses associated with their brokerage or trading activity.

Bucketing: Directly or indirectly taking the opposite side of a customer's order into a broker's own account or into an account in which a broker has an interest, without open and competitive execution of the order on an exchange. Also called **trading against**.

Bucket Shop: A brokerage enterprise that "books" (i.e., takes the opposite side of) retail customer orders without actually having them executed on an exchange.

Bull: One who expects a rise in prices. The opposite of bear. A news item is considered bullish if it is expected to result in higher prices.

Bullion: Bars or ingots of precious metals, usually cast in standardized sizes.

Bull Market: A market in which prices generally are rising over a period of months or years. Opposite of bear market.

Bull Spread: (1) A strategy involving the simultaneous purchase and sale of options of the same class and expiration date but different strike prices. In a bull vertical spread, the purchased option has a higher delta than the option that is sold. For example, in a call bull spread, the purchased option has a lower exercise price than the sold option. Also called **bull vertical spread**. (2) The simultaneous purchase and sale of two futures contracts in the same or related commodities with the intention of profiting from a rise in prices but at the same time limiting the potential loss if this expectation is wrong. In agricultural commodities, this is accomplished by buying the nearby delivery and selling the deferred.

Bull Vertical Spread: See Bull Spread.

Buoyant: A market in which prices have a tendency to rise easily with a considerable show of strength.

Bust: An executed trade cancelled by an exchange that is considered to have been executed in error.

Bunched Order: A discretionary order entered on behalf of multiple customers.

Butterfly Spread: A three-legged option spread in which each leg has the same expiration date but different strike prices. For example, a butterfly spread in soybean call options might consist of one long call at a $5.50 strike price, two short calls at a $6.00 strike price, and one long call at a $6.50 strike price.

Buyer: A market participant who takes a long futures position or buys an option. An option buyer is also called a taker, holder, or owner.

Buyer's Call: A purchase of a specified quantity of a specific grade of a commodity at a fixed number of points above or below a specified delivery month futures price with the buyer allowed a period of time to fix the price either by purchasing a futures contract for the account of the seller or telling the seller when he wishes to fix the price. See Seller's Call.

Buyer's Market: A condition of the market in which there is an abundance of goods available and hence buyers can afford to be selective and may be able to buy at less than the price that previously prevailed. See Seller's Market.

Buying Hedge (or Long Hedge): Hedging transaction in which futures contracts are bought to protect against possible increases in the cost of commodities. See Hedging.

Buy (or Sell) On Close: To buy (or sell) at the end of the trading session within the closing price range.

Buy (or Sell) On Opening: To buy (or sell) at the beginning of a trading session within the open price range.

C

C & F: "Cost and Freight" paid to a point of destination and included in the price quoted; same as C.A.F.

Calendar Spread: (1) The purchase of one delivery month of a given futures contract and simultaneous sale of a different delivery month of the same futures contract; (2) the purchase of a put or call option and the simultaneous sale of the same type of option with typically the same strike price but a different expiration date. Also called a **horizontal spread** or **time spread**.

Call: (1) An option contract that gives the buyer the right but not the obligation to purchase a commodity or other asset or to enter into a long futures position at a specified price on or prior to a specified expiration date; (2) formerly, a period at the opening and the close of some futures markets in which the price for each futures contract was established by auction; or (3) the requirement that a financial instrument such as a bond be returned to the issuer prior to maturity, with principal and accrued interest paid off upon return. See Buyer's Call, Seller's Call.

Call Around Market: A market, commonly used for options on futures on European exchanges, in which brokers contact each other outside of the exchange trading facility to arrange block trades.

Call Cotton: Cotton bought or sold on call. See Buyer's Call, Seller's Call.

Called: Another term for exercised when an option is a call. In the case of an option on a physical, the writer of a call must deliver the indicated underlying commodity when the option is exercised or called. In the case of an option on a futures contract, a futures position will be created that will require margin, unless the writer of the call has an offsetting position.

Call Rule: An exchange regulation under which an official bid price for a cash commodity is competitively established at the close of each day's trading. It holds until the next opening of the exchange.

Cap and Trade: A market based pollution control system in which total emissions of a pollutant are capped at a specified level. Allowances are issued to firms and can be bought and sold on an organized market or OTC.

Capping: Effecting transactions in an instrument underlying an option shortly before the option's expiration date to depress or prevent a rise in the price of the instrument so that previously written call options will expire worthless, thus protecting premiums previously received. See Pegging.

Carrying Broker: An exchange member firm, usually a futures commission merchant, through whom another broker or customer elects to clear all or part of its trades.

Carrying Charges: Also called Cost of Carry. Cost of storing a physical commodity or holding a financial instrument over a period of time. These charges include insurance, storage, and interest on the deposited funds, as well as other incidental costs. It is a carrying charge market when there are higher futures prices for each successive contract maturity. If the carrying charge is adequate to reimburse the holder, it is called a "full charge." See Negative Carry, Positive Carry, and Contango.

Carry Trade: A trade where one borrows a currency or commoidity commodity or currency with a low cost of carry and lends a similar instrument with a high cost of carry in order to profit from the differential.

Cascade: A situation in which the execution of market orders or stop loss orders on an electronic trading system triggers other stop loss orders which may, in turn, trigger still more stop loss orders. This may lead to a very large price move if there are no safety mechanisms to prevent cascading.

Cash Commodity: The physical or actual commodity as distinguished from the futures contract, sometimes called spot commodity or actuals.

Cash Forward Sale: See Forward Contract.

Cash Market: The market for the cash commodity (as contrasted to a futures contract) taking the form of: (1) an organized, self-regulated central market (e.g., a commodity exchange); (2) a decentralized over-the-counter market; or (3) a local organization, such as a grain elevator or meat processor, which provides a market for a small region.

Cash Price: The price in the marketplace for actual cash or spot commodities to be delivered via customary market channels.

Cash Settlement: A method of settling futures options and other derivatives whereby the seller (or short) pays the buyer (or long) the cash value of the underlying commodity or a cash amount based on the level of an index or price according to a procedure specified in the contract. Also called Financial Settlement. Compare to Physical Delivery.

CCC: See Commodity Credit Corporation.

CD: See Certificate of Deposit.

CEA: Commodity Exchange Act or Commodity Exchange Authority.

Centralized Counterparty (CCP): A clearing organization.

Certificate of Deposit (CD): A time deposit with a specific maturity traditionally evidenced by a certificate. Large denomination CDs are typically negotiable.

CFTC: See Commodity Futures Trading Commission.

CFTC Form 40: The form used by large traders to report their futures and option positions and the purposes of those positions.

CFO: Cancel Former Order.

Certificated or Certified Stocks: Stocks of a commodity that have been inspected and found to be of a quality deliverable against futures contracts, stored at the delivery points designated as regular or acceptable for delivery by an exchange. In grain, called "stocks in deliverable position." See Deliverable Stocks.

Changer: Formerly, a clearing member of both the Mid-America Commodity Exchange (MidAm) and another futures exchange who, for a fee, would assume the opposite side of a transaction on MidAm by taking a spread position between MidAm and the other futures exchange that traded an identical, but larger, contract. Through this service, the changer provided liquidity for MidAm and an economical mechanism for arbitrage between the two markets. MidAm was a subsidiary of the Chicago Board of Trade (CBOT). MidAm was closed by the CBOT in 2003 after MidAm contracts were delisted on MidAm and relisted on the CBOT as Mini contracts. The CBOT continued to use changers for former MidAm contracts traded on an open outcry platform.

Charting: The use of graphs and charts in the technical analysis of futures markets to plot trends of price movements, average movements of price, volume of trading, and open interest.

Chartist: Technical trader who reacts to signals derived from graphs of price movements.

Cheapest-to-Deliver: Usually refers to the selection of a class of bonds or notes deliverable against an expiring bond or note futures contract. The bond or note that has the highest implied repo rate is considered cheapest to deliver.

Chooser Option: An exotic option that is transacted in the present, but that at some specified future date is chosen to be either a put or a call option.

Churning: Excessive trading of a discretionary account by a person with control over the account for the purpose of generating commissions while disregarding the interests of the customer.

Circuit Breakers: A system of coordinated trading halts and/or price limits on equity markets and equity derivative markets designed to provide a cooling-off period during large, intraday market declines. The first known use of the term circuit breaker in this context was in the Report of the Presidential Task Force on Market Mechanisms (January 1988), which recommended that circuit breakers be adopted following the market break of October 1987.

C.I.F: Cost, insurance, and freight paid to a point of destination and included in the price quoted.

Class (of options): Options of the same type (i.e., either puts or calls, but not both) covering the same underlying futures contract or other asset (e.g., a March call with a strike price of 62 and a May call with a strike price of 58).

Clearing: The procedure through which the clearing organization becomes the buyer to each seller of a futures contract or other derivative, and the seller to each buyer for clearing members.

Clearing Association: See Clearing Organization.

Clearing House: See Clearing Organization.

Clearing Member: A member of a clearing organization. All trades of a non-clearing member must be processed and eventually settled through a clearing member.

Clearing Organization: An entity through which futures and other derivative transactions are cleared and settled. It is also charged with assuring the proper conduct of each contract's delivery procedures and the adequate financing of trading. A clearing organization may be a division of a particular exchange, an adjunct or affiliate thereof, or a freestanding entity. Also called a clearing house, multilateral clearing organization, centralized counterparty, or clearing association. See Derivatives Clearing Organization.

Clearing Price: See Settlement Price.

Close: The exchange-designated period at the end of the trading session during which all transactions are considered made "at the close." See Call.

Closing-Out: Liquidating an existing long or short futures or option position with an equal and opposite transaction. Also known as Offset.

Closing Price (or Range): The price (or price range) recorded during trading that takes place in the final period of a trading session's activity that is officially designated as the "close."

CO

Co-Location: The placement of servers used by market participants in close physical proximity to an electronic trading facility's matching engine in order to facilitate high-frequency trading.

Combination: Puts and calls held either long or short with different strike prices and/or expirations. Types of combinations include straddles and strangles.

Commercial: An entity involved in the production, processing, or merchandising of a commodity.

Commercial Grain Stocks: Domestic grain in store in public and private elevators at important markets and grain afloat in vessels or barges in lake and seaboard ports.

Commercial Paper: Short-term promissory notes issued in bearer form by large corporations, with maturities ranging from 5 to 270 days. Since the notes are unsecured, the commercial paper market generally is dominated by large corporations with impeccable credit ratings.

Commission: (1) The charge made by a futures commission merchant for buying and selling futures contracts; or (2) the fee charged by a futures broker for the execution of an order. Note: when capitalized, the word Commission usually refers to the CFTC.

Commitments of Traders Report (COT): A weekly report from the CFTC providing a breakdown of each Tuesday's open interest for markets in which 20 or more traders hold positions equal to or above the reporting levels established by the CFTC. Open interest is broken down by aggregate commercial, non-commercial, and non-reportable holdings.

Commitments: See Open Interest.

Commodity: (1) A commodity, as defined in the Commodity Exchange Act, includes the agricultural commodities enumerated in Section 1a(4) of the Commodity Exchange Act, 7 USC 1a(4), and all other goods and articles, except onions as provided in Public Law 85-839 (7 USC 13-1), a 1958 law that banned futures trading in onions, and all services, rights, and interests in which contracts for future delivery are presently or in the future dealt in; (2) .A physical commodity such as an agricultural product or a natural resource as opposed to a financial instrument such as a currency or interest rate.

Commodity Credit Corporation: A government-owned corporation established in 1933 to assist American agriculture. Major operations include price support programs, foreign sales, and export credit programs for agricultural commodities.

Commodity Exchange Act: The 1936 Commodity Exchange Act as amended, 7 USC 1, et seq., provides for the federal regulation of commodity futures and options trading.

Commodity Exchange Authority: A regulatory agency of the U.S. Department of Agriculture established to regulate futures trading under the Commodity Exchange Act between 1936 and 1975. The Commodity Exchange Authority was the predecessor of the Commodity Futures Trading Commission. Before World War II, this agency was known as the Commodity Exchange Administration.

Commodity Exchange Commission (CEC): A commission consisting of the Secretary of Agriculture, Secretary of Commerce, and the Attorney General, responsible for among other things, setting Federal speculative position limits administering the Commodity Exchange Act between 1936 and 1975. Among other things, the CEC was responsible for setting Federal speculative position limits

Commodity Futures Trading Commission **(CFTC):** The Federal regulatory agency established by the Commodity Futures Trading Act of 1974 to administer the Commodity Exchange Act.

Commodity Index: An index of a specified set of (physical) commodity prices or commodity futures prices.

Commodity Index Fund: An investment fund that enters into futures or commodity swap positions for the purpose of replicating the return of an index of commodity prices or commodity futures prices.

Commodity Index Swap: A swap whose cash flows are intended to replicate a commodity index.

Commodity Index Trader: An entity that conducts futures trades on behalf of a commodity index fund or to hedge commodity index swap positions.

Commodity-Linked Bond: A bond in which payment to the investor is dependent to a certain extent on the price level of a commodity, such as crude oil, gold, or silver, at maturity.

Commodity Option: An option on a commodity or a futures contract.

Commodity Pool: An investment trust, syndicate, or similar form of enterprise operated for the purpose of trading commodity futures or option contracts. Typically thought of as an enterprise engaged in the business of investing the collective or "pooled" funds of multiple participants in trading commodity futures or options, where participants share in profits and losses on a pro rata basis.

Commodity Pool Operator (CPO): A person engaged in a business similar to an investment trust or a syndicate and who solicits or accepts funds, securities, or property for the purpose of trading commodity futures contracts or commodity options. The commodity pool operator either itself makes trading decisions on behalf of the pool or engages a commodity trading advisor to do so.

Commodity Trading Advisor (CTA): A person who, for pay, regularly engages in the business of advising others as to the value of commodity futures or options or the advisability of trading in commodity futures or options, or issues analyses or reports concerning commodity futures or options.

Commodity Swap: A swap in which the payout to at least one counterparty is based on the price of a commodity or the level of a commodity index.

Confirmation Statement: A statement sent by a futures commission merchant to a customer when a futures or options position has been initiated which typically shows the price and the number of contracts bought and sold. See P&S (Purchase and Sale Statement).

Congestion: (1) A market situation in which shorts attempting to cover their positions are unable to find an adequate supply of contracts provided by longs willing to liquidate or by new sellers willing to enter the market, except at sharply higher prices (see Squeeze, Corner); (2) in technical analysis, a period of time characterized by repetitious and limited price fluctuations.

Consignment: A shipment made by a producer or dealer to an agent elsewhere with the understanding that the commodities in question will be cared for or sold at the highest obtainable price. Title to the merchandise shipped on consignment rests with the shipper until the goods are disposed of according to agreement.

Contango: Market situation in which prices in succeeding delivery months are progressively higher than in the nearest delivery month; the opposite of backwardation.

Contract: (1) A term of reference describing a unit of trading for a commodity future or option or other derivative; (2) an agreement to buy or sell a specified commodity, detailing the amount and grade of the product and the date on which the contract will mature and become deliverable.

Contract Grades: Those grades of a commodity that have been officially approved by an exchange as deliverable in settlement of a futures contract.

Contract Market: A board of trade or exchange designated by the Commodity Futures Trading Commission to trade futures or options under the Commodity Exchange Act. A contract market can allow both institutional and retail participants and can list for trading futures contracts on any commodity, provided that each contract is not readily susceptible to manipulation. Also called **designated contract market**. See Derivatives Transaction Execution Facility.

Contract Month: See Delivery Month.

Contract Size: The actual amount of a commodity represented in a contract.

Contract Unit: See Contract Size.

Controlled Account: An account for which trading is directed by someone other than the owner. Also called a Managed Account or a Discretionary Account.

Convergence: The tendency for prices of physicals and futures to approach one another, usually during the delivery month. Also called a "**narrowing of the basis**."

Conversion: A position created by selling a call option, buying a put option, and buying the underlying instrument (for example, a futures contract), where the options have the same strike price and the same expiration. See Reverse Conversion.

Conversion Factors: Numbers published by a futures exchange to determine invoice prices for debt instruments deliverable against bond or note futures contracts. A separate conversion factor is published for each deliverable instrument. Invoice price = Contract Size X Futures Settlement Price X Conversion Factor + Accrued Interest.

Core Principle: A provision of the Commodity Exchange Act with which a contract market, derivatives transaction execution facility, or derivatives clearing organization must comply on an ongoing basis. There are 18 core principles for contract markets, 9 core principles for derivatives transaction execution facilities, and 14 core principles for derivatives clearing organizations.

Corner: (1) Securing such relative control of a commodity that its price can be manipulated, that is, can be controlled by the creator of the corner; or (2) in the extreme situation, obtaining contracts requiring the delivery of more commodities than are available for delivery. See Squeeze, Congestion.

Corn-Hog Ratio: See Feed Ratio.

Correction: A temporary decline in prices during a bull market that partially reverses the previous rally. See Bear Market Rally.

Cost of Carry: See Carrying Charges.

Cost of Tender: Total of various charges incurred when a commodity is certified and delivered on a futures contract.

COT: See Commitments of Traders Report.

Counterparty: The opposite party in a bilateral agreement, contract, or transaction, such as a swap. In the retail foreign exchange (or Forex) context, the party to which a retail customer sends its funds; lawfully, the party must be one of those listed in Section 2(c)(2)(B)(ii)(I)-(VI) of the Commodity Exchange Act.

Counterparty Risk: The risk associated with the financial stability of the party entered into contract with. Forward contracts impose upon each party the risk that the counterparty will default, but futures contracts executed on a designated contract market are guaranteed against default by the clearing organization.

Counter-Trend Trading: In technical analysis, the method by which a trader takes a position contrary to the current market direction in anticipation of a change in that direction.

Coupon (Coupon Rate): A fixed dollar amount of interest payable per annum, stated as a percentage of principal value, usually payable in semiannual installments.

Cover: (1) Purchasing futures to offset a short position (same as Short Covering); see Offset, Liquidation; (2) to have in hand the physical commodity when a short futures sale is made, or to acquire the commodity that might be deliverable on a short sale.

Covered Option: A short call or put option position that is covered by the sale or purchase of the underlying futures contract or other underlying instrument. For example, in the case of options on futures contracts, a covered call is a short call position combined with a long futures position. A covered put is a short put position combined with a short futures position.

Cox-Ross-Rubinstein Option Pricing Model: An option pricing model developed by John Cox, Stephen Ross, and Mark Rubinstein that can be adopted to include effects not included in the Black-Scholes Model (e.g., early exercise and price supports).

CPO: See Commodity Pool Operator.

Crack Spread: (1) In energy futures, the simultaneous purchase of crude oil futures and the sale of petroleum product futures to establish a refining margin. One can trade a gasoline crack spread, a heating oil crack spread, or a 3-2-1 crack spread which consists of three crude oil futures contracts spread against two gasoline futures contracts and one heating oil futures contract. The 3-2-1 crack spread is designed to approximate the typical ratio of gasoline and heating oil that results from refining a barrel of crude oil. See Gross Processing Margin. (2) Calculation showing the theoretical market value of petroleum products that could be obtained from a barrel of crude after the oil is refined or cracked. This does not necessarily represent the refining margin because a barrel of crude yields varying amounts of petroleum products.

Credit Default Option: A put option that makes a payoff in the event the issuer of a specified reference asset defaults. Also called **default option**.

Credit Default Swap: A bilateral over-the-counter (OTC) contract in which the seller agrees to make a payment to the buyer in the event of a specified credit event in exchange for a fixed payment or series of fixed payments; the most common type of credit derivative; also called c**redit swap**; similar to credit default option.

Credit Derivative: A derivative contract designed to assume or shift credit risk, that is, the risk of a credit event such as a default or bankruptcy of a borrower. For example, a lender might use a credit derivative to hedge the risk that a borrower might default or have its credit rating downgraded. Common credit derivatives include credit default swaps, credit default options, credit spread options, and total return swaps.

Credit Event: An event such as a debt default or bankruptcy that will affect the payoff on a credit derivative, as defined in the derivative agreement.

Credit Rating: A rating determined by a rating agency that indicates the agency's opinion of the likelihood that a borrower such as a corporation or sovereign nation will be able to repay its debt. The rating agencies include Standard & Poor's, Fitch, and Moody's.

Credit Spread: The difference between the yield on the debt securities of a particular corporate or sovereign borrower (or a class of borrowers with a specified credit rating) and the yield of similar maturity Treasury debt securities.

Credit Spread Option: An option whose payoff is based on the credit spread between the debt of a particular borrower and similar maturity Treasury debt.

Credit Swap: See Credit Default Swap.

Crop Year: The time period from one harvest to the next, varying according to the commodity (e.g., July 1 to June 30 for wheat; September 1 to August 31 for soybeans).

Cross-Hedge: Hedging a cash market position in a futures or option contract for a different but price-related commodity.

Cross-Margining: A procedure for margining related securities, options, and futures contracts jointly when different clearing organizations clear each side of the position.

Cross Rate: In foreign exchange, the price of one currency in terms of another currency in the market of a third country. For example, the exchange rate between Japanese yen and Euros would be considered a cross rate in the U.S. market.

Cross Trading: Offsetting or noncompetitive match of the buy order of one customer against the sell order of another, a practice that is permissible only when executed in accordance with the Commodity Exchange Act, CFTC rules, and rules of the exchange.

Crush Spread: In the soybean futures market, the simultaneous purchase of soybean futures and the sale of soybean meal and soybean oil futures to establish a processing margin. See Gross Processing Margin, Reverse Crush Spread.

CTA: See Commodity Trading Advisor.

CTI (Customer Type Indicator) Codes: These consist of four identifiers that describe transactions by the type of customer for which a trade is effected. The four codes are: (1) trading by a person who holds trading privileges for his or her own account or an account for which the person has discretion; (2) trading for a clearing member's proprietary account; (3) trading for another person who holds trading privileges who is currently present on the trading floor or for an account controlled by such other person; and (4) trading for any other type of customer. Transaction data classified by the above codes is included in the trade register report produced by a clearing organization.

Curb Trading: Trading by telephone or by other means that takes place after the official market has closed and that originally took place in the street on the curb outside the market. Under the Commodity Exchange Act and CFTC rules, curb trading is illegal. Also known as kerb trading.

Currency Swap: A swap that involves the exchange of one currency (e.g., U.S. dollars) for another (e.g., Japanese yen) on a specified schedule.

Current Delivery Month: See Spot Month.

D

Daily Price Limit: The maximum price advance or decline from the previous day's settlement price permitted during one trading session, as fixed by the rules of an exchange.

Day Ahead: See Next Day.

Day Order: An order that expires automatically at the end of each day's trading session. There may be a day order with time contingency. For example, an "off at a specific time" order is an order that remains in force until the specified time during the session is reached. At such time, the order is automatically canceled.

Day Trader: A trader, often a person with exchange trading privileges, who takes positions and then offsets them during the same trading session prior to the close of trading.

DCM: See Designated Contract Market.

Dealer An individual or firm that acts as a market maker in an instrument such as a security or foreign currency.

Dealer/Merchant (AD): A large trader that declares itself a "Dealer/Merchant" on CFTC Form 40,which provides as examples "wholesaler, exporter/importer, shipper, grain elevator operator, crude oil marketer."

Deck: The orders for purchase or sale of futures and option contracts held by a floor broker. Also referred to as an order book.

Declaration Date: See Expiration Date.

Declaration (of Options): See Exercise.

Default: Failure to perform on a futures contract as required by exchange rules, such as failure to meet a margin call, or to make or take delivery.

Default Option: See Credit Default Option.

Deferred Futures: See Back Months.

Deliverable Grades: See Contract Grades.

Deliverable Stocks: Stocks of commodities located in exchange-approved storage for which receipts may be used in making delivery on futures contracts. In the cotton trade, the term refers to cotton certified for delivery. Also see Certificated or Certified Stocks.

Deliverable Supply: The total supply of a commodity that meets the delivery specifications of a futures contract. See Economically Deliverable Supply.

Delivery: The tender and receipt of the actual commodity, the cash value of the commodity, or of a delivery instrument covering the commodity (e.g., warehouse receipts or shipping certificates), used to settle a futures contract. See Notice of Delivery, Delivery Notice.

Delivery, Current: Deliveries being made during a present month. Sometimes current delivery is used as a synonym for nearby delivery.

Delivery Date: The date on which the commodity or instrument of delivery must be delivered to fulfill the terms of a contract.

Delivery Instrument: A document used to effect delivery on a futures contract, such as a warehouse receipt or shipping certificate.

Delivery Month: The specified month within which a futures contract matures and can be settled by delivery or the specified month in which the delivery period begins.

Delivery, Nearby: The nearest traded month, the front month. In plural form, one of the nearer trading months.

Delivery Notice: The written notice given by the seller of his intention to make delivery against an open short futures position on a particular date. This notice, delivered through the clearing organization, is separate and distinct from the warehouse receipt or other instrument that will be used to transfer title. Also called Notice of Intent to Deliver or Notice of Delivery.

Delivery Option: A provision of a futures contract that provides the short with flexibility in regard to timing, location, quantity, or quality in the delivery process.

Delivery Point: A location designated by a commodity exchange where stocks of a commodity represented by a futures contract may be delivered in fulfillment of the contract. Also called Location.

Delivery Price: The price fixed by the clearing organization at which deliveries on futures are invoiced—generally the price at which the futures contract is settled when deliveries are made. Also called Invoice Price.

Delta: The expected change in an option's price given a one-unit change in the price of the underlying futures contract or physical commodity. For example, an option with a delta of 0.5 would change $.50 when the underlying commodity moves $1.00.

Delta Margining or Delta-Based Margining: An option margining system used by some exchanges that equates the changes in option premiums with the changes in the price of the underlying futures contract to determine risk factors upon which to base the margin requirements.

Delta Neutral: Refers to a position involving options that is designed to have an overall delta of zero.

Deposit: See Initial Margin.

Depository Receipt: See Vault Receipt.

Derivative: A financial instrument, traded on or off an exchange, the price of which is directly dependent upon (i.e., "derived from") the value of one or more underlying securities, equity indices, debt instruments, commodities, other derivative instruments, or any agreed upon pricing index or arrangement (e.g., the movement over time of the Consumer Price Index or freight rates). They are used to hedge risk or to exchange a floating rate of return for fixed rate of return. Derivatives include futures, options, and swaps. For example, futures contracts are derivatives of the physical contract and options on futures are derivatives of futures contracts.

Derivatives Clearing Organization: A clearing organization or similar entity that, in respect to a contract (1) enables each party to the contract to substitute, through novation or otherwise, the credit of the derivatives clearing organization for the credit of the parties; (2) arranges or provides, on a multilateral basis, for the settlement or netting of obligations resulting from such contracts; or (3) otherwise provides clearing services or arrangements that mutualize or transfer among participants in the derivatives clearing organization the credit risk arising from such contracts.

Derivatives Transaction Execution Facility (DTEF): A board of trade that is registered with the CFTC as a DTEF. A DTEF is subject to fewer regulatory requirements than a contract market. To qualify as a DTEF, an exchange can only trade certain commodities (including excluded commodities and other commodities with very high levels of deliverable supply) and generally must exclude retail participants (retail participants may trade on DTEFs through futures commission merchants with adjusted net capital of at least $20 million or registered commodity trading advisors that direct trading for accounts containing total assets of at least $25 million).

Designated Contract Market: See Contract Market.

Designated Self-Regulatory Organization (DSRO): Self-regulatory organizations (i.e., the commodity exchanges and registered futures associations) must enforce minimum financial and reporting requirements for their members, among other responsibilities outlined in the CFTC's regulations. When a futures commission merchant (FCM) is a member of more than one SRO, the SROs may decide among themselves which of them will assume primary responsibility for these regulatory duties and, upon approval of the plan by the Commission, be appointed the "designated self-regulatory organization" for that FCM.

Diagonal Spread: A spread between two call options or two put options with different strike prices and different expiration dates. See Horizontal Spread, Vertical Spread.

Differentials: The discount (premium) allowed for grades or locations of a commodity lower (higher) than the par of basis grade or location specified in the futures contact. See Allowances.

Digital Option: See Binary Option.

Directional Trading: Trading strategies designed to speculate on the direction of the underlying market, especially in contrast to volatility trading.

Disclosure Document: A statement that must be provided to prospective customers that describes trading strategy, potential risk, commissions, fees, performance, and other relevant information.

Discount: (1) The amount a price would be reduced to purchase a commodity of lesser grade; (2) sometimes used to refer to the price differences between futures of different delivery months, as in the phrase "July at a discount to May," indicating that the price for the July futures is lower than that of May.

Discretionary Account: An arrangement by which the holder of an account gives written power of attorney to someone else, often a commodity trading advisor, to buy and sell without prior approval of the holder; often referred to as a "managed account" or controlled account.

DRT ("Disregard Tape") or Not-Held Order: Absent any restrictions, a DRT (Not-Held Order) means any order giving the floor broker complete discretion over price and time in execution of an order, including discretion to execute all, some, or none of this order.

Distant or Deferred Months: See Back Month.

Dominant Future: That future having the largest amount of open interest.

Double Hedging: As used by the CFTC, it implies a situation where a trader holds a long position in the futures market in excess of the speculative position limit as an offset to a fixed price sale, even though the trader has an ample supply of the commodity on hand to fill all sales commitments.

DSRO: See Designated Self-Regulatory Organization.

DTEF: See Derivatives Transaction Execution Facility.

Dual Trading: Dual trading occurs when: (1) a floor broker executes customer orders and, on the same day, trades for his own account or an account in which he has an interest; or (2) a futures commission merchant carries customer accounts and also trades or permits its employees to trade in accounts in which it has a proprietary interest, also on the same trading day.

Dutch Auction: An auction of a debt instrument (such as a Treasury note) in which all successful bidders receive the same yield (the lowest yield that results in the sale of the entire amount to be issued).

Duration: A measure of a bond's price sensitivity to changes in interest rates.

E

Ease Off: A minor and/or slow decline in the price of a market.

ECN: Electronic Communications Network, frequently used for creating electronic stock or futures markets.

Economically Deliverable Supply: That portion of the deliverable supply of a commodity that is in position for delivery against a futures contract, and is not otherwise unavailable for delivery. For example, Treasury bonds held by long-term investment funds are not considered part of the economically deliverable supply of a Treasury bond futures contract.

Efficient Market: In economic theory, an efficient market is one in which market prices adjust rapidly to reflect new information. The degree to which the market is efficient depends on the quality of information reflected in market prices. In an efficient market, profitable arbitrage opportunities do not exist and traders cannot expect to consistently outperform the market unless they have lower-cost access to information that is reflected in market prices or unless they have access to information before it is reflected in market prices. See Random Walk.

EFP: See Exchange for Physical.

EIA: See Energy Information Administration.

Electronic Trading Facility: A trading facility that operates by an electronic or telecommunications network instead of a trading floor and maintains an automated audit trail of transactions.

Eligible Commercial Entity: An eligible contract participant or other entity approved by the CFTC that has a demonstrable ability to make or take delivery of an underlying commodity of a contract; incurs risks related to the commodity; or is a dealer that regularly provides risk management, hedging services, or market-making activities to entities trading commodities or derivative agreements, contracts, or transactions in commodities.

Eligible Contract Participant: An entity, such as a financial institution, insurance company, or commodity pool, that is classified by the Commodity Exchange Act as an eligible contract participant based upon its regulated status or amount of assets. This classification permits these persons to engage in transactions (such as trading on a derivatives transaction execution facility) not generally available to non-eligible contract participants, i.e., retail customers.

Elliot Wave: (1) A theory named after Ralph Elliot, who contended that the stock market tends to move in discernible and predictable patterns reflecting the basic harmony of nature and extended by other technical analysts to futures markets; (2) in technical analysis, a charting method based on the belief that all prices act as waves, rising and falling rhythmically.

E-Local: A person with trading privileges at an exchange with an electronic trading facility who trades electronically (rather than in a pit or ring) for his or her own account, often at a trading arcade.

E-Mini: A mini contract that is traded exclusively on an electronic trading facility. E-Mini is a trademark of the CME Group, Inc.

Emergency: Any market occurrence or circumstance which requires immediate action and threatens or may threaten such things as the fair and orderly trading in, or the liquidation of, or delivery pursuant to, any contracts on a contract market.

Energy Information Administration (EIA): An agency of the US Department of Energy that provides statistics, data, analysis on resources, supply, production, consumption for all energy sources. EIA data includes weekly inventory statistics for crude oil and petroleum products as well as weekly natural storage data.

Enumerated Agricultural Commodities: The commodities specifically listed in Section 1a(3) of the Commodity Exchange Act: wheat, cotton, rice, corn, oats, barley, rye, flaxseed, grain sorghums, mill feeds, butter, eggs, Solanum tuberosum (Irish potatoes), wool, wool tops, fats and oils (including lard, tallow, cottonseed oil, peanut oil, soybean oil, and all other fats and oils), cottonseed meal, cottonseed, peanuts, soybeans, soybean meal, livestock, livestock products, and frozen concentrated orange juice.

Equity: As used on a trading account statement, refers to the residual dollar value of a futures or option trading account, assuming it was liquidated at current prices.

ETF: See Exchange Traded Fund.

EURIBOR® (Euro Interbank Offered Rate): The euro denominated rate of interest at which banks borrow funds from other banks, in marketable size, in the interbank market. Euribor is sponsored by the European Banking Federation. See LIBOR, TIBOR.

Euro: The official currency of most members of the European Union.

Eurocurrency: Certificates of Deposit (CDs), bonds, deposits, or any capital market instrument issued outside of the national boundaries of the currency in which the instrument is denominated (for example, Eurodollars, Euro-Swiss francs, or Euroyen).

Eurodollars: U.S. dollar deposits placed with banks outside the U.S. Holders may include individuals, companies, banks, and central banks.

European Option: An option that may be exercised only on the expiration date. See American Option.

Even Lot: A unit of trading in a commodity established by an exchange to which official price quotations apply. See Round Lot.

Event Market: A market in derivatives whose payoff is based on a specified event or occurrence such as the release of a macroeconomic indicator, a corporate earnings announcement, or the dollar value of damages caused by a hurricane.

Exchange: A central marketplace with established rules and regulations where buyers and sellers meet to trade futures and options contracts or securities. Exchanges include designated contract markets and derivatives transaction execution facilities.

Exchange for Physicals (EFP): A transaction in which the buyer of a cash commodity transfers to the seller a corresponding amount of long futures contracts, or receives from the seller a corresponding amount of short futures, at a price difference mutually agreed upon. In this way, the opposite hedges in futures of both parties are closed out simultaneously. Also called **Exchange of Futures for Cash**, **AA (against actuals)**, or **Ex-Pit transactions**.

Exchange of Futures for Cash: See Exchange for Physicals.

Exchange of Futures for Swaps (EFS): A privately negotiated transaction in which a position in a physical delivery futures contract is exchanged for a cash-settled swap position in the same or a related commodity, pursuant to the rules of a futures exchange. See Exchange for Physicals.

Exchange Rate: The price of one currency stated in terms of another currency.

Exchange Risk Factor: The delta of an option as computed daily by the exchange on which it is traded.

Exchange Traded Fund (ETF): An investment vehicle holding a commodity or other asset that issues shares that are traded like a stock on a securities exchange.

Excluded Commodity: In general, the Commodity Exchange Act defines an excluded commodity as: any financial instrument such as a security, currency, interest rate, debt instrument, or credit rating; any economic or commercial index other than a narrow-based commodity index; or any other value that is out of the control of participants and is associated with an economic consequence. See the Commodity Exchange Act definition of excluded commodity.

Exempt Board of Trade: A trading facility that trades commodities (other than securities or securities indexes) having a nearly inexhaustible deliverable supply and either no cash market or a cash market so liquid that any contract traded on the commodity is highly unlikely to be susceptible to manipulation. An exempt board of trade's contracts must be entered into by parties that are eligible contract participants.

Exempt Commercial Market: An electronic trading facility that trades exempt commodities on a principal-to-principal basis solely between persons that are eligible commercial entities.

Exempt Commodity: The Commodity Exchange Act defines an exempt commodity as any commodity other than an excluded commodity or an agricultural commodity. Examples include energy commodities and metals.

Exempt Foreign Firm: A foreign firm that does business with U.S. customers only on foreign exchanges and is exempt from registration under CFTC regulations based upon compliance with its home country's regulatory framework (also known as a "Rule 30.10 firm").

Exercise Price (Strike Price): The price, specified in the option contract, at which the underlying futures contract, security, or commodity will move from seller to buyer.

Exotic Options: Any of a wide variety of options with non-standard payout structures or other features, including Asian options and lookback options. Exotic options are mostly traded in the over-the-counter market.

Expiration Date: The date on which an option contract automatically expires; the last day an option may be exercised.

Extrinsic Value: See Time Value.

Ex-Pit: See Transfer Trades and Exchange for Physicals.

F

FAB (Five Against Bond) Spread: A futures spread trade involving the buying (selling) of a five-year Treasury note futures contract and the selling (buying) of a long-term (15-30 year) Treasury bond futures contract.

Fannie Mae: A corporation (government-sponsored enterprise) created by Congress to support the secondary mortgage market (formerly the Federal National Mortgage Association). It purchases and sells residential mortgages insured by the Federal Housing Administration (FHA) or guaranteed by the Veteran's Administration (VA). See Freddie Mac.

FAN (Five Against Note) Spread: A futures spread trade involving the buying (selling) of a five-year Treasury note futures contract and the selling (buying) of a ten-year Treasury note futures contract.

Fast Market: An open outcry market situation in which transactions in the pit or ring take place in such volume and with such rapidity that price reporters fall behind with price quotations, label each quote "FAST" and show a range of prices. Also called a **fast tape**.

Federal Energy Regulatory Commission: (FERC): An independent agency of the U.S. Government that regulates the interstate transmission of natural gas, oil, and electricity. FERC also regulates natural gas and hydropower projects.

Federal Limit: A speculative position limit that is established and administered by the CFTC rather than an exchange.

Feed Ratio: The relationship of the cost of feed, expressed as a ratio to the sale price of animals, such as the corn-hog ratio. These serve as indicators of the profit margin or lack of profit in feeding animals to market weight.

FERC: See Federal Energy Regulatory Commission.

FIA: See Futures Industry Association.

Fibonacci Numbers: A number sequence discovered by a thirteenth century Italian mathematician Leonardo Fibonacci (circa 1170-1250), who introduced Arabic numbers to Europe, in which the sum of any two consecutive numbers equals the next highest number—i.e., following this sequence: 1, 1, 2, 3, 5, 8, 13, 21, 34, 55, and so on. The ratio of any number to its next highest number approaches 0.618 after the first four numbers. These numbers are used by technical analysts to determine price objectives from percentage retracements.

Fictitious Trading: Wash trading, bucketing, cross trading, or other schemes which give the appearance of trading but actually no bona fide, competitive trade has occurred.

Fill: The execution of an order.

Fill or Kill Order (FOK): An order that demands immediate execution or cancellation. Typically involving a designation, added to an order, instructing the broker to offer or bid (as the case may be) one time only; if the order is not filled immediately, it is then automatically cancelled.

Final Settlement Price: The price at which a cash-settled futures contract is settled at maturity, pursuant to a procedure specified by the exchange.

Financial: Can be used to refer to a derivative that is financially settled or cash settled. See Physical.

Financial Commodity: Any futures or option contract that is not based on an agricultural commodity, a natural resource such as energy or metals, or other physical or tangible commodity. It includes currencies, equity securities, fixed income securities, and indexes of various kinds.

Financial Future: A futures contract on a financial commodity.

Financial Settlement: See Cash settlement.

First Notice Day: The first day on which notices of intent to deliver actual commodities against futures market positions can be received. First notice day may vary with each commodity and exchange.

Fix, Fixing: See Gold Fixing.

Fixed Income Security: A security whose nominal (or current dollar) yield is fixed or determined with certainty at the time of purchase, typically a debt security.

Floor Broker: A person with exchange trading privileges who, in any pit, ring, post, or other place provided by an exchange for the meeting of persons similarly engaged, executes for another person any orders for the purchase or sale of any commodity for future delivery.

Floor Trader: A person with exchange trading privileges who executes his own trades by being personally present in the pit or ring for futures trading. See Local.

F.O.B. (Free On Board): Indicates that all delivery, inspection and elevation, or loading costs involved in putting commodities on board a carrier have been paid.

Forced Liquidation: The situation in which a customer's account is liquidated (open positions are offset) by the brokerage firm holding the account, usually after notification that the account is under-margined due to adverse price movements and failure to meet margin calls.

Force Majeure: A clause in a supply contract that permits either party not to fulfill the contractual commitments due to events beyond their control. These events may range from strikes to export delays in producing countries.

Foreign Exchange: Trading in foreign currency.

Forex: Refers to the over-the-counter market for foreign exchange transactions. Also called the **foreign exchange market**.

Forwardation: See Contango.

Forward Contract: A cash transaction common in many industries, including commodity merchandising, in which a commercial buyer and seller agree upon delivery of a specified quality and quantity of goods at a specified future date. Terms may be more "personalized" than is the case with standardized futures contracts (i.e., delivery time and amount are as determined between seller and buyer). A price may be agreed upon in advance, or there may be agreement that the price will be determined at the time of delivery.

Forward Market: The over-the-counter market for forward contracts.

Forward Months: Futures contracts, currently trading, calling for later or distant delivery. See Deferred Futures, Back Months.

Forward Rate Agreement (FRA): An OTC forward contract on a short-term interest rate. The buyer of a FRA is a notional borrower, i.e., the buyer commits to pay a fixed rate of interest on some notional amount that is never actually exchanged. The seller of a FRA agrees notionally to lend a sum of money to a borrower. FRAs can be used either to hedge interest rate risk or to speculate on future changes in interest rates.

Freddie Mac: A corporation (government-sponsored enterprise) created by Congress to support the secondary mortgage market (formerly the Federal Home Loan Mortgage Corporation). It purchases and sells residential mortgages insured by the Federal Home Administration (FHA) or guaranteed by the Veterans Administration (VA). See Fannie Mae.

Front Month: The spot or nearby delivery month, the nearest traded contract month. See Back Month.

Front Running: With respect to commodity futures and options, taking a futures or option position based upon non-public information regarding an impending transaction by another person in the same or related future or option. Also known as **trading ahead**.

Front Spread: A delta-neutral ratio spread in which more options are sold than bought. Also called **ratio vertical spread**. A front spread will increase in value if volatility decreases.

Full Carrying Charge, Full Carry: See Carrying Charges.

Fund of Funds: A commodity pool that invests in other commodity pools rather than directly in futures and options contracts.

Fundamental Analysis: Study of basic, underlying factors that will affect the supply and demand of the commodity being traded in futures contracts. See Technical Analysis.

Fungibility: The characteristic of interchangeability. Futures contracts for the same commodity and delivery month traded on the same exchange are fungible due to their standardized specifications for quality, quantity, delivery date, and delivery locations.

Futures: See Futures Contract.

Futures Commission Merchant (FCM): Individuals, associations, partnerships, corporations, and trusts that solicit or accept orders for the purchase or sale of any commodity for future delivery on or subject to the rules of any exchange and that accept payment from or extend credit to those whose orders are accepted.

Futures Contract: An agreement to purchase or sell a commodity for delivery in the future: (1) at a price that is determined at initiation of the contract; (2) that obligates each party to the contract to fulfill the contract at the specified price; (3) that is used to assume or shift price risk; and (4) that may be satisfied by delivery or offset.

Futures-equivalent: A term frequently used with reference to speculative position limits for options on futures contracts. The futures-equivalent of an option position is the number of options multiplied by the previous day's risk factor or delta for the option series. For example, ten deep out-of-money options with a delta of 0.20 would be considered two futures-equivalent contracts. The delta or risk factor used for this purpose is the same as that used in delta-based margining and risk analysis systems.

Futures Industry Association **(FIA):** A membership organization for futures commission merchants (FCMs) which, among other activities, offers education courses on the futures markets, disburses information, and lobbies on behalf of its members.

Futures Option: An option on a futures contract.

Futures Price: (1) Commonly held to mean the price of a commodity for future delivery that is traded on a futures exchange; (2) the price of any futures contract.

G

Gamma: A measurement of how fast the delta of an option changes, given a unit change in the underlying futures price; the "delta of the delta."

Ginzy Trading: A non-competitive trade practice in which a floor broker, in executing an order—particularly a large order—will fill a portion of the order at one price and the remainder of the order at another price to avoid an exchange's rule against trading at fractional increments or "split ticks."

Give Up: A contract executed by one broker for the client of another broker that the client orders to be turned over to the second broker. The broker accepting the order from the customer collects a fee from the carrying broker for the use of the facilities. Often used to consolidate many small orders or to disperse large ones.

Gold Certificate: A certificate attesting to a person's ownership of a specific amount of gold bullion.

Gold Fixing (Gold Fix): The setting of the gold price at 10:30 a.m. (first fixing) and 3:00 p.m. (second fixing) in London by representatives of the London gold market.

Gold/Silver Ratio: The number of ounces of silver required to buy one ounce of gold at current spot prices.

Good This Week Order (GTW): Order which is valid only for the week in which it is placed.

Good 'Till Canceled Order (GTC): An order which is valid until cancelled by the customer. Unless specified GTC, unfilled orders expire at the end of the trading day. See Open Order.

GPM: See Gross Processing Margin.

Grades: Various qualities of a commodity.

Grading Certificates: A formal document setting forth the quality of a commodity as determined by authorized inspectors or graders.

Grain Futures Act: Federal statute that provided for the regulation of trading in grain futures, effective June 22, 1923; administered by the Grain Futures Administration, an agency of the U.S. Department of Agriculture. The Grain Futures Act was amended in 1936 by the Commodity Exchange Act and the Grain Futures Administration became the Commodity Exchange Administration, later the Commodity Exchange Authority.

Grantor: The maker, writer, or issuer of an option contract who, in return for the premium paid for the option, stands ready to purchase the underlying commodity (or futures contract) in the case of a put option or to sell the underlying commodity (or futures contract) in the case of a call option.

Gross Processing Margin (GPM): Refers to the difference between the cost of a commodity and the combined sales income of the finished products that result from processing the commodity. Various industries have formulas to express the relationship of raw material costs to sales income from finished products. See Crack Spread, Crush Spread, and Spark Spread.

GTC: See Good 'Till Canceled Order.

GTW: See Good This Week Order.

Guaranteed Introducing Broker: An introducing broker that has entered into a guarantee agreement with a futures commission merchant (FCM), whereby the FCM agrees to be jointly and severally liable for all of the introducing broker's obligations under the Commodity Exchange Act. By entering into the agreement, the introducing broker is relieved from the necessity of raising its own capital to satisfy minimum financial requirements. In contrast, an independent introducing broker must raise its own capital to meet minimum financial requirements.

H

Haircut: In computing the value of assets for purposes of capital, segregation, or margin requirements, a percentage reduction from the stated value (e.g., book value or market value) to account for possible declines in value that may occur before assets can be liquidated.

Hand Held Terminal: A small computer terminal used by floor brokers or floor traders on an exchange to record trade information and transmit that information to the clearing organization.

Hardening: (1) Describes a price which is gradually stabilizing; (2) a term indicating a slowly advancing market.

Hard Position Limit: A speculative position limit, especially in contrast to a position accountability level.

Head and Shoulders: In technical analysis, a chart formation that resembles a human head and shoulders and is generally considered to be predictive of a price reversal. A head and shoulders top (which is considered predictive of a price decline) consists of a high price, a decline to a support level, a rally to a higher price than the previous high price, a second decline to the support level, and a weaker rally to about the level of the first high price. The reverse (upside-down) formation is called a head and shoulders bottom (which is considered predictive of a price rally).

Heavy: A market in which prices are demonstrating either an inability to advance or a slight tendency to decline.

Hedge Exemption: An exemption from speculative position limits for bona fide hedgers and certain other persons who meet the requirements of exchange and CFTC rules.

Hedge Fund: A private investment fund or pool that trades and invests in various assets such as securities, commodities, currency, and derivatives on behalf of its clients, typically wealthy individuals. Some commodity pool operators operate hedge funds.

Hedge Ratio: Ratio of the value of futures contracts purchased or sold to the value of the cash commodity being hedged, a computation necessary to minimize basis risk.

Hedger: A trader who enters into positions in a futures market opposite to positions held in the cash market to minimize the risk of financial loss from an adverse price change; or who purchases or sells futures as a temporary substitute for a cash transaction that will occur later. One can hedge either a long cash market position (e.g., one owns the cash commodity) or a short cash market position (e.g., one plans on buying the cash commodity in the future).

Henry Hub: A natural gas pipeline hub in Louisiana that serves as the delivery point for New York Mercantile Exchange natural gas futures contracts and often serves as a benchmark for wholesale natural gas prices across the U.S.

Hidden Quantity Order: An order placed on an electronic trading system whereby only a portion of the order is visible to other market participants. As the displayed part of the order is filled, additional quantities become visible. Also called **Iceberg, Max Show**.

High Frequency Trading: Computerized or algorithmic trading in which transactions are completed in very small fractions of a second.

Historical Volatility: A statistical measure of the volatility (specifically, the annualized standard deviation) of a futures contract, security, or other instrument over a specified number of past trading days.

Hog-Corn Ratio: See Feed Ratio.

Horizontal Spread (also called Time Spread or Calendar Spread): An option spread involving the simultaneous purchase and sale of options of the same class and strike prices but different expiration dates. See Diagonal Spread, Vertical Spread.

Hybrid Instruments: Financial instruments that possess, in varying combinations, characteristics of forward contracts, futures contracts, option contracts, debt instruments, bank depository interests, and other interests. Certain hybrid instruments are exempt from CFTC regulation.

IJK

IB: See Introducing Broker.

Iceberg: See Hidden Quantity Order.

Implied Repo Rate: The rate of return that can be obtained from selling a debt instrument futures contract and simultaneously buying a bond or note deliverable against that futures contract with borrowed funds. The bond or note with the highest implied repo rate is cheapest to deliver.

Implied Volatility: The volatility of a futures contract, security, or other instrument as implied by the prices of an option on that instrument, calculated using an options pricing model.

Index Arbitrage: The simultaneous purchase (sale) of stock index futures and the sale (purchase) of some or all of the component stocks that make up the particular stock index to profit from sufficiently large intermarket spreads between the futures contract and the index itself. Also see Arbitrage, Program Trading.

Indirect Bucketing: Also referred to as **indirect trading against**. Refers to when a floor broker effectively trades opposite his customer in a pair of non-competitive transactions by buying (selling) opposite an accommodating trader to fill a customer order and by selling (buying) for his personal account opposite the same accommodating trader. The accommodating trader assists the floor broker by making it appear that the customer traded opposite him rather than opposite the floor broker.

Inflation-Indexed Debt Instrument: Generally a debt instrument (such as a bond or note) on which the payments are adjusted for inflation and deflation. In a typical inflation-indexed instrument, the principal amount is adjusted monthly based on an inflation index such as the Consumer Price Index.

Initial Deposit: See Initial Margin.

Initial Margin: Customers' funds put up as security for a guarantee of contract fulfillment at the time a futures market position is established. SeeOriginal Margin.

In Position: Refers to a commodity located where it can readily be moved to another point or delivered on a futures contract. Commodities not so situated are "out of position." Soybeans in Mississippi are out of position for delivery in Chicago, but in position for export shipment from the Gulf of Mexico.

In Sight: The amount of a particular commodity that arrives at terminal or central locations in or near producing areas. When a commodity is "in sight," it is inferred that reasonably prompt delivery can be made; the quantity and quality also become known factors rather than estimates.

Instrument: A tradable asset such as a commodity, security, or derivative, or an index or value that underlies a derivative or could underlie a derivative.

Intercommodity Spread: A spread in which the long and short legs are in two different but generally related commodity markets. Also called an intermarket spread. See Spread.

Interdelivery Spread: A spread involving two different months of the same commodity. Also called an intracommodity spread. See Spread.

Interest Rate Futures: Futures contracts traded on fixed income securities such as U.S. Treasury issues, or based on the levels of specified interest rates such as LIBOR (London Interbank Offered

Rate). Currency is excluded from this category, even though interest rates are a factor in currency values.

Interest Rate Swap: A swap in which the two counterparties agree to exchange interest rate flows. Typically, one party agrees to pay a fixed rate on a specified series of payment dates and the other party pays a floating rate that may be based on LIBOR (London Interbank Offered Rate) on those payment dates. The interest rates are paid on a specified principal amount called the notional principal.

Intermarket Spread: See Spread and Intercommodity Spread.

Intermediary: A person who acts on behalf of another person in connection with futures trading, such as a futures commission merchant, introducing broker, commodity pool operator, commodity trading advisor, or associated person.

International Swaps and Derivatives Association (ISDA): A New York-based group of major international swaps dealers, that publishes the Code of Standard Wording, Assumptions and Provisions for Swaps, or Swaps Code, for U.S. dollar interest rate swaps as well as standard master interest rate, credit, and currency swap agreements and definitions for use in connection with the creation and trading of swaps.

In-The-Money: A term used to describe an option contract that has a positive value if exercised. A call with a strike price of $1100 on gold trading at $1150 is in-the-money 50 dollars. See Intrinsic Value.

Intracommodity Spread: See Spread and Interdelivery Spread.

Intrinsic Value: A measure of the value of an option or a warrant if immediately exercised, that is, the extent to which it is in-the-money. The amount by which the current price for the underlying commodity or futures contract is above the strike price of a call option or below the strike price of a put option for the commodity or futures contract.

Introducing Broker (IB): A person (other than a person registered as an associated person of a futures commission merchant) who is engaged in soliciting or in accepting orders for the purchase or sale of any commodity for future delivery on an exchange who does not accept any money, securities, or property to margin, guarantee, or secure any trades or contracts that result therefrom.

Inverted Market: A futures market in which the nearer months are selling at prices higher than the more distant months; a market displaying "inverse carrying charges," characteristic of markets with supply shortages. See Backwardation.

Invisible Supply: Uncounted stocks of a commodity in the hands of wholesalers, manufacturers, and producers that cannot be identified accurately; stocks outside commercial channels but theoretically available to the market. See Visible Supply.

Invoice Price: The price fixed by the clearing house at which deliveries on futures are invoiced—generally the price at which the futures contract is settled when deliveries are made. Also called Delivery Price.

ISDA: See International Swaps and Derivatives Association.

Job Lot: A form of contract having a smaller unit of trading than is featured in a regular contract.

Kerb Trading or Dealing: See Curb Trading.

Knock-In: A provision in an option or other derivative contract, whereby the contract is activated only if the price of the underlying instrument reaches a specified level before a specified expiration date.

Knock-Out: A provision in an option or other derivative contract, whereby the contract is immediately canceled if the price of the underlying instrument reaches a specified level during the life of the contract.

L

Large Order Execution (LOX) Procedures: Rules in place at the Chicago Mercantile Exchange that authorize a member firm that receives a large order from an initiating party to solicit counterparty interest off the exchange floor prior to open execution of the order in the pit and that provide for special surveillance procedures. The parties determine a maximum quantity and an "intended execution price." Subsequently, the initiating party's order quantity is exposed to the pit; any bids (or offers) up to and including those at the intended execution price are hit (acceptable). The unexecuted balance is then crossed with the contraside trader found using the LOX procedures.

Large Traders: A large trader is one who holds or controls a position in any one future or in any one option expiration series of a commodity on any one exchange equaling or exceeding the exchange or CFTC-specified reporting level.

Last Notice Day: The final day on which notices of intent to deliver on futures contracts may be issued.

Last Trading Day: Day on which trading ceases for the maturing (current) delivery month.

Latency: The amount of time that elapses between the placement of a market order or marketable limit order on an electronic trading system and the execution of that order.

Leaps: Long-dated, exchange-traded options. Stands for "Long-term Equity Anticipation Securities."

Leverage: The ability to control large dollar amounts of a commodity or security with a comparatively small amount of capital.

LIBOR: The London Interbank Offered Rate. The rate of interest at which banks borrow funds (denominated in U.S. dollars) from other banks, in marketable size, in the London interbank market. LIBOR rates are disseminated by the British Bankers Association, which also disseminates LIBOR rates for British pounds sterling. Some interest rate futures contracts, including Eurodollar futures, are cash settled based on LIBOR. Also see EURIBOR® and TIBOR.

Licensed Warehouse: A warehouse approved by an exchange from which a commodity may be delivered on a futures contract. See Regular Warehouse.

Life of Contract: Period between the beginning of trading in a particular futures contract and the expiration of trading. In some cases, this phrase denotes the period already passed in which trading has already occurred. For example, "The life-of-contract high so far is $2.50." Same as **life of delivery** or **life of the future**.

Limit (Up or Down): The maximum price advance or decline from the previous day's settlement price permitted during one trading session, as fixed by the rules of an exchange. In some futures contracts, the limit may be expanded or removed during a trading session a specified period of time after the contract is locked limit. See Daily Price Limit.

Limit Move: See Locked Limit.

Limit Only: The definite price stated by a customer to a broker restricting the execution of an order to buy for not more than, or to sell for not less than, the stated price.

Limit Order: An order in which the customer specifies a minimum sale price or maximum purchase price, as contrasted with a market order, which implies that the order should be filled as soon as possible at the market price.

Liquidation: The closing out of a long position. The term is sometimes used to denote closing out a short position, but this is more often referred to as covering. See Cover, Offset.

Liquid Market: A market in which selling and buying can be accomplished with minimal effect on price.

Local: An individual with exchange trading privileges who trades for his own account, traditionally on an exchange floor, and whose activities provide market liquidity. See Floor Trader, E-Local.

Location: A Delivery Point for a futures contract.

Locked-In: A hedged position that cannot be lifted without offsetting both sides of the hedge (spread). See Hedging. Also refers to being caught in a limit price move.

Locked Limit: A price that has advanced or declined the permissible limit during one trading session, as fixed by the rules of an exchange. Also called Limit Move.

London Gold Market: Refers to the dealers in the London Bullion Market Association who set (fix) the gold price in London. See Gold Fixing.

Long: (1) One who has bought a futures contract to establish a market position; (2) a market position that obligates the holder to take delivery; (3) one who owns an inventory of commodities. See Short.

Long Hedge: See Buying Hedge.

Long the Basis: A person or firm that has bought the spot commodity and hedged with a sale of futures is said to be long the basis.

Lookalike Option: An over-the-counter option that is cash settled based on the settlement price of a similar exchange-traded futures contract on a specified trading day.

Lookalike Swap: An over-the-counter swap that is cash settled based on the settlement price of a similar exchange-traded futures contract on a specified trading day.

Lookback Option: An exotic option whose payoff depends on the minimum or maximum price of the underlying asset during some portion of the life of the option. Lookback options allow the buyer to pay or receive the most favorable underlying price during the lookback period.

Lot: A unit of trading. See Even Lot, Job Lot, and Round Lot.

M

Macro Fund: A hedge fund that specializes in strategies designed to profit from expected macroeconomic events.

Maintenance Margin: See Margin.

Managed Account: See Controlled Account and Discretionary Account.

Managed Money Trader (MMT): A futures market participant who engages in futures trades on behalf of investment funds or clients. While MMTs are commonly equated with hedge funds, they may include Commodity Pool Operators and other managed accounts as well as hedge funds. While CFTC Form 40 does not provide a place to declare oneself a Managed Money Trader, a large trader can declare itself a "Hedge Fund (H)" or "Managed Accounts and Commodity Pools."

Manipulation: Any planned operation, transaction, or practice that causes or maintains an artificial price. Specific types include corners and squeezes as well as unusually large purchases or sales of a commodity or security in a short period of time in order to distort prices, and putting out false information in order to distort prices.

Manufacturer (AM): A large trader that declares itself a "Manufacturer" on CFTC Form 40, which provides as examples "refiner, miller, crusher, fabricator, sawmill, coffee roaster, cocoa grinder."

Many-to-Many: Refers to a trading platform in which multiple participants have the ability to execute or trade commodities, derivatives, or other instruments by accepting bids and offers made by multiple other participants. In contrast to one-to-many platforms, many-to-many platforms are considered trading facilities under the Commodity Exchange Act. Traditional exchanges are many-to-many platforms.

Margin: The amount of money or collateral deposited by a customer with his broker, by a broker with a clearing member, or by a clearing member with a clearing organization. The margin is not partial payment on a purchase. Also called Performance Bond. (1) Initial margin is the amount of margin required by the broker when a futures position is opened; (2) Maintenance margin is an amount that must be maintained on deposit at all times. If the equity in a customer's account drops to or below the level of maintenance margin because of adverse price movement, the broker must issue a margin call to restore the customer's equity to the initial level. See Variation Margin. Exchanges specify levels of initial margin and maintenance margin for each futures contract, but futures commission merchants may require their customers to post margin at higher levels than those specified by the exchange. Futures margin is determined by the SPAN margining system, which takes into account all positions in a customer's portfolio.

Margin Call: (1) A request from a brokerage firm to a customer to bring margin deposits up to initial levels; (2) a request by the clearing organization to a clearing member to make a deposit of original margin, or a daily or intra-day variation margin payment because of adverse price movement, based on positions carried by the clearing member.

Market-if-Touched (MIT) Order: An order that becomes a market order when a particular price is reached. A sell MIT is placed above the market; a buy MIT is placed below the market. Also referred to as a board order. Compare to Stop Order.

Market Maker: A professional securities dealer or person with trading privileges on an exchange who has an obligation to buy when there is an excess of sell orders and to sell when there is an excess of buy orders. By maintaining an offering price sufficiently higher than their buying price, these firms are compensated for the risk involved in allowing their inventory of securities to act as a buffer against temporary order imbalances. In the futures industry, this term is sometimes loosely used to refer to a floor trader or local who, in speculating for his own account, provides a market for commercial users of the market. Occasionally a futures exchange will compensate a person with exchange trading privileges to take on the obligations of a market maker to enhance liquidity in a newly listed or lightly traded futures contract. See Specialist System.

Market-on-Close: An order to buy or sell at the end of the trading session at a price within the closing range of prices. See Stop-Close-Only Order.

Market-on-Opening: An order to buy or sell at the beginning of the trading session at a price within the opening range of prices.

Market Order: An order to buy or sell a futures contract at whatever price is obtainable at the time it is entered in the ring, pit, or other trading platform. See At-the-Market Limit Order.

Mark-to-Market: Part of the daily cash flow system used by U.S. futures exchanges to maintain a minimum level of margin equity for a given futures or option contract position by calculating the gain or loss in each contract position resulting from changes in the price of the futures or option contracts at the end of each trading session. These amounts are added or subtracted to each account balance.

Maturity: Period within which a futures contract can be settled by delivery of the actual commodity.

Maximum Price Fluctuation: See Limit (Up or Down) and Daily Price Limit.

Max Show: See Hidden Quantity Order.

Member Rate: Commission charged for the execution of an order for a person who is a member of or has trading privileges at the exchange.

Mini: Refers to a futures contract that has a smaller contract size than an otherwise identical futures contract.

Minimum Price Contract: A hybrid commercial forward contract for agricultural products that includes a provision guaranteeing the person making delivery a minimum price for the product. For agricultural commodities, these contracts became much more common with the introduction of exchange-traded options on futures contracts, which permit buyers to hedge the price risks associated with such contracts.

Minimum Price Fluctuation (Minimum Tick): Smallest increment of price movement possible in trading a given contract.

Minimum Tick: See Minimum Price Fluctuation.

MMBTU: Million British Thermal Units, the unit of trading in the natural gas futures market.

MOB Spread: A spread between the municipal bond futures contract and the Treasury bond contract, also known as **munis over bonds**.

Momentum: In technical analysis, the relative change in price over a specific time interval. Often equated with speed or velocity and considered in terms of relative strength.

Money Market: The market for short-term debt instruments.

Multilateral Clearing Organization: See Clearing Organization.

N

Naked Option: The sale of a call or put option without holding an equal and opposite position in the underlying instrument. Also referred to as an uncovered option, naked call, or naked put.

Narrow-Based Security Index: In general, the Commodity Exchange Act defines a narrow-based security index as an index of securities that meets one of the following four requirements (1) it has nine or fewer components; (2) one component comprises more than 30 percent of the index weighting; (3) the five highest weighted components comprise more than 60 percent of the index weighting, or (4) the lowest weighted components comprising in the aggregate 25 percent of the index's weighting have an aggregate dollar value of average daily volume over a six-month period of less than $50 million ($30 million if there are at least 15 component securities). However, the legal definition in Section 1a(25) of the Commodity Exchange Act, 7 USC 1a(25), contains several exceptions to this provision. See Broad-Based Security Index, Security Future.

National Futures Association (NFA): A self-regulatory organization whose members include futures commission merchants, commodity pool operators, commodity trading advisors, introducing brokers, commodity exchanges, commercial firms, and banks, that is responsible—under CFTC oversight—for certain aspects of the regulation of FCMs, CPOs, CTAs, IBs, and their associated persons, focusing primarily on the qualifications and proficiency, financial condition, retail sales practices, and business conduct of these futures professionals. NFA also performs arbitration and dispute resolution functions for industry participants.

Nearbys: The nearest delivery months of a commodity futures market.

Nearby Delivery Month: The month of the futures contract closest to maturity; the front month or lead month.

Negative Carry: The cost of financing a financial instrument (the short-term rate of interest), when the cost is above the current return of the financial instrument. See Carrying Charges and Positive Carry.

Net Asset Value (NAV): The value of each unit of participation in a commodity pool.

Net Position: The difference between the open long contracts and the open short contracts held by a trader in any one commodity.

NFA: National Futures Association.

Next Day: A spot contract that provides for delivery of a commodity on the next calendar day or the next business day. Also called **day ahead**.

NOB (Note Against Bond) Spread: A futures spread trade involving the buying (selling) of a Treasury note futures contract and the selling (buying) of a Treasury bond futures contract.

Non-Member Traders: Speculators and hedgers who trade on the exchange through a member or a person with trading privileges but who do not hold exchange memberships or trading privileges.

Nominal Price (or Nominal Quotation): Computed price quotation on a futures or option contract for a period in which no actual trading took place, usually an average of bid and asked prices or computed using historical or theoretical relationships to more active contracts.

Notice Day: Any day on which notices of intent to deliver on futures contracts may be issued.

Notice of Intent to Deliver: A notice that must be presented by the seller of a futures contract to the clearing organization prior to delivery. The clearing organization then assigns the notice and subsequent delivery instrument to a buyer. Also **notice of delivery**.

Notional Principal: In an interest rate swap, forward rate agreement, or other derivative instrument, the amount or, in a currency swap, each of the amounts to which interest rates are applied in order to calculate periodic payment obligations. Also called the **notional amount**, the **contract amount**, the **reference amount**, and the **currency amount**.

NYMEX Lookalike: A lookalike swap or lookalike option that is based on a futures contract traded on the New York Mercantile Exchange (NYMEX).

O

OCO: See One Cancels the Other Order.

Offer: An indication of willingness to sell at a given price; opposite of bid, the price level of the offer may be referred to as the ask.

Off Exchange: See Over-the-Counter.

Offset: Liquidating a purchase of futures contracts through the sale of an equal number of contracts of the same delivery month, or liquidating a short sale of futures through the purchase of an equal number of contracts of the same delivery month. See Closing Out and Cover.

Omnibus Account: An account carried by one futures commission merchant, the carrying FCM, for another futures commission merchant, the originating FCM, in which the transactions of two or more persons, who are customers of the originating FCM, are combined and carried by the carrying FCM. Omnibus account titles must clearly show that the funds and trades therein belong to customers of the originating FCM. An originating broker must use an omnibus account to execute or clear trades for customers at a particular exchange where it does not have trading or clearing privileges.

On Track (or Track Country Station): (1) A type of deferred delivery in which the price is set f.o.b. seller's location, and the buyer agrees to pay freight costs to his destination; (2) commodities loaded in railroad cars on tracks.

One Cancels the Other (OCO) Order: A pair of orders, typically limit orders, whereby if one order is filled, the other order will automatically be cancelled. For example, an OCO order might consist of an order to buy 10 calls with a strike price of 50 at a specified price or buy 20 calls with a strike price of 55 (with the same expiration date) at a specified price.

One-to-Many: Refers to a proprietary trading platform in which the platform operator posts bids and offers for commodities, derivatives, or other instruments and serves as a counterparty to every transaction executed on the platform. In contrast to many-to-many platforms, one-to-many platforms are not considered trading facilities under the Commodity Exchange Act.

Opening Price (or Range): The price (or price range) recorded during the period designated by the exchange as the official opening.

Opening: The period at the beginning of the trading session officially designated by the exchange during which all transactions are considered made "at the opening."

Open Interest: The total number of futures contracts long or short in a delivery month or market that has been entered into and not yet liquidated by an offsetting transaction or fulfilled by delivery. Also called **open contracts** or **open commitments**.

Open Order (or Orders): An order that remains in force until it is canceled or until the futures contracts expire. See Good 'Till Canceled and Good This Week orders.

Open Outcry: A method of public auction, common to most U.S. commodity exchanges during the 20th century, where trading occurs on a trading floor and traders may bid and offer simultaneously either for their own accounts or for the accounts of customers. Transactions may take place simultaneously at different places in the trading pit or ring. At most exchanges open outcry has been replaced or largely replaced by electronic trading platforms. See Specialist System.

Open Trade Equity: The unrealized gain or loss on open futures positions.

Option: A contract that gives the buyer the right, but not the obligation, to buy or sell a specified quantity of a commodity or other instrument at a specific price within a specified period of time, regardless of the market price of that instrument. Also see Put and Call.

Option Buyer: The person who buys calls, puts, or any combination of calls and puts.

Option Delta: See Delta.

Option Writer: The person who originates an option contract by promising to perform a certain obligation in return for the price or premium of the option. Also known as **option grantor** or **option seller**.

Option Pricing Model: A mathematical model used to calculate the theoretical value of an option. Inputs to option pricing models typically include the price of the underlying instrument, the option strike price, the time remaining till the expiration date, the volatility of the underlying instrument, and the risk-free interest rate (e.g., the Treasury bill interest rate). Examples of option pricing models include Black-Scholes and Cox-Ross-Rubinstein.

Original Margin: Term applied to the initial deposit of margin money each clearing member firm is required to make according to clearing organization rules based upon positions carried, determined separately for customer and proprietary positions; similar in concept to the initial margin or security deposit required of customers by exchange rules. See Initial Margin.

OTC: See Over-the-Counter.

Out of Position: See In Position.

Out-Of-The-Money: A term used to describe an option that has no intrinsic value. For example, a call with a strike price of $400 on gold trading at $390 is out-of-the-money 10 dollars.

Outright: An order to buy or sell only one specific type of futures contract; an order that is not a spread order.

Out Trade: A trade that cannot be cleared by a clearing organization because the trade data submitted by the two clearing members or two traders involved in the trade differs in some respect (e.g., price and/or quantity). In such cases, the two clearing members or traders involved must reconcile the discrepancy, if possible, and resubmit the trade for clearing. If an agreement cannot be reached by the two clearing members or traders involved, the dispute would be settled by an appropriate exchange committee.

Overbought: A technical opinion that the market price has risen too steeply and too fast in relation to underlying fundamental factors. Rank and file traders who were bullish and long have turned bearish.

Overnight Trade: A trade which is not liquidated during the same trading session during which it was established.

Oversold: A technical opinion that the market price has declined too steeply and too fast in relation to underlying fundamental factors; rank and file traders who were bearish and short have turned bullish.

Over-the-Counter (OTC): The trading of commodities, contracts, or other instruments not listed on any exchange. OTC transactions can occur electronically or over the telephone. Also referred to as Off-Exchange.

P

P&S (Purchase and Sale Statement): A statement sent by a futures commission merchant to a customer when any part of a futures position is offset, showing the number of contracts involved, the prices at which the contracts were bought or sold, the gross profit or loss, the commission charges, the net profit or loss on the transactions, and the balance. FCMs also send P&S Statements whenever any other event occurs that alters the account balance including when the customer deposits or withdraws margin and when the FCM places excess margin in interest bearing instruments for the customer's benefit.

Paper Profit or Loss: The profit or loss that would be realized if open contracts were liquidated as of a certain time or at a certain price.

Par: (1) Refers to the standard delivery point(s) and/or quality of a commodity that is deliverable on a futures contract at contract price. Serves as a benchmark upon which to base discounts or premiums for varying quality and delivery locations; (2) in bond markets, an index (usually 100) representing the face value of a bond.

Path Dependent Option: An option whose valuation and payoff depends on the realized price path of the underlying asset, such as an Asian option or a Lookback option.

Pay/Collect: A shorthand method of referring to the payment of a loss (pay) and receipt of a gain (collect) by a clearing member to or from a clearing organization that occurs after a futures position has been marked-to-market. See Variation Margin.

Pegged Price: The price at which a commodity has been fixed by agreement.

Pegging: Effecting transactions in an instrument underlying an option to prevent a decline in the price of the instrument shortly prior to the option's expiration date so that previously written put options will expire worthless, thus protecting premiums previously received. See Capping.

Performance Bond: See Margin.

Physical : A contract or derivative that provides for the physical delivery of a commodity rather than cash settlement. See Financial.

Physical Commodity: A tangible commodity rather than a financial commodity, typically an agricultural commodity, energy commodity or a metal.

Physical Delivery: A provision in a futures contract or other derivative for delivery of the actual commodity to satisfy the contract. Compare to cash settlement.

Pip: The smallest price unit of a commodity or currency.

Pit: A specially constructed area on the trading floor of some exchanges where trading in a futures contract or option is conducted. On other exchanges, the term ring designates the trading area for commodity contract.

Pit Brokers: See Floor Broker.

Point-and-Figure: A method of charting that uses prices to form patterns of movement without regard to time. It defines a price trend as a continued movement in one direction until a reversal of a predetermined criterion is met.

Point Balance: A statement prepared by futures commission merchants to show profit or loss on all open contracts using an official closing or settlement price, usually at calendar month end.

Ponzi Scheme: Named after Charles Ponzi, a man with a remarkable criminal career in the early 20th century, the term has been used to describe pyramid arrangements whereby an enterprise makes payments to investors from the proceeds of a later investment rather than from profits of the underlying business venture, as the investors expected, and gives investors the impression that a legitimate profit-making business or investment opportunity exists, where in fact it is a mere fiction.

Pork Bellies: One of the major cuts of the hog carcass that, when cured, becomes bacon.

Portfolio Insurance: A trading strategy that uses stock index futures and/or stock index options to protect stock portfolios against market declines.

Portfolio Margining: A method for setting margin requirements that evaluates positions as a group or portfolio and takes into account the potential for losses on some positions to be offset by gains on others. Specifically, the margin requirement for a portfolio is typically set equal to an estimate of the largest possible decline in the net value of the portfolio that could occur under assumed changes in market conditions. Sometimes referred to as risked-based margining. Also see Strategy-Based Margining.

Position: An interest in the market, either long or short, in the form of one or more open contracts.

Position Accountability: A rule adopted by an exchange requiring persons holding a certain number of outstanding contracts to report the nature of the position, trading strategy, and hedging information of the position to the exchange, upon request of the exchange. See Speculative Position Limit.

Position Limit: See Speculative Position Limit.

Position Trader: A commodity trader who either buys or sells contracts and holds them for an extended period of time, as distinguished from a day trader, who will normally initiate and offset a futures position within a single trading session.

Positive Carry: The cost of financing a financial instrument (the short-term rate of interest), where the cost is less than the current return of the financial instrument. See Carrying Charges and Negative Carry.

Posted Price: An announced or advertised price indicating what a firm will pay for a commodity or the price at which the firm will sell it.

Prearranged Trading: Trading between brokers in accordance with an expressed or implied agreement or understanding, which is a violation of the Commodity Exchange Act and CFTC regulations.

Premium: (1) The payment an option buyer makes to the option writer for granting an option contract; (2) the amount a price would be increased to purchase a better quality commodity; (3) refers to a futures delivery month selling at a higher price than another, as "July is at a premium over May."

Price Banding: A CME Group and ICE-instituted mechanism to ensure a fair and orderly market on an electronic trading platform. This mechanism subjects all incoming orders to price verification and rejects all orders with clearly erroneous prices. Price bands are monitored throughout the day and adjusted if necessary.

Price Basing: A situation where producers, processors, merchants, or consumers of a commodity establish commercial transaction prices based on the futures prices for that or a related commodity (e.g., an offer to sell corn at 5 cents over the December futures price).

Price Discovery: The process of determining the price level for a commodity through the interaction of buyers and sellers and based on supply and demand conditions.

Price Movement Limit: See Limit (Up or Down).

Primary Market: (1) For producers, their major purchaser of commodities; (2) to processors, the market that is the major supplier of their commodity needs; and (3) in commercial marketing channels, an important center at which spot commodities are concentrated for shipment to terminal markets.

Producer (AP): A large trader that declares itself a "Producer" on CFTC Form 40, which provides as examples, "farmer" and "miner." A firm that extracts crude oil or natural gas from the ground would also be considered a Producer.

Program Trading: The purchase (or sale) of a large number of stocks contained in or comprising a portfolio. Originally called program trading when index funds and other institutional investors began to embark on large-scale buying or selling campaigns or "programs" to invest in a manner that replicates a target stock index, the term now also commonly includes computer-aided stock market buying or selling programs, and index arbitrage.

Prompt Date: The date on which the buyer of an option will buy or sell the underlying commodity (or futures contract) if the option is exercised.

Prop Shop: A proprietary trading group, especially one where the group's traders trade electronically at a physical facility operated by the group.

Proprietary Account: An account that a futures commission merchant carries for itself or a closely related person, such as a parent, subsidiary or affiliate company, general partner, director, associated person, or an owner of 10 percent or more of the capital stock. The FCM must segregate customer funds from funds related to proprietary accounts.

Proprietary Trading Group: An organization whose owners, employees, and/or contractors trade in the name of accounts owned by the group and exclusively use the funds of the group for all of their trading activity.

Public: In trade parlance, non-professional speculators as distinguished from hedgers and professional speculators or traders.

Public Elevators: Grain elevators in which bulk storage of grain is provided to the public for a fee. Grain of the same grade but owned by different persons is usually mixed or commingled as opposed to storing it "identity preserved." Some elevators are approved by exchanges as regular for delivery on futures contracts, see Regular Warehouse.

Purchase and Sale Statement: See P&S.

Put: An option contract that gives the holder the right but not the obligation to sell a specified quantity of a particular commodity, security, or other asset or to enter into a short futures position at a given price (the "strike price") prior to or on or prior to a specified expiration date.

Pyramiding: The use of profits on existing positions as margin to increase the size of the position, normally in successively smaller increments.

QR

Qualified Eligible Person (QEP): The definition of QEP is too complex to summarize here; please see CFTC Regulation 4.7(a)(2) and (a)(3), 17 CFR 4.7(a)(2) and (a)(3), for the full definition.

Quick Order: See Fill or Kill Order.

Quotation: The actual price or the bid or ask price of either cash commodities or futures contracts.

Rally: An upward movement of prices.

Random Walk: An economic theory that market price movements move randomly. This assumes an efficient market. The theory also assumes that new information comes to the market randomly. Together, the two assumptions imply that market prices move randomly as new information is incorporated into market prices. The theory implies that the best predictor of future prices is the current price, and that past prices are not a reliable indicator of future prices. If the random walk theory is correct, technical analysis cannot work.

Range: The difference between the high and low price of a commodity, futures, or option contract during a given period.

Ratio Hedge: The number of options compared to the number of futures contracts bought or sold in order to establish a hedge that is neutral or delta neutral.

Ratio Spread: This strategy, which applies to both puts and calls, involves buying or selling options at one strike price in greater number than those bought or sold at another strike price. Ratio spreads are typically designed to be delta neutral. Back spreads and front preads are types of ratio spreads.

Ratio Vertical Spread: See Front Spread.

Reaction: A downward price movement after a price advance.

Recovery: An upward price movement after a decline.

Reference Asset: An asset, such as a corporate or sovereign debt instrument, that underlies a credit derivative.

Regular Warehouse: A processing plant or warehouse that satisfies exchange requirements for financing, facilities, capacity, and location and has been approved as acceptable for delivery of commodities against futures contracts. See Licensed Warehouse.

Replicating Portfolio: A portfolio of assets for which changes in value match those of a target asset. For example, a portfolio replicating a standard option can be constructed with certain amounts of the asset underlying the option and bonds. Sometimes referred to as a **synthetic asset**.

Repo or **Repurchase Agreement:** A transaction in which one party sells a security to another party while agreeing to repurchase it from the counterparty at some date in the future, at an agreed price. Repos allow traders to short-sell securities and allow the owners of securities to earn added income by lending the securities they own. Through this operation the counterparty is effectively a borrower of funds to finance further. The rate of interest used is known as the **repo rate**.

Reporting Level: Sizes of positions set by the exchanges and/or the CFTC at or above which commodity traders or brokers who carry these accounts must make daily reports about the size of the position by commodity, by delivery month, and whether the position is controlled by a commercial or non-commercial trader. See the Large Trader Reporting Program.

Resistance: In technical analysis, a price area where new selling will emerge to dampen a continued rise. See Support.

Resting Order: A limit order to buy at a price below or to sell at a price above the prevailing market that is being held by a floor broker. Such orders may either be day orders or open orders.

Retail Customer: A customer that does not qualify as an eligible contract participant under Section 1a(12) of the Commodity Exchange Act, 7 USC 1a(12). An individual with total assets that do not exceed $10 million, or $5 million if the individual is entering into an agreement, contract, or transaction to manage risk, would be considered a retail customer.

Retender: In specific circumstances, some exchanges permit holders of futures contracts who have received a delivery notice through the clearing organization to sell a futures contract and return the notice to the clearing organization to be reissued to another long; others permit transfer of notices to another buyer. In either case, the trader is said to have retendered the notice.

Retracement: A reversal within a major price trend.

Reversal: A change of direction in prices. See Reverse Conversion.

Reverse Conversion or Reversal: With regard to options, a position created by buying a call option, selling a put option, and selling the underlying instrument (for example, a futures contract). See Conversion.

Reverse Crush Spread: The sale of soybean futures and the simultaneous purchase of soybean oil and meal futures. See Crush Spread.

Riding the Yield Curve: Trading in an interest rate futures contract according to the expectations of change in the yield curve.

Ring: A circular area on the trading floor of an exchange where traders and brokers stand while executing futures trades. Some exchanges use pits rather than rings.

Risked-Based Margining: See Portfolio Margining.

Risk Factor: See Delta.

Risk/Reward Ratio: The relationship between the probability of loss and profit. This ratio is often used as a basis for trade selection or comparison.

Roll-Over: A trading procedure involving the shift of one month of a straddle into another future month while holding the other contract month. The shift can take place in either the long or short straddle month. The term also applies to lifting a near futures position and re-establishing it in a more deferred delivery month.

Round Lot: A quantity of a commodity equal in size to the corresponding futures contract for the commodity. See Even Lot.

Round Trip Trading: See Wash Trading.

Round Turn: A completed transaction involving both a purchase and a liquidating sale, or a sale followed by a covering purchase.

Rules: The principles for governing an exchange. In some exchanges, rules are adopted by a vote of the membership, while in others, they can be imposed by the governing board.

Runners: Messengers or clerks who deliver orders received by phone clerks to brokers for execution in the pit.

S

Sample Grade: Usually the lowest quality of a commodity, too low to be acceptable for delivery in satisfaction of futures contracts.

Scale Down (or Up): To purchase or sell a scale down means to buy or sell at regular price intervals in a declining market. To buy or sell on scale up means to buy or sell at regular price intervals as the market advances.

Scalper: A speculator, often with exchange trading privileges, who buys and sells rapidly, with small profits or losses, holding his positions for only a short time during a trading session. Typically, a scalper will stand ready to buy at a fraction below the last transaction price and to sell at a fraction above, e.g., to buy at the bid and sell at the offer or ask price, with the intent of capturing the spread between the two, thus creating market liquidity. See Day Trader, Position Trader, High Frequency Trading.

Seasonality Claims: Misleading sales pitches that one can earn large profits with little risk based on predictable seasonal changes in supply or demand, published reports or other well-known events.

Seat: An instrument granting trading privileges on an exchange. A seat may also represent an ownership interest in the exchange.

Securities and Exchange Commission (SEC): The Federal regulatory agency established in 1934 to administer Federal securities laws.

Security: Generally, a transferable instrument representing an ownership interest in a corporation (equity security or stock) or the debt of a corporation, municipality, or sovereign. Other forms of debt such as mortgages can be converted into securities. Certain derivatives on securities (e.g., options on equity securities) are also considered securities for the purposes of the securities laws. Security futures products are considered to be both securities and futures products. Futures contracts on broad-based securities indexes are not considered securities.

Security Deposit: See Margin.

Security Future: A contract for the sale or future delivery of a single security or of a narrow-based security index.

Security Futures Product: A security future or any put, call, straddle, option, or privilege on any security future.

Self-Regulatory Organization (SRO): Exchanges and registered futures associations that enforce financial and sales practice requirements for their members. See Designated Self-Regulatory Organizations.

Seller's Call: Seller's call, also referred to as call purchase, is the same as the buyer's call except that the seller has the right to determine the time to fix the price. See Buyer's Call.

Seller's Market: A condition of the market in which there is a scarcity of goods available and hence sellers can obtain better conditions of sale or higher prices. See Buyer's Market.

Seller's Option: The right of a seller to select, within the limits prescribed by a contract, the quality of the commodity delivered and the time and place of delivery.

Selling Hedge (or Short Hedge): Selling futures contracts to protect against possible decreased prices of commodities. See Hedging.

Series (of Options): Options of the same type (i.e., either puts or calls, but not both), covering the same underlying futures contract or other underlying instrument, having the same strike price and expiration date.

Settlement: The act of fulfilling the delivery requirements of the futures contract.

Settlement Price: The daily price at which the clearing organization clears all trades and settles all accounts between clearing members of each contract month. Settlement prices are used to determine both margin calls and invoice prices for deliveries. The term also refers to a price established by the exchange to even up positions which may not be able to be liquidated in regular trading.

Shipping Certificate: A negotiable instrument used by several futures exchanges as the futures delivery instrument for several commodities (e.g., soybean meal, plywood, and white wheat). The shipping certificate is issued by exchange-approved facilities and represents a commitment by the facility to deliver the commodity to the holder of the certificate under the terms specified therein. Unlike an issuer of a warehouse receipt, who has physical product in store, the issuer of a shipping certificate may honor its obligation from current production or through-put as well as from inventories.

Shock Absorber: A temporary restriction in the trading of certain stock index futures contracts that becomes effective following a significant intraday decrease in stock index futures prices. Designed to provide an adjustment period to digest new market information, the restriction bars trading below a specified price level. Shock absorbers are generally market specific and at tighter levels than circuit breakers.

Short: (1) The selling side of an open futures contract; (2) a trader whose net position in the futures market shows an excess of open sales over open purchases. See Long.

Short Covering: See Cover.

Short Hedge: See Selling Hedge.

Short Selling: Selling a futures contract or other instrument with the idea of delivering on it or offsetting it at a later date.

Short Squeeze: See Squeeze.

Short the Basis: The purchase of futures as a hedge against a commitment to sell in the cash or spot markets. See Hedging.

Significant Price Discovery Contract (SPDC): A contract traded on an Exempt Commercial Market (ECM) which performs a significant price discovery function as determined by the CFTC pursuant to CFTC Regulation 36.3 (c). ECMs with SPDCs are subject to additional regulatory and reporting requirements.

Single Stock Future: A futures contract on a single stock as opposed to a stock index. Single stock futures were illegal in the U.S. prior to the passage of the Commodity Futures Modernization Act of 2000. See Security Future, Security Futures Product.

Small Traders: Traders who hold or control positions in futures or options that are below the reporting level specified by the exchange or the CFTC.

Soft: (1) A description of a price that is gradually weakening; or (2) this term also refers to certain "soft" commodities such as sugar, cocoa, and coffee.

Sold-Out-Market: When liquidation of a weakly-held position has been completed, and offerings become scarce, the market is said to be sold out.

SPAN® (Standard Portfolio Analysis of Risk®): As developed by the Chicago Mercantile Exchange, the industry standard for calculating performance bond requirements (margins) on the basis of overall portfolio risk. SPAN calculates risk for all enterprise levels on derivative and non-derivative instruments at numerous exchanges and clearing organizations worldwide.

SPDC: See Significant Price Discovery Contract.

Spark Spread: The differential between the price of electricity and the price of natural gas or other fuel used to generate electricity, expressed in equivalent units. See Gross Processing Margin.

Specialist System: A type of trading commonly formerly used for the exchange trading of securities in which one individual or firm acts as a market-maker in a particular security, with the obligation to provide fair and orderly trading in that security by offsetting temporary imbalances in supply and demand by trading for the specialist's own account. Like Open Outcry, the specialist system was supplanted by electronic trading during the early 21st century. In 2008, the New York Stock Exchange replaced the specialist system with a competitive dealer system. Specialists were converted into Designated Market Makers who have a different set of privileges and obligations than specialists had.

Speculative Bubble: A rapid run-up in prices caused by excessive buying that is unrelated to any of the basic, underlying factors affecting the supply or demand for a commodity or other asset. Speculative bubbles are usually associated with a "bandwagon" effect in which speculators rush to buy the commodity (in the case of futures, "to take positions") before the price trend ends, and an even greater rush to sell the commodity (unwind positions) when prices reverse.

Speculative Limit: See Speculative Position Limit.

Speculative Position Limit: The maximum position, either net long or net short, in one commodity future (or option) or in all futures (or options) of one commodity combined that may be held or controlled by one person (other than a person eligible for a hedge exemption) as prescribed by an exchange and/or by the CFTC.

Speculator: In commodity futures, a trader who does not hedge, but who trades with the objective of achieving profits through the successful anticipation of price movements.

Split Close: A condition that refers to price differences in transactions at the close of any market session.

Spot: Market of immediate delivery of and payment for the product.

Spot Commodity: (1) The actual commodity as distinguished from a futures contract; (2) sometimes used to refer to cash commodities available for immediate delivery. See Actuals or Cash Commodity.

Spot Month: The futures contract that matures and becomes deliverable during the present month. Also called Current Delivery Month.

Spot Price: The price at which a physical commodity for immediate delivery is selling at a given time and place. See Cash Price.

Spread (or Straddle): The purchase of one futures delivery month against the sale of another futures delivery month of the same commodity; the purchase of one delivery month of one commodity against the sale of that same delivery month of a different commodity; or the purchase of one commodity in one market against the sale of the commodity in another market, to take advantage of a profit from a change in price relationships. The term spread is also used to refer to the difference between the price of a futures month and the price of another month of the same commodity. A spread can also apply to options. See Arbitrage.

Squeeze: A market situation in which the lack of supplies tends to force shorts to cover their positions by offset at higher prices. Also see Congestion, Corner.

SRO: See Self-Regulatory Organization.

Stop-Close-Only Order: A stop order that can be executed, if possible, only during the closing period of the market. See also Market-on-Close Order.

Stop Limit Order: A stop limit order is an order that goes into force as soon as there is a trade at the specified price. The order, however, can only be filled at the stop limit price or better.

Stop Logic Functionality:A provision applicable to futures traded on the CME's Globex electronic trading system designed to prevent excessive price movements caused by cascading stop orders. Stop Logic Functionality introduces a momentary pause in matching (Reserved State) when triggered stops would cause the market to trade outside predefined values. The momentary pause provides an opportunity for additional bids or offers to be posted.

Stop Loss Order: See Stop Order.

Stop Order: This is an order that becomes a market order when a particular price level is reached. A sell stop is placed below the market, a buy stop is placed above the market. Sometimes referred to as stop loss order. Compare to market-if-touched order.

Straddle: (1) See Spread; (2) an option position consisting of the purchase of put and call options having the same expiration date and strike price.

Strangle: An option position consisting of the purchase of put and call options having the same expiration date, but different strike prices.

Strategy-Based Margining: A method for setting margin requirements whereby the potential for gains on one position in a portfolio to offset losses on another position is taken into account only if the portfolio implements one of a designated set of recognized trading strategies as set out in the rules of an exchange or clearing organization. Also see Portfolio Margining.

Street Book: A daily record kept by futures commission merchants and clearing members showing details of each futures and option transaction, including date, price, quantity, market, commodity, future, strike price, option type, and the person for whom the trade was made.

Strike Price (Exercise Price): The price, specified in the option contract, at which the underlying futures contract, security, or commodity will move from seller to buyer.

Strip: A sequence of futures contract months (e.g., the June, July, and August natural gas futures contracts) that can be executed as a single transaction.

STRIPS (Separate Trading of Registered Interest and Principal Securities): A book-entry system operated by the Federal Reserve permitting separate trading and ownership of the principal and coupon portions of selected Treasury securities. It allows the creation of zero coupon Treasury securities from designated whole bonds.

Strong Hands: When used in connection with delivery of commodities on futures contracts, the term usually means that the party receiving the delivery notice probably will take delivery and retain ownership of the commodity; when used in connection with futures positions, the term usually means positions held by trade interests or well-financed speculators.

Support: In technical analysis, a price area where new buying is likely to come in and stem any decline. See Resistance.

Swap: In general, the exchange of one asset or liability for a similar asset or liability for the purpose of lengthening or shortening maturities, or otherwise shifting risks. This may entail selling one securities issue and buying another in foreign currency; it may entail buying a currency on the spot market and simultaneously selling it forward. Swaps also may involve exchanging income flows; for example, exchanging the fixed rate coupon stream of a bond for a variable rate payment stream, or vice versa, while not swapping the principal component of the bond. Swaps are generally traded over-the-counter. See Commodity Swap.

Swap Dealer (AS): An entity such as a bank or investment bank that markets swaps to end users. Swap dealers often hedge their swap positions in futures markets. Alternatively, an entity that declares itself a "Swap/Derivatives Dealer" on CFTC Form 40.

Swaption: An option to enter into a swap—i.e., the right, but not the obligation, to enter into a specified type of swap at a specified future date.

Switch: Offsetting a position in one delivery month of a commodity and simultaneous initiation of a similar position in another delivery month of the same commodity, a tactic referred to as "rolling forward."

Synthetic Futures: A position created by combining call and put options. A synthetic long futures position is created by combining a long call option and a short put option for the same expiration date and the same strike price. A synthetic short futures contract is created by combining a long put and a short call with the same expiration date and the same strike price.

Systematic Risk: Market risk due to factors that cannot be eliminated by diversification.

Systemic Risk: The risk that a default by one market participant will have repercussions on other participants due to the interlocking nature of financial markets. For example, Customer A's default in X market may affect Intermediary B's ability to fulfill its obligations in Markets X, Y, and Z.

T

Taker: The buyer of an option contract.

TAS: See Trading at Settlement.

T-Bond: See Treasury Bond.

Technical Analysis: An approach to forecasting commodity prices that examines patterns of price change, rates of change, and changes in volume of trading and open interest, without regard to underlying fundamental market factors. Technical analysis can work consistently only if the theory that price movements are a random walk is incorrect. See Fundamental Analysis.

Ted Spread: (1) The difference between the interest rate on three-month U.S. Treasury bills and three-month LIBOR; (2) traditionally, the difference between the price of the three-month U.S. Treasury bill futures contract and the price of the three-month Eurodollar time deposit futures contract with the same expiration month (Treasury Over Eurodollar).

Tender: To give notice to the clearing organization of the intention to initiate delivery of the physical commodity in satisfaction of a short futures contract. Also see Retender.

Tenderable Grades: See Contract Grades.

Terminal Elevator: An elevator located at a point of greatest accumulation in the movement of agricultural products that stores the commodity or moves it to processors.

Terminal Market: Usually synonymous with commodity exchange or futures market, specifically in the United Kingdom.

TIBOR (Tokyo Interbank Offered Rate): A daily reference rate based on the interest rates at which banks offer to lend unsecured funds to other banks in the Japan wholesale money market (or interbank market). TIBOR is published daily by the Japanese Bankers Association (JBA). See EURIBOR, LIBOR.

Tick: Refers to a minimum change in price up or down. An up-tick means that the last trade was at a higher price than the one preceding it. A down-tick means that the last price was lower than the one preceding it. See Minimum Price Fluctuation.

Time Decay: The tendency of an option to decline in value as the expiration date approaches, especially if the price of the underlying instrument is exhibiting low volatility. See Time Value.

Time-of-Day Order: This is an order that is to be executed at a given minute in the session. For example, "Sell 10 March corn at 12:30 p.m."

Time Spread: The selling of a nearby option and buying of a more deferred option with the same strike price. Also called Horizontal Spread.

Time Value: That portion of an option's premium that exceeds the intrinsic value. The time value of an option reflects the probability that the option will move into-the-money. Therefore, the longer the time remaining until expiration of the option, the greater its time value. Also called Extrinsic Value.

Total Return Swap: A type of credit derivative in which one counterparty receives the total return (interest payments and any capital gains or losses) from a specified reference asset and the other counterparty receives a specified fixed or floating cash flow that is not related to the creditworthiness of the reference asset. Also called **total rate of return swap**, or **TR swap**.

To-Arrive Contract: A transaction providing for subsequent delivery within a stipulated time limit of a specific grade of a commodity.

Trade Option: A commodity option transaction in which the purchaser is reasonably believed by the writer to be engaged in business involving use of that commodity or a related commodity.

Trader: (1) A merchant involved in cash commodities; (2) a professional speculator who trades for his own account and who typically holds exchange trading privileges.

Trading Ahead: See Front Running.

Trading Arcade: A facility, often operated by a clearing member that clears trades for locals, where e-locals who trade for their own account can gather to trade on an electronic trading facility (especially if the exchange is all-electronic and there is no pit or ring).

Trading at Settlement (TAS): An exchange rule which permits the parties to a futures trade during a trading day to agree that the price of the trade will be that day's settlement price (or the settlement price plus or minus a specified differential).

Trading Facility: A person or group of persons that provides a physical or electronic facility or system in which multiple participants have the ability to execute or trade agreements, contracts, or transactions by accepting bids and offers made by other participants in the facility or system. See Many-to-Many.

Trading Floor: A physical trading facility where traders make bids and offers via open outcry or the specialist system.

Transaction: The entry or liquidation of a trade.

Transfer Trades: Entries made upon the books of futures commission merchants for the purpose of: (1) transferring existing trades from one account to another within the same firm where no change in ownership is involved; (2) transferring existing trades from the books of one FCM to the books of another FCM where no change in ownership is involved. Also called Ex-Pit transactions.

Transferable Option (or Contract): A contract that permits a position in the option market to be offset by a transaction on the opposite side of the market in the same contract.

Transfer Notice: A term used on some exchanges to describe a notice of delivery. See Retender.

Treasury Bills (or T-Bills): Short-term zero coupon U.S. government obligations, generally issued with various maturities of up to one year.

Treasury Bonds (or T-Bonds): Long-term (more than ten years) obligations of the U.S. government that pay interest semiannually until they mature, at which time the principal and the final interest payment is paid to the investor.

Treasury Notes: Same as Treasury bonds except that Treasury notes are medium-term (more than one year but not more than ten years).

Trend: The general direction, either upward or downward, in which prices have been moving.

Trendline: In charting, a line drawn across the bottom or top of a price chart indicating the direction or trend of price movement. If up, the trendline is called bullish; if down, it is called bearish.

UV

Unable: All orders not filled by the end of a trading day are deemed "unable" and void, unless they are designated GTC (Good Until Canceled) or open.

Uncovered Option: See Naked Option.

Underlying Commodity: The cash commodity underlying a futures contract. Also, the commodity or futures contract on which a commodity option is based, and which must be accepted or delivered if the option is exercised.

Variable Price Limit: A price limit schedule, determined by an exchange, that permits variations above or below the normally allowable price movement for any one trading day.

Variation Margin: Payment made on a daily or intraday basis by a clearing member to the clearing organization based on adverse price movement in positions carried by the clearing member, calculated separately for customer and proprietary positions.

Vault Receipt: A document indicating ownership of a commodity stored in a bank or other depository and frequently used as a delivery instrument in precious metal futures contracts.

Vega: Coefficient measuring the sensitivity of an option value to a change in volatility.

Vertical Spread: Any of several types of option spread involving the simultaneous purchase and sale of options of the same class and expiration date but different strike prices, including bull vertical spreads, bear vertical spreads, back spreads, and front spreads. See Horizontal Spread and Diagonal Spread.

Visible Supply: Usually refers to supplies of a commodity in licensed warehouses. Often includes floats and all other supplies "in sight" in producing areas. See Invisible Supply.

Volatility: A statistical measurement (the annualized standard deviation of returns) of the rate of price change of a futures contract, security, or other instrument underlying an option. See Historical Volatility, Implied Volatility.

Volatility Quote Trading: Refers to the quoting of bids and offers on option contracts in terms of their implied volatility rather than as prices.

Volatility Spread: A delta-neutral option spread designed to speculate on changes in the volatility of the market rather than the direction of the market.

Volatility Trading: Strategies designed to speculate on changes in the volatility of the market rather than the direction of the market.

Volume: The number of contracts traded during a specified period of time. It is most commonly quoted as the number of contracts traded, but for some physical commodities may be quoted or as the total of physical units, such as bales, or bushels, pounds or dozens or barrels.

WXYZ

Warehouse Receipt: A document certifying possession of a commodity in a licensed warehouse that is recognized for delivery purposes by an exchange.

Warrant: An issuer-based product that gives the buyer the right, but not the obligation, to buy (in the case of a call) or to sell (in the case of a put) a stock or a commodity at a set price during a specified period.

Warrant or Warehouse Receipt for Metals: Certificate of physical deposit, which gives title to physical metal in an exchange-approved warehouse.

Wash Sale: See Wash Trading.

Wash Trading: Entering into, or purporting to enter into, transactions to give the appearance that purchases and sales have been made, without incurring market risk or changing the trader's market position. The Commodity Exchange Act prohibits wash trading. Also called Round Trip Trading, Wash Sales.

Weak Hands: When used in connection with delivery of commodities on futures contracts, the term usually means that the party probably does not intend to retain ownership of the commodity; when used in connection with futures positions, the term usually means positions held by small speculators.

Weather Derivative: A derivative whose payoff is based on a specified weather event, for example, the average temperature in Chicago in January. Such a derivative can be used to hedge risks related to the demand for heating fuel or electricity.

Wild Card Option: Refers to a provision of any physical delivery Treasury bond or Treasury note futures contract that permits shorts to wait until as late as 8:00 p.m. Chicago time on any notice day to announce their intention to deliver at invoice prices that are fixed at 2:00 p.m., the close of futures trading, on that day.

Winter Wheat: Wheat that is planted in the fall, lies dormant during the winter, and is harvested beginning about May of the next year.

Writer: The issuer, grantor, or seller of an option contract.

Yield Curve: A graphic representation of market yield for a fixed income security plotted against the maturity of the security. The yield curve is positive when long-term rates are higher than short-term rates.

Yield to Maturity: The rate of return an investor receives if a fixed income security is held to maturity.

Zero Coupon: Refers to a debt instrument that does not make coupon payments, but, rather, is issued at a discount topar and redeemed at par at maturity.

BASIC TITLES ON THE UNITES STATES

IMPORTANT! All publications are updated annually!
Please contact IBP, Inc. at ibpusa3@gmail.com for the latest ISBNs and additional information

Title	ISBN
United States Banking & Financial Market Handbook	1438751052
United States Business and Investment Opportunities Yearbook Volume 1 Strategic Information and Opportunities	143877821X
United States Business Law Handbook - Strategic Information and Basic Laws	1438771320
United States Business Law Handbook - Strategic Information and Basic Laws	1438771320
United States Chambers of Commerce Directory, Vol.1 Alaska, Arkansas, Arizona	1438751060
United States Clothing & Textile Industry Handbook	1438751079
United States Congress Guide	1438751087
United States Country Study Guide - Strategic Information and Developments Volume 1 Strategic Information and Developments	1438775865
United States Ecology & Nature Protection Handbook	1438751095
United States Energy Policy, Laws and Regulations Handbook	1438751109
United States Healthcare Sector Organization, Management and Payment Systems Handbook - Strategic Information, Programs and Regulations	9781433086045
United States Industrial and Business Directory	1438751117
United States Internet and E-Commerce Investment and Business Guide - Strategic and Practical Information: Regulations and Opportunities	1438751125
United States Investment and Business Guide - Strategic and Practical Information	1438769040
United States Investment and Business Guide - Strategic and Practical Information	1438769040
United States Justice System and National Police Handbook	1438751133
United States Medical & Pharmaceutical Industry Handbook	1438751141
United States Mineral & Mining Sector Investment and Business Guide - Strategic and Practical Information	143875115X
United States Oil & Gas Sector Business & Investment Opportunities Yearbook	1438751168
United States Privatization Programs and Regulations Handbook	1438751176
United States Recent Economic and Political Developments Yearbook	143306233X
United States Research & Development Policy Handbook	1433062909
United States Telecommunication Industry Business Opportunities Handbook	1438751184
United States: How to Invest, Start and Run Profitable Business in United States Guide - Practical Information, Opportunities, Contacts	9781433084843
United States: Importacion a los Estados Unidos	1433068826
United States: Starting Small Business In the US Handbook	1433068834
US - Korea North: Political and Economic Cooperation Handbook	9781577515517
US - Utah Investment & Business Guide	1433057972
US - Utah Small Business Assistance and Programs Handbook	1433057980
US "Green Card" How to Become US Permanent Resident Handbook	1433054035
US "War on Terror" Handbook	1433061465
US "War on Terror" Handbook	1433061465
US "War on Terror" Handbook	1433061465
US "War on Terror" Military Strategy Handbook	1433054043
US & Canada Literary Agents and Publishers	1433054051
US & International Economic Assistance to Palestine Handbook	143875244X
US & International Economic Assistance to Palestine Handbook	143305406X
US A "Spy" Guide - Strategic Information and Developments	1433054078
US A Spy" Guide"	1438752458
US Aerospace and Space Doctrine Handbook	1433068869

Title	ISBN
US Affordable Healthcare Act Handbook - Strategic Information and Implementation	9781433086045
US African Development Fund Handbook	1438752466
US African Development Fund Handbook	1433054086
US AGENCY FOR INTERNATIONAL DEVELOPMENT BUSINESS OPPORTUNITIES HANDBOOK	1438752474
US AGENCY FOR INTERNATIONAL DEVELOPMENT BUSINESS OPPORTUNITIES HANDBOOK	1433054094
US Agency for International Development Handbook	1438752482
US Agency for International Development Handbook	1433054108
US Air Force Academy Handbook	1438752490
US Air Force Academy Handbook	1433054116
US Air Force Air University Handbook	1438752504
US Air Force Air University Handbook	1433054124
US Air Force Base Conversion Agency Handbook	1438752512
US Air Force Base Conversion Agency Handbook	1433054132
US Air Force Handbook	1438752520
US Air force Handbook	1433060558
US Air Force Handbook	1433054140
US Air force Handbook	1433060558
US Air force Handbook	1433060558
US Air Force in Europe Handbook	1438752539
US Air Force in Europe Handbook	1433054159
US Air force or the Future Handbook Volume 1	1433061066
US Air force or the Future Handbook Volume 1	1433061066
US Air Force or the Future Handbook Volume 1	1433061066
US Air force or the Future Handbook Volume 2	1433061074
US Air force or the Future Handbook Volume 2	1433061074
US Air Force or the Future Handbook Volume 2	1433061074
US Air force or the Future Handbook Volume 3	1433061228
US Air force or the Future Handbook Volume 3	1433061228
US Air force or the Future Handbook Volume 3	1433061228
US Air Force or the Future Handbook Volume 4	1433061090
US Air force or the Future Handbook Volume 4	1433061090
US Air force or the Future Handbook Volume 4	1433061090
US Air Force Special Operations School Handbook	1438752547
US Air Force Special Operations School Handbook	1433054167
US Air Transportation Business Law Handbook - Strategic Information and Basic Laws	1438752555
US Air Transportation Business Law Handbook - Strategic Information and Basic Laws	1433054175
US Air Transportation Handbook: Regulations and Business Opportunities	1438752563
US Air Transportation Handbook: Regulations and Business Opportunities	1433054183
US Airport Improvement Program Handbook	1438752571
US Airport Improvement Program Handbook	1433054191
US Airports Handbook: Regulations and Business Opportunities	143875258X
US Airports Handbook: Regulations and Business Opportunities	1433054205
US Airpower and Space Security Doctrine Handbook	1433068877
US Alabama Business Registration and Incorporation Guide	1433000350
US Alabama Investment & Business Guide	1433000369

Title	ISBN
US Alabama Small Business Assistance and Programs Handbook	1433000377
US American Indians Business Opportunities Handbook	1433061856
US American Indians Business Opportunities Handbook	1433061856
US American Indians Business Opportunities Handbook	1433061856
US and Canada Literary Agents and Publishers Handbook	1438752431
US Anti SPAM Laws and Regulations Handbook	1438752598
US Anti SPAM Laws and Regulations Handbook	1433054213
US Anti Terrorism Handbook: Strategy, Operations, Programs	1438752601
US Anti Terrorism Handbook: Strategy, Operations, Programs	1433054221
US Anti-Gambling Laws and Regulations Handbook	9781577515524
US Arms Control and Disarmament Agency Handbook	143875261X
US Arms Control and Disarmament Agency Handbook	143305423X
US Arms Control and International Security Policy Handbook	1438752628
US Arms Control and International Security Policy Handbook	1433054248
US Arms Export Policy and Control Procedures Handbook	1438752636
US Arms Export Policy and Control Procedures Handbook	1438752644
US Arms Export Policy and Control Procedures Handbook	1433054256
US Arms Export Policy and Control Procedures Handbook	1433054264
US Arms Sales to Foreign Countries Handbook	1438752652
US Arms Sales to Foreign Countries Handbook	1433054272
US Army Future Combat Systems Handbook	1433062925
US Army Future Combat Systems Handbook	1433062925
US Army Future Combat Systems Handbook	1433062925
US Army Handbook	1433060701
US Army Handbook	1433060701
US Army Handbook	1433060701
US Army Modernization Plans Handbook	1433062917
US Army Modernization Plans Handbook	1433062917
US Army Modernization Plans Handbook	1433062917
US Army National Guards Handbook	1438752660
US Army National Guards Handbook	1433054280
US Army New Weapon Systems Handbook	1433062046
US Army New Weapon Systems Handbook	1433062046
US Army New Weapon Systems Handbook	1433062046
US Army Security Assistance Command Handbook	1438752679
US Army Security Assistance Command Handbook	1433054299
US Army Security Assistance Training Management Organization Handbook	1438752687
US Army Security Assistance Training Management Organization Handbook	1433054302
US Army Weapon Systems Handbook	1438752695
US Army Weapon Systems Handbook	1433054310
US Assistance to Afghanistan Handbook	1438752709
US Assistance to Afghanistan Handbook	1433054329
US Assistance to Albania Handbook	1438752717
US Assistance to Albania Handbook	1433054337
US Assistance to Angola Handbook	1438752725
US Assistance to Angola Handbook	1433054345
US Assistance to Armenia Handbook	1438752733
US Assistance to Armenia Handbook	1433054353
US Assistance to Azerbaijan Handbook	1438752741

Title	ISBN
US Assistance to Azerbaijan Handbook	1433054361
US Assistance to Bangladesh Handbook	143875275X
US Assistance to Bangladesh Handbook	143305437X
US Assistance to Belarus Handbook	1438752768
US Assistance to Belarus Handbook	1433054388
US Assistance to Benin Handbook	1438752776
US Assistance to Benin Handbook	1433054396
US Assistance to Bolivia Handbook	1438752784
US Assistance to Bolivia Handbook	143305440X
US Assistance to Bosnia-Herzegovina Handbook	1438752792
US Assistance to Bosnia-Herzegovina Handbook	1433054418
US Assistance to Brazil Handbook	1438752806
US Assistance to Brazil Handbook	1433054426
US Assistance to Bulgaria Handbook	1438752814
US Assistance to Bulgaria Handbook	1433054434
US Assistance to Burundi Handbook	1438752822
US Assistance to Burundi Handbook	1433054442
US Assistance to Cambodia Handbook	1438752830
US Assistance to Cambodia Handbook	1433054450
US Assistance to Colombia Handbook	1438752849
US Assistance to Colombia Handbook	1433054469
US Assistance to Croatia Handbook	1438752857
US Assistance to Croatia Handbook	1433054477
US Assistance to Cuba Handbook	1438752865
US Assistance to Cuba Handbook	1433054485
US Assistance to Cyprus Handbook	1438752873
US Assistance to Cyprus Handbook	1433054493
US Assistance to Czech Republic Handbook	1438752881
US Assistance to Czech Republic Handbook	1433054507
US Assistance to Dominican Republic Handbook	143875289X
US Assistance to Dominican Republic Handbook	1433054515
US Assistance to DR Congo Handbook	1438752903
US Assistance to DR Congo Handbook	1433054523
US Assistance to East Timor Handbook	1438752911
US Assistance to East Timor Handbook	1433054531
US Assistance to Ecuador Handbook	143875292X
US Assistance to Ecuador Handbook	143305454X
US Assistance to Egypt Handbook	1438752938
US Assistance to Egypt Handbook	1433054558
US Assistance to El Salvador Handbook	1438752946
US Assistance to El Salvador Handbook	1433054566
US Assistance to Eritrea Handbook	1438752954
US Assistance to Eritrea Handbook	1433054574
US Assistance to Ethiopia Handbook	1438752962
US Assistance to Ethiopia Handbook	1433054582
US Assistance to FYR of Macedonia Handbook	1438752970
US Assistance to FYR of Macedonia Handbook	1433054590
US Assistance to Georgia Handbook	1438752989
US Assistance to Georgia Handbook	1433054604

Title	ISBN
US Assistance to Ghana Handbook	1438752997
US Assistance to Ghana Handbook	1433054612
US Assistance to Guatemala Handbook	1438753004
US Assistance to Guatemala Handbook	1433054620
US Assistance to Guinea Handbook	1438753012
US Assistance to Guinea Handbook	1433054639
US Assistance to Guyana Handbook	1438753020
US Assistance to Guyana Handbook	1433054647
US Assistance to Haiti Handbook	1438753039
US Assistance to Haiti Handbook	1433054655
US Assistance to Honduras Handbook	1438753047
US Assistance to Honduras Handbook	1433054663
US Assistance to India Handbook	1438753055
US Assistance to India Handbook	1433054671
US Assistance to Indonesia Handbook	1438753063
US Assistance to Indonesia Handbook	1438753071
US Assistance to Indonesia Handbook	1433054698
US Assistance to Indonesia Handbook	143305468X
US Assistance to Ireland/Northern Ireland (UK) Handbook	143875308X
US Assistance to Ireland/Northern Ireland (UK) Handbook	1433054701
US Assistance to Jamaica Handbook	1438753098
US Assistance to Jamaica Handbook	143305471X
US Assistance to Jordan Handbook	1438753101
US Assistance to Jordan Handbook	1433054728
US Assistance to Kazakhstan Handbook	143875311X
US Assistance to Kazakhstan Handbook	1433054736
US Assistance to Kenya Handbook	1438753128
US Assistance to Kenya Handbook	1433054744
US Assistance to Kosovo Handbook	1438753136
US Assistance to Kosovo Handbook	1433054752
US Assistance to Kyrgyzstan Handbook	1438753144
US Assistance to Kyrgyzstan Handbook	1433054760
US Assistance to Laos Handbook	1438753152
US Assistance to Laos Handbook	1433054779
US Assistance to Lebanon Handbook	1438753160
US Assistance to Lebanon Handbook	1433054787
US Assistance to Liberia Handbook	1438753179
US Assistance to Liberia Handbook	1433054795
US Assistance to Lithuania Handbook	1438753187
US Assistance to Lithuania Handbook	1433054809
US Assistance to Madagascar Handbook	1438753195
US Assistance to Madagascar Handbook	1433054817
US Assistance to Malawi Handbook	1438753209
US Assistance to Malawi Handbook	1433054825
US Assistance to Mali Handbook	1438753217
US Assistance to Mali Handbook	1433054833
US Assistance to Mexico Handbook	1438753225
US Assistance to Mexico Handbook	1433054841
US Assistance to Moldova Handbook	1438753233

Title	ISBN
US Assistance to Moldova Handbook	143305485X
US Assistance to Mongolia Handbook	1433054868
US Assistance to Morocco Handbook	1438753241
US Assistance to Morocco Handbook	143875325X
US Assistance to Morocco Handbook	1433054876
US Assistance to Morocco Handbook	1433054884
US Assistance to Mozambique Handbook	1438753268
US Assistance to Mozambique Handbook	1433054892
US Assistance to Myanmar Handbook	1438753276
US Assistance to Myanmar Handbook	1433054906
US Assistance to Namibia Handbook	1438753284
US Assistance to Namibia Handbook	1433054914
US Assistance to Nepal & Pakistan Handbook	1438753292
US Assistance to Nepal & Pakistan Handbook	1433054922
US Assistance to Nicaragua Handbook	1438753306
US Assistance to Nicaragua Handbook	1433054930
US Assistance to Nigeria Handbook	1438753314
US Assistance to Nigeria Handbook	1433054949
US Assistance to Panama Handbook	1438753322
US Assistance to Panama Handbook	1433054957
US Assistance to Paraguay Handbook	1438753330
US Assistance to Paraguay Handbook	1433054965
US Assistance to Peru Handbook	1438753349
US Assistance to Peru Handbook	1433054973
US Assistance to Philippines Handbook	1438753357
US Assistance to Philippines Handbook	1433054981
US Assistance to Poland Handbook	1438753365
US Assistance to Poland Handbook	143305499X
US Assistance to Romania Handbook	1438753373
US Assistance to Romania Handbook	1433055007
US Assistance to Russia Handbook	1438753381
US Assistance to Russia Handbook	1433055015
US Assistance to Rwanda Handbook	143875339X
US Assistance to Rwanda Handbook	1433055023
US Assistance to Senegal Handbook	1438753403
US Assistance to Senegal Handbook	1433055031
US Assistance to Serbia and Montenegro Handbook	1438753411
US Assistance to Serbia and Montenegro Handbook	143305504X
US Assistance to Sierra Leone Handbook	143875342X
US Assistance to Sierra Leone Handbook	1433055058
US Assistance to Slovak Republic Handbook	1438753438
US Assistance to Slovak Republic Handbook	1433055066
US Assistance to Somalia Handbook	1438753446
US Assistance to Somalia Handbook	1433055074
US Assistance to South Africa Handbook	1438753454
US Assistance to South Africa Handbook	1433055082
US Assistance to Sri Lanka Handbook	1438753462
US Assistance to Sri Lanka Handbook	1433055090
US Assistance to Sudan Handbook	1438753470

Title	ISBN
US Assistance to Sudan Handbook	1433055104
US Assistance to Tajikistan Handbook	1438753489
US Assistance to Tajikistan Handbook	1433055112
US Assistance to Tanzania Handbook	1438753497
US Assistance to Tanzania Handbook	1433055120
US Assistance to Turkey Handbook	1438753500
US Assistance to Turkey Handbook	1433055139
US Assistance to Turkmenistan Handbook	1438753519
US Assistance to Turkmenistan Handbook	1433055147
US Assistance to Uganda Handbook	1438753527
US Assistance to Uganda Handbook	1433055155
US Assistance to Ukraine Handbook	1438753535
US Assistance to Ukraine Handbook	1433055163
US Assistance to Uzbekistan Handbook	1438753543
US Assistance to Uzbekistan Handbook	1433055171
US Assistance to Vietnam Handbook	1438753551
US Assistance to Vietnam Handbook	143305518X
US Assistance to West Bank/ Gaza Handbook	143875356X
US Assistance to West Bank/ Gaza Handbook	1433055198
US Assistance to Yemen Handbook	1438753578
US Assistance to Yemen Handbook	1438753586
US Assistance to Yemen Handbook	1433055201
US Assistance to Yemen Handbook	143305521X
US Assistance to Zambia Handbook	1438753594
US Assistance to Zambia Handbook	1433055228
US Assistance to Zimbabwe Handbook	1438753608
US Assistance to Zimbabwe Handbook	1433055236
US Aviation and Aerospace Industry Handbook Vol 2 Military Equipment	1433053616
US Aviation and Aerospace Industry Handbook Volume 1 BASIC TRENDS AND REGULATIONS	1438753616
US Aviation and Aerospace Industry Handbook Volume 1 BASIC TRENDS AND REGULATIONS	1433055244
US Aviation Industry Strategic Developments and Statistics Yearbook	1433068885
US Banking & Financial Market Handbook	1433052458
US Bankruptcy Regulations and procedures Handbook	1438753624
US Bankruptcy Regulations and procedures Handbook	1433055252
US Banks Handbook	1438753632
US Banks Handbook	1433055260
US Book Distributors Directory vol2	1438753640
US Book Distributors Directory vol2	1433055279
US Brazil Diplomatic and Political Cooperation Handbook	1438751516
US Budgeting Process Handbook	1433068893
US Business and Investment Opportunities Yearbook	1438753659
US Business and Investment Opportunities Yearbook	1433055287
US Business for Sale and Franchises Opportunities Handbook: Information by State	1433068907
US Business Intelligence Handbook	1438753667
US Business Intelligence Handbook	1433055295
US Business Intelligence Report - Practical Information, Opportunities, Contacts	1438753675
US Business Intelligence Report - Practical Information, Opportunities, Contacts	1433055309

Title	ISBN
US Business Law Handbook - Strategic Information and Basic Laws	1438753683
US Business Law Handbook - Strategic Information and Basic Laws	1433055317
US Buying and Financing Residential Real Estate in the US Handbook	1433004925
US Buying or Selling a Business in the US Handbook	1433004941
US California Business Registration and Incorporation Guide	1433004976
US California Government Handbook - Practical Information and Contacts	1433002353
US California Investment & Business Guide	1433004984
US California Small Business Assistance and Programs Handbook	1433004992
US Catalog of Federal Domestic Assistance Handbook	9781577515531
US CENTRAL INTELLIGENCE AGENCY (CIA) HANDBOOK	1438753691
US CENTRAL INTELLIGENCE AGENCY (CIA) HANDBOOK	1433055325
US Chambers of Commerce Directory, Vol.1 Alaska, Arkansas, Arizona	1433052466
US Chambers of Commerce Directory, Vol.3 Florida	1438753705
US Chambers of Commerce Directory, Vol.3 Florida	1433055333
US Chemical and Biological Weapon Strategy Handbook	1433060493
US Chemical and Biological Weapon Strategy Handbook	1433060493
US Chemical and Biological Weapon Strategy Handbook	1433060493
US Citizenship, Naturalization Regulation and Procedures Handbook: Practical Information and Contacts	9781577515548
US Civil Rights Policy Handbook	1438753713
US Civil Rights Policy Handbook	1433055341
US Clothing & Textile Industry Handbook	1433052474
US Coastal Guards Handbook	1438753721
US Coastal Guards Handbook	143305535X
US Commercial insurance Modernization Handbook	1433062933
US Commercial insurance Modernization Handbook	1433062933
US Commercial insurance Modernization Handbook	1433062933
US Commodity Futures Trading Commission Handbook	143875373X
US Commodity Futures Trading Commission Handbook	1433055368
US Companies in Russia Directory	1438753748
US Companies in Russia Directory	1433055376
US Company Laws and Regulations Handbook Volume 1 Corporate Laws and Regulations Basics	1433070804
US Company Laws and Regulations Handbook Volume 2 Non Profits	1433070820
US Congress Guide	1438753756
US Congress Guide	1433055384
US Congress Guide	1433052482
US Congress Joint Committee on Printing Handbook	1433056526
US Congress Joint Committee on Taxation Handbook	1433056534
US Congress Joint Economic Committee Handbook	1433056542
US Congressional Budget Office Handbook	1438753764
US Congressional Budget Office Handbook	1433055392
US Counterintelligence Handbook	1438753772
US Counterintelligence Handbook	1433055406
US Counterintelligence Operations against Cuba Handbook	1438753780
US Counterintelligence Operations against Cuba Handbook	1433055414
US Country Study Guide - Strategic Information and Developments	1438753799
US Country Study Guide - Strategic Information and Developments	1433055422
US Customs Broker Handbook: Regulations, Procedures, Opportunities	1433068915

Title	ISBN
US Customs Brokers Directory	1433068923
US Customs Regulations Handbook	1438753802
US Customs Regulations Handbook	1433055430
US Customs, Trade Regulations and Procedures Handbook	1438753810
US Customs, Trade Regulations and Procedures Handbook	1433055449
US Defense Advanced Research Projects Agency Handbook	1438753829
US Defense Advanced Research Projects Agency Handbook	1433055457
US Defense Agencies and Organizations Handbook	1438753837
US Defense Agencies and Organizations Handbook	1433055465
US Defense and Intelligence Abbreviations and Acronyms Handbook	1438753845
US Defense and Intelligence Abbreviations and Acronyms Handbook	1433055473
US Defense and Military Strategy Handbook	1433060973
US Defense and Military Strategy Handbook	1433060973
US Defense and Military Strategy Handbook	1433060973
US Defense Information Systems Agency Handbook	1438753853
US Defense Information Systems Agency Handbook	1433055481
US Defense Intelligence Agency Business Guide	1438753861
US Defense Intelligence Agency Business Guide	143305549X
US Defense Intelligence Agency Handbook	143875387X
US Defense Intelligence Agency Handbook	1433055503
US Defense Policy Handbook	1438753888
US Defense Policy Handbook	1433055511
US Defense Security Service Handbook	1438753896
US Defense Security Service Handbook	143305552X
US Defense Threat Reduction Agency Handbook	143875390X
US Defense Threat Reduction Agency Handbook	1433055538
US Department of Agriculture Business Opportunities Handbook	1438753918
US Department of Agriculture Business Opportunities Handbook	1433055546
US Department of Agriculture Handbook	1433055554
US Department of Commerce Handbook	1438753926
US Department of Commerce Handbook	1433055562
US Department of Defense Handbook	1438753934
US Department of Defense Handbook	1433055570
US Department of Energy Business Opportunities Handbook	1438753942
US Department of Energy Business Opportunities Handbook	1433055589
US Department of Energy Handbook	1438753950
US Department of Energy Handbook	1433055597
US Department of Health and Human Services Handbook	1438753969
US Department of Health and Human Services Handbook	1433055600
US Department of Homeland Security Handbook	1438753977
US Department of Homeland Security Handbook	1433055619
US Department of Housing and Urban Services Handbook	1438753985
US Department of Housing and Urban Services Handbook	1433055627
US Department of Interior Handbook	1438753993
US Department of Interior Handbook	1433055635
US Department of Justice Handbook	1438754000
US Department of Justice Handbook	1433055643
US Department of Labor Handbook	1438754019
US Department of Labor Handbook	1433055651

Title	ISBN
US Department of State Handbook	1438754027
US Department of State Handbook	143305566X
US Department of the Air Force Handbook	1438754035
US Department of the Air Force Handbook	1433055678
US Department of the Army Handbook	1438754043
US Department of the Army Handbook	1433055686
US Department of the Navy Handbook	1438754051
US Department of the Navy Handbook	1433055694
US Department of the Treasury Handbook	143875406X
US Department of the Treasury Handbook	1433055708
US Department of Transport Handbook	1438754078
US Department of Transport Handbook	1433055716
US Department of Veteran Affairs Handbook	1438754086
US Department of Veteran Affairs Handbook	1433055724
US Diplomatic Handbook - Strategic Information and Developments	1438754094
US Diplomatic Handbook - Strategic Information and Developments	1433055732
US Drug and Medical Devices Export-Import Regulations Handbook	1438754108
US Drug and Medical Devices Export-Import Regulations Handbook	1433055740
US Ecology & Nature Protection Handbook	1433052490
US Ecology & Nature Protection Laws and Regulation Handbook	1433075210
US E-Commerce Business Guide	1438754116
US E-Commerce Business Guide	1433055759
US E-Commerce Business Law Handbook - Strategic Information and Basic Laws	1438754124
US E-Commerce Business Law Handbook - Strategic Information and Basic Laws	1433055767
US Economic and Political Assistance to Macedonia Handbook	1438754132
US Economic and Political Assistance to Macedonia Handbook	1433055775
US ECONOMIC ASSISTANCE TO RUSSIA Handbook	1438754140
US Economic Assistance to Russia Handbook	1433055783
US Education System and Policy Handbook	1433068796
US El Salvador Diplomatic and Political Cooperation Handbook	1438751648
US Emission Trading Laws, Regulations and Programs Handbook	9781577515555
US Energy Policy, Laws and Regulation Handbook	1433072971
US Energy Policy, Laws and Regulations Handbook	1433052504
US Environmental Protection Agency Handbook	1438754159
US Environmental Protection Agency Handbook	1433055791
US Export Guide: How to Export Products and Services from the United States	1438754167
US Export Guide: How to Export Products and Services from the United States	1433055805
US Export Programs Guide	1438754175
US Export Programs Guide	1433055813
US Export-Import Bank Handbook	1438754183
US Export-Import Bank Handbook	1433055821
US Export-Import Trade and Business Directory	143305583X
US Export-Import, Investment & Financial Assistance Handbook	1438754191
US Export-Import, Investment & Financial Assistance Handbook	1433055848
US Farmers Markets Directory	1433062038
US Farmers Markets Directory	1433062038
US Farmers Markets Directory	1433062038
US Farmers Markets Directory – Volume 2 Ohio-Wyoming	1433068931
US FDA Cosmetics Products Control and Regulations Handbook	1438754205

Title	ISBN
US FDA Cosmetics Products Control and Regulations Handbook	1433055856
US FDA Drug Products Control and Regulations Handbook	1438754213
US FDA Drug Products Control and Regulations Handbook	1433055864
US FDA Food Products Control and Regulations Handbook	1438754221
US FDA Food Products Control and Regulations Handbook	1433055872
US FDA Medical Devices Control and Regulations Handbook	143875423X
US FDA Medical Devices Control and Regulations Handbook	1433055880
US Federal Bureau of Investigation (FBI) Academy Handbook	1433055899
US Federal Bureau of Investigation (FBI) Business Opportunities Handbook	1438754248
US Federal Bureau of Investigation (FBI) Business Opportunities Handbook	1433055902
US Federal Bureau of Investigation (FBI) Handbook	1438754256
US Federal Bureau of Investigation (FBI) Handbook	1433055910
US Federal Business Opportunities Handbook	1438754264
US Federal Business Opportunities Handbook	1433055929
US Federal Communication Commission Handbook	1438754272
US Federal Communication Commission Handbook	1433055937
US Federal Depository Libraries Directory	1438754280
US Federal Depository Libraries Directory	1433055945
US Federal Election Commission Handbook	1438754299
US Federal Election Commission Handbook	1433055953
US Federal Energy Sector Regulations Handbook	1438754302
US Federal Energy Sector Regulations Handbook	1433055961
US Federal Executive Government Handbook	1438754310
US Federal Executive Government Handbook	143305597X
US Federal Government Directory	1438754329
US Federal Government Directory	1433055988
US Federal Grant Management Handbook	1438754337
US Federal Grant Management Handbook	1433055996
US Federal Law Enforcement Training Center Handbook	1438754345
US Federal Law Enforcement Training Center Handbook	1433056003
US Federal Maritime Commission Handbook	1438754353
US Federal Maritime Commission Handbook	1433056011
US Federal Maritime Commission Handbooks	1438754361
US Federal Maritime Commission Handbooks	143305602X
US Federal Mine Safety and Health Commission Handbook	143875437X
US Federal Mine Safety and Health Commission Handbook	1433056038
US Federal Reserve System Handbook	1438754388
US Federal Reserve System Handbook	1433056046
US Federal Trade Commission Handbook	1438754396
US Federal Trade Commission Handbook	1433056054
US Financial Crimes Enforcement Regulations Handbook	1433060450
US Financial Crimes Enforcement Regulations Handbook	1433060450
US Financial Crimes Enforcement Regulations Handbook	1433060450
US Financial Crimes Prevention Handbook for Everybody	1433060590
US Financial Crimes Prevention Handbook for Everybody	1433060590
US Financial Crimes Prevention Handbook for Everybody	1433060590
US Fire-Safe Hotels Directory: Fire-Safe Hotels by States	9781577515562
US Food and Drug Administration Handbook	143875440X
US Food and Drug Administration Handbook	1433056062

Title	ISBN
US Food Assistance to Russia Handbook	1438754418
US Food Assistance to Russia Handbook	1433056070
US Foreign Embassies, Representations and Consulate Offices in the US Handbook	143306894X
US Foreign Policy & Government Guide	1438754426
US Foreign Policy & Government Guide	1433056089
US Foreign Trade Sanctions Handbook	1438754434
US Foreign Trade Sanctions Handbook	1433056097
US Foreign Trade Zones Handbook	1438754442
US Foreign Trade Zones Handbook	1433056100
US Free Trade Agreements with Foreign Countries Handbook	1433068958
US Free Trade and Investment Agreements and Associations Handbook	1438754450
US Free Trade and Investment Agreements and Associations Handbook	1433056119
US Free Trade and Investment Agreements and Associations with Foreign Countries Handbook	1438754469
US Free Trade and Investment Agreements and Associations with Foreign Countries Handbook	1433056127
US Future Combat & Weapon Systems Handbook	1438754477
US Future Combat & Weapon Systems Handbook	1433056135
US Gabling Industry Investment and Business Guide - Strategic and Practical Information	1438754485
US Gabling Industry Investment and Business Guide - Strategic and Practical Information	1433056143
US Gaming Industry Investment and Business Guide - Strategic and Practical Information	1438754493
US Gaming Industry Investment and Business Guide - Strategic and Practical Information	1433056151
US Gaming Industry Investment and Business Guide - Strategic and Practical Information	1433056178
US Gaming Industry Investment and Business Guide - Strategic and Practical Information Volume 1	1438754515
US Gaming Industry Law and Regulations Handbook	1438754507
US Gaming Industry Law and Regulations Handbook	143305616X
US Gaming Industry Laws and Regulations Handbook	1438754523
US Gaming Industry Laws and Regulations Handbook	1433056186
US General Service Administration Handbook	1438754531
US General Service Administration Handbook	1433056194
US George W. Bush President of the US (Leadership Vision Reforms)	1433016974
US Gourmet Food Distributors Directory vol 1	1433056208
US Gourmet Food Distributors Directory vol 2	1433056216
US Gourmet Food Distributors Directory vol 3	1433056224
US Gourmet Food Distributors Directory vol 4	1433056232
US Gourmet Food Distributors Directory vol 5	1433056240
US Gourmet Food Distributors Directory vol 6	1433056259
US Gourmet Food Distributors Directory Volume 1	143875454X
US Gourmet Food Distributors Directory Volume 2	1438754558
US Gourmet Food Distributors Directory Volume 3	1438754566
US Gourmet Food Distributors Directory Volume 4	1438754574
US Gourmet Food Distributors Directory Volume 5	1438754582
US Gourmet Food Distributors Directory Volume 6	1438754590
US Government and Business Contacts Handbook	1438754604

Title	ISBN
US Government and Business Contacts Handbook	1433056267
US Government and Special Subsidized Housing Buying Programs Handbook	1438754612
US Government and Special Subsidized Housing Buying Programs Handbook	1433056275
US GOVERNORS FEDERAL LEGISLATIVE AGENDA HANDBOOK	1438754620
US GOVERNORS FEDERAL LEGISLATIVE AGENDA HANDBOOK	1433056283
US GOVERNORS GUIDE	1438754639
US GOVERNORS GUIDE	1433056291
US GOVERNORS STATE-TO-THE STATE ANNUAL ADDRESSES AND BUDGET PRESENTATIONS YEARBOOK	1438754647
US GOVERNORS STATE-TO-THE STATE ANNUAL ADDRESSES AND BUDGET PRESENTATIONS YEARBOOK	1433056305
US Green Card" How to Become US Permanent Resident Handbook"	1438752415
US Hedge Finds Handbook	1438754655
US Hedge Finds Handbook	1433056313
US House Committee on Agriculture Handbook	1438754663
US House Committee on Agriculture Handbook	1433056321
US House Committee on Appropriations Handbook	1438754671
US House Committee on Appropriations Handbook	143305633X
US House Committee on Armed Services Handbook	143875468X
US House Committee on Armed Services Handbook	1433056348
US House Committee on Education and the Workforce Handbook	1438754698
US House Committee on Education and the Workforce Handbook	1433056356
US House Committee on Energy and Commerce Handbook	1438754701
US House Committee on Energy and Commerce Handbook	1433056364
US House Committee on Financial Services Handbook	143875471X
US House Committee on Financial Services Handbook	1433056372
US House Committee on Government Reform Handbook	1438754728
US House Committee on Government Reform Handbook	1433056380
US House Committee on House Administration Handbook	1438754736
US House Committee on House Administration Handbook	1433056399
US House Committee on International Relations Handbook	1438754744
US House Committee on International Relations Handbook	1433056402
US House Committee on Resources Handbook	1438754752
US House Committee on Resources Handbook	1433056410
US House Committee on Rules Handbook	1438754760
US House Committee on Rules Handbook	1433056429
US House Committee on Science Handbook	1438754779
US House Committee on Science Handbook	1433056437
US House Committee on Small Business Handbook	1438754787
US House Committee on Small Business Handbook	1433056445
US House Committee on Standards of Official Conduct Handbook	1438754795
US House Committee on Standards of Official Conduct Handbook	1433056453
US House Committee on Taxation Handbook	1438754809
US House Committee on Taxation Handbook	1433056461
US House Committee on the Budget Handbook	1438754817
US House Committee on the Budget Handbook	143305647X
US House Committee on the Judiciary Handbook	1438754825
US House Committee on the Judiciary Handbook	1433056488
US House Committee on Transportation and Infrastructure Handbook	1438754833

Title	ISBN
US House Committee on Transportation and Infrastructure Handbook	1433056496
US House Committee on Veterans Affairs Handbook	1438754841
US House Committee on Veterans Affairs Handbook	143305650X
US House Committee on Ways and Means Handbook	143875485X
US House Committee on Ways and Means Handbook	1433056518
US House Joint Committee on Printing Handbook	1438754868
US House Joint Committee on Taxation Handbook	1438754876
US House Joint Economic Committee Handbook	1438754884
US House of Representatives Ethics Manual	1433068966
US House Permanent Select Committee on Intelligence Handbook	1438754892
US House Permanent Select Committee on Intelligence Handbook	1433056550
US Idaho Business Registration and Incorporation Guide	1433022672
US Idaho Investment & Business Guide	1433022680
US Idaho Small Business Assistance and Programs Handbook	1433022699
US Illinois Business Registration and Incorporation Guide	1433022702
US Illinois Investment & Business Guide	1433022710
US Illinois Small Business Assistance and Programs Handbook	1433022729
US Immigration Policy and Programs Handbook Vol. 1 Basic Information and Legislation	1438754906
US Immigration Policy and Programs Handbook Vol. 1 Basic Information and Legislation	1433056569
US Immigration Policy and Programs Handbook Vol. 2 Procedures, Regulations, Application Forms	1433056577
US Immigration Policy Handbook	1438754914
US Immigration Policy Handbook; Strategic and Practical Information	1433056585
US Importing Products into the US Market Guide	1433022737
US Income Tax Treaties with Foreign Countries Handbook	1438754922
US Income Tax Treaties with Foreign Countries Handbook	1433056593
US Income Tax Treaties with Foreign Countries Handbook. Vol 2	1433056607
US Income Tax Treaties with Foreign Countries Handbook. Vol 3	1433056615
US Income Tax Treaties with Foreign Countries Handbook. Vol 4	1433056623
US Income Tax Treaties with Foreign Countries Handbook. Vol 5	1433056631
US Income Tax Treaties with Foreign Countries Handbook. Volume 2	1438754930
US Income Tax Treaties with Foreign Countries Handbook. Volume 3	1438754949
US Income Tax Treaties with Foreign Countries Handbook. Volume 4	1438754957
US Income Tax Treaties with Foreign Countries Handbook. Volume 5	1438754965
US Indian Gaming Laws and Regulations Handbook	1433061457
US Indian Gaming Laws and Regulations Handbook	1433061457
US Indian Gaming Laws and Regulations Handbook	1433061457
US Indian Reservations Casino Gaming Industry Investment and Business Guide - Strategic and Practical Information	1433056658
US Indian Reservations Casino Gaming Investment and Business Guide - Strategic and Practical Information	1438754973
US Indian Reservations Casino Gaming Investment and Business Guide - Strategic and Practical Information	143305664X
US Indian Tribal Leaders Directory	1433061449
US Indian Tribal Leaders Directory	1433061449
US Indiana Business Registration and Incorporation Guide	1433023229
US Indiana Investment & Business Guide	1433023237
US Indiana Small Business Assistance and Programs Handbook	1433023245

Title	ISBN
US Industrial and Business Directory	1433052512
US Industrial and Business Directory	1433056666
US Information Agency Handbook	1438754981
US Information Agency Handbook	1433056674
US Initial Public Offering Regulations Handbook	143875499X
US Initial Public Offering Regulations Handbook	1433056682
US Intelligence and Counterintelligence History Handbook Vol.1 American Revolution, Civil War, World War 1, Between the Wars	1433061384
US Intelligence and Counterintelligence History Handbook Vol.1 American Revolution, Civil War, World War 1, Between the Wars	1433061384
US Intelligence and Counterintelligence History Handbook Vol.2 World War 2	1433061392
US Intelligence and Counterintelligence History Handbook Vol.2 World War 2	1433061392
US Intelligence and Counterintelligence History Handbook Vol.3 Cold War Counterintelligence, 1960s,70s,80s, end of 20th Century	1433061406
US Intelligence and Counterintelligence History Handbook Vol.4 Military and Nuclear Technology, Russian Spies in the US, Defense Industry	1433061414
US Intelligence and Counterintelligence History Handbook Vol.4 Military and Nuclear Technology, Russian Spies in the US, Defense Industry	1433061414
US Intelligence and Counterintelligence Laws and Regulations Handbook	1433061430
US Intelligence and Counterintelligence Laws and Regulations Handbook	1433061430
US Intelligence and Counterintelligence Laws and Regulations Handbook	1433061430
US Intelligence Community Handbook	1438755007
US Intelligence Community Handbook	1433056690
US Intelligence Community Legal Reference Book	9781577515579
US Intelligence Community Legal Reference Handbook	9781577515586
US Intelligence Policy Handbook	1438755015
US Intelligence Policy Handbook	1433056704
US Internal Revenue Service Handbook	1438755023
US Internal Revenue Service Handbook	1433056712
US International Telephone Traffic Report	1433068974
US Internet and E-Commerce Investment and Business Guide - Strategic and Practical Information: Regulations and Opportunities	1438755031
US Internet and E-Commerce Investment and Business Guide - Strategic and Practical Information: Regulations and Opportunities	1433056720
US Internet and E-Commerce Investment and Business Guide - Strategic and Practical Information: Regulations and Opportunities	1433052520
US Investment and Business Guide - Strategic and Practical Information	143875504X
US Investment and Business Guide - Strategic and Practical Information	1433056739
US Investment and Trade Laws and Regulations Handbook	1433076837
US Investment and Trade Laws and Regulations Handbook	1433076810
US Investors' Fraud Prevention Handbook	1438755058
US Investors' Fraud Prevention Handbook	1433056747
US Iowa Business Registration and Incorporation Guide	1433023989
US Iowa Investment & Business Guide	1433023997
US Iowa Small Business Assistance and Programs Handbook	1433024004
US Iraq Strategy Handbook: new developments	1433060469
US Iraq Strategy Handbook: new developments	1433060469
US Iraq Strategy Handbook: new developments	1433060469
US Justice System and National Police Handbook	1433052539
US Largest Commercial Banks Handbook (Banks with 300+ Mill Dol. Assets)	1438755066

Title	ISBN
US Largest Commercial Banks Handbook (Banks with 300+ Mill Dol. Assets)	1433056755
US Laws for Regulation of Therapeutic Goods in the United States Handbook	9781577515593
US Legislative Process Handbook Vol. 1 House of Representatives	1433068982
US Legislative Process Handbook Vol. 2 Senate	1433068990
US Libraries and Information Science National Commission Handbook	1438755074
US Libraries and Information Science National Commission Handbook	1433056763
US Marine Corp Handbook	1433061058
US Marine Corp Handbook	1433061058
US Marine Corp Handbook	1433061058
US Marketing and Advertising Regulations Handbook	1438755082
US Marketing and Advertising Regulations Handbook Volume 1 Ecommerce and Internet Marketing Regulations	1433056771
US Medical & Pharmaceutical Industry Handbook	1433052547
US Medical Drugs Development and Approval Process Handbook	9781577515609
US Michigan Life Sciences Business Opportunities and Programs Handbook	1433069008
US Military Base Structure and Location Handbook	1433060507
US Military Base Structure and Location Handbook	1433060507
US Military Base Structure and Location Handbook	1433060507
US Military Cooperation with African Countries Handbook	1438755090
US Military Cooperation with African Countries Handbook	143305678X
US Military Cooperation with Asian Countries Handbook	1438755104
US Military Cooperation with Asian Countries Handbook	1433056798
US Military Cooperation with China Handbook	1438755112
US Military Cooperation with China Handbook	1433056801
US Military Cooperation with Eastern European Countries Handbook	1438755120
US Military Cooperation with Eastern European Countries Handbook	143305681X
US Military Cooperation with Russia Handbook	1438755139
US Military Cooperation with Russia Handbook	1433056828
US Military Forces Recruitment Handbook	143306104X
US Military Forces Recruitment Handbook	143306104X
US Military Forces Recruitment Handbook	143306104X
US Military Intelligence Handbook	1438755147
US Military Intelligence Handbook	1433056836
US Military Intelligence Interrogation Techniques Handbook	1438755155
US Military Intelligence Interrogation Techniques Handbook	1433056844
US Military Policy Toward Iraq Handbook	1438755163
US Military Policy Toward Iraq Handbook	1433056852
US Mineral & Mining Sector Investment and Business Guide - Strategic and Practical Information	1433052555
US Mining Industry Technology, Equipment and Financial Services Directory	1438755171
US Mining Industry Technology, Equipment and Financial Services Directory	1433056860
US Mining Laws and Regulations Handbook	1433078430
US Missile Defense Agency Handbook	143875518X
US Missile Defense Agency Handbook	1433056879
US Missile Defense Glossary Handbook	9781577515616
US Mobile Telecom & Data Companies Directory	1438755198
US Mobile Telecom & Data Companies Directory	1433056887
US Mortgage and Financial Companies Directory	1433056895
US Mortgage Market Handbook	1438755201

Title	ISBN
US Mortgage Market Handbook	1433056909
US Mortgage System Handbook Vol.1 : How to Obtain Mortgages for Foreigners	1433062941
US Mortgage System Handbook Vol.1 : How to Obtain Mortgages for Foreigners	1433062941
US Mortgage System Handbook Vol.1 : How to Obtain Mortgages for Foreigners	1433062941
US Mortgage System Handbook Vol.2 : How to Obtain Mortgages in the US	143306295X
US Mortgage System Handbook Vol.2 : How to Obtain Mortgages in the US	143306295X
US Mortgage System Handbook Vol.2 : How to Obtain Mortgages in the US	143306295X
US National Academy of Science and Research Policy Handbook	143875521X
US National Academy of Science and Research Policy Handbook	1433056917
US National Academy of Science Handbook	1438755228
US National Academy of Science Handbook	1433056925
US National Aeronautics and Space Administration Handbook	1438755236
US National Aeronautics and Space Administration Handbook	1433056933
US National Border Protection Strategy Handbook	1433069016
US National Counter Terrorism Center Handbook	1433061376
US National Counter Terrorism Strategy Handbook	1433061236
US National Counterterrorism Center Handbook	1433061376
US National Counterterrorism Center Handbook	1433061376
US National Counterterrorism Strategy Handbook	1433061236
US National Counterterrorism Strategy Handbook	1433061236
US National Cyber Security Strategy and Programs Handbook - Strategic Information and Developments	9781577515623
US National Drug Control Policy Handbook	1438755244
US National Drug Control Policy Handbook	1433056941
US National Educational & Social Development Policy Handbook	1433035391
US National Educational and Social Development Policy Handbook Volume 2 Social Policy	9781577515630
US National Emergency Response and Rescue Training Programs Handbook	1438755252
US National Emergency Response and Rescue Training Programs Handbook	143305695X
US National Export Strategy and Regulations Yearbook	1433069024
US National Fire Fighting Training Handbook - Strategic Information and Contacts	1438755260
US National System of Fire Fighting Handbook - Strategic Information and Contacts	1433056968
US National Governors Association Handbook	1438755279
US National Governors Association Handbook - Organization, Strategy, Contacts	1433056976
US National Guard and Reserve Management Policy Handbook	1433060477
US National Guard and Reserve Management Policy Handbook	1433060477
US National Guard and Reserve Management Policy Handbook	1433060477
US National Guard Handbook	1433061031
US National Guard Handbook	1433061031
US National Guard Handbook	1433061031
US National Homeland Security Strategy Handbook	1433060523
US National Homeland Security Strategy Handbook	1433060523
US National Homeland Security Strategy Handbook	1433060523
US National Import Strategy and Regulations Yearbook	1433069032
US National Import Strategy Handbook	1433069040
US National Institute of Health Handbook	1438755287
US National Institute of Health Handbook	1433056984
US National Plan of Integrated Airport Systems Handbook	1438755295
US National Plan of Integrated Airport Systems Handbook	1433056992

Title	ISBN
US National Science Foundation Handbook	1438755309
US National Science Foundation Handbook	143305700X
US National Security Handbook	1438755317
US National Security Handbook	1433057018
US National Security Policy Handbook	1438755325
US National Security Policy Handbook	1433057026
US National Security Strategy Handbook	1433060531
US National Strategy on Combating Terrorism Handbook	1433060515
US Naval Intelligence Handbook	1438755333
US Naval Intelligence Handbook	1433057034
US Naval Postgraduate School Handbook	1438755341
US Naval Postgraduate School Handbook	1433057042
US Navy Defense Industry Handbook	143875535X
US Navy Defense Industry Handbook	1433057050
US Navy Enlisting Handbook Vol 1 Navy Enlisted Occupational Standards	1433069059
US Navy Enlisting Handbook Vol 2 Navy Enlisted Classifications	1433069067
US Navy Handbook	1433061015
US Navy Seals Handbook	1438755368
US Navy Seals Handbook - Strategic Information and Contacts	1433057069
US Navy Total Manpower Requirements Handbook	1433069075
US Nonproliferation, Arms Control, and International Security Handbook	1438755376
US Nonproliferation, Arms Control, and International Security Handbook	1433057077
US Nuclear Energy Development Strategy: Programs and Projects Handbook	9781577515647
US Nuclear Energy Sector Laws and Regulations Handbook	9781577515708
US Nuclear Industry Handbook	1438755384
US Nuclear Industry Handbook	1433057085
US Nuclear Industry Investment and Business Guide - Strategic and Practical Information	1438755392
US Nuclear Industry Investment and Business Guide - Strategic and Practical Information	1433057093
US Nuclear Power Facilities and Power Stations Handbook	1438755406
US Nuclear Power Facilities and Power Stations Handbook	1433057107
US Nuclear Power Facilities Handbook	1438755414
US Nuclear Power Facilities Handbook	1433057115
US Nuclear Regulatory Commission Handbook	1438755422
US Nuclear Regulatory Commission Handbook	1433057123
US Ocean Transportation Companies Directory	1438755430
US Ocean Transportation Companies Directory	1433057131
US Office of Management and Budget Handbook	1438755449
US Office of Management and Budget Handbook	143305714X
US Office of Personnel Management Handbook	1438755457
US Office of Personnel Management Handbook	1433057158
US Oil & Gas Companies Directory	1433069083
US Oil & Gas Sector Business & Investment Opportunities Yearbook	1433052563
US Oil and Gas Exploration Laws and Regulation Handbook	1433079089
US Overseas Private Investment Corporation Programs Handbook	1438755465
US Overseas Private Investment Corporation Export Subsidies System Handbook	1433057166
US Pacific Air Force Handbook	1438755473
US Pacific Air Force Handbook	1433057174

Title	ISBN
US Pacific Regional Strategy Handbook	1438755481
US Pacific Regional Strategy Handbook	1433057182
US Paging and Messaging Telecom Companies Directory	143875549X
US Paging and Messaging Telecom Companies Directory	1433057190
US Payphone Telecom Service Providers Directory	1438755503
US Payphone Telecom Service Providers Directory	1433057204
US Peace Corp Handbook	1438755511
US Peace Corp Handbook	1433057212
US Policy and Legislation on Cuba Handbook	143875552X
US Policy and Legislation on Cuba Handbook	1433057220
US Political Intelligence Handbook	1438755538
US Political Intelligence Handbook	1433057239
US Ports Handbook: Structure, Location, Operation	1433057247
US Ports of Entry Handbook: Airports and Ports	1433069091
US Postal Service Handbook	1438755546
US Postal Service Handbook	1433057255
US President George W. Bush Handbook	1438755554
US President George W. Bush Handbook	1433057263
US Presidential Doctrines Handbook - Reagan, Carder, Clinton, Bush, Obama	9781577515890
US Prison Privatization Handbook: Strategic Information, Regulations, Developments	9781577515920
US Private Security Contractors in Afghanistan and Iraq Handbook - Strategic Information and Regulations	9781577515937
US Private Security Forces Regulations Handbook - Strategic Information, Basic Laws and Regulations	9781577515944
US Privatization Programs and Regulations Handbook	1438755562
US Privatization Programs and Regulations Handbook	1433057271
US Privatization Programs and Regulations Handbook	1433052571
US Privatization Yearbook: Major Programs and Projects	1433069105
US Privatizations Consulting Companies Directory	1433069113
US Professional Internet Advertising Handbook	1438755570
US Professional Internet Advertising Handbook	143305728X
US Racing Industry Laws and Regulations Handbook	1438755589
US Racing Industry Laws and Regulations Handbook	1433057298
US Radio Broadcasting Business Opportunities and Regulations Handbook	1438755597
US Radio Broadcasting Business Opportunities and Regulations Handbook	1433057301
US Real Estate Market Business Law Handbook - Strategic Information and Basic Laws	1438755600
US Real Estate Market Business Law Handbook - Strategic Information and Basic Laws	143305731X
US Real Estate Markets Analysis and Investment Opportunities Yearbook	1438755619
US Real Estate Markets Analysis and Investment Opportunities Yearbook	1433057328
US Recent Economic and Political Developments Yearbook	143306233X
US Recent Economic and Political Developments Yearbook	143306233X
US Research & Development Policy Handbook	1433062909
US Research & Development Policy Handbook	1433062909
US Residential Real Estate Investment Guide for Everybody	1438755627
US Residential Real Estate Investment Guide for Everybody	1433057336
US Residential Real Estate Investment Guide for First Time Buyers	1438755635
US Residential Real Estate Investment Guide for First Time Buyers	1433057344

Title	ISBN
US Residential Real Estate Investment Guide for Foreigners	1438755643
US Residential Real Estate Investment Guide for Foreigners	1433057352
US Residential Real Estate Investment Guide for Permanent Residents	1438755651
US Residential Real Estate Investment Guide for Permanent Residents	1433057360
US Satellite Communication Companies Directory	143875566X
US Satellite Communication Companies Directory	1433057379
US Science and Technology Policy Handbook	1438755678
US Science and Technology Policy Handbook	1433057387
US Sea and River Ports Handbook	1438755686
US Sea and River Ports Handbook	1433057395
US Sea And River Ports Handbook Vol. 2 North Carolina-Wisconsin	1433069121
US Secret Service Handbook	1438755694
US Secret Service Handbook	1433057409
US Securities and Exchange Commission Handbook	1438755708
US Securities and Exchange Commission Handbook	1433057417
US Security and Anti Terrorism Legislation Handbook	1438755716
US Security and Anti Terrorism Legislation Handbook	1433057425
US Security Cooperation Agency Handbook	1438755724
US Security Cooperation Agency Handbook	1433057433
US Security Cooperation Education and Training Center Handbook	1438755732
US Security Cooperation Education and Training Center Handbook	1433057441
US Senate Agriculture, Nutrition, And Forestry Committee Handbook	1438755740
US Senate Agriculture, Nutrition, And Forestry Committee Handbook	143305745X
US Senate Appropriations Committee Handbook	1438755759
US Senate Appropriations Committee Handbook	1433057468
US Senate Armed Services Committee Handbook	1438755767
US Senate Armed Services Committee Handbook	1433057476
US Senate Banking, Housing, And Urban Affairs Handbook	1438755775
US Senate Banking, Housing, And Urban Affairs Handbook	1433057484
US Senate Budget Committee Handbook	1438755783
US Senate Budget Committee Handbook	1433057492
US Senate Commerce, Science, And Transportation Handbook	1438755791
US Senate Commerce, Science, And Transportation Handbook	1433057506
US Senate Committee On Indian Affairs Handbook	1438755805
US Senate Committee On Indian Affairs Handbook	1433057514
US Senate Energy And Natural Resources Committee Handbook	1438755813
US Senate Energy And Natural Resources Committee Handbook	1433057522
US Senate Environment And Public Works Committee Handbook	1438755821
US Senate Environment And Public Works Committee Handbook	1433057530
US Senate Finance Committee Handbook	143875583X
US Senate Finance Committee Handbook	1433057549
US Senate Foreign Relations Committee Handbook	1438755848
US Senate Foreign Relations Committee Handbook	1433057557
US Senate Governmental Affairs Committee Handbook	1438755856
US Senate Governmental Affairs Committee Handbook	1433057565
US Senate Guide vol1	1438755864
US Senate Guide vol1	1433057573
US Senate Guide VOLUME 2. United States Senators Biographic Information and Contacts	1433061112

Title	ISBN
US Senate Health, Education, Labor And Pensions Committee Handbook	1438755872
US Senate Health, Education, Labor And Pensions Committee Handbook	1433057581
US Senate Joint Committee On Taxation Handbook	1438755880
US Senate Joint Committee On Taxation Handbook	143305759X
US Senate Joint Economic Committee Handbook	1438755899
US Senate Joint Economic Committee Handbook	1433057603
US Senate Judiciary Committee Handbook	1438755902
US Senate Judiciary Committee Handbook	1433057611
US Senate Rules And Administration Committee Handbook	1438755910
US Senate Rules And Administration Committee Handbook	143305762X
US Senate Select Committee On Ethics Handbook	1438755929
US Senate Select Committee On Ethics Handbook	1433057638
US Senate Select Committee On Intelligence Handbook	1438755937
US Senate Select Committee On Intelligence Handbook	1433057646
US Senate Small Business Committee	1438755945
US Senate Small Business Committee	1433057654
US Senate Special Committee On Aging Handbook	1438755953
US Senate Special Committee On Aging Handbook	1433057662
US Senate Veterans' Affairs Committee Handbook	1438755961
US Senate Veterans' Affairs Committee Handbook	1433057670
US Small Business Administration Handbook	143875597X
US Small Business Administration Handbook	1433057689
US Small Business Support Guide: 50 States of the United States	143306913X
US South Africa Diplomatic and Political Cooperation Handbook	1438752156
US Space Programs and Exploration Handbook	1438755988
US Space Programs and Exploration Handbook	1433057697
US Spain Diplomatic and Political Cooperation Handbook	1438752199
US Special Combat Forces Handbook	1438755996
US Special Combat Forces Handbook	1433057700
US Special Operations Command Handbook	1438756003
US Special Operations Command Handbook	1433057719
US Special Operations Forces Handbook vol 1	1433061023
US Special Operations Forces Handbook vol 2	1433061023
US Special Operations Forces Handbook vol 3	1433057727
US Special Operations Forces Handbook vol 4	1433061023
US Starting Business (Incorporating) in the US Guide	1433047209
US Starting Business (Incorporating) in....Guide	1433069148
US Starting Business (Incorporating) in....Guide	143306880X
US STATE GOVERNMENTS KEY ECONOMIC AND POLITICAL ISSUES AND PROGRAMS HANDBOOK	1438756011
US STATE GOVERNMENTS KEY ECONOMIC AND POLITICAL ISSUES AND PROGRAMS HANDBOOK	1433057735
US Stem Cell Research Policy & Programs Handbook	143875602X
US Stem Cell Research Policy & Programs Handbook	1433057743
US Submarine Force Handbook	1438756038
US Submarine Force Handbook	1433057751
US Subsidized Housing Buying Programs Handbook	1438756046
US Subsidized Housing Buying Programs Handbook	143305776X
US Tax Guide - Corporate Taxation	1433057778

Title	ISBN
US Tax Guide-Corporate Taxation	1438756054
US Taxation Laws and Regulations Handbook	1433081261
US Telecom Companies Directory	1433057786
US Telecom Laws and Regulations Handbook vol 1	1433082632
US Telecom Laws and Regulations Handbook vol 2	1433082659
US Telecommunication Industry Business Opportunities Handbook	1438756062
US Telecommunication Industry Business Opportunities Handbook	143305258X
US Telecommunication Industry Business Opportunities Handbook	1433057794
US Terrorism Prevention Regulations Handbook	1433069156
US Trade & Export Sanctions Handbook	1438756070
US Trade & Export Sanctions Handbook	1433057808
US Trade and Development Agency Handbook	1438756089
US Trade and Development Agency Handbook	1433057816
US Trade Industrial and Business Show Handbook	1438756097
US Trade Industrial and Business Show Handbook	1433057824
US Trade Representative Office Handbook	1438756100
US Trade Representative Office Handbook	1433057832
US Transportation Policy and Regulations Handbook	1433068818
US TV Broadcasting Business Opportunities and Regulations Handbook	1438756119
US TV Broadcasting Business Opportunities and Regulations Handbook	1433057840
US War Against International Terrorism Handbook	1438756127
US War Against International Terrorism Handbook	1433057859
US War Against Iraq Handbook: Political Strategy and Operations	1438756135
US War Against Iraq Handbook: Political Strategy and Operations	1433057867
US War on Terror" Military Strategy Handbook"	1438752423
US Wine Industry Investment and Business Opportunities Yearbook	1433069164
US Wireless Telecom & Data Companies Directory	1433057875
US Yugoslavia Economic and Political Cooperation Handbook	1438752407
US: Importing into the Unites States Practical Guide	1433069172
US: State of Georgia Business Financial Assistance Programs Handbook	1433069180
USA Constitution and Citizenship Laws Handbook - Strategic Information and Basic Laws	1438780168
USA Immigration Laws and Regulations Handbook - Strategic Information and Basic Laws	1438783760
USA Insolvency (Bankruptcy) Laws and Regulations Handbook - Strategic Information and Basic Laws	9781433085758
USA Labor Laws and Regulations Handbook - Strategic Information and Basic Laws	1438781962
USA Land Ownership and Agriculture Laws Handbook	143876023X
US-Argentina Diplomatic and Political Cooperation Handbook	1438751389
US-Argentina Diplomatic and Political Cooperation Handbook	1433052792
US-Argentina Economic and Political Cooperation Handbook	1438751397
US-Argentina Economic and Political Cooperation Handbook	1433052806
US-Armenia Diplomatic and Political Cooperation Handbook	1433052814
US--Armenia Diplomatic and Political Cooperation Handbook	1438751400
US-Armenia Economic and Political Cooperation Handbook	1433052822
US--Armenia Economic and Political Cooperation Handbook	1438751419
US-Australia Diplomatic and Political Cooperation Handbook	1438751427
US-Australia Diplomatic and Political Cooperation Handbook	1433052830
US-Australia Economic and Political Cooperation Handbook	1438751435

Title	ISBN
US-Australia Economic and Political Cooperation Handbook	1433052849
US-Austria Diplomatic and Political Cooperation Handbook	1438751443
US-Austria Diplomatic and Political Cooperation Handbook	1433052857
US-Austria Economic and Political Cooperation Handbook	1438751451
US-Austria Economic and Political Cooperation Handbook	1433052865
US-Azerbaijan Diplomatic and Political Cooperation Handbook	1433052873
US-Azerbaijan Economic and Political Cooperation Handbook	143875146X
US-Azerbaijan Economic and Political Cooperation Handbook	1433052881
US-Belgium Diplomatic and Political Cooperation Handbook	1438751478
US-Belgium Diplomatic and Political Cooperation Handbook	143305289X
US-Belgium Economic and Political Cooperation Handbook	1438751486
US-Belgium Economic and Political Cooperation Handbook	1433052903
US-Bosnia & Herzegovina Diplomatic and Political Cooperation Handbook	1438751494
US-Bosnia & Herzegovina Diplomatic and Political Cooperation Handbook	1433052911
US-Bosnia & Herzegovina Economic and Political Cooperation Handbook	1438751508
US-Bosnia & Herzegovina Economic and Political Cooperation Handbook	143305292X
US-Brazil Diplomatic and Political Cooperation Handbook	1433052938
US-Brazil Economic and Political Cooperation Handbook	1433052946
US-Bulgaria Diplomatic and Political Cooperation Handbook	1438751524
US-Bulgaria Diplomatic and Political Cooperation Handbook	1433052954
US-Bulgaria Economic and Political Cooperation Handbook	1438751532
US-Bulgaria Economic and Political Cooperation Handbook	1433052962
US-Canada Diplomatic and Political Cooperation Handbook	1438751540
US-Canada Diplomatic and Political Cooperation Handbook	1433052970
US-Canada Economic and Political Cooperation Handbook	1438751559
US-Canada Economic and Political Cooperation Handbook	1433052989
US-Chile Diplomatic and Political Cooperation Handbook	1438751567
US-Chile Diplomatic and Political Cooperation Handbook	1433052997
US-Chile Economic and Political Cooperation Handbook	1438751575
US-Chile Economic and Political Cooperation Handbook	1433053004
US-Chile Free Trade Agreement Handbook	1433069199
US-China Diplomatic and Political Cooperation Handbook	1438751583
US-China Diplomatic and Political Cooperation Handbook	1433053012
US-China Economic and Political Cooperation Handbook	1433053020
US-Costa Rica Diplomatic and Political Cooperation Handbook	1433053039
US-Costa Rica Economic and Political Cooperation Handbook	1438751591
US-Costa Rica Economic and Political Cooperation Handbook	1433053047
US-Croatia Diplomatic and Political Cooperation Handbook	1438751605
US-Croatia Diplomatic and Political Cooperation Handbook	1433053055
US-Croatia Economic and Political Cooperation Handbook	1433053063
US-Cuba Political and Economic Relations Handbook	1433053071
US-Czech Republic Diplomatic and Political Cooperation Handbook	1438751613
US-Czech Republic Diplomatic and Political Cooperation Handbook	143305308X
US-Czech Republic Economic and Political Cooperation Handbook	1438751621
US-Czech Republic Economic and Political Cooperation Handbook	1433053098
US-Egypt Diplomatic and Political Cooperation Handbook	143875163X
US-Egypt Diplomatic and Political Cooperation Handbook	1433053101
US-Egypt Economic and Political Cooperation Handbook	143305311X
US-El Salvador Diplomatic and Political Cooperation Handbook	1433053128

Title	ISBN
US-El Salvador Economic and Political Cooperation Handbook	1438751656
US-El Salvador Economic and Political Cooperation Handbook	1433053136
US-Estonia Diplomatic and Political Cooperation Handbook	1438751664
US-Estonia Diplomatic and Political Cooperation Handbook	1433053144
US-Estonia Economic and Political Cooperation Handbook	1438751672
US-Estonia Economic and Political Cooperation Handbook	1433053152
US-Finland Diplomatic and Political Cooperation Handbook	1438751680
US-Finland Diplomatic and Political Cooperation Handbook	1433053160
US-Finland Economic and Political Cooperation Handbook	1438751699
US-Finland Economic and Political Cooperation Handbook	1433053179
US-France Diplomatic and Political Cooperation Handbook	1438751702
US-France Diplomatic and Political Cooperation Handbook	1433053187
US-France Economic and Political Cooperation Handbook	1433053195
US-Georgia Diplomatic and Political Cooperation Handbook	1438751710
US-Georgia Diplomatic and Political Cooperation Handbook	1433053209
US-Georgia Economic and Political Cooperation Handbook	1438751729
US-Georgia Economic and Political Cooperation Handbook	1433053217
US-Germany Diplomatic and Political Cooperation Handbook	1438751737
US-Germany Diplomatic and Political Cooperation Handbook	1433053225
US-Germany Economic and Political Cooperation Handbook	1438751745
US-Germany Economic and Political Cooperation Handbook	1433053233
US-Greece Diplomatic and Political Cooperation Handbook	1433053241
US-Greece Economic and Political Cooperation Handbook	1438751753
US-Greece Economic and Political Cooperation Handbook	143305325X
US-Hungary Diplomatic and Political Cooperation Handbook	1438751761
US-Hungary Diplomatic and Political Cooperation Handbook	1433053268
US-Hungary Economic and Political Cooperation Handbook	143875177X
US-Hungary Economic and Political Cooperation Handbook	1433053276
US-India Diplomatic and Political Cooperation Handbook	1433053284
US-India Economic and Political Cooperation Handbook	1438751788
US-India Economic and Political Cooperation Handbook	1433053292
US-Indonesia Diplomatic and Political Cooperation Handbook	1438751796
US-Indonesia Diplomatic and Political Cooperation Handbook	1433053306
US-Indonesia Economic and Political Cooperation Handbook	143875180X
US-Indonesia Economic and Political Cooperation Handbook	1433053314
US-Iran Political & Economic Relations Handbook	1438751818
US-Iran Political & Economic Relations Handbook	1433053322
US-Iraq Political & Economic Relations Handbook	1438751826
US-Iraq Political & Economic Relations Handbook	1433053330
US-Israel Diplomatic and Political Cooperation Handbook	1438751834
US-Israel Diplomatic and Political Cooperation Handbook	1433053349
US-Israel Economic and Political Cooperation Handbook	1438751842
US-Israel Economic and Political Cooperation Handbook	1433053357
US-Italy Diplomatic and Political Cooperation Handbook	1438751850
US-Italy Diplomatic and Political Cooperation Handbook	1433053365
US-Italy Economic and Political Cooperation Handbook	1433053373
US-Japan Diplomatic and Political Cooperation Handbook	1438751869
US-Japan Diplomatic and Political Cooperation Handbook	1433053381
US-Japan Economic and Political Cooperation Handbook	143305339X

Title	ISBN
US-Jordan Free Trade Agreement Handbook	1433069202
US-Kazakhstan Diplomatic and Political Cooperation Handbook	1438751877
US-Kazakhstan Diplomatic and Political Cooperation Handbook	1433053403
US-Kazakhstan Diplomatic and Political Relations Handbook	1438751885
US-Kazakhstan Diplomatic and Political Relations Handbook	1433053411
US-Kazakhstan Economic and Political Cooperation Handbook	1438751893
US-Kazakhstan Economic and Political Cooperation Handbook	143305342X
US-Korea South Diplomatic and Political Cooperation Handbook	143305373X
US-Korea South Economic and Political Cooperation Handbook	1433053748
US-Kuwait Diplomatic and Political Cooperation Handbook	1438751907
US-Kuwait Diplomatic and Political Cooperation Handbook	1433053438
US-Kuwait Economic and Political Cooperation Handbook	1433053446
US-Kyrgyzstan Diplomatic and Political Cooperation Handbook	1438751915
US-Kyrgyzstan Diplomatic and Political Cooperation Handbook	1433053454
US-Kyrgyzstan Economic and Political Cooperation Handbook	1438751923
US-Kyrgyzstan Economic and Political Cooperation Handbook	1433053462
US-Latvia Diplomatic and Political Cooperation Handbook	1438751931
US-Latvia Diplomatic and Political Cooperation Handbook	1433053470
US-Latvia Economic and Political Cooperation Handbook	143875194X
US-Latvia Economic and Political Cooperation Handbook	1433053489
US-Lithuania Diplomatic and Political Cooperation Handbook	1438751958
US-Lithuania Diplomatic and Political Cooperation Handbook	1433053497
US-Lithuania Economic and Political Cooperation Handbook	1438751966
US-Lithuania Economic and Political Cooperation Handbook	1433053500
US-Mexico Diplomatic and Political Cooperation Handbook	1438751974
US-Mexico Diplomatic and Political Cooperation Handbook	1433053519
US-Mexico Economic and Political Cooperation Handbook	1438751982
US-Mexico Economic and Political Cooperation Handbook	1433053527
US-Moldova Diplomatic and Political Cooperation Handbook	1438751990
US-Moldova Diplomatic and Political Cooperation Handbook	1433053535
US-Moldova Economic and Political Cooperation Handbook	1433053543
US-New Zealand Diplomatic and Political Cooperation Handbook	1433053551
US--New Zealand Diplomatic and Political Cooperation Handbook	1438752008
US-New Zealand Economic and Political Cooperation Handbook	143305356X
US--New Zealand Economic and Political Cooperation Handbook	1438752016
US-Norway Diplomatic and Political Cooperation Handbook	1438752024
US-Norway Diplomatic and Political Cooperation Handbook	1433053578
US-Norway Economic and Political Cooperation Handbook	1438752032
US-Norway Economic and Political Cooperation Handbook	1433053586
US-Peru Diplomatic and Political Cooperation Handbook	1438752040
US-Peru Diplomatic and Political Cooperation Handbook	1433053594
US-Peru Economic and Political Cooperation Handbook	1438752059
US-Peru Economic and Political Cooperation Handbook	1433053608
US-Philippines Diplomatic and Political Cooperation Handbook	1438752067
US-Philippines Economic and Political Cooperation Handbook	1433053624
US-Poland Diplomatic and Political Cooperation Handbook	1438752075
US-Poland Diplomatic and Political Cooperation Handbook	1433053632
US-Poland Economic and Political Cooperation Handbook	1438752083
US-Poland Economic and Political Cooperation Handbook	1433053640

Title	ISBN
US-Portugal Diplomatic and Political Cooperation Handbook	1438752091
US-Portugal Diplomatic and Political Cooperation Handbook	1433053659
US-Portugal Economic and Political Cooperation Handbook	1438752105
US-Portugal Economic and Political Cooperation Handbook	1433053667
US-Russia Cooperation Against Terrorism Handbook	1438756143
US-Russia Cooperation Against Terrorism Handbook	1433057883
US-Russia Diplomatic and Political Cooperation Handbook	1438752113
US-Russia Diplomatic and Political Cooperation Handbook	1433053675
US-Russia Economic & Financial Cooperation Handbook	1438756151
US-Russia Economic & Financial Cooperation Handbook	1433057891
US-Russia Economic and Political Cooperation Handbook	1438752121
US-Russia Economic and Political Cooperation Handbook	1433053683
US-Russia Military Cooperation Handbook	143875616X
US-Russia Military Cooperation Handbook	1433057905
US-Russia Political Cooperation Handbook	1438756178
US-Russia Political Cooperation Handbook	1433057913
US-Russia Scientific & Technological Cooperation Handbook	1438756186
US-Russia Scientific & Technological Cooperation Handbook	1433057921
US-Russia Scientific Cooperation Handbook	1438756194
US-Russia Scientific Cooperation Handbook	143305793X
US-Russia Space Cooperation Handbook	1438756208
US-Russia Space Cooperation Handbook	1433057948
US-Saudi Arabia Diplomatic and Political Cooperation Handbook	143875213X
US-Saudi Arabia Diplomatic and Political Cooperation Handbook	1433053691
US-Saudi Arabia Economic and Political Cooperation Handbook	1438752148
US-Saudi Arabia Economic and Political Cooperation Handbook	1433053705
US-Serbia Diplomatic and Political Cooperation Handbook	1438752393
US-South Africa Diplomatic and Political Cooperation Handbook	1433053713
US-South Africa Economic and Political Cooperation Handbook	1438752164
US-South Africa Economic and Political Cooperation Handbook	1433053721
US-South Korea Diplomatic and Political Cooperation Handbook	1438752172
US-South Korea Economic and Political Cooperation Handbook	1438752180
US-Spain Diplomatic and Political Cooperation Handbook	1433053756
US-Spain Economic and Political Cooperation Handbook	1438752202
US-Spain Economic and Political Cooperation Handbook	1433053764
US-Sri Lanka Diplomatic and Political Cooperation Handbook	1438752210
US-Sri Lanka Diplomatic and Political Cooperation Handbook	1433053772
US-Sri Lanka Economic and Political Cooperation Handbook	1433053780
US-Sweden Diplomatic and Political Cooperation Handbook	1433053799
US-Sweden Economic and Political Cooperation Handbook	1438752229
US-Sweden Economic and Political Cooperation Handbook	1433053802
US-Switzerland Diplomatic and Political Cooperation Handbook	1438752237
US-Switzerland Diplomatic and Political Cooperation Handbook	1433053810
US-Switzerland Economic and Political Cooperation Handbook	1438752245
US-Switzerland Economic and Political Cooperation Handbook	1433053829
US-Taiwan Diplomatic and Political Cooperation Handbook	1433053837
US-Taiwan Economic and Political Cooperation Handbook	1438752253
US-Taiwan Economic and Political Cooperation Handbook	1433053845
US-Turkey Diplomatic and Political Cooperation Handbook	1433053853

Title	ISBN
US--Turkey Diplomatic and Political Cooperation Handbook	1438752261
US-Turkey Economic and Political Cooperation Handbook	1433053861
US--Turkey Economic and Political Cooperation Handbook	143875227X
US-Turkey Economic and Political Relations Handbook	1438756216
US-Turkey Economic and Political Relations Handbook	1433057956
US-Turkmenistan Diplomatic and Political Cooperation Handbook	1438752288
US-Turkmenistan Diplomatic and Political Cooperation Handbook	143305387X
US-Turkmenistan Economic and Political Cooperation Handbook	1438752296
US-Turkmenistan Economic and Political Cooperation Handbook	1433053888
US-UK Diplomatic and Political Cooperation Handbook	143875230X
US-UK Diplomatic and Political Cooperation Handbook	1433053896
US-UK Economic and Political Cooperation Handbook	1438752318
US-UK Economic and Political Cooperation Handbook	143305390X
US-Ukraine Diplomatic and Political Cooperation Handbook	1433053918
US-Ukraine Economic and Political Cooperation Handbook	1438752326
US-Ukraine Economic and Political Cooperation Handbook	1433053926
US-Ukrainian Business Contacts Directory	1433069210
US-Uruguay Diplomatic and Political Cooperation Handbook	1438752334
US-Uruguay Diplomatic and Political Cooperation Handbook	1433053934
US-Uruguay Economic and Political Cooperation Handbook	1438752342
US-Uruguay Economic and Political Cooperation Handbook	1433053942
US-Uzbekistan Diplomatic and Political Cooperation Handbook	1438752350
US-Uzbekistan Diplomatic and Political Cooperation Handbook	1433053950
US-Uzbekistan Economic and Political Cooperation Handbook	1433053969
US-Venezuela Diplomatic and Political Cooperation Handbook	1433053977
US--Venezuela Diplomatic and Political Cooperation Handbook	1438752369
US-Venezuela Economic and Political Cooperation Handbook	1433053985
US--Venezuela Economic and Political Cooperation Handbook	1438752377
US-Vietnam Diplomatic and Political Cooperation Handbook	1433053993
US-Vietnam Economic and Political Cooperation Handbook	1438752385
US-Vietnam Economic and Political Cooperation Handbook	1433054000
US-Yugoslavia Diplomatic and Political Cooperation Handbook	1433054019
US-Yugoslavia Economic and Political Cooperation Handbook	1433054027
Utah Business Registration and Incorporation Guide	1438756224
Utah Business Registration and Incorporation Guide	1433057964
Utah Investment & Business Guide	1438756232
Utah Small Business Assistance and Programs Handbook	1438756240

WORLD STOCK, FINANCIAL MARKET LAWS AND REGULATIONS HANDBOOK LIBRARY

STRATEGIC INFORMATION AND BASIC LAWS

UPDATED ANNUALLY: PLEASE CONTACT IBP, INC FOR ISBN NUMBERS

978 ISBN	COMPLETE FULL TITLE
9781433084997	Afghanistan Stock, Financial Market Laws and Regulations Handbook - Strategic Information and Basic Laws
9781433085000	Albania Stock, Financial Market Laws and Regulations Handbook - Strategic Information and Basic Laws
9781433086793	Algeria Stock, Financial Market Laws and Regulations Handbook - Strategic Information and Basic Laws
9781433085017	Angola Stock, Financial Market Laws and Regulations Handbook - Strategic Information and Basic Laws
9781433086250	Antigua and Barduba Stock, Financial Market Laws and Regulations Handbook - Strategic Information and Basic Laws
9781433085024	Argentina Stock, Financial Market Laws and Regulations Handbook - Strategic Information and Basic Laws
9781433086786	Armenia Stock, Financial Market Laws and Regulations Handbook - Strategic Information and Basic Laws
9781433085031	Australia Stock, Financial Market Laws and Regulations Handbook - Strategic Information and Basic Laws
9781433086779	Austria Stock, Financial Market Laws and Regulations Handbook - Strategic Information and Basic Laws
9781433085048	Azerbaijan Stock, Financial Market Laws and Regulations Handbook - Strategic Information and Basic Laws
9781433086762	Bahamas Stock, Financial Market Laws and Regulations Handbook - Strategic Information and Basic Laws
9781433085055	Bahrain Stock, Financial Market Laws and Regulations Handbook - Strategic Information and Basic Laws
9781433086243	Bangladesh Stock, Financial Market Laws and Regulations Handbook - Strategic Information and Basic Laws
9781433085062	Barbados Stock, Financial Market Laws and Regulations Handbook - Strategic Information and Basic Laws
9781433086755	Belarus Stock, Financial Market Laws and Regulations Handbook - Strategic Information and Basic Laws
9781433085079	Belgium Stock, Financial Market Laws and Regulations Handbook - Strategic Information and Basic Laws
9781433086748	Belize Stock, Financial Market Laws and Regulations Handbook - Strategic Information and Basic Laws
9781433085086	Benin Stock, Financial Market Laws and Regulations Handbook - Strategic Information and Basic Laws
9781433086731	Bermuda Stock, Financial Market Laws and Regulations Handbook - Strategic

978 ISBN	COMPLETE FULL TITLE
	Information and Basic Laws
9781433085093	Bhutan Stock, Financial Market Laws and Regulations Handbook - Strategic Information and Basic Laws
9781433086595	Bolivia Stock, Financial Market Laws and Regulations Handbook - Strategic Information and Basic Laws
9781433085109	Bosnia and Herzegovina Stock, Financial Market Laws and Regulations Handbook - Strategic Information and Basic Laws
9781433086236	Brazil Stock, Financial Market Laws and Regulations Handbook - Strategic Information and Basic Laws
9781433086236	Bulgaria Stock, Financial Market Laws and Regulations Handbook - Strategic Information and Basic Laws
9781433085123	Burkina Faso Stock, Financial Market Laws and Regulations Handbook - Strategic Information and Basic Laws
9781433086717	Cabo Verde Stock, Financial Market Laws and Regulations Handbook - Strategic Information and Basic Laws
9781433085130	Cambodia Stock, Financial Market Laws and Regulations Handbook - Strategic Information and Basic Laws
9781433086847	Cameroon Stock, Financial Market Laws and Regulations Handbook - Strategic Information and Basic Laws
9781433085147	Canada Stock, Financial Market Laws and Regulations Handbook - Strategic Information and Basic Laws
9781433086694	Cayman Stock, Financial Market Laws and Regulations Handbook - Strategic Information and Basic Laws
9781433085154	Central African Republic Stock, Financial Market Laws and Regulations Handbook - Strategic Information and Basic Laws
9781433086687	Chad Stock, Financial Market Laws and Regulations Handbook - Strategic Information and Basic Laws
9781433085161	Chile Stock, Financial Market Laws and Regulations Handbook - Strategic Information and Basic Laws
9781433086670	China Stock, Financial Market Laws and Regulations Handbook - Strategic Information and Basic Laws
9781433085178	Colombia Stock, Financial Market Laws and Regulations Handbook - Strategic Information and Basic Laws
9781433086663	Comoros Stock, Financial Market Laws and Regulations Handbook - Strategic Information and Basic Laws
9781433085208	Congo Democratic Republic Stock, Financial Market Laws and Regulations Handbook - Strategic Information and Basic Laws
9781433085185	Costa Rica Stock, Financial Market Laws and Regulations Handbook - Strategic Information and Basic Laws
9781433086229	Croatia Stock, Financial Market Laws and Regulations Handbook - Strategic Information and Basic Laws
9781433085192	Cyprus Stock, Financial Market Laws and Regulations Handbook - Strategic Information and Basic Laws
9781433086212	Czech Stock, Financial Market Laws and Regulations Handbook - Strategic Information and Basic Laws
9781433086656	Denmark Stock, Financial Market Laws and Regulations Handbook - Strategic Information and Basic Laws
9781433085215	Dominican Republic Stock, Financial Market Laws and Regulations Handbook - Strategic Information and Basic Laws
9781433086649	Ecuador Stock, Financial Market Laws and Regulations Handbook - Strategic Information and Basic Laws
9781433085222	Egypt Stock, Financial Market Laws and Regulations Handbook - Strategic Information and Basic Laws

978 ISBN	COMPLETE FULL TITLE
9781433086632	El Salvador Stock, Financial Market Laws and Regulations Handbook - Strategic Information and Basic Laws
9781433085239	Estonia Stock, Financial Market Laws and Regulations Handbook - Strategic Information and Basic Laws
9781433086625	Ethiopia Stock, Financial Market Laws and Regulations Handbook - Strategic Information and Basic Laws
9781433085246	European Union Stock, Financial Market Laws and Regulations Handbook - Strategic Information and Basic Laws
9781433086076	Fiji Stock, Financial Market Laws and Regulations Handbook - Strategic Information and Basic Laws
9781433085253	Finland Stock, Financial Market Laws and Regulations Handbook - Strategic Information and Basic Laws
9781433086199	France Stock, Financial Market Laws and Regulations Handbook - Strategic Information and Basic Laws
9781433085260	Gabon Stock, Financial Market Laws and Regulations Handbook - Strategic Information and Basic Laws
9781433086311	Gambia Stock, Financial Market Laws and Regulations Handbook - Strategic Information and Basic Laws
9781433085277	Georgia Republic Stock, Financial Market Laws and Regulations Handbook - Strategic Information and Basic Laws
9781433086175	Germany Stock, Financial Market Laws and Regulations Handbook - Strategic Information and Basic Laws
9781433085284	Ghana Stock, Financial Market Laws and Regulations Handbook - Strategic Information and Basic Laws
9781433086618	Gibraltar Stock, Financial Market Laws and Regulations Handbook - Strategic Information and Basic Laws
9781433085291	Greece Stock, Financial Market Laws and Regulations Handbook - Strategic Information and Basic Laws
9781433086168	Grenada Stock, Financial Market Laws and Regulations Handbook - Strategic Information and Basic Laws
9781433085307	Guatemala Stock, Financial Market Laws and Regulations Handbook - Strategic Information and Basic Laws
9781433086601	Guyana Stock, Financial Market Laws and Regulations Handbook - Strategic Information and Basic Laws
9781433085314	Haiti Stock, Financial Market Laws and Regulations Handbook - Strategic Information and Basic Laws
9781433086977	Honduras Stock, Financial Market Laws and Regulations Handbook - Strategic Information and Basic Laws
9781433085321	Hong Kong Stock, Financial Market Laws and Regulations Handbook - Strategic Information and Basic Laws
9781433086151	Hungary Stock, Financial Market Laws and Regulations Handbook - Strategic Information and Basic Laws
9781433085338	Iceland Stock, Financial Market Laws and Regulations Handbook - Strategic Information and Basic Laws
9781433086144	India Stock, Financial Market Laws and Regulations Handbook - Strategic Information and Basic Laws
9781433085345	Indonesia Stock, Financial Market Laws and Regulations Handbook - Strategic Information and Basic Laws
9781433086991	Iran Stock, Financial Market Laws and Regulations Handbook - Strategic Information and Basic Laws
9781433085352	Iraq Stock, Financial Market Laws and Regulations Handbook - Strategic Information and Basic Laws
9781433086137	Ireland Stock, Financial Market Laws and Regulations Handbook - Strategic Information

978 ISBN	COMPLETE FULL TITLE
	and Basic Laws
9781433085369	Island of Jersey Stock, Financial Market Laws and Regulations Handbook - Strategic Information and Basic Laws
9781433086724	Israel Stock, Financial Market Laws and Regulations Handbook - Strategic Information and Basic Laws
9781433085376	Italy Stock, Financial Market Laws and Regulations Handbook - Strategic Information and Basic Laws
9781433087080	Ivory Coast Stock, Financial Market Laws and Regulations Handbook - Strategic Information and Basic Laws
9781433085383	Jamaica Stock, Financial Market Laws and Regulations Handbook - Strategic Information and Basic Laws
9781433087073	Japan Stock, Financial Market Laws and Regulations Handbook - Strategic Information and Basic Laws
9781433085390	Jersey Stock, Financial Market Laws and Regulations Handbook - Strategic Information and Basic Laws
9781433087066	Jordan Stock, Financial Market Laws and Regulations Handbook - Strategic Information and Basic Laws
9781433085406	Kazakhstan Stock, Financial Market Laws and Regulations Handbook - Strategic Information and Basic Laws
9781433086120	Kenya Stock, Financial Market Laws and Regulations Handbook - Strategic Information and Basic Laws
9781433085413	Kiribati Stock, Financial Market Laws and Regulations Handbook - Strategic Information and Basic Laws
9781433086113	Korea Stock, Financial Market Laws and Regulations Handbook - Strategic Information and Basic Laws
9781433085420	Kuwait Stock, Financial Market Laws and Regulations Handbook - Strategic Information and Basic Laws
9781433086106	Kyrgyz Republic Stock, Financial Market Laws and Regulations Handbook - Strategic Information and Basic Laws
9781433085437	Latvia Stock, Financial Market Laws and Regulations Handbook - Strategic Information and Basic Laws
9781433087059	Lebanon Stock, Financial Market Laws and Regulations Handbook - Strategic Information and Basic Laws
9781433085444	Lesotho Stock, Financial Market Laws and Regulations Handbook - Strategic Information and Basic Laws
9781433087042	Liechtenstein Stock, Financial Market Laws and Regulations Handbook - Strategic Information and Basic Laws
9781433085451	Lithuania Stock, Financial Market Laws and Regulations Handbook - Strategic Information and Basic Laws
9781433086090	Luxembourg Stock, Financial Market Laws and Regulations Handbook - Strategic Information and Basic Laws
9781433085468	Macedonia Stock, Financial Market Laws and Regulations Handbook - Strategic Information and Basic Laws
9781433086083	Madagascar Stock, Financial Market Laws and Regulations Handbook - Strategic Information and Basic Laws
9781433085475	Malaysia Stock, Financial Market Laws and Regulations Handbook - Strategic Information and Basic Laws
9781433087110	Malta Stock, Financial Market Laws and Regulations Handbook - Strategic Information and Basic Laws
9781433085482	Marshall Islands Stock, Financial Market Laws and Regulations Handbook - Strategic Information and Basic Laws
9781433087035	Mexico Stock, Financial Market Laws and Regulations Handbook - Strategic Information and Basic Laws

978 ISBN	COMPLETE FULL TITLE
9781433085499	Micronesia Stock, Financial Market Laws and Regulations Handbook - Strategic Information and Basic Laws
9781433087097	Moldova Stock, Financial Market Laws and Regulations Handbook - Strategic Information and Basic Laws
9781433085505	Monaco Stock, Financial Market Laws and Regulations Handbook - Strategic Information and Basic Laws
9781433087028	Mongolia Stock, Financial Market Laws and Regulations Handbook - Strategic Information and Basic Laws
9781433085512	Montenegro Stock, Financial Market Laws and Regulations Handbook - Strategic Information and Basic Laws
9781433087011	Mozambique Stock, Financial Market Laws and Regulations Handbook - Strategic Information and Basic Laws
9781433085529	Nepal Stock, Financial Market Laws and Regulations Handbook - Strategic Information and Basic Laws
9781433086441	Netherlands Stock, Financial Market Laws and Regulations Handbook - Strategic Information and Basic Laws
9781433085536	New Zealand Stock, Financial Market Laws and Regulations Handbook - Strategic Information and Basic Laws
9781433086465	Nicaragua Stock, Financial Market Laws and Regulations Handbook - Strategic Information and Basic Laws
9781433085543	Niger Stock, Financial Market Laws and Regulations Handbook - Strategic Information and Basic Laws
9781433087004	Nigeria Stock, Financial Market Laws and Regulations Handbook - Strategic Information and Basic Laws
9781433085550	Norway Stock, Financial Market Laws and Regulations Handbook - Strategic Information and Basic Laws
9781433086205	Pakistan Stock, Financial Market Laws and Regulations Handbook - Strategic Information and Basic Laws
9781433085567	Palau Stock, Financial Market Laws and Regulations Handbook - Strategic Information and Basic Laws
9781433086564	Panama Stock, Financial Market Laws and Regulations Handbook - Strategic Information and Basic Laws
9781433085574	Papau New Guinea Stock, Financial Market Laws and Regulations Handbook - Strategic Information and Basic Laws
9781433086557	Paraguay Stock, Financial Market Laws and Regulations Handbook - Strategic Information and Basic Laws
9781433085581	Peru Stock, Financial Market Laws and Regulations Handbook - Strategic Information and Basic Laws
9781433087127	Philippines Stock, Financial Market Laws and Regulations Handbook - Strategic Information and Basic Laws
9781433085598	Poland Stock, Financial Market Laws and Regulations Handbook - Strategic Information and Basic Laws
9781433086540	Portugal Stock, Financial Market Laws and Regulations Handbook - Strategic Information and Basic Laws
9781433085604	Romania Stock, Financial Market Laws and Regulations Handbook - Strategic Information and Basic Laws
9781433086854	Russia Stock, Financial Market Laws and Regulations Handbook - Strategic Information and Basic Laws
9781433085611	Saudi Arabia Stock, Financial Market Laws and Regulations Handbook - Strategic Information and Basic Laws
9781433086533	Senegal Stock, Financial Market Laws and Regulations Handbook - Strategic Information and Basic Laws
9781433085628	Serbia Stock, Financial Market Laws and Regulations Handbook - Strategic Information

978 ISBN	COMPLETE FULL TITLE
	and Basic Laws
9781433086526	Sierra Leone Stock, Financial Market Laws and Regulations Handbook - Strategic Information and Basic Laws
9781433085635	Singapore Stock, Financial Market Laws and Regulations Handbook - Strategic Information and Basic Laws
9781433087103	Slovak Republic Stock, Financial Market Laws and Regulations Handbook - Strategic Information and Basic Laws
9781433086519	Slovenia Stock, Financial Market Laws and Regulations Handbook - Strategic Information and Basic Laws
9781433085642	Solomon Islands Stock, Financial Market Laws and Regulations Handbook - Strategic Information and Basic Laws
9781433086502	South Africa Stock, Financial Market Laws and Regulations Handbook - Strategic Information and Basic Laws
9781433085659	Spain Stock, Financial Market Laws and Regulations Handbook - Strategic Information and Basic Laws
9781433086984	Sri Lanka Stock, Financial Market Laws and Regulations Handbook - Strategic Information and Basic Laws
9781433085666	St. Kitts & Nevis Stock, Financial Market Laws and Regulations Handbook - Strategic Information and Basic Laws
9781433086496	Sweden Stock, Financial Market Laws and Regulations Handbook - Strategic Information and Basic Laws
9781433085673	Switzerland Stock, Financial Market Laws and Regulations Handbook - Strategic Information and Basic Laws
9781433086489	Taiwan Stock, Financial Market Laws and Regulations Handbook - Strategic Information and Basic Laws
9781433085680	Tajikistan Stock, Financial Market Laws and Regulations Handbook - Strategic Information and Basic Laws
9781433086472	Tanzania Stock, Financial Market Laws and Regulations Handbook - Strategic Information and Basic Laws
9781433085697	Thailand Stock, Financial Market Laws and Regulations Handbook - Strategic Information and Basic Laws
9781433085703	Togo Stock, Financial Market Laws and Regulations Handbook - Strategic Information and Basic Laws
9781433086960	Trinidad and Tobago Stock, Financial Market Laws and Regulations Handbook - Strategic Information and Basic Laws
9781433085710	Tunisia Stock, Financial Market Laws and Regulations Handbook - Strategic Information and Basic Laws
9781433086953	Turkey Stock, Financial Market Laws and Regulations Handbook - Strategic Information and Basic Laws
9781433085727	Tuvalu Stock, Financial Market Laws and Regulations Handbook - Strategic Information and Basic Laws
9781433086946	Uganda Stock, Financial Market Laws and Regulations Handbook - Strategic Information and Basic Laws
9781433085734	Ukraine Stock, Financial Market Laws and Regulations Handbook - Strategic Information and Basic Laws
9781433086939	United Arab Emirates Stock, Financial Market Laws and Regulations Handbook - Strategic Information and Basic Laws
9781433085741	United Kingdom Stock, Financial Market Laws and Regulations Handbook - Strategic Information and Basic Laws
9781433086328	Uruguay Stock, Financial Market Laws and Regulations Handbook - Strategic Information and Basic Laws
9781433085758	USA Stock, Financial Market Laws and Regulations Handbook - Strategic Information and Basic Laws

978 ISBN	COMPLETE FULL TITLE
9781433086922	Uzbekistan Stock, Financial Market Laws and Regulations Handbook - Strategic Information and Basic Laws
9781433085765	Venezuela Stock, Financial Market Laws and Regulations Handbook - Strategic Information and Basic Laws
9781433086915	Vietnam Stock, Financial Market Laws and Regulations Handbook - Strategic Information and Basic Laws
9781433085116	Virgin Islands, British Stock, Financial Market Laws and Regulations Handbook - Strategic Information and Basic Laws
9781433085772	Zambia Stock, Financial Market Laws and Regulations Handbook - Strategic Information and Basic Laws
9781433086458	Zimbabwe Stock, Financial Market Laws and Regulations Handbook - Strategic Information and Basic Laws

www.ingramcontent.com/pod-product-compliance
Ingram Content Group UK Ltd.
Pitfield, Milton Keynes, MK11 3LW, UK
UKHW051510290926
15471UKWH00008B/1536

9 780739 762028